John Feinberg's classic treatment of the p
has been a standard treatment of this p
Coming from the Augustinian/Reformed tradition, it is a vigorous defense of both
God's sovereignty and human responsibility in the area of theodicy. This new edition makes an already great book an even better one, as Feinberg has been able to incorporate new material in his debates and conversation with people like Rowe and Plantinga. This is surely one of the most important books ever written on the problem of evil. Those who ignore it will find their own understanding of this issue impoverished, especially in light of the current discussion.

—CHAD BRAND
Associate Professor of Christian Theology
The Southern Baptist Theological Seminary

This latest edition of John Feinberg's *The Many Faces of Evil* is a gem. It provides extensive analyses of various statements of the problem of evil as well as responses that can be offered from a variety of Christian perspectives. Feinberg shows that both the problem and the response to the problem will vary, depending on one's understanding of God and of evil. His own position is offered in dialogue with major classic and contemporary discussions of the problem of evil. In chapter 14, Feinberg offers a poignant and extremely helpful description of his own struggle with evil in the face of his family's medical problems. His advice on how to help others who struggle with evil in their lives is worth the price of the book.

—RONALD J. FEENSTRA
Director of Doctoral Studies
Calvin Theological Seminary

The Many Faces of Evil is a thorough, clear, and highly competent treatment of a perennial problem. At times, it is painful and moving to read. All of us can learn much from it.

—KEITH E. YANDELL
Professor of Philosophy
University of Wisconsin

This is a book about the many problems of evil and their solutions. In this updated edition, Feinberg continues to press home the message that there are various versions of the problem of evil and that, in fact, there are many successful solutions to these versions as well. For example, he claims that theonomy or Leibnizian rationalism engender distinctive problems of evil, and that these positions do solve their logical problems, though he finds their metaphysical or theological claims to be unacceptable. Feinberg's own position is a modified rationalism, in which he contends that God could not eliminate evil and still maintain his intention of having the world populated by genuine human beings. This is a thorough and technical book, fulfilling its promise of addressing the many areas involved with the problem of evil. Feinberg once again comments on his personal situation, which adds to the interest generated by the book. A valuable resource!

—WINFRIED CORDUAN
Professor of Philosophy and Religion
Taylor University

The Many Faces of Evil presents an excellent overview and response to the logical, evidential, and existential aspects of the problem. Those who expect insightful, decisive analyses from John Feinberg will not be disappointed. Crossway Books is also to be commended for its ongoing tradition of strong scholarly publications. This is a "must read" text on this issue.

—GARY HABERMAS
Distinguished Professor and Department Chairman,
Philosophy and Theology
Liberty University

The Many Faces
of Evil

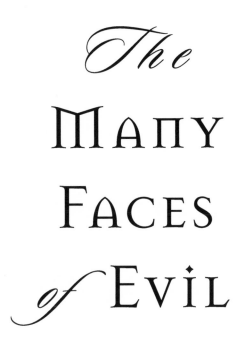

The
Many
Faces
of Evil

THEOLOGICAL SYSTEMS AND THE PROBLEMS OF EVIL

REVISED AND EXPANDED EDITION

John S. Feinberg

CROSSWAY

WHEATON, ILLINOIS

To
My Wife,
PATRICIA

without whose constant love, encouragement, and sacrifice
this volume could not have been produced, and
whose life and testimony amidst affliction
are an inspiration to all who know her

Contents

PREFACE TO THE FIRST EDITION   11

PREFACE TO THE REVISED EDITION   13

PREFACE TO THE THIRD (REVISED AND EXPANDED) EDITION   15

1   INTRODUCTION   17

SECTION I
THE LOGICAL PROBLEM OF EVIL

2   THEONOMY AND THE PROBLEM OF EVIL   33

3   LEIBNIZ AND THE PROBLEM OF EVIL   45

4   THE FREE WILL DEFENSE   67

5   SEVERAL CONTEMPORARY MODIFIED RATIONALIST THEOLOGIES   123

6   GOD AND MORAL EVIL   165

7   GOD AND NATURAL EVIL   191

SECTION II
THE EVIDENTIAL PROBLEM OF EVIL

8   EVIL AS EVIDENCE   207

9   ATHEISTIC ARGUMENTS FROM EVIL   215

10   THEISTS AND THE EVIDENTIAL ARGUMENT FROM EVIL   261

11   THEISTS AND EVIL AS EVIDENCE (II)   303

12   EVIL AND EVIDENCE   357

SECTION III
THE PROBLEM OF HELL

13   HELL AND THE PROBLEM OF EVIL   395

SECTION IV
THE RELIGIOUS PROBLEM OF EVIL

14   THE RELIGIOUS PROBLEM OF EVIL   447

15   THE RELIGIOUS PROBLEM: USES OF SUFFERING   477

APPENDIX—STRATEGY OF THEODICY AND DEFENSE-MAKING   489

NOTES   491

INDEX   533

PREFACE
TO THE
First Edition

Anyone who has ever suffered affliction or had friends or loved ones who have suffered, has probably wondered why there should be such pain if there is a God who truly loves us and has power to do something to remedy our plight. My interest in this issue is of long standing, and it stems from several factors. First, I have seen relatives and friends suffer, and I have wondered about the riddle of God and evil. Second, as a theist very heavily interested in and involved in the study of theology, I have always considered the problem of evil to be one of the most perplexing difficulties that confronts a theist who truly wants to hold a theological position that would recommend itself as both rationally and religiously acceptable. Finally, my great love for philosophy in general and philosophy of religion in particular has continued to engender my interest in the problem. Because of this interest, I was especially pleased that I was granted permission to write on it for my doctoral dissertation for the philosophy department at the University of Chicago. The work presented in the following pages represents the fruit of that study. In the book I have argued four theses. I am certain that the one which will prove to be the most controversial is the fourth. In order to establish that thesis, I have written a new defense which I have argued renders my theological position internally consistent.

There have been various people involved in the production of this volume whose help I want to acknowledge. I shall always be especially grateful for the assistance given to me by my committee at the University of Chicago. Professor Alan Donagan, who served as first reader deserves a special word of appreciation for his countless hours of advisement in my behalf, and I am also most grateful for the insights of the other two readers, Professors Warner Wick and Paul Ricoeur. Mrs. Phyllis East and Mr. Leonard Stucky deserve much thanks for their help in typing the manuscript and preparing it for publication. Bruce Ware spent many hours helping me proofread the manuscript. His help was invaluable. Finally, my deepest appreciation goes to my wife to whom this volume is lovingly dedicated for all the many ways she helped in the production of this volume.

John S. Feinberg
Portland, Oregon, 1979

Preface
to the
Revised Edition

Sometimes philosophical discussions develop very slowly over time. In other cases, there is great change over a short period of time. In the fifteen years or so since I wrote my dissertation on the problem of evil, there have been significant changes in the focus of discussions about God and evil. In addition, in the years since the first edition of this book, there have been major developments in the life of my family which have affected forever the way I think about this problem. As a result of those changes, there are significant differences in this revised edition as opposed to the first edition.

Originally, I intended only to do a stylistic revision and update bibliography. But as I reviewed the literature from the last fifteen years, I realized very quickly that much more was needed. As it turned out, I wrote seven new chapters for this edition. Five treat the evidential problem of evil, which has been the major change in the way this problem is discussed. The other two directly address the religious problem of evil. As for the original book, seven of the eight chapters remain, though the content of many has changed. For example, the chapter on the free will defense now reflects several recent developments in discussions of this defense. I have also expanded my own handling of the problem of moral evil, including responses to what seem to me the most significant objections raised against it. And, then, I have changed my mind about the best way to handle the problem of natural evil. Hence, that chapter contains more new material than old.

I should add as well that I had planned to cover other topics in this revision. For example, some important process theodicies have appeared. Treatment of David Griffin's *God, Power, and Evil: A Process Theodicy* would undoubtedly be beneficial. As it is, I have interacted somewhat with his later book *Evil Revisited*. Moreover, discussing the problem of evil as it is addressed by other world religions would broaden the horizons of those who work within the Christian tradition. Unfortunately, one cannot do everything in one book. When I saw how long the book was becoming with the additions already mentioned, I had to decide to omit certain topics. At that point, I decided to limit this book to the problems of evil as they are handled by traditional forms of Christian theism.

In the process of revising this book, many people have been especially helpful, and I want to acknowledge them. First, a special word of appreciation is due to Stan Gundry and Leonard Goss of Zondervan who believed in this project and secured permission to publish it. They granted approval, even though they only had the original volume and my proposals about how the new volume would be different. Their encouragement and patience during the process of revision is deeply appreciated. Then, I want to thank the board and administration of Trinity Evangelical Divinity School for granting me sabbatical leaves to work on this project. Special thanks is due to Kenneth Meyer and Walter Kaiser for their compassionate responses to me and my family during times of deep trouble. As you will see when you read the chapters on the religious problem of evil, their actions were significant in helping us cope with afflictions that confronted us. Others who have helped us personally in various ways are Gary Almy and Lee Schuemann, and we are deeply indebted to them. Third, various student assistants have been extremely helpful over the years in gathering bibliography and proofreading various portions of this manuscript, and they deserve recognition and appreciation for their efforts. In particular, Steve Wellum and Gregg Allison were especially helpful in these areas. Then, I want to thank those who have interacted with the first edition either in print or in classes. Their comments, suggestions, and objections have been most helpful. Finally, I owe a very special word of appreciation to my wife, Pat, to whom this volume is lovingly dedicated. Without her constant love and encouragement, this book would never have been written in the first place, nor would the revision have been completed. But beyond that, her own responses to personal tragedy say far more than anything I could write about how to cope with evil. She is living testimony that there are those who remain faithful to God no matter what happens. Her life and devotion to God are an inspiration to all who know her, and especially to her family.

John S. Feinberg
Chicago, Christmas 1992

Preface
to the Third (Revised and
Expanded) Edition

Times and cultures change, but some things remain constant. People continue to suffer and to wonder how there can be an all-loving and all-powerful God who allows such evil in our world. The problems that evil creates continue to engage philosophers and theologians as well as ordinary people who experience pain and evil. There is no evidence that these problems (and thinking about them) will go away anytime soon. They continue to be a major obstacle in the way of many people believing in any kind of theism, let alone any form of traditional, evangelical Christian theism.

Because of the import of these problems, I am a third time putting this book in print. I had originally intended to update bibliography and include a completely new chapter on hell and the problem of evil. While I have done both, I have done more. Certain theologies that were discussed in earlier editions no longer receive much attention, whereas other theologies and defenses have gained continued hearing. Moreover, some of the familiar participants in this discussion such as William Rowe have further developed their arguments for and against theism. In order to represent the current discussion adequately, I could not simply supplement footnotes with recent bibliography. Hence, there is more new in this edition than originally intended. In addition to adding new content, I have also undertaken a stylistic revision of the whole manuscript. Some chapters (or portions of chapters) are of necessity still quite technical, but my hope is that in general this volume will read less like a dissertation than it has previously.

Several words of appreciation are in order. First, to Lane Dennis and Marvin Padgett of Crossway I am deeply indebted for their willingness to undertake the revision and reprint of this volume. I am also very thankful for the careful and precise editorial work of Bill Deckard on this volume. Then, I must add a word of thanks to the board and administration of Trinity Evangelical Divinity School for granting me sabbatical time to work on this project.

As you read this work, those who have read earlier editions will note some changes in my views, but my fundamental approach to and defense against the problem of evil haven't changed. I continue to be convinced (and hope that you will be convinced) that this issue and the various intellectual problems it engenders can be successfully addressed. That doesn't mean everyone will be convinced or that even all theists will have the same answer, but it does mean that despite the difficulty of these issues, Christian theism can be successfully defended against the problem of evil in its various forms. May God grant that readers will find it useful to that end!

John S. Feinberg
Chicago, July 2003

1

Introduction

God said that Job was a righteous and blameless man, but he suffered anyway. He lost his children, his possessions, and ultimately his health. Job's friends believed that a loving, powerful, and righteous God would never punish a blameless man, so they urged Job to repent and make peace with God. Job maintained his innocence, but like his friends, he knew that God punishes the wicked, so he couldn't understand why he was suffering. Wracked by intellectual and spiritual questions and besieged by emotional and physical pain, Job wanted an opportunity to plead his case in God's courtroom. Eventually God spoke to Job out of the whirlwind and overwhelmed him with a sense of his power and grandeur. But he never explained why he hadn't used some of that power to protect Job from the evil that befell him, nor why once beset by tragedy upon tragedy, Job wasn't released from it by this omnipotent God who seemingly could do anything. Though God had bestowed his love upon Job bountifully before the affliction came and did so even more abundantly when he finally released Job from the evils he endured, he never explained how allowing those evils into Job's life squared with his love and benevolence.

Job's experience is a paradigm case for the riddle of God and evil, but it isn't the only instance of horrendous suffering and evil. And so, professional philosophers and theologians along with ordinary people wonder how God could allow such horrible things to happen and why he wouldn't stop them from taking such a heavy toll upon mankind. Doesn't he love us enough to remove these evils? Or, is the problem that he just isn't powerful enough to do so? Who hasn't asked such questions?

The problem of evil as traditionally understood in philosophical discussion and debate is stated succinctly in David Hume's *Dialogues Concerning Natural Religion*:

Is he willing to prevent evil, but not able? then is he impotent. Is he able, but not willing? then is he malevolent. Is he both able and willing? Whence then is evil?[1]

In his article "Evil and Omnipotence," written some years ago, J. L. Mackie concurred with this traditional understanding of the problem. He claimed that though traditional arguments for God's existence don't work, theists can accept the criticisms against those arguments and still maintain that God's existence can be known in some nonrational way. Perhaps they have experienced God in a vivid way, so no amount of rational argument to the contrary will likely dissuade them from their belief in God. However, Mackie argued that there is a far more devastating objection to theism. *All* forms of theism, he argued, which hold that God is omnipotent and benevolent succumb before the Epicurean trilemma stated in the portion cited from Hume. Mackie wrote:

> Here it can be shown, not that religious beliefs lack rational support, but that they are positively irrational, that the several parts of the essential theological doctrine are inconsistent with one another, so that the theologian can maintain his position as a whole only by a much more extreme rejection of reason than in the former case. He must now be prepared to believe, not merely what cannot be proved, but what can be disproved from other beliefs that he also holds.[2]

Mackie believed the traditional problem of evil deals a devastating blow to all theistic positions committed to God's omnipotence and benevolence and evil's existence. Later in life he modified his views somewhat, but he maintained to the end that the existence of evil poses an unresolvable problem for traditional theism. I believe these claims are mistaken and that it is possible to demonstrate so. That is the major burden of this book.

Many things can and will be said about why and how Mackie's and other atheists' claims err. However, I begin by pointing out that Mackie's critique ultimately rests on two false assumptions. The first is that *all* forms of theism that hold to God's omnipotence (in some sense of "omnipotence") entail that an omnipotent being *can* eliminate all forms of evil. Of course, if one defines divine omnipotence so as to allow God to actualize logically contradictory states of affairs, then God can eliminate all forms of evil. My point is that not *all* forms of theism understand omnipotence that way. Hence, not all theistic systems entail that God can remove all kinds of evil.

Mackie's second erroneous assumption is that conditions in our world which *he* considers evil are evil according to all forms of theism that hold that God is omnipotent. As we shall see, theistic systems incorporate different notions of evil. This is even true of systems committed to divine omnipotence. Moreover, it is simply wrong for Mackie, an atheist, to assume that all theological positions committed to God as omnipotent hold *his* views on the meaning and nature of evil.

These complaints about Mackie must not be misunderstood. They don't mean that the existence of evil poses no problem for theistic systems committed to divine omnipotence and benevolence. As we shall see, evil's existence poses a variety of problems for any number of theistic positions. Moreover, if a theology has an unacceptable view of divine omnipotence and/or an untenable account of evil, then the system is untenable, regardless of any alleged inconsistency between God's attributes and evil's existence as the system understands them. As Peter Geach says, any critic who attacks a theological position on the grounds of a problem of evil and any apologist who defends the system against a problem of evil are simply wasting their time, if the theology's notions of divine omnipotence and/or evil have already been shown to be untenable.[3] There is simply no need to beat a dead horse, so to speak. Nonetheless, inadequacy of a theology because it holds unacceptable notions of omnipotence and/or evil isn't the same thing as untenability for failure to solve its problem of evil.

My complaints about Mackie's view, then, don't mean that evil poses no problem for theistic belief, but rather that one must understand more accurately than Mackie has the nature of this problem and the "ground rules" for dealing with it. There are a number of theological positions with doctrines of divine omnipotence and benevolence, and the existence of evil poses a variety of serious and significant problems for those systems. Some of those problems deal with matters of internal inconsistency, whereas others question how probable it is that the theology's account of God and evil are accurate.

Granting, then, that it is legitimate for theologians and critics alike to talk about the problems that evil's existence creates for theistic belief, I want to address those problems in this book. I propose to do so by focusing my discussion around the articulation and defense of seven theses. They are: 1) The traditional understanding of the nature of the problem of evil considers it to be only one problem that attacks all theological positions in precisely the same way, but this is mistaken. There is in fact no such thing as *the* problem of evil, for at best, the expression "the problem of evil" stands for a host of distinct problems that confront theologies holding that (a) God is omnipotent (in some sense of "omnipotent"), (b) God is good in that he wills that there be no evil, in some sense of "evil," and (c) evil, in the sense alluded to in (b), exists; 2) Since a problem of evil in its logical form is about the *internal* consistency of the three propositions just mentioned (propositions [a]-[c]), anyone who attempts to discuss a logical problem of evil as it relates to a particular theology must show that the problem arises *within that system's* accounts of God and evil. It is illegitimate to criticize a theology for failing to solve a problem of evil which could arise only if the critic's notions of omnipotence and evil are incorporated into the system; 3) There are many forms of theism that can solve their logical problem of evil. Thus, the complaint that there is no rational way to demonstrate the internal consistency of *any* theological position that holds to an omnipotent and benevolent God and to evil's existence is false; 4) Evil's existence also poses an evidential problem that many theistic systems can resolve; 5) While many theologies can solve their logical and evidential problems of evil, they incorporate theological and/or philosophical commitments I find unacceptable. Thus, I shall present a theology whose intellectual commitments I accept, and I shall show how problems of evil arise for that system and how to solve them. In order to do this, I shall present an original defense that is compatible with the system's views of the divine attributes, human freedom, and evil; 6) Among the many problems of evil, one of the most challenging for theism is the problem of hell. Despite its difficulty, there are a number of systems that can solve this problem in its logical and evidential forms. I shall examine many of those answers and explain how, given my theology, I would handle this problem; and 7) The religious problem of evil is a different kind of problem from the rest; consequently, it requires a different treatment. I shall offer a variety of reflections that address that problem.

At this early point in this book the meaning of many of these seven theses is opaque to the reader. As the discussion moves along, however, each will be explained. In the rest of this chapter I want to explain the first two theses. This will allow me to set forth the ground rules for handling the problem of evil in its logical form. At the end of the chapter, I plan to present the structure for the rest of the book. In doing so, I shall indicate how I shall handle the remaining theses.

Before turning to my first thesis, I want to address two other preliminary but important matters. Readers who believe in God may be troubled by what I have said so far. Rather than resolving the problem of evil, I appear to be expanding it in that I am claiming that there is not just one problem of evil but many. This may be especially perplexing to some in light of a commonly held belief that the problem of evil is an attack on God's very existence.

To the first concern I reply that we shall see that by recognizing that there is more than one problem of evil, we don't make it harder to handle this issue. Rather, I shall show that by distinguishing the many problems of evil we make great headway in moving to their resolution. In fact, when theists do not distinguish among the many problems and identify the specific one they want to address, the likelihood of their resolving any of the problems is diminished.

As to the concern that the problem of evil is an attack on God, that isn't necessarily true. Any of the many problems of evil is actually an attack on some *theological conception* of God. To the extent that a given theology's conception of God matches the true and the living God, then, of course a problem of evil posed against *that* notion of God really does attack God. Suffice it to say that the burden of this book isn't to defend my conception of God as the correct one; I have done so elsewhere.[4] Rather, my purpose in this book is to show that many different theologies committed to divine omnipotence and benevolence can solve the many problems evil poses for them. That is a tall enough order in itself. Deciding and defending which of these theologies most likely matches the true and living God is a task for another occasion.

THESIS 1

My first thesis is that there is no such thing as *the* problem of evil. This is true in at least three distinct respects, the first of which is that it is possible to distinguish a host of different problems that can arise over the issue of God and evil. There is initially a distinction between what I shall call the religious problem of evil and the theological/philosophical problem of evil.

A religious problem of evil arises from a particular instance of suffering and evil that someone is actually experiencing. Faced with such affliction, the sufferer finds it hard to reconcile what is happening with his beliefs about God's love and power. This precipitates a crisis of faith. In the midst of this turmoil, the sufferer asks, "Why is this evil happening to me now?" "This just isn't fair. What did I do to deserve this?" "How can a loving God let this happen to me?" and, "In view of what's happening, how can I worship a God who won't stop it?"[5] It is the religious problem of evil that Job confronted.

In contrast, the theological/philosophical problem of evil is about the existence of *evil in general*, not some specific evil that someone encounters which disrupts her personal relation with God. In fact, the theological/philosophical problem of evil is sufficiently abstracted from instances of experienced evil that it could be posed even if there actually were no God and no evil at all. One could ask how the existence of an omnipotent, all-benevolent God, if he existed, would square with the existence of evil, if there were any.[6]

Attempts to solve a theological/philosophical problem of evil may not help someone at all with his religious needs. In response to the pain and suffering someone undergoes and bemoans, suppose some well-meaning but misguided friend says, "Stop your complaining; evil is just an illusion, an illusion that soon will pass."[7] Or, "I know things are hard now, but you must see that there really couldn't be less evil in the world, because this is the best of all possible worlds."

Such remarks have philosophical sense and may even have a certain philosophical plausibility for some, but they are no help to someone who wonders whether God is worthy of devotion in view of *actual* suffering being experienced. If you were suffering greatly, would such pronouncements comfort you? Of course not! As Plantinga says, after the philosophical discussion ends, the person with problems about his personal relation to God needs pastoral care, but his questions don't belong in a philosophical debate.[8]

There is also a distinction between the problem of moral evil and the problem of natural evil. Moral evil or sin is evil that arises from human or angelic actions (though the problem is normally posed in regard to human action alone). The problem of moral evil asks why there should be sin in a world created by an all-powerful, all-loving God. The problem of moral evil is actually the theological/philosophical problem of evil.

Natural evil includes various phenomena like pains and diseases, earthquakes, fires, floods, pestilences, hurricanes, and famine. Though some of these evils result from human activity, many natural evils occur apart from the direct actions of any agent. Like the problem of moral evil, this is a problem about evils in general, not about specific natural evils. If God is omnipotent and omnibenevolent, why doesn't he remove natural evils?

In addition to these problems of evil, there are also problems about the quantity, intensity, and apparent gratuitousness of evil. The problem about quantity grants that there may be a satisfactory explanation as to why God would allow evil in general. However, this problem asks why there should be so much evil in our world. Whatever God's point in allowing evil, couldn't he make it with much less evil than there is? A variation of this problem focuses not on the amount of evil produced by many different people, but the amount stemming from the actions of one person. Consider the serial killer who murders ten helpless people. Some might argue that the killer must be allowed to do these evil deeds, because it is only by the exercise of his free will that his character becomes set. However, the critic of this reply will ask why God didn't stop the killer after the fourth or fifth murder. By that point, hasn't the killer's character been determined? Why are the other five or six murders necessary to establish his character? If four or five murders would be enough to set his character, than even one more murder, let alone another five or six, is just too much evil.

The problem of the intensity of evil grants that it may be possible to justify the existence of evil in general and even in the amounts present in our world. Still, why are some evils as bad as they are? For example, if someone has to get cancer, why must it be excruciatingly painful and so resistant to any medication that would remove even some pain? In other words, why are certain evils so evil?

Then, there is the problem of the apparent gratuitousness of many evils. Some evils seem attached to some good end, but others seem to serve absolutely no purpose whatsoever. If there are evils that really are purposeless, not just apparently so, it is difficult to imagine why an omnipotent, all-loving God wouldn't remove them.

We can also identify two other distinct problems of evil. One is the problem of animal suffering and pain. Sometimes animals suffer at the hands of humans, and in other instances the cause is nonhuman, but there is no doubt that animals experience a significant amount of pain. It is hard to see the purpose of such suffering, since it can't be to punish animals or to aid in their moral growth. If the point of their suffering is to teach humans some lesson, it is difficult to understand why we could not learn that lesson through some other means. Surely, if there is an all-powerful and all-loving God, he wouldn't subject innocent animals to such treatment. In more recent years, some atheists have linked the problem of animal suffering with the problem of the apparent gratuitousness of some evil to argue that instances of animal suffering that serve no apparent purpose whatsoever surely argue against the likelihood that God exists.

A final problem of evil has received increasing attention in recent years, and it is especially challenging to theistic belief; it is the problem of hell. No one would deny the enormity of evils like the Holocaust, but as horrible as that was, neither it nor any other evil can match the horror of hell. As understood by traditional Christianity, hell is an evil that is meted out in retribution for sin, and it is a never ending punishment. How can an eternity of conscious torment, an apparently infinite punishment, be a just recompense for a finite amount of sin? Even the most heinous crimes ever perpetrated don't merit such a response. And, if that is true, how can it possibly be just for God to send otherwise noble people to an eternal hell, just because they didn't believe in Christ, even though they never heard of him? Many critics of theism (and even some theists) believe that the traditional doctrine of hell must be abandoned, for there is no moral way to justify its existence, and any God who would exact such a punishment can't be a loving God.[9]

From what I have already written, it is clear that there is not just one problem of evil. However, there is a second sense in which there isn't just one problem. Not only can we distinguish the various problems already mentioned, but even the theological/philosophical problem of evil is *not* just *one* problem. Since each theology has its own views of omnipotence, benevolence, and evil, there isn't just *one* theological/philosophical problem of evil that attacks *all* theologies in the same way. That is, there are as many distinct theological/philosophical problems of evil as there are theological systems which hold that (a) God is omnipotent, in some sense of "omnipotence," (b) God is benevolent in that he wills that there be no evil, in some sense of "evil," and (c) evil, in the system's sense of "evil," is said to exist. What this means is that not everyone holds the same account of God and evil. Each account generates a distinct theology, and a distinct theological/philosophical problem of evil confronts each theology. Some systems can solve their problem of evil, while others fail to do so, but each theology confronts its own theological/philosophical problem.

There is a final respect in which there is no such thing as *the* problem of evil. In recent years, philosophers have distinguished between a logical form of the problem of evil and an evidential form. Problems about moral evil, natural evil, the quantity of evil, evil's intensity, apparently gratuitous evil, animal pain, and the problem of hell can all be posed in either a logical or an evidential form.

The logical form of the problem is the traditional way the problem of evil has been posed for centuries. According to the logical problem, theistic systems which espouse divine omnipotence and benevolence *and* the existence of evil contradict themselves. That is, if any two of the propositions about God's attributes and evil's existence are true, the third must be false. The set as a whole is self-contradictory. Readers will immediately recognize this as the form of the problem of evil contained in the portions quoted from Hume and Mackie. Chapters 2–7 of this book address various problems of evil in their logical form.

As a result of Alvin Plantinga's masterful elaboration and defense of the free will defense, there is a general consensus among atheists and theists alike that the logical problem of evil is solvable. I shall argue that other defenses also solve that problem, but Plantinga's free will defense is surely the best-known. In spite of the success of Plantinga's defense, atheists aren't yet ready to give up the fight. Rather, they have launched the attack from another direction. They have argued that even if it is possible for theists to tell a logically consistent story about God and evil, evil in our world still offers strong evidence against the probability that there is a God. This is the evidential problem of evil. It is inductive in form and relies heavily on the notion of probability. In chapter 8, I shall explain more thoroughly the nature of this problem, and in chapters 9–12, I shall interact with contemporary discussions of this problem.

The fact that there isn't just one problem of evil has some important implications for both theists and atheists. For theists, the implication is that they must identify which problem of evil they are discussing, and they must provide an answer that is relevant to that problem. To illustrate this point, consider the following.

A man walks into his pastor's office and begins to tell the pastor his tale of woe. He explains that he is absolutely devastated. Today his wife went to the doctor and learned that she has ovarian cancer. It has been growing for some time, and as a result, the doctor wants to begin treatments immediately. Treatments will be painful, there are no guarantees about whether she can be cured, and treatments are very expensive. This last fact is especially troublesome in that the parishioner explains that because of the bad economy, people are being laid off at the plant where he works, and during layoffs, insurance benefits are not available. Today he learned that he is one of those being laid off.

If that isn't bad enough, the story gets even worse. He relates that his son was riding his bike home from school on a very busy street. He wasn't as cautious as he should have been, and a motorist accidentally ran into him. His son, thankfully, is alive, but he has a number of broken bones and is in the hospital for observation and care. When he will be released is unknown. The parishioner explains that he knows that Christians aren't guaranteed exemption from all pain and problems in this life, but he never thought something like this would happen. It is especially hard to take since he and his family are faithful followers of Christ. How could God allow this to happen? If he loves us as much as Scripture says and has the power that Christians believe he has, it is just unbelievable that he would let this happen. Why do things like this happen to people who are trying to follow God and do his will?

Suppose the pastor swallows hard and then says, "Well, dear brother, you have really been through the wringer! I know that these things are hard to handle, but you must understand why things like this happen. When God decided to create this world, he debated whether to create us as creatures with free will or not. He loves us, and he wants us to love him. But God realized that it is better if we love him because we want to than if we love him because we are forced to do so, so he gave us free will. Free will is a great gift, but it has a liability. If people are really going to be free, no one can guarantee what they will do with that freedom. Hopefully, they will use it to do good, but sometimes they choose to do evil. So, the reason that things like those that have happened to your family occur is that humans have free will, and sometimes they use it to do evil. But God isn't to blame, because he didn't do these

things to your family, and because the gift of free will is a great gift! Would
you rather be a robot?"

If you were that man, would you be comforted by what the pastor just
said? Of course not! The parishioner will probably leave the pastor's office
scratching his head, but before he goes, he may just ask the pastor, "Pastor,
what does free will have to do with my wife's ovarian cancer and the other
things that happened to my family today?" And well he should pose that question to the pastor, for the pastor has made a grave error. What is the problem
here? The problem with the pastor's "counsel" is that while the free will
defense he has just offered is an appropriate answer to the problem of moral
evil, the parishioner isn't asking that question. He is wrestling with the religious problem of evil, and an answer to the problem of moral evil simply
doesn't address, let alone solve, the religious problem. No, this man doesn't
need to hear the free will defense or any other answers to the problem of moral
evil. As Plantinga says, this man needs pastoral care, and unfortunately, his
pastor doesn't understand that. If we are going to help people as they wrestle
with a problem of evil, we must identify which problem they are raising and
offer an answer that is relevant to that problem, not some other problem.

There is also an important implication for the atheist of the fact that there
isn't just one problem of evil. It is illegitimate to reject a theist's defense
against one problem of evil on the ground that it doesn't solve all problems
of evil. Unfortunately, atheists frequently make this mistake. For example,
some critics of theism aren't sure whether the free will defense works, but
even if it does, they complain that it is inadequate, because it doesn't handle
natural evil.[10] Of course, it was never intended to do so, for it addresses a different problem, the problem of moral evil. As another example, Richard
Schoenig presents an elaborate critique of Plantinga's free will defense. In
answer to various possible objections to Schoenig's presentation, Schoenig
affirms that atheists have posed a significant challenge to theism, and theists
must explain "why it is reasonable to affirm both the existence of the theistic God and the quantity and quality of evil found in this world."[11] Indeed,
theists do need to answer the problems of the quantity and quality of evil in
our world, but not in order to address or assess Plantinga's free will defense.
That is a defense whose focus is the problem of moral evil. If Plantinga were
to extend that defense to address the problems of the quantity and quality of
evil, then we would have to assess how well it handles those problems. But
since Schoenig is evaluating Plantinga's free will defense as contained in his
God, Freedom, and Evil (as well as others of his writings), Schoenig's comments about the quantity and quality of evil are irrelevant. In other instances
if the theist offers an explanation for natural evil in general, critics complain

that this does not solve problems about the amounts of natural evil or the instances of apparently purposeless natural evil in our world.

While there is an element of truth in each of those objections, they are still misguided. They fail to recognize that there are different problems of evil and that no one defense addresses all problems of evil, nor does it intend to do so. It is wrongheaded at a very fundamental level to think that because a given defense or theodicy doesn't solve *every* problem of evil, it doesn't solve *any* problem of evil. Once we understand that there are many problems of evil, then we can avoid this mistake. In each instance, then, theists and atheists alike must identify the specific problem which is under discussion, and then decide which defenses address *that* problem and how well they handle it. An acceptable solution to one problem of evil isn't nullified because it doesn't solve any or all other problems.

Thesis 2

My second thesis deals with the "ground rules" for handling the logical problem of evil. The most fundamental rule for handling that problem is that any problem of evil posed in its logical form is about the *internal* consistency of a theological position. This means that the theistic system is accused of contradicting itself. Hence some of its views can't be true, because taken together, they generate a contradiction within the set.

This rule has implications for theists who would construct a philosophical theology, and for atheists who critique theism. As for theists, they must be careful to structure their theologies so that they don't incorporate in their system views that do contradict one another. In particular, they must be careful not to formulate a theology with a God who is *both* good *and* able to get rid of the evil present in our world. If the theist's God is both good, can get rid of evil, and has no morally sufficient reason for failing to do so, then his theology will be internally inconsistent and will collapse.

The implication of this ground rule for atheists is that they must specify a problem that actually arises *within* the views of the system they attack. If the alleged inconsistency between God and evil doesn't arise within a system theists actually hold, then it damages no position theists actually hold. Hence, atheists must ensure that when they accuse a theology of contradicting itself in regard to its handling of God and evil, they are attacking a viewpoint that some theist(s) actually holds.

J. L. Mackie is one who has broken this rule when interacting with Alvin Plantinga's free will defense. As we shall see in chapter 4, Mackie rejects the free will defense, because he believes that it is possible for God both to give us free will and to eliminate all moral evil. Of course, Mackie's attack incorporates a notion of free will that is contrary to the understanding of free will inherent in the free will defense. Nonetheless, he still thinks that he has shown the free will defense to be unable to solve its problem of evil. However, the problem under discussion is the *logical* problem of moral evil, and Mackie hasn't identified any problem *internal* to the free will defender's theology. One can always generate a problem of internal inconsistency by attributing one's own views about God, evil, and freedom to someone else. But that doesn't show that the theist contradicts *himself*. Rather, it shows that the theist and atheist have different, even contradictory views on such matters as God's attributes, the nature of evil, and human freedom. But we already knew that; that's why the atheist is an atheist and not a theist.

Mackie isn't the only one who makes this error, for other atheists and even some theists overlook this important point. Obviously, challenges to theism that commit this error fail to show that a theistic position is actually guilty of contradicting itself. However, just because some break this rule that doesn't mean that theistic systems have been vindicated. As we shall see, there are logical problems of evil that do arise within various theological systems. In those cases, the theist must explain why his apparently self-contradictory views aren't in fact genuinely contradictory. As for Mackie, because he doesn't show that any free will defender accepts his account of human freedom, his objection fails to destroy the free will defense on grounds of *internal* inconsistency!

There are other ground rules for addressing the logical problem of evil. Since the logical problem of evil accuses theistic positions of contradicting themselves, we must clarify what it means to say that a system or a set of propositions contains a contradiction. It doesn't mean that there may be a way to fit a theology's views together consistently but neither the critic nor the theist knows how. Nor does it mean that someday we shall understand, even though we don't now. It doesn't even mean that God knows how ideas fit together without contradiction, even though we don't. Instead, a charge of contradiction means that there is no possible way for *anyone ever* to harmonize these views, for they both affirm and deny the same thing at the same time and in the same way.

This is, indeed, a robust accusation. We can see why Mackie believed this attack more fatal to theism than theism's supposed inability to write a valid and sound argument for God's existence. But if this is what it means to claim that views are contradictory, then how to answer this charge should be clear. The theistic defender need only show a *possible* way for the various propositions held to be true. Hence, theists need not claim to have *the* explanation as to why an omnipotent, all-loving God would allow evil. They need only offer a possible explanation. Atheists may complain (and they do, as we shall see) that the explanation isn't very plausible, but that is irrelevant to the logical problem. When someone charges a system with contradiction, the only relevant issue is whether the defender can offer a possible explanation of how the allegedly contradictory ideas can all be true at once. If the defender does that, she answers the charge of contradiction, and her views are vindicated.

This must not be misunderstood. Armed with this ground rule, theists may offer any explanation whatsoever that removes the contradiction, no matter how fanciful the answer. Though doing so would remove the alleged inconsistency and thereby satisfy the demands of the logical problem of evil, theists should try to offer explanations that are as plausible as possible. After all, one would hope to say more than that one's theology tells a logically consistent story. Any good philosopher or theologian should know enough about logic to know how to construct a set of views that avoids contradicting itself. But that alone isn't reason enough for anyone to believe those views. To be believable, the system should espouse plausible views, not just possible ones. Still, all that is necessary to meet the demands of the logical problem of evil is to show a possible way for the theistic doctrines to fit together without contradiction.

Since theists, when addressing the logical problem of evil, need only offer a possible explanation of why God would allow evil, they needn't claim that they know God's actual reason. In line with this point, in contemporary discussions of the problem of evil a distinction is often made between a theodicy and a defense. A theodicy purports to offer the actual reason God has for allowing evil in our world. A defense is much less pretentious, for it claims to offer only a *possible* reason God might have for not removing evil.[12] As long as that *defense* does remove the alleged inconsistency in the theist's system, the theist meets the demands of the logical problem of evil. A defense is defense enough; a theodicy is not required.

Not everyone adheres to this distinction. Some use the term "theodicy" when they actually offer what they consider only a *possible* explanation of why God would allow evil. For our purposes, I shall assume that when a philosopher uses either term, he refers to the concept indicated by the term "defense." Normally, I'll use the terms interchangeably in that way. However, if a philosopher claims to know the actual reason for evil in our world and tells us that she is offering it, I'll make a point to mention that.

THE STRUCTURE OF THE BOOK

In order to elaborate and defend my theses 1–3 and 5, in chapters 2–7 I shall investigate various forms of theism in order to show that there is no *one* theological/philosophical problem of evil. Each system generates its own distinctive problem, and many of these theologies can solve their logical problem of evil. Nonetheless, I shall raise objections to these systems, objections based on grounds *external* to each system. I shall then offer my own system, and indicate how it solves its logical problem of evil.

In chapters 8–12, I turn to the evidential problem of evil (thesis 4). Chapter 8 clarifies the nature of this problem, and then chapters 9–11 present atheists' and theists' treatments of this problem, concluding with my own response to it (chapter 12). Among other things, I shall show that my point about different forms of theism is still important in handling this problem. Before leaving the evidential problem, I shall address the problem of the quantity of evil, and the problem of apparently gratuitous evil. In chapter 13, the discussion turns to the problem of hell, and I'll address it in both its logical and evidential forms (thesis 6). Finally, in chapters 14–15 I turn to the religious problem (thesis 7). I shall explain why and how this problem differs from the rest. Then, I shall present material from my own family's experience which I hope will both minister to the afflicted and help those who minister to them.

As to the next portion of the book, chapter 2 begins my treatment of the logical problem. The focus is theonomy, a radical form of theism in which theology is prior to logic, ethics, physics, etc., so that God chooses whatever laws govern those matters. If we plot theistic positions along a continuum running from those at one end which emphasize God's will and power (as the controller of all things) to those at the other end which emphasize reason as the governing principle of the universe, theonomy is located toward or at the former end. For theonomy everything depends on God's will, so reason alone cannot comprehend how things are or should be in our world; all rules must be conveyed to us by divine revelation. Theonomy immediately suggests its opposite, a radical form of rationalism, located toward or at the opposite end of the continuum. That rationalistic position is Leibnizian Rationalism, a system in which logic is prior to theology, so to speak. Whatever is logically and morally possible according to Leibnizian Rationalism is discernible by pure reason alone apart from divine revelation. Leibniz's system is the subject of chapter 3. In chapter 4, the discussion turns to Modified Rationalism, a mediating position between the two extremes. As we shall see, many traditional Christian theistic systems assume the Modified Rationalist metaphysic. My own system is one of them. Chapters 4–7 present various theologies broadly within the Modified Rationalistic approach and address in particular the logical problem of moral evil as it arises for these theologies. In chapters 6 and 7 I offer my defenses against the problems of moral and natural evil.

Section I

The Logical Problem of Evil

2

THEONOMY AND THE
PROBLEM OF EVIL

Imagine a world with no rationally necessary laws. Nothing about this world has to be the way it is, for nothing about it is inherent in its very structure. The only necessity and the only law in this universe is God's will.[1] If God wants something to be so, whatever it is, it will be so. As a result, by the light of pure reason alone, we could never know what the rules are in any area of life. Instead, whatever can be known about physics, epistemology, and ethics depends on what God chooses and reveals to be the case. If God had so chosen, things could have been (and still can be) partially or totally different. This is the nature of our world according to the theological system known as theonomy.

Theonomy is a radical form of theism in which theology is prior to logic. That is, God and his will are paramount; reason and logic are secondary. God isn't faced, for example, with the rules of logic, physics, or ethics which he didn't choose and forced to conform to them. Instead, he chooses the rules of reason, physics, and ethics that he wants, and everything and everyone must conform to his choices. Of course, he doesn't have to conform to any of these rules, unless he decides to so bind himself. If he is subject to such rules, we know that only because he reveals that to us.

Though this chapter addresses theonomy and its logical problem of evil, the mention of theonomy immediately suggests its radical opposite, Leibnizian Rationalism. It is the subject of chapter 3, but a word about it now in contrast to theonomy will help us understand both systems better. Gottfried Leibniz, unlike theonomists, held that everything happens in accord with the principle of sufficient reason. Thus, everything that is true of our universe is a necessary law; i.e., it had to be the way it is, for there is no adequate reason for it to be any other way than it is. For Leibniz, there is a certain order and logic inherent in things as they are which even God must obey; God dare not change a thing. Since there is a certain logic to the way things are, Leibniz believed that whatever is true of our world, or even possibly true, can be discovered by human reason apart from divine revelation. This is quite clearly a very different form of theism than theonomy. How does a problem of evil arise for a theonomous theology, and can the system solve it?

A BRIEF OVERVIEW OF THEONOMY

Historically, some philosophers have held some or all of theonomy's central notions. Descartes is one of the most noteworthy. Several of his letters to Mersenne (in particular, his letters of April 15, 1630; May 6, 1630; and May 27, 1630) show that he held this view of the universe. Moreover, Thomas Hobbes's writings exhibit this tendency as well. As to contemporary philosophers, P. T. Geach is one who holds theonomous views. Geach's *God and the Soul* especially echoes key theonomous ideas. At one point, Geach speaks of the relation of God's law to human moral law. He imagines someone who wonders why he should obey God's law. Geach's answer is a clear example of what a theonomist might say. He writes:

> But what if somebody asks "Why should I obey God's Law?" This is really an insane question. For Prometheus to defy Zeus made sense because Zeus had not made Prometheus and had only limited power over him. A defiance of an Almighty God is insane: it is like trying to cheat a man to whom your whole business is mortgaged and who you know is well aware of your attempts to cheat him, or again, as the prophet said, it is as if a stick tried to beat, or an axe to cut, the very hand that was wielding it. Nebuchadnezzar had it forced on his attention that only by God's favour did his wits hold together from one end of a blasphemous sentence to another—and so he saw that there was nothing for him but to bless and glorify the King of Heaven, who is able to abase those who walk in pride. To quote Hobbes again "God is King, though the nations be angry: and he that sitteth upon the cherubim, though the earth be moved. Whether men will or no they must be subject always to the divine power. By denying the existence or providence of God, men may shake off their ease, but not their yoke."
> This reasoning will not convince everybody; people may still say that it makes sense, given that there is a God, to defy him; but this is so only because, as Prichard said, you can no more make a man think than you can make a horse drink. A moral philosopher once said to me: "I don't think I am morally obliged to obey God unless God is good; and surely it is a synthetic proposition that God is good." I naturally asked him how he understood the proposition that God is good; he replied "Well, I have no considered view how it should be analysed; but provisionally I'd say it meant something like this: God is the sort of God whom I'd choose to be God if it

were up to me to make the choice." I fear he has never understood why I found the answer funny.

I shall be told by such philosophers that since I am saying not: It is your supreme moral duty to obey God, but simply: It is insane to set about defying an Almighty God, my attitude is plain power-worship. So it is: but it is worship of the Supreme power, and as such is wholly different from, and does not carry with it, a cringing attitude towards earthly powers. An earthly potentate does not compete with God, even unsuccessfully: he may threaten all manner of affliction, but only from God's hands can any affliction actually come upon us. If we fully realize this, we shall have such fear of God as destroys all earthly fear: "I will show you whom you shall fear," said Jesus Christ to his disciples.[2]

What do all these philosophers hold in common? As evident in Geach, they hold that the omnipotence, majesty, and transcendence of God are the fundamental facts about the universe. With this conception of God, the idea that someone could rationally deduce a standard of good and evil and then use it to sit in judgment of God's actions is both ludicrous and blasphemous. Moreover, God's revelation is the source of all knowledge of whatever ethical standards obtain in this universe. As for God's relation to these ethical norms, God could reveal that his actions exemplify the principles he has chosen, or he might even reveal that he is beyond good and evil (i.e., none of the rules of ethics apply to him). Consequently, anyone holding theonomy would be most presumptuous, to say the least, to complain or argue about the moral activities of this God.

Not only are some philosophers theonomists, but various theologians also hold this view. For example, the idea that humans might be allowed to argue with God about his morals or anything else is foreign to much of Orthodox Judaism. Moreover, any Jewish, Islamic, or Christian theologian who stresses above all else the utter transcendence and power of God holds views akin to theonomy.[3]

Might theonomy find any Scriptural support? At least some biblical passages can be interpreted so as to fit with theonomy. Two examples illustrate the point. One comes from the book of Job. Job suffered great pain and anguish, and he continually questioned God. Job's "comforters" had their theories, but when God finally answered Job (chapters 38–41), we learn that none of those ideas was right. God overwhelmed Job with a picture of his own power and majesty in comparison to Job's puniness. Job responded:

I know that Thou canst do all things,
And that no purpose of Thine can be thwarted.
"Who is this that hides counsel without knowledge?"
Therefore, I have declared that which I did not understand,
Things too wonderful for me, which I did not know (Job 42:2-3).

One way to understand this sees Job as saying that now he understands how powerful God is. Whatever he wants to do, he can do, and no one can stop him. But if that is true, Job was wrong to question whether this God was in control or whether he knew what he was doing. Job should have kept his mouth shut and submitted to the powerful hand of God. I am not suggesting that this is the correct way or even the only way to interpret this passage. My only point is that this interpretation surely sounds like theonomy.

Another example is Romans 9:19-21. In Romans 9 Paul discusses two types of election, election to privilege (9:1-5) and election to salvation (9:6ff.). He says God has a right to foreordain whomever he wishes to salvation or damnation. Paul then imagines an opponent's question: "If God ordains the sin and condemnation of the wicked, why then does he hold them morally responsible for doing what he decreed them to do?" (see Rom. 9:19). The stage is set for Paul to give a philosophical or theological dissertation on how to reconcile God's decree with man's moral responsibility for sin, but Paul doesn't offer that. Instead, he replies:

> On the contrary, who are you, O man, who answers back to God? The thing molded will not say to the molder, "Why did you make me like this," will it? Or does not the potter have a right over the clay, to make from the same lump one vessel for honorable use, and another for common use? (Rom. 9:20-21).

Now, one way to understand this (though not the only way) is that Paul is saying that we don't have a right to ask these questions, for they imply that God has done something wrong. God's in charge; we aren't. Our job is to be quiet and satisfied with whatever God does, not to question his ways. Such an interpretation of this passage is consistent with a theonomous theology.[4]

Both passages, then, can be interpreted as consistent with theonomy. One could argue that they teach that we have no right to haul an omnipotent God into the courtroom of human moral perceptions and put him on trial for what he tells us about his actions. Trying to put God on trial displays a ludicrously inflated view of our position as humans and a blasphemously low view of God's power and authority. All of this fits theonomy.

In considering various theonomous theologies, one realizes that there are two broad forms of theonomy. One claims that nothing whatsoever constrains God's will. Hence, if God wants, he can break the law of noncontradiction. Of course, the problem of evil in its logical form is about whether a given theology is internally consistent. Since this form of theonomy describes God as able to actualize contradictory states of affairs, logical consistency isn't important for it. This kind of theonomy isn't really of philosophical interest for those addressing the logical problem of evil.

There is, however, a second broad variety of theonomy according to which God cannot actualize contradictory states of affairs. Ethical rules (in fact, all knowledge) still depend on God's will, but God can't choose rules of ethics that contradict one another. All God's choices (ethical, epistemological, etc.) must obey the law of noncontradiction. This form of theonomy is philosophically interesting in relation to the logical problem of evil, a problem of logical consistency. Hence, this form is my focus in this chapter.

WILLIAM OF OCKHAM'S THEONOMOUS POSITION

Various medieval thinkers held theonomy, though at that time it was called voluntarism. Traditionally, William of Ockham is considered a voluntarist (in fact, one of the more famous ones). Some think he wasn't a voluntarist in all aspects of his philosophy, especially not in his ethics.[5] I do not intend to resolve that debate. However, I appeal to his writings, because many consider Ockham a voluntarist, and because his writings contain concepts that illustrate some of the central notions of theonomy.

Foundational Notions

Theonomy rests on several fundamental concepts. The starting point, at least for Ockham, seems to be the distinction between the *potentia absoluta* and the *potentia ordinata* of God. As Heiko Oberman suggests, in the nominalistic tradition, these ideas became key concepts for theological method and for understanding a number of dogmatic positions. The distinction between the two powers doesn't mean God acts sometimes with order and other times without it. It means that God can and has, in fact, decided to do certain things according to the laws which he *freely* establishes, i.e., *de potentia ordinata*. On the other hand, God has absolute power (*potentia absoluta*) to do anything that doesn't imply a contradiction, regardless of what he decides to do *de potentia ordinata*.[6]

This doesn't mean, according to theonomy, that once God ordains certain laws, he can arbitrarily violate them. Instead, it means that according to God's *potentia absoluta,* before any rules are chosen God is free to ordain any self-consistent set of rules. Once he chooses them, he acts in accord with them. If he wants to operate otherwise, then *de potentia absoluta* he may rescind the laws he has chosen, and ordain any other set of self-consistent laws. Once those new laws are in place, if God decides that all beings in the universe must follow them, then even he must obey them. Of course, God might reveal that the rules pertain to everyone but him, because he is above all obligation to

any rules. But we can only know this (or any other regulations God imple-
ments) once God tells us his decision. Gordon Leff helpfully explains the distinction between the two powers as follows:

> Now God's absolute power (*potentia absoluta*) had been used as far back
> as Peter Damian's time in the eleventh century to preserve God's freedom of
> action. It differed from his ordained power (*potentia ordinata*) in denoting
> God's omnipotence purely and simply. It was outside all space and time in
> that it was uncommitted to upholding any set order in the universe. Freedom
> to will was its only *raison d'etre*. In contrast, God's ordained power was
> directed to sustaining this world; it constituted God's law of creation, the
> eternal ordinance by which everything was governed. As given expression
> in the Bible and interpreted by the Church, it was immutable and irrevoca-
> ble. Thus while God's ordained power applied less to His own nature than
> to His creatures, His absolute power referred to Himself, and so, in the final
> analysis, it could override His ordinances. The latter were only a particular
> application of a wider authority: like an ambassador vested with certain
> rights they could be superseded.[7]

This distinction between God's powers suggests other theonomous
notions. First, theonomists insist that God be described as establishing *freely*
the laws by which he works. This means there was nothing about the set of
laws God chose that made or determined him to choose them. The only
restriction on God as he chose was that he had to function in a self-
consistent manner. Even God can't choose laws that contradict one another.

Second, God has revealed that the universe runs according to certain
laws. However, if he wants, *de potentia absoluta,* he can rescind those laws
and ordain another set. He will then reveal the new laws, and we must obey.
This is true for physical laws, the rules of ethics, and for rules in all other areas
of life.

A third principle stemming from the distinction of God's powers explains
it further. That principle is the theonomist's notion of God's freedom.
According to theonomy, God's will is absolutely free at all times. This doesn't
mean God can contradict what he has ordained, but only that he is absolutely
free to rescind his rules and will others. Moreover, theonomists also hold that
only God's free will is necessary. Anything other than God is radically contingent. This is true because everything depends on God as its cause, but also
because everything could have been (and still can be) anything else God
wants. Thus, only God's will is necessary in any sense.[8]

This may sound like God wills arbitrarily. However, Boehner says that in
Ockham's thinking, God, despite his freedom, has a will that is identical with
his intellect, wisdom, and love.[9] In other words, Ockham believed that God
had the attribute of simplicity according to which God's attributes are iden-

tical to one another and to his essence. Thus, while God can do anything that is logically possible, his goodness and intellect ensure that he won't choose or act arbitrarily either *de potentia absoluta* or *de potentia ordinata*. This is so, because God's will is identical with his intellect.[10]

Ockham's Ethics

The tenets of theonomy presented so far apply specifically to its metaphysics and epistemology. Before discussing how a problem of evil arises against a theonomous system, we must also understand its ethics. Ockham's ethics are a good example of theonomous ethics, and four basic principles are at the heart of his ethical theory.

First, Ockham held that there is only one immutable basis or standard of morality, namely, God's will. No matter what God commands, humans must obey.[11] As a result, no specific act or set of actions (such as the Ten Commandments) is the unchanging standard of morality, because God can change the rules anytime he wants. Thus, actions prohibited by the Ten Commandments may not always be evil. Certainly, they are not intrinsically so. God could just as easily have decided that humans should murder, steal, and commit adultery and that if they did, they would receive praise and rewards for those acts.[12] The implications of this view are rather startling. According to this account of ethics, rescuing a drowning swimmer isn't inherently good and pouring gasoline over a baby and lighting a match isn't in itself morally wrong. Nor is one of these acts intrinsically better or worse than the other. These acts are morally right or wrong only because God mandates or forbids them.

For most people, this is a shocking viewpoint, but it is thoroughly consistent with the basic mindset of a theonomous system. God is totally free to command us to do anything. To underscore this point Ockham wrote:

> By the very fact that God wills something it is right for it to be done. . . . Hence if God were to cause hatred of himself in anyone's will, that is, if he were to be the total cause of the act (he is, as it is, its partial cause), neither would that man sin nor would God; for God is not under any obligation, while man is not (in the case) obliged, because the act would not be in his own power.[13]

That is, if God wanted, he could order us to hate him, and even cause us to do so. It is hard to imagine exactly how we could obey this command, for obedience is a form of love. So, if we disobey the command to hate God, we would love him. If we obey the command, our obedience would be a form of love. Hence, it seems impossible to obey such a command no matter what we do. Nonetheless, Ockham was so intent on preserving God's freedom to choose any rules of ethics whatsoever that he claimed God could even ordain this rule.

Second, for a theonomous ethic there is only one obligation or precept of morality, and it isn't difficult to guess what it is. If God's will is the only basis of morality, then "Obey whatever God wills" is the only moral precept. We have no other moral obligation. Love of God is equated with obeying his will, for, as Ockham says, "To love God above all means to love whatever God wills to be loved."14 Thus, only by obedience can we prove our love for God, and, as Ockham explains, loving God is the only necessarily virtuous act:

> Thirdly I maintain that a necessarily virtuous act, in the sense explained above, is an act of will, since the act by which God is loved above all and for His own sake is such an act. For this act is virtuous in such a way that it cannot be vicious, nor can this act be caused by a created will without being virtuous. First, because everyone is bound (according to time and place) to love God above all, and consequently this act cannot be vicious; secondly, because this act is the first of all good acts.15

Third, according to this ethical theory, there is only one criterion for calling an act good or evil. What makes an act good is that God reveals that we must do it. Likewise, an act is evil because God reveals that he forbids it. The moral quality of every act depends on God's will that it be done or not be done, and nothing else.16 Thus, as Gabriel Biel, a philosopher in Ockham's tradition, argued, God's will has priority over any moral structure, for God doesn't will something because it is good or right. Something is good or right because God wills it.17 And, God is always free to change ethical rules at any time. As Ockham explains:

> Hatred of God, stealing, adultery, and the like, have sinful circumstances connected with them according to the generally accepted moral law, inasmuch as they are done by someone who is obligated by divine precept to the contrary, but as far as the absolute being of those acts is concerned, however, they may be performed by God without any sinful circumstances attached to them. . . .
> And were divine precepts standing to the contrary, such acts could not be meritoriously or well done by anyone because they cannot be done meritoriously unless they fall under the divine precept.18

What Ockham says here about acts could also be said of events, though Ockham doesn't. A clear implication of this criterion is that for theonomous ethics, all moral norms are contingent. God could, *de potentia absoluta,* change all precepts tomorrow. The only exception (the only necessary rule), of course, is the command to obey whatever God requires.

Fourth, theonomists claim that God has absolute freedom in every realm, including ethics. Humans are obligated to obey God's commands, and they sin if they don't. Only if someone is indebted to another and fails to meet his obligations, does he sin against that person. According to Ockham, God is obligated to no one, so he can't sin. Ockham affirms God's freedom in moral issues in the following way as he explains why God can't sin:

> I reply: A man never sins unless it is because he is bound to do what he does not do or because he does what he ought not to do. For this reason man becomes a debtor. However, God is not bound nor obligated to anyone as a debtor. And therefore he is not able to do what he ought not do, nor is able not to do what he ought to do.[19]

This needs clarification. In effect, Ockham is saying that God is beyond good and evil, i.e., moral rules don't apply to him at all, so he can do whatever he wants. In contrast, many theonomists hold that God must obey what he wills all rational beings, including himself, to do. If a theonomist tells us that God has obligated himself to follow his own rules, then that theonomist's theology (and his God) is in trouble only if his God reveals that he has disobeyed his own rules. In what follows I shall explain the problem this would create for a theonomous theology.[20]

THEONOMY'S PROBLEM OF EVIL

Given the preceding description of theonomy's metaphysics and ethics, how would a problem of evil in its logical form arise? Ockham never formulated a problem of evil, but from the principles I have presented it is possible to do so.

James King thinks theonomy's problem of evil might be stated as follows: Is it incompatible with (against) God's will (=evil) that God should have permitted evils to exist?[21] According to King, if this is the theonomist's problem of evil (and King thinks it is), then the very problem itself becomes a tautology, and thus, no problem at all. King thinks this interpretation "renders tautologous (and hence unanswerable) the *prima facie* valid question: Is it good to do God's will?"[22] Following King's line of reasoning, one could add that the *prima facie* meaningful question "Is it evil that there are evils?" also seems to be a meaningless tautology, because for a theonomist the question appears to mean "Is it against God's will that God has willed that evil be present in the universe?"

Despite King's claims, I think a legitimate non-tautologous problem of evil can arise for a theonomous theology. Once we see what that problem is, we see that questions like "Is it good to do God's will?" and "Is it evil that there are evils?" are neither serious problems nor meaningless tautologies for theonomy. One of King's major errors is that he apparently thinks the problem of evil for a theonomist focuses on what God has allowed to happen. Instead, the important issue is what God reveals about *his* own actions and how they relate to the moral law he has ordained. Moreover, if a logical inconsistency is going to arise, it must arise as an attack on the theonomist's system, not as an attack on God himself. King's general approach to the issue (as is true of many others) makes it sound too much like God is under attack by means of a problem of evil, when in fact it is a theological system that is under attack.23

What, then, is the logical problem for theonomy? One of the tenets of theonomy is that divine revelation is the source of all *a priori* knowledge. Hence, divine revelation is the source of our knowledge of whatever ethical norms are our obligation. Divine revelation is also our source of knowledge about whether or not God is good. God might reveal that he is beyond morality, i.e., no moral rules whatsoever obligate him. Hence, we can't call him good or evil, because those categories don't apply to him. If this is what God reveals, then a problem of evil can't arise within such a theonomous theology.

In contrast, God might instead reveal that he is subject to the specific moral norms he has ordained for this universe. If so, then a problem of evil can only attack a theonomous theology as follows: if God reveals 1) that he has ordained that all beings avoid certain actions (he has decided they are evil) and do others (he has decided they are good); 2) that his character and actions conform completely to that moral law; and yet 3) that he has done something that violates the moral law he has revealed, then clearly there is a problem of logical consistency. Not only would the scenario described create a problem of evil for theonomy, but it would also defeat that theonomous position. Remember that in a theonomous universe the one moral obligation is to obey God's will. In the situation before us, if God reveals that he disobeyed one of his own laws, then he is evil according to the ethics of theonomy.

Suppose, however, that the theonomist informs us that God has placed himself under the moral obligation of obeying whatever moral rules God has ordained for all moral beings. Suppose as well that God reveals that his actions have always conformed to the moral laws he ordained. Since he has never broken any of those rules, he has met the only moral rule he has obligated himself to follow. He is vindicated as an omnipotent and all-good God. Moreover, if this is the story the theonomist tells us about God, that story is internally consistent. Theonomy solves its logical problem of evil.

Some will object that this still leaves a lot of evil in the world, and it seems that God should be required to remove it. However, what God *should* do is what he *must* do, and removing evil is God's obligation only if he requires himself to do that. If he reveals that he is required to remove all moral and natural evil, and yet there are things in our world that God defines as evil, then he has failed to meet his moral obligations. He is either impotent or evil, and the theonomous theology that describes God in this way does fail to solve its logical problem of evil. But suppose that God hasn't obligated himself to remove all moral and natural evil (or even any of it), and suppose that he says that he has obeyed all the moral rules he has obligated himself to follow. If so, regardless of the kinds, varieties, and amounts of evil still present in our world, God is neither evil nor impotent. The theonomous theology just imagined can and does solve its logical problem of evil.

ASSESSMENT OF THEONOMY

Regardless of what one thinks of theonomy in general, it presents a very provocative conception of the universe. As to its handling of its problem of evil, everything depends on how the theologian describes God. If a given theonomist claims that God has revealed that he is beyond good and evil, then the existence of evil in our world creates no problem whatsoever for this theology. Since God isn't subject to human ethical theories or standards (in fact, there may be no moral rules of any sort that bind him), any complaint that he is morally deficient according to our moral rules is unfounded and misguided. So this kind of theonomous system is unharmed by the problem of evil.

In addition, if a different version of theonomy says God has revealed that he is bound by the moral rules he has ordained for us, and also informs us that he has never disobeyed any of those moral laws, then that theonomous system doesn't generate an insoluble problem of evil. Of course, if this version of theonomy adds that on one occasion God did break one of the rules he agreed to obey, then that system is internally inconsistent and can't solve its problem of evil. Of course, theonomists don't describe God and evil in such an internally inconsistent way. In sum, then, granting the theonomist's basic assumptions, it is possible to defend that theology's internal consistency. Theonomy can solve its logical problem of evil.

Should all theists, then, embrace theonomy as their theology? Some aspects of it are certainly attractive. Those who believe that the basic fact of the universe is the existence of an omnipotent creator who reveals that he has laid down a set of moral laws for the universe will find affinity with theonomy. Moreover, any who think it is both ludicrous and blasphemous to argue with God over matters of right and wrong or even to accuse him of moral wrongdoing because of any feature of our world will also be drawn to theonomy.

There are, however, reasons to reject theonomy as a whole, despite its ability to solve its problem of evil in its logical form. For example, one might reject its metaphysic in favor of a more rationalistic one. Or, one may disagree with its conception of God's freedom and power. Or, one might reject theonomy's account of ethics. If one holds that God wills that we do something because he knows it is right, that person will likely reject theonomy's ethics. Moreover, many would find repulsive and insupportable the view that there is no intrinsic difference between the rightness or wrongness of pouring gasoline on a child and igniting the gas, on the one hand, and rescuing a drowning man, on the other.[24]

In my opinion, theonomy incorporates both an inadequate metaphysic and an inadequate ethic. Thus, I cannot defend it as a correct theology. However, those complaints in no way suggest that theonomy succumbs to the logical problem of evil, a problem of *internal* inconsistency. Theonomy can and does solve that problem. If so, then even at this early stage of our investigation, we have shown that Mackie's claim that there is no rational way for *any* theist to solve a problem of evil is false.

3

Leibniz and the Problem of Evil

Leibnizian Rationalism is an extreme form of rationalism which is the opposite of theonomy. Gottfried Leibniz held that whatever is morally as well as logically possible is ascertainable by pure reason alone apart from divine revelation of God's will. Logic is clearly prior to theology in his system.

Though few in our day adopt Leibniz's system or his theodicy, he is still worthy of consideration. His approach to the problem of evil is important historically. Moreover, his system gives us an example of what an extreme rationalistic position looks like. As to that rationalistic metaphysic, Leibniz held that the universe runs totally on rational bases and that its creator operates according to rational calculations in everything he does. In a Leibnizian universe God exists by logical necessity, for his nature is such that it is impossible for him not to exist. The primary activity of this God is to pick the best world out of an infinite number of contingent possible worlds. Leibniz's God always operates according to the principle of sufficient reason in whatever he does, so he wouldn't create a possible world without a sufficient reason for doing so.

This certainly differs from theonomy! In a theonomous universe, God determines by his free choice what is and isn't possible, chooses which possibilities will be actual, and then reveals his choices so that we can know what he requires of us. In contrast, Leibniz believed that the possibilities already existed before God made any decision about which ones to actualize. God couldn't create the possibilities; he had to choose from among those that were already there. Whereas in some theonomous systems God's choice of rules for us and actions for himself could be arbitrary, in Leibniz's theology God's decisions are never arbitrary. They are always based on the principle of sufficient reason.[1] Since there must always be a sufficient reason for what God does (otherwise he wouldn't do it), human reason, apart from divine revelation, should be able discover that reason and ascertain what God would choose. Leibniz believed this to be so.

Leibniz believed that, given the principle of sufficient reason, there is a best possible world. This is confirmed by the fact that God created a world. God would only do so if there were a best possible world; he would have no sufficient reason to create a world less than the best. Moreover, Leibniz believed that God didn't have the option to refrain from choosing a world. God could forego creating only if he had a sufficient reason for doing so. But since there is a world, we know he had a sufficient reason for creating, and that reason could only be that our world is the best possible world. Hence, Leibniz believed that God had to create.[2]

Can Leibniz's system generate a problem of evil, and if so, how does he solve it? In this chapter I shall explain how a problem of evil arises for Leibniz's system and how he answers it. Though I believe his theology as a whole is inadequate, I shall argue that its inadequacy isn't an inability to solve its problem of evil.

THE LEIBNIZIAN SYSTEM

Leibniz on Evil

Five basic concepts are crucial for understanding Leibniz's system in general and his theodicy in particular. The first is his account of evil, which really brings us to the heart of his theodicy. Leibniz distinguished three kinds of evil: moral, physical, and metaphysical. He explained each as follows:

> Evil may be taken metaphysically, physically and morally. *Metaphysical evil* consists in mere imperfection, *physical evil* in suffering, and *moral evil* in sin. Now although physical evil and moral evil be not necessary, it is enough that by virtue of the eternal verities they be possible.[3]

According to Leibniz, metaphysical evil is simply finitude or lack of being. This isn't *moral* imperfection, but ontological imperfection or finitude. God, of course, isn't evil in any sense of the word. He isn't metaphysically evil, because his being is compossible (i.e., can exist together) with any and all possibility, and in that sense he is unlimited power to be; his actuality is in no way diminished or threatened by anything possible or actual.[4]

In the cited portion above (numbered as note 3), Leibniz says that moral and physical evil need only be possible, not necessary. He later adds the empirical premise that such evil actually exists. However, from the standpoint of his theodicy, it is only necessary that moral and physical evil be possible for there to be what Leibniz calls the best of all possible worlds.

As for moral evil (evil of will), Leibniz defines it as willing less than the maximum, metaphysically speaking. Moral evil flows from metaphysical evil, i.e., because humans are finite, they are able to fall into sin. In answering the question of evil's source, Leibniz explains the notion of metaphysical evil and its relation to moral evil as follows:

> The answer is, that it must be sought in the ideal nature of the creature, in so far as this nature is contained in the eternal verities which are in the understanding of God, independently of his will. For we must consider that there is an *original imperfection in the creature* before sin, because the creature is limited in its essence; whence ensues that it cannot know all, and that it can deceive itself and commit other errors.[5]

According to Leibniz, physical evil in an object indicates that its physical nature hasn't been realized without defect. Physical evil results either from moral evil or from its usefulness in accomplishing a greater happiness in the end.[6] Of course, since the greatest metaphysical good is the greatest compossibility of being, for the sake of that compossibility there must be at least some moral and physical evil in the universe.[7] Thus, both moral and physical *evil* ultimately stem from metaphysical evil. Moreover, moral *good* (willing the maximum metaphysically) and physical *good* (full realization of an object's nature without defect) stem from metaphysical goodness (perfection or fullness of being).

Though this may sound like a rather strange conception of ethics, Leibniz's account of "good" and "evil" follows the Platonic and Aristotelian metaphysical traditions. In those traditions, "good" and "evil" are *pros hen* (Greek for "toward one") equivocal terms. To use a term equivocally is to use it in multiple senses. The term "good" has different senses in the following sentences: 1) "Saving someone's life is a good deed"; 2) "It isn't good to drive with an expired driver's license"; 3) "If you want to avoid getting sunburned at the beach, it would be a good idea to wear some sun block lotion"; and 4) "Many people own a Mercedes Benz automobile, because they think it's a very good car." All of these sentences use the term "good," but each uses it in a distinct sense. "Good" is used in a moral sense in sentence 1), in a legal sense in 2), in a prudential sense (good prudent advice) in 3), and in a functional sense in 4). "Good," then, can be used in various senses, but which of the four senses noted is the primary one? For Leibniz and the tradition he follows, none of the four is the primary sense. Rather, these four distinct senses ultimately point toward one primary sense. That sense for Leibniz is its metaphysical sense.[8] Leibniz considered good a transcendental attribute of being (*ens*). Consequently, he believed that the fundamental sense of "good" is metaphysical. From his perspective, the greater the order and variety of being in a thing, the more metaphysically good it is.[9]

In applying this notion of good and evil to the problem of evil, we can begin to sense how Leibniz will handle that problem. Consider the following three possible worlds: 1) World 1 has moral and natural good, but neither moral nor natural evil; 2) World 2 contains moral and natural evil, but neither moral nor natural good; 3) World 3 has both moral good and evil and natural good and evil. Of these three possible worlds, which is the best, metaphysically speaking? Clearly World 3 is the richest, for, in comparing these three possible worlds, it contains the greatest number and variety of existing things. As noted above, Leibniz held that God must create, and he must create the best possible world. When we add this to the fact that Leibniz means *metaphysically* best by the phrase "best of all possible worlds," it is clear why the best of all possible worlds can't contain only moral and natural good or only moral and natural evil; it must contain both.

Necessity, Contingency, and Logical Possibility

Leibniz's views about necessary and contingent truths and logical possibility are essential to his system and its theodicy. By necessity, Leibniz didn't mean that if something is foreseen, it can't fail to exist. Instead, a necessary truth is "that whereof the contrary is impossible or implies contradiction."[10] This means that a necessary truth is true under every circumstance or true for all possible worlds[11] (the concept of a possible world will be explained shortly). On the other hand, a contingent truth is true of at least some world (perhaps the actual world), but not true of all possible worlds.[12]

Leibniz's notion of possibility is tied up with his concept of necessity. According to Leibniz, anything is possible which doesn't imply a contradiction. Whatever implies a contradiction is impossible.[13] Hence, whatever doesn't violate the law of noncontradiction is possible, i.e., logically possible. For example, round squares are logically impossible, whereas unicorns and Martians are logically possible. As to propositions, ones that are logically possible may be either true or false. If they are true, they are either necessary or contingent truths. If a proposition is a necessary truth, it is true in every possible world. If it is contingently true, it is true in some possible world, but not in every one.

The concepts of necessity, contingency, and possibility may seem very remote from theodicy, but they are very important to Leibniz's system, for when one asks what God could do about evil, one must clarify what is logically possible for God to do. Moreover, one must ascertain whether existence of moral and physical evil is necessary or contingent. If these evils are necessary, God couldn't avoid them without totally refusing to create any world. If they are contingent, God could avoid them. One must then explain why God didn't create some other possible world that omits those evils. As we shall see, Leibniz admits that moral and physical evil are contingent, but he then explains why a world with just those evils in the amount present in our world must exist.

Metaphysical and Moral Necessity, and the Absolutely Arbitrary

In his *Theodicy*, Leibniz distinguishes things that are metaphysically necessary, things that are morally necessary, and things that are absolutely arbitrary. Metaphysical or geometrical necessity corresponds to Leibniz's definition of necessity already presented. Moral necessity is the necessity that comes from the free choice of wisdom in relation to envisioned ends. Strictly speaking, something that is morally necessary in Leibniz's sense is contingent, i.e., wisdom dictates it, but one might still choose otherwise. On the other hand, something that is metaphysically necessary is necessary, i.e., true of all possible worlds. Something that is completely arbitrary depends on an indifference of equipoise. This means that nothing decisively inclines the agent toward it or against it. If an agent chooses arbitrarily, it would be impossible to explain the sufficient reason for the choice. Leibniz emphatically held that something absolutely arbitrary is imaginable but cannot exist.[14] Leibniz explained these ideas as follows:

> But provided that it is understood that necessity and possibility, taken metaphysically and strictly, depend solely upon this question, whether the object in itself or that which is opposed to it implies contradiction or not; and that one takes into account that contingency is consistent with the inclinations, or reasons which contribute towards causing determination by the will; provided that one knows how to distinguish clearly between necessity and determination or certainty, between metaphysical necessity, which admits of no choice, presenting only one single object as possible, and moral necessity, which constrains the wisest to choose the best; finally, provided that one is rid of the chimera of complete indifference, which can only be found in the books of philosophers, and on paper (for they cannot even conceive the notion in their heads, or prove its reality by an example in things) one will easily escape from a labyrinth whose unhappy Daedalus was the human mind.[15]

Possible Existents

The passages about metaphysical and moral evil (quoted above) mention the "eternal verities." That raises the idea of concepts of possibles. According to

Leibniz, there exist in God's mind what Leibniz calls forms or ideas (we would say "concepts") of everything that doesn't imply a logical contradiction. So, a concept of a possible is an idea (eternally present in God's mind) of something that doesn't imply a logical contradiction. The thing conceived is possible in two respects: 1) it doesn't imply a contradiction (hence, it is thinkable), and 2) it isn't actual, but could become actual if God chooses to actualize it. Though the *concepts* of possible things exist eternally in God's mind, the *things* of which they are concepts need never exist in an actual world and won't unless God actualizes them. In explaining how evil even happened to be a possible constituent of the actual world, Leibniz summarizes what I've just presented as follows:

> Evil springs rather from the *Forms* themselves in their detached state, that is, from the ideas that God has not produced by an act of his will, any more than he thus produced numbers and figures, and all possible essences which one must regard as eternal and necessary; for they are in the divine understanding. God is therefore not the author of essences in so far as they are only possibilities. But there is nothing actual to which he has not decreed and given existence . . . [16]

Note here Leibniz's insistence that God didn't create the concepts of the possibles or possible essences. They are coeternal with his own existence. In Leibniz's thinking, creation is the actualization of possibilities. God knows all the possibilities there are, but the possibilities are eternal by the nature of things and not themselves created. If Leibniz held that God existed first and then sometime in eternity past created the realm of possibles, we might reasonably ask why he created the concept of evil. Leibniz could answer that since God knows and can conceive of everything logically possible, he had to create the concept of evil, since it isn't logically contradictory. Still, we could justly accuse God of being involved in some way as the source of evil, since he did create (for whatever reason) the concept of evil. By claiming that God didn't create the possibles, Leibniz forestalled that objection.

At this point, the difference between Leibniz and theonomy is noteworthy. Theonomists would say that God exists first and then creates whatever verities (forms) he wants. They are not coeternal with God. A Leibnizian might accuse theonomy's God of being guilty for creating the concept of evil. Theonomists would reply that in their system God can do whatever he wants so long as it doesn't contradict anything else he does or chooses, and creating the concept of evil produces no such contradiction. Thus, according to theonomy, God is prior to the possibles, and he creates them. In Leibniz's rationalistic theology, a God prior to the possibles would produce problems for his philosophical theology. Leibniz avoids such problems by holding to the coeternality of the forms and God.

God's inability, according to Leibniz, to create the possibles may in turn draw fire from the theonomist. The theonomist might claim that Leibniz limits God's freedom too severely, and hence his views should be rejected. Of course, this in no way shows Leibniz's views to be self-contradictory. In fact, all it does is offer a good example of two conflicting metaphysical systems coming head to head. Certainly, Leibniz's God's power is limited, *if theonomy's truth is presupposed*. But why should a Leibnizian do that?

Leibniz would probably respond to this objection that God's power is simply power to actualize possibilities. The eternal existence of the possibles in no way limits that power. The only limitation on God's power is that he can't actualize self-contradictory states of affairs, but as we saw in chapter 2, even many theonomists grant that. Of course, God did actualize everything that already exists, so it hardly limits his power significantly to say he can't contradict what he has already done. Theonomists may still think all of this limits God too much, but that merely shows they have a different view of divine power than Leibniz does. It in no way proves Leibniz's doctrine wrong.

Leibniz held that concepts of possible existents have various characteristics. Understanding those qualities helps clarify his idea of a possible world. First, Leibniz held that every concept of a possible is complete in itself. For example, the concepts of the Adam and/or Eve who were created include them as sinning. Adam isn't one possible concept and Adam's sin another which God just happened to unite when he gave Adam existence. Instead, in order for God to actualize Adam at all, God had to create the Adam who sins, for the concept of *that* Adam involves him as sinning.[17] Of course, there are numerous other possible worlds in which counterparts to Adam and Eve exist. The concepts of at least some (perhaps many) of those counterparts don't include them as sinning. Although *we* might say that those possible Adams and Eves are really the same persons as the Adam and Eve God actualized, Leibniz would say they aren't identical to the Adam and Eve God actualized. Their concepts may be like the concepts of the Adam and Eve God actualized, but they differ in at least one important respect. Their concepts don't include Adam and Eve as sinning. E. M. Curley relates the idea of a concept being complete in itself to contingency as follows:

> The concept of Adam, if it is to be an individual concept, i.e., if it is to secure uniqueness of reference to a *possible* individual, must be a complete concept, in the sense that it must assign one or the other of each pair of contradictory predicates to the subject. And if it is a complete concept, then the ques-

tion of the truth or falsity of any predication about that possible individual must be purely a question of logic.[18]

We must not misunderstand this. Leibniz held that every concept of a possible is complete in itself, but that doesn't mean that every concept includes existence. Moreover, God can't change a concept of a possible, but he can give existence to that which is only in the realm of possibility. Furthermore, Leibniz held that actualizing a possible existent in no way changes anything included in its concept. Leibniz summarizes these ideas as follows:

> Since, moreover, God's decree consists solely in the resolution he forms, after having compared all possible worlds, to choose that one which is the best, and bring it into existence together with all that this world contains, by means of the all-powerful word *Fiat,* it is plain to see that this decree changes nothing in the constitution of things: God leaves them just as they were in the state of mere possibility, that is, changing nothing either in their essence or nature, or even in their accidents, which are represented perfectly already in the idea of this possible world. Thus that which is contingent and free remains no less so under the decrees of God than under his prevision.[19]

A final characteristic of a possible is that any possible existent is compossible with some other possibles, but not with all. Individual concepts are compossible if they are capable of joint realization. Two concepts are jointly realizable if they don't logically contradict each other. Compossibility is especially important for the determination of a whole interconnected world. According to Leibniz, God saw all things in their possible interconnections before he decided to actualize any particular set of compossible concepts.[20]

Possible World

With these features of concepts of possible existents in hand, we can understand Leibniz's notion of a possible world. He writes, "I call 'World' the whole succession and the whole agglomeration of all existent things, lest it be said that several worlds could have existed in different times and different places."[21] If the actual world is the whole succession and agglomeration of all *existing* things, then a *possible* world is the agglomeration of a set of compossible possibles which hasn't been actualized. According to Leibniz, only one world is actual, but there is "an infinitude of possible worlds,"[22] since there is an infinite number of ways of arranging possibles into possible worlds.

In sum, Leibniz held that there is an infinite number of contingent finite possible worlds. The notion of a possible world is explained above. To say that these worlds are finite means that each world with its "history" doesn't contain an infinite amount of objects, actions, events, etc., for to put into one world an infinite number of items would conjoin items that contradict one another. These possible worlds are contingent in that they must be brought into existence if they are to be actual, and they depend on someone else (God) for their existence.

How can there be an infinite number of these possible worlds? It isn't hard to imagine, in that even the smallest change from one world generates another possible world. So, for example, in our world, I wear contact lenses. A second possible world is identical to our world except that I need no corrective eyewear; in fact, I never need eye correction of any sort in that world. In a third possible world, I need no corrective eyewear from the age of forty to the end of my life, because I undergo laser surgery on my eyes. A fourth differs from the previous three in that I wear glasses but can't wear contact lenses. We can imagine similar variations for every characteristic of every person who ever lives, for every act in a given possible world, for every event and every person existing in a particular world. The number of possible worlds multiplies quickly to infinity.

Though Leibniz believed that there is an infinite number of these possible worlds, he also held that one of them is the best of all possible worlds. He further believed that God must create a world and that he must choose the best world. If a given world were not the best, there wouldn't be a sufficient reason for God to actualize it.

LEIBNIZ'S PROBLEM OF EVIL AND HIS THEODICY

How does a philosophical/theological problem of evil in its logical form arise in Leibniz's system? The answer appeals to both his metaphysics and his ethics. According to the former, God can't refuse to create; he must create a world, and it must be the best. According to Leibniz's ethics, the primary sense of "good," "evil," "better," and "best" is metaphysical, not moral. The metaphysically best world incorporates the greatest number and variety of existing things compossible. Leibniz held that if God doesn't fulfill his obligation to create the best world, he is *morally* reprehensible.

Given these metaphysical and ethical notions, the problem of evil for Leibniz revolves around the following question: Has God created the best, metaphysically speaking, of all possible worlds? If so, then God is morally good, regardless of the amount of moral and physical evil in the world. If not, he is evil.

Can Leibniz solve his problem of evil? I believe he can and does, and in what follows, I want to present in some detail Leibniz's solution. I begin with

Leibniz's understanding of what he needed to do to defend his system's God. Leibniz decided to defend his system by handling several interrelated issues. Theologians usually address a problem of evil only in terms of God's relation to evil, but Leibniz intended to harmonize what reason and revelation teach about evil in relation to both God *and* man.[23] He explained his task as follows:

> The *difficulties* are distinguishable into two classes. The one kind springs from man's freedom, which appears incompatible with the divine nature; and nevertheless freedom is deemed necessary, in order that man may be deemed guilty and open to punishment. The other kind concerns the conduct of God, and seems to make him participate too much in the existence of evil, even though man be free and participate also therein. And this conduct appears contrary to the goodness, the holiness and the justice of God, since God co-operates in evil as well physical as moral, and co-operates in each of them both morally and physically.[24]

Leibniz's strategy here is very interesting. The second set of problems relates to the theological/philosophical problem of evil that confronts his system. The first set is often handled as a separate problem, the problem of how human freedom and moral responsibility for sin can be upheld in light of the divine predestining decree. The double task of dealing with both sets of issues permeates Leibniz's whole work. Actually, the two sets of problems needn't be discussed together, but theologians who believe that God's providential decree includes our actions typically see these two sets of problems as interrelated. Some of these theologians use the free will defense to answer their problem of evil, and when they do, that often raises issues in the first group of difficulties mentioned.[25]

As we shall see, Leibniz accounts for moral evil in terms of human free will, but that isn't his main answer to the problem of evil. In truth, Leibniz offers a kind of double theodicy using the free will defense against the problem of moral evil, but offering his best of all possible worlds theodicy as his primary answer to the problem of evil. As we also shall see, Leibniz also has some thoughts about natural evil, but they are hardly developed enough to call them a defense or theodicy.

In understanding Leibniz's theodicy, we must know what Leibniz saw as God's purposes in creation. Leibniz raises the objection of one of his opponents that since people have abused free will, and since God knew they would, God could have saved them much misery if he had created them without free will. If God wanted to make us as happy as possible, he wouldn't have given us free will.[26] In response, Leibniz explains God's purpose in creation:

... the author is still presupposing that false maxim advanced as the third, stating that the happiness of rational creatures is the sole aim of God. If that were so, perhaps neither sin nor unhappiness would ever occur, even by concomitance. God would have chosen a sequence of possibles where all these evils would be excluded. But God would fail in what is due to the universe, that is, in what he owes to himself.[27]

This offers an initial glimpse of one answer Leibniz won't use to defend his God. Some, adopting a utilitarian ethic, say God is either not as good or not as powerful as supposed, because he hasn't made things so as to produce the greatest amount of happiness possible for man. In reply, many theists, thinking they must answer the problem of evil a utilitarian might pose, have felt obliged to show that our world truly is the happiest possible place for humankind.

In contrast, Leibniz clearly rejects a utilitarian ethic and any problem of evil that would arise by adopting such an ethic, for he says that human happiness isn't God's chief aim in creation. God has another purpose, which I'll fully explain when presenting Leibniz's theodicy. By fulfilling that purpose, God might also produce a universe which is the happiest for us. However, since Leibniz didn't hold utilitarian ethics, he wasn't particularly concerned about whether human happiness is maximized.

What, then, is God's purpose, and by what principles does he operate to achieve it? As to the latter question, Leibniz held that God operates according to the principle of sufficient reason. That is, God doesn't act from indifference or arbitrariness, but always has a sufficient reason for what he does. Moreover, that sufficient reason will always be whatever God rationally determines as the best, and whatever that is, God must do it. Leibniz explains:

> For either God will act through a vague indifference and at random, or again he will act on caprice or through some other passion, or finally he must act through a prevailing inclination of reason which prompts him to the best. But passions, which come from the confused perception of an apparent good, cannot occur in God; and vague indifference is something chimerical. It is therefore only the strongest reason that can regulate God's choice. It is an imperfection in our freedom that makes us capable of choosing evil instead of good, a greater evil instead of the lesser evil, the lesser good instead of the greater good. That arises from the appearances of good and evil, which deceive us; whereas God is always prompted to the true and the greatest good, that is, to the absolutely true good, which he cannot fail to know.[28]

God's actions, then, are always rationally determined and never arbitrary. Moreover, by his wisdom he always knows what is best, and he does it.[29]

As to God's purpose in creation, Leibniz writes:

> In truth God, in designing to create the world, purposed solely to manifest
> and communicate his perfections in the way that was most efficacious, and
> most worthy of his greatness, his wisdom, and his goodness. But that very
> purpose pledged him to consider all the actions of creatures while still in the
> state of pure possibility, that he might form the most fitting plan.[30]

Thus, God considered carefully how best to create the world so as to accomplish his purpose of best manifesting his perfections. In this he, of course, was moved by moral necessity (not metaphysical necessity) to choose the best. This brings us to the heart of Leibniz's theodicy.

Leibniz believed that when God decided to create, he decided on a whole world at once. Since Leibniz held that the concept of a possible individual contains everything true of that individual, including everything true of that person's relationships, God couldn't create a few individual possibles in isolation from all other possibles to which they relate. Because Leibniz held that each monad mirrors all of reality, if God actualizes anything, he must actualize a whole possible world.[31] Leibniz states:

> Thus God's pronouncement concerns the whole sequence at the same time;
> he simply decrees its existence. In order to save other men, or in a different
> way, he must needs choose an altogether different sequence, seeing that all
> is connected in each sequence. In this conception of the matter, which is that
> most worthy of the All-wise, all whose actions are connected together to the
> highest possible degree, there would be only one total decree, which is to cre-
> ate such a world. This total decree comprises equally all the particular
> decrees, without setting one of them before or after another.[32]

God chose the best from the infinite number of contingent possible worlds. Since Leibniz conceived of being as good in itself, a Leibnizian God who refrained from choosing any world at all couldn't himself be metaphysically perfect, and since moral necessity dictates that the wisest chooses the best, if God chose less than the best he would be morally reprehensible. Leibniz claimed that God chose the whole sequence of things at once, but how did God determine the best world? Leibniz's explanation of how God made his decision portrayed God as a great mathematician mentally scanning all possible worlds and calculating the best. Leibniz writes:

> The infinity of possibles, however great it may be, is no greater than that of
> the wisdom of God, who knows all possibles. One may even say that if this
> wisdom does not exceed the possibles extensively, since the objects of the
> understanding cannot go beyond the possible, which in a sense is alone intel-
> ligible, it exceeds them intensively, by reason of the infinitely infinite com-
> binations it makes thereof, and its many deliberations concerning them. The
> wisdom of God, not content with embracing all the possibles, penetrates
> them, compares them, weighs them one against the other, to estimate their

degrees of perfection or imperfection, the strong and the weak, the good and the evil. It goes even beyond the finite combinations, it makes of them an infinity of infinites, that is to say, an infinity of possible sequences of the universe, each of which contains an infinity of creatures. By this means the divine Wisdom distributes all the possibles it had already contemplated separately, into so many universal systems which further compares the one with the other. The result of all these comparisons and deliberations is the choice of the best from among all these possible systems, which wisdom makes in order to satisfy goodness completely; and such is precisely the plan of the universe as it is.[33]

According to Leibniz, then, God has the intelligence to know what is the best, and he, after deliberating on the matter, chose it. Throughout his *Theodicy* Leibniz maintained that the world God chose is the best world possible and couldn't be better. If there were a better world, God most assuredly would have chosen it, but since he didn't, that proves ours is the best possible world.[34]

Now, it is possible that because of the infinite number of possible interconnections among the objects and events in a given world, the best possible world *could* contain moral and physical evil. In fact, in my explanation of metaphysical good and evil, we saw that a world with the greatest variety and number of existing things is better than one with less. Since a world with both moral and natural good and evil is metaphysically richer (and such a world is compossible) than one with only good, it is clear why Leibniz's best possible world must contain moral and natural evil. By observation, we also note the empirical fact of evil in our world. Combined with Leibniz's insistence that ours is the best possible world, this means that Leibniz held that it is an empirical fact that the best possible world contains evil. Still, moral necessity dictated that God choose as he did; had he not done so, he would have sinned. Leibniz explains:

> God makes of matter the most excellent of all possible machines; he makes of spirits the most excellent of all governments conceivable; and over and above all that, he establishes for their union the most perfect of all harmonies, according to the system I have proposed. Now since physical evil and moral evil occur in this perfect work, one must conclude . . . that *otherwise a still greater evil would have been altogether inevitable.* This great evil would be that God would have chosen ill if he had chosen otherwise than he has chosen. It is true that God is infinitely powerful; but his power is indeterminate, goodness and wisdom combined determine him to produce the best.[35]

Contemporaries of Leibniz (and many after his time) thought it laughable that he believed our world to be the best of all possible worlds.[36] With all of its moral and physical evil, how could our world be the best possible? The key, of course, is what Leibniz means by "best." He seems to offer three answers as to why our world is best, but his explanation does clarify his point. His first answer (and this is really what he means by "best world") is that it doesn't matter if the world has moral and physical evil as long as the world is metaphysically the best. Leibniz writes:

> Now since everything resolves itself into this greatest perfection, we return to my law of the best. For perfection includes not only the *moral good* and the *physical good* of intelligent creatures, but also the good which is purely *metaphysical,* and concerns also creatures devoid of reason. It follows that the evil that is in rational creatures happens only by concomitance, not by antecedent will but by a consequent will, as being involved in the best possible plan; and the metaphysical good which includes everything makes it necessary sometimes to admit physical evil and moral evil, as I have already explained more than once.[37]

Clearly, for Leibniz, the best world is the one which is the richest metaphysically, and that just means it must contain both moral and natural good *and* evil, not just good. In fact, the greatest amount of these kinds of evil that is compossible with the greatest amounts of moral and natural good is best.

Some might claim that God should have created all this variety of being without including evil. Leibniz has two responses. First, he would remind us that anything as possible is a complete thing, so if God wanted to actualize some possible existent without the evil contained in its concept, he couldn't. He could actualize a counterpart which didn't contain evil, but if he decided to actualize the possible itself, he couldn't avoid the evil. God isn't responsible for evil being present in the concept, nor can he remove it from the concept.

Hearing this, one might wonder why God didn't actualize only those possibles which contain no evil in their concept. The answer is that for God to create that world, he would have to actualize much less being than he did, but then, the world created wouldn't be the metaphysically best. As less than metaphysically best, it wouldn't display God's perfections adequately. Such a world would reflect negatively on God's moral goodness.

Leibniz's second answer to why the best of all possible worlds contains moral and physical evil is that the best world is the best in toto, but not necessarily in its parts. Leibniz explains:

> What is deceptive in this subject, as I have already observed, is that one feels an inclination to believe that what is the best in the whole is also the best possible in each part. One reasons thus in geometry, when it is a question *de maximis et minimis.* If the road from A to B that one proposes to take is the shortest possible, and if this road passes by C, then the road from A to

C, part of the first, must also be the shortest possible. But the inference from *quantity* to *quality* is not always right, any more than that which is drawn from equals to similars. . . .

This difference between quantity and quality appears also in our case. The part of the shortest way between two extreme points is also the shortest way between the extreme points of this part; but the part of the best Whole is not of necessity the best that one could have made of this part. For the part of a beautiful thing is not always beautiful, since it can be extracted from the whole, or marked out within the whole in an irregular manner.[38]

Leibniz's third answer as to why there is moral and physical evil in the best of all possible worlds centers around the notion of total harmony. Leibniz claimed that "God wills order and good; but it happens sometimes that what is disorder in the part is order in the whole."[39] Many philosophers and theologians have said this about evil, i.e., when you look at evil apart from the whole plan and order of the universe, it looks like something is gravely amiss in the universe. However, if we could only see God's total plan, we would see how this little portion of evil isn't actually evil, for it promotes good in God's total plan and total creation.

This is quite similar to Leibniz's second response, but builds on it. Leibniz's second answer is that this is the best world as a whole but not necessarily in all its parts. His third answer says that even the parts shouldn't be viewed negatively, for they all contribute to the order and good of the whole.

Let me summarize the main points presented so far. Leibniz demonstrated from his metaphysical views 1) that there is a necessary and perfect being, 2) that this being must create the best of all contingent finite possible worlds, for the principle of sufficient reason demands that no other world exist, and 3) that it is at least possible that the best of all contingent possible worlds contains moral and physical evil. In addition, there is an empirical claim 4) that the world God chose actually contains moral and physical evil, but since God's benevolence is defined in terms of doing whatever is metaphysically best, the truth of 3) and 4) poses no problem for God's perfection. For Leibniz, then, as long as God actualizes the metaphysically richest of all possible worlds, metaphysical and moral goodness *in God* are compatible with moral and physical evil *in the world*. Since Leibniz assures us that God did create the best world, he solves his system's theological/philosophical problem of evil in its logical form.

Leibniz could have ended the discussion here, for his best of all possible worlds theodicy renders his theology internally consistent. However, he decided to offer a further justification for specific evils beyond his claim that they are part of the metaphysically best plan. Essential to understanding these further answers to his system's problems of moral and physical evil is his distinction between God's antecedent and consequent wills. According to Leibniz, God's will consists in the inclination to do something in proportion to the good it contains. That will is called antecedent when it is detached and considers each good apart from every other good or evil.[40] God's consequent will refers to what he has determined to do after considering each good and evil in relation to every other good and evil.[41] With this distinction in mind, we turn to Leibniz's discussion of moral evil.

Leibniz was keenly aware that some might say that since God, in actualizing an individual substance, creates an essence from which all of that substance's actions follow, God is responsible for the moral evil produced by those beings. Leibniz's answer seems, on the one hand, 1) to leave metaphysical considerations and turn to moral ones, and on the other hand, 2) to be an implicit version of the free will defense. Let me support these two claims. In regard to moral evil Leibniz writes:

> Concerning sin or moral evil, although it happens very often that it may serve as a means of obtaining good or of preventing another evil, it is not this that renders it a sufficient object of the divine will or a legitimate object of a created will. It must only be admitted or *permitted* in so far as it is considered to be a certain consequence of an indispensable duty: as for instance if a man who was determined not to permit another's sin were to fail of his own duty, or as if an officer on guard at an important post were to leave it, especially in time of danger, in order to prevent a quarrel in the town between two soldiers of the garrison who wanted to kill each other.[42]

This certainly doesn't sound like a metaphysical explanation, but rather a claim using moral concepts. Thus, when Leibniz speaks of God's actualizing a whole world, he defends God by appealing to metaphysical issues (though in Leibniz's system, as we have seen, metaphysical good and evil are moral matters), but when he speaks of specific items in that world, he turns to exclusively ethical ones. This blending of issues (and defenses) is evident in the section following the above cited passage. Leibniz summarizes his views as follows:

> But in relation to God nothing is open to question, nothing can be opposed to *the rule of the best,* which suffers neither exception nor dispensation. It is in this sense that God permits sin: for he would fail in what he owes to himself, in what he owes to his wisdom, his goodness, his perfection, if he followed not the grand result of all his tendencies to good, and if he chose not that which is absolutely the best, notwithstanding the evil of guilt, which is involved therein by the supreme necessity of the eternal verities. Hence the conclusion that God wills all good *in himself antecedently,* that he wills the best *consequently* as an *end,* that he wills what is indifferent, and physical evil, sometimes as a *means,* but that he will only permit moral evil as the

sine quo non [*sic*] or as a hypothetical necessity which connects it with the best. Therefore the *consequent will* of God, which has sin for its object, is only *permissive*.[43]

The first portion of this passage sounds like the argument that God does what is metaphysically best in regard to a whole world. The latter portion is less a reference to the world as a totality and more a reference to the specific kinds of evils within it. Those comments justify God more in terms of ethical than metaphysical concepts. For example, if Leibniz were speaking purely metaphysically about moral evil, why would he say that God wills it *permissively?* If God wants to create the metaphysically richest universe, and sees that moral evil contributes to that end, he won't merely permit its existence. He will most certainly choose a world containing it for the sake of making a metaphysically better universe. On the other hand, if Leibniz is thinking in ethical categories and evaluating ethically, not metaphysically, God's relation to our world, Leibniz definitely must show that God hasn't sinned by creating a world with sin in it. Hence, on moral grounds, Leibniz claimed that God only *permits* sin rather than positively willing its existence.

The preceding comments not only substantiate 1), but also help to establish 2). The free will defense is implicit in the following way: Leibniz wanted to claim that free will is compatible with divine determination in two ways: a) God can decree something to happen and yet humans possess genuine free will, and b) God can decree to actualize some possible person or thing without being morally responsible for its actions, since that being has free will.[44] The free will defense is implicit in b). Leibniz also says God *permits* a created will to do evil, because he knows that if God is morally responsible for the actions of his creatures (and ethical judgments are made in terms of ethical concepts, not metaphysical considerations), and those actions are good, then there is no problem for God's moral holiness. But if humans sin and God is morally responsible for their deeds, then God's holiness is stained.

Here the crucial notion has been introduced, i.e., moral evil is the product of *human willing* which is *permitted* by God. It is neither desired nor caused by him, and thus God's creatures, not God, are morally responsible for the moral evil they produce. These claims amount to the free will defense.

As to Leibniz's handling of physical evil, he again shifts the discussion from metaphysics to ethics. In explaining why God might have willed physical evil, he states:

> . . . and one may say of physical evil, that God wills it often as a penalty owing to guilt, and often also as a means to an end, that is, to prevent greater evils or to obtain greater good. The penalty serves to make us savour good the more; sometimes too it contributes to a greater perfection in him who

suffers it, as the seed that one sows is subject to a kind of corruption before it can germinate . . . [45]

While this appears to offer some explanation as to how physical evil might contribute to the best of all possible worlds, that isn't necessarily so, for the passage doesn't really explain how physical evil makes a metaphysically best world, but how it makes a morally better world. Of course, that is a different issue altogether from Leibniz's main claim about the best of all possible worlds. Again, as with moral evil, when Leibniz talks about the best possible world as a whole, he focuses on metaphysical good and evil, but when he turns specifically to physical evils in that best world, the discussion shifts from metaphysics to ethics.

ASSESSMENT OF LEIBNIZIAN RATIONALISM

Does Leibniz's theodicy solve the logical problem for his system? I think one can object to his views on many grounds, but most, if not all, of those complaints reject his views on grounds external to his system. That is, they disagree with his fundamental intellectual commitments about metaphysics, ethics, and the like. But such objections show no internal inconsistency in his views, and thus, his theodicy does adequately solve his theology's problem of evil.

In what follows, I turn to problems with his basic intellectual concepts. I begin with those of lesser import. A first objection relates to God's knowledge of the future. Does God foreknow the future because he foresees what must happen (in Leibniz's case, God foresees what might happen, for there are limitless options) and then puts his stamp of approval on one of those worlds, or does God foreknow it because he chooses what will happen and then knows what will happen? In other words, are the possibilities present before God, and then he, without being able to change any of them, just puts his stamp of approval on one set? Or, does God create the possibilities, choose the ones he wants as he wants them, and then foresee the future because he has decreed it?

Actually, the options presented offer a false dichotomy, for they suggest that God *either* has no control over what world he will choose *or* he has total control, even to the point of creating the possibilities themselves and using them to construct the multiplicity of possible worlds *before* he decides which one to actualize. Neither option quite represents Leibniz's views. While Leibniz denies that God can create or change any of the possibles (they are just there in his mind as possible), that doesn't mean he has no say about which world will become actual. All possible worlds are "before his mind," but he still must choose one of them over the others. So, there is a sense in which God knows the future because he chooses it, but that doesn't mean he has complete control to the point of creating the very concepts of the possibles. Within the realm of what is possible for him to do (in Leibniz's system, actualizing one of the possible worlds is something God can do, whereas creating the eternal verities themselves isn't), God acts.

Of course, since Leibniz's God must act according to the principle of sufficient reason when he chooses a world, and since for Leibniz the only sufficient reason for God to choose one world over another is that it is the best, some might think that Leibniz's God is "locked into" only one option after all, so it seems that we are back to the idea that God just puts his stamp of approval on what must happen anyway. This objection is understandable, but I believe it is incorrect. The very fact that Leibniz portrays God as surveying the various possible worlds and calculating which is the best shows that the decision hasn't already been made, so to speak, even before God comes to make the decision. Though Leibniz assures us that his God is morally good and so will definitely choose the best world, metaphysically speaking, that doesn't show that choosing another world is impossible for God (equivalent, say, to deciding to create a married bachelor). It only shows that it would be irrational, though not logically impossible. So, Leibniz presents this decision as a genuine choice for God, but he assures us that God is too good and too rational to do the immoral and irrational, namely, choose less than the best.

So, I believe the two options raised in this objection present a dichotomy that doesn't accurately reflect Leibniz's metaphysics. When one understands why it doesn't, one can see that this first objection in no way damages Leibniz's system,[46] and of course, it in no way suggests a failure of Leibniz's theology to solve its logical problem of evil, a problem of internal inconsistency.

A second objection is that despite Leibniz's claims that this is the best possible world, things could be better than they are. All God had to do was just make a universe that approximated his own perfection more. In fact, historically, those within the Thomistic tradition have attacked Leibniz on just this point. However, Hick claims the Thomists use a different definition than Leibniz's for "best world." Hick explains the difference, and shows that the two positions aren't necessarily at odds. He writes:

> The Thomist doctrine assumes a scale of possible universes rising from non-being to God, who is treated for this purpose as the terminal member of the series. This scale contains an infinity of steps . . . so that between any two universes it is always theoretically possible for there to be another. Thus there is always a possible universe which is superior to any given actual universe, but less than God. . . . Within this framework of thought it is correct to reject as meaningless the notion of the best possible world.

Leibniz, on the other hand, was assuming an unlimited range of possible universes, among which there is one that contains more reality than any other. This one will not necessarily be, and in fact is not, particularly close to the level of the divine perfection; but nevertheless there is no other compossible system that is as a totality superior to it. The infinite mind of the Creator has surveyed the infinite realm of world-possibilities and has selected the best. Defined in this way the notion of the best possible world is coherent and feasible.[47]

Why raise this distinction now? Because Hick later says that whichever conception one takes of the best possible world, grave difficulties arise. If one takes the Thomistic interpretation, God's love is impugned, for it could always be said that he could have made a better world, if he loved his creatures enough. If one takes Leibniz's interpretation, God's power is impugned, for no matter how much God loved us and still loves us, there are certain things he simply cannot do to change things.[48] As with the other objections about Leibniz's understanding of God's power, this one is simply mistaken. Hick's objection in no way shows Leibniz's metaphysics or his theology to be internally inconsistent. It merely offers a different notion of God's power. But offering a different understanding of divine power does not in itself prove Leibniz's views wrong.

The objections raised so far are of lesser import than others that can be raised. In particular, four seem more significant to me. None of them shows Leibniz's system internally inconsistent and thereby unable to solve its logical problem of evil. They all reject his position on grounds external to it, i.e., they attack some of the foundational notions of his system as inadequate. The preceding objections did, too, but I think a better case can be made in support of the next objections.[49]

First, Leibniz held that an infinite being must create a universe of finite beings in order for the best possible state of things to exist. Since I hold a Modified Rationalist metaphysic which says that God doesn't need to create anything because his own existence is the highest good, I don't think God must create anything to demonstrate his perfection. He is perfect and remains so, regardless of whether or not he ever does anything.

Second, as already noted, Leibniz's answer to why God isn't responsible for moral evil in the best of all possible worlds is the free will defense. As I shall show in the next chapter, the kind of freedom necessitated by that defense is incompatibilism or libertarian free will. Since I hold compatibilistic free will, I am not willing to accept the commitments Leibniz's system entails at this point, even though I agree that his account of freedom does render *his* system internally consistent.

Third, Leibniz speaks of the best of all possible worlds. But, best for what purpose? Leibniz says this world is best for showing God's perfections, and that was God's purpose for creating any world at all. Hick thinks perhaps we should see God's purpose as creating a place that is most suitable for human soul-building.[50] I think Hick's reaction isn't exactly to the point of Leibniz's claim. Suppose God's purpose in creating is to display his perfections, as Leibniz says. Leibniz thinks the only way for God to succeed in that purpose is to create the metaphysically richest world. If one accepts Leibniz's metaphysics and his account of ethics, then Leibniz is correct. However, I see no reason why one must accept Leibniz's conceptions. Couldn't there be another way for the world to reflect God's perfections accurately (benevolence in particular) other than making it the metaphysically richest world? Those, including myself, who hold different accounts of ethics than Leibniz would certainly answer affirmatively.[51]

I should also add that I do believe one of God's purposes in creating was to display his glory. However, appealing to that isn't how I answer the logical problem of evil that confronts my system. For one thing, such a response to the problem of moral evil implicitly commits one to consequentialist ethics, at least for the purpose of solving this problem. Since I reject such ethical theories, I can't adopt an answer to the logical problem of moral evil that presupposes consequentialism without thereby introducing an element into my overall worldview that will contradict something else in my system, namely, my commitment to nonconsequentialist ethics. But more on my system and its defense in chapter 6.[52]

In my opinion the worst indictment of Leibniz's theology is that his God is utterly repugnant. Leibniz portrays God as coldly calculating the metaphysically richest world and then actualizing it without any thought or concern about what that world might mean to the creatures in it. A God who personally cares about his creatures seems foreign to Leibniz's portrait. If Leibniz's God really cared about his creatures, it seems that he would look at the world he calculated, see how much sin and suffering it contains, and either refuse to actualize any world at all or actualize a world with less evil, even if doing so meant less variety of being. Of course, Leibniz's God couldn't do that, since Leibniz's system obligates God to create the metaphysically richest world, and that world must contain evil. But that understanding of God's moral obligation only further underscores how objectionable the Leibnizian world is. Surely all of this is quite foreign to the portrait of God one finds in Scripture.

In sum, I find Leibniz's theology objectionable because of the commitments it entails. I haven't proved here that those commitments are wrong, and that goes beyond the scope of this book. However, elsewhere I have presented and defended a view of God as the King who cares, and anyone reading that can see why I find Leibniz's conception of God so problematic.[53]

Where does this leave us in relation to the major concerns of this book? Actually, there is very good news for theism. My objections to Leibniz in no way show that his theology fails on grounds of internal inconsistency. This means that whether or not one adopts Leibniz's system, one must agree that Leibniz can and does solve the logical problem of evil that arises for his form of theism. Here again we see that Mackie's claim about there being no rational way for any theist to solve a problem of evil is wrong, and I take that to be good news for those who believe in God!

4

The Free Will Defense

In chapter 3, I noted that Leibniz's views actually contain two defenses, his best of all possible worlds theodicy and the free will defense. The free will defense both historically and in contemporary discussions has been the approach most frequently used. Men of such divergent backgrounds and different eras as Augustine and Alvin Plantinga have used this defense to answer the problem of evil.

Because of its importance historically and because much current literature focuses on this defense, I am devoting this chapter to it. I believe the free will defense solves the logical theological/philosophical problem of evil for its theology. However, as I shall show, theists have used this defense in support of theologies whose basic intellectual commitments contradict the free will defense.

Before turning directly to the free will defense, however, I must introduce a third broad form of theism, for the free will defense incorporates neither theonomy nor Leibnizian Rationalism. Then, I shall turn to a key historical example of the free will defense before taking up the defense in contemporary debate. As to recent discussion, key participants have been J. L. Mackie, Antony Flew, and Alvin Plantinga, but many others have contributed to this discussion as well. My critique and evaluation will be limited to the current debate and issues surrounding it.

MODIFIED RATIONALISM AND THE PROBLEM OF EVIL

The free will defense presupposes a broad form of theism that can be called Modified Rationalism. There are various distinguishable Modified Rationalist theologies, but all of them have certain things in common. Modified Rationalism takes a mediating position between theonomy and Leibnizian Rationalism. It differs from theonomy, because it claims that God's

choice of a contingent possible world is not arbitrary and is not without a specific reason. It differs from Leibnizian Rationalism, for it holds that there is
no *best* possible world. Even though God has reasons for whatever he
chooses to do, it would be perfectly acceptable for him not to create at all. In
contrast, Leibniz believed that one contingent possible world is the best, and
God is obligated to choose it.

According to Modified Rationalism, God need not create any world at
all, for his own existence is the perfect good. If he chooses to create a world,
that is a fitting thing for him to do, though not the only fitting thing he can
do. Moreover, it isn't logically necessary that he create anything or that if he
creates, he must create one good possible world as opposed to any other good
world he could have created. Modified Rationalists believe there is a series of
contingent finite possible worlds. Many are inherently evil, and thus, God had
better not create any of them. However, there is more than one good possible world, and God has power to create any of those good worlds, if he
chooses to create at all. There is no best possible world.[1] Finally, in a
Modified Rationalist world some things are known only by divine revelation
whereas others are knowable by reason.

As to their ethics, Modified Rationalist theologies incorporate one or the
other of two general approaches. They hold either a nonconsequentialist or
a consequentialist account of ethics.[2] For Modified Rationalists committed
to nonconsequentialism, if God creates a world that is inherently evil, that is
evidence that he isn't good. Thus, nonconsequentialists hold that the world
as created by God was good, but was corrupted by the creatures in it. On the
other hand, Modified Rationalists who are consequentialists claim that it isn't
wrong for God to create a world which, as created, contains evil, as long as
that world is one in which good is maximized. Often, these theologians argue
that the existence of evil is justified, because God will use it ultimately to max-
imize good. As for the free will defense, it presupposes the Modified
Rationalist metaphysic and incorporates a nonconsequentialist account of
ethics.

When we join this conception of metaphysics with its ethics, we can see
where God's obligation in regard to creating a world resides. He isn't obligated to create at all, but if he decides to create, he must create one of the good
possible worlds. From this, we can state the problem of evil for a Modified
Rationalist theology in the form of the following question: Is the evil in our
world (evil as the Modified Rationalist theologian conceives it, i.e., according to a consequentialist or a nonconsequentialist ethical theory) of such a
nature as to refute the Modified Rationalist's claim that our world *is* one of
those good possible worlds God could have created? To solve this problem

the Modified Rationalist must explain why the evil in our world doesn't make our world one of the evil possible worlds. That is, the Modified Rationalist must explain what it is about our world, despite its evil, that makes it a good world. If the Modified Rationalist can't specify what makes our world a good world, then the Modified Rationalist's God isn't a good God, and the theology in question doesn't solve its logical problem of evil. On the other hand, if the Modified Rationalist can explain what makes our world a good one, then the God in question is good, for he has fulfilled his obligation (i.e., create a good possible world if you create at all) as the Modified Rationalist understands it. The theology solves its logical problem of evil.

Free will defenders believe that human creatures with free will make our world one of those good possible worlds that God could have chosen. Let us turn now to this defense and see how it is expressed and defended.

AUGUSTINE ON FREE WILL

Augustine's formulation of the free will defense is an appropriate place to begin. He is one its earlier proponents, and we can see in his work the essentials of this defense. Augustine encapsulates the basics of this defense when he writes:

> If man is a good, and cannot act rightly unless he wills to do so, then he must have free will, without which he can not act rightly. We must not believe that God gave us free will so that we might sin, just because sin is committed through free will. It is sufficient for our question, why free will should have been given to man, to know that without it man cannot live rightly. That it was given for this reason can be understood from the following: if anyone uses free will for sinning, he incurs divine punishment. This would be unjust if free will had been given not only that man might live rightly, but also that he might sin. For how could a man justly incur punishment who used free will to do the thing for which it was given? When God punishes a sinner, does He not seem to say, "Why have you not used free will for the purpose for which I gave it to you, to act rightly"? Then too, if man did not have free choice of will, how could there exist the good according to which it is just to condemn evildoers and reward those who act rightly? What was not done by will would be neither evil doing nor right action. Both punishment and reward would be unjust if man did not have free will. Moreover, there needs be justice both in punishment and in reward, since justice is one of the goods that are from God. Therefore, God must needs have given free will to man.[3]

Though this sketches the main features of Augustine's free will defense, there is more to it than this. Augustine begins *On the Free Choice of the Will* by asking whether God is the cause of evil. He answers that God isn't. Instead, each of us is the cause of the evil we willfully commit.[4] This answer tells us immediately that this defense incorporates a nonconsequentialist account of ethics. In the rest of book I, Augustine discusses the nature of God, and then turns to a lengthy consideration of the various kinds of evils (how they arise and how they relate to the will). As to how evils arise, Augustine says the problem stems from our desires. Desires in themselves need not be problematic, but we get into trouble when we desire temporal things rather than eternal things, and when we do so excessively.[5] Once excessive desires are present in us, we will in accord with them and bring evil into the world.

Toward the end of book I Augustine introduces the question of why God gave us free will, if he knew we could and would abuse it. Augustine's imagined opponent says:

> But I question whether free will—through which, it has been shown, we have the power to sin—ought to have been given to us by Him who made us. For it seems that we would not have been able to sin, if we did not have free will. And it is to be feared that in this way God may appear to be the cause of our evil deeds.[6]

Augustine begins book II with his basic answer to this question. His answer appears in the passage cited above (numbered as note 3). The rest of his books II and III fill in further details of that answer. Early in book II Augustine says the discussion should focus around the following three questions: 1) how it is proved that God exists, 2) whether all things insofar as they are good are from God, and 3) whether free will is to be considered a good. Augustine says that once these questions are answered, it will be clear whether free will was rightly given.[7] As he answers these questions, Augustine delineates three types of goods: the highest, the lowest, and intermediate goods. He writes:

> Therefore the virtues, by which men live rightly, are great goods, while all kinds of physical beauties [species], without which no one can live rightly, are the intermediate goods [media bona] between these two. No one uses the virtues for evil. However, the other goods, the lowest and the intermediate ones, can be used not only for good, but also for evil.[8]

According to Augustine, all three kinds of goods come from God. Free will is an intermediate good, because it can be used to do either good or evil.[9]

Since free will is an intermediate good and can be used for evil, should God have given it to us? Augustine answers that God definitely should have given it, because we can use it to do good. If we abuse our free will, that isn't God's fault, and the possibility of abusing free will is worth it in view of the possibility of using free will for good.[10]

In book III Augustine discusses whether God is responsible for evil produced by free will, since he foreknew that we would abuse it when he gave it. In other words, does God's foreknowledge of our abuse of free will make that sin necessary, and does it make God morally responsible for our sin, since God knew what we would do and ordained it anyway? Augustine emphatically argues that God's foreknowledge of our sins does not make them necessary. Moreover, we are responsible for our sin, because we could have done otherwise. Our decision to sin is voluntary.[11] Augustine explains that God is just in punishing us for these sins which he foreknows must happen. He explains:

> Because unless I am mistaken, your foreknowledge that a man will sin does not of itself necessitate the sin. Your foreknowledge did not force him to sin even though he was, without doubt, going to sin; otherwise you would not foreknow that which was to be. Thus, these two things are not contradictories. As you, by your foreknowledge, know what someone else is going to do of his own will, so God forces no one to sin; yet He foreknows those who will sin by their own will.
>
> Why cannot He justly punish what He does not force to be done, even though he foreknows it? Your recollection of events in the past does not compel them to occur. In the same way God's foreknowledge of future events does not compel them to take place. As you remember certain things that you have done and yet have not done all the things that you remember, so God foreknows all the things of which He himself is the Cause, and yet He is not the Cause of all that He foreknows.[12]

According to Augustine, the human will is the radical root of all evil.[13] Human beings sin voluntarily, and thus are worthy of punishment. Of course, one might ask how this defense squares with the case of innocent children who suffer. Augustine was aware of this problem and answered as follows:

> Hence they ask: "What evil have they done that they should suffer so?" But what reason is there to believe that anyone should be rewarded for innocence before he could do harm? Since God works some good by correcting adults tortured by the sickness and death of children who are dear to them, why should this suffering not occur? When the sufferings of children are over it will be as if they had never occurred for those who suffered. Either the adults on whose account the sufferings occurred will become better, if they are reformed by temporal troubles and choose to live rightly, or else, if because of the hardships of this life they are unwilling to turn their desire toward eternal life, they will have no excuse when they are punished in the judgment to come. Moreover, who knows what faith is practiced or what pity is tested when these children's sufferings break down the hardness of parents? Who knows what reward God reserves in the secret place of his judgment for the children who, though they have not acted rightly, are not, on the other hand, weighed down by sin? For it is not in vain that the Church commends as martyrs the infants who were slaughtered when Herod sought to slay Jesus Christ our Lord.[14]

Augustine's defense of God on this point essentially amounts to saying that God uses the suffering of innocent children to work good in the lives of their parents who have used free will to sin. This explanation presupposes that everything that occurs in the universe is interrelated and thus occurs so as to produce more overall good, order, and harmony than would otherwise be possible.

Though this answer is probably not very convincing or satisfying to many people, it is possibly true. Since a defense purports to explain a possible reason (not a reason one knows is *the* reason) for God's permission of evil, Augustine's answer does render his theology internally consistent. As a result, his system doesn't succumb to a problem of evil.[15]

Before leaving Augustine, I note that his defense, like most expositions of the free will defense, doesn't defend God against physical evil. Some atheists think this is a devastating deficiency, but as I shall argue, their complaint is misguided.

THE FREE WILL DEFENSE IN CONTEMPORARY DISCUSSIONS

Most free will defenders follow Augustine's basic approach. Of course, through the centuries there have been various amplifications and refinements of his notions. This is especially true of contemporary treatments of the free will defense. Three of the main combatants in the contemporary debate are J. L. Mackie and Antony Flew, who attack the free will defense, and Alvin Plantinga, who has answered Mackie and Flew and has developed the free will defense significantly. There are other participants in the debate,[16] but much of the recent discussion centers around the work of these three. We begin with Flew.

Antony Flew

Flew distinguishes four basic moves in the free will defense. The theist initially claims that God's omnipotence doesn't mean he can do anything, even the logically contradictory, but it does grant him power to do the logically consistent.[17] The second move is to say that God gave humans free will and that free will implies the possibility of doing evil as well as good.[18] The theist will then "point out that certain good things, viz. certain virtues, logically presuppose: not merely beings with freedom of choice (which alone are capable of either virtue or vice), and consequently the possibility of evil; but also the actual occurrence of certain evils."[19] The theist finally argues that unfortunately we have used our freedom of choice to choose evil, but nevertheless, all the evil that is chosen is "more than offset by the actually achieved sum of those higher goods of which the capacity to choose is the logically necessary condition."[20]

Flew next argues that there is an essential assumption underlying the whole free will defense, an assumption he wants to attack. As Flew states, the issue at stake is:

> ... the idea that there is a contradiction involved in saying that God might have made people so that they always in fact *freely* choose the right. If there is no contradiction here then Omnipotence might have made a world inhabited by wholly virtuous people; the Free-Will Defence is broken-backed; and we are back again with the original intractable antinomy.[21]

Flew's attack on the free will defense rests on the belief that "God made people so that they always choose the right" is logically compatible with "humans have free choice." If these two claims are compatible, then one could say without contradiction that God could make people so that they always *freely* choose the right.

In order to clarify the issue, Flew, in his article "Compatibilism, Free Will and God," distinguishes two senses of freedom that are crucial to understanding the debate between Flew and Plantinga. One sense of "free" means "unconstrained," while the other is libertarian free will. Flew's distinction is as follows: to say someone acted freely in the unconstrained sense means "there are contingently sufficient non-subsequent conditions for a person's being such that he chooses to act, and acts, in one particular way and not another."[22] In other words, his acts are causally determined. Still, Flew insists that when the agent so acts, he could have acted or chosen otherwise.[23] Though Flew could be more explicit on this matter, it becomes apparent that he thinks that as long as the agent makes a choice without being forced to choose a particular option (and thus could do otherwise), he acts freely.

What does it mean, according to this notion of compatibilistic freedom, to do something unfreely? Here Flew employs the term "constraint," but what does this mean? Flew helps us understand his point by distinguishing the following two sentences: "My arm moved, but I did not move it" and "I moved my arm." The first speaks of a motion, and the second of a moving.[24] A moving likely results from causal conditions that precede the agent's decision to move his arm and also succeed in getting him to move the arm, i.e., his moving is causally determined. Such an act is still a free action, according to Flew's understanding of compatibilism, because the agent could have done otherwise and did make a choice. In contrast, a motion (e.g., the moving of my arm without me moving it) likely occurs as a result of someone else's action or something else's movement which causes my arm to move. My arm moves under constraint, and since I don't control that motion, I am not in a position to choose or do something else (such as keep my arm still). In fact, my constrained motion really doesn't even qualify as an action.

In contrast, Flew explains the libertarian sense of free will as follows:

> This is the sense in which the point of saying that someone acted freely is: not to bring out that he did not do what he did under constraint; but to imply that there were no contingently sufficient non-subsequent conditions for his choosing to act in this particular way and no other.[25]

Put simply, this means that a free act isn't causally determined. Flew calls those who hold the first notion of freedom compatibilists, for they believe that human freedom is compatible with certain non-constraining conditions that determine actions. It is the compatibilist who thinks there is no contradiction in saying that God might have made people so that they always freely choose the right.

On the other hand, those who hold libertarian free will are incompatibilists, for they believe that human freedom is incompatible with any contingently sufficient non-subsequent conditions of an action. These people think it is contradictory to assert that God could have made us so that we would freely do one thing or another. If God makes us that way, that is a contingently *sufficient* non-subsequent condition of our actions. But conditions that decisively incline the will (i.e., those which in Flew's terms are sufficient conditions to produce our actions) are incompatible with free will as defined by incompatibilists.[26] Clearly compatibilism and incompatibilism contradict each other. The former says that an act can be free even though it is causally determined, whereas the latter says that if the act is free it can't be causally determined.

Flew's claim, in essence, is that those who use the free will defense assume the accuracy of incompatibilism. However, Flew thinks compatibilism is the correct view of freedom. But according to compatibilism, it is possible for God to make people so that they always freely do what is right. Hence, there can be freedom without evil, contrary to the free will defender's claims, and that just means that creating beings with free will doesn't justify the evil present in our world. Thus, our world with free will and evil isn't a good world, and God shouldn't have created it. The free will defense fails, and the theology it presupposes collapses from internal inconsistency.

Flew argues that the compatibilist's interpretation of freedom is not only the correct one but is also representative of the more common usage of "free will." Moreover, choices and actions that aren't free in the libertarian sense of freedom are still genuine choices and true actions. Flew offers two cases to show that a compelled action and a constrained action differ, and that the compelled action is free, though not, of course, in the libertarian sense of freedom. Flew writes:

> Suppose that, threatened by a man with a gun, the Bank Manager opens the safe and reluctantly hands him the contents. Called to account for the losses involved, the Bank Manager pleads compulsion; and this plea in this case is, very properly, accepted as a complete excuse. Nevertheless, although he was forced to do what he did not want to do, although he thus acted not freely but under compulsion, still he did act. His situation was in this respect entirely different from that of a man who is seized by main force and projected through a shop window. The latter, as a human missile, is a victim not an agent. Reproached by the shopkeeper about the breaking of the window the missile man's reply should be: not that he acted under compulsion, and is therefore to be excused; but that it was not he who broke the window but the toughs who threw him through it.

Here we come to understand better what Flew means by a compatibilistically free act, and we also see what, given his compatibilism, he means by an unfree deed. To act under compulsion is, therefore, still to act and to do so freely. The same holds, with appropriate alterations, for choice. And whenever it is correct to say that someone acts or chooses, Flew holds that it must be equally correct to say that, in some fundamental sense, he could have acted or chosen otherwise.[27]

All of this needs explanation, because Flew's use of terminology here is a bit unusual. Many use "compelled" *and* "constrained" to mean the same thing, namely, to be forced to do something against one's wishes. Flew uses "constrained" to mean forced to do something so as to do it without any willing whatsoever—the case of the "missile man." "Compulsion" means, for Flew, to be causally moved to choose one thing over another, even if one's choice is contrary to one's wishes. Although the choice is made contrary to one's wishes, at least the agent exercises his will, and so could have chosen otherwise. Though it would be unwise for the bank manager to refuse to give the robber the money, he could still decide not to give it. In contrast, in a case of constraint, the person doesn't exercise his will at all.

Flew, then, seems to suggest that to act under compulsion is still to act freely, whereas when one is constrained, as in the case of the missile man, in no sense can that person be said to act, so no question can arise about whether she "acts" freely. A proponent of libertarian free will would grant that there is a difference between the cases of the bank manager and the missile man, but would add that these two instances of compulsion or constraint (the libertarian would probably not distinguish the two) are instances of causal determinism and hence aren't examples of free choice or action.

As for compatibilists other than Flew, at least as "compatibilism" is understood and used in more recent discussions, they also grant that there is a difference between the bank manager and the missile man, but maintain that both are still instances of constraint. The missile man is more severely constrained than the bank manager, but both are constrained. Since acting under constraint or compulsion (the terms are used synonymously by most compatibilists, including myself) is acting contrary to one's wishes, it isn't free action. For compatibilists an act is free if it is determined by causes which decisively incline the will without constraining it, i.e., without moving it to choose and the agent to act against the agent's wishes.[28]

Hence, Flew's use of terminology and especially his illustrations are somewhat confusing, in part because they understand these concepts differently than do recent compatibilists. Compatibilists other than Flew, including myself, would contend that neither of his two examples is an instance of someone acting freely (in the compatibilist sense of "free"). Though his illustrations are problematic, we must not miss the basic point he is making. His basic contention is that an act can be causally determined and yet free. Though both incompatibilists and compatibilists would agree that Flew's examples are instances where the person doesn't act freely, the compatibilist would still agree with Flew that there are instances where a person is causally determined to do what she does, but she does it freely, because she chooses and acts in accord with her wishes. And (the key point for the free will defense), if such freedom is possible, then it seems that God could have created humans with compatibilistic free will and so arranged things in our world that we would always use our freedom to do good. Thus, the compatibilist's objection to the free will defense stands.[29] There can be free will and no moral evil.[30]

J. L. Mackie

Mackie begins by distinguishing what he calls first order and second order good and evil. Pain and misery are examples of first order evil. In contrast to those evils, there are first order goods like pleasure and happiness.[31] Typically, those who try to justify the existence of first order evil claim that second order good exists "which somehow emerges in a complex situation in which evil (1) is a necessary component—logically, not merely causally, necessary."[32] This means that there couldn't be the second order good without the first order evil. For example, if courage is a second order good, no one could ever develop that character trait if there were never any first order pains and evils that cause fear.

Mackie also notes that just as first order good has a counterpart in first

order evil, so does second order good. Second order evil includes "malevo-
lence, cruelty, callousness, cowardice, and states in which good (1) is decreas-
ing and evil (1) is increasing."[33] Mackie argues that many theists claim that
in order to have second order goods, there must also be certain first order
evils. Mackie's attack on the free will defense initially focuses on this notion
of different levels of good and evil. He claims that in essence the free will
defense rests on the belief that freedom, even though it entails committing certain evils, is a third order good, and the goods it produces are of greater value
than any second order goods produced in a wholly determined way. Mackie
writes:

> The free will solution also involves the preceding solution at a higher level.
> To explain why a wholly good God gave men free will although it would
> lead to some important evils, it must be argued that it is better on the whole
> that men should act freely, and sometimes err, than that they should be inno-
> cent automata, acting rightly in a wholly determined way. Freedom, that is
> to say, is now treated as a third order good, and as being more valuable than
> second order goods (such as sympathy and heroism) would be if they were
> deterministically produced, and it is being assumed that second order evils,
> such as cruelty, are logically necessary accompaniments of freedom, just as
> pain is a logically necessary pre-condition of sympathy.[34]

After making this preliminary point, Mackie turns to his major criticism
of the free will defense. We might call it Mackie's "good choosing argument,"[35] but whatever it is called, it rests on the notion of compatibilistic free
will. Mackie writes:

> I should ask this: if God has made men such that in their free choices they
> sometimes prefer what is good and sometimes what is evil, why *could he not
> have made men such* that they *always freely choose the good?* If there is no
> logical impossibility in a man's freely choosing the good on one, or on sev-
> eral occasions, there cannot be a logical impossibility in his freely choosing
> the good on every occasion. God was not, then, faced with a choice between
> making innocent automata and making beings who, in acting freely, would
> sometimes go wrong: there was open to him the obviously better possibility
> of *making beings who would act freely but always go right.* Clearly, his fail-
> ure to avail himself of this possibility is inconsistent with his being both
> omnipotent and wholly good.[36] [Italics mine]

The only way that what Mackie suggests (as indicated in the italicized portions) could be true is if humans possess compatibilistic free will. This becomes
even clearer when Mackie raises a further objection to the free will defense.
He says some may reply that his objection is absurd, because the making of
some wrong choices is logically necessary for freedom. However, Mackie
claims, they are thinking of freedom as complete randomness or indetermi-

nacy, including randomness with regard to the alternatives good and evil.[37] Mackie says this means men's choices can be free, then, in this sense only if they aren't determined by their characters. However, if freedom is randomness, it can't be a characteristic of will. Moreover, if it is mere randomness, it can't be the most important good, a good worth having at the expense of the evil it produces, for what value could there be in such free choices, if they were random actions and thus not determined by the nature of the agent?[38]

Mackie's claims amount to a twofold objection to the free will defense. First, the free will defender must hold incompatibilism, but compatibilism is the correct view of freedom. Given compatibilism, the free will defender can't explain why God didn't make us so that we would always choose good on every occasion. Second, the free will defender is committed to incompatibilistic freedom, but that view of freedom makes freedom nothing but randomness. However, if freedom is randomness, it isn't a good of any order, and God is doubly blameworthy in giving free will, for he not only gave something that is used to produce evil, but what he gave shouldn't even be considered a good. Thus, according to Mackie, the free will defense is thoroughly inadequate as a way to solve a problem of evil.[39]

One of the issues that grew out of Flew's and Mackie's attacks centers around what Ninian Smart calls the Utopia Thesis. According to Smart, if Flew and Mackie are correct, their arguments involve two assertions. The first is that causal determinism is compatible with free will—the Compatibility Thesis. The second is that God could have created men wholly good—the Utopia Thesis.[40] Smart's intention is to show that, despite appearances, the Utopia Thesis doesn't follow from the Compatibility Thesis. In fact, Smart believed that the notion of a utopia is altogether unclear. Moreover, it isn't at all certain that a utopia, if one could give it content, would be superior to our universe.[41]

Mackie's response to Smart is threefold. First, the Utopia Thesis does follow from the Compatibility Thesis. Second, Smart's essay misses the point of Flew's and Mackie's objections, which is how the Compatibility Thesis relates to the free will defense. Moreover, the burden of proof can't be removed from the free will defender by holding that the Compatibility Thesis does or doesn't entail the Utopia Thesis and then claiming that the Utopia Thesis can't be given any content. Finally, as to the issue of the content of the Utopia Thesis, Mackie says it seems obvious that it does have content, since traditional Christian theists always speak of a Kingdom of God on earth.[42] As Mackie says:

> I should have thought, indeed, that the concept of a state of affairs in which men were wholly good, that is, of a Kingdom of God on Earth, was an

orthodox theist one, and if that concept is empty or unintelligible, so much the worse for theism. If the theists tell us that God will eventually bring this utopia into being, the critics can hardly be blamed for wondering why he has gone such a long way round about it, and it is a curious defence of theism to say that the critics have not made this concept clear.[43]

My concern now isn't to solve or even assess the issue raised by the Utopia Thesis, for I shall return to it later in this chapter. The point of mentioning it now is to show that the free will defense has engendered discussions among philosophers that have led in various directions, one of them being the issue of a utopia.

Alvin Plantinga

No contemporary philosopher has done more to develop and defend the free will defense than Alvin Plantinga. He not only answers Flew and Mackie but also gives the free will defense its most complicated and sophisticated expression, an expression that has convinced many. Whether one agrees or disagrees with Plantinga, one dare not overlook his work on this issue.

In his earlier work, Plantinga discusses the logical aspects of the problem of evil. He begins by pointing out what must be done to answer the charge of contradiction that Mackie and others make. He says that to answer the atheists' attack, one needs a premise to the effect that "God creates a world containing evil and has a good reason for doing so."[44] That premise will solve the logical aspects of the problem of evil, but of course only if the premise is true. To prove its truth one must propose what God's reason might have been for creating a world containing evil, and then argue that his reason proves that ours is a good world and exonerates God from having to remove moral evil.[45] It is at this point that Plantinga introduces the free will defense.

The very way Plantinga states the free will defense helps to clarify the point of his disagreement with Flew and Mackie. The disagreement is ultimately over what each one means by "freedom" or "free will." That this is so is evident from what Plantinga says about freedom and the free will defense. In relation to freedom, Plantinga writes:

> What is relevant to the Free Will Defense is the idea of *being free with respect to an action*. If a person is free with respect to a given action, then he is free to perform that action and free to refrain from performing it; no antecedent conditions and/or causal laws determine that he will perform the action, or that he won't. It is within his power, at the time in question, to take or perform the action and within his power to refrain from it. Freedom so conceived is not to be confused with unpredictability. You might be able to predict what you will do in a given situation even if you are free, in that situation, to do something else. . . . Secondly, I shall say that an action is

morally significant, for a given person, if it would be wrong for him to perform the action but right to refrain or *vice versa.*[46]

It seems rather clear that Plantinga's notion of freedom is incompatibilism. If
there are any doubts about that, or about whether Flew and Mackie disagree
with Plantinga's concept of freedom, all doubt is removed when Plantinga
states:

> Given these definitions and distinctions, we can make a preliminary state-
> ment of the Free Will Defense as follows. A world containing creatures who
> are significantly free (and freely perform more good than evil actions) is
> more valuable, all else being equal, than a world containing no free creatures
> at all. Now God can create free creatures, but He can't *cause* or *determine*
> them to do only what is right. For if He does so, then they aren't significantly
> free after all; they do not do what is right *freely.* To create creatures capa-
> ble of *moral good,* therefore, He must create creatures capable of moral evil;
> and He can't give these creatures the freedom to perform evil and at the same
> time prevent them from doing so. As it turned out, sadly enough, some of
> the free creatures God created went wrong in the exercise of their freedom;
> this is the source of moral evil. The fact that free creatures sometimes go
> wrong, however, counts neither against God's omnipotence nor against His
> goodness; for He could have forestalled the occurrence of moral evil only
> by removing the possibility of moral good.[47]

In view of Plantinga's claims about freedom in general and the free will
defense in particular, it isn't hard to imagine how he answers Flew and
Mackie. Plantinga takes issue with Flew first, and considers his objection the
lesser difficulty. To answer Flew, Plantinga simply points to his own incompatibilist view of freedom. Plantinga says it isn't possible for all of a person's
actions to be causally determined while some of them are free. Causal determinism and freedom are incompatible.[48]

In *God, Freedom, and Evil* Plantinga goes no further than this in answer-
ing Flew. He does address Flew's concerns in more detail in "The Free Will
Defence" and *God and Other Minds,* but still concludes that Flew is wrong.
Interested readers are welcome to consult that material,[49] but Plantinga takes
Mackie's objection as much more serious, so I shall focus on it.

Plantinga takes Mackie's argument seriously enough to give it a logical
reconstruction.[50] The key premise in Plantinga's reconstruction is the one he
labels (5). It says "God can create free men such that they always do what is
right."[51] Plantinga believes premise (5) is true only if "(5a) God creates free
men such that they always do what is right" is consistent.[52]

The problem, according to Plantinga, is that there are two possible ways
to interpret (5a). (5a) is equivalent either to (5b) "God creates free men and
brings it about that they always freely do what is right" or to (5c) "God cre-

ates free men and these free men always do what is right."[53] The difference is that with interpretation (5b) God must intervene to get the desired result, whereas on interpretation (5c) God need do no more than create the world that contains these creatures; they will on their own always use their freedom to choose good. Mackie, of course, had granted that if it were possible on one occasion for someone to use her freedom to choose good, it must also be possible for her to do so on every occasion. In such cases, her actions would not be causally determined; she just happens to prefer doing good in every instance where there is a choice, and so she chooses the good deed. Thus, by (5a) Mackie may well mean (5c). Of course, Mackie also espouses compatibilism, so by (5a) he may mean (5b).

Plantinga is correct in pointing out this ambiguity in (5a), but he does more than that. He assesses Mackie's argument on both interpretations. Plantinga explains that if (5a) is taken to mean (5b), then it isn't consistent, because "if God *brings it about* that the men He creates always do what is right, then they do not do what is right *freely*."[54]

Why does Plantinga think this is inconsistent? Isn't it because Plantinga's claim incorporates *incompatibilism* and so rejects the compatibilistic notion of freedom that (5b) seems to require? If (5) or (5a) is equivalent to (5b), and if (5b) is what Mackie claims in his argument (and indeed Mackie's good choosing argument does presuppose compatibilism), then the disagreement between Mackie and Plantinga is about compatibilism vs. incompatibilism.

Let us continue, though. Suppose that the second interpretation of (5a), i.e., (5c), is Mackie's claim. Then, what follows? Plantinga thinks (5c) is clearly consistent, for it expresses what is logically possible.[55] Of course, Plantinga views it as consistent, because it doesn't contradict incompatibilism. Still, Plantinga thinks even (5c) has problems. Plantinga says that (5), if interpreted as (5c), may be meant to express (5d) "The proposition '*God creates free men and the free men created by God always do what is right*' is consistent." Plantinga says that if (5) is equivalent to (5d), then (5) is true[56] (again, of course, because it presupposes incompatibilism). However, (5), understood as (5d), leads to (6) "If God can create free men such that they always do what is right, and if God is all good, then any free men created by God always do what is right,"[57] or more specifically, in view of (5d), (6) should be stated as (6') "If God is all good and the proposition '*God creates free men and the free men He creates always do what is right*' is consistent, then any free men created by God always do what is right." The problem with (6) or (6'), according to Plantinga, is that there is no reason for assuming that (6') is true at all, let alone necessarily true.[58] If God gives humans libertarian free will, how can he (or anyone else) be sure that on their own they will always freely choose good? While it is possible for this to happen, there is no guarantee that it will, so Plantinga claims that there is no reason for thinking this even to be true, let alone necessarily so. Plantinga summarizes the difficulty he sees with Mackie's good choosing argument as follows:

> Put in a nutshell the difficulty with the argument is the following. Proposition (5a) (God creates free men such that they always do what is right) is susceptible of two interpretations ((5b) and (5c)). Under one of these interpretations (5) turns out to be false and the argument fails. Under the other interpretation (6) turns out to be contingent, and again the argument fails.[59]

Plantinga thinks he has clarified the issues between himself and Mackie and clearly destroyed Mackie's position, but, as already argued, that isn't necessarily so. As to (5b) (the interpretation Mackie really has in mind),[60] Plantinga considers it wrong, because he rejects compatibilism in favor of incompatibilism. As to (5c), I agree that if it does lead to (6) or (6'), there are problems, for (6) or (6') is problematic in the way Plantinga suggests. However, it is very important to see why Plantinga even accepts (5c) as consistent and then moves on. Clearly, it is because (5c) rests on incompatibilism which he accepts. Since that is so, Plantinga must move on to (6) or (6') in order to answer Mackie, for (5), taken as (5c), is certainly possible and has much to commend it to proponents of incompatibilism. It should be clear, then, that whether Mackie by (5a) means (5b) or (5c), the fundamental issue between Mackie and Plantinga is the compatibilism/incompatibilism issue.

Though he believes he has answered Mackie, Plantinga sees something else in Mackie's argument which suggests a further issue. Plantinga agrees that it is at least logically possible that someone would always do what is right (i.e., what [5c] asserts could possibly happen). Since God knows everything, he knows if a person he proposes to create will or won't commit evil. Moreover, for every person who would commit evil, there is another possible person like the first person in every respect except that he wouldn't do evil. God could have created those persons, and if he were truly benevolent, he would have done so, since they wouldn't do any evil.[61]

Once Plantinga states matters this way, he raises the whole issue of possible worlds and possible persons. Doing so gives him the opportunity to introduce and combine Leibnizian notions with the free will defense. Plantinga explains the concepts of possible persons and possible worlds. Briefly stated, a possible world is a world which isn't actual but might have been. In a possible world either a state of affairs or its opposite will obtain, and this is true for a whole series of states of affairs. Thus, a possible world is the conjunction of every state of affairs which obtains for that world, even though that world has never been actualized. The actual world is also a conglomeration of every state of affairs which obtains for it, but of course the world formed by the aggregation is actual, not potential.[62]

In regard to possible persons, the same principles hold true. Every person has a set of properties and those properties entail the exclusion of their opposites. This is true of a person in the actual world or in a possible world. The difference between the two is that the possible person with his properties hasn't been actualized, whereas the actual person with his properties has been actualized.[63]

Once Plantinga introduces the concepts of possible worlds and possible people, he turns to answer a more sophisticated version of Mackie's argument (a version Plantinga constructs). Plantinga argues that Mackie's claims that 1) there is a possible world in which everyone does right and that 2) it is logically possible for God to create that world rest on the Leibnizian assumption that God can actualize any possible world he pleases. Plantinga sets out to prove that this thesis, i.e., God can actualize any possible world he pleases, is false. This claim isn't right in the first place, Plantinga argues, because there are logically conceivable worlds in which God doesn't exist, and of course, if he doesn't exist in those worlds, he couldn't actualize them as a whole or any state of affairs they contain.[64] However, Plantinga's point is much more subtle and significant. He argues that there are even worlds where God does exist but still can't create just any possible world he pleases. How this becomes significant for supporting the free will defense will become evident shortly, but Plantinga first explains and illustrates his point by offering (in *God, Freedom, and Evil*) a series of examples that show that God cannot actualize just any state of affairs or any possible world whatsoever. It is instructive to look at one of his examples.

Plantinga asks us to suppose that someone named Maurice will at some time in the future be free (of course, Plantinga means "free" in the libertarian sense of that term) with respect to having freeze-dried oatmeal for breakfast. Of course, being free with respect to that matter means he might choose shredded wheat instead. The state of affairs, S', which pertains in the actual world at time t, the time of the decision, contains all the conditions relevant to his choice, but S' doesn't contain Maurice's either taking or rejecting oatmeal. According to Plantinga, God knows that one of the following is true in relation to Maurice: either 1) If S' were to obtain, Maurice would freely take the oatmeal, or 2) If S' were to obtain, Maurice would freely reject it. Plantinga then claims that there is clearly a possible world God couldn't create, even though he is omnipotent. That is, there is a possible world in which Maurice freely chooses oatmeal, and another in which he freely rejects oatmeal, so each of these worlds is internally consistent. However, depending on whether 1) or 2) is true of Maurice when he is in state of affairs S', God will either not be able to create the possible world with 1) or the possible world where 2) occurs. To see why this is so, we need to return to Plantinga's explanation.

Suppose 1) is true. Suppose also that there is a possible world W which contains S' but is a world in which Maurice freely rejects oatmeal. Now, reasons Plantinga, God cannot actualize W since Maurice freely *rejects* oatmeal in W when S' obtains, but we are supposing instead that when S' obtains Maurice chooses oatmeal (i.e., 1] is true). So, if God actualizes S' (which he must do to actualize W), and leaves Maurice free in regard to the action in question, Maurice will take oatmeal, and so W will *not* be actual.

Suppose again that 1) is true, and that God tries to actualize W by *causing* Maurice at S' to *refrain* from choosing oatmeal. If God does this, he still can't actualize W, for God's *causing* Maurice to refrain means Maurice doesn't refrain (incompatibilistically) *freely*, whereas we have seen that in W Maurice is *free* (incompatibilistically) either to take or reject the oatmeal.

Of course, if 2) is true rather than 1), then *mutatis mutandis,* Plantinga's argument arrives at the same results. We must be careful not to misunderstand what this illustration shows. It doesn't show that W is an impossible world, i.e., that W after all contains states of affairs that contradict one another. W is definitely a possible world. The lesson from this example is that there are circumstances in which God cannot actualize just any possible world he wants, in spite of Leibniz's belief to the contrary (Plantinga calls this error Leibniz's Lapse). Of course, accepting Leibniz's supposition that God could actualize any possible world he wants is foundational to Mackie's assertion that God could actualize any possible world, including one where no one does evil and refrains from it freely.[65] Since Leibniz's assumption is wrong, Mackie's objection which rests on it is wrong.[66]

Still, if atheists like Mackie accept Leibniz's assumption, they will also believe that the proposition "God is omnipotent, and it was not within his power to create a world containing moral good but no moral evil" is false. Plantinga thinks atheists are wrong for rejecting this proposition even as they are wrong in holding Leibniz's Lapse. Rejecting Leibniz's Lapse, however, doesn't in itself show that the above-mentioned proposition is true. In order to prove it true and atheists wrong, one must show that among the *possible* worlds God could *not* actualize are all the worlds containing moral good but no moral evil (and Plantinga agrees that there are such possible worlds with moral good but no moral evil). Plantinga offers a lengthy but important argument for this notion, and I shall summarize it. Again, he explains by way of an illustration, and it is parallel to the Maurice illustration, but it involves a morally significant decision rather than an amoral one like choosing or rejecting oatmeal.

Suppose an imaginary person L. B. Smedes offers Curley Smith, a politician, a bribe in return for political favors. Smedes offers $35,000, and Curley takes it, but Smedes wonders if he could have bought Curley for $20,000. Plantinga tells us that in fact if Smedes had offered Curley $20,000, he would have taken it (Smedes, of course, doesn't know this). Thus, Plantinga says there is a state of affairs S' which 1) includes Curley being offered $20,000 as a bribe, 2) doesn't include either his acceptance or rejection of the bribe, and 3) is otherwise as much as possible like the actual world. Now, there is at least one possible world W' in which S' obtains and in which Curley *rejects* the bribe. Of course, we already know that if S' were *actual,* Curley would accept the bribe.[67] Hence, we know that W' can't be the actual world. Plantinga now presents a dilemma analogous to the Maurice and the oatmeal case. Plantinga writes:

> This means, of course, that God could not have actualized W'. For to do so He'd have been obliged to bring it about that S' is actual; but then Curley would go wrong with respect to A [the action of taking the bribe—my insert]. Since in W' he always does what is right, the world thus actualized would not be W'. On the other hand, if God *causes* Curley to go right with respect to A or *brings it about that* he does so, then Curley isn't free [incompatibilistically—my insert] with respect to A; and so once more it isn't W' that is actual. Accordingly God cannot create W'. But W' was just any of the worlds in which Curley is significantly free but always does only what is right. It therefore follows that it was not within God's power to create a world in which Curley produces moral good but no moral evil. Every world God can actualize is such that if Curley is significantly free in it, he takes at least one wrong action.[68]

Again we see that there is a possible world which God cannot actualize, contrary to Leibniz's assumption that God can actualize any possible world whatsoever. Having read the above account of Curley and Smedes, one might agree with Plantinga's assessment but still say that there are other possible worlds in which Curley is significantly free and doesn't accept the bribe. In fact, there must be some possible world in which both Curley and everyone else who ever lives freely chooses only to do morally good deeds; hence those possible worlds contain no moral evil. And, the critic of theism maintains, if God is omnipotent, he could create one of those worlds, and if he is omnibenevolent he would have done so.

Prima facie this sounds like a good reply to Plantinga's example of Curley, but Plantinga has a counter reply. Suppose, says Plantinga, Curley suffers from a malady Plantinga labels transworld depravity. Plantinga defines it as follows:

> ... A Person P *suffers from transworld depravity* if and only if the following holds: for every world W such that P is significantly free in W and P does only what is right in W, there is an action A and a maximal world segment S' such that
> (1) S' includes A's being morally significant for P
> (2) S' includes P's being free with respect to A
> (3) S' is included in W and includes neither P's performing A nor P's refraining from performing A
>
> and
>
> (4) If S' were actual, P would go wrong with respect to A.[69]

The important thing about transworld depravity is that if someone suffers from it, it isn't within God's power to actualize any world where that person is significantly free but does no wrong. Moreover, Plantinga says it is possible that everybody suffers from transworld depravity, and if this possibility were actual, "then God, though omnipotent, could not have created any of the possible worlds containing just the persons who do in fact exist, and containing moral good but no moral evil."[70]

Some may reply that while it is possible that everyone may suffer from transworld depravity, it is also possible that only some or even none suffer from it. If either some or none suffer from it, then it still seems that God could have created one of the possible worlds in which free creatures do only what is morally good (or at least most or many free creatures—those without transworld depravity—do only good). But this objection is simply misguided. Plantinga could grant these possibilities, but they are beside the point. The point with the logical problem of evil is that the atheist accuses the theist's theology of being internally inconsistent. That is, the atheist claims that there is no *possible* way everything the theist holds could be true since some things the theist holds contradict other things she holds. Since the complaint is "no possible way," all that is incumbent on the theist is to show a possible way. And that is precisely what Plantinga is doing. It is surely *possible* that everyone suffers from transworld depravity, and if so, then it wouldn't be possible for God to create any world with free creatures who do only moral good and never do moral evil. If someone replies that this is possible but not very plausible, the proper response is that we must remember Plantinga's distinction between a theodicy and a defense. The theodicy purports to offer God's actual reason for not removing evil. In that case, the story the theist tells had better be plausible. But a defense doesn't claim to know the actual reason God hasn't removed evil, only a possible one. Plantinga nowhere claims that he is offering a theodicy; rather he offers a defense, so his explanation needs only to be possible, and it is.

The upshot of incorporating transworld depravity into the free will defense is that the price for creating a world in which people freely produce moral good is that they also produce moral evil. Thus, Mackie's notion of God being able to create a world where people always do moral good but never evil cannot stand. He hasn't destroyed or refuted the free will defense.

Though the free will defense addresses moral evil, Plantinga knows that nothing said so far addresses natural evil. Prior to Plantinga, few theists, if any, applied the free will defense to natural evil. Plantinga, however, believes it is possible to solve the problem of natural evil by means of the free will defense as he expounds it. The only difference is that we must think in terms of Satanic and demonic free will, not human freedom. Plantinga writes:

> Satan, so the traditional doctrine goes, is a mighty nonhuman spirit who, along with many other angels, was created long before God created man. Unlike most of his colleagues, Satan rebelled against God and has since been wreaking whatever havoc he can. The result is natural evil. So the natural evil we find is due to free actions of nonhuman spirits.[71]

Plantinga knows this sounds strange to modern ears, so he reminds us that he isn't offering a theodicy, but a defense. And it is certainly possible, even if not plausible, that natural evil in our world stems from abuse of Satanic and demonic free will.[72] The line of argument to vindicate God against the existence of natural evil follows the same pattern that Plantinga used in appealing to human free will as the cause of moral evil.[73]

CONTEMPORARY INTERCHANGE OVER THE FREE WILL DEFENSE

As one would expect, the free will defense in general and Plantinga's version in particular have received much attention. Rather than rehashing all of it, I want to raise what seem to me the more significant concerns. I shall first address matters that specifically pertain to Plantinga's form of the free will defense. Then, I plan to handle other challenges to the free will defense in any form. As we shall see, many of the objections raised are wrong because they ignore the fundamental ground rules for handling a problem of *internal* consistency in general and for dealing with the logical problem of evil in particular. On the other hand, other objections, though capable of answer, are more significant.

On Plantinga

Because of the philosophical sophistication and richness of Plantinga's presentation, much ink has been devoted to interacting with him. My comments are fundamentally positive, because I think his free will defense succeeds.

DAVID GRIFFIN'S OBJECTION

David Ray Griffin raises an objection which I think is clearly wrong, but I mention it because it is instructive generally about the nature of the logical problem of evil. Griffin chides Plantinga for offering a defense rather than engaging in theodicy. He thinks Plantinga should offer the reason (not just a possible reason) for God to allow both moral and natural evil. Griffin is particularly disturbed by Plantinga's claims that a defense

> need be neither true, nor probable, nor plausible, nor believed by most theists, nor anything else of that sort. . . . The fact that a particular proffered *r* is implausible, or not congenial to "modern man," or a poor explanation of *q*, or whatever, is utterly beside the point.[74]

Griffin considers this thoroughly unconvincing to any modern person and hence inadequate. Plantinga says that to rebut the charge of contradiction one needs only to offer a hypothesis that renders the system internally consistent, even if the hypothesis is improbable or untrue. Griffin (including quotes from his earlier work) replies:

> . . . while that attitude may have been justified at the time of Leibniz and especially earlier, when the existence of God was not widely questioned, an approach based on that attitude is not adequate in our time. We need "a 'global argument,' the purpose of which is to show that a theistic interpretation can illuminate the totality of our experience, including the experience of evil, better than nontheistic interpretations." . . . For that purpose, the hypotheses reconciling God with evil must be plausible, not simply possible. It was to this discussion that I referred in saying that the hypothesis about Satan and his cohorts "returns us to the previous point about the general illumination that theism needs to provide to render itself plausible in our day."[75]

As the quote suggests, Griffin finds Plantinga's handling of natural evil especially disturbing. He argues that no twentieth-century person will find it even vaguely plausible, but if we want nonbelievers to become believers, we must offer them an explanation of God's ways that not only meets formal demands of the problem of evil, but is plausible. Hence, a defense like Plantinga's is inadequate to solve the real problem of evil people face.[76]

Plantinga, then, should offer a theodicy, not a defense. In fact, the task of a philosophical theologian, according to Griffin, isn't to provide possible though implausible answers, but plausible answers that touch people where they really live.[77] Griffin says:

> Why should anyone, therefore, think that Plantinga and others who take the same line have done anything worth doing, insofar as they invent merely possible hypotheses that show the existence of the God of traditional theism not to be logically inconsistent with the existence of evil? Does it have any relevance to the problem of evil as humans actually grapple with it? . . .
>
> Some critics of traditional theism have, to be sure, presented the case against it as if a strictly logical inconsistency were the crux of the matter. That presentation has provided defenders of traditional theism the opportunity for an easy victory. But what the critics should have meant, if they did not, is that there is no *plausible* way to portray the consistency of the existence of that God with the evil in the world. Only with this interpretation would the critics be speaking on behalf of the problem of evil as it is widely experienced in our culture; and only with this interpretation would the philosophical theologian's attempted defense of the traditional God have any relevance to the wider culture.[78]

This objection may appear devastating,[79] but it is wrongheaded. The fundamental problem is that it ignores the basic ground rules I set forth in chapter 1 for handling the issue of God and evil in general and the logical problem of evil in particular.

When someone decides to evaluate a conceptual scheme (theological, philosophical, or otherwise), there are several items to check. The system can be checked for logical consistency (does it contradict itself?), factual adequacy (does it square with the data of reality so that it is likely to be true, in a correspondence sense of "true"?), and practical applicability (can one live in the world in accord with such views?). As I argued in chapter 1, the first issue relates exclusively to the logical form of the problem of evil. As we shall see in later chapters, the second item relates to the evidential form of the problem. As to the third item, I submit that it relates to the existential dimension of the problem of evil. That will be my focus in the chapters on the religious problem of evil.

With this explanation, I think Griffin's errors become clear. For one thing, the problem of evil isn't just one problem, but a series of problems. However, Griffin tends to conflate the problems. He talks about the logical consistency of theism, but he also talks about a plausible way to explain God's relation to evil. This implicitly conflates the problem of evil in its logical and evidential forms. Moreover, he speaks of the problem of evil "as people really grapple with it." This invokes the religious problem of evil, a different problem again. As I argued in chapter 1, one gets nowhere if one mixes these problems. Complaining that a given defense is worthless because it doesn't address all problems of evil is illegitimate. Just because a defense doesn't solve every problem of evil doesn't mean it resolves none.

Griffin's complaint that Plantinga offers only a possible answer to evil (one which Griffin thinks implausible) evidences an even more fundamental misunderstanding of the ground rules of the problem of evil. Plantinga appeals to those rules (and Griffin quotes him),[80] but Griffin (like many others) seems to miss the point.

As argued in chapter 1, the *logical* problem of evil (and that is clearly what Plantinga's free will defense addresses!) accuses a theistic system of contradicting itself. Specifically, it says that propositions about God's existence and evil's existence contradict one another. To assert that a set of propositions is self-contradictory means there is *no possible way* to fit those claims together consistently—not now, not ever!

Now, if this is what the logical problem of evil charges against theism, to meet the charge the theist need only offer *a possible way* to harmonize the propositions consistently. But since that is the rule of this "game," why should Griffin or anyone else complain when Plantinga sticks to the rule and offers a possible way? Griffin may think Plantinga's free will defense is implausible and doesn't meet the needs of modern people, and he may be right.[81] But the most that would show, if correct, is that Plantinga's version of the free will defense may be of little help in handling the evidential problem of evil where the probability of theism is at issue, and of little help in handling the religious problem of evil where one's personal struggles with evil are the concern. It does *not* show that the free will defense is inadequate for handling the logical problem of moral evil! Plantinga has done precisely what the atheistic challenge demands. He has offered a possible way to render his theology consistent.

One further word about plausibility. Just because Plantinga doesn't offer arguments for the plausibility of the free will defense doesn't mean it can't be done. For example, anyone who holds libertarian free will (even if he or she is an atheist) will think it possible to support convincingly at least the libertarian notion of freedom. As to Plantinga's appeal to Satan and demons abusing their free will as the cause of natural evil, regardless of whether Plantinga would defend the existence of such creatures, there are many traditional theists who hold the free will defense who could and would support the existence of Satan on biblical grounds. Though those biblical grounds might impress few, the evidence shouldn't be ruled out on question-begging anti-supernaturalistic presuppositions. The theist's case should be given fair hearing.[82]

I conclude, then, that though we should take seriously the plea to offer not only possible defenses but plausible ones, that in no way undermines the success of Plantinga's free will defense. Thankfully, many theists and atheists alike have understood the rules covering the logical problem of evil, and so have agreed (even if somewhat grudgingly on the part of atheists) that Plantinga has met the demands of the *logical* problem of moral evil. Unfortunately, Griffin's objection ignores several fundamental rules of procedure for the logical problem, and thus fails.

FLEW, MACKIE, AND PLANTINGA

Unquestionably, the key to the Flew, Mackie, and Plantinga exchange is the meaning of free will. In fact, it is at the heart of any discussion of the free will defense. Philosophers and theologians have debated the question of determinism vs. indeterminism for centuries without reaching a conclusion that satisfies all parties. It is probably unlikely that there will ever be a resolution of the problem that convinces everyone. Furthermore, it isn't my purpose to try to solve this problem in this book.[83]

My reason for raising this issue is to make several points about the free will defense as an answer to the logical problem of moral evil which confronts some Modified Rationalist theologies. My initial point is that both incompatibilism and compatibilism are possible accounts of freedom. That is, neither view is self-contradictory, so either could be correct. If there is a complaint about one of these views not being self-consistent, it is usually raised with respect to compatibilism. However, the objection typically amounts to the question-begging claim that freedom and causal determinism can't fit together consistently, because freedom just means that the act isn't causally determined. Thankfully, there are many indeterminists as well as determinists who recognize that both views are logically possible.[84] Of course, if both compatibilism and incompatibilism are possible, then the free will defense can't be rejected as incorporating a self-contradictory notion of free will.

If the free will defender's notion of freedom is logically consistent, then what follows? What follows is that Mackie's and Flew's objections to the free will defense fall flat. Let me explain. The key is that the logical problem of evil is about the *internal* consistency of a given theological position, and that just means that the crucial question is whether the theist's views contradict one another. We know they contradict the atheist's views; that's at least part of why the atheist is an atheist! But that isn't the point of the logical problem of evil. I believe that it is of utmost importance to see that the objections of Flew and Mackie aren't really that the free will defense still leaves its theology self-contradictory. Their complaint is that it incorporates an inadequate account of free will. Of course, if compatibilism is forced into the free will defender's system, then Flew's and Mackie's objections succeed in destroying the system. But free will defenders don't hold compatibilism, nor should it be forced on them. If one holds incompatibilism and adopts the free will defense to explain moral evil, the demands of the logical problem of moral evil are met for the theologies using the defense, because the free will defense explains why God would allow evil, and does so in a way that leaves such theologies internally consistent. It simply breaks the ground rules of the logical problem when Flew and Mackie force their compatibilism on Plantinga (or any other free will defender) and then tell him that he can't solve a problem of logical consistency that is *internal* to his theology. If it's their view and not his, it isn't *internal* to his theology, and they can't make it internal to his theology just because they think they have a better account of free will.

Flew's and Mackie's objections don't defeat the free will defense, but those who, like Flew and Mackie, are convinced that compatibilism is the correct account of free will should reject incompatibilism, the free will defense, and any theology that incorporates it. However, rejecting the free will defense on those grounds shows no internal inconsistency with the defense itself or any theology that uses it. It simply refuses to pay the price for the system's fundamental intellectual commitments.

On the Free Will Defense in General

Some objections relate to most if not all versions of the free will defense, and I want to interact with the major ones. Some question the internal consistency of the defense, whereas most object on grounds external to the system. I believe the challenges to internal consistency are answerable. As to external objections, some are misguided, whereas others raise problems that lead many, including myself, to reject this theology and its defense altogether. But, of course, that shows no inability to solve the logical problem of evil.

GRIFFIN'S OBJECTIONS

In *Evil Revisited,* David Griffin poses a series of objections to the free will defense which he believes not only show that it is inadequate, but help to make his case that a process theology and theodicy is the best option for those who want to remain theists. I shall present his objections and respond to them, but before turning directly to them, we must see how Griffin portrays the free will defense, since some of his objections stem from his understanding of it. Griffin explains the free will defense as follows:

It offers the hypothesis that reliable laws of nature and genuine human free-dom *vis-a-vis* God, which are seldom if ever interrupted, are necessary aspects of God's overall purpose for the creation which is a good purpose (perhaps the "best conceivable" one). This purpose is to encourage the formation of beings who freely develop moral-spiritual character. Given this perspective, the occurrence of natural and moral evil is said not to contra-dict God's goodness and power. God *could,* of course, interrupt the laws of nature to alter the otherwise inevitable spatiotemporal features of physical things (bullets, bombs, cancerous cells) or the decisions of free subjects that would otherwise lead to massive suffering. . . . But to have done this to avoid momentary pain and suffering would actually have hindered the realization of the long-term purpose, the development of moral and spiritual qualities through free decisions. This is the case not only because this purpose requires genuine freedom and regular laws of cause and consequence, but also because pain and suffering are essential conditions to the realization of many of the most important moral and spiritual qualities. Without suffer-ing, for example, there cannot be courageous endurance of suffering. Although some forms of suffering seem counterproductive to this purpose, because they seem to defeat rather than to stimulate the process of soul-making, it is often precisely the most horrendous evils, those that seem least capable of being understood as contributing to any moral-spiritual purpose, that evoke the deepest compassion in others. They are thus not counter-productive after all.[85]

It should be clear that this isn't the free will defense as traditionally pre-sented and as described in this chapter. Actually, it combines two different defenses, the free will defense and the soul-building theodicy which we shall discuss in the next chapter. The free will defense justifies God in terms of his giving us an extremely valuable gift, free will. Unfortunately, we use it to bring moral evil into the world. Still, God isn't guilty, for he hasn't done the evil, and his gift, free will, is something good. On the other hand, the soul-building theodicy adopts a consequentialist ethic according to which ours is a good world because of how God uses it. God is good because he uses this world with its evil to bring about our spiritual growth.

These are two separate defenses with two different reasons for calling ours a good world. I raise this point because several of Griffin's objections actually attack the soul-building part of the defense, not the free will part. For example, Griffin's first complaint asks if it is plausible to believe, "granting that virtue often presupposes suffering, that *every* basic structural aspect of the world can be justified as necessary to the promotion of creatures with moral and spiritual qualities?"[86] Griffin thinks not. Regardless of how we would answer his question, his objection clearly attacks the soul-making aspect of his understanding of the free will defense. It is not, in fact, an objec-tion to the free will defense per se.

Griffin's second objection suffers from the same problem. He notes that much suffering in our world doesn't promote virtue, but the opposite. Faced with evil and suffering, many people turn from God, not to him. Hence, God's plan for producing virtuous beings appears to have backfired.[87] As we shall see, John Hick raises this same issue in regard to the soul-building theodicy, and offers an answer. For now, it should be clear that the objection can't harm the free will defense, because it attacks the soul-building theodicy instead.

A third objection has the same malady. Griffin complains that the free will defense "requires an excessive belittling of the importance of enjoyment and suffering in comparison with virtue and vice."[88] Griffin agrees that values like character enhancement are more important than enjoyment, and sin is worse than suffering. His objection, however, is that

> . . . the degree to which the traditional free-will defenders are forced to go in making the sin-virtue spectrum virtually all-important and the enjoyment-suffering spectrum virtually irrelevant, seems excessive. They are forced into this extreme position by their basic premise. Because God, by hypothesis, built the capacity for so much suffering into our world deliberately, for the sole purpose of stimulating moral and spiritual virtues, the theologian must conclude that the question of suffering is very trivial in comparison with the question of virtue.[89]

Clearly, this rejects the soul-building aspect of Griffin's understanding of the free will defense. It doesn't touch the free will aspect of it. I needn't continue with these arguments, for the point is clear enough; many of Griffin's objections to the free will defense fail, because they don't really address it![90]

Griffin also complains that the traditional free will defense doesn't explain animal pain and suffering. Some animal pain may offer opportunity for us to express compassion, but not most of it. Moreover, the free will defense emphasizes only human development, but how can that justify the vast amount of pain in animals that can't develop moral or spiritual qualities?[91] We might also add that it just isn't true that all animal suffering results from abuse of human free will.

Though Griffin's attack again conflates the soul-building theodicy and the free will defense, his general objection about animal suffering raises a significant problem. It is true that the free will defense doesn't handle animal suffering, but then it wasn't intended to do so. That problem is a separate problem of evil, and clearly, the free will defense isn't useful in handling a lot of animal suffering. On the other hand, the free will defense *does* address the problem of moral evil, and it handles it successfully. Failure to answer every problem of evil doesn't mean it solves no problem of evil!

Another problem for the free will defense, according to Griffin, involves the evolutionary process. Traditional theists believe God's purpose in creation was to produce human-like creatures possessing free will. According to evolution, it took God billions of years to bring things to where humans appeared on the scene. Griffin wonders why God would use a method that took so long. It is problematic that "God devoted over 99.9 percent of the history of creation thus far to that which was mere preparation for the only part of it having any intrinsic value."[92]

Any free will defenders who hold evolution (or even theistic evolution) may feel uncomfortable as a result of this challenge. However, the objection is totally irrelevant to free will defenders who don't believe in evolution. Since the logical problem is about consistency of the views *internal* to the theist's own system, if a free will defender doesn't hold evolution, Griffin's objection creates no problem for the internal consistency of his system. Griffin offers no evidence that most or even any free will defenders believe in evolution. It is safe to say some do. They should take his objection seriously. Those who don't shouldn't.

Griffin also complains that the free will defense offers no explanation of natural evils that result from nonhuman agency. Plantinga's suggestion that they might result from Satan and demons is, of course, dismissed as implausible. As a result, Griffin thinks free will defenders either have no answer or they tend to think this evil is only apparently evil, not really evil.[93]

This is a more substantial objection than many of Griffin's. As for Plantinga, Griffin's objection is beside the point. All that is needed to meet the charge that these natural evils contradict God's existence is a possible way to fit them together. Appeal to the free will of spirit beings is a possible way, regardless of how plausible anyone thinks the suggestion.

Apart from Plantinga's suggestion, the free will defense doesn't cover natural evils that occur without someone's action. But that shouldn't surprise us, because the problems of moral evil and natural evil are separate problems, and the free will defense addresses the problem of moral evil alone. This objection is a prime example of what happens when we forget that there are many problems of evil, not just one. The fact that the free will defense doesn't handle all problems of evil doesn't mean it solves none.

Another problem with the free will defense, according to Griffin, is that it tends to deny that there is really any genuine evil in the world. The reason is that theists believe God has so ordered things that everything eventually works for good. If anything genuinely, unredeemably evil occurs, that would look bad for God. But the problem with these views is that they ultimately trivialize the evils people experience. We do, in fact, believe there are real evils; we believe we have experienced some ourselves. That the free will defense minimizes and even eliminates the existence of genuine evils shows its inadequacy.[94]

It is important here to note how Griffin defines genuine evil. He clearly sees it as evil which is unattached to any subsequent good. I shall discuss in a later chapter this problem in detail as the problem of gratuitous evil, but let me offer two comments now. First, I see no reason why this is the only type of evil that counts as genuine evil. Moreover, I doubt that any free will defender thinks of evils that are instrumental in producing good as less than genuine. Those who do must face the brunt of Griffin's criticism. Those who don't needn't worry.

My other reply is that this objection again confuses the free will defense and the soul-building theodicy. The free will defense doesn't justify God by claiming all things work out well in the end. That's what the soul-building theodicy says. The free will defense justifies God on the basis of the origin of moral evil, not on its use. Of course, Griffin can respond that this misses his point that an evil is really only evil if it is unredeemable (i.e., unattached to some subsequent good). Since many of the evils produced by free will do attach to some subsequent good, they are not genuinely evil, so his objection still stands. The problem with this response, however, is that it just begs the question again on what it means for an evil to be "genuine."

Two more objections from Griffin remain, and both relate to his process notion of freedom as opposed to the free will defender's understanding of power and freedom. According to Griffin's process theism, each actual entity is its own center of power and freedom. God doesn't have all the power and then decide to delegate some to the rest of us. On the other hand, Griffin believes that traditional theism in general holds that ultimately all power belongs to God. One form of traditional theism (Griffin labels it all-determining theism) puts all the power in God's hands and says he shares none of it with us. We may think we have power vis-à-vis God, but we don't. The other form of traditional theism (Griffin calls it traditional free-will theism) says God has all the power, but he chooses to delegate some of it to us. He does this by unilaterally deciding not to use his power on various occasions to make room for human freedom. However, it is always understood that our freedom and power are derivative from God's power, and God can override our freedom at any time.[95]

Griffin thinks this view of power creates problems for the free will defense. Free will defenders say God gave us genuine freedom to go against his will. However, Griffin wonders why God didn't make us so as to be like we are in every respect except that we would have no freedom vis-à-vis God. He could have allowed us to enjoy all the valuable things we enjoy, even if we didn't have this freedom. Griffin knows free will defenders will answer that this leaves out one important value, namely, the sense that we have freely avoided sin and developed spiritual virtues. Griffin says the way around this dilemma is for God to have created us so that we would think we are genuinely free, even though we aren't. Traditional theists will complain that deception on God's part is unacceptable, for it counts against his perfect goodness. Griffin suggests, however, that a God who creates an earthly paradise and deceives his creatures into thinking they are free is less morally reprehensible than a God who unilaterally made all forms of evil in our world possible solely for the value that would accrue to himself from beings who genuinely freely love him and develop spiritually.[96]

Of course, Griffin believes the way out of this problem is to adopt process theism, which says that each actual entity is its own center of underived power. While I agree that this might be a reason for rejecting the free will defense and its theology as a whole, it shows no internal inconsistency in the free will defense's theology.

What about the specific attack, though? Many free will defenders will probably contend that the kind of utopia Griffin envisions can't be created. However, for the sake of argument, assume that it can be. If so, this objection complains that God could have made a better world than he did; therefore, he is reprehensible.

Now, even if the free will defender agrees that Griffin's envisioned world would be a better world, that doesn't obligate God to create it. Remember the basics of a Modified Rationalist theology. There is no best world, only good and bad possible worlds. The Modified Rationalist's system demands only that if God creates, he create a good world. Has he done so? If not, the problem of evil destroys the system, for God is shown to be evil on the system's own grounds. But the free will defense points to free will as the item that makes this world a good world. Free will defenders don't have to prove our world is better than some other worlds God could create in order to show that their system is *internally* consistent. All they must do is show that our world is one of the good possible worlds God could create, and they have done so. Hence, Griffin's objection uncovers no internal inconsistency in the free will defense or its theology, and thus doesn't make the free will defense inadequate.[97]

As to the other aspects of Griffin's suggestion, they are unacceptable. Griffin wants free will defenders to choose between one reprehensible God and another. He asks which God would be less reprehensible. That is beside the point. A God who is morally reprehensible at all contradicts the theist's claim that God is good and absolutely holy. Hence, to buy Griffin's sugges-

tion forces free will defenders to incorporate into their theology notions that
do contradict their other beliefs about God (e.g., God is a God of truth).
Griffin would probably reply that all of this is so much the worse for traditional theism; the remedy is process theism. Maybe so (though I doubt it), but
that is beside the point of whether the free will defense resolves its logical
problem of moral evil, a problem about the internal consistency of views free
will defenders actually hold.

Griffin's final objection also relates to power. Since Griffin believes the
traditional God has all the power, he argues that this God could retake power
at any moment to prevent all sorts of evil. The problem, says Griffin, is that
the free will defender's God could do something, but he doesn't. Griffin says:

> But after all the qualifications are made, and after all the reasons are
> rehearsed as to why it is good for God not to interrupt, it is hard to still the
> thought, when confronted with a concrete case of horrendous evil: "In *this*
> case God should have done something!"[98]

For Griffin, of course, the answer is to adopt process theism, which holds that
God can't intervene because he doesn't have all the power.

What about this objection? I note initially that if one thinks it cogent, one
might be inclined to drop free will theism altogether. But none of that shows
any internal inconsistency in the free will defender's system. It is still true that
if God wants to give us incompatibilistic free will, he can't stop the evils
Griffin wants stopped without removing that freedom. Hence, if the free will
defense is adopted, God cannot do what Griffin suggests.

Griffin might reply that God could just remove freedom when it would
lead to evil, but otherwise let it be. This would remove all the evils God could
and should stop. In regard to my own system (chapter 6), I contemplate what
God would have to do to remove evil, and I point out the difficulties with
God doing that. I think many of the problems that would arise for my God
also arise for the free will defender's God if he tries to remove evil.
Fundamentally, though, if God created such a world, it isn't abundantly clear
that we would use this freedom much. It is not always possible to know when
one's actions would lead to evil. However, in the world imagined, we would
know that if an action leads to evil, God would do something to stop it. If so,
I submit that we would be fearful of even doing things we would think God
would allow. It isn't at all clear that life as we know it wouldn't come to an
end. Hence, it isn't at all clear that the free will defender's God can do what
is requested without eliminating the use of free will (if not free will itself)
entirely. And, it seems rather odd for God to bother to give us free will only
to have to spend so much time counteracting it.

In addition, if God did what Griffin requests, it would mean our world would be a very different world. But as argued above, God isn't obligated to create a better world than other good worlds. His obligation in a Modified Rationalist system is only to create a good world, and free will makes ours one of those good worlds. Hence, God has done what he is required to do.

Still, Griffin might reply that God should at least stop horrendous evils. I note in response that this shifts the discussion from the problem of moral evil to the problem of the intensity of evil. The free will defense may be inadequate to handle that problem of evil, but that isn't at issue here. What is at issue is whether it handles adequately the logical problem of moral evil for its theology, and it does. Moreover, I believe the free will defender can appropriately respond that the things which make it problematic for God to stop evil in general also make it troublesome for him to stop it in specific instances. God could restrict himself to only the horrendous evils (of course, it is always debatable as to which are the horrendous ones). However, what he would need to do in those cases (I think there would be many more than Griffin suspects) to stop the evil would again make ours a different world. Perhaps that would be a better world, but it is only God's obligation, according to Modified Rationalism, to create a good possible world, and the free will defense explains why God has done so. I conclude, then, that this objection (as the others) doesn't destroy the free will defense.

THE BOËR PROPOSAL

Some years ago Steven Boër raised another objection to the free will defense in his article "The Irrelevance of the Free Will Defence." Boër claimed that the free will defense is irrelevant, because all that is needed for people to have free will is that they have the ability to choose freely, not the ability to succeed in effecting what they intend to accomplish. In other words, God could allow us to choose evil, but intervene so that the consequences of our choices never befall anyone. Some might object that God's intervention would be so overt that it would clarify that there is a God, and then it would make no sense to defy him. But then, there would be no *freedom* to follow or reject him because of the knowledge that he exists and might punish us if we defy him. The way around this, according to Boër, is for God to stop the consequences of evil actions by means of coincidence miracles. That kind of miracle would hide the fact that God is at work, but still accomplish the intended goal of keeping evil from befalling anyone.[99] As Frank Dilley explains, this would also have the further value of "preserving the illusion that it is meaningful to try to do evil."[100]

The net result of this objection is that free will per se is an inadequate justification of moral evil, because God could so arrange the world that we would have incompatibilistic free will, and still avoid evil. Boër thinks that doing this would make only minor adjustments to our world.

In the years since Boër made this proposal, some have defended his views, while others have attacked them.[101] I think Dilley's objections are most helpful, and I shall present several of his strongest arguments.

Boër's proposal assumes that God could create a world with incompatibilistic free will and no evil. However, for reasons Frank Dilley offers, it isn't at all clear that God could do that. Of course, if he can't do it, he isn't obligated to do it.

Dilley rightly argues that for God to do what Boër requires, the world would change far more than Boër thinks. God wouldn't only have to perform coincidence miracles to overcome evil intentioned actions, but would have to do the same for good-intentioned actions that result in evil (even though the agent didn't intend or anticipate evil). This means the world would be interrupted far more frequently than Boër thinks.[102] But then, argues Dilley, what happens to free will? After seeing coincidence miracles occur enough times, people would get the message that evil-intended actions can't succeed, and that would be a great hindrance to their free decision to choose evil. Moreover, since even good-intentioned acts might be interrupted, might we not be hesitant to choose even those acts? It seems so, but then, this seems to paralyze human action of any sort. Laws of nature which describe the regularities of the natural order would change so as to reflect interruption of actions by coincidence miracles. But then, if someone does choose to act, her choices will no doubt be decisively influenced by what she has learned from past experiences of trying to perform those acts. If so, what becomes of undetermined action, i.e., what happens to incompatibilistic free will? Remember that Boër's claim is that his proposal still leaves free will in place in the world. Under the circumstances imagined, that is doubtful.[103]

Another problem with Boër's proposal is that it won't allow people to be cognitively free with respect to God. That is, in Boër's world, people would surely conclude that there is a God. But then, this would force belief in God upon them whether they wanted it or not. How could they dare refuse? But this isn't incompatibilistic freedom! As Dilley explains:

> Could even the fool continue to say in his heart 'there is no God' if every time he intended to harm himself or others some coincidence occurred which prevented it? Suppose that Gertrude is determined to find out whether there is a beneficent providence and takes to intending to jump from tall buildings. The first time she might discover that she could not find any windows to jump through. The second time she might find a window but discover it was barred. The third time someone intending to rob her might prevent her

from jumping. . . . Make her as dumb as you will, the hundredth or the thou-sandth or millionth time she tries to kill herself, it will occur to her that her failure to come to harm is not mere coincidence, that there is something about the universe which prevents her from coming to harm. Unless Boër could counter with some hitherto unmentioned feature of reality which would prevent her from ever learning from experience, God's secret could not be kept.[104]

Again, it appears that God could not actualize Boër's suggested world.

There is another respect in which God couldn't do what Boër asks. In the world imagined, people have incompatibilistic free will. But, given this sort of freedom, many have argued that God can't know the future, because he can't predict what sort of actions people will do. His prediction of those actions wouldn't *cause* them to occur, but it would guarantee that they occur. But, with libertarian free will of the sort the incompatibilist imagines, there can't be any guarantees.

This is a problem many indeterminists have recognized and tried to address in one way or another. But why must God know the content of free choices? He must know so that he can know the outcome in order to prepare a coincidence miracle to counteract the consequences. Since with incompat-ibilism it appears that he can't foreknow the choice, God's only option is to wait to see its outcome. However, on Boër's proposal, God isn't supposed to know the evil outcome, because the coincidence miracle is supposed to keep the outcome from occurring. So, God is supposed to prepare a coincidence miracle to counteract the evil choice, but given incompatibilism, it seems that he can't know to do that until the consequences have already occurred, con-sequences the miracle was to have precluded. Dilley explains the problem as follows:

> The tradition answers this question, at least sometimes, by claiming that God observes "future" free choices *as they occur.* That is how St. Thomas, for example, reconciles liberty of causes with "foreknowledge." However, this option is not available to Boër because in *his* view God has by coinci-dence miracles *prevented* the occurrence of the very effect that would have followed from the content of that free choice! God cannot observe the occur-rence of an effect which God prevented from happening. That effect never happened, it was never an actual event which could have been observed. Now, not knowing what effect was to occur, how could God arrange the appropriate coincidence miracle? Let me go over the ground again.
>
> The contracausalist outcome is not the product of antecedent causes, but rather is the outcome of a free choice. God, however, does not know the con-tent of that free choice, he supposedly only knows the outcome of it. But that outcome *is precisely what does not occur because God has prevented its occurrence*! On the basis of what knowledge did God take preventive action? The situation is plainly absurd.[105]

It seems that the only way out of this dilemma is for God to perform a miracle as he sees the action take place,[106] but that kind of miracle won't be a coincidence miracle. It will be a major intervention on his part. The problem with that is that it will do further damage to cognitive freedom about belief in God. Those miracles will make it abundantly clear that there is a God, and then, there will be tremendous pressure to believe in him. That seems clearly incompatible with incompatibilism.

I conclude from the preceding that it is dubious that God could create the kind of world Boër requests. Hence, any failure to do so counts in no way against the traditional free will defense. Boër's objection fails.

FLEW, FRANKFURT, AND THE FREE WILL DEFENSE

As we saw in discussing Flew's complaints about the free will defense, he held that causal determinism is compatible with free choice and action. Hence, he believed that with compatibilistic free will, God could guarantee that humans do only good even though they act freely. Typically, incompatibilists have held that one is not free (and hence, not morally responsible) in a given instance unless one has access to an alternate course of action.

In an important article which has gained increasing attention in recent years, Harry Frankfurt has argued that even if an agent doesn't have access to alternate courses of action, he may still be morally responsible for what he does.[107] He illustrates his point with a series of situations in which the person involved decides freely to do a certain act which, if he had chosen otherwise, he would have been forced to do anyway. The fact that he couldn't have done otherwise if he had wanted to isn't a sufficient reason to relieve him of moral responsibility for what he chose. Andrew Eshleman describes the common structure of such Frankfurt-type examples as follows:

> An agent decides upon a course of action and proceeds to act in a normal responsibility-conferring manner. Unbeknownst to the agent, circumstances are such that if the agent had shown signs of choosing a course of action other than the one she did, some coercive factor would come into play and guarantee that she perform her originally intended action. Significantly however, this coercive factor never comes into play.[108]

In a case of this sort, Frankfurt argued that despite the fact that the agent really couldn't have done other than he did, that isn't reason to relieve him of moral responsibility for what he did.

Eshleman notes that while Frankfurt-type examples have received much attention in scholarly philosophical literature, there has been very little application of this issue to the free will defense. Eshleman's article makes that application. He begins with Flew's objection to the free will defense, and notes that Flew proposed that with compatibilism, one could still hold that the agent could have done otherwise. Flew argued that "could have done otherwise" claims could be given a conditional analysis, i.e., to say that an agent is free so that she could have done otherwise just means that if she had chosen to do otherwise, she would have been able to do so.[109]

Now one doesn't have to agree with Flew's conditional analysis of "could have done otherwise" to use his basic ideas to attack the free will defense. Eshleman argues that it may be possible to resurrect Flew's main objection to the free will defense by appealing to Frankfurt-type cases. If Frankfurt-type examples do show that one can still be free and morally accountable even though the agent can't do otherwise, Eshleman believes that would be a strong argument in favor of compatibilism. And if freedom and moral responsibility are compatible with determinism, then, following Flew's initial objection, "God could have created a world inhabited by free and responsible agents who nevertheless were causally determined to always act rightly."[110]

Eshleman devotes the rest of his article to evaluating various strategies incompatibilists have suggested for blunting the force of Frankfurt-style examples. He argues that none of those strategies is successful, and as a result, he believes "that Frankfurt-style examples provide grounds for a Flew-like objection to the free will defence."[111]

What should we say about this objection to the free will defense? Elsewhere I have discussed Frankfurt-style examples in relation to the debate between libertarian free will and compatibilism.[112] I am inclined to view that argument as a significant help in making a case for compatibilism. However, making a case for compatibilism is beyond the purpose of this book, and that in itself should be a good hint as to why Eshleman's use of Frankfurt-style examples doesn't damage the free will defense.

Put simply, the *logical* problem of moral evil isn't about whether one thinks the basic theological commitments of a given position are right or wrong, plausible or implausible. Rather, it is about whether the theologian holds views which are *self*-contradictory. It is a problem about the internal consistency of the theology under consideration. Once we understand this, we also recognize that even if Frankfurt-style examples are helpful in establishing compatibilism as the correct view of free will, appeal to them is irrelevant, since free will defenders don't hold compatibilism, and the logical problem isn't about whether compatibilism is superior to incompatibilism or not. At most, then, appeal to Frankfurt-style examples counts as grounds *external* to the free will defender's theology for rejecting that theology as a whole; it uncovers no problem of internal inconsistency in the free will defender's position.

The relation of incompatibilism to divine foreknowledge of future contingent actions is an important issue in itself, but it also has significant implications for the free will defense. According to the free will defense, God isn't guilty of the moral evil in the world, for it happens as a result of the free and independent actions of human beings. But as Joseph Runzo explains:

> But as Augustine saw, the success of the free will defense is logically dependent on the solution to another difficulty: viz., if an omniscient God foreknows what I shall do—and surely, it seems, He must—then I cannot act other than I do and, consequently, I do not act freely. Hence, the insistence that God is omniscient seems logically incompatible with the free will defense against the problem of evil.[113]

This is no small problem. It appears that the free will defense resolves the apparent inconsistency between evil's existence and that of an all-powerful and all-benevolent God. But libertarian free will seems to contradict God's omniscience. Hence, the free will defender resolves the apparent contradiction at one point in his system only to find that the solution creates an apparent contradiction at another point in the system. If so, any theistic position committed to an omnipotent, omnibenevolent, *and* omniscient God can't solve its problem of evil by appeal to the free will defense. Unfortunately, this means many traditional Christian systems which appeal to incompatibilism would be destroyed.

Indeterminists have for centuries wrestled with the freedom/foreknowledge problem, but before turning to answers, we must be clear about the nature of this problem. No one is saying God's knowledge of future actions *causes* (or even causally determines) them to occur. Rather, the point is that since God really *knows* the future, there is no way for something else to occur. But then, the agent really couldn't do other than what God knows she will do. This doesn't mean she will be forced to do what she does by some antecedent sufficient conditions. It simply asks how, if incompatibilism is correct so that there aren't any antecedent conditions sufficient to produce the action, it can be true that God really *knows* an act will happen? How can there be this guarantee?

Indeterminists have proposed five basic solutions to this problem. Before analyzing those options, however, we must clarify what is meant by omniscience. As Runzo explains, there are three senses of "know." The first means to have a competence, i.e., know how to. The second means to be acquainted with, and the third is to know a truth, i.e., to know that. Claiming that God is omniscient means specifically that he has knowledge of this third sort. If that is so, it also means God knows every true proposition, and he also knows if a proposition is false. If it is false, he won't believe it. In essence, this means God knows everything that is logically possible for a being with his attributes (all of which are perfections) to know.[114]

In turning to specific answers to the freedom/foreknowledge problem and relating them to the logical problem of evil, we needn't decide whether any of the answers is true, but only whether any self-consistent solution actually removes the apparent contradiction between free will and God's omniscience. The first option is one that Runzo favors, as have many other indeterminists. According to this solution, God's omniscience means God knows everything there is to know. The future just isn't something that can be known. As Runzo argues, if incompatibilists claim that God knows the future, they must explain how God could know it. Runzo considers and refutes various alternatives, and ultimately concludes that God couldn't know the future.[115]

A major point in Runzo's argument that God can't know the future is the definition of knowledge. Knowledge is typically defined as justified true belief. This means God can't *know* something (nor can anyone else) unless it is true. But, *before an act or event occurs,* a proposition about it is neither true nor false. That is, at time T_1 any proposition of the form "x will do A at T_2" is neither true nor false. Of course, if that is so, that means God can't *know* it ahead of time. In fact, according to Runzo, God might not even believe it ahead of time. On what grounds would he be inclined to believe it? He might believe it or know it, because he knows everything now and knows how each thing will logically or even causally entail something later. But this can't be so for an indeterminist, for if God knows the logical and/or causal antecedents of an act, the act isn't incompatibilistically free. Hence, with incompatibilism, there simply is no future to *know,* because knowledge requires true belief, but prior to an act's occurrence, there is no true belief about it.[116]

While this answer to the freedom/foreknowledge problem has most frequently been held by secular philosophers, many of whom aren't theists, let alone evangelical Christians, over the last decade or so this view has been and continues to be espoused by those committed to open theism. Proponents of open theism are fully committed to humans possessing libertarian free will. They recognize that such freedom removes any guarantees about what free creatures will do with their freedom. But if there are no guarantees, then even God can't know what we will freely do in the future. Open theists call this view of divine foreknowledge presentism. Presentism is the view that God exhaustively knows the past and the present, including whatever tendencies each of us has, but he can't know what we will do in the future. He knows whatever he plans to do unilaterally in the future, but he can't predict how that will impact whatever we do. Open theists, contrary to their critics, believe that presentism is not only biblically defensible, but is the most biblical of all the ways to handle the freedom/foreknowledge problem.[117]

Whether or not one agrees with Runzo and open theists, does this answer solve the freedom/foreknowledge problem? If one adopts it, one can still hold the free will defense with its incompatibilism and also legitimately claim that God is omniscient. Of course, omniscience is now defined as knowing everything that is knowable; the future just isn't something that can be known. Hence, this answer does resolve the apparent contradiction between omniscience and freedom, so any free will defenders who deny that God knows the future can solve their problem of moral evil.

There is a further advantage of adopting this option. As Runzo explains, adopting this approach eliminates the complaint that God could have and should have created a better world than ours. It does so, because the objection assumes that God would know of a better world. But if libertarian free will is true, and if sentences about the future can't be true or false in the present, there is no way for God to know of a better world. And, if he cannot know of a better world, he cannot be expected to produce it. Runzo makes the point nicely as follows:

> Imagine the actual moment, T_0 at which God decides to instantiate a created world. Which world would He create? Presumably a world containing as little moral evil as possible. But which world is that? For any morally responsible agent which God creates, He could not foreknow how much evil—or good—that *actual* moral agent would produce. Moreover, given human free will acts of reproduction, God could not even foreknow how many human moral agents there would be—each agent acting for evil and/or good. And finally, God could not even have a sure foreknowledge that if He creates certain conditions, then *some* human agents or other will commit evil acts, even though the identity of the actual malefactors is dependent on the free, interpersonal relations among the human agents. For if every particular moral act of every human agent is indeed a freely-committed act, then it must be causally possible—however improbable—that no human agent ever in fact commits an immoral act. Therefore, at T_0, for any possible world W containing free moral agents, which God instantiates, He could not foreknow the eventual incidence of morally evil versus morally good actions in W.[118]

Indeed, there are many advantages to this resolution of the freedom/foreknowledge problem. But there is a major disadvantage for any free will defender who believes God knows the future. Many traditional theists (determinists and indeterminists) hold that God has revealed various biblical prophecies about the future. They believe those prophecies will come true, and they believe God knows these things about the future. He isn't merely telling us his hunch. Hence, this answer to the freedom/foreknowledge problem maintains the internal consistency of the free will defender's theology, but only at the expense of giving up another key doctrine. Any free will theology committed to the belief that God knows the future dare not adopt this solution.

Many free will defenders do believe God knows the future, so they have answered the freedom/foreknowledge problem in a way that affirms God's knowledge of the future. There are four answers of this sort: the Boethian answer, simple foreknowledge, the Molinist answer, and the Ockhamist answer.

According to Boethius, God as eternal is outside of time. He sees all of time at once, and he sees it as present. Hence, he knows our future as present to himself, and this allows him to know our future while it leaves the future open from our perspective. This is so, in part at least, because what he knows doesn't cause anything to happen. Moreover, since we don't know what he knows about our future, we can't be influenced by that information when we make choices in the future.[119]

This approach to the problem does allow God to know our future, and so upholds omniscience as traditional theism understands it. The problem with this solution is that it still contradicts incompatibilism. To say that God sees everything at once as present sounds good, but it won't solve the problem, for he sees things that *from our perspective* are still future. Since he really *knows* our future actions, how can they be avoided? Contracausal free will is still compromised. So, the Boethian resolution upholds divine foreknowledge of our future deeds, but does so at the expense of incompatibilistic free will. Hence, it doesn't adequately solve the freedom/foreknowledge problem, and consequently doesn't rescue the free will defense.

A further libertarian solution to this problem invokes what is called simple foreknowledge. According to this view, God exhaustively knows everything that will ever happen in our world once he decides to create a world at all. Thus, he knows every act his creatures will do. He simply sees them doing these acts freely (in a libertarian sense) once he decides to create a world. How does God knows this? He doesn't infer it from antecedent conditions at each point in time; he just directly and clearly sees what will occur.[120]

Simple foreknowledge can be thought of along the lines of ordinary perception of an object. The difference here, of course, is that the "object" is a future which doesn't yet exist. Nevertheless, advocates of this view hold that God can see what will occur, much as someone might claim to see something when looking at a crystal ball or through a telescope.[121] As Hasker explains, we must understand that such knowledge isn't knowledge of propositions about what will occur, but rather knowledge (we might even call it prevision) of events and acts that will actually occur.[122]

Now it is important not to confuse this with middle knowledge, the next resolution to be considered. According to middle knowledge, God knows all possible worlds, and in doing so, he knows what would happen in every possible world, if he were to put someone in a given situation. Armed with such knowledge, God makes a decision about which outcome he prefers, and then actualizes the possible world that contains the situations and following outcomes he wants. In contrast, simple foreknowledge holds that God just decides whether he will create a world or not, and having decided to create, he does and then sees directly what will happen in that world. He doesn't first see every possible world and then choose one of them. Since God doesn't know exactly what sort of world he will get until he creates, David Basinger argues that a God with simple foreknowledge is somewhat of a gambler. The initial gamble is whether to risk creating at all. Basinger suggests that before God creates he might think through how he might respond in the various situations that could arise in this world. For example, God might say to himself, "if after I create this world I see that there will exist in it Joe and Sue who will fall in love and marry, but the outcome will be sad because a year later Joe will run off with another woman, in that case I'll try to encourage Sue not to marry Joe in the first place. On the other hand, if I see that they will fall in love and have a long, happy life together, I will encourage Sue to accept Joe's marriage proposal when it is offered."[123] Though Basinger raises this possibility, simple foreknowledge proponents normally say that God first creates, then sees what will happen, and then decides how to respond and react.

Although appeal to simple foreknowledge can be used to address the freedom/foreknowledge problem, in contemporary discussions that hasn't been the primary concern with simple foreknowledge. Rather the key issue has been whether a God who possesses it would be able (and how he would be able) to put that knowledge to practical use in his providential control of the world. We can evaluate simple foreknowledge in relation to both issues, but I begin where contemporary discussions do, i.e., with the practical value and use of such knowledge if God has it. If the doctrine runs into incoherence here, as many argue, then there is little need to ask whether this incoherent doctrine could save the day for indeterminists on the freedom/foreknowledge issue.

Three basic questions have been raised about the practical use of simple foreknowledge (if God should have it), though the second and third are very similar. Before raising any of them, however, we must note what simple foreknowledge includes. According to this concept, God knows everything that will ever occur, including his own future actions, simply by directly apprehending it. If something will happen that he doesn't foresee, then he doesn't have simple foreknowledge of everything, but only of some things. But, given divine omniscience and the interconnection of events and acts, including how various acts of a given set of agents will impact others in that set, it is hard to see how God could actually see the future without seeing all of it.

With this clarification, we are ready for objections to simple foreknowledge as serving any positive advantage to God. The first is called the "Doxastic Problem." Simple foreknowledge portrays God as making his decisions about what to do in our world after viewing the future. That future, of course, includes his own future decisions. Thomas Kapitan explains the problem by offering what he calls the doxastic principle:

> It is impossible for a rational, self-reflective agent to consciously entertain the belief that he/she will perform an action A while, at the same time, deliberating about whether to perform A.[124]

In order to be able to deliberate about a decision, doing the act or refraining from it must be genuine options for the one deliberating. But if God already knows via simple foreknowledge that he will perform a given action, it is impossible for him to do anything other than what he foresees. If he can genuinely deliberate and make a different choice than the one he foreknows he will make, then he doesn't have simple foreknowledge of that matter after all. Since simple foreknowledge says God just sees all actions, including his own, in advance, there can be no deliberating about whether to do or refrain from doing any of them. If God can't deliberate and choose in light of what he knows about the future, this information can't help him plan responses to what he sees.[125]

David Hunt calls a second objection to the practical use of simple foreknowledge the metaphysical problem. This can perhaps best be explained by an example. Imagine that God through simple foreknowledge knows that a person (call him Osmo, as in the example Hunt takes from Richard Taylor) will find a winning lottery ticket worth millions. He will find it at the intersection of 7th and Elm Streets on May 8. For whatever reason God has someone record all the events of Osmo's life in a book, and somehow Osmo finds this book. Osmo reads about his impending good fortune, and gets very excited. He also sees that for this to happen, he must walk by 7th and Elm on the appointed day. This seems a bit odd to Osmo, because while he normally walks to work, he has never taken this route before. Nonetheless, armed with this information, Osmo decides to walk by 7th and Elm on May 8, and finds the winning lottery ticket.

All of this means that Osmo's belief that if he walks the appointed route he will find the ticket, and the very decision to walk by 7th and Elm both depend on his knowledge (thanks to God's simple foreknowledge) that he will find the ticket. So the decision to go the appointed route depends on his belief, and the discovery of the ticket depends on his decision. Moreover, the belief depends on his knowledge that he will discover the ticket. If he doesn't have that belief and make that decision, he won't get the lottery ticket. But unless he believes already that he will get the lottery ticket, he won't believe there is a reason to go by 7th and Elm, nor will he decide to do so. Hunt explains the apparent problem as follows:

> It looks like Osmo's discovery of the ticket involves a circle of dependence in which his foreknowledge helps bring about the very future that he fore-knows. But the assumption that such a metaphysical "loop" is possible might well be incoherent. The principle at stake—call it the 'Metaphysical Principle'—can be stated as follows:
>
> > (MP) It is impossible that a decision depend on a belief which depends on a future event which depends on the original decision.
>
> I shall call the conflict between the Metaphysical Principle and the providential use of foreknowledge the 'Metaphysical Problem.'[126]

Now if Osmo has the metaphysical problem, then there must also be a similar metaphysical problem for a God possessing simple foreknowledge. For, fore-knowing all that will occur, how could he then decide to make a decision that he foresees he already has decided to make, in that it leads to certain ends he also foresees? In my judgment, this is a major problem for simple foreknowledge, and implicit in it also is the doxastic problem, for if Osmo foresees that he will win the lottery, he will also foresee some of the means to that end, namely, believing that if he goes by 7th and Elm on May 8 he will find the lottery ticket. But then, he can't really decide, after foreseeing all of this, to go the appointed route, for he will already have foreseen that he would make that decision.

William Hasker has raised an objection that plays on many of the same themes as the metaphysical problem. He contends that if God has simple fore-knowledge, it is utterly useless to his providential control of anything. Simple foreknowledge gives God complete knowledge of actual events and actions that will occur, but then, it includes all the causal antecedents to those events and acts. If all of this is foreknown, however, and God doesn't like what will happen, he can't intervene to change anything he knows will happen, for doing so would bring a different future, but there can't be a different future from the one he foresees. On the other hand, if God likes what he foresees,

but it is to come about by factors other than his intervention, he can't intervene to try to guarantee the result, for doing so might change the result, which
is impossible, since the result is already certain. Moreover, even if his action
wouldn't change the result, he still can't do anything he didn't already foresee himself doing. Hence, whether or not God likes what he sees via simple
foreknowledge, he can't use the information to do anything he wouldn't
already do.[127]

Hasker adds (I believe correctly) that the uselessness of simple foreknowledge to providence would accrue with either libertarian free will or
determinism, for it depends on neither. It depends on the fact that one can't
change what one infallibly sees will happen, nor can one change means to that
end when one already foresees what the means will be.[128] Of course, this isn't
a problem for a determinist like myself who believes that God foreknows on
the basis of what he foreordains.[129]

What should we conclude about simple foreknowledge? As to the usefulness of simple foreknowledge for divine providential control, I think the
doxastic and metaphysical problems, plus the problems raised by Hasker, cast
serious doubts about whether simple foreknowledge would help a God who
had it control the world. Hence, even if it solves the freedom/foreknowledge
problem for systems committed to libertarian free will, it still seems inconsistent with those same systems' claims about God's providential dealings in
our world to accomplish his general goals. If God via simple foreknowledge
doesn't already foresee those general goals being achieved, simple foreknowledge won't help him to reach them.

What about simple foreknowledge as a solution to the freedom/fore-
knowledge problem? We must ask this question from the standpoints of logical consistency and factual adequacy. If God has simple foreknowledge of
everything that will occur, this surely upholds the foreknowledge end of the
equation, but we run into problems on the freedom side of things. For this
solution to be internally consistent we must grant that God foreknows the
free (in a libertarian sense) deeds of his creatures; he knows them all plus all
that aren't free in this sense. But we must first ask, in virtue of what does he
see these free actions? If he foresees them in virtue of seeing the antecedent
causal conditions that bring them about, that is determinism, not libertarian
free will. If he supposedly just infallibly sees people freely (in a libertarian
sense) making such choices, this is no answer at all, for if these people are free
in the libertarian sense, they must be able both to do the acts and refrain, but
how can they refrain from doing what God infallibly sees they will do? To
say that God just sees them doing these actions freely doesn't explain how it
could be so; it just reasserts that freedom (libertarian) and foreknowledge do

after all fit together consistently with one another. However, simple fore-knowledge was intended at least in part to explain how that can be so. Asserting that it is without explaining how it could be so won't do.

In light of these considerations, I believe that while simple foreknowledge upholds divine foreknowledge, it doesn't explain how that fits with libertarian free will. If one holds both, they certainly seem to be logically consistent, but until the incompatibilist explains how such foreknowledge allows our actions to be free in the libertarian sense, we don't know that this freedom and simple foreknowledge can fit together. Hence, appeal to simple fore-knowledge won't resolve the apparent contradiction in the free will defender's system.

Another attempt by incompatibilists to solve this problem stems from Luis de Molina. It appeals to what is known as middle knowledge. Thomas Morris explains that according to Molina and his followers:

> The range of divine knowledge is thought of as divided into three types: *natural* knowledge—knowledge God has prior to (conceptually prior to) any act of creation, concerning what all the possibilities of creation are; *free knowledge*—knowledge of everything that will actually happen in the world *given* God's free choice of which possibilities of creation to actualize; and *middle knowledge*—comprehensive knowledge of what contingently, as a matter of fact, *would* result from any creative decision he might make.[130]

According to middle knowledge, God knows the future, for he knows all possible future states of affairs. He knows this by knowing the contents of every possible world, and in knowing that, he sees the connection of every possible state of affairs to what might happen next. Middle knowledge is expressed in one of two forms. According to the less common formulation, God's middle knowledge means God knows that if x were to occur, y *could* follow. The more typical formulation says that if x were to occur, y *would* follow.

How does this solve the problem of freedom and foreknowledge? The point is that in having middle knowledge, God knows the future by knowing all the possible things that can happen. However, by knowing the possibilities, but not knowing until he chooses to create a particular possible world which will become actual, there still seems to be room for incompatibilistic free will. Moreover, even after God chooses the world he wants to actualize, his creatures don't know which world he has chosen, so that information can't influence their decision making.

Though this is a more promising approach than the Boethian resolution and simple foreknowledge, I think it still has problems. Even if one agrees that

God has middle knowledge (and not all do),[131] I don't believe this solves the problem. This resolution, on one construal of the conditional proposition, really upholds incompatibilism, but it is dubious that it maintains divine foreknowledge. As to the second construal, it supports divine foreknowledge, but seems to compromise libertarian freedom again. Let me explain.

The first construal of the conditional claim is "if x happens, y could occur." With this interpretation of middle knowledge what God knows is pure possibilities. Hence, even if God actualizes a possible world which otherwise meets with his approval, he still doesn't know which possibility will follow each "if" situation. Since this is so for all conditionals relating to this whole possible world, it is hard to see how God really knows the future that will occur. It would be hard, for example, for him to guarantee any prophecy about the end times which involved human choices (and the majority of these prophecies do), since such scenarios would be one among numerous other possible things that could happen. Such uncertainty about the future surely fits libertarian free will but doesn't support divine foreknowledge of our future deeds.

On the second construal, middle knowledge talks about what *would* happen, so once God chooses the possible world he wants to actualize, he knows in every situation what his creatures would freely do. Divine foreknowledge is upheld. However, if incompatibilism is correct, how can he *know* what *would* happen if any given x occurred? That is, if y is an incompatibilistically free human action, it must be indeterminate, but if so, it is impossible for God to know in advance of our free choice which y would actually occur in any given "x situation."[132] In virtue of what would he know the particular y that would follow? In virtue of causal conditions that confront the agent at the time of decision making and move him to choose as he does? If so, that is determinism, not libertarian free will. In virtue of a hunch based on his thorough knowledge of the person's character and tendencies? Hunches may turn out to be correct, but they don't qualify as *knowledge* (even if they are right), and they certainly aren't infallible *divine* knowledge.

The result is that the middle knowledge solution on either construal of the conditional proposition doesn't solve the freedom/foreknowledge problem. The first construal of the conditional leaves incompatibilism intact, but at the expense of God really knowing the future. The second allows God to know our future actions, but in a way that seems possible only with some form of determinism.

A final approach to the freedom/foreknowledge problem that incompatibilists have used stems from the work of William of Ockham. Thomas Morris's general description of this approach is a helpful place to begin:

Suppose God has always believed that in exactly five minutes my right index finger will lightly scratch the tip of my nose. God is necessarily omniscient and so, as a believer, he is absolutely infallible. He cannot be wrong. Does it follow that no one is in a position to prevent it from being the case that, nearly five minutes hence, my finger will scratch my nose? Does it follow, in particular, that I am not free with respect to scratching? No, the Ockhamists insist, all that follows is that I *shall* scratch, not that I *must,* or that I lack the power to refrain from scratching. I can prevent the event in question. I can refrain from scratching. This option is open to me. I shall not take it, as a matter of fact, but the alternative is there. And, the Ockhamists add, if I did refrain from scratching, I would not prove God wrong. For if I were to exercise this option and leave the tip of my nose alone, God would have held a belief different from the one he in fact holds—he always would have believed that I would, at the appointed time, have done something else with my right index finger rather than scratching my nose. So the Ockhamists hold that for this event *x,* I am in a position to prevent *x,* but as a matter of fact will freely perform *x* instead.[133]

This may sound confusing, so let me explain. This approach relies on Ockham's notion of accidental necessity and his distinction between hard and soft facts. According to Ockham, the past is necessary in a sense he refers to as accidental necessity. He says:

> I claim that every necessary proposition is *per se* in either the first mode or the second mode. This is obvious, since I am talking about all propositions that are necessary *simpliciter.* I add this because of propositions that are necessary *per accidens,* as is the case with many past tense propositions. They are necessary *per accidens,* because it was contingent that they be necessary, and because they were not always necessary.[134]

Something that is accidentally necessary didn't have to occur, but once it happened, it can't be changed. But this can be true of any proposition, regardless of whether it is past, present, or future. For example, any future action or event doesn't have to occur, and hence, any proposition about the future doesn't specify what must occur. There is still the possibility for an agent to do other than the future-tensed proposition states. At some point in the future, if the agent does what is predicted, the proposition becomes accidentally necessary, i.e., once the action it specifies occurs, no one can change it, but that doesn't mean it had to be done.[135]

Ockham also distinguished between hard and soft facts. A proposition that is a hard fact is a genuine fact about the past. This means that what the proposition asserts has occurred and is completely finished. Moreover, a hard fact is exclusively about a past finished event. A proposition that mixes past and present or past and future (from our present perspective) is a soft fact, not a hard fact. Examples help to make the point. The proposition "Frank is a high school student during all of April 2005," if true, isn't a hard fact if Frank is in high school during April 2005 and that month hasn't ended. Once April 2005 passes, a corresponding proposition "Frank was a high school student during all of April 2005" will not only be true, but accidentally necessary and a hard fact.

Consider another proposition: "Frank was a junior high school student in May 2001." Assuming that the proposition is true, then since we are past May 2001, the proposition is a hard fact and accidentally necessary.

Now, consider one more proposition: "Frank correctly believed in June 2002 that he would graduate from high school in June 2005." Since Frank really did believe this in June 2002 and June 2002 is now past, one might think this proposition is a hard fact. However, it isn't, because it is about both the past and the future. Since the future hasn't yet happened, the proposition is a soft fact. Moreover, though hard facts about the past are accidentally necessary, soft facts aren't necessary in any sense, so this one isn't either. Of course, if that is so, it is still possible for Frank to do something that will keep him from graduating in June 2005. Graduation in June 2005 isn't necessary and unavoidable, though he and his parents might wish otherwise.[136] Moreover, since Frank's belief was correct, we can expect him to graduate in June 2005, but this belief won't be true and a hard fact until Frank actually graduates in June 2005.

Let us now apply this to God's foreknowledge and human freedom. If God has *fore*knowledge, then we can construct a proposition about that knowledge that is tensed as follows: "God believed (believes, or will believe)[137] at time T_1 that x will do A at time T_2." It should be clear that no matter how one tenses the verb "believe" in this proposition, the proposition expresses a soft fact, not a hard fact. It isn't now accidentally necessary, though after T_2 it will be, assuming that it occurs.

To make matters more specific consider the following proposition: "God believed in 1980 that I shall mow my lawn in April 2005." If God foreknows the future, then of course, it must be possible that this proposition is true. Moreover, I note that this proposition is a soft fact, because as I edit this, it is 2003, so the proposition says something about the future (from my current perspective). As a soft fact, the proposition isn't accidentally necessary. Should I mow my lawn in April 2005, the proposition will be both true and accidentally necessary after that. Of course, it isn't necessary (in the sense that it must happen and is unavoidable) that when April 2005 comes, I'll mow my lawn. Hence, it is contingent as to whether I'll do so or not, but that just means I am free as to whether to do it or not. The freedom side of the freedom/foreknowledge dilemma is upheld.

Suppose April 2005 comes and goes, and I don't mow my lawn. In that case, the proposition in question will never be necessary in our world and never a hard fact. But then, will God be wrong (and thereby not omniscient) for believing that I'll mow my lawn in April 2005? This brings us to the crux of the Ockhamist strategy. The Ockhamist answers the question negatively, and explains that if it turns out that I don't mow the lawn in April 2005, God never would have believed that I would. He would have believed (in the past) and now believes (in the present) something different about my future. What that is, *we* won't know until we get to the future. At that time, we shall be in a position to speak accurately about what God believed in the past about our future. If I do mow my lawn, then I'll know that I was correct in thinking that God in 1980 believed I would mow my lawn in April 2005. If I don't mow it then, I'll know that in 1980 God had a different belief about my lawn mowing in April 2005.

Someone may ask, "if God believes about the future only what actually will happen, doesn't that belief still necessitate its occurrence?" The answer is no, because on the one hand, God's beliefs have no causal power to make an event or act happen (determinists also agree with this). Moreover, given Ockham's claims, any proposition about the future will be a soft fact, and hence, cannot before the future be accidentally necessary. Furthermore, I don't yet know the truth or falsity of the proposition about God's belief about my mowing, so even though I can write that proposition, that hardly guarantees that the proposition in any way will causally *determine* me to mow my lawn. The proposition, if I think it true, may influence what I do in April 2005, but it guarantees nothing about what I shall do. I can still decide to do otherwise. In fact, I might be paralyzed, dead, or just out of town during all of April 2005 so that I couldn't decide to mow the lawn. Hence, there is no necessity that I mow my lawn in April 2005; I'm free to do what I want.

It is crucial here to realize that the Ockhamist answer does *not* say God doesn't know what the future really will be. It says that since *we* don't know, we don't know exactly what *he* knows about the future. Hence, we can write any number of propositions about God's knowledge of the future only to find out later that most or even all of them were wrong. Our errors don't mean he didn't know the truth. We just won't know what he actually believed until we see it happen (unless he tells us beforehand what will happen). And, since God's knowledge doesn't cause actions, and since we can't be causally determined by what God knows about the future, because we don't yet know what he now knows about it, we are *free* (incompatibilistically) to do other than what God knows we shall do, even though he knows we won't do otherwise.

The Ockhamist answer, then, is that God definitely knows the future, but given the distinction between hard and soft facts, *our* propositions about what he knows express soft facts and thus are not accidentally or otherwise necessary. Human freedom and divine foreknowledge of our future actions seem compatible.

Some may still be puzzled about how God actually knows the future. Ockham doesn't entirely explain, but one passage gives us a clue about how God knows our futures. He writes:

> Despite [the impossibility of expressing it clearly], the following way [of knowing future contingents] can be ascribed [to God]. Just as the [human] intellect on the basis of one and the same [intuitive] cognition of certain non-complexes can have evident cognition of contradictory contingent propositions such as 'A exists,' 'A does not exist,' in the same way it can be granted that the divine essence is intuitive cognition that is so perfect, so clear, that it is evident cognition of all things past and future, so that it knows which part of a contradiction [involving such things] is true and which part false.[138]

How does the Ockhamist approach fare in handling the freedom/foreknowledge problem? I believe this is the most promising approach for one who wants to maintain that God really knows the future and at the same hold that we are incompatibilistically free. The Ockhamist strategy really does seem to allow human actions to be undetermined by God's foreknowledge. Hence, the answer seems to be *self*-consistent. If so, then when it is applied to the free will defender's theology, it renders it internally consistent as a whole.

In response to this approach, one might still complain that it is hard to see how God can just intuitively know the future, when actions and events aren't causally connected (given incompatibilism) to causally sufficient antecedent conditions. That is, on what basis can God know in advance that one act follows after another? Ockham just says God knows intuitively, but doesn't explain how that can be so when there are no sufficient antecedent conditions connecting any two actions or any event and a subsequent action. To my knowledge, no other indeterminists explain that satisfactorily either. However, that shows no internal inconsistency in the Ockhamist solution or in the free will defender's theology. It shows that there are some significant questions about how anyone can know the future with all its interconnections unless some form of causal determinism is true. But those are objections about incompatibilistic free will, not about the Ockhamist resolution to the freedom/foreknowledge problem. To reject the system as holding an inadequate view of freedom is not to reject it on grounds of *internal* inconsistency.

In sum, the freedom/foreknowledge problem is a genuine problem for those who use the free will defense to solve the logical problem of evil. However, we have seen two satisfactory ways to resolve this apparent contradiction. One denies that God knows the future. The other, which upholds God's foreknowledge, is the Ockhamist approach.

ON SMART'S UTOPIA

In discussing some of Griffin's objections to the free will defense, we saw that he is really asking God to make a better world. If God did that, he would make some sort of utopia. Ninian Smart also raised the matter of a utopia, and I want to discuss more fully the interchange between Smart and Mackie over the utopia thesis.

Smart claims that it is impossible to give content to the idea of the utopia that would result if God created a world wherein everyone freely chooses good and never chooses evil. Mackie responds that if that is so, it's all the worse for theism, since theists speak of a Kingdom of God on earth.

Let me address Mackie's comment first. It is important to compare the biblical concept of the Kingdom of God on earth with Mackie's notion. Since he invokes traditional theistic belief, let's see if he really portrays that belief accurately. Scripture portrays the Kingdom as a time of unparalleled peace and justice on earth. This happens not because people freely choose to do good and refrain from evil, but because God's Messiah is on earth to enforce peace and justice. Even during the Kingdom there will be those who choose evil, but they will be punished swiftly.

That is quite different from the picture of no Messiah present or even needed, because none do evil of their own free will. The picture invoked by Mackie is much more like the scene in the early chapters of Genesis before Adam and Eve sinned. The main difference between the Edenic Paradise and the utopia demanded by Mackie's claims is that whereas the inhabitants of Eden did choose evil freely, the inhabitants of the imagined utopia never choose evil. The question in relation to this utopia is whether it can be given enough content for it to make sense. Mackie claims that the Compatibility Thesis entails the Utopia Thesis, and I agree with him. Let's assume that it does and that compatibilism is the correct view of freedom so that we can get to the Utopia Thesis. Given these assumptions, does it make sense to speak of such a utopia?

Smart offers a series of arguments to show that the notion of a utopia is contentless. First, Smart argues, when we claim that someone is good, we normally give reasons for that claim. For example, we say she resists temptations, is courageous, is generous to her friends, etc. Smart claims that to ensure that people would be wholly good in relation to temptation, they would have to be built differently than they are so that they either wouldn't be tempted, or luck would have it that they don't fall to temptation, or God would have to intervene each time to keep them from falling to temptation.[139] As for courage, people would also have to be made quite differently to guarantee that they would never be afraid, panic, or show cowardice.[140] Smart's conclusion in regard to these kinds of examples is:

> These examples, then, are meant to indicate that the concept *goodness* is applied to beings of a certain sort, beings who are liable to temptations, possess inclinations, have fears, tend to assert themselves and so forth; and that if they were to be immunized from evil they would have to be built in a different way. But it soon becomes apparent that to rebuild them would mean that the ascription of goodness would become unintelligible, for the reasons why men are called good and bad have a connection with human nature as it is empirically discovered to be. Moral utterance is embedded in the cosmic status quo.[141]

Smart's next line of argument imagines several cosmomorphic utopias and a noncosmomorphic utopia, and asks whether they have any content. In Cosmomorphic Utopia A people are never seriously tempted to harm or injure anyone, because no one has any serious desires that likely conflict with those of others. It wouldn't be correct to say of people in this utopia, claims Smart, that they are good, because they don't resist temptations, act courageously, or act generously. Their utopia demands none of these qualities. Thus, it would be meaningless to say of them that they always do good and never do evil.[142]

In Cosmomorphic Utopia B circumstances would always combine to make men good. For example, Hitler might be somewhat anti-Semitic, but those tendencies would never overwhelm him. Any other possibilities for evil would be avoided, because circumstances would luckily eliminate them. Smart replies that this utopia is either a version of A or it is a dream. Things don't just happen to go right by luck and chance. Hence, this utopia is also meaningless.[143]

Cosmomorphic Utopia C is a world where people are always virtuous because of frequent miraculous intervention. Smart thinks it is hard to make sense of this utopia, but he offers the following explanation. Suppose that in this utopia causal factors C usually give rise to actions of a certain empirical type, type-A. However, sometimes type-A actions are wrong, and in those cases C wouldn't have type-A effects because of miraculous intervention.[144] Smart concludes the following:

> Hence either we have to count rightness and wrongness as empirical differences in order to formulate a causal law here or we must confess that no

strict causal laws of human behavior could be formulated in this cosmos. The former alternative is baffling and unacceptable, while the latter is incompatible with determinism. Hence Cosmomorphic Utopia C provides no support for the Utopia Thesis.[145]

As for a noncosmomorphic utopia, it is possible that God could create one, but Smart thinks this wouldn't solve the problem. The problem with a cosmos so unlike ours is that we have no idea of what sapients in that world would be like. As a result, it's impossible to say what it would mean to call them good, impossible to say what that world would be like, and impossible to say whether it would be superior to ours.[146] Thus, Smart concludes that no matter how one tries, one can't give content to the notion of a utopia. Therefore, it is difficult to know what it would mean if God were to create people who freely do only good and no evil.

In response to this issue, I agree that the noncosmomorphic utopia notion isn't too helpful. However, my major point is that there is something right and wrong about what both Mackie and Smart say. I am not so sure the idea of a utopia is as contentless as Smart thinks. So long as one accepts a compatibilistic account of freedom, it seems that God could create Cosmomorphic Utopias A, B, C, or some other utopian situation. And, Mackie asks why God doesn't create a utopia, since he can.

If asked to specify such a utopia, I believe I could. Suppose, for example, God did whatever is necessary so that people would freely never do evil but only good. Suppose as well that doing good involves doing what God commands and refraining from what he forbids, and doing evil involves disobeying God. This seems to give content to the notion of a utopia. Moreover, given compatibilism, God could create this utopia. Perhaps words like "courage," "generosity," etc., would have no meaning in this utopia. But why is that a problem, since there is no need for those virtues, and since we can still describe the nature of life in general and the meaning of "good" and "evil" in particular in this utopia? Thus, in favor of Mackie and against Smart on the utopia issue, I think content can be given to the idea of a utopia, if one accepts a certain account of ethics and a certain account of freedom.

In spite of my agreement with Mackie on this point, I disagree with him in favor of Smart's views in another respect. Smart doesn't explicitly voice this complaint, but one senses throughout his discussion that Smart not only thinks these utopias are without meaningful content but also that they would be *undesirable* even if they had meaningful content. Of course, that is a different issue than whether one can *speak* meaningfully of a utopia. Anyone who believes in the eternal state as portrayed in Scripture (let alone the other utopian situation I described above) should believe that it is possible to speak meaningfully of a utopian situation. But these utopias are different worlds than ours, and our ability to describe them doesn't prove that it would be desirable for God to have created any of them instead of our world. Of course, since God can produce that kind of world, Modified Rationalist theologians like myself who hold compatibilism must show why it would be undesirable for God to do so. I plan to address that matter when I offer my answer to the problem of moral evil that arises for my system. It isn't, however, a matter for this chapter on the free will defense. What *is* a question for this chapter is whether the notion of a utopia is meaningful, and I answer affirmatively.

IS INCOMPATIBILISM WORTH IT?

One final objection to the free will defense is worthy of attention. The free will defense claims that incompatibilistic free will is a value of the first order. In fact, it is such a great value, that even though freedom's abuse results in evil, it is still worthwhile to have such free will.

Is libertarian free will really worth it? If the choice is between being a robot and being free (in the libertarian sense), most, if not all, of us would opt for freedom. However, suppose the choice is between incompatibilism and evil, on the one hand, and compatibilistic freedom and no evil, on the other. Is it then altogether clear that having incompatibilistic freedom is worth it? Anyone who uses the free will defense must answer affirmatively. However, many, including myself, think that kind of freedom isn't worth the evil that results.

Those who think incompatibilism isn't worth it should reject the free will defense. Of course, rejecting the free will defense on that ground demonstrates no problem of internal inconsistency in the theologies that use the free will defense to solve their problem of evil. It only shows that one isn't willing to pay the price for this kind of free will.

FINAL ASSESSMENT

In this chapter, I have examined the free will defense in a historical and a contemporary form. Whether formulated by Augustine or Plantinga, the defense is a rationally consistent way of handling the logical problem of moral evil which arises for the Modified Rationalist theologies that use it. There are significant objections to the defense, but as we have seen, the defense does render theologies that adopt it internally consistent.

Despite its success in solving its logical problem of evil, I can't adopt the free will defense or the theology it presupposes. My reasons (as with theonomy and Leibnizian Rationalism) are external to the system. In particular, I am unwilling to accept the commitment to incompatibilistic freedom; I hold compatibilism instead. In this respect, I side with Mackie and Flew, and agree as well that in principle God can both give us freedom and create a world without evil. Of course, this means that any theist, including myself, who sides with Flew and Mackie in favor of compatibilism must find some other solution to their system's logical problem of moral evil. In chapter 6, I shall offer such a solution.

In concluding this chapter on the free will defense, I have several comments. First, there are many theists who hold the free will defense but are actually inconsistent in doing so. That is so because they hold such a strong view of God's sovereign control over the world that they must be committed to some form of determinism. On the other hand, when they come to the problem of evil, they use the free will defense. Of course, the free will defense incorporates incompatibilism whereas their notion of God's sovereignty logically necessitates either compatibilism or no freedom at all. Hence, their theology as a whole is internally inconsistent, since incompatibilism contradicts both compatibilism and harder forms of determinism.[147]

This is an old mistake and a very common one. In fact, I believe Augustine himself made this error. His free will defense clearly commits him to indeterminism, and yet his other treatises about God's control of the world necessitate some form of determinism.[148] Theists who take this approach need either to change their views on freedom or modify their notion of divine sovereignty.

Second, from the free will defense and the issues that arise from it I take some insights that will be important in formulating my own defense. As seen in regard to the utopia issue, it isn't at all clear that it would be desirable for God to do what is necessary to create a utopian situation. In fact, I shall argue that even if God could create a utopia, he shouldn't.

And finally, of the theologies and approaches to answering the logical problem of evil that have been discussed so far, this one more than the others solves its problem of evil by looking at some problem in human beings, rather than by placing all the emphasis on what God has or hasn't done. As a nonconsequentialist, I think that is the correct approach. Hence, in answering the logical problem of moral evil for my theology, I emphasize something about human nature (not human free will, but something about what it means to be human). As I intend to show, that approach can produce a rationally consistent theology that involves intellectual commitments which theists who are Modified Rationalists and also compatibilists can accept.

5

Several Contemporary Modified Rationalist · Theologies

In chapter 4, I discussed the free will defense and its theology. There are other Modified Rationalist theologies which don't invoke the free will defense to handle the logical problem of evil. In this chapter I want to consider several of those systems to see how they handle their respective problems of moral evil. In particular, I shall examine four contemporary Modified Rationalist theologies: 1) Schlesinger's Greatest Happiness Argument, 2) the Greater Good Defense as presented by Keith Yandell, 3) John Hick's Soul-building Theodicy, and 4) Marilyn Adams's Christian Solution. As we shall see, some succeed and others fail in solving their problem of evil. Why that is so, plus other issues each raises, are reasons to examine each in some depth.

SCHLESINGER'S GREATEST HAPPINESS ARGUMENT

As one reads Schlesinger's work, it becomes very clear that he thinks there is only one theological/philosophical problem of evil. Early in his discussion he announces that the way to dissolve the problem of evil is to recognize that the notion of infinity is involved in the problem of evil in a way that hasn't previously been understood. Moreover, he thinks the problem of evil disappears once that issue is explained.[1]

Schlesinger selects a criterion of morality from human affairs, and claims that atheists will insist on a criterion of this sort. If theists reject this criterion as inapplicable to God because it comes from human affairs, then they have no meaningful criterion of morality for God. If the criterion doesn't come from human affairs, where else could theists get one?[2] According to Schlesinger, the usual criterion of morality taken from human affairs is:

> . . . if I have the opportunity to cause a person extreme happiness without harming anyone, without any expense or effort on my part, and I am aware of this, (even though *he* may not be) then if I refrain from doing so, I am morally reprehensible.[3]

Schlesinger claims that even if all the evil in the world were removed so that no one suffered, the problem of evil could still be posed. Using the above-mentioned principle of morality, atheists could still ask why God hasn't made people much happier than they are.[4] Here I note that Schlesinger's acceptance of this criterion shows that his theology incorporates a consequentialist account of ethics. Schlesinger believes that the above-mentioned dilemma (and also the problem of evil) dissolves when we realize that this moral criterion may apply to humans, but it can't logically apply to God because of the notion of infinity.[5] His argument for this view is as follows: the happiest man on earth could still make a list of requirements which, if met, would increase his happiness. In fact, everyone could be made as happy as this happiest man. However, in light of this moral criterion, God still wouldn't have discharged his moral responsibilities to mankind. He would always know of much greater possible happiness for his creatures, even if they felt totally satisfied.[6]

Next Schlesinger offers the crucial claim of his argument. Normally, when addressing a problem of evil, if there is talk about infinity, it refers to God's power, but Schlesinger emphasizes another aspect of infinity. He claims that there is no *prima facie* case for thinking that the possibility for greater happiness is infinite.[7] We may think that because of God's infinite power, he is obligated to produce infinite happiness. In fact, I think Schlesinger implies that this is just what atheists require of God. Moreover, by accepting consequentialism, Schlesinger seems to agree that God must produce infinite happiness. However, Schlesinger says God isn't obligated to do this, because it is impossible to create an infinite happiness.[8] Thus, as Schlesinger argues:

> . . . God's inability to create the greatest state of happiness is seen to be no different from his inability to create the greatest integer. Neither diminish His might, if we agree that He need not accomplish what is logically impossible. We cannot ask that He go against the laws of logic for we do not know what it is we are asking of Him; and when He does not do what is logically impossible, there just is no feat which we can say He failed to accomplish.[9]

In view of this point, Schlesinger believes that we must conclude that the amount of pain and joy in our world is irrelevant, and can't be introduced as evidence concerning the moral nature of God.[10] He further concludes that the problem of evil arose in the first place because it was assumed that if the universe were different than it is now, there would be no problem. But we now see that this is wrong. Nonetheless, just because the problem can't be solved by God merely removing the evil that does exist, that doesn't mean a problem still remains. In fact, in light of the problems with the very notion of the greatest possible happiness, the problem dissolves. It dissolves, because we have seen that while the principle "'It is morally wrong, when it does not interfere with the welfare of others, not to do as much as one *possibly can* to make others happy' may apply to humans, it *logically* cannot apply to an Omnipotent Being."[11]

Schlesinger and His Critics

Winslow Shea and Jay Rosenberg wrote responses to Schlesinger's proposal, and Schlesinger answered them. Schlesinger later offered a revised statement of his views, and there have been responses to that as well.[12] Before offering my own evaluation of Schlesinger's views, I want to sketch the exchange between Schlesinger and his critics. I begin with Rosenberg and Shea.

Rosenberg is far more favorable to Schlesinger than is Shea. In fact, Rosenberg agrees that the phrase "best of all possible worlds" doesn't represent a consistent concept. Hence, he further agrees that "there is no possibility of applying moral censure to an agent for his failure to create the best of all possible worlds."[13] Rosenberg thinks Schlesinger has disposed of the argument from evil along these lines, but hasn't disposed of it altogether. Rosenberg delineates two different types of morally wrong acts. The first are actions one ought to do but doesn't ("sins of omission"). The second are acts one does which shouldn't be done ("sins of commission").[14] Rosenberg then says he can offer examples of moral principles which, if violated, will produce sins of omission and sins of commission. The first principle (clearly based on consequentialism) is "One ought, *ceteris paribus,* to do all one can to make others happy."[15] The second principle is "One ought not condone unnecessary suffering."[16] Rosenberg draws the following conclusions:

> Ethical principles of the first sort are *prescriptive*; those of the second sort, *prohibitive.* To sin by commission is to do what is morally prohibited. The classical argument from the existence of evil to the radical falsity of theism presents itself as an argument of the first sort. What Schlesinger has shown us is that we cannot assess God *by an argument of the first sort.* This is no small achievement. But it is a philosophical mistake of the first order to conclude on this basis that we cannot assess God *at all,* and, unfortunately, precisely this is what Dr. Schlesinger has done.[17]

The thrust, then, of Rosenberg's reply to Schlesinger is that while he agrees with Schlesinger that we can't state what kind of world God should have created, we can tell the kind of world he should have prohibited. He shouldn't have created a world that contains intrinsic evil, i.e., evil which isn't merely a privation but evil which is per se bad. Rosenberg believes our world does contain intrinsic evil.[18] The second type of world that shouldn't be created is one in which the actual amount of happiness falls short of the potential amount (however much that is) of happiness for that world. Rosenberg thinks our world is of this type.[19] Hence, Schlesinger hasn't disposed of the problem of evil altogether, because he hasn't shown that our world isn't one of those worlds God shouldn't have created.

Shea is much less optimistic about Schlesinger's views than is Rosenberg, for he finds reasons to reject Schlesinger's greatest happiness argument altogether. Shea believes three main questions must be answered in regard to Schlesinger's position: 1) Isn't there some reason why, contra Schlesinger, happiness is or may be finite? 2) Does the problem of evil disappear if God isn't obligated to create as much happiness as possible? and 3) Is that all that follows, if the greatest happiness argument succeeds?[20] Shea thinks the second question can be answered affirmatively, if the greatest happiness argument is successful. However, he thinks there are reasons why the greatest happiness argument fails, and they center around the notion that happiness could be finite. Moreover, he also says that if the greatest happiness argument does succeed, other things follow from it which would be unacceptable to many theists.[21]

Shea attempts to ascertain what Schlesinger means when he speaks of infinite happiness. He concludes that Schlesinger must mean that "there is an infinite number or set of (possible) kinds, degrees, or values of happiness, and that because this set is infinite it cannot contain even one maximum or optimum degree of value of happiness."[22] Shea thinks Schlesinger bases his argument on a mathematical conception of infinity.[23] Schlesinger must be thinking of a linear picturing of points of happiness according to which happiness increases as one moves from left to right on the line. However, no matter how far to the right we go on the line, we cover only part of an abstract infinite geometrical line. Therefore, regardless of where we place happiness on a linear portrayal of states of happiness, since the line is infinite, we can never specify a state of greatest possible happiness.[24]

In response to Schlesinger, Shea says that even if we think of infinity in mathematical terms (as he believes Schlesinger does), there is more than one way to interpret the mathematical metaphor. Whichever way one interprets it, one need not reach Schlesinger's conclusions. Shea explains the two possible interpretations as follows:

First, if we view the line before us as Schlesinger seems to, we may see it as but a finite segment of an imaginary line that extends endlessly in each direction. This view I call the "macroscopic illusion of infinity." But second, just as every infinitely "long" line contains an infinity of points and line segments within it, so does every segment itself, including the finite segment represented as "co-extensive" with our drawn line. Viewing it thus, not as a line infinitely extended, but as a finite segment infinitely divisible, is what I call the "microscopic illusion of infinity."[25]

Shea thinks Schlesinger shifts back and forth between these two notions of infinity. Sometimes Schlesinger speaks of our happiness or misery being insignificant in relation to possible happiness or misery (macroscopic view). At other times he speaks of a specific amount of happiness as being as far from the end of the line where the greatest happiness is as it was at another point on the line.[26] Even to speak of an end to the line, claims Shea, invokes the microscopic notion of infinity. Shea draws the following conclusions: if we take the microscopic view of infinity whereby a line is infinitely divisible, we can say of any part of the line segment not identical with the end that it is "infinitely remote" from the end, and yet there is an end. Thus, the line represents the possibility of a greatest misery and a greatest happiness, and as long as there is such a limit, an omnipotent being could have, and possibly should have, created it.[27] On the other hand, if we take the macroscopic view, there are two possibilities. Shea explains:

One is that the finite line "extends" to such a great length beyond any happiness or goodness we have experienced, or can even imagine, that we are (though again in the "infinitely divisible" sense) "infinitely remote" from its right end. Only God knows what such supreme bliss is, and only He could create it. On the other view, which I prefer, we may regard the happiness line or value scale as relatively "short," and the greatest happiness as something which, if never fully experienced, we can nevertheless envision, even (and especially) under the conditions of the world as we know it. Here the extent of possible happiness is only as long as we can imagine it to be. And perhaps we can, on our own, more or less approximate the end envisioned, though with increasingly diminishing returns for our efforts.[28]

From this discussion of macroscopic infinity Shea concludes that we have some conception of it, and even if we don't have a complete understanding of it, God does. Since he is omnipotent, he could have and should have placed us there.[29] So, whichever meaning of infinity one takes, Shea thinks a greatest possible happiness is logically possible. Hence, an omnipotent being could have and perhaps should have created it.[30]

In sum, Schlesinger believes God can't create a greatest possible happiness, because we can't even specify what it would be. Shea in essence says

Schlesinger's views are internally inconsistent because he uses conflicting notions of infinity. Moreover, even if Schlesinger's argument were internally consistent, it wouldn't solve his problem of evil, because on either account of infinity, the notion of a greatest possible happiness does make sense.

These objections cut at the central notions of Schlesinger's position, but Shea also rejects the view, because it entails some negative consequences. In particular, if Schlesinger is right, two main things are lost. First, God is lost, if by "God" we mean a perfect or best possible being. Shea explains the point as follows:

> But if God cannot be the embodiment of Sufficient Reason and create a best possible world insofar as there cannot be a greatest happiness, neither can God himself be a happiest being. We cannot ever share in God's supreme bliss because there can be no such thing. But the same result occurs when we predicate of God any exclusive property that has a logic of comparatives, that admits or generates a continuum of better and worse, or of more and less. For as soon as you put such a property on a Schlesinger line, that line and that property zooms out without limit to infinity. So in any exclusive sense, the notion of a "greatest conceivable being" reduces to nonsense.[31]

If Schlesinger is correct, Shea also thinks God becomes as little adorable and morally praiseworthy as he is blameworthy. As Shea says, "if He cannot be blamed for not creating more happiness than He did create, on the ground that otherwise no matter how much happiness He created He could still be blamed for not creating more of it, then it seems to me He cannot be praised for having created any happiness at all."[32] Schlesinger says any amount of extra happiness is relatively small in comparison to any other state of happiness or misery because of the infinite possibilities for either happiness or misery. But if that is so, Shea argues that God can neither be blamed nor praised for whatever amount of happiness or lack of it there is. As Shea explains:

> One cannot therefore praise Him for being a better deity than He might have been, for in that case one could just as deservedly blame Him for not being better than He is. Pessimistically viewed our deity is infinitely inferior to what He or other deities might have been; or, if you like, the deity has created a world infinitely worse than millions of worlds He could have made. But most hideous of all, suppose He overnight turned our world into one of those monstrous hells, that he decided, in Schlesinger's words, to "multiply the amount of pain in the world by a billion." As Schlesinger would say: "We *still* could not blame Him." What should we not do to such a one, especially if he continued to praise and worship such a being?[33]

In a later refinement of his views[34] Schlesinger offered two illustrations intended to convince us that the aforementioned moral principle is correct and applicable to humans but not to God. He first appeals to the dictum that it is better to be Socrates and dissatisfied than to be a satisfied pig. Since the degree of desirability of state represented by a dissatisfied Socrates could be increased infinitely by a God with infinite power, it really makes no sense to expect God to bring about the most desirable state possible since there really is no coherent idea of what that would be like. Schlesinger believes that the degree of desirability of state of being is "a two-valued function depending both on the potentials of the individual and the extent to which his needs are being taken care of."[35] Schlesinger's first example proposes a situation in which a person's potential is increased at the expense of his happiness, and argues that because it would be immoral to refuse to increase the person's potential just because it would decrease his happiness, we should see that the demand for increased happiness doesn't always make sense. Here is the first example:

> I have under my care a retarded child who is completely content in his con-
> dition. The opportunity exists to let him undergo a risk-free operation guar-
> anteed by the best physicians to endow the child with normal intelligence. If
> I should leave him as he is, and not surgically correct his brain, he will remain
> incapable of acquiring even the most basic skills and thus will never be able
> to support himself by earning a livelihood; nor will he ever have a social or
> cultural life. Unfortunately, however, if he is subjected to the operation then,
> like any normal person, he will be subject to the ups and downs of life, some-
> times suffering and therefore no longer completely happy. In his present state,
> he is assured of lifelong contentment and hardly any suffering.[36]

In this case, Schlesinger argues that refusing to do the operation on the grounds that it would decrease the child's happiness would be morally rep-rehensible. Hence, producing the greatest happiness isn't always possible, and in a case of this sort, increase in potentiality offsets decrease in happiness.

A second example takes just the opposite approach. That is, it imagines a case in which happiness is increased but potential limited. Presumably, all of us should agree that it would be wrong to increase happiness in the way proposed, but then again, how can we demand that God make a "happiest" world when to do so might require changes to our lives which would pro-duce unwanted decreases in our potential? Schlesinger's example is as follows:

> Fred is an adult of normal intelligence, with an average amount of problems
> and worries, and a normal lack of complete happiness. I have the opportu-
> nity to hook him up to a machine which will stimulate electrically the plea-
> sure centres of his brain, putting him, without his prior permission, into a
> state of perpetual, supreme, passive bliss. I have also the means to see to it
> that all Fred's bodily needs will be met for the rest of his days, without his
> ever being unhooked from the machine.[37]

Stephen Grover has responded to Schlesinger's revised argument in some detail, and at least some of his objections are worth noting. First, Grover explains that apart from the unreality of the first example, a major problem is the unreality of the choice it offers. Children who are seriously retarded are not "completely content" in the sense we normally use that phrase; that is, they aren't just human versions of satisfied pigs. When we speak of contentment, happiness, and absence of suffering, we think of those qualities in terms of people of normal intelligence and potential. So, Grover's first complaint is that the first example compares a severely retarded child to a satisfied pig, but that comparison doesn't work. Moreover, the first example plays upon concepts of contentment, etc., that just don't apply to someone who is seriously retarded. We simply don't know how such a person sees the world or evaluates his own condition. Moreover, without knowing the degree of retardation and its effects on the child's mental processes and emotions, we are further uncertain as to how contentment and happiness relate to this child.[38] Schlesinger says that the operation will make the retarded person a different kind of person, but Grover disagrees. He writes:

> But this is not how we think of it at all, and such a consideration plays no role in our response to this example. The seriously retarded are not a particular kind of people, as careless or friendly or well-educated are, but rather those who are prevented from realising to the full the kind of people they are. It is because of this that we seek to remove the cause of retardation in so far as it lies in our power to do so. For who knows what kind of person this child is? He could be clever, kind, dull, selfish, athletic, loving, cowardly. If he is none of these because of his illness, that does not show that he is another kind of person (the "seriously retarded kind") but shows instead that he is so damaged a person that we do not know how to ascribe anything more to him than what seems to us like contentment and the absence of pain.[39]

As to the second example, Grover notes that here there is again a supposed trade-off between pleasure and potential, except that in this case potential will be decreased. In fact, the description of Fred makes his situation sound not unlike a "vegetable-like" existence, but how, asks Grover, does it make sense to call such a state bliss? Moreover, this situation isn't parallel to that of the satisfied pig, for the pig presumably can engage in normal activities of pigs, whereas Fred is stuck on this machine. And, it isn't clear that Fred's state is equivalent to that of the severely retarded child, for the child may not understand his situation, whereas Fred presumably has enough intelligence left to understand how diminished his life is while being hooked up to the machine.[40] If he really does understand how much he has given up by being on the machine, rather than being very happy because of the pleasure centers of his brain being stimulated, he is likely to be very sad. Moreover, this sort of experience is arguably not one wherein happiness lies.[41]

Grover sums up his problems with these two examples as follows:

> Schlesinger's examples are supposed to elicit from us the recognition that it is not mere satisfaction which is involved in determining the degree of desirability of someone's state. But they show nothing of the kind. Given what we normally mean by satisfaction in relation to children (as opposed to pigs), it is simply not true that any seriously retarded child is properly thought of as satisfied. Equally, no one hooked up to a machine which does things to their brain has been given happiness as we normally think of it; they have been deprived of the opportunity of ever finding happiness again. The imaginary child . . . loses nothing by undergoing the operation. Fred gains nothing by being hooked up to the machine. Neither of these examples show that degree of desirability of state is a two-valued function in which one value, satisfaction, may pull against another, potential.[42]

In spite of all of this, as Grover notes, Schlesinger's use of these examples ultimately rests on a belief that being Socrates dissatisfied is better than being a pig satisfied, and that being a "super-Socrates" dissatisfied is better than being a Socrates satisfied, and so on for further comparisons that move toward a "super-super-Socrates" ad infinitum. There are really two main problems with this line of argument, according to Grover. The first is that it relies on making sense of the relation "better than" as it is used in these examples and Schlesinger's argument. However,

> Nothing in *Example 1* shows that it is better to be a dissatisfied Socrates than a satisfied pig, because a seriously retarded child is not to be likened to a pig, and because such a child is not properly described as satisfied. Nothing in *Example 2* shows this either, for again we do not have the required contrast between a being analogous to a pig which is satisfied and another being which is akin to a dissatisfied philosopher, but only the contrast between someone who lacks all happiness and all opportunity to seek it, and someone who lacks complete happiness.[43]

The other problem with this line of argument is that it isn't clear that the notion of "super-Socrates" even makes sense, especially in light of the way Schlesinger describes him. Schlesinger claims that he "has much higher intelligence [than Socrates] and many more than five senses through which to enjoy the world, and . . . stands to Socrates as the latter stands to the pig."[44] How this shows that the state of being "super-Socrates" is better than being Socrates, regardless of how satisfied Socrates is, isn't clear. Grover discusses a variety of enhanced senses that this might involve and shows that they aren't necessarily more desirable than the five senses we have which function as they do. For example, Grover imagines that we all are super-human in that we have telepathy added to our five senses. This would mean that falling in love with someone would involve both of them hearing every thought the other is thinking as if it were spoken aloud. How can we say that this enhancement would be better than our current life without such abilities?[45]

In sum, Schlesinger's argument depends on our agreeing that various comparative states are truly better than lesser states, but neither his examples nor his explanation of the differences between Socrates and "super-Socrates" succeeds in making his point.

Assessment of Schlesinger's Position

Schlesinger's argument is an ingenious handling of the problem of evil, but not a successful one. Let me make some general comments about Schlesinger's presentation, and then I shall turn to objections on grounds internal and external to his theology.

I begin with two initial points. Neither indicates that Schlesinger's theology fails to solve its problem of evil, but both suggest that Schlesinger needs to be clearer about what he is doing. First, Schlesinger errs in thinking there is only one problem of evil and that he addresses and removes it. Rosenberg and Shea also err in assuming there is only one problem of evil. As I have shown, there isn't even just one theological/philosophical problem of evil, and there are other problems of evil as well.

A second error is Schlesinger's belief that his greatest possible happiness argument makes it impossible for there to be a problem of evil. That is also clearly false. I have already specified how a problem of evil arises for any Modified Rationalist theology. The best one could say for Schlesinger's solution, if it were acceptable, is that it renders his theology internally consistent and thereby solves his logical problem of evil. Unfortunately for Schlesinger, I can't even make that claim, for his solution leaves his system internally inconsistent.

Schlesinger's theology is internally inconsistent on two accounts, and in other regards simply doesn't work. As for internal consistency, as Shea argues, Schlesinger uses contradictory notions of infinity. Hence, he doesn't offer an acceptable solution to his problem of evil.

A second internal problem is suggested by Shea's complaint that even if Schlesinger is right about either notion of infinity, his argument succeeds in removing God, an infinite being. My argument is simply this: on the one hand, Schlesinger's theology clearly includes a greatest conceivable being, God. On the other hand, if he is right that a proper understanding of infinity makes the notion of "a greatest possible x" (happiness, integer, being, etc.)

logically impossible and thereby meaningless, then he can't (logically) believe in a greatest conceivable being, though he does. Thus, even if Schlesinger's claims about infinity were correct, he would wind up with a self-contradictory theology.

Then, I believe Grover's interaction with Schlesinger's refinement and elaboration of his position is compelling. I agree, for example, that his examples don't prove his point because the beings that he compares and concludes are analogous aren't in fact similar enough to make his point. I also agree that it isn't clear that Schlesinger's understanding of what would make someone even happier than she is (e.g., his understanding of the "advantages" of being "super-Socrates") or even content in the first place is correct.

My most fundamental complaint with Schlesinger's views is that they ignore the nature of the logical problem of evil as it arises in Modified Rationalist theologies and what the Modified Rationalist needs to do to solve his logical problem of evil. Nowhere does Schlesinger tell us that he is a Modified Rationalist, but there is nothing in his presentation that suggests he is either a theonomist or a Leibnizian rationalist. His understanding of ethics seems to fit best with the type of ethical theories one finds with Modified Rationalist systems.

But what, then, should a Modified Rationalist do to solve his logical problem of evil? Modified Rationalists say that there is no best world, but more than one good world, and God, if he decides to create at all, must create one of those good worlds. Hence, Schlesinger doesn't need to show us that it is impossible for God to create the best possible world (and clearly, Schlesinger isn't using this notion in the Leibnizian sense of metaphysically best). Rather, he needs to tell us what feature of our current world makes it one of those good worlds that God could have created. Nothing in Schlesinger's presentation suggests what makes our world a good possible world. Instead, Schlesinger tries to convince us that we can't even pose the problem of evil in a meaningful way, but we have already seen that for each broad form of theism we have considered there is a particular way that the problem of evil confronts it. Schlesinger's attempt to stop the discussion before anyone can even offer a solution that would fit the theologian's brand of theology badly misunderstands the nature of the problem of evil and how various forms of theism should go about addressing it.

Because Schlesinger has decided not to answer the logical problem in a way that his broad form of theism requires but has rather decided to make a case that the problem of evil can't even be posed, everything hinges on his ability to prove it can't be posed. As already noted, his approach doesn't address the nature of the logical problem for a Modified Rationalist, let alone try to solve it, and since we have also seen that neither his earlier nor his later statement of his views actually makes the problem evaporate, his position has failed on a number of accounts.

In addition to these problems, Schlesinger's position is objectionable on grounds external to the system. First and foremost, his claim that the idea of a greatest possible happiness makes no sense is simply false. As Shea argues, on either a microscopic or a macroscopic account of infinity, one can speak sensibly about a greatest possible happiness. Thus, Schlesinger's theology is inadequate, because it incorporates assumptions about infinity that are false.

Second, when Schlesinger's argument is viewed from the perspective of his emphasis on degrees of happiness or misery, the argument becomes irrelevant as an answer to the logical philosophical/theological problem of evil (i.e., the logical problem of moral evil). Schlesinger generates his argument in part by focusing on the issue of degrees of evil in the universe. However, this emphasis conflates problems of evil. The theological/philosophical problem of evil isn't about the amount of evil or good, but about the existence of any evil at all. Everyone probably could be happier, and some things that appear evil from one perspective appear good in a broader perspective and vice versa. But these matters are not germane to a theological/philosophical problem of evil. Schlesinger thinks he can remove a theological/philosophical problem of evil by relativizing the meaning of good and evil by placing them on an infinite continuum and then arguing about degrees or amounts of happiness and pain. However, that raises the problem of the amount of evil (perhaps also the intensity of some evils), and that just isn't the same problem as the theological/philosophical problem of evil.

Third, Shea points out the problems with Schlesinger's notion of infinite happiness. I want to add another point about this matter of infinite happiness. Schlesinger says God's inability to create the greatest state of happiness is in the same class as his inability to create the greatest integer. However, Schlesinger also claims that no matter how happy someone is, God would always be aware of much greater possibilities of happiness for that person, even if she felt totally satisfied.[46]

I find this very troublesome. It seems that Schlesinger is saying that while God can't create the greatest possible happiness, he can conceive of it. If Schlesinger is actually saying that, it is problematic, for it means God is omnipotent and yet can't do what is logically possible. Of course, there is question about whether this is what Schlesinger actually means. But the tenor of these claims seems to be that God can at least conceive of the greatest possible happiness, even if he can't create it. If Schlesinger isn't making that claim, he should be clearer about what he holds.

A final objection to Schlesinger is suggested by Shea's comments that Schlesinger's system allows us neither to praise nor to blame God no matter what kind of universe he creates. I think Schlesinger's argument results in an even further ludicrous consequence. It allows God to create a hell on earth in which he continually inflicts harm on his creatures without that state of affairs raising a problem of evil at all. Schlesinger said that no matter how we multiply the amount of good or evil, the existence of evil doesn't effect a problem of evil, and a problem, therefore, doesn't arise in the first place.[47] This conclusion makes his greatest possible happiness argument utterly unacceptable, for it allows God to do totally repulsive acts without incurring any moral censure. Schlesinger may embrace a theology with that sort of God, but I doubt that many will follow him. In sum, Schlesinger's handling of the logical problem of evil is unsatisfactory on grounds internal and external to the system.

THE GREATER GOOD DEFENSE

The greater good defense isn't a new defense, but it has been revived and refined in recent years. It presupposes a Modified Rationalist theology which incorporates a consequentialist account of ethics. This defense argues that evil is causally and logically tied to some subsequent good which justifies the evil's existence.

The Greater Good Defense

Keith Yandell sets forth this defense in his article "The Greater Good Defense." He begins by noting that orthodox theists agree that "(1) God exists, and is an all-knowing, all-powerful, all-good Creator and Providence,"[48] and that "(2) There is evil in the world."[49] Yandell reasons that because everything is under God's control, in view of (2) theists must also agree that "(3) Every evil is such that God has a morally sufficient reason for creating or allowing it."[50] Premise (3) isn't the greater good defense, but is the basis for it. We need to see how the proposition which is the greater good defense comes from (3).

Yandell begins his explanation by referring to what I referred to in the preceding chapter as the notion of first order/second order good and evil. Certain evils like fear are related to goods like courage by logical necessity.[51] That is, one cannot be courageous if there is nothing to fear. Of course, not every evil that is tied to a good by logical necessity is justified by the good. If the good neither counterbalances nor overbalances the evil to which it is logically connected, the being that produced the evil is morally culpable.[52] Thus, as Yandell explains:

So an evil E open to greater-good treatment is such that: (a) there is a good G such that G exists entails that E *exists,* and (b) G at least counterbalances E. A good G counterbalances an evil E if and only if G *exists* and if an agent who creates or permits E for the sake of G performs a morally neutral action (is neither praiseworthy nor blameworthy). A good G overbalances an evil E if and only if G *exists* entails E *exists* and an agent who creates or permits G for the sake of E [sic] is morally praiseworthy.[53]

With these notions in mind, Yandell says the greater good defense can be stated in one of two ways:

(4) Every evil is logically necessary to some good which either counterbalances or overbalances it, and some evil is overbalanced by the good to which it is logically necessary . . .

(4') Every evil is logically necessary to some good, some evil is overbalanced by some good to which it is logically necessary, and *no* evil overbalances the good to which it is logically necessary.[54]

In order to move from (3) to (4), Yandell says we must return to certain ideas involved in (1). In particular, "God is all good" entails that he wills that each of us will attain our greatest good, and "God is providential" entails that he controls the course of history so that we all have maximal opportunity to attain our greatest good.[55] These claims seem to indicate a commitment to some form of consequentialism. Using all of these notions, Yandell explains that the move from step (3) to (4) requires a pattern of thought on the order of the following:

1. (3) Every evil is such that God has a morally sufficient reason for creating or allowing it. (from (1) and (2)).
2. God wills that each man attain his greatest good. (entailed by *God is all-good*).
3. Man's greatest good is his realization of his capacities as one made in the *imago dei* and one who is to act always in *imitatio dei*. (Part One of an outline interpretation of theistic ethics).
4. God controls the course of history so that each man has maximal opportunity to attain his greatest good. (entailed by *God is providential*).
5. Logically necessary conditions of attaining moral maturity are: (1) free moral agency, where an agent A is free with respect to a choice x or not-x if and only if A can in fact choose x or choose not-x; (b) the existence of states of affairs which are evil (in the sense that it would be blameworthy to allow them without morally sufficient reason) and which are logically necessary to states of affairs which are both good (in the sense of being virtues which comprise, or are logically necessary to, mature moral character) and at least counterbalancing. (Part Two of an outline interpretation of theistic ethics).

6. Some good overbalances the evil to which it is logically necessary. (entailed by the theistic claim that God's creation of men is a good state of affairs).

So: 7. (5) Every evil that God allows is logically necessary to some at least counterbalancing state of affairs, and some evil is overbalanced by the good to which it is logically necessary, where one applicable criterion for a state of affairs being good is that it furthers the growth to moral maturity of some moral agent, and where the evils occurring to each agent are so arranged as to provide him maximal opportunity for moral maturity.[56]

Having presented this version of the greater good defense and having explained the thinking behind it, Yandell then asserts that the free will defense is really a form of the greater good defense, for it is said that it is a greater good that humans have free will, even if misused, than for them not to be free.[57] Thus, even if an agent Andrew doesn't respond to fear by becoming more courageous, our evaluation of his moral failure should be described as follows, according to Yandell:

It is better that Andrew be given opportunity to respond freely (and so creatively or destructively) to his fears than that he not have this opportunity—there is justificatory value in even the wrong exercise of moral agency.[58]

Evaluations of the Greater Good Defense

I begin with a small but not insignificant point about Yandell's claim that the free will defense is a form of the greater good defense. I believe Yandell is mistaken here, for while it seems true enough that free will is logically necessary for there to be *moral evil,* it isn't true that moral evil is logically necessary for there to be free will. That is, in order for there to be free will there need not be antecedent moral evil. Moreover, as we saw in chapter 4, it is at least logically possible (unless, of course, everyone suffers from transworld depravity), though unlikely, for someone to be free without doing evil. Hence, there is no *logical* tie between moral evil and free will.

Though this may appear insignificant, I don't think it is, because it reveals something important about any use of the greater good defense. It suggests that in order for evil to be *logically* necessary to some good in the way that the first-order/second-order schema requires, the good must be a subsequent (to the evil) good. In fact, those who use this defense or some version of it invariably justify evil's existence in terms of something it produces for which it is the logical precursor. This, at least in part, is how one knows that the greater good defense incorporates consequentialist ethics. If a greater good defense justified evil's existence in terms of something subsequent to the evil, but the greater good defender held a nonconsequentialist ethic, that would generate a contradiction in the theologian's system.

One result of this point about the greater good defense is that the free will defense and the defense I shall offer in chapter 6 are not versions of the greater good defense, even though some have thought they are. They aren't versions of the greater good defense, because they justify moral evil in terms of something that precedes the evil and produces it, though not with logical necessity but only as its cause. I don't see how there can be a logical tie of the sort the greater good defense demands between an evil and something that precedes it and even produces it. Moral evil is neither logically necessary nor causally necessary to produce libertarian free will (the free will defense) or the non-glorified human beings God created when he made our world (my defense presented in chapter 6). Unlike the greater good defense, these defenses justify God not in terms of what evil produces, but in virtue of what produces evil.

Let me turn now to other comments about the greater good defense. Some seem more relevant to Yandell's formulation of it than to the defense in general. I believe the greater good defense is internally consistent, though there is reason for concern about Yandell's version.

First, some might argue that while the greater good defense handles many evils, it won't work for every evil, for it seems impossible to show that every evil is logically necessary to some good. Obviously, this is a very moot point, and a lot depends on what one thinks is the good to which the evil is tied. For example, if the good is soul-building, then, as Hick argues, every evil is logically tied to that good. However, trying to find a good to which each instance of evil is tied in order to exonerate the greater good defense errs in a rather fundamental way. As mentioned in chapter 1, a theological/philosophical problem of evil in its logical form (that is what this defense addresses) is a problem about the logical consistency of God's existence and the existence of evil *in general*. In order to solve that problem, one need not justify every individual instance of evil. Instead, one needs only to show that evil in general isn't incompatible with an all-benevolent, all-powerful God. And the greater good defense does that.

Stanley Kane raises a second objection which seems much more to the point. It shows no internal inconsistency in the position, but instead, directly attacks one of the defense's fundamental notions. Kane argues that while we value virtues like courage and fortitudinous pain bearing, that doesn't prove they have intrinsic worth. It may only underscore that fear and pain are so prevalent in our lives that we must value these virtues, if we are to survive and get along in the world.[59] However, all along one wonders if these second-order goods are really worth or really justify the first-order evils they logically presuppose. As Kane explains:

> Do human beings as a matter of fact really value more highly the existence of second-order goods than the non-existence of first-order evils? I venture to suggest that if thoughtful men were asked what kind of world they would prefer—whether they would prefer a world in which there was not fear or pain or suffering or disease, even though this would mean that such virtues as courage and fortitudinous pain-bearing would no longer be possible; or whether they would prefer a world in which it was still possible to manifest these virtues, even though this would require the existence of at least some fear or pain or suffering or disease—I venture to suggest that everyone would prefer the first kind of world as having the greater value. Indeed the building of such a world is the final goal of a great deal of concentrated human effort today. Mankind generally recognizes a duty to eliminate first-order evil because in that way and only in that way a better world—a world having greater than the present one [sic]—can be achieved.[60]

Kane's argument is essentially that it isn't really worth it to have the first-order evils just to get second-order goods. Hence, second-order goods don't justify the first-order evils.

Yandell offers several answers to this argument. He thinks Kane is wrong, because *reducing* fear and pain in our world is an intelligent goal, but *eliminating* them isn't. Yandell writes, "I do a man no favour if I prevent him from feeling a pain that warns of disease or remove his healthy fear of foaming canines."[61] Yandell thinks this "error" is merely a slip on Kane's part, but Kane is arguing something more significant that requires an answer. Yandell sees the issue as follows:

> Presumably he is contending that (1) It is good that some pains and fears be eliminated entails (2) Some pains and fears are evils for which the theist should be able to provide explanation but cannot. But (1) does not entail (or even provide evidence for) (2). For (1) is compatible with (1a) The point (justification of every pain and fear that it would be better to eliminate) is that the compassion exercised in their elimination be possible. If the compassion is a great enough good, (1) and (1a) will entail not (2). So (1) alone does not entail (2).[62]

In my judgment, Kane's point is well taken. For example, it seems that while it is true that pain is helpful in warning of disease and fear is helpful when confronted by foaming canines, there is reason to wonder why God doesn't just remove altogether diseases, foaming canines, and anything else that causes pain and fear. That is, if it is a choice between no pain or fear because of no disease or cause for fear, on the one hand, and pain and fear accompanying disease and causes for fear, on the other hand, why opt for the

latter? As to compassion, is it worth it to suffer first-order evil just so someone gets a chance to express compassion? I agree with Kane in all of these
cases that the second-order goods aren't so valuable as to make it worth it to
have the first-order evils. Moreover, do we really need either first-order evil
or second-order good? Couldn't the world get along quite well without second-order good, if it also didn't have to put up with first-order evil? It may
be that it is desirable to have both first-order evil and second-order good, but
the greater good defense doesn't tell us why.

Before leaving this objection, I note that it shows no internal inconsistency in the greater good defender's system, but suggests one reason why
someone might reject the greater good defense and its theology altogether.

In response, Yandell might answer that if there were no first-order evils
and second-order goods, the world wouldn't be as opportune a place as it is
for character development. This claim seems to be part of Yandell's argument,
as can be seen from his proposition 7 presented above. However, that
response rests on two problematic notions. For one thing, it seems to assume
that the only way God has to build character is through the use of first-order
evil. I don't see that God has no other means at his disposal for character
building. Moreover, the reply also assumes that the purpose of the world is
character building. Of course, if that is so, then the greater good defense must
be justified not by itself, i.e., not by evil being logically necessary to some
greater good per se, but in terms of something outside the defense, namely,
the idea that the purpose of the world is to build character.

If the greater good defense is supported by this line of thinking, there are
some obvious problems. For one thing, the greater good defense surely
doesn't rest on nor prove the claim that the world's purpose is character building. In addition, if the greater good defense must ultimately be justified by the
notion of character building, then we have left the greater good defense and
turned to Hick's soul-building theodicy. In other words, the greater good
defense's adequacy or inadequacy reduces to a decision on some version of
the soul-building theodicy. But then we are really saying the greater good
defense is inadequate in itself to solve its problem of evil. I don't believe it is
inadequate per se, but some may think Yandell's version of the defense leaves
that impression by mixing it with the soul-building theodicy.

There is a final objection to the greater good defense as Yandell presents
it. Yandell argues that for there to be moral agency, there must be moral freedom, but moral agents use their freedom to choose evil sometimes. However,
that evil is justified because of the greater good to which it is logically tied,
namely, moral agency as a result of moral freedom.[63]

If this defense sounds familiar, it should, for it is just the free will defense brought in under the umbrella of the greater good defense. In response to Yandell, one could repeat Mackie's objection that God should have created us so that we would always freely choose only good. That seems like a way to allow people to mature morally without introducing evil into the world. Of course, Yandell would answer that God couldn't *make* it the case that we would *freely* do anything.

This line of argumentation returns us to the debate over compatibilism and incompatibilism. I believe I can show that by quoting a portion from Yandell in which he talks about moral agency:

> This view of moral agency, of course, assumes (what seems to be true) that moral agents are necessarily free agents, and that free agents are necessarily not determined. Alternately, one could hold that (a) in one sense of "free" (say, $free_1$) libertarianism and determinism cannot both be true with respect to any particular choice or action, (b) in another sense of "free" (say, $free_2$) libertarianism and determinism can be co-true, (c) correspondingly, there are two possible sorts of moral agents, those who are $free_1$ and those who are $free_2$ with respect to the choices for which they are morally responsible, and (d) it is vastly more valuable that there be $free_1$ agents than that there be $free_2$ agents.[64]

It seems that Yandell is discussing here the compatibilism/incompatibilism issue and opting for incompatibilism. If so, then as was the case when Yandell rested the greater good defense on the soul-building theodicy, resting the greater good defense on the free will defense is unnecessary and really removes us from the greater good defense. In addition, combining these two defenses produces an internally inconsistent position. The inconsistency is that the free will defense rests on nonconsequentialism, while the greater good defense assumes a consequentialist account of ethics. Hence, an attempt to blend the two defenses results in a self-contradictory theology, because the theology as a whole adopts contradictory accounts of ethics.

In assessing the greater good defense as a whole, I conclude that the *basic defense* preserves the internal consistency of the theology that incorporates it, even if Yandell's form of it raises the internal problems mentioned. However, in spite of the greater good defense's ability to solve the logical problem of moral evil, I am unwilling to accept the commitments it entails. I don't hold a consequentialist ethic, but in addition, I am not convinced that either the goods or the evils that the goods logically presuppose are worth it. Since the greater good defense per se doesn't explain why I should be convinced about this, I am unconvinced by this defense and unwilling to accept the theological position that uses it. Still, I am pleased to find another theistic system which can and does solve its logical problem of moral evil.

JOHN HICK'S SOUL-BUILDING THEODICY

Thanks to John Hick's *Evil and the God of Love,* the soul-building theodicy has become very influential during the last half of the twentieth century. Hick's approach presupposes a Modified Rationalist metaphysic with a consequentialist account of ethics. His position also incorporates incompatibilistic free will.

Hick's Theodicy

Throughout his book Hick discusses two traditions of theodicy, which he labels the Augustinian Tradition and the Irenaean Tradition. While much of Christendom has followed the former, Hick believes much can be learned from the latter. Before offering his own theodicy, Hick delineates the areas of agreement and difference between the two approaches.[65] Two items of disagreement in particular offer significant clues as to what Hick does in his own theodicy.

The first major difference is the motivating interest of each tradition. As Hick explains:

> The main motivating interest of the Augustinian tradition is to relieve the Creator of responsibility for the existence of evil by placing that responsibility upon dependent beings who have willfully misused their God-given freedom. In contrast the Irenaean type of theodicy in its developed form, as we find it in Schleiermacher and later thinkers, accepts God's ultimate and omni-responsibility and seeks to show for what good and justifying reason He has created a universe in which evil was inevitable.[66]

According to this distinction, theodicies following the Augustinian tradition hold a nonconsequentialist account of ethics, whereas those in the Irenaean tradition usually incorporate a consequentialist ethic. As already noted, Hick's theology does incorporate consequentialism.

Hick says that a second major distinction between the traditions is that the Augustinian tradition sees God's relation to his creation in predominantly impersonal terms, whereas the Irenaean tradition emphasizes the personal relation of God and the creature. In speaking of the Irenaean approach, Hick writes:

> According to the Irenaean type of theodicy, on the other hand, man has been created for fellowship with his Maker and is valued by the personal divine love as an end in himself. The world exists to be an environment for man's life, and its imperfections are integral to its fitness as a place of soul-making.[67]

This notion of soul-making is, of course, the key to Hick's theodicy.

Hick begins his theodicy by claiming that according to the Augustinian view, God created humans in a finished finitely perfect state, but they fell disastrously away from this. The Irenaean tradition, on the other hand, doesn't see people as created perfect. Instead, they are still in the process of creation.[68] Hick, referring to and quoting Irenaeus on this issue, states:

> Irenaeus himself expressed the point in terms of the (exegetically dubious) distinction between the 'image' and 'likeness' of God referred to in Genesis i.26: "Then God said, Let us make man in our image, after our likeness." His view was that man as a personal and moral being already exists in the image, but has not yet been formed into the finite likeness of God. By this 'likeness' Irenaeus means something more than personal existence as such; he means a certain valuable quality of personal life which reflects finitely the divine life. This represents the perfecting of man, the fulfillment of God's purpose for humanity, the 'bringing of many sons to glory,' the creating of 'children of God' who are 'fellow heirs with Christ' of his glory.[69]

Hick sees this notion in the writings of the apostle John in terms of the movement from mere animal life (*Bios*) to a higher level of existence, namely, eternal life (*Zoe*).[70] According to Hick, for God to create humans on the first level of life was very easy, but the second stage of the creative process is of a different kind. It cannot be performed by omnipotent power alone, because "personal life is essentially free and self-directing. It cannot be perfected by divine fiat, but only through the uncompelled responses and willing cooperation of human individuals in their actions and reactions in the world in which God has placed them."[71]

What kind of world would God have created, then, in view of this desire to "bring many sons to glory"? Certainly not the hedonistic paradise that many atheists request. Hick answers:

> But if we are right in supposing that God's purpose for man is to lead him from human *Bios,* or biological life of man, to that quality of *Zoe,* or the personal life of eternal worth, which we see in Christ, then the question that we have to ask is not, Is this the kind of world that an all-powerful and infinitely loving being would create as an environment for his human pets? or, Is the architecture of the world the most pleasant and convenient possible? The question that we have to ask is rather, Is this the kind of world that God might make as an environment in which moral beings may be fashioned, through their own free insights and responses, into 'children of God'?
>
> Such critics as Hume are confusing what heaven ought to be, as an environment for perfected finite beings, with what this world ought to be, as an environment for beings who are in the process of becoming perfected.[72]

Thus, the value of our world shouldn't be measured primarily in terms of the amount of pleasure and pain occurring in it at any given moment, but rather by its fitness for what Hick claims is its primary purpose, soul-making.

This is the major thrust of the soul-building theodicy, but Hick has a few additions. For example, he discusses how his theodicy relates to the free will issue. In particular, he responds to the Flew-Mackie attack on the free will defense. Hick says we must remember that it is God's desire not only that people freely act rightly toward one another, but that "they shall also freely enter into a filial personal relationship with God Himself."[73] We must ask, then, whether it is logically possible for God to make people so that they will always freely do right not only in relation to one another (something Hick thinks God *can* do), but will also freely respond to him in love, trust, and faith. Hick thinks the answer is no, and he argues his case by an analogy to a hypnotist and his patient. If a hypnotist suggests that his patient do a certain act, after waking, the patient would have the sense of doing it freely, but he would actually be the hypnotist's puppet. Hick says the same is true of God making us so that we would respond to him in love. Such emotions would be unauthentic.[74] In relation to God fixing our responses, Hick writes:

> . . . He would have pre-selected our responses to our environment, to one another, and to Himself in such a way that although these responses would from our point of view be free and spontaneous, they would from God's point of view be unfree. . . . if we proceed instead from the Christian view that God is seeking man's free response to Himself in faith, trust, and obedience, we see the necessity for our fourth question and for a negative answer to it.[75]

Hick's ultimate conclusion from this is:

> But if human analogies entitle us to speak about God at all, we must insist that such a universe could be only a poor second-best to one in which created beings, whose responses to Himself God has not thus 'fixed' in advance, come freely to love, trust, and worship Him. And if we attribute the latter and higher aim to God, we must declare to be self-contradictory the idea of God's so creating men that they will inevitably respond positively to Him.[76]

Hick also addresses physical evil. He doesn't give a full analysis of all the types of natural evil, but focuses primarily on pain and suffering. He considers the possibility of God removing pain from the world in order to make it a better place, but he says we must ask the question, "Better for what?" According to Hick, the purpose of the world isn't to grant us maximal pleasure but rather to grant us maximal opportunity for soul-building. Since soul-building couldn't be effected in a world devoid of pain, Hick thinks it necessary to have a human environment like ours in order to build souls.[77]

While this is Hick's general answer to natural evil, he knows there is still the question of why there must be as much pain as there is in order to build souls. He refuses to answer that this excessive evil is due to demonic beings, as some in the Augustinian tradition have argued.[78] Hick's answer is that the solution is a mystery. Still, there is a positive value of mystery. He explains:

> Such suffering remains unjust and inexplicable, haphazard and cruelly excessive. The mystery of dysteleological suffering is a real mystery, impenetrable to the rationalizing human mind. It challenges Christian faith with its utterly baffling, alien, destructive meaninglessness. And yet at the same time, detached theological reflection can note that this very irrationality and this lack of ethical meaning contribute to the character of the world as a place in which true human goodness can occur and in which loving sympathy and compassionate self-sacrifice can take place. 'Thus, paradoxically,' as H.H. Farmer says, 'the failure of theism to solve all mysteries becomes part of its case!'[79]

Hick thinks his theodicy only works if soul-making succeeds. He recognizes, however, that so far as we can see, "the soul-making process does in fact fail in our own world at least as often as it succeeds."[80] Since that is so, Hick adds one more element to his theodicy, an eschatological item. Hick says that according to Christian belief, the ultimate life of man lies in the Kingdom of God which is depicted in Jesus' teachings as a state of exultant bliss and happiness. Hick believes Christian theodicy must point to that time of final blessedness, expecting a resolution to the problem of evil in the ultimate triumph of God's good purpose. As Hick argues:

> We must thus affirm in faith that there will in the final accounting be no personal life that is unperfected and no suffering that has not eventually become a phase in the fulfillment of God's good purpose. Only so, I suggest, is it possible to believe both in the perfect goodness of God and in His unlimited capacity to perform His will. For if there are finally wasted lives and finally unredeemed sufferings, either God is not perfect in love or He is not sovereign in rule over his creation.[81]

Some think of this resolution as a kind of book-keeping matter according to which each person will be rendered compensation equal to the trials undergone. However, Hick says this is wrong, because:

> As distinct from such a book-keeping view, what is being suggested here, so far as man's sufferings are concerned, is that these sufferings—which for some people are immense and for others relatively slight—will in the end lead to the enjoyment of a common good which will be unending and therefore unlimited and which will be seen by its participants as justifying all that has been endured on the way to it. The 'good eschaton' will not be a reward or a compensation proportioned to each individual's trials, but an infinite

good that would render worthwhile *any* finite suffering endured in the course of attaining to it.[82]

Some might agree that without this eschatological dimension Hick's theodicy would be in grave difficulty. I disagree. It is true that for a consequentialist evil is instrumental in maximizing good. However, even if most people don't respond to evil by growing more spiritually mature, that isn't God's fault. Given incompatibilism he can't make them love him. Still, some people's souls will be built through suffering, and the fundamental point of the soul-building theodicy is that without suffering souls can't be built. So if God's purpose in creating our world is to make it a venue for soul-building, he has succeeded. There is no other way to build souls, according to this theodicy, but even if there were another way, that wouldn't mean that God's purpose for this world fails. Our world is one of those good worlds the Modified Rationalist speaks about, because it offers a good environment in which to build souls. Just because not everyone responds, that doesn't make our world a bad one.

My point, then, is that the traditional Irenaean theodicy still solves its problem of moral evil even without Hick's eschatological addendum. Of course, it can succeed with it, too.

Evaluations of Hick's Soul-Building Theodicy

Hick's theodicy is very appealing in many respects. It seems to explain a maximal amount of evil in our world, and does so in a rather plausible way. There have, of course, been objections to it, and in what follows I want to raise various objections and then give a final assessment.

Some of the most substantial objections to Hick's version of the soul-building theodicy are found in two articles by G. Stanley Kane. In fact, Hick thought them sufficiently significant that in a revised edition of *Evil and the God of Love* he raised and addressed those objections.[83] Let me turn to those objections first.

In "The Failure of Soul-Making Theodicy," Kane raises five major objections to Hick's project. I shall present what seem to me the most significant. Hick lumps Kane's second and fifth objections together as involving the same basic point (and error, in Hick's opinion). Both objections presuppose that Hick claims that the existence of evil is logically necessary in order for there to be epistemic distance between God and us. Epistemic distance means that there isn't such clear evidence of God's existence available to us that we have no choice but to believe he exists. If it were abundantly obvious to everyone that God exists, belief wouldn't result from a free decision to believe. However, without choosing freely to trust God, mankind can't grow spiritually.

Is it true, however, that Kane accuses Hick of holding that evil is logically necessary to maintain epistemic distance? Listen to Kane himself. In regard to his second objection against Hick, he writes:

> A second way that soul-making theodicy seeks to justify the existence of evil is by holding that the existence of evil is logically necessary to the establishment of epistemic distance between men and God. Hick never explicitly states that the existence of evil is logically necessary to the establishment of epistemic distance but it is clearly part of his theodicy.[84]

As for his fifth objection, Kane writes:

> Hick, as we have seen, believes that the existence of evil is necessary in order for man to be set at an epistemic distance from God. We have found strong reason for rejecting this method of justifying the existence of evil, but for the purposes of our discussion in this section, let us accept it. Now it would seem that evil could serve this function in helping to establish *epistemic* distance only if its existence constituted evidence against the existence of God. But theodicy is an effort to show that in reality evil is not evidence against the existence of God. Hick seems thus led into the clutches of a paradox. If his theodicy succeeds qua theodicy, the existence of evil is not evidence against the existence of God. But since one of the pillars of his theodicy is the notion of epistemic distance, *his* theodicy cannot succeed unless the existence of evil *is* evidence against the existence of God. Now, the existence of evil is either evidence against the existence of God or it is not. But in either case Hick's theodicy fails.[85]

Clearly, Kane thinks Hick believes that evil is logically necessary to epistemic distance between God and man. Kane's fifth objection rests on this notion. His second objection is that this idea is simply wrong. That is, there can be epistemic distance without evil.[86]

Thankfully, Hick responded to these complaints, and his answer is rather simple. Hick never claimed that evil is logically necessary to epistemic distance from God. He believes that natural and moral evil contingently reinforce our epistemic distance from God, but they aren't logically necessary to it. Instead, Hick's point is that epistemic distance is required for freedom in our relation to God. And freedom is required in order to build souls. But evil isn't required for epistemic distance. As Hick says, "So far as this consideration is concerned, however, man could be created at an epistemic distance from God in a world containing no challenges or physical perils of any kind."[87]

Kane believes his fourth objection is utterly devastating. Hick claims that the purpose of enduring this world's struggles is to develop spiritual and moral character. Kane thinks that it is more important to be able to *use* those qualities than to acquire or merely possess them. But here is where the problem arises. In Hick's total worldview,

> the final state of man, which is the fully perfected state of man, is one in which there will be no call for the actual showing of such traits in behavior. The final state will be one from which all evil has been banished and, according to Hick, it is logically impossible to show any of these traits in actual behavior when there is no evil.[88]

Why should God structure a world where we have to put up with all sorts of pain and misery in order to develop virtues that will never be used throughout most of our existence?

William Hasker defends Hick on this point. He answers that it isn't entirely clear that these virtues will be useless in the afterlife. We know very little about conditions in heaven, so it isn't out of line for Hick to think that perhaps there will be challenges and tasks, problems and pains in heaven. In that case, these virtues would be very valuable.[89]

While it is true that we know little of the afterlife, I think what Hasker and Hick suggest is mere speculation. Certainly, Scripture is clear enough that pains, etc., arise from sin, and that in our glorified state we shall be removed from sin in all its forms and influence. Hence, I don't see that the eternal state, for example, as described in Revelation 21–22, will require these virtues.

Hasker's other defense seems more convincing, but even here, Kane might have a counter response. Hasker complains that Kane's objection commits him to believing that acquired virtues aren't valuable if conditions change so that they can't be used. Hasker says:

> But this is a view which is clearly inconsistent with Christianity, and I would argue that it is also inconsistent with common morality. Heroes in many walks of life are often prized, esteemed and honored long after age and/or changed circumstances have made a repetition of their heroic achievements impossible, and the honor given them, insofar as it is sincere, cannot be solely for the sake of inspiring the coming generation. Such persons are valued for what they *are* and for what they *have done,* rather than for what they may yet do.[90]

I think Kane could grant Hasker's point, but argue that it essentially misses his point. That is, if the ultimate value of developing these virtues is just to serve as an example or hero for all eternity, that is small recompense for what some people have to endure in this life.

What about Hick's response? It strikes me as more convincing than Hasker's. In relation to Kane, Hick writes:

He takes, as it seems to me, too narrowly moralistic a view of 'soul-making'. This is not primarily a matter of acquiring certain specific moral virtues, such as courage and compassion, but of entering into a certain relationship with God. The path to this end-state has the moral life as one of its indispensable aspects; but it need not be assumed that the various particular moral quali- ties which relate to man's pilgrimage through time continue as such in eternity. The central work of moral and spiritual growth is the overcoming of egoity, the transcending of individual self-interest in a common human life in relation to God.[91]

In essence, Hick's reply is that these virtues may not be useful in a future life and they needn't be. However, we need to develop them in this life, for they are instrumental in preparing us for communion with God in the next life. This seems more clearly to justify the soul-making process than other answers to this objection do.

I have saved Kane's initial objection until now, because I think it is the most significant, and so does Kane. According to the soul-building theodicy, maturing morally and spiritually involves developing traits like courage, com- passion, and fortitude. But the soul-building theodicy tells us that the exis- tence of evils is logically necessary to the development of these traits. Kane disagrees, because "we can imagine situations where these traits could be dis- played even though there is no actual evil existing."[92] For example, Kane argues that courage and fortitude could manifest themselves as persistence and perseverance in accomplishing difficult tasks like writing a doctoral dis- sertation or preparing for and competing in the Olympic Games. Compassion could develop in the form of fellow-feeling and sympathy on the part of those who watch others engaged in these projects. Kane writes:

> It is hard to see why a man or a woman cannot develop just as much patience, fortitude and strength of character in helping his or her spouse complete a doctoral dissertation as in caring for a sick child through a long and serious illness. It is hard to see why people cannot learn just as much of the spirit of help and cooperation by teaming together to win an athletic championship as by coming together to rescue a town leveled by a tornado or inundated by a flood.[93]

Hick responds that Kane's examples underestimate matters. As a matter of fact, even the situations Kane imagines contain risks of serious evils. The doctoral student and his wife may have to undergo some significant poverty in order to complete his program. They may find that the dissertation is rejected so that he never gets the degree. Or, he may get the degree but not be able to get a job. As to the athlete, no one competes without recognizing that there is risk of physical injury and even tragically fatal accidents. Hick believes that if these risks are removed for both the doctoral student and the athlete, it is impossible any longer to assume that these activities would have any soul-making value.[94] Hick concludes:

> It therefore does not seem to me that there is a viable possibility of a 'soul-making' world from which we exclude all risk of severe hardship and injury, with desperate and even suicidal misery as the extreme point of the one continuum, and death as the extreme point of the other. The world, as a person-making environment, does not have to include the *particular* perils that it contains, but it does have to contain some particular perils and challenges which are real and which inevitably have, to us, an arbitrary and sometimes threatening character which is beyond our control.[95]

Fundamentally, Hick (and the soul-building theodicy) is saying that the risk and experience of evils is the only way to build souls. I shall return to this matter in my final assessment of Hick's position, but let me turn now to handle one more objection Kane raises in his "Soul-Making Theodicy and Eschatology." Kane's complaint centers around Hick's contention that every soul will eventually be built. If this is so, then what becomes of free will? Isn't it at least possible that some people will choose forever to reject God? If that is possible, it seems that the only way Hick can guarantee that all will be saved is for God to override the freedom of inveterate sinners and force them to comply.[96]

This is a serious objection, because if it is right, it appears that Hick's system is self-contradictory. His soul-building explanation demands that we have incompatibilistic free will, but his stipulation that all souls will be built seems to necessitate either compatibilism or a harder form of determinism. Hick recognizes the importance of this objection and addresses it in his book *Death and Eternal Life*.

There are several elements in Hick's response to this problem. Initially, he notes that the objection assumes that God can accomplish this goal only if he overrides the wayward wills of human beings. However, this overlooks the point made by Augustine that "in creating our human nature God has formed it for himself, so that—to draw upon another strand of Augustine's thought—our hearts will be restless until they find their rest in him."[97] In other words, the process of reforming our souls won't be as hard as it seems, because God has created us so that there is an inherent gravitation toward him.

Some may reply that if this is so, then God has "stacked the deck" in his favor. This sounds like determinism after all. Hick anticipates the objection and answers that it assumes wrongly "that human beings have or could have chosen their own basic nature."[98] This is simply not true, according to Hick. No matter how mankind originated on this earth, human nature is the product of various forces other than ourselves. God couldn't, for example, have made us with no specific nature and no dispositions toward anyone or anything. Moreover,

> our freedom can only be a freedom within the basic situation of our being the kind of creatures that we are in the kind of world in which we are. It can only be the freedom of beings who are—without their choice—of a certain determinate kind. . . . That the basic conditions of our existence are thus set by forces beyond ourselves must be presupposed in any viable concept of human freedom. The problem of free will does not hinge upon whether we are created beings (i.e. the product of forces other than ourselves) but upon whether as created beings we have any significant freedom. For any human actions exemplifying our concepts 'free' and 'responsible' must in the nature of the case be the actions of beings who have been created and formed by forces beyond themselves.[99]

For those who are still unconvinced, Hick asks what the alternatives are. God could have created us religiously neutral, or he could have made us religious beings but then refrained from drawing us to himself. As to the former option, Hick says it isn't clear that this sort of being would be any freer with respect to God than we now are. This sort of human would be free *from* God, but not free *for* God (as we now are). Hick argues that this isn't a freer state than we already have; moreover, it would certainly be less desirable, since we would be disinclined to believe in God even though he exists.[100]

As to the second option, Hick claims this is unthinkable. It doesn't square with the Christian message that God would create us to be positively disposed toward him, but then do nothing to perfect and redeem us. Moreover, "the question is now whether we should in this case be more truly free in relation to God than we are if he is actively trying to save us by every means compatible with our existence as free personal beings."[101] To ask this question is to answer it, according to Hick. As long as God's saving activity doesn't undermine freedom, we should rejoice that God is at work to redeem us.

All of this sounds appealing, but it still may be all for naught. After all, God's saving activity doesn't achieve its desired end in this life in many cases. If death ends our chances at moral reform, then God still can't succeed. Hick knows this, and it leads to his next crucial point. There is simply no reason to think that soul-building ends with physical death. "We must suppose that beyond this life the process continues in other environments offering other experiences and challenges which open up new opportunities of response and growth."[102]

Hick likens God's attempts to build our souls to the work of a therapist trying to help her patient. Reform won't come immediately, but over time if the therapist is skillful, she will succeed in helping her patient. The therapist isn't omniscient, so she may err along the way, but this can never be true of God. Hick writes:

> We have to suppose, not a human but a divine therapist, working not to a limited deadline but in unlimited time, with perfect knowledge, and ultimately controlling instead of being restricted by the environmental factors. In so far as we can conceive of this, do we not find that it authorizes an unambiguously good prognosis?[103]

Here we have our answer. It isn't a Protestant purgatory Hick envisions. Rather, God, who knows our natures and knows what it will take to convince us to turn to him, will eventually succeed. No one knows how long it will take, but God has all eternity, so eventually he will succeed, and he will do so without destroying our freedom.

Though this all may sound convincing, I find it fundamentally flawed. It would work if we were talking about compatibilism, because the arguments, circumstances, experiences, etc., that God could bring into our life could eventually decisively incline our will to choose him. However, this isn't so with incompatibilism. Incompatibilists don't deny that God can arrange circumstances and give us arguments in favor of a course of action. What they do deny is that any of those factors or combination of those factors can decisively incline the will to choose. If the will is so inclined, it is causally determined and thus, not (incompatibilistically) free. The kind of activity Hick foresees on God's part guarantees that eventually he will persuade us all. With libertarian free will there can be no guarantees. Hence, if Hick is serious about his notion of freedom, he can't guarantee that all souls will be built. If he is serious about maintaining his universalism, he must back down on his notion of freedom. The problem still remains.

Despite this problem, we must be clear about what it proves. It does show that Hick's total set of views do contain a contradiction. Nonetheless, that doesn't mean there is no way to reform his position or to rescue the soul-making theodicy in general. As already explained, the soul-making theodicy can succeed even without Hick's eschatological addendum. Moreover, if Hick feels he must add that element, a slight modification will save his position. That is, all Hick needs to do is claim that it is likely under the conditions imagined that most souls will be built. Some souls may be lost, and that will be tragic, but it surely doesn't disprove the claim that evil in our world is instrumental to producing an abundance of good. Our world is still a good world, because it allows the possibility of soul-building, even if every soul isn't in fact built. Once these changes in Hick's views are made, the logical inconsistency evaporates, and the theology can solve its problem of evil.

Let me now offer some final words of assessment. My comments about Hick on freedom are relevant to a further point about his views. It is indeed strange that Hick finds no inconsistency in siding with Mackie in favor of compatibilism when it comes to God determining our free choices in regard to other humans, and then siding with incompatibilism when the discussion turns to man's relation to God. If there is a problem at all with compatibilism, it will be there whether the subject is our relation to God or our relation to other humans. Likewise, if compatibilism is acceptable in one case, it is hard to see why it can't apply in the other as well. It is hard to see how an incompatibilist with very specific views about how causal determinism destroys freedom could consistently agree that the normal state of affairs as we relate to one another is just as the compatibilist describes them. Hick should be consistent by siding either with incompatibilism or with compatibilism in both cases. This problem is easy enough to fix, but until it is fixed, Hick's overall theology is internally inconsistent.

Second, Hick briefly addresses the quantity of evil in our world, and his treatment is problematic. It is problematic because it assumes that the problem of the quantity of evil is just part of the theological/philosophical problem of evil. These two problems, however, are distinct, so Hick's handling of them improperly conflates them.

Though I agree that the soul-building theodicy can solve its theology's logical problem of moral evil, I believe there are reasons for rejecting it as inadequate. My next objections deal with external grounds for rejecting it (Hick's version in particular). The first matter involves Hick's eschatological addendum. He says evil will be justified, because everyone will ultimately make it to the Kingdom of God. This will happen no matter how long it takes to reform each soul and even if it involves work after physical death. Hick has every right to hold these views, even though they are difficult, if not impossible, to support biblically. Nonetheless, I can't accept these views, because they are contrary to biblical teaching. Scripture says a great deal about judgment of the wicked that indicates that many people won't wind up in the Kingdom of God.

Second, I find something fundamentally unsatisfying in any approach that essentially says that if all else fails, everything will work out in the future even though we won't be able to prove that until the future. Again, this belief is thoroughly consistent with Hick's view that religious assertions can be and are to be verified eschatologically.[104] Nonetheless, if a position is correct, I would like to be able to show that now, not in some distant future that is so far removed from the present that it makes the question of whether a theological position as a whole is correct impossible to determine now. My complaint isn't against theologies that incorporate an eschatology. It is with theologies that ultimately rest their truth or falsity on issues that are future.[105]

Finally, what I find most objectionable about the soul-building theodicy as expressed by any theologian harkens back to Kane's objection about the necessity of evil to build souls. Central to the soul-building theodicy are the notions that the purpose of our world is to build souls *and* that evil is necessary for that project. It is that latter claim that I find especially problematic. I can state my objections in the form of two questions. First, must there be difficulties to overcome in order for us to learn to love God? I don't see that the only way God has for building souls is through difficulties. Hick's response to Kane suggests that there must be risk (even if there is never any evil) in order to build souls. Perhaps this is true of the examples Kane offers, but there is a more fundamental issue that Kane's objection raises. That issue is whether God has no other way to build our souls than through our victory over difficulties. Thinking this is the only way to build souls just assumes that a relation of love and devotion can't be built through one party showering blessing upon another. Hick surely hasn't shown that. Hence, it isn't at all clear that there must be difficulties in order to build souls.

Despite one's response to the first question, there is a second. Even if, for the sake of argument, we grant that the only way to build souls is to have people overcome difficulties, must there be moral evil in order for there to be difficulties? Here the answer must be no. So long as there are situations that test one's character and develop it by that testing, a soul can be built by overcoming difficulties. Hick's answer to Kane amounts to saying there must at least be the risk of evil. Perhaps so, but that is different from what the soul-building theodicy demands, for it claims that *actual* moral and natural evil in our world are logically necessary to build souls. I disagree, because even if difficulties are necessary to build souls, it isn't true that there must be evil in order for there to be difficulties.

My point here is easy enough to illustrate. Many of us have children. We desire not only that they grow physically but also that they will grow mentally, emotionally, and spiritually. In helping them, for example, to develop a sense of responsibility, we assign them various chores. While these chores aren't as "exciting" as playing with their friends, the "assignments" we give them are not evil.

Consider another illustration. Other colleagues and I have the privilege of teaching graduate students. Our goal is to help them develop both their knowledge and their ability to reason and evaluate what they hear and read. To those ends we assign them books to read, tests to take, and papers to write. Certainly, such assignments are difficulties to overcome, and some may see them as evil, but in truth these assignments aren't intended as evil, nor are they evil.

So, people can be challenged to grow in various ways and can grow by confronting and overcoming difficulties, but there is no reason to think those challenges must be evils. Similarly, even if we grant that it is impossible to build souls without confronting difficulties, that doesn't prove that there must be evils in order for there to be difficulties. Of course, my complaint here doesn't uncover any internal inconsistency in the soul-building theodicy (it can solve its logical problem of evil). Instead, it explains in part why I find it and the theology it presupposes unacceptable.[106]

Marilyn Adams's Christian Approach

In two influential articles, Marilyn Adams has offered her solution to the problem of evil. "Horrendous Evils and the Goodness of God" was written after "Redemptive Suffering: A Christian Solution to the Problem of Evil," but the latter article contains the fuller explanation of her views. In my presentation of her views, I plan to focus primarily on the more complete statement, but materials from both articles will be helpful.

Redemptive Suffering Defense

Adams begins by explaining that most discussions of the problem of evil have dealt with the logical problem and have asked about the existence of evil in general. She agrees that recent work on these more global and/or general problems has succeeded in attempting to satisfy the requirements of the logical problem. However, the various defenses and theodicies used to address evil in general cannot successfully be applied to problems that arise in terms of truly horrific evils that individuals experience, evils that utterly challenge their continued belief in God at all. Hence, we need to separate two issues and handle two distinct problems: one deals with the goodness of God on a more global and generic level, whereas the other deals with the defeat of evil by good within the life and experience of individuals.[107] Adams notes that theists have spent much time dealing with the former, but little time and effort on the latter. She proposes to address the latter problem, and believes that in doing so, those who are Christians must and can find within the richness of their religious tradition concepts that help to answer this problem and thereby meet the pastoral needs of believers wrestling with terrible evils.[108]

Several things about Adams's approach are good, but others are problematic. It is commendable that she recognizes that there is more than one problem of evil. It is also encouraging that she sees that the personal dimensions of evil need pastoral care in addition to whatever one might offer as an answer to the sufferer's intellectual problems. Adams's repeated references to specific evils people actually suffer and to the case of Job as a prime example of this problem are correct in that the more personal problem with evil is in fact the religious problem. She is absolutely correct that defenses and theodicies marshaled against evil in general won't work when dealing with the religious problem. What is problematic is thinking that there is some intellectual answer we must have in order to deal with the religious problem. In my handling of the religious problem in later chapters, I plan to show that while the religious problem raises intellectual questions, it isn't predominantly an intellectual problem, and the search for some defense or theodicy to address the religious problem misunderstands to a certain extent the nature of this problem.

Setting aside the point I have just made, I want to present and evaluate Adams's own answer to this problem. Though she doesn't apply her defense to the more generic problems of evil, we need to ask whether it would be relevant to them or to any other problem of evil. If it is, we need to see how it would address those problems. Such questions are of significance in that those who discuss her views often do so to evaluate how well it serves as a defense or theodicy against various logical problems of evil.

In presenting her views, Adams nowhere identifies the exact form of theism she holds other than to note that it is distinctively Christian. Nor does she clearly identify her account of ethics. However, it is hard to classify her metaphysics as Leibnizian, and her views don't seem to fit a theonomous theism either. Hence, it seems most likely that she holds a form of Modified Rationalism. As to her ethics, there are elements of both consequentialism and nonconsequentialism in her defense, but the overarching solution she proposes (and the rationale behind it) appeals most frequently to consequentialist concerns.

How, then, does Adams address these personal, (even) horrendous evils that disrupt people's relationships with God? She begins by reminding us that within the Christian tradition the place to begin to grapple with the problem of evil isn't in relation to evils outside of us, but in relation to sin and evil within us. In fact, until we are willing to confront God's way of dealing with our own sin, we may be unable to appreciate how God handles other evils or the best way for us to live with such evils.[109]

To explain why this is so, Adams reminds us of some basic Christian doctrines. God's intent in creating humans was to make creatures who can "enter into nonmanipulative relationships of self-surrendering love with himself and relationships of self-giving love with others."[110] However, Adams assures us that God can't get the relationships he wants with us unless he gives us libertarian free will. Otherwise, the surrender of love would be forced, and that is no bargain for either God or us. Moreover, God couldn't hold us accountable for sin, if our responses (whatever they are) are forced. Of course, if God gives us libertarian free will, he can't guarantee that we won't use it to do evil.[111]

While this sounds like the free will defense, that isn't Adams's strategy. Rather, she turns to what follows our misuse of freedom, and that is God's judgment. While God has every right to judge us and make us face what we have done, God's purpose in judging isn't punitive. Rather, it is to drive us to repentance and reconciliation with him. But how is God most likely to succeed in moving us to repentance? Certainly not by sending us some horrendous punishment. Like a thunderbolt, that would grab our attention, but most people don't respond positively when someone makes a point by "banging them over the head" with it! God needs to use instead a strategy of indirect pedagogy, an approach that entices the sinner to participate in arriving at the verdict that we need to repent and return to him. Even an indirect strategy, however, won't always work. Jesus taught in parables, but his listeners (especially the Pharisees), if they got his point, didn't make the needed changes. When that happens, Adams explains, God must turn to a different noncoercive strategy, and he does. God chooses the more expensive strategy of redemptive suffering as epitomized in martyrdom and the cross. By forcing us to see our own evil through the unjust torment we heap upon others, God wants and hopes that we will get the message that we need to repent and reform.[112]

To be a martyr is to be a witness. It is to take a stand for what one believes is right, even if one must give his life in support of that cause. The witness that a martyr gives can have a threefold value, all of which is relevant to demonstrating God's goodness. First, for those who are onlookers to the event of martyrdom, it can serve as a prophetic picture. They can see in the martyr the person they should be and be moved to a deeper level of commitment to God. Alternatively, they can see themselves in the persecutor and be moved to repent.[113]

Martyrdom, according to Adams, can also be redemptive for the persecutor. In the martyr's sacrifice, God, so to speak, draws the persecutor an external picture of what he is really like. The more innocent the victim, the clearer the portrait of the persecutor's own evil. He can't rationalize what he is doing by saying that the victim deserves the torture. Christ's martyrdom is the prime example of such an external picture. This is so because Christ is a completely innocent victim and hence allows no room for rationalization (it serves as a very clear vehicle for informing the persecutor that he deserves judgment), and because the cross is the chief expression of God's love for the persecutor. As Adams says, "if the persecutor is moved to repentance by the love of the martyr, it is the martyr whom he will thank and love. According to Christian belief, God was so eager to win our love that he became incarnate and volunteered for martyrdom himself (John 3:16-18)."[114] Of course, this example of love must be noncoercive, given libertarian free will, and it doesn't always work. However, the clearer the picture, the more likely that the persecutor will get the message that he needs to change.

Martyrdom can also be a vehicle of God's love and goodness for the martyr. It offers the martyr an opportunity for testing and judgment as he views his life and relationship to God in the light of what he is experiencing. It also affords him an opportunity to grow in his relationship with God. Adams uses the various tests and trials of Abraham as an example of how this can work on an individual level. And, because God in Christ has suffered martyrdom for the sake of redeeming others, when we suffer from terrible evils, we have an opportunity to identify with Christ in his suffering. We learn not only what martyrdom is like for Christ; we learn what it is to be that person. Only when one has suffered severely can she fully appreciate and identify with what happened to Christ. So, in martyrdom there is positive benefit for the martyr.[115]

Though all of these positive benefits may accrue from suffering, Adams knows that things don't always turn out that way. When confronted by evil, there is no guarantee that the onlooker, the persecutor, or the martyr will repent of evil and grow in his or her relationship with God. And Adams certainly wouldn't claim that the only way to grow in our relationship with God is to suffer intense and excruciating affliction. Hence, she states clearly that what she presents doesn't mean that there is some logically necessary connection between these positive results and martyrdom. In the case of some people, trials and suffering are causally involved in moving the afflicted to grow (though, of course, not so as to guarantee that growth—which would remove libertarian free will) in their relationship to God. But there is no guarantee that with affliction growth must result, nor that the only means for growth is affliction.[116]

How does all of this relate to addressing the problem of evil? Adams admits that on the surface, redemptive suffering doesn't appear to be the wisest strategy for God to employ since it doesn't always work. Though Adams doesn't say it, it also suggests that redemptive suffering isn't likely to offer a satisfactory justification of God in the face of evil. However, redemptive suffering must be viewed within the larger context of a Christian worldview. When we do, we see that the ultimate result for those who grow closer to God in the midst of suffering is the beatific vision of God. This, affirms Adams, is a good that is incommensurate with anything else. Hence, those who receive it won't see it as slightly (or more) outweighing and making up for all the evils the sufferer has endured. Rather it is so blessed that there will be no comparison possible or needed. Talk of whether this result from a life of suffering is a morally sufficient reason for God not to remove suffering will be unnecessary and irrelevant, for such talk again plays on the notion of trying to balance out or overbalance good with the evil we have experienced. The beatific vision, however, is such an overwhelmingly blessed benefit that questions of overbalancing evil and morally sufficient reasons for God not removing such afflictions won't make sense and won't even be worth asking.[117]

Moreover, redemptive suffering also gives the sufferer a glimpse into the inner life of God by allowing the sufferer to see experientially what it means and how it feels to suffer unjustly for the sake of others. These two values, the beatific vision and a glimpse into God's inner life, don't explain why God allows the various evils, including horrendous ones, that people undergo, but once the sufferer realizes that these are the ultimate results of this process, he can live with the affliction and still praise and serve God. None of this means that the evils encountered and endured aren't really evil, but only that those who grow in their relation to God through experiencing these evils can conclude that the blessed outcome goes well beyond anything they have had to put up with along life's way.[118]

As Adams summarizes and concludes her presentation, she notes that none of this means that Christians will think the evils people endure are really insignificant. Even so, in spite of how horrid the experiences of many sufferers are, Christians

> see in the cross of Christ a revelation of God's righteous love and a paradigm of his redemptive use of suffering. Christian mysticism invites the believer to hold that a perfectly good God further sanctifies our moments of deepest distress so that retrospectively, from the vantage point of the beatific vision, the one who suffered will not wish them away from his life history—and this, not because he sees them as the source of some other resultant good, but inasmuch as he will recognize them as times of sure identification with and vision into the inner life of his creator.[119]

Evaluation

Many of the themes found in Adams's views echo things seen in other defenses and theodicies (in particular, the free will defense and the soul-building theodicy). However, her defense isn't just a rehash of other solutions; she adds her own element of originality, and that is commendable. It is also encouraging to read the work of a first-rate philosopher who willingly embraces and utilizes the resources of her religious tradition, rather than running from them. And, I think there are elements of her views that are helpful in addressing some aspects of some problems of evil. However, there are also some substantial problems which suggest that she isn't entirely successful in solving the problem of evil. Let me explain.

Earlier I alluded to an initial problem, and it is worth noting again in more detail. Adams rightly distinguishes the more (in her terms) generic answers (and respective problems) from the more personal struggles with evil. Unfortunately, she seems to think that while these are distinct problems, they are, generally speaking, two of the many predominantly intellectual questions evil's existence raises. The problem here is that her focus is really the religious problem of evil, and that problem differs from all the rest. All of the predominantly intellectual problems can be posed in either a logical or evidential form. Such categories don't even apply to the nature of, let alone the solution of, the religious or existential problem of evil. The religious problem isn't at root concerned about the logical consistency of the sufferer's theology or about whether her theological beliefs are supported by the facts of the world. Sufferers are, of course, not totally unconcerned about such issues, but anyone who thinks the religious problem is exclusively or even primarily about such matters has either not suffered serious tragedy or has but hasn't learned much from it about the nature of this very personal problem.

All of these points about the nature of the religious problem will be elaborated and illustrated in my chapters on the religious problem. For our purposes now, I only note that what Adams offers as a solution might at very best help someone to live with the God who isn't stopping the suffering, but it won't per se solve, for example, the problems of moral evil, the amount of evil, or the intensity of some evils either in their logical or their evidential form. Answers to such problems purport to explain either the reason or a possible reason why God allows such evil. In contrast, Adams says that we don't have answers to the *why* question for they are inaccessible to us,[120] and so her offering isn't intended as the answer to such questions.[121] But if that is so, then all the more so her views don't seem fitted for solving the more intellectual problems, the why problems. And yet one senses that she sees the religious problem as one of the many intellectual problems, distinct though it is, and sees herself as offering a solution to it.

If several different problems are conflated by Adams, as I am arguing, one might think there is nothing more to say. That is, one might think that before anything else can be said Adams needs to untangle the different problems, tell us exactly which problem she is addressing, and explain how she sees her material solving that problem. Rather than demand that, however, let us simply evaluate her defense from the distinct perspectives of the moral problem of evil and the religious problem. I turn first to the more intellectual dimension of things and evaluate her material from that standpoint.

An initial point worth noting is that though she doesn't tell us what her ethical theory is, the whole presentation embodies consequentialist notions. Adams points repeatedly to the results of redemptive suffering both temporally and eternally, and those consequences seem to be the "justifying" factors in explaining why God is good even though he permits such evils. In light of her ethics, one might think that her defense is just another version of the greater good defense, but that isn't so. The greater good defense does rest on consequentialism, but it demands that evil is logically necessary to some subsequent good. As we saw in describing Adams's views, she isn't ready to argue for such a logical tie between redemptive suffering and ultimate eternal goods. Actually, her views are quite reminiscent of soul-building theodicies, and arguably, her defense is a variation of that approach. As such, it has both the advantages and the disadvantages we noted when discussing the soul-building theodicy.

And yet it would be too hasty to categorize Adams's defense as nothing more than a variation of soul-building approaches. One ponders why, according to Adams, God must suffer so that we will get the message, grow closer in our relationship to him, and suffer redemptively for the sake of others. Couldn't God more directly order us to love him and get us to do so with threatened and implemented punishments? Adams's answer is that such an approach would be coercive, and in order to uphold the integrity of our libertarian free will, God won't coerce us to love him. But now it seems that the discussion has turned from redemptive suffering and soul-building to the free will defense. Adams's defense doesn't, however, reduce to the free will defense (nor does Hick's, even though he incorporates and appeals to libertarian free will), for the overarching emphasis of her position isn't what produced evil in the first place, but the results or outcome of the process of redemptive suffering. So, while her defense isn't simply a repetition of the soul-building theodicy, it is closest to that view and reaps the rewards and problems that accrue to that view.

Having said the preceding, however, I am not entirely sure that this is a convincing defense; it isn't really clear that Adams's position shows ours to be a good world. Adams places great emphasis on Christ's example of redemptive suffering, but I am not convinced that adding Christ as our fellow sufferer justifies God's permitting evil in our world. This approach is similar to other defenses which purport to show that God has a morally sufficient reason for allowing evil in our world because he hasn't made us suffer alone. In Christ, God has identified with us and our suffering. Because he was willing to endure the evils that we confront, that is supposed to make this a good world. It's as if the theist is telling us that it's all right that God doesn't get rid of evil so long as he willingly suffers along with us. I don't see how that demonstrates that ours is a good world or that God is justified in implementing such an order in this world. It does, however, increase the number of victims of evil, but why anyone thinks that solves the problem of evil in either its logical or evidential form is hard to understand.

In fairness to Adams, she isn't exactly saying that God is justified in allowing evil to stay in our world since he is willing to suffer along with us. However, invoking Christ as the prime example of redemptive suffering is all part of a larger picture that sees suffering as acceptable as long it is used (or at least intended) to draw people closer to God. What the critic of theism will want to know, and here I agree with this challenge, is why an omnipotent God would use such a strategy when it seems abundantly possible to draw us closer to himself without us having to experience horrendous evils.

My point isn't simply that I don't happen to think the various elements in Adams's story agree with the facts, for that wouldn't show any internal inconsistency in her theology. My point is twofold. At the most fundamental level I am concerned about whether this justification of evil really shows that our world is a good world. Granting Modified Rationalism, Adams needn't show that ours is the best world, but her reason for thinking this is a good world (and hence, God is justified for creating it) must convince us that this truly is a good world and that if it is, the only way for God to achieve the positive values that make this a good world is through redemptive suffering.

It is just at this point (and this is my second point), the point of showing us why we must have redemptive suffering as the means for preparing us for the beatific vision, that I think there is reason to challenge Adams's views. Adams admits that there is no logical tie between redemptive suffering and attaining the beatific vision, but then friend and foe alike will want to know if redemptive suffering in relation to horrible evils and not so horrific evils is the only means at God's disposal for helping our relationship with him grow.

A good part of the reason for raising such a question is that there are in fact some believers who have grown close to God and will someday enjoy the beatific vision who have never had to endure horrendous evils. Since they will receive the desired goal while escaping the trauma of horrendous evils, why shouldn't others? My point here must not be misunderstood. Some may think I am complaining that there must be another world (a best world) where most, if not all, of those who achieve the beatific vision do so without encountering and coping with horrible tragedy, and that God cannot be deemed good unless he creates that world. However, that isn't my point; I recognize that a

Modified Rationalist doesn't believe there is a best world, and I am not attempting to force Adams to hold that belief anyway and show that our world is the best. My point is that I am not sure that our world even qualifies as a good world, given the fact that many who suffer horrible evil turn from God and won't receive the beatific vision and given the fact that many who will have the beatific vision will do so without having experienced in this life horrendous evils. Are the relatively few who like Job do draw closer to God (and hence are made all the more ready and deserving to receive the beatific vision) as a result of coping with horrible tragedies enough to show that our world is in fact a good world?

Adams really doesn't explain how she knows that our world is a good world, despite the fact that only a few use affliction to prepare for the beatific vision while others use it to turn from God, and still others are prepared for that vision without undergoing horrendous evils. Some may think that Adams's description of our world does show it to be a good world, because, after all, some things do go right in it, including the preparation by affliction of some for the beatific vision. However, even in an evil possible world some things can and do go right. Perhaps then, even granting Adams's explanation of the positive use in our world of suffering for some, ours still isn't one of those good possible worlds that the Modified Rationalist talks about. Perhaps it is even so a good world, but my problem is that I don't find in Adams's presentation an explanation of why ours isn't an evil world where some good things occasionally happen, rather than it being a good world where bad things (even occasionally horrendous things) happen. I fear as well that attempts to meet my challenge, if successful, are likely to fall back either on the soul-building theodicy or the free will defense. If so, then her solution doesn't succeed on its own but has to be bolstered by a more fundamental one that does.

In sum, if we see Adams's solution as a justification of God's goodness, I think she hasn't made her case. But how does her proposal fare if seen as a response not to the more intellectual problems evil raises but to the religious problem? Here I find myself unconvinced again that this will help the sufferer with his or her religious crisis. In the midst of the shock, horror, and sense of abandonment and helplessness that one feels when dealing with a tragedy, can we really think that such a sufferer will be comforted with the knowledge that onlookers, persecutors, and even he or she will benefit from this experience? Will those possible positive outcomes lead her to say, "Yes, God, now I see why you are putting me through this, and I'm fully comfortable with what you are doing; I'm no longer angry at you for letting this happen to me"? Will the knowledge that Christ, too, suffered unjustly for the sake of redeeming others comfort her in her hour of need? Will she remove her anger at God for letting this happen to her because now she understands that she isn't alone in her pain; Christ has been there, too? Those who think such facts will assuage the pain and anger and repair the breach in their relationship to God either haven't suffered great tragedy themselves or haven't been around many who have. Offered such information as an attempt to comfort her, the sufferer is just as likely to ask why, then, if so many positive things can flow from affliction, hasn't God similarly afflicted others (believers and nonbelievers). Since God hasn't thought this necessary to *their* spiritual growth, why must *she* endure these evils? Offered the information that God understands and suffers too, she is at least as likely, if not more likely, to think, "Oh, great, now he's miserable too; just what we needed, more victims, more who feel as wretched as I do," as she is to be comforted. Isn't there a better way than this for God to run the world?

Thus, I think it is dubious that Adams's solution actually succeeds in its current form as an answer to the logical problem of moral evil, horrendous evils, and other intellectual problems of evil. Adams is correct in identifying as a distinct problem the religious or existential problems of individual sufferers, but she is mistaken in thinking that what she offers solves or even is the way to go about solving that problem. The religious problem, as we shall see in chapter 14, is more distinct from the more generic problems than she suggests.[122]

CONCLUSION

In this chapter, I have presented and evaluated four Modified Rationalist theologies.[123] The first doesn't successfully answer its problem of evil, and there is reason to question whether the fourth does. The other two can succeed. Yandell's and Hick's formulations of their defenses produce some internal problems in their respective theologies, but the greater good defense and the soul-building theodicy per se can solve the logical problem of moral evil. This further refutes Mackie's claim that no theist can solve a problem of evil.

With the completion of this chapter, I have examined seven different theologies. Though five of them successfully solve their problem of evil in its logical form, I have rejected them as inadequate in their metaphysics, ethics, or views on human freedom. It is now time for me to offer my own theology and show how it solves its logical problem of moral evil. That is the task of the next chapter.

6

GOD AND MORAL EVIL

In previous chapters I have examined various theologies and their responses to the logical problem of evil. In each case, I rejected the theology. In this chapter, I shall present my own theology and show how it can answer its problem of evil. My focus in this chapter is moral evil, whereas in the next chapter, I shall address more directly physical evil.

In this chapter I intend to set forth a defense, not a theodicy. Though I think a case can be made for my theological position and its answer to moral evil, I don't intend here to argue that my explanation offers *the* reason for God allowing evil in our world. Instead, my aim is to offer a possible explanation why God might allow moral evil.

At the outset, I must identify my theology's metaphysics and ethics. Because of my problems with theonomy and Leibnizian Rationalism, I hold a Modified Rationalist position. As to ethics, I am a nonconsequentialist. In particular, I hold that what makes an act good or evil is not its consequences but God's prescription about it. But this alone is indistinguishable from theonomous ethics. Hence, I hold that while acts are right because God prescribes them, God doesn't prescribe arbitrarily or without reason. Instead, his moral law reflects his character or nature as God.

The difference between my ethics and theonomy's is as follows: both a theonomist and I make a metaphysical and an epistemological point. The epistemological point concerns how people learn what the rules of ethics are. Theonomy says this information is conveyed through divine revelation, and I tend to agree. The fundamental difference between us is a metaphysical matter, namely, why the laws of ethics are what they are. For a theonomist ethical norms are what they are simply because God says so. There is nothing inherently good or evil about any action. In contrast, I believe that actions are inherently good or evil, because they reflect or fail to reflect something about God's nature. Consequently, God prescribes moral norms as a reflection of his character. For example, he is a God of truth, so he commands us not to lie. He is a God of love; to murder someone or steal from him isn't an act of love, so God forbids us from doing either.

Broadly speaking, my ethical theory is an example of a Modified Divine Command theory.[1] It fits what Frankena describes as metaphysical moralism. Frankena writes:

> A theologian might claim that "right" means "commanded by God"; according to him, then, saying that Y is right is merely a shorter way of saying that it is commanded by God. On all such views, ethical and value judgments are disguised assertions of fact of some kind. Those who say, as Perry does, that they are disguised assertions of empirical fact are called *ethical naturalists,* and those who regard them as disguised assertions of metaphysical or theological facts are called *metaphysical moralists.* Many different theories of both kinds are possible, depending on the definitions proposed.[2]

Given my theological and ethical commitments, one might suspect that I would answer my problem of evil by the free will defense. However, this isn't so, because I hold a compatibilistic account of free will. The resultant theology is a moderate form of Calvinism.

Now, it seems that any theological position in confronting the problem of evil must face three fundamental questions: 1) Must God eradicate evil?— a question about obligation; 2) Can God remove evil?—a question concerning ability and power; and 3) Should God eliminate evil?—a question about prudence or wisdom. Clearly, the second question is the most significant, for if God cannot remove evil, then he isn't obligated to do so, and it would be foolish for him to try.[3] I plan to argue that God can't eradicate evil without producing various problems I shall specify. Thus, he isn't obligated to remove evil. Though this strategy may sound strange (arguing that God can't remove evil), it actually isn't, for many defenses and theodicies use the same approach. What is unique in my defense are the reasons I offer (and the explanation I give) as to why God can't remove moral evil. Those interested in a further explanation of this general strategy employed by many theologies should consult the appendix to this book, where that strategy is presented.

Still, I suspect that my claim that God cannot remove moral evil seems odd, since God is omnipotent. Granted, God is omnipotent, but my view of divine omnipotence is that God can do whatever is logically consistent and whatever squares with his nature as God. Given this definition, I agree that if God's only goal is to remove evil, he can do so. But if he has other goal(s) he wants to accomplish in our world (and I believe he does), the achievement of those goals may conflict with removing evil. I shall argue that they do. Of course, if God can't both remove moral evil and accomplish his other goal(s) for our world (i.e., it is logically impossible to do both), he isn't obligated to do both.

My general approach here follows a strategy that is basic to other defenses and theodicies against evil. For example, the free will defender agrees that God can remove evil, if that is his only goal. However, the free will defender argues that God can't guarantee that if he gives us incompatibilistic free will, he can also remove evil at the same time. Likewise, for Hick God can remove evil if that is all he wants to do with our world, but if God also wants to build souls, he can't both build souls and remove evil. Since God's omnipotence doesn't allow him to do the logically impossible, he isn't guilty for failing to give us freedom and remove evil or build souls and remove evil. He can't do both conjointly, so he isn't required to do so. No one can justly be held accountable for failing to do what he couldn't do, or for doing what he couldn't fail to do.

My approach adopts this same strategy. God can remove evil if that is all he wants to do in our world. However, he can't remove evil without 1) contradicting other valuable things he has decided to do, 2) casting doubts on or directly contradicting the claims that he has all the attributes predicated of him in Scripture, and/or 3) performing actions which *we* would neither desire nor require him to do, because they would produce a greater evil than we already have in our world. Of course, if I can point to some valuable aspect of our world and show that God couldn't both put it into our world and at the same time remove evil without one or all of 1)-3) happening, then I shall have shown that ours is one of the good worlds God could have created, in spite of the evil in it.

THE DEFENSE

What Is Man?

My defense has several stages. The first poses and answers the following question: What sort of beings did God intend to create when he created human beings? Here I'm not referring to the kind of actions God envisioned us doing or even the character traits he wanted. Instead, I am referring to the basic abilities and capacities God gave us, i.e., a list of the ontological constituents of our being as humans. Without offering an exhaustive analysis of what it means to be human (that is beyond my purpose and need), I can point out several things God intended when he created the race. At a minimum, he intended to create a being with the capacity to reason (that capacity obviously varies from individual to individual), a being with emotions, a will that is free (compatibilistically free, though freedom isn't the emphasis of my defense), a being with desires, intentions (formed on the basis of one's desires), and the capacity for bodily movement. Moreover, he intended for us to use those capacities to live and function in a world that is suited to beings such as we are. Hence, he created our world which is run according to the natural laws we observe, and he evidently didn't intend to annihilate what he had created once he finished his creative work.

In addition, God didn't intend each human being to be identical in respect to these capacities. For example, some might have certain desires to the same degree as other humans, but in no two people would all these qualities of humanness be conjoined so as to obliterate individuality of persons. My claim is more than that no two people are numerically one; it is that the character traits of any two people wouldn't be so similar as to make them stereotypes of one another. Then, God intended to make a being who is finite both metaphysically and morally (as to the moral aspect, our finitude doesn't necessitate doing evil, but only that we don't have the moral perfection of an infinite God). In other words, God intended to create human beings, not superhuman beings or even gods. Finally, though it is true that those who have trusted and followed God will someday be given a glorified body, God's intention is that all of us would go through the first phase of our existence (starting with conception) in natural or non-glorified bodies.

At this point, I must add that none of these features were negated by the fall of the race into sin. Sin had and has negative effects on us and our world, but it didn't result in the removal of desires, intentions, free will, bodily movement, and the like. Because of our fall into sin, I don't believe these capacities function as well as they would have without sin, but that doesn't mean we no longer have them. Likewise, I don't see that the fall overturned the basic laws of nature and physics according to which our world runs. The fundamental features of humanity and of our world are still as God created them.

A natural question is how I know that this is what God intended. After all, I wasn't privy to his thinking when he decided to create, nor can I or anyone else probe his mind now to discover what his intentions were when he created. I respond that we don't need privileged access to God's thought life to discern what he intended. All we have to do is look at the sort of being he created when he created mankind, and observe as well that there is a world in which we live that is suited to our capacities.

Someone might respond that this same line of thinking could be used to say that God also intended for there to be moral evil, because we have it. However, that is not so. Moral evil isn't a substance that God created when he created other things. It isn't a substance at all. God created substances, including the world and the people in it. That God intended that we should be able to act is clear, for he made us capable of acting. But he neither created our actions themselves nor does he perform them. Hence, we can't say that God must have intended for there to be moral evil because we have it in our world. God intended to create and did create agents who can act; he didn't create or do their acts (good or evil). *They* do them.

How do we know, though, that God really intended to create the sort of being specified? Again, look at what he has done, and that will show what he intended. But don't other beings often act without fully knowing what they intend to do? How can we be sure just by looking at the effect (human beings as created) that we really know what God intended when he created us?

While it is true that human beings don't always know what they intend to do, that cannot be the case with an omniscient being's awareness of his intentions. Moreover, there is no reason to wonder if an omnipotent being could or did carry out what he intended to do. Thus, while it is valid to doubt that the way to know what human beings intend is to look at what they have done, that can't be so in regard to an omniscient and omnipotent God. We can see what he did and be sure we know what he actually intended to do.

Whether my claims are right or wrong, how are they relevant to the issue at hand? They are relevant as follows: if God intended to and did create the sort of being I have described, then I believe God cannot eradicate moral evil without contradicting his intentions in producing that being. That is, for God to fulfill both goals (eradicate evil and create human beings as I have described them) would be impossible, for accomplishing one goal would foreclose his achieving the other.[4] This is why I answer the "Can" question negatively. Of course, I must explain how this is so. But before doing that, I turn to the second stage of my defense.

How Does Sin/Moral Evil Arise?

If humans are the sort of creatures I have described, then how do they fall into sin? This brings me to the second stage of my defense, a consideration of the ultimate source of evil actions. My answer isn't free will, though of course I agree that free exercise of our will is instrumental in bringing about moral evil. However, I don't appeal to free will in part because that might appear to invoke the free will defense, but as a compatibilist I dare not do that. Instead, I go "behind" will to desires. In accord with James 1:13-15, I hold that morally evil actions ultimately stem from human desires. This doesn't mean desires in and of themselves are evil or that the desires do the evil. What it means will become apparent shortly. In James 1:13-15 the author describes how in a concrete case temptation arises and leads to moral evil (sin). James 1:13-15 says:

> Let no one say when he is tempted, "I am being tempted by God"; for God cannot be tempted by evil, and He Himself does not tempt any one. But each one is tempted when he is carried away and enticed by his own lust. Then when lust has conceived, it gives birth to sin; and when sin is accomplished, it brings forth death.

The English translation somewhat blurs the meaning of the passage in the Greek. The word translated "lust" is *epithumia,* which has the basic meaning of "desire." Often lust is thought of only in terms of sexual desire, but *epithumia* refers to desires of any kind. According to verse 14, desires are *exelkomenos* (carried away) and *deleazomenos* (enticed). The first word comes from *exelko,* and has the meaning of being moved from one's original position (in this case, a mind-set against doing moral evil). The second word comes from *deleazo,* and has the meaning of alluring. The idea is that the thing desired acts as "bait" or a lure on the one who desires it and draws him to it.

Verse 15 claims that at some point in this process, the attraction becomes so strong that sin (moral evil) is actually committed (conceived).[5] I think many moral philosophers would agree that the point of sin's "conception" is when a person wills to do the act if she could. Once that choice is made, then it remains only for her to translate that choice into overt public action. This interpretation of the point of sin's conception certainly squares with the tenor of Jesus' teachings, when he claimed that sin is committed in a person's thoughts first and made public later. Think, for example, of Matthew 5:27-28, where we find Jesus' teaching that if a man desires a woman in his heart, he has already committed adultery with her even before he does any overt act.

Morally evil acts, then, ultimately begin with our desires. Desires alone are not evil, but when they are drawn away and enticed to the point of bringing us to choose to disobey God's prescribed moral norms, we have sinned. Desires aren't the only culprit, for will, reason, and emotion, for example, enter into the process. But James says that individual acts of sin ultimately stem from desires that go astray.

To sum up, then, as to how an evil action comes to be, an individual has certain basic desires or needs which aren't evil in themselves. He initially doesn't purpose to sate those desires in a way that disobeys ethical norms. However, a desirable object comes before him, and he is attracted to it. He forms the intention to have it, even though acquiring it is prohibited by moral precept. Then, when the allurement becomes strong enough, he wills to acquire or do the thing he desires. At that point sin is committed. Then, bodily movement (whatever it might be) to carry out the decision occurs. Once the act is done, it is public knowledge that the moral law has been broken. As to the willing of the action, I hold that it is done with compatibilistic free will, for there are causally sufficient non-subsequent conditions that decisively incline the will without constraining it to choose. Some of the conditions surrounding the decision may involve God's bringing about the state of affairs in which the decision is made. However, temptation to evil and the actual willing of evil stem not from God but from man.

Carl F. H. Henry complains that appealing to desires as the ultimate source from which moral evil stems overlooks biblical teaching about angelic sin and Satanic and demonic influences in human affairs. He writes:

> According to the Bible, those angels who sinned did so prior to man's creation; Feinberg's appeal to human desire as the ultimate cause of moral evil therefore seems to ignore satanic and demonic influence in human affairs and cannot, moreover, account for racial guilt.[6]

Though this objection is mistaken, it offers an opportunity to clarify my point. Henry's objection seems to suggest that the topic is the origin of sin in the universe, i.e., who was the first to commit a sin at all, and also somewhat who is to blame for sin. Moreover, his comment about racial guilt suggests that he is thinking of the first human sin and the race's connection to it. I agree that sin was introduced into the universe in the angelic realm. I also agree that Satan and demons do some of the evil deeds that occur in our world. And, on the basis of Romans 5:12 I hold that the whole race is credited with the first sin of Adam. Nowhere in any edition of this book have I denied any of those things.

But all of this misses my point. My point isn't about who first committed sin, nor about whether satanic and demonic forces are guilty of any of the evil in our world. My point is about how, in any given instance when any human being (including Adam and Eve before the fall) commits an intentional act of sin, he or she comes to commit that sin. Does the problem stem from will, bodily movement, desire, or what? Hence, Henry and I are talking about two distinct topics.

Henry, however, somewhat seems to catch my point by referring to satanic and demonic influences in human affairs. That comment *is* relevant to the issue of how a person falls into sin. However, I don't see that Henry's suggestion squares with the point of James 1:13-15. I don't deny that Satan and his cohorts do evil and are also involved in the temptation process. But James's claim is that the temptation process in *us* doesn't begin apart from something in us. Satan may encourage us to do what we are tempted to do, but we can resist him. If we don't, it is ultimately not his fault (though he isn't without culpability); it is ours. No one will be able to stand before God on judgment day and successfully plead innocence for sinning because "the devil made them do it." God won't buy that excuse, because he knows the problem stems ultimately from us, and he calls us to resist the temptation.

What Price Utopia?

If humans are the kind of creatures I have described, and if moral evil arises in the way outlined, what would God have to do to get rid of moral evil? If he wanted to do it, would it be desirable for him to do so? In order to see why it would be undesirable for God to turn our world into a utopia, we must see what God would have to do to produce a utopia. If he can't create a utopia without producing further and greater problems, then he isn't obligated to do so. It is at this point that I hope to show that if God did what is necessary to remove moral evil from our world, he would either contradict his intentions to create man and the world as he has, cause us to wonder if he has one or more of the attributes ascribed to him, and/or do something that we wouldn't expect nor desire him to do, because it would produce greater evil than there already is.

Some may think all God needs to do to remove moral evil is merely arrange affairs so that his compatibilistically free creatures are causally determined to have desires only for the good and to choose only good without being constrained at all. With respect to each of us, God should know what it would take, and he should be powerful enough to do it.

However, this isn't as simple as it sounds. If people are naturally inclined to do what God wants, God may need to do very little rearranging of our world to accomplish this goal. If people are stubborn and resist his will, it may take a great deal more rearranging of events and circumstances than we might think. God would have to do this for every one of us every time we decide to resist his will. Moreover, changes in circumstances for one of us would affect circumstances for others, for none of us lives in isolation. But what might be a necessary change to get *us* to do good might be a change that disrupts someone else's life, constrains them to do something that serves God's purposes in regard to us, and perhaps even turns them toward doing evil. The fact is that we really don't know what we are asking when we ask for God to rearrange circumstances. If God leaves our fundamental capacities as they are, it isn't clear what he would have to do to rearrange our world so that circumstances would causally incline all of us to do right on every occasion. That being so, it isn't at all clear that the rearranged world would be better than our world.

Though we might think the rearranging required is minimal, there is reason to think otherwise. God didn't create us with a positive inclination toward sin, but even Adam in ideal surroundings and circumstances did sin. According to biblical teaching, the race inherited from Adam a sin nature which positively disposes us toward evil. In light of that sin nature, it isn't at all clear that a minimal rearranging of events, actions, and circumstances would achieve the goal of getting us to do good without constraining us. It might turn out that God would have to constrain many people to do things he needed to have done in order to rearrange circumstances to convince a few of us to do the right thing without constraining us. Of course, that would contradict compatibilistic free will for many of us, and would likely do so more frequently than we might imagine. And that would contradict God's intention to create creatures who are compatibilistically free and get to exercise that freedom more often than not.

Consider, for example, what it might take for God to bring even one person to the point of freely choosing good. To convince one person to do right would probably require rearrangements in other people's lives, changes that would require that they do things they don't want to do. If God wants those other people to do what he wants unconstrainedly, he may need to rearrange even other people's lives. To get that third group of people to do what he wants unconstrainedly may require yet more people to do something they don't want to do. I could continue, but the picture is clear. To leave everyone's freedom intact may be a lot more difficult than we suppose. It is more likely that the free will of many will be abridged as a result of God's attempts to convince certain people to do good.

In light of how hard it is, because of our sin nature, to convince many of us to do right, the amount of convincing without constraining that God will have to do likely will require much more dramatic change in our world than we can envision. In some cases, given our stubborn sinful nature, it may not be possible to get us to do good without constraining us. As one reflects on all of this, one begins to realize that God may not in fact be able to actualize such a world. Moreover, if he can, it will likely be a much different world than ours, and there is no clear guarantee that this other world will be even as good as our world, let alone better. In addition, one begins to wonder how wise this God is if he must do all of this just to bring it about that his human creatures do good. Why not just make a different creature who would be unable to do evil? But of course that would contradict God's decision to make nonglorified humans, not subhumans or superhumans.

So far, we have imagined that God could get us to do right by rearranging the world. This method, of course, assumes that if God rearranged the world, all of us would draw the right conclusion from our circumstances and do right freely. This is quite dubious, given our finite minds and wills as well as the sin nature within us that inclines us toward evil. Perhaps there is a simpler, more direct way for God to get rid of evil. In what follows I want to consider eight other ways God might get rid of evil. I don't think any of them would work, but we need to consider each individually to see why it wouldn't succeed.

First, God could eliminate moral evil by doing away with mankind. In addition to being a drastic solution that none of us would think acceptable, this would also contradict his intention to create humans who are not then annihilated by his or anyone else's actions.

A second way to remove moral evil is for God to eliminate all objects of desire. If there were no objects of desire, no "bait," it is hard to see how human desires could be led astray to do moral evil. However, to eliminate all objects of desire God would have to destroy the whole world and everything in it, including human bodies (obviously, they are often objects of desire). Minds would remain, unless minds could be objects of desire that might lead someone to do evil. If minds aren't objects of desire, then there would be minds, but no material world. If minds are objects of desire, all of them would have to be destroyed, or at least all except one (assuming that it couldn't sin by desiring itself inappropriately).

Objections to this option are obvious. What this would mean to human life and well-being makes it unacceptable. Moreover, the God I have described would have to reject it, because adopting it would mean he would contradict his intentions to create human beings and put them in our world, a world he didn't intend to destroy once created.

Third, God could remove moral evil by eliminating all human desires, since sin ultimately stems from desires. The problems with this solution again are obvious. Since God intended to create creatures who have desires, if he removes all human desires, that contradicts his intentions about the creature he wanted to create. Moreover, removing desires would also remove the ultimate basis of action so that people wouldn't act. However, that would contradict God's intention to create beings who perform the various actions necessary just to remain alive. In addition, removing all desires would create a greater evil than there already is, for if we had no desires, we wouldn't even desire things necessary to remain alive (desires for food, water, self-preservation would no longer be present, so these needs wouldn't likely be fulfilled). Surely, that would be less desirable than the world is now.

A fourth possibility seems to be one of the more likely things God could do. He could allow us to have desires but never allow those desires to be aroused to the point where they would produce moral evil (perhaps not even to the point where they would result in the forming of intentions to do evil). Since any desire can lead to evil, this would mean that we would retain all our desires, but God would eliminate or neutralize them once they approached or reached a degree of arousal that would result in intending or willing an act of moral evil. If God had chosen this option, he could have accomplished it in one of two ways. He could have created us with all the capacity for our desires to run rampant, but then performed a miracle to stop them whenever they started to do so. Or, God could have created us with the capacity to have desires aroused only to a certain degree, a degree that would never be or lead to evil. I shall address the former option, the miracle situation, shortly, when I discuss more generally the option of God removing evil by performing a miracle. The latter option concerns us now.

As for that option, there are several problems. For one thing, it contradicts the idea that God intended to create people so as not to be stereotypes of one another. Let me explain. I am not saying that people would always desire the same things. Rather, whenever someone's desires were allured toward something forbidden, those desires could be enticed only up to a point that wouldn't be evil or lead to it. What would be true of one person would be true of all. This might appear to leave much room for individuality, but that isn't necessarily so. Any desire can lead to evil, and God knows when a given desire, if pursued, would do so. In every such case, we would have to be preprogrammed to squelch the desire before it went too far. That would seem to make us stereotypes of one another more often than might be suspected.

There is another problem with God making us this way. Imagine what life would be like. The picture that comes to mind is one where our daily routine is constantly interrupted (if not stopped altogether), so that we could pause long enough to formulate new desires, intentions, etc., that wouldn't lead to evil. If this is what our world would be like, I am not sure we would want or expect God to make us this way. Would we really want our lives to be interrupted constantly and our plans to be changing so continuously as would be necessary if God made the world as we are imagining? Whenever a desire would start to run amuck, one would have to stop having the desire (or at least not follow it), change desires and begin a new course of action. The picture that comes to mind is one wherein courses of action are constantly interrupted and new courses are implemented only to be interrupted and new ones implemented and interrupted *ad infinitum*. I suspect that life as we know it would come to a standstill. The world envisioned would be a different world (perhaps radically different), but I don't see that it would be better or even as good as our world. Moreover, it would apparently contradict God's intention to create us so as to function and get along in this world.

Perhaps the greatest objection to this fourth option is that to make us this way God would have to make us superhuman both morally and intellectually. This doesn't necessarily mean we would have to be divine or angelic, but we would have to be much different morally and intellectually than we now are. Let me explain. In order to make us so that our desires would never "get out of hand," God would have to make us capable of squelching them whenever they would lead us to evil (a hard enough thing to do). Moreover, to do this we would also have to *know* when desires would lead to evil, so that we could stop them from being overly enticed. Whatever God would need to do to make us this way, it seems that it would involve making us more than human. Of course, if that is so, then God would have to make us in a way that would contradict his intention to make human beings and not superhuman beings.

Some might reply that God wouldn't have to make us superhuman, but only equal to our capacities in a glorified state. Traditional Christian theology maintains that the people of God in their glorified state will be incapable of sinning. Scripture doesn't clarify whether this will be done by making us mentally and morally superhuman or by some other means, but it does teach that this will be the final state of the righteous. Since God will do this eventually, why not sooner? I shall address this in more detail in a later section, but for now suffice it to say that if God did this it would contradict his intention to create humans in an unglorified state.

Given all these considerations, this fourth option, while having a degree of plausibility, is still problematic in the ways mentioned. Perhaps a fifth option would remove evil in an acceptable manner. Suppose that God allows desires of any sort and allows us to form intentions for actions based on those desires, unless the intentions would lead to evil. God could remove these intentions in either of the ways mentioned for handling evil-producing desires (by miracles or by making us so that we would never develop intentions that would lead to evil). However, removing evil by handling intentions this way would run into the same problems we saw in regard to handling desires. So this fifth option doesn't sound promising.

A sixth possible way to eliminate evil would be to remove any willing of evil. People could still will good things freely (compatibilistically), but whenever they contemplated willing something evil, the willing would be eliminated. God could stop it either by miraculous intervention (to be discussed later) or by making us so that we would never will anything that would be evil. However, removing evil this way faces the same kinds of objections that confront the desire and intention options.

Seventh, God could remove the public expression of moral evil by stopping human bodily movement whenever the agent attempts to do the evil deed. God could do this either by miracle or by making us as needed to stop bodily movement when it would lead to evil. This would probably mean bodily movement would be halted or eliminated quite often. This option, however, is objectionable for the same kinds of reasons raised in regard to the desire, intention, and will options.

If God couldn't eradicate evil in one of these seven ways because of the problems mentioned, couldn't he still eliminate evil by miraculous intervention at any point in the doing of an action (i.e., at desire, intention, willing, or bodily movement) or before the negative results of the action can impact the victim of an evil deed? There seem to be several basic problems with this method of eliminating moral evil. First, if God did this, it would greatly change life as we know it. At any moment, desires, intentions, willing, or bodily movement could be miraculously stopped by divine intervention. In fact, they *would* be stopped, if God knew they would lead to evil. Since people wouldn't always know when their actions would lead to evil,[7] they wouldn't know when to expect God to interfere. But eventually even the least perceptive would, it seems, get the message that they couldn't succeed in doing an evil deed or at least not in having the ill consequences of that act befall their intended victim. A possible result could be that people would be too fearful to do, try, or even think anything, realizing that at any moment their movements or thoughts could be eliminated. Under those circumstances, life as we know it might well come to a virtual standstill, and of course, that would be inconsistent with God's desire to create people who live and function in this world. Moreover, it isn't at all clear that a world in which there is a constant threat of removing our thoughts, willing, or bodily movements would be a better world or even as good a world as the one we have.

Second, it is one thing to speak of God miraculously intervening to eradicate desires, intentions, willing, or bodily movements that lead to evil. It is another to specify exactly what it would mean for God to do this. As for stopping bodily motion intended to do the evil deed, God would probably have to paralyze a person as long as necessary (perhaps indefinitely) to stop him from carrying out the evil deed. Of course, stopping bodily movement this way even momentarily would alter the nature of life altogether. Every few moments, series of people would be paralyzed while trying to do an action. Once they are ready to change their course of action, they would begin to move again while yet other people would be paralyzed. Would this not make a worse world than ours? And, wouldn't such a world contradict God's intention to make creatures who can live and function in this world?

Though it is difficult to comprehend how a world where bodily movements are stopped by miracle is better than our world, it is even more difficult just to imagine what miracle God would have to do to remove a desire, intention, or act of willing that would lead to evil. It hardly makes sense to talk about paralysis of intention, desire, or will. Instead, God would likely have to knock us unconscious or cause us to lose our memory for as long and as often as needed in order to remove our evil-producing thoughts. The picture one gets is of a world of people who fall in and out of consciousness and undergo periodic spells of amnesia. Wouldn't such states of affairs virtually bring life to a standstill and thereby be inconsistent with God's intention to make us so that we can live and function in this world? Moreover, I highly doubt that any of us would expect or want God to intervene miraculously in these ways. The price for removing evil in this way seems certainly more than we should be willing to pay. Miraculous intervention of the sort imagined seems to involve a kind of manipulation that would produce more evil than we already have.

A final objection to eliminating evil miraculously is that it would give us reason to question God's wisdom. If God goes to all the trouble he did to make human beings as he has made them, but then must perform all the miracles mentioned just to counteract them when they express that humanness in ways that would produce evil, then there is reason to wonder if God was wise in making us as he did. Of course, if God had made us differently so that he wouldn't have to eliminate evil by miracles, that would contradict his intention to make the sort of beings he has made.[8] So, either God must perform the miracles mentioned and thereby cause us to question his wisdom, or he must change our nature as human beings, but that would contradict his intention to make non-glorified humans rather than glorified humans, superhumans, or subhumans.

Up to this point, I have been discussing evil that is voluntarily produced. But one senses that even if God implemented a world without such evil, that still wouldn't satisfy critics of theism, because there would still be evil consequences that befall people as a result of others' actions which unintentionally harm these victims. However, if a world where God removes those evil-intentioned acts is problematic in the ways already suggested, there is even more reason for concern about the kind of world we would have if God also took steps to remove involuntary and reflex actions which unintentionally inflict evil on others. If it would disrupt normal life to remove our evil-intentioned acts, it would be even more disruptive to remove our good-intentioned actions and reflex actions that unintentionally produce evil consequences. Regardless of someone's intentions, God would know when an act would bring evil to someone else. In order to rid our world of all evil, God would have to remove those actions as well.[9] If life would likely come to a standstill if we knew evil-intentioned acts would be interrupted, think of how much more paralyzing it would be to know that potentially *any* action at any time could be stopped![10]

The upshot of this discussion about what God would have to do to remove moral evil is that God *can't* remove it without 1) contradicting his desires to make the kind of creature and world he has made, 2) causing us to doubt the accuracy of ascribing to him certain attributes like wisdom, or 3) producing a world we wouldn't want and would consider more evil than our present world. Perhaps someone will suggest that the way to avoid all these problems is for God simply to make a different sort of creature than man. In other words, why not make creatures without desires, intentions, will, and/or bodily movement?

I take it that God could have done this, and if he had, it would likely have removed moral evil. The problem is that it would also remove human beings as we know them. It is hard to know what to call the resultant creature since it could neither move nor think—even "robot" seems too "complimentary." I doubt that anyone who thinks there is any worth in being human and in God creating humans would find it acceptable if God did this.

Someone else might object that God shouldn't have made us the subhumans just imagined, but moral evil could be avoided if he had just made us superhumans, instead. Again, I agree that God could have done this. However, my contention is that humans as we know them are a value of the first order. Scripture refers to humans as created in the image of God (Gen. 1:26-27). When God finished his creative work, he saw that all of it, including man, was very good (Gen. 1:31). Psalm 8:5-8 speaks of God crowning man with glory and honor and giving him dominion over the other parts of his creation. In light of this evaluation by God, who are we to say that human beings as created by God aren't valuable? And remember that as a Modified Rationalist all I need to show is that our world is one of those good possible worlds God could have created. I don't have to show that our world is a better world than other good possible worlds. God's creation of this world with non-glorified human beings in it makes ours a good world.

Can God remove moral evil from our world? I believe he can, if he creates different creatures than human beings. I also believe he can if he creates humans and then removes evil in any of the ways imagined. But if he wants to do more with our world than just make it devoid of evil, then it isn't clear that he can both remove evil and accomplish some other worthy goals at the same time. If that other worthy goal is to create the sort of human creatures I have been discussing, then there are only so many ways at God's disposal to remove evil. In considering those possible ways, we have seen the various problems God would have in maintaining the integrity of those creatures as created if God took any of the options discussed for removing moral evil. Hence, even if humans possess compatibilistic free will, so long as God doesn't constrain our wills, it isn't clear that he can get us to choose only good without creating one or more of the problems mentioned. So, while I agree in principle with J. L. Mackie's compatibilistic notion of free will, if God wants to do more with our world than simply make it a place immune to and from evil, it isn't clear that he can do so. Mackie's claim that God can both give us free will and remove evil is incorrect, though it is incorrect for different reasons than those proposed by the free will defense. In short, there is a price to pay for a utopia, regardless of whether it is populated by incompatibilistically or compatibilistically free human beings.

I conclude, then, that God cannot both produce a utopia and create human beings as we know them. Though sinning isn't inevitable for us as humans, nor are we usually compelled against our wishes to do evil,[11] it is empirically true that we have freely used our capacities to sin. Adam did the same, and according to Scripture, we inherited a sin nature from him. That sin nature positively disposes us toward evil and makes sin harder to resist and righteousness easier to disobey. For God to stop our disobedience would result in the problems already mentioned.

Has God done something wrong in creating human beings? Not at all when we consider the great value man has and the great worth God places upon us. As an empirical fact, moral evil has happened as a concomitant of a world populated with human beings. Still, it is one of those good possible worlds God could have created. God is a good God; our world of nonglorified human beings demonstrates his goodness.

OBJECTIONS

In the years since I first wrote this book, readers have raised some objections. In what follows, I want to address what seem to me the most significant objections.

Isn't This a Form of the Greater Good Defense?

Some have asked if my defense isn't really just a form of the greater good defense. After all, it seems to say that God decided not to create a utopia, because a utopia would have omitted human beings, and God believed that a world with human beings was a greater good than a utopia with some other kind of creature. So, in order to achieve the greater good, he made our world rather than a utopia. If this defense is just another form of the greater good defense, then why not adopt the greater good defense and skip the details of my defense?

At first blush, my defense may appear to be a form of the greater good defense. Likewise, one might think the free will defense is a form of the greater good defense. After all, the free will defender says God gave us free will rather than remove evil, because a world with free creatures is a greater good than a world with no evil but no freedom.

Despite any similarity of these defenses to the greater good defense, my defense and the free will defense are not variants of the greater good defense. As I noted in discussing the greater good defense, it rests on consequentialist ethics. As a consequentialist defense, it claims that evil is *logically necessary* to produce some *subsequent* good. Neither the free will defense nor my defense says that. In both cases, the defenses point to some antecedent good as the cause of evil. Hence, the evil doesn't produce the good as in the greater good case; the good precedes the evil.

In addition, the good isn't logically tied to the evil. As we have seen, it is *possible* that incompatibilistically free creatures would never do wrong, though it is unlikely that they won't. But this just means there is no logical necessity to sin just because one has incompatibilistic free will. Moreover, no one could rightly claim that the existence of moral evil is logically necessary for us to have free will in a parallel manner to the logical necessity of having something to fear in order to develop courage. As to compatibilistically free creatures, it is possible that they will always do right, though, given our sin nature, it is unlikely that God could get all of us always to do good without constraining us. If God really did what he would have to do in cases where we resist his will, he would create the sorts of problems I have outlined. But this again shows that there is no logical necessity to sin just because one is compatibilistically free. In addition, no one could rightly argue that the existence of moral evil is logically necessary in order to have compatibilistically free creatures or to produce causally such freedom.

I conclude, then, that neither the free will defense nor my defense is a form of the greater good defense. This is so because in neither case is the good subsequent to and produced by the evil, nor is there a tie of logical necessity between the good and the evil.

If There Are Angels Who Have Never Sinned, Why Couldn't God Have Made Humans Who Never Sin?

Carl Henry raises this objection. He notes that according to Christian theology "God created a morally accountable angelic host of whom many did not and do not sin, and who in fact are now so confirmed in righteousness that they cannot sin."[12] If God could create angelic beings who wouldn't sin, why can't he create human beings who never sin?

I agree with Henry's analysis of angelic beings. Likewise, I concur that God could have made us so that we wouldn't sin. In fact, I earlier suggested a number of different ways God might do that. However, my contention is that in order for God to make the necessary changes in our nature so that we wouldn't do evil, he would in fact have to make us different than we are (glorified humans, superhumans, or subhumans) or interrupt our attempts at evil with miracles. I have explained the problems with any of those options. Hence, I don't deny in principle that God could have done what Henry requests. I only claim that he couldn't do it and make us the sort of beings he intended to make and did make and make ours the kind of world he wanted.

There is another problem with this objection. Even granting that God could have made us incapable of sinning, asking the theist to justify God for not doing so misses the point of the nature of the problem of evil in general and of Modified Rationalism in particular. The problem of evil is not about showing that God is justified in terms of what he *didn't* do but could have done. Rather, the task is to justify what God *has done*. Hence, even if it is granted that God could have made a better world, the theist's task in relation to the logical problem of evil is to show that God has done nothing wrong in creating *this* world.

Hence, the complaint that God could have and should have made a better world misses the point of what a theist must do to defend his conception of God in the face of the problem of evil. It also misses the point of Modified Rationalism. Modified Rationalism claims that there are good and bad worlds, but no best world. It also holds that God doesn't have to create at all, but if he does, the only obligation he must meet is to create one of the good worlds. So, for Modified Rationalism, the only significant issue is whether our world is one of those good possible worlds, not whether it is better than other good worlds. To force a Modified Rationalist to prove that this world is better than some, most, or even all other possible worlds is to impose upon Modified Rationalism something foreign to its metaphysics. We have seen this error before when dealing with the logical problem of evil; it is the error of attributing to the theist views she doesn't hold and then telling her that she has a problem of inconsistency *internal* to her theology. Once we understand that we have no right to impose upon Modified Rationalists the requirement that they show that God has created a better world than other good possible worlds, we realize that this objection is misguided.

Doesn't This View Make Sin Inescapable?

Henry argues that my defense amounts to saying that "if in fact man's fall into sin follows from the structure of human life as God created it, then Adam's fall was inevitable and Adam was not morally culpable."[13]

Here I must disagree. My point was to explain the process whereby human beings fall into sin (moral evil). That doesn't mean that anyone has to do so. The empirical facts are that people from Adam onward have used their capacities to do evil. However, there is nothing fatalistic about this arrangement, for God could have created a completely different world wherein we wouldn't sin, though that world wouldn't have had the sort of human beings in it that he created in our world. But sin isn't even inevitable in our world, for each person, though causally determined to do what she does, still has the ability and opportunity to choose otherwise than she has. And, when she chooses evil, she does so in accord with her wishes. Compatibilistic freedom is still freedom; it isn't compulsion.

What would God have to do to stop us from committing evil? I have mentioned a variety of things God could do, but then I noted the problems with each option. But none of this means our sins are necessary in the sense that there is no way we can avoid sinning or in the sense that when we are confronted with temptation, yielding or resisting aren't both genuine options.[14]

Wouldn't Superhumans Still Be Humans?

Bruce Reichenbach correctly notes that my defense places great emphasis on God creating human beings, not subhuman or superhuman beings. My claim is that for this sort of being to avoid evil desires, intentions, etc., that would lead him astray, he would need capabilities beyond what human beings have. Reichenbach argues that if the requirement is for human beings, then it is hard to see why humans with superhuman powers wouldn't still be human beings. Hence, God could have made humans and could still have given them the requisite ability to guarantee that they would resist evil successfully. Reichenbach writes:

> But why would creating humans as superhuman (or better, with superhuman powers) make them not to be human beings? Is there something unhuman about giving humans more persistence in resisting evil, more knowledge about what is evil and how to overcome it, and more desire to obey God? Indeed, though Feinberg does not deal with this, according to the orthodox perspective (which he advocates) in Heaven human beings do not sin. Indeed, Augustine argued that in that state humans cannot sin. But if they have the moral power, knowledge, or whatever to be able not to sin in Heaven and yet remain human, why should it be thought that there is a contradiction in instituting that sinless condition in the first place, on earth?[15]

This objection actually contains two separate objections. One is about why God didn't institute the heavenly state now rather than later. I shall cover that below as the final objection. The other is that humans with superhuman powers are still human.

My response is that this is both true and false. It is true that Reichenbach's envisioned humans have many qualities in common with non-glorified human beings as we know them. But they would also have qualities that go beyond humans as God created them. Using terminology from chapter 3, we would have to say that they are counterparts to human beings. But as we saw in that chapter, counterparts aren't the same as the "original" even if they have much in common with the "original." Would Reichenbach's imagined creatures still qualify as human beings? Perhaps so, but perhaps not, depending on how one defines what it means to be human. It isn't my intent to enter a debate about which qualities are necessary for a creature to qualify as a human being. Still, my point is that God intended to create non-glorified human beings as we know them. Superhumans or humans with superhuman powers may qualify as counterparts to non-glorified humans, but God intended to create the latter not the former, so God can't do what Reichenbach asks without contradicting his intentions about the sort of being he wanted to create.

Reichenbach's point about our abilities in heaven also misses my point. I agree that in heaven people won't be able to sin. But, and this is the crucial point that Reichenbach doesn't mention, that is because they will be in their glorified state. Scripture doesn't tell us a lot about life in a glorified body, but it tells us enough so that we can tell that while there will be a certain continuity with who we are in our non-glorified state, there will also be significant differences.[16] And, it seems that those differences may well require much more overhaul of our nature than we might think. The fact is, we don't know exactly how much God will have to change our natures to guarantee that we won't sin. It may involve way more than any of us suspect. But, again, speculating about how much will have to change is somewhat beside my point. My point is that God evidently intended to create non-glorified people to populate this world. God could have created us in a glorified state, but that would have contradicted his intentions to make us as he has.

Reichenbach may still object that slightly different humans would have been better. If so, he is welcome to reject my defense and my theology, but the complaint in no way suggests any internal inconsistency in what I have proposed. His objections simply reject my system's fundamental commitments.

Human Beings Are Instrumentally Valuable, Not Intrinsically Valuable

Reichenbach might agree that my theology and defense are internally consistent, and still complain that God's choice to create humans (as I describe them) isn't worth the evil that results, because human beings as we know them aren't such a great value. In fact, Reichenbach does raise this sort of argument, though the way he makes the objection is noteworthy.

According to Reichenbach, Calvinist theologians claim that God works out things with the ultimate intention of bringing glory to himself. But if that is God's ultimate goal, then the creation of superhumans might suffice just as well as the creation of humans. After all, human beings aren't intrinsically valuable, but only instrumentally valuable in an overall divine program to bring God glory. Of course, if that is so, then, it really should have made little difference to God whether he created superhumans or humans. He could fulfill his intention to bring himself glory either way, and if he had decided on superhumans, it would have saved *us* a whole lot of trouble. Reichenbach writes:

> That is, let us agree with Feinberg that this scenario of more persistent and knowledgeable beings conflicts with God's intent to make human persons. The atheologian could rightly wonder why this particular divine purpose should be part of the picture used to determine the contradiction relevant to omnipotence. If, as Calvinist theologians maintain, God's chief end is to bring himself glory, and his ultimate end in creating is to communicate his good to his creation, could not God achieve these ends by creating super-human beings? *It is not that humans are intrinsically valuable. Rather, they are instrumentally valuable in the glory they render God and in being the object of the divine grace* [italics mine]. Could not God achieve these ends through free, sinless, superhuman beings? Where something which brings about a greater good conflicts with a present intention, if that intention is not necessary or is not directed to the chief or an ultimate good, the intention can be altered.[17]

Several responses are in order. I begin with the comments I have italicized. It isn't entirely clear whether this is Reichenbach's opinion, or whether he thinks this is the Calvinist's opinion. In either case, it is problematic. If Reichenbach thinks this is the Calvinist's opinion, he is wrong. Calvinists do believe that the chief end of man is to bring God glory. But that doesn't mean they think humans as humans have no intrinsic worth. Reichenbach offers no example of any Calvinist who says this about human beings. Calvinists think that the chief end not only of man but of all of creation is to bring God glory, but none of them think this means our universe is only instrumentally valuable with no intrinsic worth to it. Even if Reichenbach were to produce an example of a Calvinist who holds this view, I surely don't, and after all, it is my system that is under discussion. The internal problem, if there is one, must be demonstrated in my system, not some other system.

Perhaps, however, the italicized sentences represent Reichenbach's opinion. One becomes suspicious about this when Reichenbach later says, "The point here is that Feinberg attempts to set up the contradiction *vis-a-vis* God's intentions to create human persons. But this isn't the place to establish the contradiction; rather it has to be generated *vis-a-vis* God's nature or some intrinsic good or chief end."[18] I take it that the comment about "some intrinsic good" refers to something other than humans as created. Hence, this seems to suggest that Reichenbach doesn't think humans as created are an intrinsic good. Whether or not this is his view, I strongly disagree with it. Earlier in the chapter I appealed to Scriptures which teach the dignity and worth of human beings. Humans as created are made in the image of God. That being so, I fail to see why they aren't inherently valuable. If Reichenbach thinks otherwise, he is entitled to think so, but his thinking so just shows that we disagree. It explains in part why he wouldn't accept my theology. It shows no inability on the part of my system to solve its logical problem of evil.

The objection is also problematic because it seems to suggest either that God has only one intention in what he does (namely, bring himself glory), or at least that this ultimate intention is the only one that really matters. Hence, so long as God achieves that goal, the means really don't make much difference. Here I must object again. It is true that Calvinists hold that God's chief end is to bring himself glory. But that doesn't mean God has no other intentions along the way about the means to an ultimate end, or that the means are unimportant to him so that his intentions about them can be altered at will. The steps along the way do matter to God. My contention is that while God intended to bring himself glory through his created order, he also had very specific intentions about the creatures he would create to accomplish that goal. He also wants things to happen in our world that are for our benefit, not just for his. Thus, in creating humans, God can and did intend to accomplish something of value in itself as well as something that is instrumentally valuable in giving him glory. Even as we can have and fulfill more than one intention with a given act, so can God. Moreover, he desires that we should come to trust him and spend eternal life with him, not just for his glory but also for our sake.

Despite the preceding, there is a precaution implicit in Reichenbach's objection that is worth noting. It is a message to Calvinists who would adopt an answer to the problem of evil by appealing to God's desire to bring himself glory. I note that a defense against the problem of evil which attempts to justify God by claiming that God uses it to bring himself glory rests on a consequentialist ethic. For Calvinists who are nonconsequentialists this should rule out this defense as the way to solve their problem of evil. Hence, while I do believe that God somehow is able to bring himself glory even through a world with evil, as a nonconsequentialist I can't affirm that this truth is what makes our world one of those good possible worlds God could have created. That is, I can't appeal to God's ultimate glory as that which justifies him as benevolent and all-powerful.

Suppose that one is both a Calvinist and a consequentialist. In that case adopting the glory of God defense won't generate a contradiction in one's theology. But, in order to show how this world brings him glory through both the good and evil in it, such a Calvinist will have quite a challenge. The challenge isn't that unless he can explain how evil brings God glory, the Calvinist's theology is self-contradictory. Rather, the challenge is to so explain the relation of God's glory to evil's existence that this sort of Calvinistic theology becomes at all believable. In chapter 3, we noted that a God who seemed only to care about calculating the metaphysically richest world without any apparent concern about what living in such a world would be like for his human creatures is morally repugnant. I fear that many would react the same way to a theology that says evil in our world is justified, because God uses it to bring himself glory!

Since God Will Create a Better World Eventually, Why Not Sooner?

Another objection lurks in the background of Reichenbach's concerns. However, he isn't the only person to raise it. It is, I think, a significant objection.

The objection is as follows: theists, including myself, often say our world is a good world because of some feature in it. However, those same theists believe in a future state (call it the Kingdom of God or the Eternal State) where there will be no evil. It is part and parcel of Christian belief that God will someday bring this to pass, and it is agreed that, morally speaking, this will be a better world than our present world. Since God not only can create this better world but in fact will do so some day, why didn't he do it in the first place? Why not simply forego this current world altogether and create that other world from the beginning?

Several responses are in order. First, this objection confronts not only my theology but many other theologies, including Reichenbach's free will theology and Hick's soul-building theodicy. As to the free will defense, many of its proponents (especially those whose theology is some form of Arminianism) agree that there is a future world where people will only do good. Free will defenders aren't always clear about whether inhabitants of that world will have incompatibilistic free will. Nonetheless, they agree that God will eventually bring that world to pass and that God could have created it instead of ours. As for Hick, he believes that someday everyone will make it to the Kingdom of God. He doesn't tell us whether there will be sin there, but one suspects that there won't be. At any rate, Hick not only believes this ideal state is possible; he believes that some day it will be actual.

It should be clear, then, that this objection confronts not only my theology but others as well. My second comment is that the objection in no way demonstrates an internal inconsistency in my theology, the free will defender's theology, or the soul-building theodicist's theology. A critic of theism might reject all of these theologies on this ground, but it wouldn't be an objection on grounds of inability to solve a logical problem of evil, a problem of internal inconsistency.

Specifically, how should one answer this objection? I reply initially that the objection contains a confusion. The confusion centers around what is required of a Modified Rationalist theology to solve its logical problem of evil. Modified Rationalists don't claim that there is a best world, but they do claim that there is more than one good possible world. Moreover, Modified Rationalism doesn't demand that God create the best world or even a better world than some good world. It only requires God to create a good possible world.

Hence, it isn't up to me (or the free will defender or the soul-building theodicist) to show that our world is the best or even better than some other good world God might have created. It is only my task to show that ours is one of those good worlds God could have created. I have done that by pointing to human beings. Free will defenders show that by pointing to incompatibilistic free will. Soul-building theodicists do it by noting that souls are built in our world. It isn't our task to justify God by showing that our world is better than some other world God might have created. The task is to look at the world God *did* create and explain why it is a good world in spite of the evil in it. We have done so, and hence, we have solved our theologies' logical problems of evil.

Still, some will ask why God didn't begin with the world he eventually will create. I respond that the most any of us can say (free will defender, soul-building theodicist, and myself) is that it pleased God to create our world prior to and perhaps even as preparatory to that next world. Beyond that, God simply hasn't told us why. *But, we don't have to explain that ultimate reason in order to solve our logical problem of evil.* The urge behind wanting that ultimate answer is that then we will know for sure that God had a morally sufficient reason for creating our world rather than another. But again, this is wrongheaded. The Modified Rationalist must explain what it is about our world that makes it a good world, but having done that, the Modified Rationalist has offered God's morally sufficient reason for creating this world. To complain that this isn't a good enough explanation because there are better worlds is to attempt to impose upon Modified Rationalism a metaphysic and an ethic it doesn't espouse. Since the logical problem of evil is about what the theologian *does espouse,* demanding that the Modified Rationalist explain why this world is better than other good worlds is to impose upon it beliefs that are external to it. If one stays within the ground rules for handling the logical problem, then the free will defense, the soul-building theodicy, and my defense solve the logical problem of moral evil for their respective theologies. All three explain what makes our world a good world, and that's all they need to show!

Finally, it seems that implicit in this objection is the idea that everyone can see that some other world (the eternal state or whatever) would be better than ours. Therefore, God should have created it. But, better for what purpose? Presumably, God had many things he wanted to accomplish when he decided to create a world. There is no way for us to know that any other world would have accomplished those goals better than our world. Moreover, even if we think God's only purpose is to bring himself glory, we don't know that dispensing with our world in favor of creating the eternal state from the outset would bring God more glory than he receives from this world plus the next.

Perhaps someone will reply that the point isn't better for what purpose, but just that this other world would be better morally, regardless of its purpose. I agree that it would be better morally, because there will be no moral evil in it. However, by now it should be clear that God can't make that world and also make non-glorified human beings as he has made them. Likewise, free will defenders will probably say God can't make the eternal state and incompatibilistically free human beings at the same time. And the soul-building theodicist will say God can't make that world and also build the souls of free creatures, for in the eternal state all souls will already be built. Was God wrong to have other goals than just creating a sinless eternal state? Only if those goals are evil themselves, and they aren't. So, my response is that the eternal state would be better morally, but God can't create it and also accomplish the goals he has achieved by creating our world. And, according to Modified Rationalism, God is free either to create or not create at all. If he creates, he is free to create any good possible world available, but isn't obligated to forego our world in favor of the eternal state, as long as our world is a good world. Free will defenders, soul-building theodicists, and I have all shown why ours is a good world.

CONCLUSION

I conclude, then, that God must not, cannot, and should not eliminate moral evil for the reasons mentioned. Hence, the moral evil in our world is justified. It is a concomitant of a world populated with non-glorified human beings. Our world is one of the good possible worlds God could have created.[19] That means my theology can solve its logical problem of moral evil.[20] Again we see the error of Mackie's claim that no theist can solve the problem of evil.

As with other theological systems, there is, of course, an intellectual price tag that comes with mine. Some will reject my nonconsequentialism or its commitment to compatibilism. Likewise, one must agree that human beings as God made them are of enough value to make it worth it to have a world populated with them, even though being human and being individual means the possibility of evil as well as the actualization of it. Finally, this theology assumes that we can know what God intended to create when he created us and that, once having made us human, he shouldn't do things that make it impossible for us to function in accord with those human capacities. These are some of the major commitments that come with this theology. Any who accept these commitments can solve the logical problem of moral evil for this theology.

7

GOD AND NATURAL EVIL

In chapter 6, I presented my answer to the logical problem of evil that confronts my theology. That defense handled moral evil, but didn't address natural evil per se. As I examined various defenses in earlier chapters, I noted that some critics reject them because they don't address natural evil. Though this doesn't make the defenses inadequate as answers to the problem of moral evil, there is still a need to address natural evil. That is the topic of this chapter.

One of the reasons theists must address physical evil is that invariably it is this evil that atheists complain about most and theists find most difficult to justify. As we shall see in subsequent chapters on the evidential problem, natural evil has become the focus of much of the most recent literature on the problem of evil. I also want to discuss natural evil, because I can show that natural evil generates more than just one problem for theistic systems. This is so because natural evils don't present a homogeneous group. Some natural evils can be handled by a defense typically used to address moral evil, but others cannot be.

For all of these reasons, before turning from the logical problem to the evidential problem, I must address natural evil. In this chapter, I shall argue that some natural evils present a problem which actually reduces to the problem of moral evil, some don't and hence require a different solution, and specific instances of natural evil raise the religious problem of evil. I begin by reviewing the kinds of things that are classed as physical evil.

VARIETIES OF NATURAL EVILS

Many, if not most, natural evils are what people like Mackie and H. J. McCloskey call first order evils. John Stuart Mill vividly describes some of these evils as follows:

In sober truth, nearly all the things which men are hanged or imprisoned for doing to one another are nature's every-day performances. Killing, the most criminal act recognized by human laws, nature does to every being that lives, and in a large proportion of cases after protracted tortures such as only the greatest monsters whom we read of ever purposely inflicted on their living fellow creatures. If by an arbitrary reservation we refuse to account anything murder but what abridges a certain term supposed to be allotted to human life, nature also does this to all but a small percentage of lives, and does it in all the modes, violent or insidious, in which the worst human beings take the lives of one another. Nature impales men, breaks them as if on the wheel, casts them to be devoured by wild beasts, burns them to death, crushes them with stones like the first Christian martyr, starves them with hunger, freezes them with cold, poisons them by the quick or slow venom of her exhalations, and has hundreds of other hideous deaths in reserve such as the ingenious cruelty of a Nabis or a Domitian never surpassed. . . . Even when she does not intend to kill, she inflicts the same tortures in apparent wantonness. In the clumsy provision which she has made for that perpetual renewal of animal life, rendered necessary by the prompt termination she puts to it in every individual instance, no human being ever comes into the world but another human being is literally stretched on the rack for hours or days, not infrequently issuing in death. Next to taking life . . . is taking the means by which we live; and nature does this, too, on the largest scale and with the most callous indifference. A single hurricane destroys the hopes of a season; a flight of locusts, or an inundation, desolates a district; a trifling chemical change in an edible root starves a million of people. . . . Everything, in short, which the worst men commit either against life or property is perpetrated on a larger scale by natural agents.[1]

The list also includes earthquakes, pains, droughts, floods, physical deformities such as misshapen limbs, blindness, mental retardation or deficiency, insanity, fires, and diseases of seemingly limitless variety.

Reflection should convince one that this is a very diverse list of items that fall under the label of physical or natural evil. I believe they can be divided into four basic categories. The first contains evils that are attributable to human agency. It includes many of the pains we have. Moreover, fires are often caused by human agency, and sometimes misshapen limbs, blindness, and/or mental deficiency result from something one person does to another. Of course, sometimes these problems result from genetic malfunctions over which no one has control, but in other instances "birth defects" result from something evil done by the parents during pregnancy (e.g., an expectant mother's use of drugs or alcohol can negatively affect the developing fetus).

As for insanity, some say it is hereditary, and others say it is environmental. Without resolving that debate, we can say there are cases of insanity whose cause at least in part stems from things done by other people that contribute to that insanity. Think, for example, of cases where someone is severely mentally and physically abused as a child. As a defense mechanism, the child develops multiple personalities to cope with the abuse. Even when the child becomes an adult, the multiple personality disorder can continue.

There are also diseases that fall into this category. I am not thinking of cases where germs are passed by coincidental contact where there is no intention to spread disease. Rather, I am thinking of instances where someone deliberately infects another person in order to harm her.

A second category of natural evils includes all the disorders caused by some genetic malfunction. Nothing the expectant parents do prior to or during pregnancy causes the problem. Genetic processes just malfunction somehow. These disorders may result from a harmful genetic mutation that is passed down through generations, or reproduction in a specific case may somehow produce a defective gene. Whatever the exact nature of the problem or its exact cause, it doesn't happen as a result of intentional wrongdoing on anyone's part. Some of the physical deformities that can occur in this way are misshapen or malformed parts of the body, blindness, deafness, mental retardation or deficiency, and various genetically controlled diseases.

A third category includes all those natural disasters produced by some process within nature but outside of human beings (genetics is a natural process, but within us). These are events over which we have no control. In this category are items like fires caused by a bolt of lightning, earthquakes, floods, droughts, plagues or pestilences, and crop failures and famine that result from floods, droughts, or pestilences.

The final category of natural evil includes diseases. For some diseases, we don't yet know the cause. However, in many cases, we know that bacteria or viruses of some sort are the cause. These diseases may be transmitted intentionally or unintentionally, but that isn't the focus of this category. Instead, the emphasis is just that there are such diseases which result from bacteria or virus.

Upon minimal reflection, one sees that there is a significant difference between the first category and the latter three. The first category of natural evils contains evils that result from specific acts of moral evil (sin), whereas the evils in the other three categories aren't direct results of any specific act of moral evil that one person does to produce them. In what follows, I shall refer to these latter evils as *unattached natural evils*.

These two broad categories of natural evil represent two different problems of natural evil. Both problems are about the existence of natural evils in general. In addition, one can also address individual instances of natural evil that befall particular people.

With these distinctions in mind, I can make some preliminary comments about how to handle natural evil. If the question is why some specific natural evil happens to someone at a given time and place, that problem reduces to the religious problem of evil. This is so because the problem of natural evil is a problem about physical evils in general, not about specific instances. When the discussion shifts to specific instances of either moral or natural evil, it shifts to the religious problem. I shall address that problem at the end of the book.

As to natural evil in general, there is one problem about natural evils that result directly from specific acts of moral evil; that problem reduces to the problem of moral evil. Since many natural evils in our world fall within this category, a defense against the problem of moral evil covers a large portion of natural evil in our world. In chapter 6, I presented my answer to the problem of moral evil, and it also covers this category of natural evil.

The second broad group of natural evils, unattached natural evils, poses a distinct problem of natural evil. In the first edition of this book, I argued that all natural evils of any sort can be handled either under the problem of moral evil or the religious problem. In intervening years, I have come to see that my perceptions were wrong. It is true that many natural evils result from moral evil and can be handled by a defense against the problem of moral evil. It is also true that any specific instance of natural evil, regardless of its cause, may generate a religious crisis for the sufferer. However, none of that defends God against natural evils in general which don't reduce to moral evils. Since these evils don't have desires, intentions, will, etc., I can't invoke my defense against moral evil to handle them. A separate defense is needed to cover those natural evils, and that is my focus in the next section.

A Defense Against Unattached Natural Evil

In subsequent chapters when I discuss the evidential problem of evil, I shall present some other defenses against natural evil. However, at this point, I want to present my own handling of unattached natural evil. Since I am considering this problem in its logical form, all that is needed is a possible way to fit my system's God with these evils so as to remove any apparent contradiction. My defense against these evils relies on some familiar Christian doctrines, but it also borrows and adapts some ideas from Bruce Reichenbach's handling of natural evil.[2]

There are really three aspects to my handling of these evils. I begin with an appeal to the Christian doctrine of the fall and its results. In chapter 6, I noted some of the effects of the fall upon the human race. I claimed that as a result of the fall, all of us inherit a positive disposition toward sin. Though that sin nature doesn't make sin inevitable, it makes it more difficult for us to resist evil than before the fall.

In addition to this result from the fall, the Bible teaches that there were other consequences. Two are of particular relevance to my handling of natural evil. God told Adam and Eve that if they disobeyed him, they would die (Gen. 2:16-17). When they disobeyed, God confirmed that they would die (Gen. 3:19). According to this passage, then, people ultimately die because the race fell into sin. The apostle Paul confirms this in Romans 5:12.

The Genesis account also says that because of the fall there are negative consequences for the natural order. Mankind must work harder to grow crops, for thorns and thistles infest the land (Gen. 3:17-19). Though the Genesis account focuses specifically on negative consequences for agricultural endeavors, other Scriptures teach that the natural order more generally has gone awry because of sin. The apostle Paul says (Rom. 8:18-22) that the whole creation was subjected to futility and awaits the time when it will be set free from its slavery to corruption. While it waits, the whole creation groans and suffers in anticipation of a new order God will eventually institute that will overcome sin and all its effects. When Paul speaks of the created order being subjected to futility, it is hard to think he refers to anything other than the effects of the fall.

Why do I appeal to the race's fall into sin? Because in a fallen world people die as God said they would, and if they are going to die, they must die of something. One of the causes of death is disease. Some of those diseases may be contracted early in life and others may arise only later. Some diseases may kill slowly while others kill quickly. Some diseases are genetically based, while others result from germs in our world. People may also die in fires, floods, earthquakes, or famines. Had sin not entered the world, I take it that biblical teaching implies that natural processes wouldn't function in ways that contribute to or cause death.[3]

What this means is that the ultimate reason for these unattached natural evils is that we live in a fallen world. This must not be misunderstood. It doesn't mean there is some particular sin committed by each person after birth that is later punished by some particular evil that befalls him. God may on occasion mete out that kind of direct judgment against a specific sin, but that isn't my point. My point is that because we all have disobeyed God in Adam as well as during our time on earth, things like disease and death can and do occur. Even people whose basic pattern of life is to follow God may suffer from these evils (think of Job). None of us is sinlessly perfect.

The Christian doctrine of the fall and its consequences on mankind and our world means that all of us are ultimately responsible through our sin for these sorts of evils. God isn't guilty, for he doesn't do the evil. Moreover, he gave us the capacities I mentioned in chapter 6, capacities we could use for good or evil, and he warned us of what would happen if we used them for evil. To have stopped us from doing evil would have created the problems mentioned in my defense against the problem of moral evil. Surely, God has a right to establish moral governance over this universe and to mete out punishment when we break his laws. In fact, in light of the rules and the punishment God promised for breaking those rules, it is only a matter of his grace that we don't suffer more of these natural evils and die sooner.

Does this explanation justify God in allowing these evils to befall us? I believe it does. When these evils occur, it is because we live in a sinful, fallen world. When God forestalls these evils from happening, it is an expression of his grace. But God owes no one grace, only justice. Hence, I can't see any reason why God is obligated to remove these natural evils in order to show that he is good. His grace keeps more evil from happening than does, and that demonstrates his goodness since his grace isn't owed. When he doesn't extend grace but allows justice to take its course, he doesn't fail on any obligation necessary to show that he is good.

Is our world a good world, despite these evils in it? Yes, it is. It is because it contains human beings. As a result of using our good, God-given capacities to do evil, ours is a fallen world wherein these sorts of evils occur, but as already argued, the only other options are subhuman or superhuman beings. Both of those options are problematic in the ways spelled out.

In offering this explanation of unattached natural evils, I realize I appeal to doctrines that have little credence in contemporary society. It isn't my purpose to build a case for them, though I think one could be made in a broader apologetic for evangelical Christianity. However, in order to solve the logical form of the problem of unattached natural evils, all that is needed is an explanation that is possible and that would remove the apparent inconsistency between God and these evils. What I have presented already accomplishes those goals.

Though I believe the preceding is enough to handle the problem of unattached natural evils, I have more to say. This brings me to the second aspect of my defense against unattached natural evils. In my defense against moral evil, I noted that God not only created a certain sort of being when he created humans, but he also created a world in which they could live and function adequately. That world is run by various natural processes that fit the creatures God placed in it. Sometimes those processes produce unattached natural evils, so perhaps a way to get rid of these evils is for God to change natural processes.

Though this option may sound promising, there are serious objections to it. For one thing, there is no guarantee that new processes would be incapable of going awry and producing natural evils that are just as bad as or worse than those we already have. A second problem is that it is foolish to jettison processes that work well most of the time for the sake of the relatively few times they malfunction and result in evil, especially when we have no idea of what we might get in their place. In no way do I mean to minimize the severity of evil when things go wrong. My only point is that most of the time natural processes don't malfunction, but serve our needs quite well. Why, then, get rid of them?

To illustrate my point, let me briefly consider the three kinds of natural ills that fall under the broad rubric of unattached natural evils. One group contains problems that are attributable to genetic malfunction. God could get rid of these evils by removing genetic processes, but how can we seriously request that? To do so is to request a very different sort of creature than human beings as we know them, and of course, that would contradict God's desire to create non-glorified human beings. But beyond that, genetic mutations and combinations that result in physical deformities and diseases aren't the norm. That is, these evils don't occur every time or even most of the time when there is reproduction, so why should God remove processes that work wonderfully well the majority of the time even in a fallen world? Moreover, in light of what I have said about living in a fallen world, the fact that genetic mechanisms produce no evil most of the time may well be a sign of God's gracious intervention to ensure that they don't malfunction! Why, then, should God change these processes?

Consider as well the next group of unattached natural evils. These are evils that are attributable to processes in the natural order outside of human beings. The earth and its atmosphere are made in such a way that any of the natural evils in this category can occur. For example, since there is rain in our world, there can be too much rain (floods result and crop failures can stem from those floods) or too little rain (drought results, and from drought there may come crop failures which cause famine). Since the earth's crust can move, it can move enough to cause an earthquake of any magnitude. God can get rid of these problems by ridding our world of these natural processes, but why would we want that? We do need rain, sunshine, and the like to survive in our world. Most of the time when there is rain, wind, sunshine, etc., it isn't harmful. Moreover, not even every earthquake or flood is harmful to us or to other life forms. So why should we expect God to remove these processes altogether? We need them to sustain life as we know it, and there is no guarantee that life as we know it could survive with different natural processes.

The final group of unattached natural evils consists of difficulties attributable to disease or at least to the forces (bacteria or whatever) that cause disease. Should we expect God to get rid of these? Not necessarily. Bacteria are the cause of much disease, but they don't always lead to it. In fact, in our world various bacteria perform helpful functions like breaking down ingested food so that it can be digested. Moreover, bacteria don't always result in disease (some people are more disease resistant than others). For us to expect God to remove these micro-organisms, then, seems somewhat unreasonable, especially since we don't know how the positive functions they serve would be accomplished in a different world. Moreover, in light of what I have said about the relation of sin to disease and death, God is certainly not obligated to remove this category of natural evils. And, the fact that we don't have more disease more frequently can also be interpreted as a sign of God's grace in preserving us from that harm.

What I am saying about God removing unattached natural evils by changing natural processes is a point Reichenbach makes very well. As he explains, in order to avoid these natural evils, the world would have to run according to different natural laws. But if that happened, it would really require that there be different sorts of creatures than the ones God created when he created us. Reichenbach explains:

> The introduction of different natural laws affecting human beings in order to prevent the frequent instances of natural evil would entail the alteration of human beings themselves. Human beings are sentient creatures of nature. As physiological beings they interact with Nature; they cause natural events and in turn are affected by natural events. Hence, insofar as humans are natural, sentient beings, constructed of the same substance as Nature and interacting with it, they will be affected in any natural system by lawful natural events. These events sometimes will be propitious and sometimes not. And insofar as man is essentially a conscious being, he will be aware of those events which are not propitious and which for him constitute evils. Therefore, to prevent natural evils from affecting man, man himself would have to be significantly changed, such that he would be no longer a sentient creature of nature.[4]

I believe Reichenbach is right in saying that to request different natural laws (and processes) would necessitate different sorts of creatures than human beings. In my handling of moral evil, I suggested problems with creating different creatures than human beings.

There is a further reason that requesting different natural processes is unwise. I hinted at it already in my comments that various natural processes don't always produce natural evils. The point is that with many natural processes and natural phenomena, the very thing that is beneficial about them can also be detrimental. However, the beneficial aspects are so essential to life as we know it that we dare not request removal of the process or the phenomena. F. R. Tennant explains the point well when he writes:

> To illustrate what is here meant: if water is to have the various properties in virtue of which it plays its beneficial part in the economy of the physical world and the life of mankind, it cannot at the same time lack its obnoxious capacity to drown us. The specific gravity of water is as much a necessary outcome of its ultimate constitution as its freezing point, or its thirst-quenching and cleansing functions. There cannot be assigned to any substance an arbitrarily selected group of qualities, from which all that ever may prove unfortunate to any sentient organism can be eliminated, especially if . . . the world . . . is to be a calculable cosmos.[5]

In short, to rid the world of the negative results that can accrue from these natural phenomena we must also forego the benefits they bring. Hence, it isn't wise to request their removal, especially when we have no idea of what might replace them.

From the preceding, I conclude that unattached natural evils are also justified in that they stem from natural processes which most of the time don't produce natural evils and which are necessary to life as we know it. In a fallen world, it is possible for these processes to malfunction, and empirically, we know that they occasionally do. Still, to remove these processes from the world would remove life as we know it without any guarantee that what would replace these processes would avoid natural evil. Our world, then, is a good world, because it includes natural processes which make life for human beings possible.

Someone might object that this second aspect of my defense shows why our world with its natural processes is a good world, but that still doesn't explain why God allows the processes to go wrong *on specific occasions.* Indeed, this is true, but I note that if one asks for justification of each specific instance of unattached natural evil, one shifts the discussion from the more general problem of unattached natural evil to the religious problem of evil. The first two aspects of my defense justify God in the face of these evils in general, and that is all that is required in order to solve this general problem. Demanding that I explain each instance of evil shifts the discussion to a different problem of evil. And, no one is required to solve every problem of natural evil in order to solve any such problem, especially the one his solution is designed to address.

I come now to the third aspect of my defense. This phase relies heavily on Bruce Reichenbach's natural law defense. Suppose someone responded to what I have already said as follows: "Yes, I can see that these things happen because we live in a fallen world, and I can see that it makes little sense to ask God to change natural processes. But, still, on those occasions when natural processes malfunction or when people get diseases, why can't God just miraculously intervene so that these natural evils don't happen at all?"

This sounds like a reasonable request as well as a legitimate objection. However, several things mitigate against it. I note initially that in virtue of what I have said about our culpability for having a fallen world, God surely isn't obligated to perform miracles to forestall the negative consequences of our sin. God may graciously do so, but since his doing so is of grace, it isn't obligated. Hence, God's failure to stop these evils by miraculous intervention doesn't show that he is a bad God or that ours is an evil world.

In addition, I return to my point about God's gracious preserving of the universe in general and his guarding of specific individuals from specific natural evils in particular. The critic asks that God miraculously intervene to stop these evils. But isn't it possible that it is God's miraculous intervention that keeps more of these evils from happening than do? Just because we don't see the miracle doesn't mean God isn't working to preserve us. There is no reason that his intervention (miraculous or otherwise) must be observable in order for it to be actual, anyway.

I recognize that this is unprovable, since what I am saying means the world would seem the same in many instances whether or not God intervenes. However, that is beside my point. My point is not to "prove" that God is intervening, but only to say that it is possible that he intervenes more than we suspect. And that just means the critic shouldn't suppose that he has raised a devastating blow to theism when he asks why God hasn't intervened.

This doesn't end the matter, however. Even granting what I have already said in reply to this objection, none of it offers a reason why God might not graciously intervene miraculously in the cases in question. It is here that I appeal to Reichenbach for a possible explanation which, if adopted, seems to resolve the apparent difficulty. Reichenbach argues that God created a world with incompatibilistically free human beings. God also put those creatures in a world run by various natural laws. Since nature runs according to these observed regularities, it is possible for people to have some idea of the consequences of their actions. Without knowledge of the effects of actions and events, it is hard to see how rational free choice is possible. One might set out to accomplish a certain end by doing a given action and yet be frustrated by changing natural processes that make it impossible to do the action (or at least achieve the envisioned result from the action). If so, then even though God gave us free will, it wouldn't amount to much, because we wouldn't know what to choose from one moment to the next. Only in a world run by natural processes governed by natural laws can freedom be meaningfully exercised. Of course, as we have seen, sometimes natural processes go awry and the result is natural evil. But a world governed by natural laws, even though natural evil can occur, is necessary to a world with free beings. And, of course, a world with free beings is a world of great value.[6]

Though Reichenbach offers his defense in terms of incompatibilistically free beings, I see no reason that it can't apply to compatibilistically free humans. After all, in a world where there are decisive factors that incline the will to choose one way or another, it seems all the more necessary for people to have a predictable world of cause and effect if they are to make free decisions about their actions.

Even so, why couldn't God eliminate these instances of unattached natural evils by miraculous intervention? Reichenbach replies that if we are asking for a world run by miraculous intervention, then things will be too unpredictable for us to know enough to make informed free choices.[7] But what about a world run partly by miraculous intervention and partly by natural laws? Clearly, Reichenbach doesn't want to deny that God can perform miracles at all. However, to rid the world of all instances of unattached natural evil by miraculous intervention, we are talking about more miracles than just a few. Reichenbach's response is significant, so I quote him at length:

> But what would such a world be like? Presumably, a world which was only partially operated by miracle would be one in which God would allow events at some times to follow a "regular pattern," and at other times not. That is, sometimes causal conditions x and y would result in effect z, and at other times they would be followed by an effect of a different sort. For example, heavy snowfall in the mountains and collapse of snow walls will cause an avalanche to proceed down the mountain slope according to the law of gravity when no sentient creature is in its path; but should a climber be present, either that which causes the avalanche "regularly" will not have this effect this time, or the avalanche will still occur but will swerve around the climber or halt at his feet. But natural laws such as the law of gravity assert universal and necessary connections between phenomena. Then if events sometimes followed a "regular pattern" and sometimes not, there would be no natural laws regarding that particular event. But then the appeal to a "regular pattern" is specious, for "regular pattern" presupposes that there are normative natural laws which describe or govern the course of events, so that one can distinguish what is regular from what is irregular. Furthermore, if this absence of universal and necessary connections is widespread, as would seem to be required in order to prevent all natural evils, the world would have few if any natural laws: it would, in effect, be governed by miraculous intervention. Thus, though this so-called middle ground would remove the contradiction with respect to the possibility of human action vis-a-vis being free, the consequences of it still would be such as to make rational prediction and rational action impossible, and hence to make moral action impossible.[8]

Reichenbach's natural law defense is meant to address all natural evils, i.e., those that result from moral evil and those that are unattached natural evils. I believe his natural law defense is most convincing against natural evils that result from moral evil, though as I have argued, those natural evils should really be handled by a defense against the problem of moral evil. Still, his defense is also relevant to unattached natural evils, for in order to be able to exercise free will (of any kind or variety) one must understand the relation of cause and effect. In order to do so, one must know how natural processes function and expect them to function in a consistent way. Anything that consistently interrupts that natural order will only serve to confuse things when one tries to determine what to do.

One may not see this as a problem, since we could all quickly enough learn that miracles will occur only to stop unattached natural evils from happening. However, if God intervenes in this way, what is to stop him from intervening to stop *moral evil* that leads to natural evil? Wouldn't atheists complain if he didn't? Some might say God couldn't intervene to stop moral evil in these cases, because it would destroy freedom. But as we saw in chapter 4, Steven Boër has an answer to that. Let people make their free choices, but miraculously intervene to stop the consequences from befalling anyone.

I have already shown in chapter 4 the problems with the Boër proposal, but suppose for the sake of argument that we grant that God could do what Boër proposes. If so, then, God can rid the world both of natural evils that stem from moral evil and all unattached natural evils. But that covers a lot of actions and a lot of events interrupted by miraculous intervention. At that point, I believe Reichenbach's argument that the world would be so topsy-turvy that rational free action would be difficult or impossible becomes a very powerful objection to expecting God to remove natural evils in this way.

I conclude, then, that Reichenbach's natural law defense with my modifications does offer an explanation of why God doesn't remove unattached natural evils by miraculous intervention. There is no logical impossibility about this explanation, and when it is added to my theology as a whole, it renders it internally consistent with respect to the matter of unattached natural evils. Some may complain that since God graciously exempts some from particular natural evils, he should do so for others (either by miracle or otherwise). However, wondering why in specific cases God doesn't perform a miracle or otherwise intervene to overturn unattached natural evil shifts the discussion from unattached natural evil in general to the religious problem of evil, and handling the religious problem differs significantly from dealing with other problems of evil.

Some will undoubtedly reject my defense as a whole because of its commitment to the notion of a fall and natural evil as resultant from that sin. Others will believe God should have created a different world with different creatures and a different natural order. Still others won't think a world with natural laws that safeguard free will is worth the evil that results. I note, however, that none of these objections points out an internal inconsistency in my theology. They are all objections on grounds external to the system. Moreover, many of these objections amount to a complaint that God didn't make a better world than ours. As explained in chapter 6, all a Modified Rationalist must do is explain why ours is a good world. There is no need to prove that ours is a better world than some other good world God could have created. I have done that, and hence I have shown that my system's God is a good God in spite of the unattached natural evils in our world.

CONCLUSION

In sum, when addressing natural evils, one must first divide between those that result from moral evil and those that are unattached to specific sinful acts that produce them. The former evils should be handled by one's answer to the logical problem of moral evil.

As for unattached natural evils, they result from living in a fallen world. God could have avoided our disobedience only by creating subhumans or superhumans, and neither is what he wanted. Moreover, unattached evils result from malfunctioning natural processes, but those processes function without harming anyone most of the time, and they are necessary for the survival of the creatures God created to populate our world. In addition, God wants his human creatures to be able to exercise freedom in order to function in this world. But the exercise of freedom requires a natural order that is predictable. Hence, God forgoes performing a miracle on some occasions in order to maintain that regularity. For all we know, on many occasions he may intervene to keep more of these evils from occurring. Since these evils stem from living in a fallen world, a world for which all of us are ultimately responsible, God isn't obligated to remove any of them by miracle or otherwise. His preservation of us from more maladies is solely a function of his grace.

Complaining that this defense doesn't cover every instance of unattached natural evil fails to see that the problem of unattached natural evils is about those evils in general. Asking for further explanation about why this evil happens to one person and not another changes the discussion to the religious problem of evil. Finally, whether dealing with natural evils that result from moral evil or with unattached natural evils, the defenses offered render my theology internally consistent and thereby solve its problems of natural evil.[9]

Section II
The Evidential Problem of Evil

8

EVIL AS EVIDENCE

The problem of evil may be posed not only in a logical form, but also in an evidential one. Thanks largely to Alvin Plantinga's elaboration and defense of the free will defense, in recent years many critics of theism have conceded that the logical problem is solvable. Even J. L. Mackie in *The Miracle of Theism* (published posthumously) agreed and conceded "that the problem of evil does not, after all, show that the central doctrines of theism are logically inconsistent with one another."[1] For this concession theists should be rightly grateful.

Of course, in solving the logical problem theists have only shown that it is *possible* to imagine a set of conditions under which the existence of an all-powerful, all-loving God is compatible with evil's existence. That alone doesn't show that any of the solutions offered explain God's actual reason for allowing evil,[2] nor that they are even plausible. It only shows that there are many theists who can tell a logically consistent story when they talk about God and evil.

Despite the success of theists in handling the logical problem, atheists aren't ready to retreat, so they attack theism on a different front. They still believe that evil poses an insuperable problem for theism, but now they claim that even though evil's existence doesn't contradict any traditional theistic beliefs, it counts as strong evidence against the likelihood that God exists. If critics are right, then theists aren't irrational in that they believe what is logically incoherent, but they are unreasonable for believing what is highly improbable. Moreover, if theism is as improbable as atheists suggest, atheists are entirely within the bounds of reason in rejecting belief in God. In addition, some have argued that defenses against the logical problem are implausible and that their implausibility becomes especially clear when one tries to use them to handle actual evil in the world. Hence, theistic defenses and theodicies don't likely offer the actual reason that God hasn't removed evil in our world.[3]

In the next few chapters, I want to discuss the evidential problem. In this chapter, I shall explain the nature of this problem. Once that is done, I shall examine the major ways this attack on theism is posed and the main answers to it, including my own responses to the evidential problem. Key participants in this debate are William Rowe, Alvin Plantinga, Richard Swinburne, Bruce Reichenbach, and Michael Peterson, but contributions of others will also be presented.

THE NATURE AND FORMS OF THE PROBLEM

The Nature of the Problem

This version of the problem of evil is most frequently referred to as the inductive, probabilistic, or evidential problem.[4] Each term points to a different aspect of this problem, so these terms are not synonymous. As to induction, there are different kinds of inductive arguments.[5] However, Max Black suggests that induction can be used to signify "all cases of nondemonstrative argument, in which the truth of the premises, while not entailing the truth of the conclusion, purports to be a good reason for belief in it."[6] Since the premises don't logically entail the conclusion, an inductive argument won't be a lock-sure proof. Instead, the evidence offered in the premises confirms the conclusion with a certain degree of probability.

The classical notion of induction understands it as generalization from particular instances. A repeatedly observed phenomenon (e.g., seeing a sunrise each morning of one's life) leads to the generalization that in all like circumstances, the same phenomenon will be observed (i.e., there will be a sunrise each future morning of one's life). Since this kind of argument doesn't guarantee the truth of the conclusion (hence, on some future day it is possible that the sun won't rise), the most it can affirm is the likelihood or probability that the phenomenon in question will happen again.

This kind of inductive argument isn't the only type there is, and it surely isn't the kind in view when discussing the problem of evil. If this type of inductive argument were in view, then the most one could conclude from all the instances of evil one has seen is that one can expect to see more. Of course, *that* inductive generalization per se, regardless of its probability, is hardly an argument against theism.

The kind of inductive argument in view with the inductive problem of evil follows the pattern of arguments used to confirm a theory or hypothesis. The inductive argument from evil questions how well the hypothesis of theism explains the facts of our world, especially the fact of evil. The atheist charges that evil in our world renders theism an improbable explanation of the world as we know it.

As Peterson explains, this sort of reasoning includes a hypothesis (H), factual data (T), and whatever assumptions (A) are brought to the task of theory confirmation.[7] Initially, we can portray the general structure of a confirmative inductive argument as follows:

1. If (H) is true, then, assuming (A) is true, (T) will be true.

2. (T) is the case.

---

3. Therefore, (H) is probably true.[8]

A similar argument can be written to disconfirm the hypothesis by substituting '(T) is not the case' as the second premise. The conclusion is only "probably" true for several reasons. It is only probable, because (T), while true, may be consistent with other hypotheses. Likewise, there may be other evidence not mentioned in the argument which argues against the hypothesis. Moreover, the probability of the conclusion is influenced by whether the assumptions are or are not true. Clearly, this type of inductive argument is highly inferential, and the correctness of the inference may depend on a number of assumptions being correct and on many different kinds and pieces of evidence.[9]

Plantinga offers an illustration that shows why it is difficult to determine what this kind of inductive argument actually proves. Suppose that we want to calculate the probability that Feike, a Frisian, can swim (here, the hypothesis is that Feike can swim). We know two pieces of evidence which are relevant to the situation: (1) 9 out of 10 Frisians can't swim, but (2) Feike is a Frisian lifeguard, and 99 out of 100 Frisian lifeguards can swim. The hypothesis that Feike can swim is improbable on (1) but highly probable on (2). Hence, it is reasonable to believe that he can swim. As Plantinga notes, this shows how crucial it is to have all the relevant evidence before making a probability judgment. It also shows that some evidence can be consistent with one hypothesis while other evidence favors another hypothesis.[10] Plantinga further explains the tenuousness of this kind of induction by noting that we may not *know* (2), but we may *know* (1) and also just happen to *know* that Feike can swim (we have seen him swim at the local health club). Though (1) is evidence against the supposition that Feike can swim, it doesn't amount to much, since we know he can swim. Similarly, Plantinga argues, we might know on the basis of various evidences that God exists (or at least that the probability is very high). In that case, evil in our world may be evidence against God's existence, but that wouldn't amount to much in itself.[11]

Using this inductive argument form, what would the evidential argument from evil look like? Suppose the following: G = the hypothesis that an all-powerful, all-knowing, all-loving God exists; A = the assumption that this God removes every evil insofar as he can; E = there is evil in the world (one might even say large amounts of evil or apparently gratuitous evil). Using these symbols, the evidential argument from evil against God's existence is as follows:

1.   If G is true, then, assuming A, -E will be true.

2.   -E is false (i.e., E is true).

3.   Therefore, G is probably false.

Note that the only kind of evidence included in this argument is appeal to instances of evil (A is a kind of evidence, but it isn't an appeal to facts known to be true; it amounts to saying that *if* God exists, then he would be inclined to remove evil insofar as he could). Moreover, the existence of evil can be evidence not only to assess the likelihood of God's existence. It can also be the basis for inferring any of the following: there exists an evil "God"; there exists a good but impotent God; or there exists an omnipotent, all-loving God with a morally sufficient reason for allowing evil. Furthermore, evil might be used in an inductive argument *instead* in an inference for any of the following: all evil stems from human action, and all humans are radically inclined toward evil; some evil stems from human action, and all humans are radically inclined to evil; all evil stems from human action, and everyone is moderately inclined to evil; all evil stems from human action, and most are moderately inclined to do evil while some are radically inclined to it; etc. All of this suggests a need to tread very carefully when dealing with this kind of argument.

The preceding discussion sets forth the structure of this kind of inductive argument, but there is more to the evidential problem than that. This argument also invokes the notion of probability, but how does one determine the probability that evil disconfirms God's existence? In contemporary discussions of theism's probability in light of evil, philosophers have invoked and applied Bayes' Theorem, a theorem for determining the probability of any hypothesis.[12] Using symbolic notation where A refers to the hypothesis, B refers to the background information (commonly held knowledge that relates to the hypothesis without necessarily being evidence for or against it), C refers to evidence, and P(A/B) means the probability of A on (with respect to) B, note the following notions:

P(A/B)   ==   the *prior probability* that the hypothesis is true, given background information.

P(A/B&C) == the probability that the hypothesis is true, given background information and the evidence.

P(C/A&B) == the probability that there will be instances of the kind of occurrence in question, given the truth of the hypothesis and the background information.[13]

Using this symbolism, Bayes' Theorem for calculating the probability of any theory is:

$$P(A/B\&C) == \frac{P(A/B) \times P(C/A\&B)}{P(C/B)}$$

This says that the probability of a hypothesis, given the background information and available evidence, *equals* the hypothesis's prior probability *times* the probability that there will be evidence of the sort in the world that there is (given the truth of the hypothesis and the background information), *divided* by the probability that there will be the sort of evidence we have, given the background information we know. Each expression in the theorem may be assigned a numerical value, and then probability is determined from the results of working the math problem. Probabilities range between 0 and 1, and any theory with a probability greater than .5 is said to be confirmed in the sense that it is more likely true than not.

Let us now apply this information about probability to the question of the probability of theism, given the facts of evil in our world. The atheist's claim is that the probability that theism is correct, given background information and the existence of evil, is less than the probability that atheism is correct, given those same factors, i.e., P(G/A&E) < P(-G/A&E). If we apply this idea to the inductive argument presented earlier, premise 1 of that argument then states that the likelihood that there will be *no* evil in our world, given God's existence and other background information we know, is greater than .5. We may represent this symbolically as P(-E/G&A) > .5. The whole inductive argument from evil then is:

1.   P(-E/G&A) > .5
2.   But P(-E) = 0 or < .5   (or P[E] = 1 or > .5)
_____

3.   Therefore, P(G/A&E) < .5

As it stands, this looks bad for theism, but it isn't the whole story. Premise

1 assumes a certain probability for one of the items in Bayes' Theorem. However, in order to work Bayes' Theorem one must also know, for example, the prior probability (in this case) of theism. The inductive argument above presupposes that theist and atheist agree on all the probability judgments (including the one made in premise 1) needed to work Bayes' Theorem. If they do agree, the assumption is that they will see theism's improbability (given the fact of evil) and accept premise 1 as true. If they disagree, then they are likely to disagree about the truth of premise 1. The key point for us now is that so far no argument has been offered as to why anyone should agree with the first premise. The inductive argument per se offers no such argument. An independent argument for the truth of premise 1 is needed, but it isn't at all clear that theists and atheists will agree on the numerical value of the probability judgment that premise 1 makes or on the numerical value of the other items involved in Bayes' Theorem. However, unless they can agree on these matters, they will get different results from working Bayes' Theorem, and if that happens, it is highly dubious that they will agree on theism's probability or the accuracy of premise 1.

A further problem with this inductive argument's conclusiveness arises in regard to premise 2. That premise appeals to evidence, but it cites only one kind of evidence. Before making a judgment on the probability of theism and atheism, one must have all the evidence of any kind for both. Using Bayes' Theorem terminology, this other evidence would likely be part of our background information, and as can easily be seen from looking at Bayes' Theorem, it is impossible to calculate the probability of a given hypothesis without incorporating background information. But it may well turn out that something in that background information makes the probability that theism is correct so high that the fact of evil can't make it improbable. One simply doesn't know until all evidence is taken into account. As Plantinga explains:

> So the atheologian must show that G is improbable with respect to the relevant body of total evidence, whatever exactly that is. To do this, he would be obliged to consider all the sorts of reasons natural theologians have invoked *in favor of* theistic belief—the traditional cosmological, teleological and ontological arguments, for example. He would also have to consider more recent versions of the moral argument as developed, for example, by A. E. Taylor, and still more recently by Robert Adams, along with the sorts of broadly inductive arguments developed by F. R. Tennant, C. S. Lewis, E. L. Mascall, Basil Mitchell, and others; and he'd have to show either that these arguments don't really produce any evidence for G at all, or that, if they do, that evidence is outweighed by the evidence *against* G furnished by E. This would be a substantial and difficult project—one no atheologian has undertaken so far.[14]

A final point about the difficulty of constructing a compelling evidential argument from evil is also worthy of note. The attempt to show theism improbable in light of evil's existence isn't likely to succeed since theists and atheists alike now agree that evil's existence is *logically consistent* with God's existence. Since theists have offered reasons God might have for including evil in the world, reasons that remove the alleged *inconsistency* between God's and evil's existence, how likely is it that evil can be compelling evidence that God's existence is improbable? As Plantinga argues:

> We have agreed that G and E are consistent; it *could* be that God could not have actualized a world as good as this one with less evil. On what grounds, then, are we to hold that though G and E are consistent, G is improbable on E? Surely the atheologian needs an argument here. If he simply *asserts* this claim the theist can simply retort that he doesn't think so.[15]

The upshot of all of this is that there is much more to making an evidential case against theism than merely pointing to the existence of evil. Induction and probability aren't the same thing (induction is a method of argument while probability addresses the likelihood that inductive and deductive arguments and their conclusions are correct), and there are rules with respect to both that pertain to the evidential problem of evil. None of this means there isn't a genuine evidential problem for theism on the basis of evil. It only means that there are specific ground rules for handling this problem and that much is involved in producing a successful inductive argument from evil against theism.[16]

Forms of the Evidential Problem

Though atheists might appeal to evil in general as evidence against God's existence, they typically take a different approach. They usually point to either the sheer amount of evil or the apparent gratuitousness of some evil. These two items, the quantity and the apparent gratuitousness of evil, actually generate two distinct evidential problems, though frequently neither theists nor atheists distinguish the two.

Someone who asks about the quantity of evil may assume that evil in general has a purpose, but wonder why that purpose can't be accomplished with less evil. For example, if evil's purpose is to provide an environment for soul-building, the atheist may ask why that goal couldn't be accomplished with less evil. Moreover, some claim there really is too much evil, because some instances have no apparent purpose whatsoever. If the argument about the amount of evil is shaped in this way, then it really is the problem of the gratuitousness of evil. Nonetheless, there is still a distinction between the problems of the quantity of evil and the gratuitousness of evil, for one may claim either that there is too much evil because some is gratuitous or that all evil has a purpose, but God could achieve that goal with less evil.

As to gratuitous evil, the point is that no matter how hard one tries, one can't discover any morally sufficient reason for God to allow certain evils. They seem to serve no purpose whatsoever. In contemporary discussions, more often than not it is this evil that atheists raise as the strongest evidence against traditional theism. If some evil serves no apparent purpose, surely God, if he exists, would remove it. The fact that our world contains such evil seems strong evidence against the existence of an all-loving, all-powerful God.[17]

Finally, in treatments of the evidential problem the emphasis on moral as opposed to natural evil is less significant than it is for the logical problem. The reason at least in part is that most often evidential problems are stated in terms of natural evil. Moral evil can always be attributed to the free agency of God's creatures, so God apparently isn't responsible for it. He can be defended, for example, on the grounds that he doesn't do it, and he allows it in order to make room for freedom. On the other hand, the evil that seems to be just too much or to have no purpose is the natural evil that is unattached to anyone's freedom. It can't be attributed to humans, and it is hard to show that Satan or his cohorts are the culprits. While God doesn't do such evil, critics of theism ask why he allows it. Though I shall consider moral and natural evil (in their quantity and apparent gratuitousness) as evidence against God's existence, clearly the most troublesome form of the evidential problem for theism focuses on apparently gratuitous *natural* evil. Because the logical problem of evil more often emphasizes moral evil and because atheists believe natural evil is the strongest evidence against theism, recent discussions of the problem of evil have typically centered on natural evil.[18]

9

Atheistic Arguments from Evil

In chapter 8, I described the nature of the evidential problem of evil, clarifying the structure of inductive arguments of the sort involved in this discussion. However, no specific example of an argument from evil as evidence against God's existence was offered. In this chapter my focus is specific examples of how atheists have used the facts of evil against theism.

The most extensive and the most thoroughly discussed attack on theism via the evidential problem of evil comes from William Rowe. Most of this chapter focuses on his formulations of the argument. However, I shall include other examples of atheistic arguments from evil to give a feel for the kinds of arguments raised in current discussions. My intent in this chapter is to describe these arguments. In subsequent chapters I shall offer theistic responses to the evidential problem, including my own.

J. L. MACKIE

In *The Miracle of Theism* J. L. Mackie begins by rehearsing the logical form of the problem of evil. He agrees that there is no explicit contradiction between claims that God is omnipotent and all-loving and that evil exists. However, if omnipotence means there are no limits to what an omnipotent being can do, and if good and evil are opposed so that a wholly good being eliminates evil insofar as he can, then a contradiction arises.[1]

Mackie notes that theists have tried to solve this problem in various ways. Those who refuse to give up or change their conception of any of the attributes of the classical notion of God frequently handle this dilemma in one of two ways. The first claims that "evil is often necessary as a means to good."[2] This means that something considered evil is deemed *causally* necessary to some good end. Human agents are often willing to put up with or even bring about actions/events which in themselves are evil, because they lead to a good end. However, Mackie is unimpressed with this response to the problem, because he believes God isn't subject to these causal laws. As Mackie explains,

> If there is an omnipotent creator, then if there are any causal laws he must have made them, and if he is still omnipotent he must be able to override them. If there is a god, then, he does not need to use means to attain his ends. So it is idle to refer, in a theodicy, to any ordinary, factual, means-end, or in general causal, relationships.[3]

Mackie thinks a second approach to the problem of evil is more interesting and promising. According to this approach, things that are evil in themselves may contribute to the good of an overall whole in which they are found. Here Mackie appeals again to his first-order evil, second-order good analysis. According to that analysis, evil doesn't just happen to be connected to producing goods (means to ends). There is a logically necessary tie between the evil and the good. That is, without the existence of the first-order evil, there can't be the second-order good which is parasitic on it.[4] Of course, as Mackie says, one can't merely note that second-order good is logically tied to first-order evil. One must also hold that the second-order good "is greater in magnitude or importance than the first-order evil which is logically necessary for it, that the good outweighs the evil it involves."[5]

Mackie concedes that this second solution is formally possible, and hence, it meets the logical dimensions of the problem of evil. However, that doesn't end the discussion. Mackie says that all evil that can be justified by a first-order, second-order analysis may be called *absorbed* evil. But then, the problem of evil reappears as follows:

> But then the vital question is this: can the theist maintain that the only evils that occur in the world are absorbed evils? When this question is squarely put, it is surely plain that he cannot. On the one hand there are surplus first-order evils, suffering and the like which are not actually used in any good organic whole, and on the other there are second-order evils; these will not be incorporated in second-order goods, but will contrast with them: malevolence, cruelty, callousness, cowardice, and states of affairs in which there is not progress but decline, where things get worse rather than better.[6]

The problem of evil, then, recurs as the problem of unabsorbed evils, but what kind of problem is it, and is there any hope of solving it? Mackie does not himself turn this into an evidential problem. Instead, he says theists, when confronted with this problem of unabsorbed evils, typically appeal to the free will defense. They say free will is a third-order good which is parasitic upon second-order and first-order evil. Mackie then discusses the likelihood of the free will defense's success, and concludes that in the final analysis, it doesn't resolve the problem of unabsorbed evil.[7]

Though Mackie doesn't pursue this matter any further in terms of an evidential problem, the problem of unabsorbed evil can easily be formulated as either the evidential problem about the quantity of evil or the apparent gratuitousness of evil. If some evil is unabsorbed, then indeed, there seems to be too much evil. Of course, in this case the quantity is too much, because it is apparently purposeless. As purposeless, it is evidence against a God who would likely eliminate evil of this sort if he existed.[8]

WILLIAM L. ROWE

Unlike Mackie, William Rowe explicitly states that there is a strong argument for atheism, and that it is evidential. Rowe grants that Plantinga's free will defense solves the logical problem of evil (if one accepts incompatibilism), but he believes the evidential problem of evil provides *rational support* for atheism.[9] Over the years since his first statement (1979, "The Problem of Evil and Some Varieties of Atheism") of this argument, many have critiqued his argument, and he has made various modifications. While my main concern is in clarifying the basic points Rowe is making in this argument, in fairness to him I shall note major changes he has made in his statement of the argument. I begin with the original formulation in his 1979 article.

Rowe raises the problem in terms of the intensity and great plenitude of human and animal suffering. Actually, his treatment of this issue blurs together several different problems of evil. They are: 1) the problem of the quantity of evil; 2) the problem of the intensity of evil; and 3) the problem of animal suffering. Despite invoking these three separate problems, Rowe so structures his argument that it actually amounts to the problem of apparently gratuitous evil.

Rowe begins by claiming that the strongest case for atheism can be made in terms of intense human or animal suffering. He admits that if suffering is tied to some greater good which couldn't be achieved without the suffering in question, then we might conclude that the suffering is justified, even though it is still evil.[10] However, because human and animal suffering occur with great frequency, it is unlikely that all instances of it are attached to some greater good that would be lost without the evil. As a result, Rowe says atheists can posit the following argument against theism:

1.   There exist instances of intense suffering which an omnipotent, omniscient being could have prevented without thereby losing some greater good or permitting some evil equally bad or worse.

2.   An omniscient, wholly good being would prevent the occurrence of any intense suffering it could, unless it could not do so without thereby losing some greater good or permitting some evil equally bad or worse.

3.   There does not exist an omnipotent, omniscient, wholly good being.[11]

Since the argument is formally valid, Rowe argues that if there are rational grounds for accepting it, to that extent there are rational grounds for accepting atheism. He then looks at the premises individually, beginning with premise 2. He says this premise is both true and generally accepted by atheists and theists alike. All it really amounts to is that if God permits intense suffering, he has a good reason for it, namely, he knows that by allowing it he can produce some outweighing good.[12]

The crux of the issue, then, is premise 1. Theists may doubt it, but Rowe believes it is true, and he supports it with an example that he thinks shows it is reasonable to believe it. He writes:

> Suppose in some distant forest lightning strikes a dead tree, resulting in a forest fire. In the fire a fawn is trapped, horribly burned, and lies in terrible agony for several days before death relieves its suffering. So far as we can see, the fawn's intense suffering *is pointless* [italics mine]. For there does not appear to be any greater good such that the prevention of the fawn's suffering would require either the loss of that good or the occurrence of an evil equally bad or worse. Nor does there seem to be any equally bad or worse evil so connected to the fawn's suffering that it would have had to occur had the fawn's suffering been prevented. . . . Since the fawn's intense suffering was preventable and, so far as we can see, *pointless* [italics mine], doesn't it appear that premise (I) of the argument is true, that there do exist instances of intense suffering which an omnipotent, omniscient being could have prevented without thereby losing some greater good or permitting some evil equally bad or worse?[13]

The italicized words in the quote show that Rowe is really raising the problem of apparently gratuitous evil, not a problem about the quantity or intensity of evil.[14] Moreover, Rowe says this suffering is *apparently* pointless. That is, it appears to be so to us, but that doesn't prove it is. God may have some good reason for allowing it. Maybe it is tied to some good in a way we can't see. Nonetheless, our inability to *prove* that the evil is gratuitous (and our coordinate inability to *prove* that premise 1 is true) doesn't mean we have no *rational grounds* for believing it is true. As for the fawn, it seems unreasonable to believe there is some good logically tied to its suffering such that God couldn't eliminate it without removing that good. Likewise, it is equally unreasonable to think a worse evil would occur if the fawn didn't suffer.[15]

Even if someone thinks these things *are* reasonable, Rowe says, "we must then ask whether it is reasonable to believe either of these things of *all* the instances of seemingly pointless human and animal suffering that occur daily in our world. And surely the answer to this more general question must be no."[16] Though in his earlier work he offers only the suffering of the fawn as an example of pointless suffering, in later years (e.g., in his "Evil and Theodicy," published in 1988) he added examples of pointless human suffering, most notably the case of a five-year-old little girl who was brutally beaten, raped and strangled in Flint, Michigan, on New Year's eve within a few years of his 1988 article.[17] All instances of intense suffering which seem apparently pointless, while not demonstrating that premise 1 is true, surely make it reasonable (rational) to believe it is. Since premise 2 is true, since there is rational support for premise 1, and since the conclusion (premise 3) follows from the premises, this evidential argument for atheism apparently provides rational support for atheism.[18]

Rowe thinks theists can respond with any of three strategies, but he is dubious about all of them. First, the theist may say the reasoning in support of premise 1 is defective either because it alone doesn't justify premise 1, or because other things we know don't justify premise 1. Rowe thinks this approach is unfruitful for the theist since the argument from evil is valid, and the theist is likely to accept premise 2. Hence, the only way this approach could rebut the atheist's argument is for the theist to show premise 1 to be false, but all the theist has said is that there is no good reason for it.[19]

A second theistic response attacks premise 1 directly by noting goods to which the suffering is tied, goods which would be lost if God removed the evil. Rowe thinks this won't work for various reasons, but the general problem is:

> First, it cannot succeed, for the theist does not know what greater goods might be served, or evils prevented, by each instance of intense human or animal suffering. Second, the theist's own religious tradition usually maintains that in this life it is not given to us to know God's purpose in allowing particular instances of suffering. Hence, the direct attack against premise (I) cannot succeed and violates basic beliefs associated with theism.[20]

Before going any further, I note that Rowe has a habit of changing the focus of the problem and thereby shifting to a different problem. This is unfortunate, because there is little hope of a fair debate about God and evil if the problems are blurred together and the discussion shifts among several of those problems. Here we see Rowe making this kind of shift again. He moves back and forth between animal and human suffering and between the problems of evil's intensity and the apparent gratuitousness of some of it.

He also shifts back and forth between specific instances of apparently gratuitous suffering and gratuitous suffering in general (the portion cited above
focuses on specific instances, whereas other parts of his discussion focus on
gratuitous suffering in general).

I raise this point because looking at specific instances of gratuitous
human suffering seems to shift the discussion to the religious problem of evil.
As I shall show when I discuss that problem, it is a very different kind of problem than the other problems of evil. Of course, one might argue that the problem of gratuitous evil in general just reduces to the religious problem of evil.
However, the two problems are invariably perceived as distinct, and I contend that they are—for reasons that will become apparent when I discuss the
nature of the religious problem of evil.

Rowe offers a third strategy a theist might take in response to the atheistic argument from evil. Rowe thinks this is the most promising strategy, but
he personally is unconvinced. This approach indirectly attacks premise 1 in
an attempt to change the focus of the debate.[21] It involves negating the conclusion of the argument (premise 3) and turning it into the first premise of a
new argument. Premise 2 remains the same, but the original premise 1 is
negated and becomes the new argument's conclusion. The theist then notes
that the argument is formally valid, and further contends that there are rational grounds for the new first premise (this premise now says an omnipotent,
omniscient, wholly good being exists), so he accepts it as true. Since the conclusion of this new argument is the negation of the first premise of the atheist's argument, the first premise of the atheist's argument is wrong, so the
atheist's argument must be wrong.[22] Though Rowe believes this third theistic response is the most promising, he is dubious about its success, because
he doubts that the theist can offer convincing evidence for the first premise
of the new argument.[23]

In a later article ("God and Evil"), Rowe entertains several other
responses a theist might offer to his argument from evil, and finds none of
them acceptable. The first attacks premise 1 and argues that it is an argument
from ignorance. The theist may say that the atheist has only shown that we
don't know the good for which God allows horrendous evils like the death
of the fawn and the savage rape and murder of the little girl. But that doesn't
prove that there is no reason God has for allowing it; it only shows that we
don't know what that reason is. And we shouldn't be surprised at our lack of
knowledge of God's reasons, for God's mind infinitely transcends ours. Just
as a young child won't always understand the rules and punishments his parents implement, so it isn't unlikely that we shouldn't know why God allows
horrendous evils to occur. In fact, if he does exist, our inability to know his

reasons for such terrible evils is exactly what we would expect, given what we believe about his divine attributes.[24]

In reply, Rowe asserts that we must distinguish between goods we know of and those that are beyond our ken. As to the former, these goods don't have to be only those we have experienced. They can include goods we have never personally experienced and maybe never will, but we at least understand what they are. Rowe believes that there is no good we know of that could possibly justify God in allowing the brutal rape and killing of the little girl in Flint, Michigan. This is so, because as we think through the goods we can conceive, we find "either that it isn't good enough to justify God in permitting that evil, or that the good in question cannot justify God because it is never actualized, or that the good in question could likely be actualized by God without his having to permit the horrendous suffering of that little girl."[25]

What about goods we can't conceive of? Might some of them justify God's inaction with respect to the little girl? Theists may think so and argue their case on the analogy of the difference between a child's and its parents' knowledge. Rowe has two responses. He believes the argument from analogy might work if it is drawn between good parents and a good but finitely powerful God. This is so because both parents and a deity finite in power and knowledge might think the only way they can produce a certain good for someone is by allowing a particular evil to befall him or her. However, an infinite God is unlimited in power and knowledge and hence surely knows how and has power to prevent or remove horrendous evils like Auschwitz.[26]

Rowe believes there is a second problem in appealing to the good parent analogy. In a case where good parents permit their child to suffer for the sake of some long-range good, invariably the parent is present during times of the child's suffering to offer love, comfort, and concern. Similarly, we should expect God's presence and care during times when we are put through affliction for the sake of goods beyond our comprehension. However, countless numbers of humans have had no such experience with God during times of intense suffering. His absence all the more drives them to believe either that he doesn't exist or that if he does, he doesn't care about what's happening.

The net result is that the argument for premise 1 of the atheistic argument isn't an argument from ignorance. Rather, in light of goods we know of and in light of what we know a being of infinite power, intelligence, and goodness would likely do when his creatures encounter horrible evil, we have reason to believe premise 1 is true. Of course, Rowe adds, God still may have some reason we don't know for allowing these evils, but at most this shows one can't *prove* that premise 1 is true. However, what we know makes it more likely than not that it is true.[27]

Theists may adopt a second strategy in response to Rowe's argument from evil. Rather than telling atheists that they haven't given a good enough argument for premise 1, they may instead claim that theists have offered various theodicies which offer explanations as to why God allows evil. He does so in order to produce the good(s) each theodicy invokes in justifying God for creating this world. Rowe responds that none of the traditional defenses and theodicies solves problems about the excessive amounts and intensity of the worst evils. Even Hick's soul-building theodicy, which Rowe thinks is the most promising of all theodicies, fails on this point. Though his theodicy can explain the existence of moral and natural evil in general, it can't handle the fact that much evil in our world seems to bear no relation whatsoever to soul-building.[28]

Hick's response to this objection is that if God only allowed enough evils for soul-building and everyone knew that, then there would be no effort to fight and overcome evil (and to fight evil surely seems to us to make sense). It is only when there are evils that seem to go beyond what is needed for soul-building that we are inclined to fight them. And, of course, as we fight evil, at least part of what happens to us is that our character develops (our souls are built). So, paradoxically (but not incoherently, according to Rowe), Hick argues that in order to build souls, there must be more evil than is needed to build souls. Hence, it must be rational to believe that excessive amounts of evil occur in our world.[29]

Rowe believes this is an ingenious argument, but thinks it doesn't work. That is, he doesn't believe it solves the problem of the amount and intensity of evil in our world.[30] This is so, because the amount of evil in our world is certainly more than an omnipotent God needs to build souls, and it is more than he would need to permit in order for us to be rational in believing there are excess evils. To support this claim Rowe argues that if only five million had perished in the Holocaust, that would still be enough evil to build souls, and it would be enough to cause us to believe that there is excessive evil in our world, and that we should fight it. So, Hick's theodicy, even with his ingenious addition noted above, still doesn't solve the problems of the intensity and amount of evil.[31]

Returning to Rowe's 1979 article, I note that he concludes it by claiming that atheists like himself who are unconvinced by theistic arguments may respond to the *rationality* of theistic belief in one of three ways. They may hold that no one is rationally justified in believing the theistic God exists ("unfriendly atheism"). They may, instead, have no belief about whether any theist is rationally justified in believing in God's existence ("indifferent atheism"). Or, they may think some theists are rationally justified in thinking God exists ("friendly atheism").

Rowe defends the position of friendly atheism. He notes that a position need not be true for someone to be rational in believing it. One may be rationally justified, so long as one has rational grounds for belief. Hence, in espousing friendly atheism, Rowe doesn't mean the theist's beliefs are true. He just thinks some theists do have rational grounds for their belief in God. They may appeal, for example, to the traditional arguments for God's existence or to certain aspects of their own or others' religious experience. Those grounds make their belief rational without necessarily making it true. Hence, the atheist can admit that theists with reasons for belief are rational in their belief, while believing that theists' beliefs are wrong and rejecting those beliefs on rational grounds. Those rational grounds for rejecting theism show that atheists are rationally justified in rejecting it.[32]

Wykstra and Rowe

Rowe's version of the evidential problem of evil has occasioned much reaction. In particular, Stephen Wykstra's initial response to Rowe ("The Humean Obstacle to Evidential Arguments from Suffering: On Avoiding the Evils of 'Appearance'") has generated considerable discussion.

ROWE/WYKSTRA I

Wykstra begins with premise 2 of Rowe's argument, and concludes that theists and atheists alike can accept it.[33] Hence, as Rowe suggests, the crux of the debate is the first premise. Rowe supports it with empirical evidence, and says that since it is reasonable to think the first premise is true, the argument as a whole is rational support for atheism. Wykstra interprets Rowe as saying that the evidence of suffering strongly supports or confirms premise 1. By "strongly supports" Wykstra means that the evidence increases the likelihood of the premise's truth sufficiently to make it reasonable to believe by someone who appreciates the evidence.[34] Since Rowe believes the evidence of evil strongly supports atheism, Wykstra thinks Rowe rests his position on the claim that "'there does not appear to be any outweighing good' of a God-justifying sort served by (say) the fawn's suffering."[35]

Wykstra thinks it is critical to understand what Rowe means by "appears" when he says there appears to be no outweighing good from the fawn's suffering. Rowe doesn't clarify what he means, but Wykstra thinks he can explain what Rowe means by way of an illustration. He writes:

> Imagine two teachers, Ken and Nick, discussing their young colleague Tom, whom [sic] Ken thinks has mentally snapped under the stress of job-seeking. Ken tells Nick of a recent incident: Tom had abruptly excused himself from

an important departmental meeting, saying he had urgent personal business. As it was later learned, he spent the next hour out by the parking lot, digging up earthworms and making, of all things, a fat sandwich with them. "So it appears," Ken says, "that Tom has gone off the deep end." If Nick resists this conclusion, saying "But perhaps Tom had some sane and rational reason for needing a worm sandwich," Ken might adduce other bizarre episodes of Tom's recent behavior. Of each he says: "Here again, it does not appear that Tom had a rational and sane reason for so behaving;" and the instances together he puts forward as clinching a cumulative case: "It is almost beyond belief that we could be mistaken about each of these instances."[36]

As Wykstra notes, Ken wouldn't think it necessary to make a detailed argument that Tom's behavior evidences a mental disorder. Anyone hearing the story should just see the evidential import of it. Likewise, Wykstra thinks Rowe uses "appears" in the same sense. Of course, none of this means "appears" claims of this sort can't be disputed, for there are two ways of doing so. One is to grant that the situation as explained does present *prima facie* evidence for a given conclusion, but then to argue that other evidence outweighs or defeats this *prima facie* evidence. The other way "is to argue that the adduced situation does not even have the *prima facie* evidential import imputed to it by the 'appears' claim."[37] Wykstra chooses the second and more radical approach.

Wykstra begins his attack by asking how we are to judge whether someone is within his epistemic rights when using "appears" in the way mentioned. He says we must judge it by whether it meets a condition (necessary but not sufficient) which entitles one to claim that on the basis of some situation of which one is aware, p is the case. What is at issue here is whether there is epistemic access to p through some situation s. Hence Wykstra labels this condition the Condition of Reasonable Epistemic Access (CORNEA). He defines CORNEA thus:

> On the basis of cognized situation s, human H is entitled to claim "It appears that p" only if it is reasonable for H to believe that, given her cognitive faculties and the use she has made of them, if p were not the case, s would likely be different than it is in some way discernible by her.[38]

In applying CORNEA to Rowe's "appears" claim, Wykstra says it doesn't satisfy the condition. Rowe's comments about the suffering fawn suggest there is no outweighing good we know of that the suffering serves. However, Wykstra believes the crucial issue is whether it would likely be apparent to us if some good were connected to the fawn's suffering. Wykstra thinks not. If there is such a good, it is purposed by a God whose vision and wisdom are greater than ours. God's wisdom in comparison to ours is like the difference between an adult human's wisdom and that of a one-month-old infant. But, if that is so, then even if outweighing goods are connected to instances of apparently pointless suffering, we might know some of them, but it is highly unlikely that we would know what they are in most cases. Hence, for any specific instance of intense suffering, it is reasonable to believe that if an outweighing good attaches to it, we have no epistemic access to it.

The upshot of this argument is that anyone, including Rowe, who knows Wykstra's argument about whether outweighing good is within our knowledge should recognize that it is unreasonable to think Rowe's "does not appear" claim satisfies CORNEA. Hence, the claim that there doesn't appear to be any outweighing good that attaches to the suffering of a fawn carries as little weight as a ceramics teacher's comment who knows no philosophy that a sentence of philosophy uttered by a philosopher doesn't appear to have any meaning. Moreover, the difference between our knowledge and God's also means that even if an instance of intense suffering were intimately tied to some outweighing good, there is no guarantee that if we knew about the intense suffering, we would also know the good to which it is tied.

In addition, Rowe admits that traditional theism believes God's purposes for allowing suffering will usually be beyond our knowledge. In fact, Rowe says that if theism is true, it is reasonable to believe God's purposes for suffering are typically beyond our knowledge. But, claims Wykstra, if Rowe grants this, it is fatal to his case. His "does not appear" claim not only fails to satisfy CORNEA (and hence, he has no right to think it true), but he also agrees that it is reasonable to believe that if there is a God, we wouldn't know what divinely purposed good is connected to suffering. But if it is unlikely that we would know God's purposed good, then the case for there really being instances of intense suffering that have no purpose is undercut. There could be a purpose without us knowing it at all. Of course, if the case for there being genuinely purposeless instances of suffering is damaged, then Rowe's premise 1 isn't likely true, and his evidential argument against theism collapses.[39]

Thankfully, Rowe responded to Wykstra's paper, so we know what he would say. Rowe begins by defining *standard theism* as any view committed to the existence of an omnipotent, omniscient, omnibenevolent being who created the world (Rowe abbreviates this as "O"). He then distinguishes two versions of standard theism, *restricted* and *expanded* theism. Expanded theism is the view that O exists plus other religious claims about sin, redemption, future life, etc. Restricted theism is the belief that O exists, unaccompanied by any other independent religious claims.[40] Rowe then sets forth two propositions essential to his argument:

1. There exist instances of intense suffering which an omnipotent, omni-
    scient being could have prevented without thereby losing some greater
    good or permitting some evil equally bad or worse.

2. It appears that the fawn's suffering is pointless—i.e., it appears that
    the fawn's suffering does not serve an outweighing good otherwise
    unobtainable by an omnipotent, omniscient being.[41]

Rowe claims that Wykstra's objection actually has two steps. The first is
to say that in the situation described, we may affirm proposition 2 only if the
following is true:

3. We have no reason to think that were O to exist things would strike
    us in pretty much the same way concerning the fawn's suffering.[42]

The second step in Wykstra's objection is to deny proposition 3. Wykstra
thinks 3 is false, because he believes that if O exists, the outweighing good to
be achieved by allowing the fawn's suffering would be beyond our knowledge. Hence, things would strike us just as they would if O didn't exist. What
this ultimately means is that if O *does* exist, we would expect things to strike
us precisely the way they do now with respect to human and animal suffering. Hence, instances of apparently purposeless suffering can't disprove God's
existence.

Rowe restricts his discussion to the second part of Wykstra's response.[43]
It boils down to arguing that proposition 3 is false, and thus, CORNEA isn't
satisfied. Rowe's fundamental answer to Wykstra is simple but significant. He
believes Wykstra's line of reasoning assumes that either the outweighing
goods haven't occurred (though the suffering has) and thus are beyond our
knowledge (though not beyond God's), or that if they have occurred, they
remain unknown to us. Rowe replies that the mere supposition that God
exists gives no reason to think either of these assumptions is true. In other
words, before the suffering occurs or even immediately after it happens, God's
reason (the outweighing good) for it may be totally beyond our knowledge.
However, that doesn't at all mean that the good will occur so far in the future
that we won't likely know what it is. Nor does it mean that if the good happens shortly after the suffering, its purpose will remain hidden from us indefinitely. Rowe puts the point as follows:

> If O exists it is indeed likely, if not certain, that O's mind grasps many good
> states of affairs that do not obtain and which, *prior to their obtaining,* are
> such that we are simply unable to think of or imagine them. That much is
> reasonably clear. But the mere assumption that O exists gives us no reason
> whatever to suppose *either* that the greater goods in virtue of which he per-
> mits most sufferings are goods that come into existence far in the future of

the sufferings we are aware of, *or* that once they do obtain we continue to be ignorant of them and their relation to the sufferings.[44]

In light of the preceding, Rowe concludes that Wykstra hasn't provided adequate justification for the second step in his objection, and thus, the objection fails. Rowe's point is that just because we may not know at some time the good to which suffering is attached doesn't mean that if God exists we will never know. The fact that we continue in ignorance is more likely on the supposition that there is no God than on the assumption that there is one but this information will always remain beyond our knowledge.

After responding to Wykstra's objection, Rowe returns to his distinction between restricted and expanded theism. With respect to restricted theism, his objection to Wykstra is telling against it. That is, restricted theism alone gives no good reason to think things would appear just as they do if O existed. As to expanded theism, it may include the Pauline doctrine that the sufferings of this world bear no comparison to the blessing yet to be revealed at the end of the world. Expanded theism of this sort can rightly claim that what we see now would be no different if there was a God, for not until the end of the world will the outweighing good appear. When it does, it will far exceed the suffering now experienced. Hence, restricted standard theism can't meet Rowe's objection, but expanded standard theism can. That is, Wykstra's original objections to Rowe succeed if expanded theism is in view, but apparently fail if restricted theism is under consideration.

In light of the preceding, Rowe argues that the crucial issue is whether restricted theism implies expanded theism. If it does, then Wykstra's objection is decisive against Rowe's claim that suffering renders restricted theism unlikely. Rowe is convinced, however, that there is no entailment. Nonetheless, he believes Wykstra thinks the notion that the goods for which God allows suffering are beyond our knowledge is *part of* the theistic hypothesis, a logical extension of theism. If that is so, then restricted standard theism already includes the concepts that make the expanded version of theism plausible against Rowe's objection. On the contrary, Rowe says that all that is implicit in restricted theism is that God grasps goods beyond our knowledge, but as he already argued, that doesn't prove those goods will always be beyond our knowledge. Hence, restricted theism doesn't include the notion that the goods for which God allows suffering are beyond our knowledge. As a result, restricted standard theism can't successfully answer Rowe's objection.

Rowe concludes that Wykstra has included in his notion of the logical extension of restricted theism ideas which actually belong only to an expanded version of theism. As he says,

My own best judgment is that the crucial proposition Wykstra claims to be implicit in theism is in fact an added postulate that produces a version of expanded theism, a version that is not rendered unlikely by the facts about suffering that I claim to render restricted standard theism unlikely.[45]

Rowe ends his response to Wykstra by noting that even Wykstra concedes that believers and nonbelievers alike persist in sensing that inscrutable suffering somehow disconfirms theism. Rowe thinks this is so because our intuitions about suffering make it hard to understand how so much apparently pointless suffering is what we would expect if God exists. Wykstra argues that even if God exists, much of the world's suffering would appear just as it does. Rowe replies that

if I am right, what Wykstra has done is "read into" the theistic hypothesis a proposition that is part of the story of traditional theism, thus creating a version of expanded theism. He has, unwittingly, changed the question. The crucial question is whether the facts about suffering in our world tend to disconfirm the hypothesis that O exists. That question cannot be shown to deserve a negative answer merely by showing that we can supplement the hypothesis that O exists with other propositions such that the supplemented result is not disconfirmed by the facts that are claimed to disconfirm the hypothesis that O exists.[46]

ASSESSMENT OF ROWE/WYKSTRA I

In assessing this interchange between Rowe and Wykstra, several things strike me. First, Rowe talks about the amount of suffering in our world being inconsistent with what we should expect if God exists. My response is that it is difficult to see how either Rowe or Wykstra *knows* what we should expect or whether their expectations are correct. It seems that Rowe's expectations come from a sense that if he were God, he would have no reason for allowing so much suffering, so he wouldn't allow it; and therefore, God, if he exists, shouldn't and wouldn't either. But this sounds like pompous speculation, for it purports to know what one would know and do if one were God.

Isn't Wykstra guilty of the same error? I think not, for he doesn't purport to know what God would think or do. He merely looks at our world and explains why it is consistent with the theistic hypothesis. His reason isn't that it is consistent with what he would do if he were God. It is consistent with what we know about God as conceived by traditional theism. Rowe, on the other hand, suggests that the suffering in our world isn't what God should have allowed, because it fails to meet our expectations, given what we know about God. But perhaps Rowe has misinterpreted the implications of our concept of God. That is, maybe he thinks God's omnipotence and omnibenevolence obligate him to remove much of the evil in our world (perhaps even all of it), just because he can (omnipotence) and should want to do so (omnibenevolence). After all, if we had that kind of power and were that good, wouldn't we use our power to get rid of the evil?

The problem with such views is that God's power and love don't obligate him to do every good thing possible. They only necessitate that whatever he does must be good, and that if he fails to do something good which he apparently should do, he must have a morally sufficient reason for not doing it. Rowe's discussion implies that there are no morally acceptable reasons for failing to remove the great amounts of evil in our world. However, he doesn't consider any theistic defenses that explain why God doesn't remove such evil, nor any defenses as to why apparently gratuitous evil is only apparently so. I noted above that in his "God and Evil" (1997–1998) he does discuss Hick's soul-building theodicy. However, that isn't a defense against the problems of the amount and apparent gratuitousness of evil, but rather addresses most directly the problem of moral evil. In addition, Rowe doesn't consider the rest of the evidence (theistic proofs, etc.) for theism. On one item alone that seems inconsistent with theism, he rejects theism. I think he does so at least in part because he assumes he knows what God should do.

Rowe might respond that his claims aren't so strong as my objection suggests. My objection may appear to claim that Rowe thinks he has *proved* theism wrong. Rowe never claimed to have done that. He only thinks his argument from evil shows that the atheist has grounds for being an atheist, but then, he admits many theists have grounds for their theistic belief, too. The problem here, however, is that Rowe says the theist is rationally justified in believing in God (he has grounds for his belief), *but his belief is wrong.* This is a problem because it moves beyond the question of whether the theist is rational in his belief to make a judgment about whether his belief is correct. If all that is at stake in this debate is whether atheists and theists are rational in their views (i.e., they have grounds for what they believe), then this is a rather tame debate over something that is significant, but nowhere near as significant as whether God actually exists. As soon as one claims that theism is wrong and that the evidence either proves or strongly confirms that it is wrong, that changes the focus of the discussion from whether the participants are rational to whether God exists. And, if the issue is whether God exists and one tries to decide that question on the basis of evidence, then one must consider all relevant evidence. Unfortunately, Rowe entertains only the evidence that it doesn't appear that there is any outweighing good connected to instances of intense suffering in our world. While this evidence is relevant to the question of God's existence, it isn't the whole story. Too much further evidence in favor of and against each side remains untouched to think that a convincing case about the probability of theism or atheism has been made on the sole basis of appeal to evil.

ROWE/WYKSTRA II

In more recent years the dialogue between Wykstra and Rowe has continued. We needn't cover all the details, but a glimpse at one of Wykstra's more recent papers would be helpful. Wykstra's "Rowe's Noseeum Arguments from Evil" initially clarifies many of the ground rules for dealing with an argument such as Rowe's. He clarifies what CORNEA means, and how it applies to this issue.[47] In the latter portion of his paper, Wykstra turns to the substantive objection Rowe poses against Wykstra's views, namely his rejection of Wykstra's parent analogy.

As Wykstra notes, Rowe's objection to the parent analogy makes two key moves. The first imposes Rowe's restriction to the argument. That restriction distinguishes between what can be called "Core Theism" (i.e., in the terminology of earlier essays, restricted standard theism) and expanded versions of theism. The former includes only belief that O (an omnipotent, omniscient, wholly good being) exists, unaccompanied by any other religious claims. Expanded theism adds to Core Theism further religious belief about matters such as salvation, the afterlife, the end times, etc. Rowe believes that it might be possible to make a case, using some version of expanded theism, that despite appearances to the contrary, the God of this expanded theism probably has purposes for those evils even though those purposes are unseen. Rowe's restriction is that Wykstra needs to show that the situation is likely the same, if the theist holds nothing more than Core Theism and agrees that there are evils that seem purposeless. Rowe believes that if one invokes only Core Theism, then it is improbable that God has unseen purposes for evils that seem purposeless. Wykstra says that we can here distinguish two questions as follows:

(Q1)   Is E expectable from the *mere* hypothesis of H? That is, does H make E tautologously expectable?

(Q2)   Is E expectable from H *together* with other things which we know independently of commitment to H, and which are not themselves adverse to H in relation to its rivals. [sic] That is, does H contingently make E expectable?[48]

Rowe's restriction requires that theists must base their case to defeat his argument from evil on Q1, not Q2.

Rowe's second move argues that Wykstra's parent analogy argument rests on an assumption which, given the restriction to Core Theism alone, "is gratuitous." How does Rowe make this point? He argues that Wykstra's line of reasoning proceeds as follows:

(1)   O can grasp goods beyond our ken

moves to

(2)   It is likely that the goods in relation to which O permits many sufferings are beyond our ken.

and concludes with

(3)   It is likely that many of the sufferings in our world do not appear to have a point; we cannot see what goods justify O in permitting them.[49]

If one adopts Core Theism, Rowe believes (1) is true, because an omniscient God is likely to know many things we don't know, including the purpose(s) of seemingly purposeless evils. The problem, in Rowe's judgment, is making the move from (1) to (2), because this assumes that the goods in question either haven't occurred, or if they have occurred, they remain unknown to us. In addition,

the mere assumption that O exists gives us no reason to think that either of these is true. If O exists, it is indeed likely, if not certain, that O's mind grasps many good states of affairs that do not obtain and that *prior to their obtaining* we are simply unable to think of or imagine. That much is reasonably clear. But the mere assumption that O exists gives us no reason whatever to suppose *either* that the greater goods in virtue of which he permits most sufferings are goods that come into existence far in the future of the sufferings we are aware of *or* that, once they do obtain, we continue to be ignorant of them and their relation to the sufferings.[50]

Wykstra agrees that the key is how one moves from (1) to (2), according to Rowe. Making that move, Wykstra argues, rests on an assumption that the goods for which God allows many known sufferings are goods that are future and thus unknown to us. Wykstra calls this the "Futurity Assumption," and explains that Rowe's complaint with moving from (1) to (2) is that Core Theism alone gives us no reason to think the Futurity Assumption is true. Premise (1) alone, then, isn't reason enough to think there are purposes for evils that go beyond our knowledge, and if that is so, then the parent analogy argument fails.[51]

Wykstra also argues that God could have created one or another of two different types of universes. The first one (call it a "shallow" universe) contains evils whose purpose is within our knowledge, and the latter (call it a "deep" universe) has evils whose purpose is beyond our ken. Wykstra argues that it is reasonable to expect God to create the latter sort,[52] but Rowe complains that Wykstra offers us no reason as to why this is likely.[53] Wykstra replies that he did in fact offer a reason to expect God to create a deep universe, namely, the Parent Analogy argument. Rowe believes the Parent Analogy argument doesn't work (even if we add that ours is a "deep universe") because to move from (1) to (2), you must also support the Futurity Assumption, and Rowe believes that from Core Theism alone one isn't entitled to believe the Futurity Assumption.[54]

Wykstra disagrees with Rowe's assessment, and explains why. Initially, he rejects Rowe's demand that we stick only with Core Theism, for if one wants to make a probability judgment on evidence, it must rest on all relevant evidence. Wykstra doesn't ask us to consider everything we know that might be relevant to this issue. He appeals only to what we know about human cognitive capacities, and asks how likely it is, with what we know about our cognitive abilities, that God's reasons and purposes for the evils in question would be beyond our ken. Wykstra believes we can answer this by appeal again to the Parent Analogy.[55]

Wykstra asks us to consider the likelihood that an evil that parents allow in their child's life is connected to some unforeseen future good. He argues that the probability that the parents would be thinking in such terms depends on their intelligence, their character (in particular, their care about their child and its future), and their ability (in particular, their financial ability) to do something now that would have positive results in the future. The less intelligent, the less caring, and the less able they are, the more unlikely that when they allow their child to endure an evil that has no foreseeable good, they really are thinking about the child's future. Conversely, the more intelligent, caring, and able the parents are, the more likely that what they do and allow now will be done with a view to future benefit for their child. If that is so, Wykstra argues, how much more so in relation to our "divine parent" and his hand in our lives. Wykstra isn't claiming that this line of argument justifies God in allowing the evil to befall us. Rather, his point is merely to explain why, given even, say, minimally expanded theism, it is reasonable to think the Futurity Assumption is believable (and coordinately, why it is reasonable to think God created a deep universe rather than a shallow one).[56]

In all of this, Wykstra understands that a lot depends on one's starting point. Suppose that one begins with a belief in what Wykstra labels "Core Naturalism," a belief that the universe is run by totally naturalistic processes so that there is no ultimate purpose to life and no future purposes for the various experiences we have each day; everything happens as a result of the coincidental, accidental co-location of atoms. Given a belief in Core Naturalism, it is certainly most reasonable to believe that evils for which there are no seen purposes in fact have none. On the other hand, suppose that a proponent of Core Naturalism changes her views to Core Theism. Wouldn't that shift in perspective make it much more reasonable to think that evils with no seeable purposes do have unseen (perhaps even future) purposes? Wykstra thinks so, and believes that when we add to Core Theism our knowledge of our own cognitive capacities plus his Parent Analogy argument, Rowe is wrong in thinking that there is no reason whatsoever to believe that one is justified in moving from (1) to (2).[57]

ASSESSMENT OF ROWE/WYKSTRA II

Here I can be brief for I find Wykstra's argumentation quite compelling. In particular, I find Rowe's restriction of theistic belief to Core Theism unacceptable. In light of the difference it would make for someone to move from Core Naturalism to Core Theism, I'm not sure that Rowe is right when he thinks that holding Core Theism alone would offer no reason for believing (2). However, the more fundamental point is that we are talking about an inductive and probability argument, and such arguments and their assessments of the evidence need to be based on total evidence. Hence, even if we are convinced by Rowe that if you begin with Core Theism you shouldn't believe the Futurity Assumption or premise (2), there is so much more of the story to tell, so to speak, that agreeing with Rowe on this point doesn't seem to accomplish much in favor of atheism.

On the other hand, if the theist is allowed to hold some version of expanded theism, then even Rowe seems to believe that it is more probable (than on Core Theism alone) that God does have some unseen purpose related to some as yet unseen good which he intends to accomplish by allowing us to undergo what seem to be purposeless evils. Does the increase in this likelihood that comes with some version of expanded theism make theism on the whole more probable than atheism or even itself more probable than not? To this point in the discussion, I don't think we are ready to make an assessment one way or the other on that issue. But what does seem clear in light of Wykstra's arguments (especially the Parent Analogy) is that if one is assessing a form of theism some theist actually holds (it will be some expanded version), Rowe is mistaken in thinking that there is no reason whatsoever to accept the Futurity Assumption and to believe that there are in fact unseen goods that will eventuate from evils that now seem purposeless.

Reichenbach and Rowe

Bruce Reichenbach, responding to Rowe's earlier version of his argument from evil, raises two objections. First, he interprets Rowe's claims about apparently pointless evil to mean that what appear to be gratuitous instances of suffering "are in fact or likely pointless, for we do not know of any higher good to which they are a means. But this constitutes an appeal to ignorance; that we know of no higher good does not entail that there is no higher good or that one is unlikely."[58]

Does Rowe's argument against theism actually rest on an appeal to ignorance? Wykstra thinks not. He says Reichenbach thinks the key premise of Rowe's argument is that "we know of no higher good." Wykstra asks whether this is the same as "it does not appear that there is any outweighing good," the stopping point of Rowe's argument. Wykstra believes the two aren't equivalent; the key is the placement of the "not". Consider the following sentences:

1.   It does not appear to me that x is f.
2.   It appears to me that x is not f.

Claims in the form of 1, including Rowe's, may be interpreted in one of the following two ways:

1a.   It is not the case that it appears to me that x is f (the "strict sense" of "does not appear").

or

1b.   It appears to me that x is not f (the "ordinary sense" of "does not appear," equivalent to 2).

Claims like 1a are weaker than claims like 1b, because the former focuses on what one knows about the case, whereas the latter makes a comment about what is the case. According to Wykstra, Reichenbach interprets Rowe as saying the equivalent of 1a. If Reichenbach is right, Rowe is appealing to ignorance. However, Wykstra says Rowe's point is like 1b. Rowe's view is that it appears that instances of suffering are pointless, and thus, they are likely pointless. He isn't saying "it isn't the case that I know of no point, and thus, it is reasonable to think this suffering has no point." Why would he want to say that, since it merely appeals to his ignorance? Wykstra concludes that Rowe isn't appealing to ignorance but to what appears to be the case, namely, that these instances of suffering have no point. From that observation Rowe thinks it reasonable to believe that they have no point, but that is no appeal to ignorance. As Wykstra explains, this sort of move by Rowe (from "it appears that x is not f" to "it is reasonable to believe that x is not f") is licensed by what many philosophers believe a proper and indispensable principle of justification, the Principle of Credulity, as Richard Swinburne calls it. That principle is the belief that if something *appears* to be the case, that is *prima facie* justification for believing it *is* the case. That is far different from an appeal to ignorance.[59]

Reichenbach's second objection to Rowe's argument appears to be more on target. Rowe does grant that in the case of the suffering fawn there possibly is some higher good to which it is attached, despite appearances. Nonetheless, Rowe believes there really is no such higher good, and thinks it unreasonable to believe that all instances of apparently pointless suffering really are attached to outweighing goods. Reichenbach thinks this just begs the question. One must first show that there are *any* cases of *genuinely* pointless suffering before we can believe that some of the many instances of *apparently* pointless suffering are really pointless.[60] Rowe might answer as he responded to Wykstra that if there are no genuinely pointless instances of suffering, then we should have seen their point by now. However, the problem with that response is that it speculates about why we have no explanation of the suffering's purpose, i.e., it tries to interpret the silence. But it can't show that the suffering actually has no point. Until Rowe actually produces instances which he can show are genuinely pointless, I believe Reichenbach's objection is telling.

In addition, I think Reichenbach's objection suggests something about a theistic strategy for handling the problem of apparently gratuitous evil. Theists should require atheists to offer an instance of suffering which they can prove is genuinely pointless. That will be a hard challenge to meet, especially because of our limited knowledge. Atheists won't likely do better than produce some evidence that a specific evil is probably genuinely pointless, but "probably pointless" isn't enough to answer Reichenbach's objection about question begging.

Lewis and Rowe

Delmas Lewis raises two further objections against earlier versions of Rowe's project. He agrees that some instances of suffering (like the fawn's case) appear to be pointless. However, there is a logical gap between *appears to be* pointless and *is genuinely* pointless. In order for Rowe to succeed, he must "show how the former fact provides good reason to believe that the latter assertion is true."[61] Lewis claims that with arguments like Rowe's there are only two ways to move from apparently pointless evil to genuinely pointless evil. He calls them the Epistemological Slide and the Inductive Slide. However, he thinks neither legitimately supports Rowe's claim that there are instances of suffering which God could have prevented without losing any greater good or producing some worse evil.[62]

The Epistemological Slide relies on the following:

(E)   If there is a morally sufficient reason which explains why an omniscient, omnipotent being could not prevent some instance of evil without thereby losing some greater good or permitting some evil equally bad or worse, then we would know it.[63]

If one grants (E), it is easy to construct an argument for Rowe's claim that there is suffering which God could have prevented. It will look something like the following: 1) there are instances of apparently pointless suffering; 2) but from (E), if these are really only *apparently* pointless, we would know the reason for the suffering; 3) we don't know the reason, so the instances must be genuinely pointless; 4) if an omnipotent, omniscient being exists, he can and should remove genuinely pointless evil; therefore, there are instances of suffering God could have and should have prevented.

As Lewis notes, Rowe doesn't use the Epistemological Slide argument, and it is good that he doesn't, for it rests on (E). But (E) is false, at least from the perspective of theists who believe God's ways are beyond human knowledge. To assume that (E) is true merely begs the question in favor of atheism, for it ignores theistic claims that God's ways are above human knowledge.[64]

Rowe doesn't use the Epistemological Slide, but what about the Inductive Slide? Lewis claims it is important for Rowe's argument. Rowe's argument moves from the likelihood that some single instance of apparently pointless suffering is *really* pointless to the assertion that it is extremely likely that *some* of *all* apparently pointless suffering is in fact genuinely pointless. This argument in its bare essentials is:

(1)   There are terribly many instances of apparently pointless suffering in our world every day.

(2)   There is good reason to believe that some of these instances of apparently pointless suffering are instances of genuinely pointless suffering.[65]

Lewis says that even if one grants (1), (2) doesn't follow as a matter of logic from it. The move from (1) to (2) requires an additional assumption. Lewis suggests the following:

(P)   If a thing of kind X appears to lack property Y (but still have [*sic*] Y), and there are very, very many things of kind X which appear to lack Y (but still may have Y), then it is extremely likely that at least some things of kind X really do lack Y.[66]

Applying (P) to the argument at hand, we derive:

(3)   If an instance of suffering appears to lack a morally sufficient reason
        (but still may have one) and there are very, very many instances of
        suffering which appear to lack a morally sufficient reason (but still
        may have one), then it is extremely likely that some instances of suf-
        fering really do lack a morally sufficient reason.[67]

This argument is an example of the Inductive Slide, and Lewis says it is
problematic on two grounds. First, its use of induction is problematic. In
order to justify a claim that it is quite likely that some of a given number of
things which have quality F also have quality G, one must appeal to background knowledge as the basis for the high prior probability that one's claim
is correct.[68] How might one establish prior probability? One might take a
random sampling of instances of apparently pointless evil and count the number which are genuinely so. Of course, that would necessitate having a
method for identifying instances that are genuinely pointless. As Lewis notes,
Rowe offers no such method, and any critic's claim to know the distinguishing mark(s) will be dubious. But without a means of identifying genuinely gratuitous evils as such, the Inductive Slide argument is useless. On the other
hand, if one really had a way of knowing which evils are genuinely pointless,
then taking a random sampling by induction would be unnecessary. All that
would be needed is to produce one instance (using one's criterion), and the
point would be made.[69]

Prior probability could also be established if one possessed some background information which makes it extremely unlikely that there are no
instances of pointless suffering. However, this suggestion raises Lewis's second argument against (3). He writes:

> It seems that the only way to satisfy this requirement would be to have inde-
> pendent grounds on which the non-existence of God is extremely likely. If
> this is correct, then Rowe's argument is both circular, and its conclusion
> uninformative, for anyone who is in the epistemic position to offer it.[70]

Lewis concludes from his considerations that neither the Inductive Slide
nor the Epistemological Slide can provide grounds for Rowe's claim that
instances of suffering exist which God could have prevented without losing
any greater good or causing a worse evil. Hence, anyone who uses an inductive argument like Rowe's argument against theism must offer a good reason
apart from evil's existence for believing that God doesn't exist. Lewis thinks
it is unlikely that there is such an argument against God's existence. But, without it, appeal to evil's existence alone accomplishes nothing more than rein-
forcing a foregone conclusion.[71]

In addition to Lewis's objections to Rowe's argument, he adds an argument analogous to Rowe's argument, except that it favors theism. Lewis considers it objectionable on the same grounds he raised against Rowe, but if Rowe's argument is conclusive, then so is his, since the two are strictly analogous. Here Lewis is using a typical strategy for attacking an opponent's position—write an argument of the same form and structure as one's opponent's, but an argument whose conclusion contradicts that of the opponent's argument. Lewis's argument is:

(1) There are very many instances of numinous experience.
(2) While any one instance of numinous experience may be delusory, it is unlikely that all are.
(3) It is likely that one instance of numinous experience is non-delusory.
(4) If one instance of numinous experience is non-delusory, then God exists.
(5) God exists.[72]

In "The Empirical Argument from Evil," Rowe responded to Lewis. He addresses the Epistemological Slide argument and finds it problematic. Lewis notes that Rowe's argumentation moves from the fact that there is *apparently* gratuitous suffering to the belief that there actually is genuinely gratuitous suffering. In fact, Rowe takes the former fact (there are apparently gratuitous instances of suffering in our world) as a good reason for believing that there are genuinely gratuitous instances of suffering. Lewis argues that the problem here is that the fact that there are apparently gratuitous instances of suffering isn't a good reason for thinking there are genuine instances of this sort of suffering. Or, at least Rowe hasn't shown us why the former is a good reason to believe the latter. Rowe believes that this requires too much. In order for his argument to work *apparently* gratuitous evils must *be* a good reason for believing there are genuinely gratuitous evils. But proving that the former is a good reason for believing the latter is another project, one that Rowe believes he isn't required to fulfill in order for his argument from evil to succeed. He doesn't want to downplay the importance of that second project, but only to affirm that he doesn't need to address it in order for his belief that there are apparently gratuitous evils to be rational grounds for believing that there are genuinely gratuitous evils.[73]

Rowe turns next to address Lewis's claim that in order to be entitled to move from a belief in apparently gratuitous suffering to genuinely gratuitous suffering, we must accept the principle Lewis calls (E). Lewis thinks there is no good reason to adopt (E), and that doing so without establishing its truth begs the question against theism. Rowe disagrees. As to the matter of question begging, Rowe answers that adopting (E) begs no questions against restricted standard theism, for such a position doesn't include beliefs about God's providential handling of the world, including the evil in it. And, any who have good reason for rejecting restricted theism will also have good reason for rejecting expanded theism of one sort or another. Moreover, anyone who has grounds for accepting (E) will also have reason to reject expanded theisms like Christianity, Judaism, and Islam. But all this shows is that critics of these theistic positions would be unwise to attempt to get adherents of such religions to accept (E). It doesn't, however, show that there are no good reasons for believing (E).[74]

Rowe also disagrees that one must have good reason for holding (E) in order to move legitimately from apparently to genuinely gratuitous evil. This is so because the fact that something appears to us a certain way is itself justification that things are as they seem. He agrees that this justification can be defeated, but apart from such defeat the fact that things appear to us a certain way is rational grounds for believing that they are that way. Rowe adds that if in order to be entitled to believe that how things appear is how they are we must support some auxiliary principle (in this case (E)), we would wind up being skeptical of most things.[75]

As to (E) itself, Rowe believes that there are good reason to accept it. For one thing, it is reasonable to believe that the goods for which God allows these instances of intense suffering either are or include the good experiences of those who suffer. If so, we know many who suffer, so if the goods for which they suffer include conscious good experiences for the sufferer, we are likely to know that. While it is possible that some of these good experiences won't occur until the afterlife, it is reasonable to believe that much of that good could be realized during the lifetime of those who suffer. However, in the majority of cases involving such suffering we don't see in this life that the afflictions lead to conscious good experiences for the sufferer. Thus, there are good and rational reasons for believing in (E) and thereby bridging the logical gap between *apparently* and *genuinely* gratuitous suffering. So, even though Rowe doesn't think he must offer good grounds for accepting (E) in order to move from apparently to genuinely purposeless evils, he believes he has offered rational grounds for holding (E).[76]

Andre and Rowe

Shane Andre also wrote a response to Rowe, and in it he focuses on Rowe's espousal of friendly atheism. Andre distinguishes two types of atheism which he calls special grounds atheism (SGA) and paradoxical atheism (PA). Both are varieties of friendly atheism. SGA holds that the theist has limited knowledge, and according to that knowledge, is justified in being a theist. On the contrary, the atheist is less limited in knowledge, and as a result, has rational grounds for being an atheist. PA says the theist and atheist have the same information, and yet both are rationally justified in believing what they do.[77] Andre argues that SGA is coherent but uninteresting, while PA is interesting but incoherent.

As to SGA, the challenge is for the atheist to make good the claim that he has a superior evidential position than the theist. Atheists have tried to show this, but their success is dubious. Andre says Rowe's evidential argument against theism tries to do so, but he doubts its success. Andre argues:

> Rowe himself makes a contribution to this venture when he argues from the amount and variety of human and animal suffering that it is extremely unlikely that all of this apparently pointless evil should turn out to be morally justified. But why should we accept this inference? It is not a necessary truth that a great number and variety of cases of suffering make it probable that the world contains morally gratuitous evil, and it is not a truth which Rowe or, as far as I know, any atheist has demonstrated. Perhaps it is "reasonable" to accept the inference; at any rate, it is not demonstrably unreasonable, but that is cold comfort for the atheist, for it doesn't appear to be demonstrably unreasonable to reject the inference either.[78]

Rowe's argument may strengthen atheists in their atheism, but it is unlikely to convince sophisticated theists.

Andre says atheists often think their privileged position is like that of someone who sees a clock that says it is 3 o'clock but knows the power has been off for an hour. Someone unaware of that really thinks it is 3 o'clock. However, Andre believes the case of the theist and atheist is normally different. Atheists think instances of apparently unjustified suffering are grounds for rejecting theism, but when they point to such suffering, theists (unlike someone who really thinks it is 3 o'clock) remain unconvinced. Theists already know atheists' special "evidence," but interpret it differently. Andre concludes that "the atheist's position is dissimilar in an important respect to the familiar case where one party stands in a privileged evidential position to another party. The grave weakness of SGA is its failure to account for that difference."[79] Hence, SGA makes sense, but the one who holds it can't make a convincing case that he really is in a privileged evidential position.

As to PA, Andre argues that it is more than paradoxical; it is incoherent. Rowe illustrates PA by two people who add up a list of numbers. The first adds them three times and arrives at sum x. The second adds them twice on a calculator and gets y as the answer. However, he doesn't know that the calculator is damaged and thereby unreliable; the first person does. In this case, the first person is justified in believing 1) the sum is x, 2) the second person has access to the first person's evidence that the sum is x, and yet 3) the second person is rational in believing the sum is y.[80]

Though this sounds plausible, Andre says it doesn't work. If the first person adds the numbers three times and gives the sum to the second, they share the same evidential position at that point. However, if the second person uses the calculator and gets a different answer *but doesn't know the calculator is damaged,* then there is a difference in the evidential position of the two people. The first knows the calculator is damaged, so he can believe the second is mistaken, but agree that the second is justified in (has reasons for) his belief. However, the two no longer have the same evidence. In other words, now we are dealing again with SGA, not PA. All of this means that Rowe "fails to establish the general possibility of a position such as PA."[81] Andre's final conclusion on this whole matter is:

> We are left with the conclusion that, as far as PA is concerned, the atheist can be too friendly for his own good. He cannot admit that the theist is justified in rejecting atheism and yet has all the grounds that he, the atheist, has for accepting atheism, without undermining his own claim to be justified in accepting atheism. To make his position tolerable, the atheist must, as Rowe does, find some basis for differentiating between his grounds and those of the theist. But to do this is to abandon the paradoxical for the special grounds form of friendly atheism. The problem then is to defend the claim to be in a privileged evidential position against the attacks and counterclaims of theists and agnostics. As far as I know, neither Rowe nor any other atheist has solved that problem.[82]

Snyder and Rowe

Daniel Snyder discusses Rowe's argument from evil, but his purpose isn't merely to object to Rowe but to reform his argument into a stronger one. In this section, I shall discuss his objection to Rowe. In a later section, I'll present his corrective to Rowe. As Snyder says, Rowe's argument amounts to saying that the propositions 1) "God exists" and 2) "there are preventable pointless evils" are incompatible, and hence, gratuitous evil constitutes decisive evidence against theism. Snyder agrees with theists who think it possible to show 1) and 2) compatible. If so, Rowe's argument as presented fails. Let me explain Snyder's reasoning.

Snyder believes the case for the compatibility of 1) and 2) can be made using the free will defense. According to the free will defense, it is good for a person to be free (indeterministically) with respect to choices that bear on character development and relationships with others, including God. Having this freedom requires that each person has a *range of possible futures* from which to choose, including the possibilities of becoming both good and bad.

However, to have this range of possibilities, it isn't necessary that *any particular one* of those possibilities be realized. That is, to be free it is necessary to have a range of possibilities which include, for example, harming someone or treating someone well, but *actually choosing* to harm someone isn't necessary in order to have a range of possible actions. Hence, I must have the possibility to harm someone in order to be free, but I don't have to actualize it to be free. Suppose I do choose that possibility, i.e., I harm someone. Snyder explains what this all means:

> Now, given that the value of my possessing that range is at least comparable to the disvalue of my bringing about any possibility within it, my having that range justifies God in permitting me to harm you. None the less, my harming you does not result in a good that requires my harming you (since my having that range does not require that I harm you). Nor is my harming you necessary to prevent some equally bad or worse evil (since, were I to refrain from harming you or were I to treat you well, these would be good things). But surely, God could have prevented me from having that range, hence my harming you. My harming you, therefore, is preventable and pointless.[83]

The first sentence of the cited portion explains why evil is compatible with God's existence. The rest of the portion explains why such evil is preventable. As Snyder says, for someone to have a range of possibilities and thereby be free, God doesn't have to give that person any particular range of choices, nor does the person have to actualize any particular choice within the range God gives. Hence, Snyder says, God could have set things up so that we would be free (we would have some range of possible choices) and yet avoid particular evils (those evils wouldn't be within the realm of our possibilities). As a result, despite Rowe's claims, there exist preventable pointless evils, but their existence is justified because they are necessary to human freedom. God's existence is compatible with preventable pointless evil.[84]

Though Snyder's argument is intriguing, I am not convinced it entirely works. The key is his claim that "God could have prevented me from having that range, hence my harming you." I think everyone can agree in principle that God could prevent a specific instance of harm by giving an individual a range of choices that excludes that instance as a possibility. The significant question, however, is whether in everyone's case, God could give a range of choices that includes *no possible choice of any* instance of evil. God *can* do that by omitting choices of evil from everyone's range of possibilities. However, if God does that, he leaves out freedom as the free will defender and Snyder define it. Snyder has admitted that the kind of freedom in view requires possible choices that are bad as well as possible choices that are good.

It appears, then, that though God could prevent some specific evil by leaving it out of the possibilities, he must offer all some choices of evil if they are to have this free will. It is possible that no one would choose any of those evil actions, but God can't guarantee it, given the nature of incompatibilistic free will. He can't make it the case that each person freely chooses only the good options from the range of available choices. This makes it likely that some evil choices will be made, and if one invokes Plantinga's transworld depravity, it is likely that everyone will choose some evil.

What all of this means is that while some particular instance of evil is preventable by leaving it out of the possible choices, given indeterminism, it is impossible to guarantee prevention of all evil. The net result is that the free will defender says God's existence is compatible with evil (even pointless evil) because it is *un*preventable. He doesn't say (as Snyder claims) the evil is preventable, but compatible with God's existence, anyway. It is compatible because it is necessary to free will, a good of the highest order. To remove it all removes free will.

How does the preceding relate to Rowe's argument? Rowe's argument concludes that preventable pointless evil is incompatible with God's existence. Snyder's argument shows that specific instances of such evil are compatible with God's existence. Rowe can't answer Snyder as I have, for that would commit Rowe to the free will defense, and the free will defense answers Rowe's basic argument from evil.[85] He dare not solve one problem (Snyder's objection) by adopting a resolution which refutes his position.

Snyder thinks Rowe might respond by objecting that Snyder's example of pointless preventable evil is an instance of *moral* evil, whereas Rowe's example of the fawn is a case of *natural* evil, and thus Snyder's argument is irrelevant to Rowe's point.[86] Snyder thinks this won't save the day for Rowe for two reasons. Snyder says theists don't all agree on their account of natural evil, so it is possible the fawn case might result from human choices after all. If so, then his argument is relevant to Rowe.[87] While I have argued that some natural evil is reducible to moral evil, I think Rowe's explanation of the fawn case makes it rather clear that this natural evil has no connection to human agency. If the example doesn't rule out human participation in the act, the example can be easily adjusted to exclude any hint of moral evil. And if moral evil isn't at all involved, it is hard to see how Snyder's argument damages Rowe's case. Of course, as we noted earlier, in Rowe's further development of his argument he did offer an example of moral evil, the rape and murder of the little girl. Hence, Snyder's complaint is relevant to that example, even if it doesn't relate to the fawn example.

Snyder's second response is that even if the fawn case isn't an instance of moral evil, his objection to Rowe's argument still destroys it. Snyder says Rowe seems to think that as long as the fawn's suffering is preventable pointless evil, that is enough for it to be an instance of intense suffering which God could have prevented without losing some greater good. Snyder disagrees. He thinks his own argument shows that the fawn's suffering could be preventable and pointless without being something an omnipotent being could prevent without losing some greater good.[88] Snyder thinks the only way Rowe's argument can succeed is to show that the fawn's suffering serves neither free will nor any other possible good that would be removed if the fawn didn't suffer.[89]

In response, I find Snyder's argument here unconvincing. The fawn's suffering could be preventable and pointless and yet not something an omnipotent being would remove. This could be God's response if he doesn't remove the evil because he wants to safeguard human freedom or some other value. Since the fawn's case involves natural evil unconnected to moral evil, Snyder hasn't shown why or how letting it happen safeguards human freedom. Of course, some have argued that even natural evil is necessary to ensure free will, i.e., it is a concomitant of freedom that helps to make freedom possible. I shall consider those arguments later, but they are somewhat beside the point now. My point here is that unless Snyder can show that the fawn's suffering is a *result* of some human action (and in his 1979 article Rowe defines the case so as to exclude that possibility), not just a concomitant of a world in which people make free choices, it is hard to see how God's removal of the fawn's suffering would damage some exercise of freedom that produced the suffering, since no use of freedom did!

Well, maybe God fails to remove this pointless, preventable suffering to safeguard some value other than freedom. But what other value? A suitable environment for building souls? How would a world without the fawn's suffering be a less auspicious environment for soul-building? What other value could there be that would be lost or damaged by removing the fawn's suffering? That seems to be Rowe's ultimate point. Until Snyder offers an example of some counterbalancing or overbalancing value and explains how it would be lost if God removed this preventable, pointless evil, his argument doesn't damage Rowe's case.

Rowe Again, and Plantinga

In a more recent article ("The Evidential Argument from Evil: A Second Look"), Rowe has taken the evidential argument a step further. He begins by outlining his latest statement of the argument prior to his "second look" article.[90] Understanding that E1 refers to the death of the fawn in the forest fire and E2 is the beating, rape, and killing of the five-year-old little girl, that argument is:

P: No good we know of justifies an omnipotent, omniscient, perfectly good being (a perfect being) in permitting E1 and E2; therefore,

Q: No good at all justifies an omnipotent, omniscient, perfectly good being in permitting E1 and E2; therefore,

not-G There is no omnipotent, omniscient, perfectly good being.[91]

Rowe clarifies the meaning of P and Q and then raises various objections that have been and could be brought against this argument. After considering them, he proposes to abandon this particular argument in favor of a simpler argument. The new argument bypasses Q altogether, moving directly from P to -G. The argument is again a probability argument, so Rowe invokes Bayes' Theorem to make his case. As I noted in chapter 8, one of the elements in Bayes' Theorem is the prior probability of a hypothesis. Prior probability refers to the likelihood that the hypothesis will be true, based solely on background evidence. Rowe proposes that in this case background evidence (k) includes almost entirely information that is shared by both theists and atheists who have reflected on the problem of evil. He believes that the only way to avoid begging the question in favor of either theism or atheism is to assign P (G/k) the probability of .5. Exactly why this assignment avoids question begging and truly represents the probability of theism solely in light of background information isn't explained. But Rowe thinks that this assignment is fair to both sides. As to the other items in Bayes' Theorem as it applies to this argument, Rowe proposes that P (P/G&k) (where P stands for proposition P above, which can be abbreviated as "No good we know of justifies God in permitting E1 and E2") is also .5; and P (P/k) is .75.[92] Bayes' Theorem is:

$$P(G/P\&k) == \frac{P(G/k) \times P(P/G\&k)}{P(P/k)}$$

Using the numerical values Rowe suggests, we have:

$$P(G/P\&k) == \frac{.5 \times .5}{.75} == .333333 \text{ or } 1/3$$

Now since the prior probability of theism (G) is .5 and the probability of theism in light of evidences such as E1 and E2 is .333333, it should be clear that the facts of such evil alone lower the probability of theism and do so to the extent that theism on the whole is less likely than not to be true (a probability of 1/3 shows it to be unlikely). That means, of course, that Rowe apparently can move directly from P to -G without bothering with Q. Hence, this simpler version of his evidential argument from evil, Rowe believes, succeeds in showing that the evidence of horrendous evils such as E1 and E2 makes theism improbable.[93]

Of course, Rowe understands that lowering theism's probability to 1/3 may not be enough to warrant moving from agnosticism to square atheism; in fact, this is what Rowe believes Wykstra would say.[94] Even if we grant Wykstra this point, Rowe claims, we still can say that it has now been shown that it is more rational to hold atheism than theism.[95]

Next Rowe turns to Wykstra's argument that if there are justifying reasons for God to permit evils like E1 and E2, it is likely that we wouldn't know what those reasons are. In Wykstra's "Rowe's Noseeum Arguments from Evil," he again takes up the parent/child analogy argument and attempts to strengthen it. Rowe believes it still won't work. He argues that the most basic problem with it is that when a parent allows a child to undergo significant suffering for the sake of future goods, the parent makes a point to be with the child, comfort her, and assure her that this trial is for her ultimate good. Similarly, we would expect God to show the same kind of comfort and concern for those undergoing horrible trials. Since there are many instances of intense suffering where God's care and concern are nowhere evident, it is most reasonable to believe either that there is no God or that if there is one, he doesn't have reasons that would justify putting his creatures through horrible afflictions.[96]

Rowe concludes by considering whether P is true or false. He believes that it is true, and that we can agree when we reflect on various goods that God might intend when he allows his creature to endure evils such as E1 and E2. No matter what good we think of, Rowe believes that upon reflection we will agree either that it isn't good enough to warrant evils like E1 and E2, or that an omniscient and omnipotent being could bring about such goods without having to permit E1 and E2.[97]

In "Degenerate Evidence and Rowe's New Evidential Argument from Evil," Alvin Plantinga addresses this revised form of Rowe's argument. Plantinga raises a variety of objections to Rowe's new argument, including questioning why the appropriate probability for the prior probability of theism is .5 and how Rowe's assessment of the numerical values of other elements in Bayes' Theorem is reached.[98]

When Plantinga turns to address Rowe's argument directly, he finds it problematic. Plantinga explains that there are theistic arguments of a similar form and nature that can be constructed. Hence, if Rowe's argument makes atheism more probable, then these theistic arguments shift things in favor of theism. To make this point, Plantinga asks us to consider several propositions like P which claim something positive toward theism. For example:

P*:   Neither E_1 nor E_2 is such that we know that no known good justifies a perfect being in permitting it.

P**:   No evil we know of is such that we know that no perfect being is justified by some known good in permitting it.

P***:   No evil we know of is such that we know that no perfect being would permit it.[99]

Using P*, Plantinga constructs an argument using Bayes' Theorem that has the same form as Rowe's. Moreover, following Rowe's assignment of numerical values to the various items in Bayes' Theorem, Plantinga plugs those values into his own argument. The result is that now, using Bayes' Theorem, we have an argument that shows that theism is more probable than not. Since this argument is relevantly similar to Rowe's, Plantinga believes we can see this as a counterbalancing argument to Rowe's.[100]

Plantinga explains that using the same argument form and some other fact about the world (e.g., that you are barefoot or that some specific person wins the lottery), we can construct a series of arguments in favor of theism and a counterbalancing set of arguments favoring atheism.[101] This should strike us as odd and cause us to wonder if there isn't some basic problem with all of these arguments. Plantinga believes that there is a problem with the barefoot and lottery arguments, and it is that they are arguments from degenerate evidence. He explains the nature of such arguments as follows:

> to give an argument from degenerate evidence, you propose to support a proposition A by showing that A is probable with respect to a part of your evidence which is such that there is an isomorphic part of your evidence with respect to which -A is at least equally probable. Clearly no argument from degenerate evidence will be of much use to anyone: clearly I don't advance the discussion by pointing to some proper part of my total evidence with respect to which G is probable, if there is a structurally isomorphic proper part of my total evidence with respect to which -G is probable.[102]

Plantinga affirms that he believes the ultimate problem with Rowe's argument is that it is in fact an argument from degenerate evidence. If so, then it will be of little or no use to anyone, and it certainly can't serve as adequate grounds for dismissing theism as improbable.[103]

Rowe has briefly responded to Plantinga's essay on degenerate evidence. He raises various points, but I focus on two which relate to what I have described above from Plantinga's paper. Plantinga argued that we can write arguments that are parallel to Rowe's argument from P to -G, but arrive at the opposite conclusion. Rowe considers whether his own arguments do in fact parallel precisely the reasoning in Plantinga's barefoot argument, and he argues that there is a significant difference. In regard to the barefoot argument, whether or not one is barefoot is *"evidentially irrelevant* to whether God exists or does not exist."[104] Suppose that our background information, k, tells us that one is barefoot about half of the time. Hence, the probability of (B/G and k) is .5, just as is the probability of (B/-G and k). From this the nonbeliever uses addition to infer (-G or B) from B and produces a statement that lowers the probability of God's existence; the theist uses addition to infer (G or B) from B and produces a statement that lowers the likelihood of God's nonexistence.

In contrast, Rowe asks us to compare what happens in his argument, and we'll see that the reasoning differs from Plantinga's barefoot arguments. We reflect on the goods we know of and also on E1 and E2, and we come to see that none of them justifies E1 and E2. If so, we have every reason to believe X ("No known good has J to E1 and E2"—here J stands for "has a justifying relation to"). But from X we can logically infer that "No good we know of justifies God in permitting E1 and E2," and since that proposition is logically equivalent to P, it is entailed by -G and hence lowers the probability of G.[105] It should be clear, Rowe thinks, that this line of reasoning doesn't proceed as the reasoning in the barefoot argument does. The difference is that while B is evidentially irrelevant to whether or not God exists, X is evidentially very relevant to that question. B is as likely regardless of whether or not God exists, because it is evidentially irrelevant to whether he exists. In contrast, X makes -G more probable. Hence, the reasoning in Rowe's argument significantly differs from that in Plantinga's barefoot and lottery arguments, and thus offers us reason to reject the belief that Plantinga's line of argument damages Rowe's evidential argument from evil.[106]

What about Plantinga's charge that Rowe's argument is an argument from degenerate evidence? Rowe disagrees, because X alone, given our background information k, is enough to render God's existence less likely than it was apart from X, and that shows that this argument isn't an argument from degenerate evidence. Rowe explains:

> For Plantinga stresses that in an argument from degenerate evidence a part of your evidence (e.g., B or G) makes a certain proposition (G) probable when there is "an isomorphic part of your evidence" (B or ~G) with respect to which (~G) is at least *"equally probable."* But, as we've seen, neither (P) nor (X), from which we directly inferred (P), is such that it makes G anywhere near as probable as ~G. For unlike B, which leaves G as probable as ~G, X makes ~G more likely than G.[107]

In chapter 12, I plan to offer my own responses to the evidential argument from evil. For now, I offer several comments about the Rowe/Plantinga interchange. In interacting with Plantinga's barefoot argument, etc., Rowe repeatedly claims that Plantinga said that the reasoning in the barefoot argument *"precisely"* parallels that in Rowe's evidential argument from evil. Since B is evidentially irrelevant to either G or ~G, Rowe complains that his argument doesn't *precisely* parallel the reasoning of the barefoot argument.[108] However, Plantinga doesn't use such language. Rather he says that the reasoning in the barefoot and lottery arguments is "relevantly similar" to that in Rowe's argument.[109]

This difference in wording may seem unimportant, but I think not. Rowe repeats that Plantinga thinks the reasoning in his barefoot argument is *precisely* parallel to that in Rowe's argument. Doesn't that suggest that the reasoning had better be "identical" or very close to it? It seems to do so, but then all Rowe has to do is show some difference between the two arguments and they aren't precisely parallel. On the other hand, two arguments can be relevantly similar without being precisely parallel. Plantinga's point isn't that they are identical, anyway. The point about each that concerns him is the argument form and strategy, and the assignment of numerical values to the various items in Bayes' Theorem. Plantinga's and Rowe's arguments are similar for they follow the same form and strategy, and assign the same numerical values to the different items in Bayes' Theorem. But there is a difference, the one Rowe notes about the nature of the evidence invoked in each argument. However, while that difference may suggest that the two arguments aren't precisely parallel, it doesn't refute Plantinga's claim that they are similar and relevantly so. Typically, when one can write two arguments whose conclusions contradict one another and yet they both use the same argument form, this suggests that there is something wrong with this line of reasoning altogether. And I take this to be at least part of what Plantinga is saying in offering these barefoot and lottery arguments. He takes that to be damaging to Rowe's claims that his argument succeeds, and I agree.

What I find also to be troubling here is that Plantinga's argument that his P* makes theism more probable doesn't get the treatment it deserves. That is, Rowe complains that Plantinga's barefoot and lottery arguments don't proceed precisely as does his argument from evil. However, before Plantinga introduces those arguments, he constructs an argument from P* which shares the same form as Rowe's evidential argument from evil, and assigns the same numerical values to each element in Bayes' Theorem as does Rowe's evidential argument from P. It is this argument from P* which Plantinga presents as the counterbalance to Rowe's argument from P. The two arguments come to contradictory conclusions, use the same form and strategy, and assign the same numerical values to the various items in Bayes' Theorem. Rowe certainly can't dismiss Plantinga's argument from P* as he did Plantinga's barefoot and lottery arguments, because P* is definitely evidentially relevant to whether or not God exists. So, how does Rowe respond? His answer is that P* has its own counterbalancing argument, but his argument from evil (argument from P) isn't that argument. I find myself unconvinced by this assessment; hence I don't see that Rowe's response adequately addresses Plantinga's point in raising his argument from P*.

Finally, I find Plantinga's claims that Rowe's argument is one from degenerate evidence more compelling than Rowe's avowal that it isn't. However, in the background is a very fundamental point that Plantinga has made repeatedly in discussing the evidential argument, namely, that in order to construct a convincing probability argument, one must make the probability judgment on the basis of total evidence. Isn't that at least in part Plantinga's complaint that moving from P alone to -G isn't sufficient to make the case? Of course, one can water down background knowledge to the point of making it totally innocuous to any and all views and then choose one type or piece of evidence from the sum total of all relevant evidence and make a case for one's preferred conclusion. But that surely can't be taken as a conclusive argument on the matter. Plantinga claims that in simplifying the argument from evil, Rowe has made it weaker than earlier versions. That is so, because "an analysis of purely formal features of the argument shows that it is counterbalanced by other arguments of the same structure and strength for a conclusion inconsistent with Rowe's conclusion, and hence for the denial of Rowe's conclusion."[110] I believe that Plantinga's paper successfully shows this to be true, and I agree with him. Moreover, I add that since to my knowledge none of Rowe's statements of the evidential argument incorporates *total evidence,* Rowe's argument in its various forms cannot be convincing. But more on all of this in chapter 12 when I offer my own views on the evidential argument.[111]

MICHAEL MARTIN

For many years Michael Martin has critiqued various theistic attempts to answer the evidential problem of evil. In fact, Martin was one of the earlier contemporaries to argue that evil is evidence against God's existence, and it is instructive to see how he argued his case.

Martin begins by admitting that 1) "God is all-powerful"; 2) "God is all-good"; and 3) "evil exists in great abundance" are logically compatible. And he admits that proposition 3) per se doesn't contradict 1) and 2). However, he thinks that unless certain assumptions are added, evil in great abundance does conflict with God's existence. Those assumptions involve the notions that God has a morally sufficient reason for allowing the evil and/or that the evil is logically necessary. Barring those assumptions, however, evil in great abundance is *prima facie* evidence against God's existence.[112]

Propositions 1)-3) don't entail a contradiction. However, Martin thinks those three *plus* 4) ("the existence of evil in great abundance isn't logically necessary and there is no sufficient reason for God to allow evil in great abundance") entail a fifth proposition. That proposition is "evil doesn't exist in great abundance." Of course, that conflicts with proposition 3), so the set appears to generate a contradiction.[113] So evil in abundance appears to be *prima facie* evidence against God's existence.

Despite these logical difficulties for theism, Martin admits that they offer no *inductive* reason to doubt God's existence, unless there is good reason to think proposition 4) is true. Martin sees no *a priori* way to prove it true, but notes that all attempts to show it false have failed. That is,

> apologists down through the ages have failed to specify a sufficient reason for God allowing evil; they have failed to show that this is the best of all logically possible worlds. These failures should give us some confidence in (4). For if every attempt to specify a needed explanation fails over a long period of time this failure gives one good grounds to suppose that an explanation is *impossible* [italics mine].[114]

This is strong language indeed, but Martin goes even further. He says that even if failure to offer a sufficient reason for God allowing evil provides indirect evidence for God's nonexistence, theists might still save the day by offering other positive evidence for God's existence that would outweigh the negative evidence (i.e., evil in abundance) against his existence. Martin, however, responds with the truly amazing claim that "it is generally acknowledged even by many religious persons that the traditional arguments for the existence of God are bankrupt. There is no positive evidence for belief in God that could outweigh the negative evidence."[115]

It is quite a jump in logic to move from the bankruptcy of arguments for God's existence (and of course, that claim is debatable) to the conclusion that no evidence for belief in God could outweigh the negative evidence. Without mentioning any other positive evidence, it is hard to see how Martin is justified in his claims. One would at least like to entertain some of that positive evidence and hear Martin's argument as to why it can't possibly ("no positive evidence *could* outweigh") outweigh the negative evidence. Martin never offers a hint about what the other positive evidence is or why it can't outweigh the negative evidence.

Having offered the preceding line of argument, Martin then presents a more formal statement of his argument from evil as follows:

(1)   If (a) there is no positive evidence that P, and
            (b) unless one assumes that R, evidence E would
                  falsify that P, and
            (c) despite repeated attempts no good reason has
                  been given for believing that R,
       then on rational grounds one should believe that P is false.
(2)   There is no positive evidence that God exists.
(3)   The existence of evil in great abundance would falsify the existence
       of God unless one assumes either that God has sufficient reason for
       allowing the existence of evil in great abundance or that evil in great
       abundance is logically necessary.
(4)   Despite repeated attempts to do so, no one has provided a good rea-
       son to believe that God has sufficient reason to allow evil to exist in
       great abundance or that evil in great abundance is logically necessary.
       _____
(5)   ∴ On rational grounds one should believe that God does not exist.[116]

Martin grants that this argument is formulated as a deductive argument, but then recasts it as an inductive argument as follows:

(1) Evidence E falsifies H unless R.
(2) Repeated attempts to establish R have failed.
(3) There is no positive evidence that H.
     _____
(4) - H.[117]

In this case, the conclusion isn't established by the premises, but is made prob-able relative to them.

Martin concludes by raising and answering three objections that might be lodged against his argument. First, some might complain that Martin offers only two kinds of explanations relevant to rescuing the theist's posi-tion. Those explanations are that God has a sufficient reason for allowing evil and that evil is logically necessary. Some might argue that there could be other reasons why evil is present, reasons compatible with God's existence. Martin responds that it is hard to see what other considerations there could be since he thinks these two handle all the possibilities. Nonetheless, Martin welcomes theists to offer some other reasons compatible with theism that evil might be in our world. However, he believes theists' failure to provide other explana-tions is good grounds for thinking no others exist.[118]

A second possible objection is that though God's existence doesn't explain evil's existence, his nonexistence explains nothing either, including evil. Martin's initial response is that while God's nonexistence doesn't explain evil's existence, that misses the point. The point is that God's existence not only fails to explain why evil exists, but the facts of evil also count as inductive evidence for disbelief in God. Evil becomes especially significant evidence, since there is no positive evidence for theism, and since theism's assumptions that God has a morally sufficient reason for allowing evil and/or that evil is logically necessary seem wrong in light of inductive evidence to the contrary.[119]

Martin then thinks it necessary to return to the claim that God's nonexistence explains nothing. He agrees, but thinks various nontheistic hypotheses can explain evil. He writes:

> Natural evil can be explained in terms of certain natural laws; for example, the birth of a defective baby by genetics. Moral evil can be explained in terms of certain psychological or sociological theories; for example the murder of an innocent bystander by the police in terms of motives and beliefs. There need be no general explanation for all evil.[120]

Martin grants that some naturalistic explanations may not be too compelling, but he still thinks "there is *no* reason to suppose, however, that *all* such explanations would be false."[121] This is again truly amazing. Without much consideration of any, let alone all, naturalistic explanations, Martin wants us to believe that some of them must be true. On the other hand, without any argument as to why traditional arguments for God's existence are totally bankrupt and without offering and assessing any other theistic evidences, Martin wants us to agree that the traditional theistic arguments don't work, and no other positive evidence for theism could outweigh the negative evidence of evil. I see no reason to accept Martin's assessment of the plausibility of naturalistic explanations of evil or of the value of theistic arguments. If he, with intellectual imperialism, can dismiss all theistic evidences without consideration, then the theist should be allowed to "return the compliment"!

Finally, Martin says some might reject his argument, because thinking evil's existence in great abundance is *prima facie* evidence against God's existence relies on an intuitively grasped relation between evil and God's nonexistence. But such intuitions are unreliable and can't be trusted. Martin thinks it enough to respond that he has shown that "the *prima facie* conflict between the existence of God and the existence of evil can be defined and defended without appeal to intuition. The relation was defined in terms of entailment under certain conditions."[122]

Basinger and Martin

David Basinger thinks Martin's argument is problematic and that its problems are symptomatic of difficulties that beset inductive arguments from evil more generally. After reconstructing Martin's basic argument, Basinger claims that it ultimately rests on a belief that an omnipotent, omniscient, wholly good God could have done better. In fact, without that assumption, it is hard to see how the existence of evil (even in abundance) is good inductive evidence against God's existence.[123]

If atheists believe that God could have done better, says Basinger, it is because they normally assume that one or both of the following are true:

(1)   An omnipotent, omniscient, wholly good God can create any logi-
       cally possible state of affairs—for example, he could have created a
       world in which moral agents would as a matter of fact always freely
       choose to do what is right;

(2)   An omnipotent, omniscient, wholly good God, by benevolently inter-
       vening in the lives of individuals and/or in the natural environment
       could greatly reduce the amount of evil in our present world—for
       example, he could cure small children of cancer.[124]

Basinger agrees that if either proposition is true, the atheist is right to think God could have created a better world. But Basinger thinks neither is right. The first is wrong, because granting indeterminism, God can't create the world envisioned. Basinger argues this point by simply restating Plantinga's free will defense argument that God can't create a world in which he makes agents freely choose good (see my chapter 4 for details of Plantinga's argumentation).

Some might grant the point of the free will defense, but then respond that God should have created no world at all or a world with automata who always do what is right. Basinger replies that while God could have chosen either of those options, the atheist must offer evidence that either of those creative options would have produced a more valuable state of affairs than the option God chose (a world with indeterministically free beings and the evil they produce). Since no argument to that effect is forthcoming, it is dubious that God could do what proposition (1) suggests or that he should have opted for any of these other creative alternatives.[125]

What about proposition (2)? If it is true, the atheist can still complain that there is a better world God could have and should have made. Basinger believes it is false as well. As it relates to moral evil, it runs into the same problem that confronts proposition (1). But, what about natural evil?

Basinger offers two reasons why (2) fails if natural evil is in view. His initial reason is that (2) would involve God intervening in our natural world repeatedly to overturn or circumvent the natural order to avoid evil. The only other way for God to do what (2) says is to change the natural system in some significant fashion. With either option there is a problem. Basinger explains:

> it seems extremely doubtful that God could continually circumvent or modify natural (including psychological) laws in a widespread manner without destroying our belief that anticipated consequences will normally follow given actions—that is, without destroying our belief in predictable regularities. But if we can no longer have the assurance that given consequences will normally follow given actions, we must seriously question whether we can retain a meaningful concept of "free choice."[126]

This is a refrain we have already heard and shall hear again in subsequent chapters, so I needn't belabor it here. It simply says we need the natural order as is in order to ensure the exercise of human freedom.

In addition, Basinger raises a second challenge to (2). He claims that even if God modified the natural system so as to remove isolated instances of natural evil, that wouldn't necessarily result in a significant increase in the net amount of good present in the world. Thus, the atheist must show that "in the context of the entire world system of which it would be a part, such modification would actually result in a significant increase in the net amount of good in comparison to the actual world."[127] Basinger thinks no atheist has yet met this challenge. Until someone does, his objection is good reason to think proposition (2) is false.

The net result, according to Basinger, is that the atheist cannot prove that there is some better world than ours which God could have created. But unless the atheist can show that, pointing to the evil in our world cannot serve as convincing evidence against God's existence. Martin's evidential argument (and others that incorporate the idea that God could create a better world) can't succeed.

Before turning to Basinger's other objections to Martin's project, a brief comment is in order. While I don't hold the free will defense nor use it with respect to either moral or natural evil, I believe Basinger's appeal to it demonstrates some major problems in Martin's argument against theism. Martin says there is no positive evidence for God's existence which outweighs the negative evidence of evil. He also says theists have failed to offer a good reason why God would allow evil in the world. However, both of those claims are made apart from presenting and critiquing any theistic evidences. Basinger could have responded to Martin's complaints by saying nothing more than "yes, there is evidence, and yes, there are good reasons." Had he done so, his "case" would be no better or worse than Martin's support for his views. But Basinger chose a better path. He offered specific evidence and reasons why God couldn't create a better world. Whether or not one agrees with his views, one must grant that if indeterminism is accepted, then Basinger's explanations offer reasons why there is evil in the amount in which we find it in our world. Those reasons are at least good enough to show God's existence logically compatible with evil. From an indeterminist's perspective, they do even more; they show that it is probable God exists and has a morally sufficient reason for allowing the evil in our world.

My complaint with Martin in this matter, then, is that he is ready to end the debate and declare atheism the winner too quickly. He should have entertained evidence of the sort Basinger offers and explained why it is wrong before he concluded that theists have offered no good reasons to think God has a morally sufficient reason for allowing the evil in our world. Though Basinger wrote after Martin's article appeared, Basinger's work is based on Plantinga's free will defense, and that material was certainly available to Martin when he wrote his article.

Perhaps Martin would reply that he would have considered this kind of evidence more specifically, but it doesn't offer *good* reasons for God allowing evil. This brings us to Basinger's final complaint with Martin and with inductive arguments from evil in general. Basinger argues that key terms in these arguments are extremely ambiguous, and that ambiguity makes it very hard to believe the arguments succeed. Basinger explains:

> Martin and other atheologians who utilize such argumentation continually use such phrases as "positive evidence," "good reasons" and "rational grounds" throughout their discussions. But what exactly are these phrases to mean in the present context? What exactly, for example, must be true concerning a piece of data before it can be considered "positive evidence" for or against God's existence? And who is to make such a decision? The theist? The atheologian? Both? Or let us consider the concept of "rationality." Must the atheologian agree that the theist has plausible responses to (supposed) difficulties such as evil before theistic belief can be considered rational? Or is theistic belief rational as long as it is self-consistent and the atheologian has not conclusively demonstrated its implausibility? Martin appears to adopt the former criterion, but why is this superior to the latter? In short, a great deal of ambiguity surrounds the key terms in the general atheological argument in question.[128]

As Basinger explains, this ambiguity wouldn't necessarily be devastating if theists and atheists could agree on how to use these terms and evaluate various arguments and evidences. But they don't. Instead, they are both likely to evaluate arguments and evidences in light of their presuppositions—in particular, their commitment to either theism or atheism. For example, in the thinking of some atheists, the undeserved suffering of even one person outweighs any amount of good present in our world. A theist might say (as Basinger does) this suffering occurs as a result of the exercise of human freedom, and freedom is a value that outweighs the suffering produced when people abuse that freedom. That is God's reason for allowing the evil, and it is a good enough reason to exonerate God. In response, don't be surprised if the atheist responds (given his belief about how bad unjust suffering is) that human freedom isn't a good reason (or good enough reason) for God to allow evil. But then, who is right, the atheist or the theist? How can we decide without begging the question? Basinger thinks there is no way to do so, but then evidential arguments from evil can't succeed. He concludes:

> In short, it seems to me that inductive inter-world view discussions concerning metaphysical issues ultimately come down to a "difference of opinion." Accordingly, I must agree with Alvin Plantinga, who has recently argued that, since the probability with respect to belief or disbelief in God is relative to one's noetic structure, the whole program of an atheologian attempting to demonstrate that belief in God is irrational (or vice versa) is totally misconceived.[129]

I'm not ready to go as far as Plantinga, but the fundamental point Basinger and Plantinga make seems hard to dispute. That is, arguments based on probability and conclusions that are probability judgments are likely to reflect one's presuppositions. Hence, it will be very hard to avoid begging the question when using or assessing such arguments. This is detrimental to a theistic case that theism is probable, but it is also destructive of inductive arguments from evil against theism. Since the atheist points to evil as evidence against the probability that God exists, in this case the problem of question begging most directly hampers the chances of *the atheist's* project succeeding. He may convince atheists, but that may be all. If so, that isn't much, since they already reject theism.

DANIEL SNYDER AND SURPLUS EVIL

As already noted, Daniel Snyder begins with Rowe's argument from evil. Snyder believes it doesn't succeed as Rowe formulated it, but he thinks it can work if it is reformulated in terms of surplus evil. The key premise in Rowe's argument is his first premise: there exist instances of intense suffering which an omnipotent being could have prevented without thereby losing some greater good or permitting some evil equally bad or worse. Snyder believes surplus evils are instances of such evils.

What does Snyder mean by surplus evil? He offers first an illustration and then a definition. Snyder believes cases of serial killing involve surplus evil. He uses as an example Harrison Graham's slaying of seven women in Philadelphia a few years ago. Graham lured the women to his apartment with a promise of drugs, and then strangled them during sex. Appealing to his argument against Rowe, Snyder says that according to the free will defense, none of those particular murders per se was necessary for Graham to have a hand in shaping his character. However, Graham's having the power to bring them about (even if unused) was necessary.[130]

Now Snyder is ready to make his point about surplus evil. Granting what he has said about Graham having power to bring about these murders in order to have a significant hand in shaping his own character, is it really true that he must commit all seven for that to be so? Suppose Graham has already committed five murders (all instances of pointless suffering), and has lured the sixth victim to his apartment. Snyder says:

> Presumably, the free-will theodicist would have us believe that if God restricts the range of possible actions open to Graham so as to prevent him from killing his sixth and seventh victims, God would prevent him from having as significant a role as is good for him to have in becoming the man he wills to be. Furthermore, it is of at least as great a value that Graham have this particular range of possibilities open to him than that he be prevented from having that range; indeed, the value of his having that range is at least comparable to the disvalue of his raping and strangling his sixth and seventh victims.[131]

According to Snyder, in a case like this, there is something deeply wrong in thinking that Graham needs to be allowed to commit the sixth and seventh murders in order to have freedom to shape his character. Whatever value for shaping one's character there is in having freedom to kill others, it has already been achieved by the time the first five victims are killed. "Despite the value attending Graham's having it within his power to slay his sixth and seventh victims, that goodness is outweighed by the disvalue of his raping and strangling his sixth and seventh victims."[132] Before Graham killed anyone, having the freedom and exercising it may have been values that outweighed the evil such abuse of freedom brought. But by the time Graham killed his fifth victim, there is no way the power to kill the next two is a value so great that it outweighs the evil to be done. God should have stopped the sixth and seventh killings. If he had, he wouldn't have hampered Graham's character development. Those killings, therefore, are surplus pointless evils, and they show that the first premise of Rowe's argument is true.

After offering the example, Snyder turns to definition. He defines surplus evil as follows:

> E is a *surplus evil* just in case the disvalue of E outweighs the value of the range of real possibilities to which E belongs. In the context of free will, E is a surplus evil just in case the disvalue of E outweighs the value of E being within the range of possible actions performable by someone.[133]

Snyder then says that all surplus evils are pointless, but not all pointless evils are surplus evils. That is, suppose there was *one* instance of a given evil act. That evil act might be necessary as a possibility in order to ensure that its doer is allowed freedom to make choices that will contribute to her character development. And so she does it, but the evil she does is still a pointless evil. In this case, the pointless evil isn't surplus. However, if she does many of those same pointless acts, then some of them are not only pointless but surplus.[134] What strikes us about a pointless but non-surplus evil act is that it isn't required for any good end, i.e., it is simply pointless. What strikes us about a surplus evil is that it is too much, that it isn't worth it.[135]

Before returning to Rowe's argument, Snyder notes that the free will defender dare not admit the existence of surplus evils. To do so would admit that there are some evils whose disvalue exceeds the value of having the freedom to produce them. But to admit that would be to admit that free will does not in fact justify these surplus evils.[136] Hence, whereas Snyder believes the free will defense can possibly defeat the problem of gratuitous evil, it can't successfully answer the problem of surplus evil.

At this point, the corrective to Rowe's argument is obvious. Preventable pointless evil is compatible with God's existence, but preventable surplus evil is not. Thus, Rowe's argument succeeds once it is rewritten in terms of preventable surplus evil. Snyder argues that it is clearly true that there are surplus preventable evils that God could eliminate. An omniscient and wholly good being would prevent any surplus evil he could. So, it follows that an omniscient, omnipotent, and wholly good being does not exist.[137]

I plan to respond later to this argument from surplus evils, but I believe it is a good point at which to end this chapter. This argument raises a clearly different challenge to theism than does a problem about the apparent gratuitousness of evil. Whether the problem of surplus evil is ultimately different from the problem of the quantity of evil or any of the other problems of evil addressed in this book remains to be seen. Likewise, a crucial question is whether there actually are any instances of surplus evil. Snyder thinks so, and thinks their existence destroys the free will defense. I doubt the free will defender, let alone other theists, will be ready to give up so easily. Moreover, it seems that at the end of the discussion, we may wind up right where Basinger says inductive arguments of this sort typically do. Convinced atheists will believe there are genuinely surplus evils, while convinced theists will disagree. More on this and the other evidential problems in subsequent chapters.[138]

10

THEISTS AND THE EVIDENTIAL ARGUMENT FROM EVIL

As with the logical problem of evil, Alvin Plantinga is the theist who has addressed the evidential problem in the greatest detail. Plantinga has discussed the evidential problem in three general ways. Each raises issues that are both philosophically significant in general and broaden our understanding of the evidential problem in particular.

Because Plantinga's treatment of the evidential problem is so significant, I shall devote this chapter entirely to it. However, I shall present only his first two approaches, for the third leaves the evidential argument per se and asks whether belief in God is properly basic for the theist. If it is, Plantinga thinks theists are within their epistemic rights in believing in God, apart from how the existence of evil affects that belief.[1]

PLANTINGA'S *NATURE OF NECESSITY* DISCUSSION

In *The Nature of Necessity* Plantinga discusses the evidential problem briefly, and focuses on what it means to confirm or disconfirm something by evidence. According to Plantinga,

> A proposition *p confirms* a proposition *q* if *q* is more probable than not on *p* alone; if, that is, *q* would be more probable than not-*q*, with respect to what we know, if *p* were the only thing we knew that was relevant to *q*. And let us say that *p* disconfirms *q* if *p* confirms the denial of *q*.[2]

Plantinga then offers the following propositions:

> (37) All the evil in the world is broadly moral evil; and every world that God could have actualized and that contains as much moral good as the actual world displays, contains at least 10^{13} turps of evil.

(39)   Every world that God could have actualized and that contains less than 10^{13} turps of evil, contains less broadly moral good and a less favourable over-all balance of good and evil than the actual world contains.

(40)   There are 10^{13} turps of evil.

(41)   God is the omnipotent, omniscient, and morally perfect creator of the world; all the evil in the world is broadly moral evil; and every world that God could have actualized and that contains as much moral good as the actual world displays, contains at least 10^{13} turps of evil.

(42)   God is the omnipotent, omniscient, and morally perfect creator of the world; and every world that God could have actualized and that contains less than 10^{13} turps of evil, contains less broadly moral good and a less favourable over-all balance of good and evil than the actual world contains.[3]

Given his definitions of confirmation and disconfirmation, Plantinga argues that (40) disconfirms neither (37), (39), (41), nor (42). But if one proposition confirms another, then it confirms every proposition the other entails. Likewise, if one proposition disconfirms another, it disconfirms all propositions the other entails. Propositions (41) and (42) entail proposition (1) ("God is omniscient, omnipotent, and wholly good"), but since (40) disconfirms neither (41) nor (42), it can't disconfirm (1).[4]

This doesn't end the matter, however, for (41) and/or (42) may be improbable with respect to (40) *plus* our total evidence. Plantinga says (41) involves the notion that evil not due to human agency is due to the free agency of *other* free (incompatibilistically speaking) creatures. Though others may believe this is absurd, that doesn't mean they have evidence against it. If there is evidence against it, Plantinga doesn't know what it is, so modern *predispositions* against believing in angels and demons can't count for much in an evidential argument.[5]

According to Plantinga, we shouldn't conclude from the preceding that total evidence *doesn't* disconfirm (41) or (42). There is so much evidence, and it is so amorphous that it may in fact disconfirm theism. Plantinga, however, says there is no reason to think it does. This is, of course, a more modest claim than saying total evidence definitely doesn't disconfirm theism.

The net result is that neither by itself nor with other things we know can evil render God's existence impossible or even improbable. There is no good evidential argument from evil against theism. Evil may create a religious problem for individuals, but that requires pastoral care, not philosophical discussion.[6]

Chrzan, Langtry, and Plantinga

Keith Chrzan sets forth Plantinga's *Nature of Necessity* argument, and then proposes to draft an argument of the same form which incorporates patently absurd premises. This, he believes, will show that Plantinga's argument is flawed. In particular, he believes both Plantinga's argument and his own counterexample contain three logical errors which doom them.[7]

Chrzan portrays Plantinga's *Nature of Necessity* argument as follows:

(1)   "p disconfirms q if not-q is more probable than q on p;"

(2)   "if p disconfirms q, p disconfirms every proposition that entails q;"

(3)   "All the evil in the world is broadly moral evil; and every world that God could have actualized and that contains as much moral good as the actual world displays, contains at least 10^{13} turps of evil;"

(4)   "God is the omnipotent, omniscient, and morally perfect creator of the world; all the evil in the world is broadly moral evil; and every world that God could have actualized and that contains as much moral good as the actual world displays, contains at least 10^{13} turps of evil;"

(5)   (E) does not disconfirm (3);

(6)   Therefore, (E) does not disconfirm (4);

(7)   (4) entails (G);

(8)   "therefore, the existence of the amount of evil actually displayed in the world does not render improbable the existence of an omnipotent, omniscient, and wholly good God."[8]

Adopting Plantinga's argument structure, Chrzan offers a counterexample. Chrzan introduces us to Bobby. Bobby is a good boy who wouldn't disobey his mother (proposition B), but Mom catches him stealing cookies after barring him from the cookie jar (proposition C). Bobby's mother tells him he isn't a good boy, because he disobeyed her demand about the cookies. Bobby reminds her that she knows, however, that he is a good boy.[9] The following, says Chrzan, is Bobby's argument which uses a form like Plantinga's argument about evil:

(1)   p disconfirms q if not-q is more probable than q on p;

(2)   if p disconfirms q, p disconfirms every proposition that entails q;

(9)   Mischievous invisible gnomes dragged me to the cookie jar and forced cookies down my throat;

(10)   I am a good boy and would never deliberately disobey; unfortunately, mischievous invisible gnomes dragged me to the kitchen and shoved the cookies into my mouth;

(11)   (C) does not disconfirm (9);

(12)   Therefore, (C) does not disconfirm (10);

(13)   (10) entails (B);

(14)   Therefore (C) does not disconfirm (B).[10]

Chrzan thinks Bobby's mother shouldn't fall for his argument. It is infected with the same three errors that beset Plantinga's defense. First, Chrzan claims that Plantinga subtly withdraws G and E from the debate. He does this by presupposing they are compatible and smuggling them into premises (3) and (4). Consider, for example, (3) (Plantinga's [37]). Chrzan complains that this premise entails E, so E can't disconfirm it. It is just E augmented by enough mitigating circumstances to accommodate G with logical consistency.[11] Since that is so, however, Chrzan's further claim is that Plantinga has simply added G to (3) to invent (4) (Plantinga's [41]). Since (4) implies both E and G, neither can disconfirm it. Chrzan then adds,

> To the extent that he suggests that the atheist must deny (5) and (6), however, Plantinga distorts his opponent's case. As the conjunction of (E) and (G), (4) is just the unlikely entity that drives the atheological induction in the first place. The atheist argues not that (E) renders (3) or (4) improbable, but that (3) and (4) are internally improbable.[12]

In other words, the atheist doesn't claim that evil renders (3) and (4) improbable (as [5] and [6] assert). They are already improbable even before one considers their probability in light of evil's existence.

Chrzan believes this means Plantinga's strategy is to shift the burden of proof to the atheist. Plantinga tries to establish (4) by lack of disproof. All of this, however, makes this an all or nothing case (no middle ground of probability is allowed at all). Either the atheist's "argument succeeds with strict deductive rigor or it fails completely. Plantinga does not so much defeat induction as he denies its very existence."[13] There is no reason the atheist should accept (4) any more than Bobby's mom should accept (10). The burden of proof must rest on Bobby (and Plantinga), not on Mom or the atheist. Hence, "Plantinga totally misconstrues the atheistic project."[14]

Chrzan's second objection is that even if Plantinga is allowed to use (4), he can't assert (6) without help from the following implicit premise which Chrzan thinks is false:

(1.5)   q is not less probable than not-q on p if possibly p and q co-pertain.[15]

This implicit premise allows Plantinga to make more out of the logical consistency of G and E. However, Chrzan believes he can describe a possible world in which the logical compatibility of two propositions doesn't make them probable. Instead of p and q, substitute the following:

(T)   Rex holds one of the 1,000,000 tickets to the $1,000,000 state lottery; and
(W)   Rex will win the lottery.[16]

It should be obvious, claims Chrzan, that though (T) and (W) are logically compatible, the two together aren't probable, for the probability of (W) on (T) is one in a million. Chrzan concludes:

> What Plantinga needs, but fails, to supply for (6) is
> (1.5') q is not less probable than not on p if the probability of q given p equals or exceeds 0.5.
>
> He needs more than the bare logical co-possibility of (G) and (E) [via (1), (1.5) and (4)]; again, he must show probability [via (1), (1.5'), and (4)] to assert non-disconfirmation. This he has not done.[17]

Chrzan offers a third objection to Plantinga. Plantinga says one proposition disconfirms another if, given the first, the denial of the second is more likely than its affirmation. If this account of disconfirmation is correct, Chrzan thinks there is a problem. Consider the example of the lottery ([T] and [W]). Rex's ticket, on Plantinga's notion of disconfirmation, disconfirms hopes of winning the lottery, because "not-(W) is exactly 999,999 times as likely as (W) on (T)."[18] Clearly, something has gone wrong, for buying a lottery ticket increases rather than decreases the chances of winning the lottery, but on Plantinga's notion of disconfirmation it decreases it.

For Chrzan, the lottery example shows that Plantinga's account of confirmation and disconfirmation is wrong. What is needed, instead, is

> (1') p disconfirms q if $P(q) < P(q/p)$
> where $P(q)$ is the probability that q pertains and $P(q/p)$ is the probability that q pertains given that p pertains. Thus (T) disconfirms (W) only if (W) seems more likely before taking (T) into account than after. This account preserves the logic of the lottery.[19]

Of course, this ruins Plantinga's defense against atheistic induction, according to Chrzan. Even if Plantinga could show that God's nonexistence isn't more likely than God's existence, given evil's existence, he still wouldn't have shown that evil doesn't disconfirm God's existence. That is, given evil's existence, God's existence might be less than .5 probable, even if his nonexistence is even less probable than his existence. So long as God's existence, given evil, is less than .5, evil apparently disconfirms God's existence. In order to show that evil doesn't disconfirm God's existence, Plantinga must argue that the probability of God's existence considered apart from the fact of evil isn't greater than the probability that he exists, given evil's existence, but he hasn't done so.[20]

Bruce Langtry has argued that Chrzan's analysis of Plantinga is problematic, but that doesn't mean Plantinga's handling of the evidential problem is without problem. Langtry claims initially that though Plantinga considers in *The Nature of Necessity* whether God's existence is improbable in light of the great amount of evil in the world, it isn't at all clear that such evil tells us much about the probability of God's existence.

Langtry makes his point by way of an illustration. Consider the claims "Elephants exist" and "There is a great amount of iron ore in the world." It would be hard to assess the probability of the former on the latter. The same is true of propositions about God's existence and the great amount of evil in the world. This shows that in trying to discern the probability of a given proposition on the basis of everything we know, many things we know are irrelevant to the proposition. Hence, we must select a subset of what is known, a subset relevant to the proposition in question. However, there are potential problems at this point. For example, will we always know that a given piece of information is relevant to the probability of a specific proposition in question? Will the atheist agree with us? Moreover, in regard to propositions thought to be background information, mightn't there be disagreements about which ones are actually common knowledge? The theist might say it is common knowledge that God exists, while the atheist may claim that it is common knowledge that he doesn't exist. If either theist or atheist demands that his claim is common knowledge and must be included in the totality of what we know before we can judge any probability claims about God and evil, the question will obviously be begged in the direction of either theism or atheism.[21]

Langtry then turns to Plantinga's account of confirmation and disconfirmation and Chrzan's criticisms. As Langtry notes, Plantinga's arguments about theism's probability answer the following two questions negatively: 1) Is God's existence improbable with respect to the great amount of evil that we find? and 2) Is God's existence improbable with respect to the totality of what we know?[22] Chrzan has many problems with Plantinga's argumentation, but Langtry says he is mistaken. In order to understand Langtry's objections, I must set forth his reconstruction of Plantinga's arguments, for it differs some from Plantinga's and Chrzan's presentations. Langtry reconstructs Plantinga's arguments as follows:

(1)   There exists an omnipotent, omniscient and perfectly good God
(2)   There are 10^{13} turps of evil
(3)   All the evil in the world is broadly moral evil; and every world that God (if he exists) could have actualised and that contains as much moral good as the actual world displays, contains at least 10^{13} turps of evil.
(4)   There exists an omnipotent, omniscient and perfectly good God; and all the evil in the world is broadly moral evil; and every world that God (if he exists) could have actualised and that contains as much good as the actual world displays contains at least 10^{13} turps of evil.

Plantinga reasons as follows:

(a)   It is not the case that -(3) is more probable relative to (2) than (3) is.
(b)   Therefore it is not the case that -(4) is more probable relative to (2) than (4) is.
(c)   (4) entails (1).
(d)   if -q is more probable relative to p than q is, and r entails q, then -r is more probable relative to p than r is.
(e)   Therefore it is not the case that -(1) is more probable relative to (2) than (1) is [from (b) and (c), via (d)].[23]

This means that the answer to whether the amount of evil in our world makes it improbable that God exists is no. The next phase of the argument shows that the totality of what we know doesn't make it improbable that God exists:

(f)   If -(1) is more probable relative to the totality of what we know than (1) is, then -(4) is more probable with respect to the totality of what we know than (4) is.
(g)   There is no reason to suppose that -(4) is more probable relative to the totality of what we know than (4) is.
(h)   Therefore there is no reason to suppose that -(1) is more probable relative to the totality of what we know than (1) is.[24]

Chrzan appeals to the case of Bobby to show that Plantinga's argument that God's existence isn't improbable in light of the amount of evil in the world is wrong. Langtry thinks Chrzan's argument doesn't prove its point. Bobby's attempt to get out of trouble by arguing that it is more probable that he is a good boy than not (despite his mother catching him taking the cookies) is mere sophistry, for it evades the issue of whether his mother's accusation is well founded and true. Even though his piece of sophistry might be true, it is irrelevant to the issue at hand, i.e., it may be more *probable* that Bobby is a good boy than not *relative to* the evidence of his mother catching him with the cookies, but that is beside the point of whether Bobby's mother's accusations are correct. According to Langtry, then, Bobby's mother shouldn't accept his defense, because it evades the issue, not because it contains a wrong probability judgment. Likewise, Langtry thinks Chrzan's example can't show any problem with *the probability judgment* involved in Plantinga's argument about the existence of God relative to the amount of evil in the world.[25] Something else may be wrong with Plantinga's claims, but Chrzan's argument doesn't destroy them.

Langtry next turns to Chrzan's objection that Plantinga shifts the burden of proof from the theist to the atheist. As Langtry notes, the premise of Plantinga's argument Chrzan labels (4) (also premise [4] in Langtry's reconstruction of Plantinga) is really at issue. Chrzan says it is internally improbable, but what does that mean? Langtry thinks it is most likely that Chrzan just asserts that -(4) is probable relative to all we know, and then puts the burden of proof on Plantinga to show otherwise. Langtry responds:

> Now disputes about where the burden of proof lies are often turgid and ster-ile. But as I read Plantinga's words on his page 195, he is not asserting that (4) is true and is not asserting that (4) is more probable relative to the total-ity of what we know than -(4) is. Plantinga's claim is more modest, *viz* (g) ("There is no reason to suppose that -[4] is more probable relative to the totality of what we know than [4] is"—my insertion of premise [g] in Langtry's reconstruction of Plantinga's argument). The passage quoted from Chrzan is a feeble response to (g).[26]

Despite his responses to Chrzan, Langtry still has some doubts about Plantinga's argument at this point. He wonders if (b) is true. Without argu-ment Plantinga asserts that the existence of so much evil doesn't disconfirm (3) and then infers that it doesn't disconfirm (4) either (these claims are rep-resented by Langtry's premises [a] and [b]). Langtry notes that (3) and (4) each entail another proposition (5) "All the evil in the world is broadly moral evil." That being so, the probability of (3) on (2) and (4) on (2) can't be greater than the probability of (5) on (2). Langtry then asks what he thinks is the key question:

> So is the probability relative to (2) of (5) at least as great as the probabil-ity relative to (2) of -(5)? Which of 'All the trees in the world are eucalypts' and 'There are trees which are not eucalypts', is more probable, relative to 'There are 10^{13} trees in the world' alone? I find it very hard to say. It is far from evident to me that Plantinga is correct in his claim that (a) and (b) are true. Hence Plantinga's argument (a)-(e) falls short of convincing me that (e) is true.[27]

Langtry finally turns to Plantinga's argument about the probability of God's existence in light of all we know (this argument is represented by premises [f]-[h] on Langtry's reconstruction of Plantinga). The key premise is (g), which involves the belief in the possibility of the existence of angelic beings. Langtry cites Plantinga's claim that it is hard to see how our total evi-dence discredits belief in these beings. In *God and Other Minds* Plantinga dis-cussed the possibility that the Lisbon earthquake was caused by a fallen angel. Though modern man may think the idea foolish, that is no evidence against it. Langtry thinks the key here is evidence and disconfirmation. He notes that in our context the question "Is proposition p disconfirmed by our total evi-dence?" just means "Is -p more probable than p, with respect to the totality of what we know?"[28] Langtry says:

But the question 'Do we have evidence against the truth of p?' should not be taken as equivalent to 'Is there some q, known to be true and such that -p is more probable than p, with respect to q?' For one thing, for almost any contingent proposition p we can find *some* q fulfilling the condition. It would be obvious that you and I have evidence against the Lisbon earthquake's being caused by demons— e.g., 'Most geologists do not believe that earthquakes are caused by demons'. It might be suggested that 'Do we have evidence against the truth of p?' should be taken as equivalent to 'Is there some q, known to be true, and such that -p is more probable than p relative to the conjunction of q with some suitably related body of background knowledge?' But this suggestion too runs into major problems. Exactly how talk of evidence for and against hypotheses is to be related to statements of epistemic probability is very hard to tell.[29]

Despite this problem, Langtry says we don't have to solve all issues in order to doubt Plantinga's argument with respect to fallen angels and natural evil. Langtry asks us to consider four mutually exclusive hypotheses:

(6)   The Lisbon earthquake was caused by the free action of a disaffected fallen angel.

(7)   The Lisbon earthquake was caused by the unfree action of a disaffected fallen angel.

(8)   The Lisbon earthquake was caused by the well-intentioned but bungling action of an unfallen angel.

(9)   The Lisbon earthquake was caused not by an angel but by a robot from a distant planet.[30]

Though it might be false to say there is evidence against any of (6)-(9), Langtry says probability assures us that at least three of the four are less probable than their negations with respect to all we know. "Even though we have no evidence against the truth of a hypothesis, it may be less probable than its negation with respect to the totality of what we know."[31] Langtry focuses in on (9), but could just as easily have made his point with respect to the others (though he might have been accused of question begging in regard to whether angelic beings exist, if he had). He says we have no evidence for (9), but other things we know allow us to explain things in scientific, geological terms. Does that mean (9) is less probable than its negation? Langtry says we can't answer without a full-fledged theory of epistemic probability. From all of this Langtry draws the following conclusion with respect to (9) and by analogy with respect to Plantinga's claims about the likelihood of (4):

But if we cannot make such an inference, either deductively or nondeductively, then it is hard indeed to see how talk of the probabilities of propositions is linked to argument, acceptance and rational belief in science, history and other empirical disciplines. Hence, assuming that there is such a thing as the probability of (9) relative to the totality of what we know, there seems to me some reason to suppose that (9) is less probable than its negation, relative to the totality of what we know.

Similarly there seems to me some room to suppose that -(4) is more probable relative to the totality of what we know than (4) is.[32]

The upshot of the preceding is *not,* according to Langtry, that atheists are right in claiming that the amount of evil in the world, taken in conjunction with all we know, makes theism improbable. Langtry believes the atheist's claim is actually false. But Langtry thinks "Plantinga is short-sighted when he says that he sees no reason to think that the atheological claim is true."[33]

How should we assess this interchange between Plantinga, Chrzan, and Langtry? Most of my comments relate to Chrzan, for I think his attack on Plantinga is most problematic. However, I shall begin with Langtry's complaints about Plantinga. His objections are much milder than Chrzan's, since he seems in fundamental agreement with Plantinga that atheists will have a hard time making a convincing argument against theism on the basis of evil.

Langtry thinks Plantinga is wrong that there is *no reason* to think the atheist's claim correct that the amount of evil in the world makes theism improbable. Plantinga might agree and say that his claim was hyperbole to make the point that the atheist's argument fails. There are reasons to think the atheist's claim true, but those reasons are nowhere near strong enough to make a convincing case against theism. On the other hand, if Plantinga really does believe there is no reason to think the atheist's claim true, then I think he has overstated the case. However, such overstatement wouldn't destroy his argument; it would merely suggest the need for a more moderately stated conclusion.

More significant is Langtry's claim that it is far from clear, contra Plantinga, that (3), (4), and (5) are more probable, given (2), than is their negation. Hence, Langtry doubts whether (a) and (b) are correct. Now, it strikes me that there is something correct about what Langtry says, but something wrong with it, too. The problem with Langtry's comments is that he portrays matters as though Plantinga has offered no argument for the truth of (a) and (b) whatsoever, and no argument to the effect that (3) and (4) are more probable, given (2), than their negation. This simply isn't true. Plantinga doesn't merely stipulate that (a) and (b) are right apart from any argument. Earlier in *The Nature of Necessity* he offers an extended treatment of the free will defense, and shows why that defense resolves an alleged problem of logical inconsistency for his theology. But the same defense that resolves the logical problem of evil also shows that it isn't clear that evil is convincing evidence against God's existence. If the evil in the world is a concomitant of free will, and if God is right in giving us free will, then it seems that the case in favor of (a) and (b) is made. Moreover, (3) and (4) are likely more probable than their negations, if the free will defense is correct.

Langtry might reply that the "ifs" in my defense of Plantinga are the problem. Until we know that the free will defense is right, we can't agree with Plantinga's assessment of (a) and (b), etc. The problem with that reply, however, is that it fails to recognize that the free will defense is a defense, not a theodicy. That is, it doesn't purport to know the exact reason God allowed evil. It suggests, instead, a possible reason, and that possible reason, if adopted, would show God's existence and evil's existence to be logically compatible. I believe that if it were true, it would also show that God's existence isn't improbable, even though there is evil in the world. Understood as a defense and not a theodicy, it seems that Plantinga's free will defense does offer grounds for Plantinga to think (a) and (b) are true and that (3) and (4) are more probable than their negations. Hence, I think Langtry's attack on Plantinga's case at this point is in error.[34]

On the other hand, I think there is something correct about what Langtry says. Even granting that Plantinga offers a defense rather than a theodicy, does Plantinga have a right to be so certain about his claims about (a) and (b) and (3) and (4)? Plantinga is certain, because the free will defense convinces him. For someone who rejects the free will defense because he rejects its account of freedom, it won't be certain that Plantinga's assessment of the probabilities is right. Moreover, someone who holds indeterministic free will and basically agrees with the free will defense might still think other arguments and evidence against God's existence make theism less probable than atheism. Even if that person is inclined to agree with Plantinga's assessment of (a), (b), (3), and (4), she surely won't agree with (1). Hence, what seems to be correct about Langtry's objection is that it isn't always easy to determine the probability of a given proposition or for atheists and theists to agree on probabilities. As we shall see, Plantinga argues just this point in his later work.

The net result of this point is far less damaging to Plantinga's *Nature of Necessity* argument than to the atheist's program. Plantinga merely needs to be a bit less certain that he has proven his case. The atheist, on the other hand, must realize that it will be very hard to point to evil and use it to make a convincing case that evil disconfirms theism. Plantinga's arguments weren't meant to make a case to prove theism; they were meant to rebut the atheist's claims against theism. They do so by answering that if the free will defense is correct, it isn't at all likely the atheist can make a probability case against theism. Plantinga need do nothing more than this, but atheism, in trying to make a positive case against theism, must demonstrate that its probability judgment is correct. It isn't clear that atheism will succeed in doing that. Langtry's uneasiness about Plantinga's probability judgments should also apply to the atheist's. But if those judgments are debatable, then the atheist has lost more, for he tried to use them to demonstrate that theism is improbable.

In turning to Chrzan, there are significant problems beyond those Langtry raises. First, Chrzan complains that Plantinga actually smuggles (G) and (E) into propositions (3) and (4) in such a way as to render them compatible. Plantinga includes (E) in (3), so (3) must entail (E). He then adds (G) to (3) to create (4). Since (4) implies both (G) and (E), neither can disconfirm it. In essence, this amounts to accusing Plantinga of question begging. Do Plantinga's (3) and (4) beg the question? I don't think so. If Plantinga merely asserts in (4) without any proof that God and evil are compatible, then he is guilty. However, Plantinga doesn't do that. He has already presented in great detail his argument for the compatibility of God and evil. That argument is the free will defense. Now, Chrzan may reject the free will defense and the theology that goes with it, but he must admit that the free will defense does render its theology internally consistent. If that is so, then it is also likely that evil won't serve as conclusive evidence that there is no God. The free will defense demonstrates that there can be a God, in spite of the evil in our world. If that is so, then Plantinga has a right to structure propositions (3) and (4) as he has. No question is begged.

Second, Chrzan complains that Plantinga's argument shifts the burden of proof from the theist to the atheist, whereas it should be on the theist. The truth is that a burden of proof falls on both the theist and atheist, but I think the atheist has the greater burden. Who "picked this fight," anyway? It isn't the theist who tried to make a case for theism or against atheism. The atheist appealed to evil as evidence against theism. This means the theist can assume a basically defensive posture. He needs only to rebut the atheist's charge. He can do this in one of two ways. He can go on offense and try to present positive evidence for theism's probability. This will be quite an ambitious undertaking, and hard to accomplish. If it succeeds, then, of course, the atheist's case against theism won't amount to much. The other theistic strategy is much more modest. It is completely defensive and involves explaining why the atheist's evidence against theism doesn't make theism *improbable* (theism might still be improbable, but all the theist tries to show is that evil alone doesn't make it so). If the theist adopts the former strategy, he assumes a heavy burden; if the latter, a burden of proof is still there, but it is much lighter.

What I am saying is that it is harder to demonstrate that there is positive evidence for the probability of a position than to show that an opponent's evidence against it doesn't make it improbable. Plantinga has chosen the second strategy. The atheist, on the other hand, must demonstrate that evil really does make theism improbable. As we saw in chapter 9, it will be very hard for the atheist to make a case by merely pointing to evil and expecting everyone to agree that it makes theism improbable. His burden of proof will be as heavy as that which falls on a theist who tries to prove theism is probable by offering positive evidence for it.

What does this mean about Chrzan's objection? I believe it shows it to be wrong. Plantinga doesn't shift any burden of proof. The atheist already has a heavy burden of proof, one which the atheist chose to carry by "picking this fight"; Plantinga adds nothing to it. Chrzan may think Plantinga needs to adopt the first strategy to defend theism. By opting for the second strategy, it may appear that Plantinga shifts the burden of proof to Chrzan, but this simply isn't so. Plantinga is totally within his rights to choose to defend theism by the second strategy.

Third, Chrzan thinks his example of Bobby and the cookies ruins Plantinga's argument. I agree with Langtry's complaints against it. I also think there are other problems with Chrzan's argument. Chrzan says the atheist shouldn't accept premise (4) on the basis of (3) just as Bobby's mother shouldn't accept Chrzan's premise (10) on the basis of (9). But are the two cases parallel? I don't think so, and this ruins Chrzan's attempted rejection of Plantinga's argument. Let me explain two important respects in which the cases are dissimilar.

As to Bobby and his mother, even if (9) is true, that wouldn't prove/confirm that Bobby is a good boy. Bobby could really be a bad boy, but it just happens in this case that gnomes actually forced him to take the cookies. If so, then his taking the cookies proves nothing one way or the other about whether he is a good boy or not. Likewise, if (3) is true, that wouldn't necessarily confirm/prove that there is a God (4). There might be no God after all, but it just happens that all possible worlds contain as much moral good as ours with at least as much as 10^{13} turps of evil. Hence, the amount of evil in our world would prove nothing about whether or not God exists.

So far, the two cases are similar, but what comes next shows their difference. While (9) and (10) are logically compatible (even though Chrzan doesn't show how), the main problem is that Chrzan offers no reason to think gnomes exist. That seems to be a large part of the reason Bobby's mother shouldn't buy (10), even though she might agree that (9) and (10) are consistent. On the other hand, Plantinga has shown by means of the free will defense that (3) and (4) are compatible, but he has also shown that there is such a thing as free will. So, that which renders God's existence compatible with evil (free will producing evil) has been shown to exist, and thus, the theist's case is believable. What makes Bobby's being a good boy compatible with the stolen cookies is the activity of the gnomes, but no one has offered a reason to believe in gnomes. Hence, Bobby's mother's skepticism (and ours) is more understandable.

There is another respect in which the two cases are dissimilar. Chrzan says that (3) doesn't confirm (4) just as (9) doesn't confirm (10). However, this matter isn't as simple as Chrzan supposes. As to Bobby, it is clear that stealing the cookies makes it less probable that Bobby is good, because presumably, good boys don't disobey their mothers. If good boys do disobey, then the stolen cookies don't conclusively prove that Bobby is a bad boy. If the presumption is correct, then (9) clearly can't confirm (10). However, Chrzan thinks (3) doesn't confirm (4), because the existence of evil makes it less probable that there is a God, presumably because if there were a God, he would remove evil. Since there is evil, there must be no God, or so the atheist reasons. But we have already seen that the atheist's assumption that if there is a God, he would remove evil, isn't necessarily true. If there were a God, he might not remove evil, because doing so might eliminate free will, the possibility of soul-building, or some other value. But then, we must ask again how the sheer facts of evil make God's existence less probable (disconfirm it)? At best, it is inconclusive as to whether evil does or doesn't disconfirm it. Hence, (3) may in fact confirm (4) or it may not; the evidence isn't entirely conclusive. But this seems to illustrate Plantinga's ultimate point, namely, that if one takes seriously what it actually takes to disconfirm a proposition, then it isn't clear in regard to God and evil that the atheist has the necessary evidence to make the case. In sum, (9) can't confirm (10) in light of the presumption that good boys don't disobey their mother, but (3) may still confirm (4), for it isn't clear that the presumption is true that if there is a God, he would remove evil. Hence, Bobby's case and Plantinga's argument are dissimilar in this second respect, and the dissimilarities suggest that Chrzan hasn't refuted Plantinga's argument.

One final comment on Chrzan and the lottery. Chrzan thinks his example shows Plantinga's notion of confirmation and disconfirmation to be wrong. I'm not convinced, because I think Chrzan has misinterpreted his example. Chrzan complains that with Plantinga's notion of confirmation, if one buys the ticket, his chances of winning diminish, and this goes against our intuitions. I disagree. For one thing, if Rex buys no lottery ticket, it is impossible for him to win. If he buys a ticket, his chances are slim, but now it is no longer impossible for him to win. So, he has increased his chances of winning by buying the ticket. Plantinga's notion of disconfirmation says that given T, -W will be more probable than W. But this assumes that T lowers the probability of W with respect to the probability of -W. In Rex's case as properly interpreted, T doesn't lower the probability of W with respect to -W. Buying the ticket makes W more probable than it was and -W less probable. Of course, W was never probable and -W was never improbable. Chrzan seems to focus on this last fact as disproof of Plantinga's notion of disconfirmation. I disagree. It is true that W was never probable and -W never improbable, but that doesn't mean buying a lottery ticket makes W less probable and -W more probable. It just means that in spite of Rex's increased chances of winning the lottery by buying the ticket (without the ticket they are zero), it is still a long shot that he will win. When one properly understands what buying the ticket and not buying it do to Rex's chances, I don't see that Plantinga's account of disconfirmation is shown to be inadequate.

In sum, I don't think Chrzan's objections to Plantinga are correct. Plantinga's account of confirmation and disconfirmation seems adequate, and Chrzan's counterexample doesn't refute Plantinga's argument.[35] My fundamental concern with Plantinga in what we have seen so far is that, as Langtry suggests, he is perhaps too confident about the accuracy of his probability judgments. As I have suggested, there is reason to think probability judgments are based on a degree of subjectivity. Hence, theists and atheists may disagree about the accuracy of some of Plantinga's probability claims. But that doesn't mean Plantinga hasn't successfully rebutted the atheist's case against theism.

Moore, Wierenga, and Plantinga

Harold Moore and Edward Wierenga have also interacted over Plantinga's views expressed in *The Nature of Necessity*. Moore reformulates Plantinga's propositions about confirmation and disconfirmation as follows:

1. A proposition p confirms a proposition q just in case q is more probable than not on p alone.
2. A proposition p disconfirms a proposition q just in case it confirms the denial of q.
3. If a proposition p confirms a proposition q it confirms every proposition q entails.
4. If a proposition p disconfirms q, p disconfirms every proposition that entails q.[36]

After offering Plantinga's argument that evil's existence doesn't disconfirm God's existence, Moore complains that the argument rests on a notion of confirmation and disconfirmation whose unqualified use generates contradictions. Suppose two hypotheses share a given piece of evidence and yet have further incompatible consequences. On Plantinga's principles of confirmation and disconfirmation it wouldn't be possible for two otherwise incompatible hypotheses to share any evidence, and that seems odd. Moore illustrates his point with an example. Suppose two hypotheses (H_1 and H_2) share one piece of evidence (E_1). Suppose also that H_1 entails a piece of evidence (E_2) and H_2 entails the denial of E_2. With Plantinga's principles, Moore claims we generate the following:

10.   Since E_1 confirms H_1 and since H_1 entails E_2, then E_1 confirms E_2, and because E_1 confirms E_2, it disconfirms the denial of E_2.

10'.   Since E_1 confirms H_2 and since H_2 entails the denial of E_1 [sic], then E_1 confirms the denial of E_2, and because E_1 confirms the denial of E_2, it disconfirms E_2.[37]

Of course, 10 contradicts 10', but that means two incompatible beliefs can't have some evidence in common, and that seems clearly false.

Moore raises a second problem. Moore thinks Plantinga would argue that the following proposition (call it C) is false: "'God does not exist' must be more probable than not on the evidence." Moore says that even though Plantinga's belief that C is false is crucial to Plantinga's argument, Plantinga offers no argument that C is false. Plantinga thinks C is false, according to Moore, because Plantinga believes a proposition like the following:

God is omniscient, omnipotent, and morally perfect; God has created the world; all the evil in the world is broadly moral evil; and there is no possible world God could have created that contains a better balance of broadly moral good with respect to broadly moral evil.[38]

Moore says this seems to be the only reason Plantinga would think C is false, but it is unacceptable, "for it renders virtually any belief impregnable to disconfirmation; in short 'confirmation' is emptied of the content that makes it important."[39] This happens, according to Moore, because it presupposes a view like the view that a given hypothesis isn't rendered improbable by a piece of evidence, so long as one can formulate the hypothesis in a way consistent with the evidence. Of course, then, any hypothesis that can be formulated in a way logically consistent with the evidence can escape being improbable with the same maneuver. The problem, however, is that this notion of confirmation and disconfirmation is so broad as to trivialize confirmation and disconfirmation.[40]

Moore thinks there is a more charitable way to interpret Plantinga. Perhaps he means that for all we know, there is no way to choose between theistic and nontheistic explanations of evil. Moore agrees, but not because he thinks the evidence is neutral on the question. He agrees because he thinks the concept of evidence can't be applied to issues like God's existence. To make his point, Moore distinguishes between merely positive instances of a hypothesis and a confirming instance. He writes:

Confirmation is not just supplying positive instances of a hypothesis; additional reliable background knowledge of some relevant kind must be supplied to justify the more substantial claim that the positive instances are confirming ones.[41]

Here is where the problem enters, however, with evidential arguments for God's existence, according to Moore. This is so,

> for *we have no idea* of what kind of universe an omnipotent, loving, omniscient God would create to produce the greatest balance of moral good over moral evil. And since this is so, then indeed there is little to choose between theistic and non-theistic explanations of evil, but not because evidence is neutral, but because it can't be applied.[42]

Of course, if evil can't be applied as evidence in this situation, it can't count as evidence against God's existence.

Edward Wierenga interacts with Moore's article and finds each of his arguments lacking. As to Moore's first complaint that Plantinga's view of confirmation and disconfirmation leads to contradictions, Wierenga is dubious. He compresses Moore's 10 and 10' into the following (Wierenga labels it 4):

4.   There are propositions E, H_1 and H_2 such that E confirms H_1 and E confirms H_2 and H_1 entails the denial of H_2.[43]

According to Moore, either Plantinga's principles of confirmation and disconfirmation (propositions 1-4 on Moore's analysis) are inconsistent or they make it impossible for incompatible beliefs to have some evidence in common. Wierenga says Moore's argument doesn't show that Moore's propositions 1-3 (propositions expressing Plantinga's concepts of confirmation and disconfirmation) are inconsistent. Instead, Moore's argument shows that 1-3 are inconsistent with Wierenga's proposition 4. But then, we must ask if proposition 4 is true.[44]

Wierenga considers whether his proposition 4 is true. He says Moore takes it to mean "There are incompatible propositions which have some evidence in common." This is a plausible claim, but Plantinga understands confirmation to be a stronger relation than the relation of being some evidence for something. Wierenga illustrates his point by distinguishing two concepts of confirmation. He expresses them as propositions 7 and 8:

7. p confirms q just in case $Pr(q/p) > Pr(q)$.

8. p confirms q just in case $Pr(q/p) > 1/2$.[45]

The second notion of confirmation is clearly stronger. According to the first, p confirms q if q is more probable on evidence p than q is with no evidence or on tautological evidence. However, on this notion of confirmation, p could confirm q even if the probability of q on p is very low. For example, if the probability of q alone is .1 and the probability of q on p is .2, then p is some evidence for q and confirms it on this notion of confirmation, but q is still not very probable. On the other hand, the second notion of confirmation says the probability of q on evidence p must be greater than .5 for p to confirm q. In that case, p would confirm q, and the probability of q on p would be rather high. Wierenga thinks Plantinga invokes the second notion of confirmation, not the first. He further claims that if proposition 4 (Wierenga's) assumes the second concept of probability, then 4 is incompatible with probability calculus. In that case, Wierenga's 4 can be discarded, and the difficulty Moore raises evaporates. Wierenga explains:

> It is a theorem of the probability calculus that if H_1 and H_2 are logically incompatible (and $Pr(E) \neq 0$), $Pr(H_1/E)$ and $Pr(H_2/E)$ sum to at most 1. Thus, it cannot happen that both conditional probabilities are greater than 1/2. So Plantinga's premisses [*sic*] (1), (2), and (3) are none the worse for conflicting with (4) under this interpretation, unless we have some reason to reject the relevant theorem of the probability calculus.[46]

When Wierenga speaks of conditional probabilities, he means the probability that H_1 or H_2 is true on the condition that E is true. His point is that if H_1 and H_2 are logically incompatible, the probability of these theories (taken together) on the evidence can't total more than 1. However, the second notion of confirmation requires that each be more than .5, so together they would total more than 1. Since the probability of the two mutually exclusive theories can't together be more than 1, there must be something wrong with 4. Hence, if Plantinga's premises (1-3) incorporate the second notion of confirmation, then 1-3 are inconsistent with 4, but it doesn't matter, since premise 4 is false on the second notion of confirmation.[47]

Suppose we interpret Wierenga's 4 according to the first notion of confirmation (Wierenga's 7). Wierenga says that in that case 4 appears to be true. However, on that interpretation the claim "E disconfirms H_1, and E disconfirms H_2" (Wierenga's proposition 5) no longer follows from 4. But, if that is true, then there is no contradiction between 4 and 5, and it was that alleged contradiction that led Moore to question whether Plantinga has an adequate account of confirmation. The upshot, then, is that whether one interprets confirmation along the lines of 7 or 8, Plantinga's notions of confirmation and disconfirmation don't generate contradictions. Moore's first objection to Plantinga is mistaken.[48]

Moore's second objection is that Plantinga's argument must implicitly involve the idea that if one can formulate a hypothesis so as to be *consistent* with the evidence, then the evidence can't render it *improbable.* Wierenga responds that if Plantinga's argument does contain that idea, it is defective, but Wierenga sees no reason to believe the argument assumes it. Wierenga thinks Moore misunderstands the structure of Plantinga's argument. From premises 2 and 3 (two of Plantinga's propositions about confirmation and disconfirmation) it follows that "If p disconfirms q, then p disconfirms every proposition entailing q."[49] Plantinga argued that evil doesn't disconfirm the notions that God is omniscient, omnipotent, morally perfect, and created the world, that the evil in the world is broadly moral evil, and that there is no possible world God could have created with a better balance of broadly moral good and broadly moral evil. But these notions about God and his creative activities entail that God exists. In light of the principle that a proposition that disconfirms another also disconfirms every proposition entailing that second one, it is clear that if evil's existence doesn't disconfirm a proposition about God and his creative activities, it doesn't disconfirm the proposition that God exists. But, this is all Plantinga's argument says. It nowhere incorporates the notion that no hypothesis becomes improbable on the evidence so long as the hypothesis is formulated to be consistent with the evidence. Hence, Moore's second objection fails.[50]

This doesn't end the matter, for Moore wrote a reply to Wierenga. Moore returns only to the objection just discussed. Moore complains that all Wierenga does is reconstruct Plantinga's argument, not really interact with whether or not its premises are true. Moore contends that if claims like Plantinga's premise about God and his creative activities producing a world with a balance of good over evil are allowed to save other claims from disconfirmation, then confirmation and disconfirmation become trivial, for it is possible to render almost any belief impregnable to disconfirmation. Wierenga's restatement of Plantinga's argument doesn't address that issue, because it doesn't consider whether its premises are really plausible. Hence, Moore accused Plantinga of implicitly believing that so long as evil can be shown compatible with God's existence, God's existence isn't rendered improbable by evil. Nothing Wierenga says indicates that Plantinga doesn't hold that view, because nothing Wierenga says assesses the plausibility of the claim about God and his creative activities. Until we see an argument for its plausibility, for all we know Plantinga invoked it just because it renders God's existence consistent with evil. But consistency of God's existence with evil doesn't prove there actually is a God who created this world. One can write propositions that say it is so, but that doesn't prove it. Hence, Moore believes his second objection still stands.[51]

In assessing the debate between Moore and Wierenga over Moore's second objection, I must side with Wierenga. Moore essentially repeats his original objection. Wierenga explained the logic of Plantinga's argument, i.e., he explained why Plantinga isn't guilty of doing what Moore thinks he does. However, Moore thinks none of that counts until Wierenga shows Plantinga's premise about God and his creative activities to be plausible. This simply will not do. Wierenga explained how Plantinga's argument works. In so doing, he explained why Plantinga isn't guilty of incorporating the illicit premise. Now, Moore wants to stipulate that the argument really includes the illicit premise until it is shown that Plantinga's argument is plausible. This ad hoc determination of what counts as a satisfactory answer to his objection after Wierenga has explained why the objection is wrongheaded won't do.

Moore's complaint is problematic on other grounds as well. Suppose we must accept his new rule about how to exonerate Plantinga's argument. Even granting that Plantinga's premise about God and his creative activities must be shown plausible, I don't think Plantinga's argument fails. The reason is Plantinga's detailed exposition of the free will defense. That defense against the logical problem of evil also explains why it is at least plausible that there is a God who created the world we have. So Plantinga has already done what Moore requires, but Moore ignores it. What should Wierenga do? Rehash Plantinga's exposition of the free will defense to show why it is plausible that God should exist and our world have the evil it does? If Moore didn't agree with Plantinga's presentation, why would he be convinced if Wierenga repeated it? The main point, though, is that even if we must accept Moore's stipulation about how to exonerate Plantinga's argument, what Moore requires has already been offered.[52]

I conclude, then, that Moore's second objection doesn't work, and Wierenga's answer to Moore's first objection seems to answer it adequately. In sum, I don't think Moore's complaints damage Plantinga's argument. What about Moore's claim that ultimately one can't apply evidence to questions about God's existence? I am nowhere near as skeptical about that as is Moore. However, suffice it to say for this discussion that if Moore is right, that doesn't damage Plantinga's presentation nor theism in general. Plantinga wasn't trying to produce a positive evidential argument for theism's probability. He was merely trying to rebut the atheist's claim that evidence can make a strong case *against* theism. If Moore wants us to believe that evidence can't apply to questions about God's existence, so much the worse for atheistic attempts to use the evidence of evil to disprove theism!

In summing up this whole section on Plantinga's treatment of the evidential problem in *The Nature of Necessity,* it seems that Plantinga's argument emerges relatively unscathed by the critics' complaints. Of course, as I have argued, accepting Plantinga's argument requires agreeing with his probability judgments. Plantinga's free will defense offers reasons for agreeing that evil doesn't make theism improbable. Still, that doesn't mean we can demonstrate that theism is probable. My point here is that without the free will defense theism might have a probability of .1. With it, its probability might rise to .35. But a probability of .35 is still improbable. Someone might respond that while this is true, theism might instead have a probability of .4 without the free will defense, and a probability of .7 with it. That is true, but which of the probability assessments are we to accept, the first or the second? It isn't clear that even theists will agree on this matter, let alone a theist and an atheist. But all of this just illustrates my point about the element of subjectivity in probability arguments of this sort.

Hence, while Plantinga's argument seems successfully to rebut the atheist's probability argument against theism, it doesn't make a conclusive probability argument *for* theism. Of course, Plantinga wasn't trying to do that, and it may actually be very difficult to do. One suspects that Plantinga agrees that a probability case for or against theism will be extremely difficult to make, because of the approach he takes in his later handling of the probabilistic argument from evil. It is to that treatment we now turn.

PLANTINGA'S "THE PROBABILISTIC ARGUMENT FROM EVIL" DISCUSSION

Plantinga says that though the atheist thinks God's existence is improbable because of evil, evil alone cannot make theism improbable. As the case of Feike the Frisian shows, what may be improbable on one piece or set of evidence may be probable on another. Hence, the atheist must show theism improbable on some relevant body of *total* evidence. If it is improbable on the atheist's body of evidence, then the atheist has good reason to reject theism. If it is improbable on the theist's total evidence, the theist is irrational in maintaining belief in God. Of course, to show theism improbable on total evidence would involve considering all the traditional theistic proofs as well as other evidence for theism, along with all the atheist's evidence against theism.[53]

After making this point about total evidence and arguing that it isn't easy to show God's existence improbable on total evidence, Plantinga turns to a narrower question. Specifically, is God's existence improbable on the basis of evil's existence? Since it isn't clear that this is so, Plantinga believes the atheist must produce an argument to that effect. Moreover, he must recognize that having granted that God's existence is consistent with evil (i.e., theists can solve the problem of evil in its logical form), it will only be harder to make the case that God's existence is improbable.[54]

Plantinga considers several arguments that evil makes theism improbable (he represents this as G is improbable on E), and concludes that Rowe's is the strongest example of this kind of argument. As Plantinga sees it, Rowe thinks theists are committed to the following:

(8)   For each evil state of affairs E that obtains, there is a good state of affairs G such that (a) G outweighs E, and (b) God, though omnipotent and omniscient, could not have brought about G without permitting E.[55]

Plantinga says Rowe argues that (8) is exceedingly improbable in view of the amount and variety of evil in our world. Plantinga thinks what is at issue is whether God could have produced a world just as good as our world but with less evil overall. This means the theist would be committed to one of the following:

(11)   God is omnipotent, omniscient and wholly good; and every world God could have actualized that contains less evil than the actual world, contains a less favorable overall balance of good and evil than does the actual world;

(12)   God is omnipotent, omniscient and wholly good; and the actual world is a better world than any world God could have actualized that contains less evil than the actual world.[56]

According to Plantinga, Rowe probably believes theists hold something like (12). Rowe likely thinks (12) is improbable with respect to E, but is that right? Plantinga isn't sure it is. The first conjunct of (12) surely doesn't entail the second (if Rowe thinks it does, he is mistaken), but beyond that Plantinga says it isn't clear that there is such a thing as *the* best world or even *a* best world. However, for the sake of argument, Plantinga will assume that the theist is committed to (12) and that G entails (12). In that case, Rowe would say (12) is improbable with respect to E, and if G entails (12), then G is improbable with respect to E. However, Plantinga asks why we should think (12) improbable with respect to E. It isn't clear that there are grounds for making that claim, and it is unclear how we should judge whether (12) is improbable with respect to E.

Plantinga suggests turning to the calculus of probabilities. He invokes various axioms used in probability theory, including Bayes' Theorem. The atheist argues that G (God is omnipotent, omniscient and wholly good) is improbable on E (there are 10^{13} turps of evil), because G entails (12), but (12) is improbable on E. In this whole discussion, however, how probable one thinks a proposition is will rely heavily on how one interprets probability calculus. As it turns out, there are three main interpretations of probability, the *logical* interpretation, the *frequency* interpretation, and the *personalist* interpretation.[57]

According to the personalist interpretation, probability statements record the degree to which someone accepts some proposition or other. This approach holds that each person has a *credence function*. This is "a function from the set of propositions believed by S into the real numbers between 0 and 1. $Ps(A) = n$, then, records something like the degree to which S believes or accepts A.[58] $Ps(A/B)$ measures S's *conditional* partial belief, i.e., his partial belief that A, given the condition that B.

Plantinga asks how to construe on the personalist interpretation the atheist's claim that $P(G/E) < 1/2$. If all it tells us is a truth about the atheist (e.g., $Pa[G \& E]/Pa[E] < 1/2$, i.e., the probability for the atheist that G and E are true on the probability for the atheist that there is evil is less than 1/2), then it is nothing more than biographical information about the atheist. But we already knew he doesn't believe in God. Surely, this tells us nothing about whether God exists, nor does it offer an argument for atheism.[59]

If we construe the personalist atheist's claim to mean that '$P(G/E) < 1/2$' is *rational*, i.e., it can be embedded in a coherent set of beliefs, this isn't of great relevance. The theist can respond that '$P(G/E) > 1/2$' is also rational in that it also can be embedded in a coherent set of beliefs. This, too, is of no great relevance in determining how likely it is that theism is true.[60] The net result, according to Plantinga, is that the personalist interpretation of probability doesn't help the atheist make an argument against theism on the basis of evil.

Does the atheist's argument fare any better with the logical concept of probability? According to this interpretation, probability is a "quasi-logical relation of which entailment is a special case."[61] As Plantinga explains about the logical interpretation of probability:

> It's [*sic*] truth in no way depends upon anyone's belief or knowledge, or upon any other contingent state of affairs. From this point of view, the probability relation may be thought of as *partial entailment*, with entailment *simpliciter* the limiting case where $P(A/B) = 1$.[62]

This means that unlike the personalist interpretation, this interpretation doesn't rest on anyone's belief or knowledge. It simply states the logical relations between the propositions involved. In that case, a probability claim like $P(G/E) < 1/2$ states necessary truths that don't depend on anyone's beliefs.

Plantinga applies the logical notion of probability to the question of *a priori* probability, the probability of a hypothesis on a tautology. He questions whether contingent propositions have any degree of probability in the logical sense on a tautology. As he states, to ask for the probability of G or E on a tautology "might be like asking for the temperature of the number nine. The temperature of nine isn't zero (F, C or K): it *has* no temperature. Similarly, perhaps G and E have no *a priori* probability."[63] Plantinga then considers what might determine the *a priori* probability of a proposition. He rejects Swinburne's suggestion that simpler propositions have greater *a priori* probability, and he also objects to Carnap's suggestion that the greater the content of the proposition, the less likely it is to be true, because more could go wrong.[64] He concludes that there is no reason to think a contingent proposition has an *a priori* probability or to think that if it did, we would know how to determine what it is. The implication of this for the atheist is that it is hard to see how he could work out his probabilistic argument using the logical notion of probability. Moreover, even if this concept of probability is correct, there is no reason to think the probability of "God is wholly good and all-powerful and yet could not have actualized a world with less evil" is less than half the *a priori* probability of E. Thus, there is no reason to think E disconfirms G.[65]

Plantinga finally turns to the frequency notion of probability. According to it, probabilities are ratios, "proportions of events of one kind among events of another kind."[66] An example is the probability of getting heads a certain number of times when flipping a coin a series of times. In trying to apply the frequency notion to the atheist's probability argument from evil, the initial problem is that G and E are propositions, not classes of events or objects. Hence, one wonders what is the relevant infinite series of events to which these propositions belong. Perhaps the way to proceed is to talk of possible worlds. In that case, the atheist may be claiming that $P(G/E) < 1/2$ represents the relation between the class of possible worlds in which G holds and the class of worlds in which E holds. If this is so, however, there are problems. Is it possible to count the number of E worlds?

The biggest problem, however, is that even if one could count those worlds, with a countably infinite class of things there are many sequences associated with that class and any subset of it. How do we know which sequence to choose? As Plantinga says, "Granted that there are only countably many E-worlds, which of the many associated sequences is the right one to pick to determine $P(G/E)$?"[67] Even beyond that, "how shall we appropriately associate a class and attribute with G and E in such a way that we can speak of the probability, in the frequency sense, of G with respect to E?"[68]

After discussing these and many other problems with the frequency interpretation, Plantinga says one way to determine the probability of propositions G and E is to associate them with the broadest homogeneous reference class containing them. However, taking this approach, one will normally estimate the probability of given propositions in terms of all one's beliefs (one's noetic structure). As for the theist, G will be associated with the class of *true* propositions as the appropriate broadest homogeneous reference class. But in that case the prior probability of G will be 1, and the posterior probability of G on E will also be 1 for the theist. On the other hand, the atheist will evaluate the probability of G against his noetic structure. When he chooses the broadest homogenous reference group for G, that will be the class of false propositions (since he thinks G is false). Of course, then the prior probability of G will be 0, and so will the posterior probability of G on E. Both the theist and atheist are within their rights in making these claims. We aren't after all talking about the actual truth of G or E. We are talking about the theist's and atheist's assessments of the probabilities of the truth of G and G on E, and of course, those will appear different depending on each's noetic structure.[69] The net result of this discussion of the frequency notion of probability is that it offers little help in determining the actual probability of G on E. Hence, it offers the atheist little help in making a probabilistic argument against theism.

From all of the preceding Plantinga concludes that the atheist's program is totally misconceived. He writes:

> If prior probabilities are thus relative to noetic structures, it is no wonder that theist and atheologian will assign different values to $P(G)$ and $P(E)$; and hence it is no more than a bit of intellectual imperialism for the atheologian to insist that the theist accept the atheological estimate of $P(G/E)$. One who offers this sort of inductive argument as an objection to theism is like a theist, who offers as an objection to atheism, the fact that we all agree that there are 10^{13} turps of evil, together with the claim that the probability of G with respect to that evidence is high. What atheist should pay any attention to that? Such an argument of course, is thoroughly silly; but from the present perspective the atheolotical [sic] argument from evil is really no more sensible.[70]

Plantinga admits that some might object that while he raises doubt about the probability argument in virtue of difficulties with the various analyses of probability, still, we often do know that a proposition is improbable with respect to total evidence. Plantinga agrees, but explains that in those cases there is an agreed upon body of knowledge against which we judge the probability of a given claim. Such isn't the case in the current discussion. Hence the atheist's "probabilistic argument from evil is totally misconceived."[71]

As Plantinga ends his article, he says we are often told that a religion should be accepted only if it accords with the evidence. However, what is the evidence? Normally, those who raise this demand believe there is a set of propositions which is universally accepted, propositions of common sense, self-evident propositions, and a host of perceptual beliefs. To this many would add some of the deliverances of the sciences. Religious faith will be rational, then, only if it is probable with respect to these evidences. Likewise, probability, using Bayes' Theorem, will be estimated in terms of these propositions. In other words, these beliefs are foundational, and the truth of other claims must be judged in terms of them. With respect to these beliefs (Plantinga calls them B) Plantinga asks:

> why suppose theistic belief must be probable with respect to B, to be rationally acceptable? What's so special about B? B, we are told, contains the propositions I *know*, the propositions with respect to which I am to judge the acceptability of other propositions. How do propositions get into B anyway? B contains propositions implying that there are other persons, that the world is more than 10 minutes old, and that there are material objects that persist when no one is looking. What makes these good candidates for being in B? Clearly there is no way they can be proved or established with respect to the sorts of propositions either classical or modern foundationalists are prepared to accept in the foundations of a rational noetic structure: that is the central lesson of the development of modern philosophy from Descartes to Hume. So how are they epistemologically superior to, say, the central tenets of Christianity?[72]

All of this leads to the point Plantinga has repeatedly argued in recent years about belief in God. If one accepts this sort of foundationalism, why can't belief in God be part of the theist's noetic foundation? That is, why must the probability of G be judged in terms of some other supposedly more foundational propositions? Why can't G be properly basic for the theist and hence part of the noetic structure against which the probability of other statements must be judged?[73]

Adams and Plantinga

Robert M. Adams, well-known theist, discusses Plantinga's probabilistic argument at some length. He notes initially that Plantinga isn't arguing that evil doesn't count at all as evidence against theism. Instead, his point is that the existence of evil doesn't make theism improbable. Hence, evil may count as evidence against theism while theism still remains probable as a whole on other grounds.[74] Adams rehearses the basic structure of Plantinga's argument against the various interpretations of probability, and agrees that on any understanding of probability, it is hard to determine prior probabilities for P(G/E), because our noetic structure will influence what we think on that matter. However, Plantinga thinks this means the atheist's program is totally misconceived. Adams isn't so sure, and it is that matter he discusses.

Adams asks what the atheist's program is. If atheists are trying to produce an argument of coercive force which will compel all reasonable people to reject theism as irrational, then indeed their program is misconceived. Adams thinks Plantinga attacks this atheistic agenda in his article.[75] On the other hand, the atheist's goals might be more modest. The atheist may appeal to evil not to coerce but to persuade theists and agnostics that atheism is more attractive than they thought, and to shore up the belief of atheists. As Adams says, "Theist and atheist can reason together about the existence of God without either trying to prove that the other has been foolish or irrational."[76] Much philosophy is of this noncoercive sort, and on occasion leads to changes in opinion. Adams thinks Plantinga hasn't shown that a probabilistic argument from evil with this goal is illegitimate or useless.

This may sound plausible, but one wonders how to construct such an argument. Adams replies that one of the conceptions of probability must be used, and for the sake of discussion, he chooses the personalist approach. Adams says that for a personalist atheist a probabilistic argument from evil may be more than mere autobiography. On the one hand, it may offer the reason for his unbelief. On the other hand, it may offer a way to get some theist "to admit that his credence function is incoherent."[77] The first use of the argument is obvious, but the second may not be so evident. Adams illustrates his point by appeal to a comparative form of Bayes' Theorem. He writes the comparative form as follows:

$$(9) \quad \frac{P(G/E\&C)}{P(-G/E\&C)} == \frac{P(G/C)}{P(-G/C)} \quad X \quad \frac{P(E/G\&C)}{P(E/-G\&C)}[78]$$

Adams imagines an atheist and theist who agree in their assessment of the probability that there will be evil in the world, given background evidence, on the views that there is and isn't a God. Apart from the problem of evil, the theist believes theism's probability is greater than atheism's, but not by a great margin, for he also agrees that evil's existence is less probable on the theistic hypothesis (plus background information) than on an atheistic one. Assume that in the theist's noetic structure, he holds the following: $P(G/E\&C)=.7$, $P(-G/E\&C)=.3$, $P(G/C)=.9$, $P(-G/C)=.1$, $P(E/G\&C)=.00001$, and $P(E/-G\&C)=.01$. If we substitute these values in the comparative form of Bayes' Theorem, we derive the arithmetical impossibility

$$\frac{.7}{.3} == \frac{.9}{.1} \quad X \quad \frac{.00001}{.01} == \frac{.000009}{.001} == \frac{9}{1000}$$

In this case, the theist has an incoherent credence function and should feel a tug in the direction of atheism. That doesn't mean he must capitulate to atheism. He might change the relative status that the probabilities of the various conditionals have for him.[79]

A theist might respond in a different way. He might try to construct a defense against the probabilistic argument from evil. As to this defense, Adams explains:

> It would propose a hypothesis about God's reasons for permitting the evils there are. This hypothesis would not have to be true or even probable in order for the Defense to be successful. For the Defense is not a Theodicy; that is, it does not purport to tell us what God's actual reasons are for permitting the evils, but only what His reasons *might have been*. But whereas in the purely logical context, as Plantinga insists, it is enough if the hypothesis of the Defense is logically possible, and consistent with G and E, here the hypothesis must also be credible—it must not be too improbable—if the Defense is to be successful.[80]

As Adams explains, the purpose of this defense would be to move us "to assign to P(E/G&C)/P(E/-G&C) a value far enough from zero to keep it from overwhelming any other theistic inclinations we may have."[81] On the personalist interpretation of probability, the prior probability of theism must significantly exceed atheism's prior probability. If so, then a defense could be successful for the theist, making theism more probable than atheism on evil and background information, even if the probability of evil on the hypothesis of atheism and background information is greater than the probability of theism on the same conditions.[82] All in all a defense would explain why a good God might permit evil. As a result, the probability that there will be evil, given God's existence and background conditions, will be higher than without the defense.

Adams adds that theists need not have a successful defense against the probabilistic argument from evil to be rational in believing in God. In fact, theists need not have any hypothesis about why God would permit evil in order to be rational. They can say God has a reason, but it is beyond us. That would be consistent with Christianity's belief that God's knowledge is far beyond ours. It isn't irrational thinking either, because we often rationally continue to believe something without knowing exactly how to explain it. For example, one may reasonably trust the laws of chemistry, even if a particular experiment went awry and one can't explain why. Likewise, theists may respond rationally to the probabilistic argument from evil in one of two ways, even if they have no idea of why God allows evil. They might maintain belief because God's wisdom is above us, and thus, we aren't likely to know why he does one thing or another unless he reveals the reason. Or, theists might claim that assigning any values to the probabilities involved in the problem of evil is dubious. In fact, the theist's trust in God may far exceed his trust in any assignment of values to the probability of evil's existence on the conditions of theism and atheism.[83]

Suppose a theist did invoke a defense, however. What might it look like, and how might it relate to the probabilistic problem of evil? Adams suggests trying the free will defense. He begins by appealing to the disagreement in assessment (according to Plantinga) of the probability of the following form of the free will defense:

> (5)   All natural evil is due to the free activity of non-human persons; there is a balance of good over evil with respect to the actions of these non-human persons; and there is no world God could have created which contains a more favorable balance of good over evil with respect to the free activity of the non-human persons it contains . . . [84]

Plantinga says theists and atheists will disagree about the truth of (5), because belief in the existence of demons isn't fashionable. Nonetheless, that isn't evidence against (5)'s truth. Adams, however, says we do have some evidence against some natural evils being caused by demons. There is reason to believe that many calamities, pains, and diseases result from the processes of nature. Some may think demons control these processes, but Adams believes such a dualistic interpretation (God and demons control the course of nature) won't likely be very attractive to many theists.

As Adams further notes, Plantinga believes other considerations like beliefs about Christ and his suffering and about life after death should affect estimates of (5)'s probability. Adams thinks those considerations aid a Christian defense against the probabilistic argument from evil, and thinks atheists should grant that, even though they hold none of those beliefs. Adams writes:

> I doubt that they provide grounds for disagreement between Christians and atheists about the force of that argument, or about the priori [sic] probabilities of G and E. In particular I do not think that these considerations should lead Christians and atheists to disagree about the success of a Free Will Defense based on (5) against the probabilistic argument from evil. Let us recall that the success of such a Defense depends on the value of $P((5)/G\&C)$ and $P(E/(5)\&G\&C)$. Plantinga has argued in effect that Christian and atheist should be expected to disagree about the overall probability of (5). But that is because the probability of (5), given the Christian's views, which include G, differs from the probability of (5), given the atheist's views which include -G. And that difference does not obviously lead to any disagreement about the probability of (5), given G and C, or of E, given (5) and G and C.[85]

Adams ends this part of his discussion by arguing that there is no reason for Christians and atheists to disagree about the bearing of beliefs in Christ and life after death on the probability of (5). They will disagree about the truth of many of those beliefs, but that doesn't mean they must disagree about the probability of (5) on the hypothesis that God exists, Christ is Savior, and there is life after death plus all the background conditions. Hence, considerations like life after death, etc., shouldn't make Christians and atheists disagree about the success of a Free Will Defense based on (5), if success means lessening the value of evils as evidence against Christian theism.[86]

The final part of Adams's discussion of Plantinga evaluates one aspect of the defense based on (5). Adams asks how plausible it is that God couldn't have obtained morally better free creatures than those that actually exist. This claim presupposes the falsity of determinism and the truth of incompatibilism, as we saw in the chapter on the free will defense. However, it also assumes that counterfactuals of freedom can be true. Adams agrees with Plantinga about incompatibilism, but disagrees that counterfactuals of freedom can be true. He says Plantinga's hypothesis is in effect:

(11)   If God had permitted less evil than He has actually permitted whatever free creatures He had would have acted less well than His actual free creatures actually do.[87]

Though Adams disagrees with (11), he says it might be true that

(12)   It was antecedently *probable* that whatever free creatures God had would act better, on the whole, if He permitted as much evil as He has actually permitted than if He did not.[88]

Now (12), Adams agrees, might give God a good reason for permitting as much evil as he has. Adams then says that in trying to assign a probability to either (11) or (12), it can be probable "that a certain sort of person would act in a certain way in certain circumstances, even though the action would not be causally or logically necessitated."[89] Since that is so, Adams asks what the probability of (11) or (12) is with respect to nonhuman free creatures and with respect to human actions.

In answering this question about nonhuman creatures, Adams says the problem is that we know so little about them that it is hard to judge what the probability of (11) or (12) would be. This is true of both evil and good angels. As for good angels, it is hard to see how they would have been less good if God had eliminated natural evils. Likewise, we simply can't be sure that any given evil is unimportant to some good in the angelic realm. All of this leads Adams to conclude that the most significant contribution the hypothesis about nonhuman free creatures can make to a defense against the probabilistic argument from evil is:

if there are free creatures that we do not see, then evils that look as if they could have been eliminated without the loss of any good that we see may still have been important for goods that we do not see. But this is hardly more than an amplification of the general theme that God may have good reasons that we do not see for permitting the evils that we see.[90]

As to free human action, Adams thinks we are in a better position to evaluate the plausibility of the following:

(13)   It is true (or was antecedently probable) that *human* actions would be morally worse on the whole if God did not permit as much evil as He has actually permitted, than if He did.[91]

According to Adams, (13) is objectionable. Even if indeterminism is true, human actions are often rather predictable. Thus, certain unfavorable circumstances like illness, oppressive poverty, and the like lead predictably to morally worse behavior. Even if indeterminism is correct and God can't know counterfactuals of freedom, he surely could have predicted that certain kinds of circumstances would generally lead to morally worse behavior, and he could have done something to remove those circumstances. Likewise, it is likely that there are hereditary factors that make it more likely that each of us will do wrong in certain ways. Hence, "it is plausible to suppose that an omnipotent deity could tamper with these hereditary factors in such a way as to get human creatures whose free behavior would probably be morally better than ours is."[92] None of this, says Adams, makes (13) false or logically impossible, but it does suggest that it isn't very plausible. Thus, he concludes:

But I think the objections do show that a hypothesis such as (13) is not of much use for a Defense against the probabilistic argument from evil. The fuction [sic] of a Defense is to *explain,* by sufficiently plausible hypotheses, *how* God could have a good reason for permitting the evils there are. It will be successful in raising the value of P(E/G&C) for us to the extent that it suggests fairly plausible reasons for permitting evils that we could previously see no good reason for permitting. (13) does not offer such explanations at the points where they are needed; for in the difficult cases we still lack explanations of *how* it could be likely that preventing this or that evil would lead to a poorer belance [sic] of moral good over moral evil. Those explanations, if we had them, would serve the function of a Defense. But (13) only promises them; it does not give them.[93]

From the preceding, Adams concludes that possibly the best defense against the probabilistic argument from evil will be partial defenses. One defense might plausibly explain some evils and another handle others. Those explanations might increase the value of P(E/G&C), even if some evils have no explanations. Thus, it is better not to use a hypothesis like (13) which tries to explain all evils but doesn't do so very well. It is better to offer specific reasons for specific evils or sets of evils.[94]

ASSESSMENT OF THE DISCUSSION

Let me first turn to Adams, for I find his treatment more troublesome. First, Adams believes Plantinga's assessment of the atheistic argument from evil is overly harsh. Though the atheist's argument doesn't have coercive force, it isn't totally misconceived, because it may have a certain persuasive force. It may state reasons for the atheist's beliefs, shore up an atheist in his beliefs, and even show a theist that he has an incoherent credence function.

In response, Plantinga is probably a bit harsh in saying the atheistic probabilistic argument is totally misconceived, if one takes that at face value. An evidential argument of the sort Adams envisions can have the functions Adams notes. Likewise, even though the argument may not render theism improbable, in an overall case for or against theism, the existence of evil must count as evidence against theism. Still, even granting Adams's point, I don't see that his *persuasive* personalist version of the argument escapes Plantinga's fundamental criticism. That is, if the atheist uses the argument to tell why he is a nonbeliever, that is still autobiographical data. Others may be persuaded by what is said, and a theist may realize that his credence function is incoherent, but still nothing the atheist says will settle the issue decisively as to whether theism is improbable, given the fact of evil. Moreover, since the argument is a piece of autobiography, listeners may recognize that and may not even be *persuaded*. Hence, Plantinga is correct that on the personalist understanding of probability, the atheist doesn't make a successful coercive case against theism, and it isn't even clear he succeeds persuasively. Adams seems more optimistic about this argument's success than is warranted.

Second, Adams says that if theists realize they hold an incoherent credence function, they may reassign probability values to the various conditional probabilities. On the other hand, they might offer a defense which gives a reason why a good God would allow evil. To solve the logical problem of evil, one needs a defense which is only logically possible. To answer the evidential problem Adams believes the defense must also be credible.

My problem is with the requirement that the defense be credible or plausible. Credible from whose perspective? Is there any hope of convincing the atheist that *any* defense is credible? Adams apparently thinks theists can latch onto a defense everyone will agree is credible. This seems to be just wishful thinking. As Plantinga suggests, whether the atheist and theist perceive the defense as plausible will largely be a function of their noetic structure. Moreover, their assessment of theism's probability and the defense's plausibility will likely be nothing more than autobiographical comment. But if that is so, it is dubious that the atheist will find any theistic defense plausible. As for theists, it is dubious that they need this defense to convince them that theism is probable. As theists, they already think it is. A defense may shore up their faith, but it is unlikely that they need it to convince them of theism's truth.

Where does this leave us? If Plantinga's intuitions about beliefs being a function of noetic structure are right, and if his criticisms of the various notions of probability have credence, then offering a defense to render theism probable will surely have no coercive force on the atheist, and it won't likely have much persuasive effect either. The atheist will probably be no more convinced by the theist's defense than the theist is convinced by the atheist's probabilistic argument from evil. And the defense will be unnecessary for the theist.

On this basis alone, one wonders what the point would be of offering a defense. Moreover, if Plantinga is right about accepting beliefs on the basis of noetic structure, then I doubt the theist can ever do what Adams requires, namely, offer a defense which theist and atheist alike deem credible (let alone persuasive or coercive). In order to convince us that there is a point in offering a defense, Adams must demonstrate one of two things. He must 1) show that, in spite of Plantinga's reformed epistemology and his assessment of the various notions of probability, it is still possible to offer a defense which will be judged plausible (and even persuasive or coercive) by theist and atheist alike, or he must 2) argue against Plantinga's epistemology and for an epistemology according to which theist and atheist can be objective enough to agree on the plausibility both of a theistic defense and of the atheist's argument from evil. Neither option will be easy to accomplish, but until Adams does one or the other there seems little point in having the theist offer a defense. The theist may offer it and say it is plausible; the atheist need only retort that he doesn't think so.

Third, Adams also says theists really don't have to offer atheists a defense, because theists can always say God has a reason for evil, but his wisdom is so far above us that we aren't likely to know it. Or, theists may just say they trust God so much it doesn't matter whether they can figure out his reason for allowing evil. Nothing will shatter that trust.

I agree that a theist may offer one of these responses, but it is hard to see what that would accomplish in regard to the evidential argument from evil. The first response hardly provides evidence for theism's probability, since it appeals to other claims about God that are also under debate. As to saying one trusts God so much that nothing can shake that trust, it appears that no amount of reason or evidence will make any difference. If so, it no longer makes sense to discuss evidence and probabilities. But how can that be a defense against the evidential argument from evil for anyone who isn't already a theist? These responses appear to be (in Plantinga's terms) nothing more than autobiographical information. As such, they resolve nothing about whether evil really makes theism improbable. The upshot of all of this is that while Adams agrees with Plantinga's assessment of the various interpretations of probability, his appeal to the personalist interpretation and his claims that theists may offer the responses noted don't seem to take seriously enough that on a personalist interpretation theists and atheists are just stating their own private opinions. Hence, I am nowhere near as optimistic as Adams about the value of the defenses and responses he offers to the argument from evil.

Fourth, Adams says theists will want to bring belief in Christ and in life after death into a discussion of theism's probability on evil. He thinks atheists should have no problem agreeing with theists about how those beliefs affect the probability of theism. Atheists can agree that if those beliefs are true, theism becomes more probable, but still maintain that none of that matters since those beliefs are false.

Adams's point about atheist and theist agreeing on how these beliefs affect theism's probability may be right for some theists and some atheists, but I don't agree with it in general. Since atheists normally reject those views, they may not think those views, if true, would help raise the probability of theism. How theist and atheist assess the impact of these beliefs on theism's probability is partly a matter of the logic of how these beliefs do relate to theism, but also partly stems from psychological factors. That is, one normally tends to place a higher value on claims one believes true than on claims considered false.

My point here is relevant not only to how theist and atheist might evaluate these claims in terms of theism's probability. It is also relevant to how different theists assess matters. For theists who hold these views and believe they entail other beliefs which provide strong evidence for theism, these beliefs, if true, would significantly raise the probability of theism. On the other hand, for a theist who thinks they are true but sees no particular connection to other claims that increase theism's probability, belief in Christ and in life after death may not appear to raise the overall probability of theism as much as the first theist thinks. From all of this I conclude that while there is a certain sense in which Adams is right that theist and atheist can agree on how these beliefs would affect theism's probability, I think some factors suggest they may disagree on that matter and suggest that if they disagree, no one is being irrational.

Fifth, the preceding objections are, I think, significant, but I am even more troubled by Adams's handling of the free will defense. I believe it contains confusions that beset not only his presentation but other handlings of the evidential problem of evil. Adams claims that in order to uphold the free will defense, Plantinga must reject determinism and believe that counterfactuals of freedom can be true (Plantinga accepts the proposition Adams labels [11]). Adams agrees about determinism, but disagrees about counterfactuals. Hence, he rejects (11) in favor of (12). I think this raises some significant flaws in his discussion of the free will defense and what is probable. Let me explain.

Let us first look at this matter from the perspective of a determinist (even a compatibilist) theist and/or atheist. A compatibilist may or may not initially have an opinion about the probability of either (11) or (12), but he will recognize that both presuppose incompatibilism which he rejects. On that ground alone, he will probably not find either (11) or (12) very probable or helpful in responding to the evidential problem.

Someone may object that what the compatibilist thinks is irrelevant, because here we are discussing and testing the incompatibilist theist's views. As I have argued, this is the proper response when handling the logical problem of evil (a problem about the *internal* consistency of a theist's beliefs). But I don't believe it is the proper response to the evidential problem of evil. Here the issue is how probable it is that the form of theism in question is true. Plantinga and Adams argue for the plausibility of a theism incorporating incompatibilistic free will. I don't see that any compatibilist (theist or atheist) will think *that* form of theism is very probable, since compatibilists reject incompatibilism. Hence, an atheistic and theistic compatibilist may think the free will defense makes a free will theism like Arminianism more probable, but since they both reject incompatibilism, I doubt that even the theist, let alone the atheist, will think such a theism has a probability greater than .5. In fact, because it incorporates incompatibilism, compatibilists may think Arminianism's probability is close to 0.

In order to convince compatibilists that a free will theology incorporating the free will defense is more than .5 probable, Plantinga and Adams must demonstrate, among other things, that incompatibilism is the correct view of freedom, but it isn't very likely the compatibilist will agree on that matter. Hence, there is little hope, contrary to Adams's claims, that a determinist (theist or atheist) can agree with an indeterminist theist on the probability of any free will theism, even if that theism incorporates the free will defense. But if that is so, it is dubious that the defense will really settle much of anything between determinists (theists and atheists) and indeterminists.[95]

What if the indeterminist theist offers the free will defense, and the atheist is an indeterminist? Can they agree on theism's probability in light of the free will defense? They may, but there is still potential problem. In fact, there is potential difficulty even among indeterminist theists. The difference between Adams's (11) and (12) points to the problem. (12) presupposes that God doesn't know the future. (11) presupposes that he knows it via middle knowledge. As we saw in the chapter on the free will defense, other indeterminists use simple foreknowledge and the Boethian and Ockhamist strategies to explain how God knows the future and yet leaves room for indeterministic freedom. For someone like Adams who holds (12), it is dubious that the free will defense like the one expressed in (11) or a free will defense that incorporates any of these other answers to the freedom/foreknowledge problem will appear very probable. For someone who holds (11), the probability of (12) or a free will defense using the Boethian strategy won't seem very high.[96]

My point here about indeterminist theists is that just as Arminianism is opposed to Calvinism in general, there are also various forms of free will theism and even varieties of Arminianism. Some free will theists believe God knows the future; some (e.g., open theists) don't. How they evaluate the probability of propositions like (11) and (12) and the theologies those forms of the free will defense presuppose will depend on the form of free will theism they hold.

As to atheistic indeterminists, they most likely deny that anyone can know the future. They may agree with Adams about the probability of (11) and the theism it presupposes. If nothing else, they will at least probably agree with Adams's views about whether God knows the future. However, they will probably disagree with *Plantinga* (or any other indeterminist theist who thinks God knows the future) about the probability of (11) and the free will theism it presupposes.

The upshot of all of this is that even among indeterminists, it is dubious that there will be unanimous agreement about the plausibility of the free will defense and of the theism that incorporates it, for there are different forms of indeterminism. This just means that a particular indeterminist theist's defense will seem probable to theists who hold that form of theism. It may also have some appeal to atheistic indeterminists whose form of indeterminism is that of the theist's in question. However, it won't likely settle the debate with many atheists or even with theists who hold different forms of indeterminism. And this just means little will be settled conclusively about the plausibility of any given formulation of the free will defense and the probability of the theism that incorporates it.

What I have just argued about agreeing on the probability of (11), (12), and the like mustn't be misunderstood. Nothing I have said about determinists' or indeterminists' evaluations of those propositions or the free will defense means the free will defense is implausible as a response to the evidential problem of evil, nor does it make any free will theism improbable. It only shows that if one agrees with Plantinga's analysis of probability and his comments about beliefs and their relation to one's overall noetic structure, (11) or (12) or free will theism in general will be probable if one holds those views about freedom, God, and evil; otherwise they will be improbable. But none of that destroys all forms of classical theism. Nor does it destroy any free will theism. It just shows that neither theists nor atheists are likely to get much mileage out of a probabilistic attack or defense (via the free will defense) of theism on the basis of evil.

The points I am making about various forms of free will theism in general and various forms of deterministic (whether compatibilist or hard determinist) theism in general underscore what I believe is a crucial point in this discussion of the probabilistic problem of evil, just as it is critical in handling the logical problem of evil. Unfortunately, it is a point that is repeatedly overlooked. Specifically, theists and atheists alike ask about the probability of God's existence, given evil. However, that question cannot be handled apart from specifying the conception of God in view. Hence, to the question "Is God's existence improbable, given evil?" one should first respond "Is the existence of *which* God improbable, given evil?" For a determinist, the existence of, for example, the Arminian God will never seem very probable, regardless of whether or not one invokes evil as evidence against that God and regardless of whether the theist defends that God with the free will defense. But then, appeal to evil as evidence in this case is somewhat beside the point, just as is appeal to the free will defense in this instance. The theist and atheist must first settle a far more fundamental disagreement between them (a disagreement over determinism and incompatibilism) before a discussion of evil as evidence and the free will defense as a support for an Arminian theology can ever be taken very seriously by *both* of them. Obviously, they won't likely agree on a resolution to the determinism/incompatibilism issue, but that just shows how hard it will be even to get to a point where a determinist atheist can raise a significant evidential argument *on the basis of evil* against an indeterminist theist. Of course, since it is the atheist who tries to make the case against theism, the considerations I've just raised should be more troublesome to his project than to the theist.

Suppose, on the other hand, that both atheist and theist are indeterminists. In that case, both may agree that evil's existence is significant evidence against a free will theist's God, and both may agree that the free will defense is important counterevidence. When these evidences are evaluated, however, they may still disagree over the overall probability of the theism in question. But, at least in this case, it makes sense for atheist and theist to ask whether evil is evidence against that God's existence and whether the free will defense raises the probability of his existence, because they agree on the notion of freedom.

In sum, my point is that just as one must specify the form of theism in view when discussing the logical problem of evil, one must do the same when handling the evidential problem. Evil might be strong evidence against one conception of God, but not against another. And, if atheists and theists disagree on fundamental metaphysical and/or ethical notions, appeal to evil by the atheist and appeal to some sort of defense by the theist won't get them to agree on the probability of the theism the theist holds. Since they hold different views on metaphysics and ethics, their disagreement goes much deeper than a difference of opinion about what the facts of evil mean for the probability of a particular form of theism.

A final set of objections emphasizes Adams's handling of (13). Adams says (13) is problematic, because there are instances and kinds of evil it doesn't justify. His comments about specific instances of evil suggest that (13) won't handle the religious problem of evil. Comments about there being leftover evils for which there seems no solution raise the problem of apparently gratuitous evil. To solve those problems, we may need specific defenses, according to Adams. In fact, we may need several partial defenses, rather than just one (like [13]).

Now, there is something right about what Adams says and something wrong. He is surely right that (13) won't cover all forms of natural evil. He is wrong in apparently thinking that it handles no problem of evil because it doesn't handle all evidential problems of evil. The error is one we have seen repeatedly, namely, failure to recognize that there are different problems of evil, each of which has its own answer. (13) is relevant to the abstract, general, evidential theological/philosophical problem of evil. But that is *not* a problem about specific instances of evil. Adams complains that (13) is inadequate because it doesn't cover specific instances of evil, but Adams wrote (13) in general terms; (13) talks about the world being "worse on the whole." It doesn't talk in terms of specific instances of evil or apparently gratuitous evils. Since that is so, Adams should have realized that (13) is one of those partial defenses he asks for. Its failure to cover every problem of evil doesn't mean it is worthless as a response to any problem of evil.

As to Adams's specific interaction with the free will defense as it relates to human action (I believe his comments about angelic action are correct), I see further problems. Adams says that even if counterfactuals of freedom can't be true, God surely can know that certain kinds of circumstances lead predictably to worse moral behavior, and he could have eliminated those circumstances. But is that really true? I'm not sure it is for someone who rejects the idea that God knows the future. There are plenty of instances of people in oppressive situations, for example, who turn to morally evil behavior, but there are also many instances of people overcoming their circumstances only to lead moral lives. So, then, how can God really predict which instances will lead to morally worse behavior, unless he knows the future? For any indeterminist theist who thinks God can't know the future, Adams's suggestion about what God should have done, given his ability to predict outcomes, won't amount to much.

If that is so, however, then to accommodate Adams's concern, God would have to remove all instances of oppressive background, etc., to insure removal of those that would lead to morally bad behavior. I suspect that Plantinga and many other committed free will defenders would object that to do that (to remove all instances of oppressive situations, etc.) would ultimately remove free will. Since much natural evil results from abuse of human freedom, I am inclined to agree with free will defenders who would object to Adams's request by saying that to fulfill it would remove freedom. Surely, theists like Reichenbach who argue for the necessity of natural evil in order to have free will would be unhappy with this request.

In his discussion of (13), Adams also says some forms of human evil action are attributable to human heredity. To eliminate those evils, God need only change our heredity. Perhaps God could do this by preprogramming people (tampering with their heredity in that way) not to have tendencies to do evil, or if they have those inclinations, never to act on them. The difficulty with these suggestions is that for an incompatibilist they eliminate what he means by freedom. It no longer seems possible for agents to do other than what they do (if otherwise is choosing evil) in the contracausal sense of "could do otherwise." Internal heredity includes causes which guarantee that they can't choose evil, but that's not incompatibilism!

For a compatibilist like myself, this request is also problematic. Granted, God could do what Adams asks, and a compatibilist could talk about man acting freely. The problem for someone like myself (as explained in chapter 6) is that this would mean God didn't create human beings but moral superhumans, but that wasn't what God intended. I agree that a world of moral superhumans would be morally superior to our world, but a Modified Rationalist isn't required to prove that our world is the best possible world or even better than other good worlds. He only needs to show that it is a good possible world. The free will defender cites free will as evidence that ours is a good world. My defense shows, by pointing to human beings as created, that it is, too. I conclude, then, that what Adams suggests about changing heredity should be objectionable to both free will defenders and to compatibilist theists like myself.

Turning to Plantinga, I see fewer problems, but let me begin with two points of agreement. First, Plantinga is surely right that to assess the probability of theism (or atheism) one must assess it on total evidence. If atheists can emphasize only one kind of evidence (evil), they may build a strong case against theism, and if theists can focus on only one kind of positive evidence, they may build a strong case for theism. However, such arguments only show that on one kind of evidence theism is probable or improbable. That may be an interesting piece of information, but it settles nothing with respect to whether theism as a whole is probable or improbable. Plantinga's example of Feike the Frisian makes the point abundantly clear.

The implication of this point, moreover, is twofold. On the one hand, if one must consider total evidence in order to make probability judgments about theism, that complicates matters for the atheist who would use a single evidence like evil to build a case against theism. On the other hand, the same is true for theists. Theists who appeal, for example, solely to the traditional arguments for God's existence must realize that if they are building a case for theism's probability, there is more evidence they must consider. The good news in all of this for theism is that atheists who think appeal to evil alone will settle the matter of theism's probability are mistaken.

Second, Plantinga doesn't appeal to the free will defense, because he chooses a different strategy. Instead, he questions whether it is possible to determine probabilities in a way that is objective enough so that theist and atheist alike can agree on probabilities and work Bayes' Theorem in regard to theism's probability. Though I am not entirely convinced that his critique of the various notions of probability makes this an impossible project, I agree with his underlying point that assigning numerical values to the probabilities that are parts of Bayes' Theorem involves a significant degree of subjectivity. It isn't at all clear that theists and atheists will agree on these matters, and hence, it is dubious that atheists can convince anyone other than themselves with a probabilistic argument against theism based on evil. In this respect, I think Plantinga's discussion in "The Probabilistic Argument from Evil" is a significant advance over his handling of the evidential problem in *The Nature of Necessity*.

On the other hand, if one can determine the requisite probabilities, then it seems hard to deny that the free will defense makes free will theism more probable. Even atheists who are indeterminists should agree on this point. As

Plantinga argues, if atheists agree that the free will defense can solve the logical problem of evil for free will theisms, they should recognize that it will also raise the probability of those systems in the face of evil as evidence against theism. Of course, atheistic agreement that the free will defense raises the probability of these theologies doesn't commit atheists to believing they are true or even probable. They may still believe that without the free will defense Arminianism, for example, is .1 probable whereas with it, Arminianism becomes .3 probable. Arminian theists may claim that without the defense their theism is .5 probable, and with it Arminianism becomes .8 probable. Though atheist and theist disagree on assignment of probability values, the atheistic indeterminist can't deny that the defense raises Arminianism's probability and therefore offers more grounds for holding that theology. I think Plantinga would agree, but repeat his concern about whether theist *and* atheist can agree on probability values, and note that if they can't, not much is resolved in regard to theism's probability by appealing either to evil or to the free will defense as evidence for or against God's existence.

As to problems with Plantinga's presentation, I find only one worth noting. First, Plantinga, as others, treats the probabilistic problem of evil as just one problem, but it actually involves many problems. This is true because there are various kinds of evidential problems of evil, but also because even the philosophical/theological probabilistic problem of evil isn't just one problem. As already argued, if asked whether evil is evidence against God's existence, one should respond "evidence against which God?" Because Plantinga's strategy attacks our ability to agree on probabilities in light of problems with each understanding of probability, his discussion doesn't directly address this issue. However, most of what he does say suggests that he assumes there is only one probabilistic problem of evil.

In the next chapter, I shall discuss Richard Swinburne's, Bruce Reichenbach's, and Michael Peterson's responses to the evidential problem. Though they appreciate Plantinga's approach, they have adopted different strategies for handling this problem, including invoking various defenses against evil to show that theism is more probable than not.

11

Theists and Evil as Evidence (ii)

Alvin Plantinga's contribution to the probabilistic argument from evil is extremely significant, but other theists have also addressed this issue. In this chapter I want to consider the contributions of Richard Swinburne, Bruce Reichenbach, and Michael Peterson. Each wrote around the time Plantinga wrote "The Probabilistic Argument from Evil," but each handles the problem differently from Plantinga.

RICHARD SWINBURNE

During the last half-century Richard Swinburne has contributed a number of significant works in philosophy of religion, including his trilogy *Faith and Reason, The Coherence of Theism,* and *The Existence of God.* All three contain materials relevant to the problem of evil, but *The Existence of God* most directly addresses it. In addition, he has discussed the issue in "The Problem of Evil,"[1] "Natural Evil,"[2] and more recently in "Does Theism Need a Theodicy?"[3] While one can see a development in Swinburne's thought, I believe these works represent a unified, coherent position.

There are several stages in Swinburne's argumentation about the problem of evil. Some of his argument relates to the logical problem of evil, but his major concern is the probabilistic problem, especially as it relates to natural evil. In what follows I present the major phases of his argument, as well as reactions to his views.

Theism and Prior Probabilities

In *The Existence of God* a central theme is that there are evidences for God's existence which make it probable that theism is the most likely model for explaining our world. Swinburne begins with chapters about the nature of inductive arguments, the nature of explanation, and the justification of explanation. He distinguishes between scientific explanations (explanations of phenomena in terms of covering laws and initial conditions) and personal explanations (explanations appealing to intentional actions of rational agents).[4] In trying to determine the probability of an explanatory hypothesis (whether scientific or personal), one must calculate the probability of the hypothesis prior to considering the evidence for or against it, calculate the probability that the evidence will obtain on the assumption that the theory is right or wrong, and calculate the posterior probability, i.e., the likelihood that the hypothesis is true, given background information and available evidence.

As we have already seen, calculating the prior probability of theism and atheism is significant to the inductive problem of evil. Hence, Swinburne begins by considering the whole question of the prior probability (or, to use his term, the "intrinsic probability") of theism. He invokes Bayes' Theorem to determine both the prior and posterior probability of theism.[5]

According to Swinburne, prior probability of a theory rests on its simplicity, fit with background knowledge, and scope, but Swinburne thinks simplicity is the most significant.[6] By simplicity Swinburne means that the less complicated a hypothesis, the more likely that it is true, for there are fewer details to account for than in a complex theory. For example, if one can explain why an event happened by referring to one agent, that is a simpler explanation than one which appeals to several people.

The second criterion is how well a theory fits with other things we know. Theories that fit well with known conditions and/or require postulating no unknown entities are more likely true than those that are out of step with what is known and/or require postulating new entities. As to scope, the narrower a theory's scope, the more probable. Swinburne explains that the more objects involved and purportedly explained by a theory, the less likely it is to be true, for the more one asserts, the more there is to prove, and the greater the room for error.[7] Of course, theories that have the narrowest scope and fit best with background knowledge are most likely the simplest, so simplicity is really the key. Swinburne doesn't mean that no complex theories, no theories of broad scope, and no theories that don't appear to fit what we already know could possibly be true. His point is that in figuring the probability of a theory, especially its prior probability, the simplest theories have the greatest probability.

Though Swinburne does assess theism's plausibility in light of various evidences, he begins building his case for theism by arguing that as an explanatory hypothesis for our world, it has a higher probability than other rival hypotheses. For one thing, prior probability depends mainly on a theory's simplicity, and Swinburne thinks theism has considerable simplicity, more than its competitors.[8] He argues this by noting that theism holds to a God whose essence contains qualities like infinity, omniscience, freedom, necessary being, and eternity. He thinks such qualities make God the "simplest kind of person that there could be."[9] Normally one thinks of a majestic God as much more complex than man, but Swinburne illustrates his point in relation to God's infinity:

> To start with, theism postulates a God with capacities which are as great as they logically can be. He is infinitely powerful, omnipotent. That there is an omnipotent God is a simpler hypothesis than the hypothesis that there is a God who has such-and-such limited power (e.g. the power to rearrange matter, but not the power to create it). It is simpler in just the same way that the hypothesis that some particle has zero mass, or infinite velocity is simpler than the hypothesis that it has a mass of 0.34127 of some unit, or a velocity of 301,000 km/sec. A finite limitation cries out for an explanation of why there is just that particular limit, in a way that limitlessness does not.[10]

As Swinburne proceeds, he enumerates various divine attributes, and explains why each is the simplest form of the attribute there could be. Along the way, he argues that God is omniscient and perfectly free and that "God's perfect goodness follows deductively from his omniscience and his perfect freedom."[11] As omniscient, God knows what is morally wrong and what is morally obligatory, and as perfectly free, he cannot be caused to do wrong. Moreover, as supremely rational, he will act according to some reason. However, if doing an act would overall be worse than refraining, then there is reason for refraining. God, being supremely rational, will understand that, and being free, he won't be forced to violate what reason dictates. Hence, he will always choose to do what is morally good and obligatory, and never choose moral wrong. As a result, he will be perfectly good.[12]

Swinburne concludes this portion of his argument by summing up why he thinks theism has great simplicity. It is simple in that it postulates a person of a very simple kind. Moreover, it is simple in that all explanation is reducible to personal explanation. That is, the operation and causation of the various factors in scientific explanation are always explainable in terms of acts of persons. God may be that person in some instances, but other persons may be the explanation in other cases. Whoever the person is, the explanation is still simple, for it reduces things to the agency of a person. As to how scientific and personal explanations relate, Swinburne says there are three tenable views on this matter. He writes:

> One is the theist's view described above that the operation and causal effi-
> cacy of the factors cited in scientific explanation have a full personal expla-
> nation; a second is the materialist's view that the operation and causal
> efficacy of the factors cited in personal explanation have a full scientific
> explanation; the third is that the operation and causal efficacy of neither
> can be given full explanation in terms of the other. On the third view,
> which we may call explanatory dualism, there are just two kinds of expla-
> nation of goings-on in the world and neither can in any way be reduced
> to the other.[13]

Swinburne says the dualist's approach is the most complex of the three. The materialist's and personalist's (personalist theist in this case) views are equally simple, and hence, more probably true than the dualist's view. In a later chapter, he raises problems with the materialist's view,[14] but at this point in his book his main point is that either personalism or materialism is simpler than dualism, and thus, more likely true.

Swinburne concludes with what he claims is a further important factor about theism. He notes that in considering arguments for God's existence (as he does later in his book), the key is how certain phenomena in our world are best explained. If one appeals to God as originator of those phenomena, one needn't then ask how God came to be. In other words, appeal to God ends the explanation.[15] The implication of this (though Swinburne doesn't explicitly say it) is that if one thinks a cause other than God brought about a given phenomenon, one may still need to ask for the cause of that cause in order to explain fully the phenomenon in question. If God, however, is the cause, then explanation ends. Hence, the theistic explanation will be simpler.

In sum, Swinburne concludes that theism is a simpler hypothesis than its rivals for explaining our world, and that means it has greater prior proba-bility than other hypotheses. Swinburne admits that it seems *"a priori* vastly improbable, if one thinks about it, that there should exist anything at all log-ically contingent. But, given that there does exist something, the simple is more likely to exist than the complex."[16] Thus, even if theism's prior proba-bility is low, it will be greater than that of other theories because of its great simplicity.

Theism and Probability

Even if theism has greater prior probability than its competitors, that doesn't mean it is more probable than those theories when all are evaluated on the evidence. Hence, in *The Existence of God,* Swinburne assesses theism in light of all theistic evidences for God's existence, and in view of the existence of evil. Before seeing Swinburne's handling of evil as evidence, we can see what he thinks about the overall probability of theism. Not only does he discuss that matter in *The Existence of God,* but also more recently in "Does Theism Need a Theodicy?" My focus is the more recent article.

Swinburne distinguishes different notions of rationality. For our purposes two will suffice. A belief is rational$_1$ if it is consistent with other beliefs one holds. A belief is rational$_2$ if it is based on evidence so that other inquirers with the same empirical evidence would reach the same conclusion.[17] According to Swinburne, on the logical theory of probability, someone's belief is rational$_2$ insofar as evidence renders it probable, for the logical theory (as opposed to the personalist or frequentist) is concerned with the extent to which one proposition makes another probable.[18]

After invoking Bayes' Theorem, Swinburne makes the same basic point about prior probability he made in *The Existence of God.* In answer to Plantinga's complaints about his idea that mere simplicity of a theory makes it more probable, he offers the following explanation:

> I must make clear, as I did not in earlier writing, that the 'simplicity' of a proposition h in my sense is a matter of the simplicity in a more normal sense of the simplest proposition logically equivalent to h. (For example, conjoining to h a complicated necessary truth makes a proposition no less simple, and so no less likely to be true, than the original h.) . . .
> He [Plantinga—my insertion] selected pairs of propositions, logically equivalent (and thus of equal content) yet greatly differing in 'simplicity,' and pointed out that it was an axiom of the calculus that logically equivalent propositions always have the same probability. I ought to have said, but did not say (because I did not adequately appreciate), that the 'simplicity' of a proposition h in my sense was to be taken as the simplicity in a more normal sense of the simplest proposition logically equivalent to it. It is a matter of the simplicity of the world, whose existence it entails.[19]

After offering this amendment, Swinburne says he doesn't think Plantinga's objections destroy his claims or the ability of probability calculus, construed according to the logical theory, to calculate the probability of a large-scale theory on evidence.[20]

Swinburne then explains how all of this relates to the idea that evils in the world are incompatible with God's existence. Since evil's existence and God's existence seem incompatible, how can a theist be rational$_1$ if he holds both? The answer depends on several factors, according to Swinburne. If, for example, background knowledge logically entails that a given theory is correct, the prior probability will be 1, but then the theory is deemed correct. Counterevidence can't falsify it, but will be considered misobservation. On the other hand, if the prior probability of a theory (like theism) on background information is not 1, and there is strong evidence that doesn't fit the hypothesis, then the probability of the hypothesis being correct, given background information and evidence, will be very low, possibly even 0. These principles hold true for scientific theories, but also apply when considering religious beliefs.[21]

What should we conclude about theism, then? Swinburne admits that background knowledge (even including theistic proofs) doesn't logically entail theism. Hence, $P(h/k) < 1$. Moreover, evils (e) in the world appear incompatible with God's existence. Apparently, the rational man must judge that $P(h/e.k) = 0$, unless some reason says otherwise. According to Swinburne, the reason for not coming to this conclusion is that theodicy has "proved to have a good track record in making evils at first sight apparently inconsistent with the existence of God not to appear so subsequently."[22] Past success of theodicy in showing a reason for apparently useless evil is grounds for rationally$_1$ believing there will be a theodicy that handles other instances of apparently purposeless evils. Hence, theists will be rational$_1$ in maintaining their theistic belief. Swinburne says theists must, then, do one of two things. They must either show of each apparently useless evil that it makes possible a greater good, or, they must point to the track record of theodicy in clarifying the point of seemingly useless evil and argue that past successes make it likely that there is a theodicy for each evil that could eventually be found. If theists can do neither, then they must either produce other evidence for God's existence which makes it probable, or must give up theistic belief, if they want to hold rational$_1$ and rational$_2$ beliefs.

As for Swinburne, he believes theism does need a theodicy,[23] and he believes it can be provided. His approach, then, is to state this theodicy and appeal to its track record in making sense of apparently senseless evil.[24] All of this means that at the end of what I am calling the second stage of Swinburne's argumentation, he would claim that not only theism's prior but also its posterior probability are sufficiently high to render it confirmed and thus reasonable to hold. Of course, none of this says what Swinburne's theodicy is. If it fails, his whole program is in trouble.

Swinburne's Theodicy and the Probability of Theism

In "The Problem of Evil," "Natural Evil," and *The Existence of God* Swinburne offers his answer to the problem of evil. Since he argues it more completely in *The Existence of God*, I shall focus on that. Swinburne offers the free will defense in response to moral evil, and then turns to natural evil.[25]

Swinburne offers several arguments as to why God would allow natural evil. However, he labels his major argument the argument from the need for knowledge. Given God's decision to give us free will (incompatibilistic), Swinburne says natural evil is logically necessary if agents are "to have the *knowledge* of how to bring about evil or prevent its occurrence, knowledge which they must have if they are to have a genuine choice between bringing about evil and bringing about good."[26] This may sound strange, so Swinburne explains it at length.

The theodicy begins by asking how agents are to gain knowledge, especially knowledge of which actions lead to pleasant results and which to unpleasant for themselves and others. Swinburne answers that the normal route is induction from similar past actions. If on one occasion one places a hand on a hot stove and gets burned, that is reason to infer inductively that the same thing will happen if one does it again. Moreover, the more past instances of an action followed by its consequence, the more accurate one's claim to know what will happen in the future. In addition, the closer an action and its consequences are to one's experience, the more certain will be one's knowledge with respect to them. Hence, to use Swinburne's example, if you want to know the results of drinking eight double whiskeys, you will know most certainly if you do it yourself, less certainly if you observe others doing it, less surely yet by observing the result in different circumstances (as when you drink them more quickly, when you are extra tired, or when you drink eight beers rather than whiskey), and least certainly if you infer the result from actions that are only remotely similar to drinking eight double whiskeys (e.g., taking several doses of a tranquilizing drug).[27] Moreover, one is more likely to be cautious about things one has personally experienced, rather than things only heard about. Someone who experiences a fire in his home is more likely to take precautions against another than someone who only hears about it.

It is also important to realize that for any evil inflicted knowingly upon others, there must have been a first instance of that evil in history. Without that instance and others, there would be no knowledge of how to inflict or avoid that evil. For example, until someone is poisoned by cyanide, no one would know that could happen. Swinburne sums up the matter as follows:

> There must be naturally occurring evils (i.e. evils not deliberately caused by men) if men are to know how to cause evils themselves or are to prevent evil occurring. And there have to be *many* such evils, if men are to have sure knowledge, for as we saw, sure knowledge of what will happen in future comes only by induction from many past instances.[28]

Swinburne also claims that what applies in the short run, also applies for long-term consequences of actions. For example, how will city planners know whether to build a city in areas prone to earthquakes or in areas not subject to such disasters unless they know where earthquakes are likely to occur? But they can't know where that is unless there have been earthquakes in the past and their consequences have been observed. Without those natural evils, long-term planning to avoid earthquakes can't be done.

Why, though, do we need this knowledge? Swinburne answers that it is essential to a world where people have free will which allows them the genuine choice of either bringing about evils or preventing them. It is an empty freedom if people have freedom to do good or evil, but have no idea of which actions are good and which evil, and what consequences stem from both. Without that knowledge, people won't know how to choose. But if the only way to get that knowledge is to infer it inductively from past evil events, then ours must be a world where evil happens. Swinburne explains:

> My main argument so far has been that *if* men are to have the opportunity to bring about serious evils for themselves or others by actions or negligence, or to prevent their occurrence, and if all knowledge of the future is obtained by normal induction, that is by induction from patterns of similar events in the past—then there must be serious natural evils occurring to man or animals. I have argued earlier that it is good that men should have the former opportunity.[29]

Knowledge of evil gained inductively from past experiences requires natural evil. However, what if God gave that knowledge in another way? What if God gave it verbally? Why couldn't God, for example, just say out loud to anyone nearing the edge of a cliff that if she walks too near the edge, she will fall over? Giving information this way would have the twin advantages of avoiding natural evils and convincing everyone that there is a God. Swinburne says that in a world where everyone knows God exists, all would realize that he knows our every thought and deed. Knowing that he is just, we would expect punishment for evil deeds. The inclination to disobey would be greatly reduced. Moreover, all would consider God good and worthy of worship. As a result, there would be little temptation to evil. Prudence and reason would demand doing what is good.[30]

This may sound like a good alternative to our world, but Swinburne claims it isn't. In such a world, God is too close to us. Knowledge would surround mankind, but in such a way that no one could work things out for oneself and in such a way as to stifle one's own choice of destiny. Swinburne writes:

> Yet a man only has a genuine choice of destiny if he has reasons for pursuing either good or evil courses of action; for, as I argued in Chapter 5, a man can only perform an action which he has some reason to do. Further, in such a world, men could not choose whether to acquire knowledge for themselves or future generations, or what kinds of knowledge to seek, but

knowledge would surround them. In this way too men would have no choice of destiny.

I conclude that a world in which God gave to men verbal knowledge of consequences of their actions would not be a world in which men had a significant choice of destiny, of what to make of themselves, and of the world. God would be too close for them to be able to work things out for themselves. If God is to give man knowledge while at the same time allowing him a genuine choice of destiny, it must be normal inductive knowledge.[31]

There is another problem with verbal knowledge. It requires language, but a description often fails to capture details and bring home to a person how an experience feels. It abstracts from reality and renders things impersonal. A description of an action and its consequences can never be as vivid as an experience of the same. Thus, the experience is closer to reality, and as Swinburne has argued, the closer to the experience, the more certain the knowledge. Without certainty of knowledge, it is hard to know how to act when wanting to cause or prevent evils. So, even if verbal knowledge allows freedom to choose one's destiny, it still would be less adequate than knowledge gained by experience.[32]

Natural evil, then, is justified, according to Swinburne, because it is necessary in a world where people must know certain things in order to have freedom to make significant choices (good and evil) which will shape their destiny. This is Swinburne's main theodicy against natural evil, but he offers two supplemental reasons why God might allow that evil. First, God might allow it because some of these evils are attached to higher-order good. This is the familiar argument we have already seen about the logically necessary tie between certain first-order evils and second-order goods. A second reason is that some natural evils are necessary for people to have a full range of possible experiences. Knowledge of the logical possibilities of evil is beneficial to those who have it. Swinburne explains:

> Why do we value watching a tragedy? Because we are glad of the small dose of emotional crisis, which second-hand participation gives us. If a parent had a drug which he could give to a child, which could ensure that the child would never feel pain, or desolation, or desertion, or maiming, in which he would never know the hard realities, he might for this reason alone well hesitate to give it.[33]

Before leaving the question of theodicy, Swinburne raises what he sees as just an extension of the problem of natural evil, but it is actually another evidential problem of evil. Swinburne thinks someone could agree with everything he has said about God's reasons for permitting moral and natural evil, and yet still be unsatisfied about the probability of theism on the evidence.

One might simply feel that everything God wants to accomplish could be attained with much less evil. Though certain benefits can be gained from evil's existence, those benefits aren't worth the amount of evil present in our world. As Swinburne explains:

> This is, I believe, the crux of the problem of evil. It is not the fact of evil or the kinds of evil which are the real threat to theism; it is the quantity of evil—both the number of people (and animals) who suffer and the amount which they suffer. If there is a God, he has given man too much choice, the objection in effect says. He has inflicted too much suffering on too many people (and animals) to give knowledge to others for the sake of the freedom of the latter; he has given to man too much opportunity to do evil, and used too powerful deterrents to certain bad actions instead of just stopping men from doing them by force. With the objection that if there is a God, he has overdone it, I feel *considerable initial* sympathy. The objection seems to count against the claim that there is a God.[34]

All of this means, according to Swinburne, that critics are saying there should be a limit to how much evil there must be in order for God to accomplish his purposes, and yet certain things that happen exceed that limit. The limit should never have allowed Hiroshima, the Lisbon Earthquake, the Black Death, or the atrocities of Belsen, Dachau, and Auschwitz. Swinburne replies:

> But the trouble is that the fewer natural evils a God provides, the less opportunity he provides for man to exercise responsibility. For the less natural evil, the less knowledge he gives to man of how to produce or avoid suffering and disaster, the less opportunity for his exercise of the higher virtues, and the less experience of the harsh possibilities of existence; and the less he allows to men the opportunity to bring about large-scale horrors, the less the freedom and responsibility which he gives to them. What in effect the objection is asking is that a God should make a toy-world, a world where things matter, but not very much; where we can choose and our choices can make a small difference, but the real choices remain God's. For he simply would not allow us the choice of doing real harm, or through our negligence allowing real harm to occur. He would be like the over-protective parent who will not let his child out of sight for a moment.[35]

What should we conclude from this? According to Swinburne, it should be clear that God has a reason for making a world with the amount of evil ours contains, but he also has a reason for not doing so. That being so, the existence of evil doesn't count against God's existence. Really, everything ultimately depends on a quantitative moral judgment about the amount of evil it is justifiable to bring about or allow to occur. But, Swinburne reasons, quantitative moral judgments are the hardest for reaching a sure conclusion. Not only is it hard to make decisions about such things, but our evaluations are prone to change from time to time. Since quantitative moral judgments are so hard to make, and since how much evil God could justifiably allow is a quantitative moral judgment, it will be impossible to make a good inductive case against God on the basis of how much evil is in the world.[36]

Reactions to Swinburne

Most notably, Michael Martin and Eleonore Stump have taken issue with some of Swinburne's major claims. Martin challenges the claim that theism has the highest prior probability, because it is the simplest hypothesis. Martin thinks Swinburne's error is failing even to consider the possibility of a rival hypothesis, namely, the hypothesis of an omniscient, omnipotent, free and perfectly evil being. As for Stump, her focus is Swinburne's defense or theodicy for theism, which she feels is inadequate.

MARTIN AND SWINBURNE

Martin notes that Swinburne thinks God's perfect goodness follows from his omniscience and perfect freedom. As perfectly good, God will do actions that are morally obligatory, if there are any, and there are. Martin reconstructs Swinburne's argument as follows:

(1)   P is omniscient. (By hypothesis)
(2)   Act A is morally good all things considered. (By hypothesis)
(3)   Act A is morally important. (By hypothesis)
(4)   If P is omniscient then P knows everything that it is possible to know. (By definition)
(5)   It is possible to know (2) and (3). (By hypothesis)
(6)   P knows that act A is morally good all things considered and that act A is morally important. [By (1), (2), (3), (4), (5)]
(7)   If P knows that act A is morally good all things considered and that act A is morally important, then P has a morally obligatory reason to do A. (By definition)
(8)   P has a morally obligatory reason to do A. [By (6) and (7)]
(9)   If P has a morally obligatory reason to do A and P is completely free, P will do A if P can. (By definition)
(10) It is possible to do A. (By hypothesis)
(11) P is completely free. (By hypothesis)
(12) P is omnipotent. (By hypothesis)
(13) ∴ P will do A. [By (8), (9), (10), (11), (12)][37]

Martin thinks this argument is problematic, and once one sees that, the prior and posterior probabilities of theism appear no greater than those of a belief in a perfectly evil being.

Martin begins by analyzing what it means to have a reason for an action (this also includes a personal explanation for an action), and says it involves two distinct aspects, the belief aspect and the intentional aspect. If someone raises a hand, and someone else asks why that happened, the answer involves both a belief and an intention. He raised his hand because he believed that would get someone's attention, and he wanted to get that person's attention. Martin believes the same distinction applies to cases where moral considerations are at issue. If someone says she did something because it was her moral obligation, she shows that she believes the act is morally obligatory, and she also shows she intends to fulfill that obligation.[38]

After this initial explanation, Martin says that someone may act from a variety of moral, immoral, and nonmoral reasons. Normally, someone doing wrong won't intend to do evil, but is just ignorant that the act is evil, or simply acts that way irrationally. On the other hand, someone might believe a given act is wrong but intend to do it anyway, just because it is evil. That person would be fundamentally evil. He would have a reason$_I$ for what he does just as the rest of us do, but his reason would be different, because he is fundamentally evil. Though this person might refrain from doing the evil because of considerations like fear of punishment, no such hindrances would confront someone who was perfectly free. All of this suggests the possibility of a being who is omniscient, omnipotent, free, and perfectly evil.[39]

Even if no one had ever believed in such an absolutely evil being, that wouldn't make his existence either impossible or improbable. In fact, the hypothesis that this being exists is just as probable as the hypothesis that a perfectly good being exists. One must explain good and design in the world on this hypothesis, but on the theistic hypothesis one must explain the existence of evil. As to prior probabilities of both hypotheses, they seem to be the same. Martin explains:

> . . . the prior probability of h_2 would seem equal to h_1, since, according to Swinburne, the prior probability of h_1 is based primarily on the simplicity of h_1 which in turn is based on purely logical and tautological considerations. The simplicity of h_1 and h_2 are identical with respect to all crucial factors. They both postulate an omnipotent, omniscient and completely free Being. These three attributes are, according to Swinburne, simpler than any finite attributes of power, knowledge or freedom. Further, there does not seem to be a difference between the simplicity of a Being that is perfectly evil and a Being that is perfectly good other things being equal.[40]

The net result is that Swinburne's belief that the idea of an absolutely evil being is incoherent is wrong. The hypothesis that this being exists is just as probable as that of a good God. Martin grants that Swinburne's argument has a degree of plausibility, because normally, one does not knowingly do evil just because it is evil. His argument also seems plausible, because it rests on an ambiguity. Once that is cleared up, the problem with Swinburne's argument becomes very clear. Martin says the key is premise (7). Though Swinburne thinks it is necessarily true, it is open to at least two interpretations as follows:

(7') If P knows that Act A is morally good all things considered and that Act A is morally important, then P has a morally obligatory reason$_I$ to do A.

(7") If P knows that act A is morally good all things considered and that Act A is morally important, then P has a morally obligatory reason$_B$ to do A.[41]

As to (7'), it is false, for "P could know that Act A is morally good all things considered and that Act A is morally important yet not have the intention to do what is morally obligatory."[42] An absolutely evil being wouldn't intend to do the act.

As for (7"), Martin says it is true, given Swinburne's meaning of moral obligation. However, this interpretation of (7) affects the truth of (9). Premise (9) becomes:

(9') If P has morally obligatory reasons$_B$ to do A and P is completely free, P will do A if P can.[43]

According to Martin, (9') is false, for the absolutely evil one has morally obligatory reasons$_B$ to do A, but has no reason$_I$ (intention) to do it.

The result of this whole discussion for Swinburne is as follows. Swinburne thinks theism is well on its way to winning the probabilistic argument, because its prior probability is higher than any competing theory. However, Martin believes he has shown that there is no impossibility in the hypothesis of an absolutely evil being and that its prior probability is the same as that of theism. Both hypotheses have equal simplicity. Hence, Swinburne's assessment of prior probabilities is wrong.[44]

STUMP AND SWINBURNE

Eleonore Stump also challenges Swinburne's probabilistic argument, but on grounds other than its assessment of prior probability. Stump objects to Swinburne's theodicy for the nature and quantity of natural evils.

First, Stump claims that a key premise in Swinburne's theodicy is false. He says people gain knowledge of their actions' consequences only by induction from past experiences. However, God could just as easily provide that information to us without us having to undergo evil. Swinburne considers this option and rejects it, and Stump thinks he rejects it too quickly. Swinburne sets forth what he feels are negative consequences if God reveals this information by speaking out loud and meeting people face-to-face. Stump responds that even if Swinburne is right about how this would eliminate freedom, it isn't the only avenue of revelation open to God. God could give this information to people in dreams. The dreams could be extremely vivid, but even if that weren't enough to convince the one who receives the dream, that person could test the dreams' messages by animal experiments, for example. If people regularly had such dreams and tested them, they would come to accept the dreams' messages as true and be adequately forewarned. Moreover, these dreams wouldn't compel belief in God, for the dreams wouldn't have to include God in them. Hence, all the problems Swinburne raises with God directly giving this information are removed. In addition, there are other ways to reveal this information without speaking directly to people, namely, through visions, inanimate objects correctly predicting the future, and animals which speak.[45] From this line of argument it is clear that experience of natural evil and natural evil itself aren't needed to uphold freedom with respect to choosing good or evil. Knowledge of this evil is available in other ways that don't limit human freedom.

Second, Stump argues that for some kinds of evil, we need neither experience nor supernatural revelation to warn us. For example, knowledge that exposure to asbestos is dangerous to human health is available in purely natural ways like scientific testing. Swinburne might respond that we would test the results of exposure to asbestos only after people had suffered from such exposure. Stump thinks scientific understanding of biology is sufficient to warrant concern over any significant altering of our biological or chemical environment.[46] Nonetheless, Stump argues that even if Swinburne is right that we need experience of these natural evils to inform us of the consequences of certain actions, there is still a problem for Swinburne's theodicy. She explains:

> But even if Swinburne were right that we need natural evils to call our attention to the dangerous effects of biological and chemical pollution, such a claim justifies natural evil only until the time men recognize the danger and the need to test in advance for harmful effects. Once that recognition has been achieved, and we know we need to be cautious about altering an individual's biological or chemical environment, there is no need for knowledge which hinders God from preventing, for example, all cases of accidental lead poisoning (that is, cases in which the victim's suffering is not a result of his choice or negligence regarding exposure to lead).[47]

In response to this objection, Swinburne might say there are just victims of the system. For people to know the consequences of their actions, natural laws must operate with regularity, but then there will be victims of the system. Stump asks why this must be so in all cases. Even if God doesn't touch any instances of suffering where humans *could* save the sufferer even if they don't (e.g., fires where victims could be saved by humans), why couldn't God rescue victims when they can't escape and no one can help them to escape (e.g., an infant or someone completely paralyzed can't escape a fire, but no one else is around to help them)? Intervening in those cases would remove countless amounts of injury and death, but it wouldn't stop the regular operation of natural laws, and it would leave many opportunities for people to learn the consequences of their actions.[48] In effect, Stump is saying that while Swinburne's theodicy may answer why natural evil in general exists, it can't adequately account for the quantity or the apparent gratuitousness of much of it.

Fourth, Swinburne believes that people need inductive evidence from experience of natural evils because experiential knowledge is better than secondhand knowledge. Such knowledge is supposedly better, because people are inclined to take precautions against evils in direct proportion to the nearness of their experience of disaster. Stump says this confuses knowledge with the inclination to act on that knowledge. Being closer to a disaster by personal experience may motivate us more to avoid that danger, but it won't make our knowledge of the danger any more certain. For example, if we know someone who has died of lung cancer as a result of heavy smoking, that may be a greater motivation not to smoke, but we can be just as certain about the negative consequences of smoking if we read statistics correlating smoking with lung cancer, even though we personally know none of the victims.[49] It just isn't necessary to acquire this knowledge by personal experience in order to know the consequences of actions that lead to the evil.

Stump realizes this doesn't end the matter, for she says Swinburne might reply that whether knowledge is more certain or whether only motivation is increased by being closer to the evil, it is still a good thing. Stump answers that in all of this we must remember that the point is to justify God's actions. Granted, people may have greater motivation to avoid evil if they come close to the disaster as opposed to God merely informing them of danger. But, argues Stump, doesn't morality dictate that God warn us, anyway?

Suppose I know that if you walk near the river's edge at a certain point along its bank, you will likely fall in and drown. I know the river bank isn't very solid at that point, and I know the river currents in that part of the river are very strong and that it is hard for even good swimmers to avoid drowning if they fall in. Suppose I also know you are a happy-go-lucky sort who won't likely heed my warning even if I give it. Under those circumstances I decide not to warn you, figuring that some lessons must be learned the hard way. If you then walk by the river's edge and fall in, am I not culpable for failing to warn you? Stump says in this case if I warn you and you walk too close to the river's edge and fall in, it's your fault. But if I don't warn you, it's my fault. Granted, my warning may be less vivid than your personal experience of the disaster, but I am still morally obliged to tell you. Likewise, if God says nothing and lets us learn by experience, the experience will be more vivid, but God is guilty. If he warns us rather than letting us learn by experience, our motivation may be less, but if we do what we have been warned against, the results are our fault, not God's. And, after all, the point of the discussion is to discover whether God is wrong in his handling of the world and the evil in it.[50] Thus, contrary to Swinburne, God not only could give us the requisite knowledge in ways other than direct experience, but should do so. Hence, Swinburne's theodicy is deficient.

Fifth, Stump sees another problem even if experiencing natural evil is either necessary or better for producing knowledge of consequences of action. That knowledge is valuable only if there are evils to avoid. But why must there be these evils to begin with? If things like earthquakes, rabies, etc., never happened, there would be no knowledge of them which would help us avoid them and their consequences in the future, but why would any of this be a loss? Is it really worth it to have this knowledge if the price is the occurrence of and experience of natural evils? Without these natural evils the variety of experiences open to us wouldn't be as rich, but would that really be a significant loss? Moreover, is God really right in allowing natural evil just because it has the valuable side-effect of imparting knowledge which we find useful in our world? Stump thinks not, and illustrates the point as follows:

> If you conceal traps in my front yard, then my repeated attempts to get from my front door to my car parked at the curb will produce in me knowledge about the consequences of my movements. And this knowledge will be useful to me, if I live long enough to acquire it, because it will enable me to avoid traps in the future. So this knowledge is good, it is gained from experience of the evil which you have introduced into my yard, and without this knowledge I could not avoid the evils of the traps. But *you* are not morally justified in setting traps in my front yard—no matter how good and useful the knowledge about the consequences of my actions may be and no matter how dependent that knowledge is on my experiencing the jaws of the trap.[51]

Finally, Swinburne's ultimate concern is to uphold human freedom. The problem, however, according to Stump, is that his theodicy tries to justify not only moral evil which does relate to human freedom but also natural evils, many of which don't stem from human freedom. The concentration camp at

Bergen Belsen was the work of men's hands (moral evil), but "evils of that magnitude with the serious choices they entail are still possible even if God were to prevent all hurricanes, earthquakes, mental retardation, birth defects, and so on."[52] Hence, if God leaves man-made evils alone, that would uphold human freedom, but there is no reason for him to leave alone all natural evils unattributable to human agency. Why are those evils necessary to impart knowledge relevant for human freedom, when human freedom has no control over them (it can neither produce nor prevent them)? Swinburne's theodicy can handle some forms of natural evil (those which reduce to moral evil), but is inadequate as a justification of natural evil in general.

Assessment of Swinburne

In my opinion, there are significant problems in Swinburne's views. I begin with his handling of prior probabilities. Swinburne thinks the key to prior probability is the simplicity of competing theories. As he explains it, I think simplicity is very important, but I'm not sure it is the key. Fit with background knowledge is at least as important in determining prior probability of a theory. This seems especially true when one considers Martin's hypothesis of an absolutely evil being. From the standpoint of simplicity, it is hard to distinguish that theory from the theistic hypothesis. But then, if there is to be any way of deciding which theory does best on prior probability, something other than simplicity must be considered. Background evidence is at least as crucial as simplicity, for even when one theory is simple and another complex, if the complex theory fits background knowledge better than the simpler one, its prior probability would seem to be greater. Hence, I'm uneasy with Swinburne's key criterion for determining prior probability.

The relation of background knowledge to prior probability raises a further crucial point, namely, what should be included in background *knowledge* for *all* theories and included in *evidence* for the theory under consideration.

Several issues make this a difficult matter. On the one hand, one can always say that something that is usually considered evidence for a theory is part of our background knowledge. I can increase the prior probability of my theory by this maneuver, but if there is debate about whether the information is actually knowledge, my considering it as such and using it to calculate the prior probability of my theory will be more optimistic than it should be. Likewise, if there is information which is generally understood to be true that supports my theory, my opponent can artificially lower the prior probability of my theory by saying the information isn't background *knowledge,* but only evidence to be considered later in calculating posterior probability. Of course, either of these moves can greatly affect the prior probability of a theory, and in some cases where evidence for the theory isn't especially strong, manipulating prior probability becomes very significant.

My point here suggests another about background knowledge and prior probability. There is no guarantee that theists and atheists will agree on which pieces of information are background knowledge and which are merely evidence to be used later in calculating posterior probability. However, if atheists and theists disagree on that matter, it may ultimately be impossible to decide which theory has greater prior probability and/or posterior probability.

Two illustrations make my point. Swinburne might want to include theistic arguments as part of the background knowledge for theism. However, it is dubious that any atheist considers those arguments knowledge. If the arguments were known to be correct (knowledge), wouldn't they also be background knowledge for any theory that tried to explain the existence of our world and all in it? It seems so, but then, these arguments, if knowledge, would make the prior probability of atheism 0, and the debate might end. Hence, no atheist could allow those arguments to count as knowledge, but then they can't affect prior probabilities. This just illustrates my point, namely, the whole project of calculating prior probability may falter on the question of what to include in background knowledge.[53]

A second example also illustrates the point. Suppose there is a debate over creation and evolution as explanatory hypotheses for the origin of life forms. Does the fossil record with the dates scientists attach to it become background knowledge for calculating prior probability of the two theories, or is it evidence to be considered later in calculating posterior probability? Evolutionists want us to agree that not only the fossil remains but also evolutionists' dates and interpretations of those fossils are part of the background knowledge of this discussion. Creationists can't deny the existence of fossils, but it is dubious that they would uncritically accept evolutionists' dates of all the fossils or their interpretation of what the fossils prove about origins.

The preceding discussion underscores two points. First, determining what is background knowledge as opposed to mere evidence isn't easy, and that issue also suggests that something other than a theory's simplicity (contra Swinburne) is crucial for determining prior probabilities. The second point relates to all discussions of the probabilistic problem of evil. It is that in order to calculate the prior and posterior probability of theism and its opponents, all sides must agree on what is background knowledge and what is evidence adduced to confirm or disconfirm the theories in question. None of this means it is impossible for rival theories to agree on these matters. It only means this is a very important but often difficult issue to decide, and it has significant impact on our ability to calculate prior and posterior probability. My concern with Swinburne's views is that what he says really offers us no help on these matters.

Though I am skeptical about simplicity as the key to prior probability, let us grant Swinburne the point for the moment for the sake of argument. Why is Swinburne's theory about God simpler than Martin's theory about an equally powerful but absolutely evil being? Swinburne might argue that it is, because the idea of an absolutely evil being is incoherent. If a being knows everything, is free to do as he chooses, and has power to accomplish what he chooses, he will be perfectly good.

On this point, I must side with Martin. Nothing Swinburne says adequately explains why Martin's omniscient, omnipotent, totally free being must have an inherently good will. Swinburne seems to believe the whole problem in doing good is knowing what it is and being free to do it. All of this underestimates the possibility of a perverse will. As Martin says, it is thoroughly possible to have a being with all the knowledge and power Swinburne suggests, and yet that being can be inherently evil. Swinburne might reply that such a being would be supremely rational, and it is just irrational for someone who knows good and is free to do it to do otherwise. However, if irrational means having no reason, then the absolutely evil one isn't irrational. He would have reasons for what he does; they just wouldn't be the normal ones we think of. If, instead, Swinburne's point is that only good action is rational, that begs the question by equating rationality with moral goodness. All in all, I agree with Martin that the notion of an absolutely evil being isn't incoherent, and that notion is no more complex than the theistic hypothesis.

Not only is Martin's absolutely evil being a simple hypothesis, but so also is matter as the ultimate explanation of the universe. Even Swinburne agrees that both matter and God as ultimate explanations are equally simple. Only dualism, which combines the two, is less simple. Perhaps Swinburne might answer that matter isn't as simple as God, because once one invokes God, explanation ends, whereas once one invokes matter, one must still explain its origin. As a theist, I am very sympathetic to the point, but many atheists wouldn't be. They would claim that appeal to matter is explanation enough. To ask for more explanation requires more for an adequate explanation than we normally do. In fact, this is precisely what some have said in response to theistic arguments like the cosmological argument. Moreover, in response to the demand to explain the origin of matter, some atheists would demand that theists explain the origin of God. To say that God is self-caused or uncaused hardly sounds like a simple theory, since everything in our experience has a cause. Hence, appeal to matter as an ultimate explanation of the world invokes a theory apparently just as simple as the theistic hypothesis, and it has just the same kinds of problems as theism for offering an adequate explanation.

Where does this leave matters? It gives the distinct impression that Swinburne thinks theism is a simpler hypothesis (and thus, has greater prior probability), not because he has seriously considered the alternatives, but at least in part because he is a theist to begin with. Likewise, atheists will probably think their views are simpler at least in part because they are atheists. The net result seems to be that we must say either 1) the theistic and atheistic hypotheses are at a standoff as concerns their simplicity, and if simplicity is the key criterion for prior probability, then both have equal prior probability, or 2) theism has greater prior probability on background knowledge. In case 1) the debate between theism and atheism must be resolved on appeal to evidence. In case 2), simplicity isn't the key, and one must be ready for a debate over what counts as background knowledge and what counts as evidence to be used in confirming or disconfirming the theories. In neither case 1) nor case 2) will simplicity make much difference.

One final point on prior probability. Swinburne spends much effort trying to establish that theism has greater prior probability than any other hypothesis. But why must theism have greater prior probability in order to be more probable overall? So long as theism's prior probability isn't 0 nor its opponents' 1, it hasn't lost the debate even if an atheistic hypothesis has greater prior probability. As long as on total evidence theism has greater probability than its opponents, there is no problem. In fact, as long as the posterior probability of theism exceeds .5, theists are completely within their epistemic rights for holding it. After all, the atheistic challenge isn't merely that atheism is more probable than theism. The atheistic argument from evil is that evil is evidence that theism is so improbable that there isn't rational warrant for holding it. But, on the contrary, it is clear that one might not be able to show theism to be as probable as some atheistic alternative, but still could show it probable enough (greater than .5, for example) in virtue of evidences to meet the complaint that it is so improbable as not to warrant belief in it. The lesson from all of this is that winning the battle at the stage of calculating prior probability isn't quite as significant as Swinburne thinks. This is encouraging for theism, since the prior probability of some forms of theism may be rather low. Thankfully, the final judgment isn't made until total evidence is considered.

As to Swinburne's handling of theism's probability overall, I also see difficulties. Swinburne says theism's probability vis-à-vis evil will be high if the theist either shows that each apparently gratuitous evil is tied to some greater good, or points to the track record of theodicy for handling apparently gratuitous evil and then argues that, given past success, we can assume there are answers for other apparently gratuitous evils. Swinburne knows the second avenue will be the more likely approach of theistic argument. Though this may sound attractive, I find some serious problems.

An initial problem is that Swinburne conflates problems of evils. In appealing to the track record of theodicy, Swinburne would probably appeal to the free will defense. In fact, until Swinburne offers his defense that natural evil is necessary to provide knowledge requisite for human freedom, no other defense is in view. However, the free will defense responds specifically to the problem of moral evil. It is not per se a response to the problem of apparently gratuitous evil in general, though in recent years Michael Peterson, for example, has applied it to that problem. It surely isn't intended as an answer to what I called unattached natural evils in chapter 7.[54] It should be clear by now that defenses for the problem of moral evil, regardless of how successful they are, don't necessarily tell us anything about a track record for resolving the problem of apparently gratuitous evil, especially if that evil is unattached natural evil. So, if Swinburne wants to appeal to a defense's track record for solving cases of apparently gratuitous evil, he must offer a defense that addresses apparently gratuitous evils and show us its successful track record. Appealing to defenses that address other problems of evil won't suffice.

One may grant my point, but reply that Swinburne does offer a theodicy which can handle many apparently gratuitous evils. Moreover, others have addressed apparently purposeless evil and have successfully shown that many instances of apparently purposeless evil do have a purpose. Isn't that a sufficient enough track record to make Swinburne's case that there is a theodicy for the rest? At this point, the atheist may attack Swinburne's theodicy on grounds that it is too new for us to have a "track record," or on grounds that it isn't as adequate as Swinburne thinks. However, a simpler reply is that the number of cases Swinburne and others have shown to have a purpose isn't enough to warrant the inductive leap that all other cases of apparently gratuitous evil can also be solved. There are too many instances of unexplained apparently pointless evil for theists to think they have explained enough cases to warrant the inductive leap that unexplained cases are solvable. If there were only a few of these cases, Swinburne's appeal to the track record might seem sufficient. But neither atheists nor many theists believe there are only a few unsolved cases left.

Here Swinburne might reply that he needs only to show that apparently gratuitous evil in general can be handled in order to make his case. But if he

said that, it would again conflate several problems of evil. There is the problem
of apparently gratuitous evil in general, and there is a problem of the quantity
of apparently gratuitous evil. Though Swinburne's theodicy might cover the former problem (though many atheists would probably say the number of cases
it covers isn't enough to cover apparently gratuitous evil *in general*), it doesn't
cover the latter. And Swinburne himself says that the problem about quantity
is the most troublesome for theism. Hence, I don't see that Swinburne's theodicy has a good record in handling the problem of evil he deems most troublesome for theism, let alone the others he tries to solve with it.

What about Swinburne's theodicy itself? Here I find several problems.
For example, Swinburne says God couldn't reveal by direct speech information about evil, because he would be too close to us. Knowing there is a God,
knowing what he wants, and recognizing the consequences of disobedience,
there would be little temptation to evil.

Here I believe Swinburne overestimates the goodness of man and underestimates the perversity of the human heart. As with Swinburne's God, we get
the impression that the main problem for us in doing right is knowing what
it is. This simply underestimates the perversity of the human will. Biblical
writers like the apostle Paul have a much different view of human nature. In
Romans 1:19-32 Paul argues that everyone has some knowledge of God, but
willfully suppresses the truth and goes another way. By the end of the chapter (v. 32), Paul states that even though people know certain acts are wrong
and worthy of punishment, they not only do them, but encourage others to
join in their folly. I conclude, then, that giving people direct knowledge of evil
consequences of actions wouldn't guarantee that they would avoid evil, nor
would it remove freedom to do good or evil. It would, however, be a way to
inform people about the consequences of their actions without there having
to be natural evil.

In addition, I don't find Swinburne's handling of the problem of the quantity of evil very convincing. I note again that his defense primarily addresses
apparently gratuitous natural evil in general. However, Swinburne thinks it
can apply to the question of quantity. He argues that removing much evil
wouldn't give us enough choices for exercising free will. But, as Stump
responds in general to Swinburne's approach, many natural evils have nothing to do with human choices. God could remove those and still leave plenty
of choices that would lead to natural evils. Moreover, even with man-made
natural evils, God could remove many of them (e.g., the most atrocious like
Auschwitz) and still leave plenty of opportunity to produce evil.[55] This suggests problems for Swinburne's handling of the quantity of evil.

As to other values Swinburne thinks come from the quantity of evil, it is true that some evils can be tied to goods that justify their existence (if one is a consequentialist, of course), but the question is whether values like the exercise of higher virtues and awareness of the harsh possibilities of existence (it is hard to see this as a value per se, but Swinburne says so) are worth it. Granted, if this were an answer to a logical problem of evil, my rejection of Swinburne's theodicy on this point wouldn't show it to fail in rendering his theology internally consistent. It would merely show my unwillingness to pay the price tag for his theodicy. The problem, though, is that we are discussing the evidential problem of the quantity of evil, and Swinburne must show that his answer makes theism probable, not internally consistent. It is just at this point that even some theists like myself are inclined to say theism would be more believable if God had foregone those higher order goods by eliminating the lower order evils. Those higher order values just aren't worth the evils they presuppose, and God should have seen that. Being good and all-powerful, he could have and should have removed them. And, if we must have those goods, that could be accomplished in satisfactory quantity with much less evil.

From what I have said, it should be clear that I agree with Stump that the benefits of the knowledge evil provides aren't worth it. Moreover, I also agree with Stump that God has other ways to get us knowledge of consequences of our actions without us having to undergo natural evil.

Swinburne's handling of the probabilistic problem of evil, then, is problematic. Though he provides useful insights into the nature of this problem (especially on the matter of prior probabilities), in the end his case for theism even in regard to natural evil in general, let alone the amount of it in our world, seems unconvincing.

BRUCE REICHENBACH

Bruce Reichenbach's work on the inductive problem of evil appeared first in a journal article and later in his *Evil and a Good God*. Since atheists use Bayes' Theorem to argue against theistic arguments like the teleological argument, Reichenbach proposes to use Bayes' Theorem to reconstruct the atheist's claim that evil makes it improbable that God exists. As Reichenbach sets forth the problem, it is clearly a problem about the *amount* of evil in the universe, not the mere fact of evil, or the apparent gratuitousness of some evil.[56] Moreover, he proposes to discuss natural evil, since the evidential problem is most frequently posed that way. However, he thinks that using Bayes' Theorem, an inductive argument can be made based on either moral or natural evil.[57]

After presenting the mechanics of Bayes' Theorem and explaining the meaning of various symbols, Reichenbach asks how one can determine the prior probabilities of theism and atheism. He replies that there are two ways to do it, but each approach yields a different answer. According to the first approach, the atheist thinks none of the traditional arguments for God's existence establish his existence, whereas the theist may think some succeed. In terms of the total evidence available, neither atheist nor theist would grant the other's conclusion concerning God's existence. Hence, the atheist might be willing to say the value of the prior probabilities $P(G/N)$ and $P(-G/N)$ (N represents, in Reichenbach's terms, the furniture and structure of the world, i.e., background information) is 1/2 each. Reichenbach then explains:

> If we assign a value of 1/2 to these *prior probabilities,* it follows that the value of $P(G/N\&E)$ will depend upon the relation of $P(E/N\&G)$ to $P(E/N\&-G)$. If $P(E/N\&G) < P(E/N\&-G)$, then $P(G/N\&E) < 1/2$; and if $P(G/N\&E) < 1/2$, the atheologian has a prima facie case with respect to natural evil, i.e., the existence of an omnipotent, omniscient, good and loving God is improbable. Indeed, the greater the disparity between the two probabilities in favor of $P(E/N\&-G)$, the more improbable God's existence is, prima facie.[58]

In virtue of this argument, the atheist will conclude that natural evil disconfirms God's existence, i.e., the probability of God's existence is less than 1/2.

The atheist might take a second approach, but it is weaker, according to Reichenbach. The atheist can argue that the prior probability of theism is unimportant, so long as it is neither 0 nor 1. With this approach, the atheist focuses solely on the role of natural evil with respect to disconfirming God's existence. "That is, does the amount of pain and suffering found in the world tend to disconfirm—i.e. make it less probable—that God exists?"[59] As long as theism's prior probability is neither 0 nor 1 (the exact probability doesn't matter), the argument about theism's probability, given evil and background information, will still obtain, though in a weaker form. As Reichenbach explains:

> Whatever the value of the *prior probabilities,* if $P(E/N\&G) < P(E/N\&-G)$, then the resulting value of $P(G/N\&E)$ will be less than the prior probability of $P(G/N)$. Thus the atheologian has a prima facie case with respect to existent natural evil, i.e. it makes belief in an omnipotent, omniscient, good and loving personal God *less* probable. Indeed, the greater the disparity between the two probabilities in favor of $P(E/N\&-G)$, the less probable God's existence is, prima facie.[60]

With this second approach the atheist will claim natural evil *tends to disconfirm* (lessen the probability of) God's existence.

Though the two arguments are similar, they aren't identical, and the difference is important. It is really the first form of the argument that is crucial to the atheist's case, for it alone, if successful, clearly disconfirms the claim that God exists. As Reichenbach explains, the second argument might succeed inductively but still not disconfirm God's existence. God's existence might have such high prior probability based on various evidences that evil won't so lower theism's probability on total evidence that God's existence is disconfirmed. This argument can succeed in disconfirming God's existence only if theism's prior probability is extremely low, or if the probability that evil will exist, given background conditions and no God, far exceeds the probability of evil's existence, given the furniture of the world and God's existence.[61]

Reichenbach asks if there is disparity between $P(E/N\&G)$ and $P(E/N\& -G)$. Atheists think there is, because they believe that if God exists, the probability that there will be evil in the world should be very low. An omnipotent, good God would probably do something about it. We expect other good persons to remove evil or prevent evil as they can, so why not expect the same of God? And, God could intervene in the natural order to overturn the laws of nature or at least introduce factors that would keep natural evil and/or its consequences from befalling us. In fact, some atheists claim that a good God could have instituted different laws in the first place so that there would be less suffering than there is.[62] The result of this line of argument is that atheists believe that if there really is a God, we should surely expect less evil than there is. As a result, Reichenbach explains:

> ... one has good reason to believe that $P(E/N\&G) < P(E/N\&-G)$. And if the *prior probability* $P(G/N)$ be put at 1/2, the result is that $P(G/N\&E) <$ 1/2, and depending on the degree to which one thinks this deity can intervene in particular cases, can alter the original natural laws, or could have created other natural laws, the disparity between $P(E/N\&G)$ and $P(E/N\&-G)$ might be so great that the value of $P(G/N\&E)$ might be *much* less than 1/2. In this manner the atheologian can give some specificity to his inductive claim that the natural evil present in our world disconfirms God's existence.[63]

As to the second form of the argument, the atheist will say that since the probability of evil, given God, is less than without God, the probability that God exists, given the furniture of our world and evil's existence, is less than the prior probability of theism. Hence, evil in the world tends to disconfirm God's existence.[64]

Having set forth the atheist's argument from evil, Reichenbach turns to theistic responses. He believes theists should offer four responses. First, as to the first form of the argument, the atheist hasn't considered total evidence in assigning prior probabilities to theism. That God's existence is improbable on background information doesn't mean it is improbable on total evidence. Total evidence includes the various theistic proofs, and atheists shouldn't exclude them from background information when considering all evidence. According to Reichenbach, if these arguments are included in the background information or total evidence, then the prior probability of theism (or alternately, its probability on total evidence and background information) is much more than 1/2.[65] Reichenbach illustrates his point with an example like Plantinga's Feike the Frisian and his ability to swim.

Reichenbach admits that atheists may say these theistic proofs don't work, so they don't recognize them as evidence. However, that settles nothing, but only raises the bigger question of how to assign prior probability in disputed cases. Reichenbach suggests several possible ways to do so, and notes the problems with each. Of course, one might simply assign probabilities of 1/2 in disputed cases, but that won't do. As Reichenbach explains,

> If a mathematician and a young student were disputing whether 24 x 566 yielded 13584 or 13564, and if the student were stubbornly unconvinced by the mathematician's answer and argument, one would not then deign to assign the probability of 1/2 to both answers on the grounds that they could not agree on the matter. Mere disagreement is no basis for assigning such a (or any) probability.[66]

Moreover, probabilities can't be assigned on the basis of what theists and atheists both know. To illustrate this point, just because one knows about optics but one's friend doesn't has nothing to do with establishing a prior probability for light traveling in waves, not photons. Moreover, we can't make probability assignment depend solely on one's noetic structure, for then the objectivity of the atheist's argument disappears. This is just Plantinga's argument in slightly different form that probability assignments run the risk of being no more than pieces of autobiographical information. Reichenbach considers no other ways of determining prior probability, but from the insufficiency of these other methods, he concludes that

> the inductive argument from natural evil considered in argument (I) fails in that it provides no way of establishing the prior probability of G on N in any objective manner or at the very least in any manner agreeable to both theist and atheologian. But unless one knows the prior probability of G on N, it is hard to see how any value can be assigned to $P(G/N\&E)$.[67]

Reichenbach reminds us that this objection doesn't attack the second form of the argument, for that form doesn't consider prior probabilities, but only theism's probability, given evil in the world. So, the atheist may still succeed with the second argument (the weaker), but the stronger argument fails.

Reichenbach's first response really contains two objections. The first is that the atheist's argument doesn't take into account total evidence. If it did, then the prior probability of theism would be much more than 1/2. Reichenbach doesn't tell us how he knows that, but he claims it is so. The second objection is that whether or not the atheist agrees to consider total evidence in assigning prior probabilities, there simply is no way for atheists and theists to agree on how to assign those probabilities objectively when there is dispute about the evidence and its value. Both objections are significant, but they aren't the same.

Reichenbach's second reply questions whether it is really true that the probability of evil is less on the assumption that God exists than on the assumption of atheism. Atheists thinks so, because they believe good persons will remove evil, and God, as the supremely powerful and good person (if he exists), would remove much evil. Reichenbach counters that this isn't necessarily so, for sometimes the activity of good persons isn't enough to alter situations where there is or would be pain and suffering. Sometimes good persons can't do anything about pain and evil. As for God, this means it is reasonable to expect that

> (S) An omnipotent, omniscient, good and loving personal God will eliminate as much evil as he can without losing a greater good or bringing about an equal or greater evil.[68]

According to Reichenbach, from (S) it doesn't follow that the probability of evil's existence on the assumption of theism is less than on atheism. This is so because (S) is compatible with

> (T)   God eliminates all the evil he can without losing a greater good or producing an equal or greater evil.[69]

However, (T) entails

> (U) $P(E/N\&G) - < P(E/N\&\text{-}G)$

> for since (T) affirms that God *eliminates* all evil for which there is no morally sufficient reason, the evil that does exist is the evil which is consonant with God's existence and nature, whereas if God did not exist, one would expect to find more evil, i.e., the evils which currently are eliminated by God.[70]

The net result is that (S) is compatible with (U) and (U) contradicts (V) $P(E/N\&G) < P(E/N\&\text{-}G)$. Since that is so, (S) doesn't entail (V), and the atheist hasn't shown by the probabilistic argument from evil that (V) is true. Unless (V) is true on other grounds, there is no way the probabilistic argument from evil can succeed.

As to Reichenbach's third response, he appeals to three other propositions, (Q), (E), and (E*). They are :

(Q)   There will be less evil as the result of God's activity than if he were not active.

(E)   There are 10^6 turps of natural evil in the world.

(E*)   There are more than 10^6 turps of natural evil in the world.[71]

Suppose the theist concedes that (Q) is true. In that case, Reichenbach says the atheist will say that if God really exists, there would be less evil in the world than there is. Hence, it appears that (Q) entails (V), and if (V) is true, E disconfirms or tends to disconfirm God's existence.

In response, the theist can assert that if God didn't exist, we would expect more evil than there is, i.e., (E*) would obtain. If so, then (V) is *not* true, because God's existence would make it more likely that (E), not (E*), would obtain. This all means, however, that (Q) entails (U), not (V), but if that is so, then (E) doesn't disconfirm or tend to disconfirm God's existence. Thus, even granting (Q), it isn't clear that this will guarantee disconfirming God's existence. Reichenbach concludes:

> What this suggests is that the position one adopts depends on one's noetic structure, for it would seem that it is one's noetic structure which would account for the fact one draws from (Q) (V) rather than (U), and vice versa.[72]

Reichenbach offers no evidence that one's noetic structure is what leads one to think (Q) leads to (V) rather than (U). He simply says it is so. In his later work, he says "it would seem that it is one's noetic structure which would account for the fact"[73] that one draws (V), not (U) from (Q). Though this explains Reichenbach's point better, it doesn't prove it. Reichenbach leaves us to wonder why he thinks one's noetic structure apparently leads to (V) rather than (U) and vice versa. Couldn't it be, for example, that theists are led to draw (U) from (Q) not in virtue of their noetic structure but because of a defense against the problem of evil which they believe explains a morally sufficient reason for God not removing more evil? In other words, theists arrive at their conclusion not simply from presuppositions but from an argument that explains why (E) is true given that God exists. Reichenbach doesn't consider that possibility.

Reichenbach begins his fourth rejoinder by asking if there is any other way to determine whether the probability that there will be evil, given the world's furniture and theism, will be less than the probability of evil, given background knowledge and atheism. We might expect atheists to argue for this on the ground that it is unreasonable to believe (T). However, even if it is unreasonable to believe (T), that doesn't itself prove (T) false and -(T) true. At best, the atheist's argument would show that one should be agnostic about the truth of (T). Hence, (T)'s mere unreasonableness doesn't mean (V) is true. To show that, the atheist must show that it is reasonable to believe (T) is false, and to show that, he must prove that it is reasonable to believe another proposition, (X):

> (X)   There are instances of evil which, if God did exist, he could have eliminated without losing a greater good or producing an equal or greater evil.

Suppose we grant that (X) is true. Still, Reichenbach says (X) alone won't get us to (V). (X) alone says nothing about how much evil to expect in the world. One must add another premise like (S) to get to (V).[74]

But why should we think (X) is true? Atheists often support it by appeal to individual cases or classes of suffering that are apparently pointless. Reichenbach cites Rowe's fawn as an example. However, Reichenbach believes this won't make the atheist's case. He argues:

> But individual cases or classes of cases of apparently pointless suffering do not help us to decide the truth or falsity of (X), for they cannot provide the evidence needed to show that God *could* have prevented the suffering without losing a greater good. For one thing, the atheologian's argument seems to proceed along the illicit lines that since *we* could have prevented the suffering, *God* could have prevented the suffering [in the morally relevant sense of could specified in (X)]. For another, the atheologian's argument claims that instances of suffering which are seemingly or apparently pointless are in fact or likely pointless, for we do not know of any higher good to which they are a means. But this constitutes an appeal to ignorance; that we know of no higher good does not entail that there is no higher good or that one is unlikely. And even if the "unlikely" were granted, this argument would only establish the unreasonableness of believing (T), which as we have seen is insufficient to make the atheologian's case.[75]

Of course, Rowe claims that even if one instance isn't really pointless, it is hard to believe that all instances of apparently gratuitous evil have a point. As I noted when discussing Rowe, Reichenbach thinks this just begs the question of whether there really are any cases of genuinely gratuitous evil. Though he raises this doubt, Reichenbach believes the theist should agree that there are genuine cases of gratuitous evil.

Granting the point, however, isn't enough to prove (X) true. (X) involves a principle specified in (S). That principle is that God's existence and goodness are incompatible with failing to remove or prevent as much evil as he can without losing a greater good or bringing a greater evil. But if that is so, then if a greater good comes with the evil, then the evil must be present. Hence, evils that are logically or causally necessary for there to be the greater good must be present. Of course, Reichenbach knows that if those evils are logically or causally necessary to some greater good, then they aren't gratuitous evils (in the sense that "gratuitous" evils are those that have no logical or causal connection to some subsequent good). Hence, he must make a further point. He claims:

> This also entails that *evils whose possibility* is logically necessary for there being this greater good are such that their presence is consistent with the existence of a good God, for if God would prevent these evils from being actual, he would be making their being-actual impossible, and to make their being-actual impossible is to make impossible this greater good for which their possibility was necessary. If we define pointless or gratuitous evils as evils which are not logically or causally necessary for there being a greater good, it follows that some instances of pointless or gratuitous evils, i.e. those whose possibility is necessary for there being a greater good or preventing a greater evil, are compatible with God's existence and goodness.[76]

This may sound confusing, but the point can be explained. On Reichenbach's definition, a gratuitous evil is one which isn't logically necessary for or causally tied to some *subsequent* good. When he refers to an evil whose possibility is logically necessary for some greater good, he means an evil which isn't logically tied to some *subsequent* good, but which must be *possible* to insure some *antecedent* great good that might result in producing the evil (by "antecedent" I mean it exists prior to the doing of the evil action). Though Reichenbach doesn't specify the antecedent good that makes the evil possible, it isn't hard to see what he has in mind. As an indeterminist, Reichenbach is thinking of free will. This is the great good that makes possible the evil action (as well as making possible refraining from that action). Now, sometimes people do use their freedom to do evil, but the evil they do isn't logically necessary (or even causally connected) to some further, subsequent good. Hence, on Reichenbach's definitions, that evil is gratuitous, and yet its possibility would be connected to an antecedent great good, namely, free will, and that connection would, according to the free will defense, justify it.

Upon hearing this explanation, one might reply that it works if the gratuitous evil is tied to a greater good like free will, but what if the gratuitous evil is an unattached natural evil? In that case, what would be the greater good for which this evil's possibility is logically necessary? Presumably, Reichenbach might offer the answer we saw when I discussed his handling of natural evil, or he might offer something like Swinburne's explanation of natural evil. However, at this point in Reichenbach's presentation, he offers no answer. Still, he says this principle (namely, a gratuitous evil's possibility may be logically necessary to some greater good) means that natural evils like the fawn's suffering will be possible, and should they occur, they will be justified by the antecedent great good to which they are tied. Thus, Reichenbach concludes:

> The suffering of the fawn may be pointless or gratuitous, but the possibility of it is a necessary condition of there being that greater good. Thus, the existence of pointless suffering whose possibility is necessary for there being a greater good or preventing a greater evil is compatible with the necessity that God eliminate as much evil as he can without losing a greater good or bringing about a greater evil, and hence with God's existence and goodness. Consequently, merely presenting instances of pointless suffering will not establish that there are instances of evil which God could have prevented, such that no overriding good would have been negatively affected by their prevention, i.e., that (X) is true or reasonably true. What the atheologian has to show is that this pointless suffering is not such that its possibility is necessary for there being the greater good—a tall order indeed.[77]

What must atheists do, then, to establish (X) as true? According to Reichenbach, they must show *both*

> that the theodicies and defenses proposed by the theist to show that there are no gratuitous evils other than those whose possibility is necessary for there being some greater good or preventing some greater evil are not sound, and that there is good reason to expect that God would not have other good reasons for not eliminating more evil than he does.[78]

Such theodicies and defenses are all part of the total evidence that must be consulted when atheists try to make their probabilistic case against theism. However, if those theodicies and defenses are included in the discussion, there seems no reason to think (X) is true. To prove (X) true, atheists must first show those theodicies and defenses to be false. But even if they do, they have a further task. They must then show that there is good reason to think God has no other good reasons for failing to eliminate more evil than he does. In other words, having disproved all theodicies and defenses theists have offered, atheists must show that there are no other *possible* defenses that might exonerate God in regard to gratuitous evil. It is very hard to see how they would show this. Pointing to individual instances of evil doesn't make the atheist's case. Such pointless evil may be logically tied to some antecedent good. Hence, these instances don't show that mere pointless evil (if it really is gratuitous) counts against (T).[79]

Assessment of Reichenbach

Though I agree with much that Reichenbach says, my agreement isn't total. As I described his views, I raised some questions. Let me address other issues of concern.

An initial matter has to do with Reichenbach's handling of prior probabilities. His discussion illustrates some of the problems I raised with Swinburne about calculating prior probabilities. Reichenbach says the probabilistic argument can be stated in one of two forms, depending on whether one thinks it is possible to calculate prior probabilities. What he says about the stronger form of the argument illustrates the problem I raised about background knowledge. As a theist, Reichenbach would like to include the traditional theistic proofs in the background information, but he knows atheists won't likely agree. By the time Reichenbach completes his first response to the atheist, he admits that there may be no objective way for theists and atheists to assign prior probabilities, because they may disagree about what is background knowledge and what is only purported knowledge. This, of course, just illustrates the problems I raised with Swinburne's treatment of prior probabilities and underscores why I believe neither side in this debate can rest much of the overall case on prior probabilities. I am not saying atheists and theists must totally disagree on what is background knowledge, but I doubt both will include the theistic arguments. What they can agree to call background information will probably not tip the scales in favor of one position or the other.

This problem of what counts as background knowledge and how that affects assignment of probabilities is further amplified by Reichenbach's claim that on total evidence, the prior probability of theism is more than .5. This suggests several points. First, I believe Reichenbach and others are correct in demanding that if theism's probability is to be calculated, it must be figured on total evidence, not just on the evidence of evil.

However, and this is the second point, why does Reichenbach think this will affect the prior probability of theism? Demanding that all theistic evidences except one's answer to the problem of evil be included in the background information (even knowledge) requests what atheists won't allow. Moreover, this demand makes it nearly impossible for atheists and theists to agree on prior probabilities.

Third, I agree that if these evidences are used only to calculate the posterior probability of theism and atheism, theists and atheists won't agree that traditional arguments for God's existence work any better than if they were adduced as background information. However, this evidence is probably better used in calculating the posterior probability of theism than in determining prior probability, for at least the theist then doesn't make the claim (which atheists won't accept) that these arguments are part of our common knowledge. Moreover, even though these traditional theistic proofs are not conclusive arguments, they do provide some evidence for theism, but that suggests they are best used as evidential support for it, rather than as part of our background knowledge.

Of course, atheists may think these arguments don't count at all as evidence for theism. If so, then atheist and theist won't likely agree on what the evidence shows about the overall probability of theism. If that happens, it will be more harmful to atheism, since it was the atheist who appealed to evidence to make a case against theism. Without some objective way for theists and atheists to agree on what is and isn't evidence and how that evidence affects the probability of theism, I see no way for atheists to convince anyone but themselves by their evidential case against theism.

My point, then, is that if Reichenbach expects atheists to allow arguments for God's existence as part of background information (even knowledge), he is expecting too much. On the other hand, if atheists won't even let those arguments count as evidence for calculating theism's posterior probability, then they should realize that theists and atheists can never objectively agree on whether theism is improbable. And that just means that atheists' probabilistic argument against theism fails.

Before leaving this point, I note that Reichenbach says that on total evidence, the prior probability of theism will be greater than .5. This, of course, isn't only because he thinks there are many evidences for God's existence, but because he thinks at least some of the traditional theistic arguments are successful to some degree. I agree in general. The problem is that Reichenbach merely asserts that the probability will be greater than .5 without proving it. In order to prove this, he would need to explain to what degree the traditional theistic proofs are successful, and then show how each success raises theism's probability. This is no easy task, but without it, it is hard to see the warrant for his claim that theism's prior probability is more than .5. Surely, atheists will require proof. Without it, his claims seem little more than autobiographical reports of his own assessments, but those reports resolve nothing.

As to Reichenbach's second response to the argument from evil, I agree. I also note that it implicitly assumes that theists can offer theodicies or defenses that explain why God hasn't eliminated any more evil than he has.

In his chapters on the evidential problem of evil, Reichenbach offers no defenses, but from what he says elsewhere, he would presumably offer the free will defense to handle the problem of moral evil. His answer to the problem of natural evil, as noted earlier, appeals to the need for natural laws to govern the processes of nature and to the fact that as natural processes function according to those laws, sometimes natural evil occurs. I agree that these defenses raise the probability of an Arminian form of theism.

I have already raised one difficulty with Reichenbach's third response, but several other concerns stem from that response. Reichenbach agrees that theists believe that if there were no God, there would be more evil than there is. Likewise, atheists claim that if there really were a God, there would be less evil than there is. It seems that theists have a response to this challenge, though Reichenbach doesn't raise it. Though theists must answer why there is so much evil if there is a God, atheists must answer a counter question. Atheists need to explain why, if there is no God, anything ever goes right in the world. Even if theists can't use this issue to build an evidential case *for theism,* it is appropriate in an evidential case *against atheism.* For atheists to make a convincing case for atheism, they must do more than raise objections to theism. They must offer positive evidence for their view and answer counterevidence. And, a major counterevidence is the good our world contains.

Atheists may attribute the good in our world to human goodness, but common sense suggests that human beings, left to themselves, won't necessarily produce a good world. Moreover, human goodness may explain some moral good in our world, but it explains nothing about natural good that is unconnected to human agency. Normally, atheists ask theists to explain why natural evils like tornadoes, earthquakes, and floods occur. These are troublesome for theism, but likewise, atheists must explain why more of these disasters don't occur, if there is no God. If there is no God, then why do natural processes ever work right? In fact, why doesn't the physical universe as we know it simply collapse?

Despite my challenge to atheism, theists must still address whether evil disconfirms theism. Although I think there would be more evil if there were no God, I don't think that claim, if true, really answers atheists' objection to God's existence based on evil. Atheists point to the evil in our world and ask theists why it should be there, if there is a God. One can't justify that evil's presence by saying that if God didn't exist, there would be more of it. Theists need a defense or theodicy which explains why God allows the evil we have. Saying there would be more without God in no way justifies the evil there is.

A further concern with Reichenbach's treatment itself is that he seems to go back and forth between the problem of the quantity of evil and the problem of the apparent gratuitousness of evil. By the end of his discussion, he appears to be handling the problem of gratuitous evil, whereas earlier in his treatment the emphasis seems to be the quantity of evil. These problems are not the same, but Reichenbach seems to treat them as one general problem. Moreover, he overtly treats these issues as they relate to natural evil, but he doesn't seem to distinguish between natural evils that result from human activity (and thus, might be best handled by a defense against the problem of moral evil) and those that are unattached.

Finally, Reichenbach's treatment of the problem of gratuitous evil is both interesting and incomplete at the same time. As I suggested, he prepares the way for a defense against it, but doesn't actually offer one. Though I am tempted here to discuss gratuitous evil at some length, I shall wait until my handling of Michael Peterson's views. Peterson makes gratuitous evil the focus of his discussion, and he offers a detailed defense of God against it. Suffice it for now to say that a key issue in discussing gratuitous evil is how one defines it. We have seen how Reichenbach defines it, but that isn't necessarily the only way the term can be used.

In sum, on some points Reichenbach is surely correct. However, he needs to distinguish clearly between the problem of the quantity of evil and the problem of apparently gratuitous evil. In regard to gratuitous evil, there needs to be a further distinction between natural ills that result from human agency (these evils really raise the problem of apparently gratuitous *moral* evil) and those that don't. This means there are at least three evidential problems Reichenbach's discussion raises (this is true for others we have discussed as well). Beyond distinguishing each problem, Reichenbach needs to offer a defense for each. As he explains, even if atheists can't make their stronger case against theism because there is no objective way for atheists and theists to agree on prior probabilities, that doesn't mean they can't make their weaker case that evil tends to disconfirm theism. If only to answer the challenge of the weaker argument, Reichenbach needs to offer defenses and show how they resolve each evidential problem he raises. This isn't an impossible task for Reichenbach. It only suggests that he has correctly set up the general framework for handling the evidential problem. But more than the framework is necessary. We need the evidence (in the form of a theodicy, defense, or whatever) that shows theism probable in spite of evil.

MICHAEL PETERSON AND GRATUITOUS EVIL

In *Evil and the Christian God* Michael Peterson considers the problem of evil from a number of angles, but his major emphasis is the evidential problem. He quickly passes over evidential problems about the existence of any evil and

the existence of the quantity of evil in the universe and comes to the evidential problem of apparently gratuitous evil.[80] In his opinion, the strongest evidential problem (most difficult for theism to rebut) is the problem of
apparently gratuitous evil.

Peterson cites statements of this problem found in Rowe's work and
James Cornman and Keith Lehrer's *Philosophical Problems and Arguments:
An Introduction*.[81] Peterson then sets forth this problem in a more formal
way. He says it not only involves claims (G), "An omnipotent, omniscient,
wholly good God exists," and (E_3), "Gratuitous or pointless evil exists," but
also an auxiliary assumption Peterson labels the principle of meticulous providence. That principle (MP) is "An omnipotent, omniscient, wholly good God
would prevent or eliminate the existence of really gratuitous or pointless
evils." Though (MP) apparently implies that (E_3) is false, empirical evidence
suggests otherwise.[82] Given these data, Peterson formulates the problem of
gratuitous evil as follows:

1. If (G) is true, then, assuming that (MP) is true, ($\sim E_3$) should be true.
    (theological premise)

2. It is probable that (E_3) is true. (factual premise)

-----

3. Therefore, it is probable that (G) is false. (logical conclusion)[83]

Since this argument's form or structure is proper, the only option for the
theist is to assess whether its premises are true. Peterson initially considers the
factual premise. He notes that since many theists and atheists assume that
(MP) is correct, the debate often surrounds the question of whether there are
any genuine instances of gratuitous evil.[84] In this debate, atheists and theists
both err, according to Peterson. Atheists err in thinking that by adding suc-
cessive instances of apparently pointless evil they raise the likelihood that
there really is gratuitous evil. However, one must investigate separately each
instance of purported gratuitous evil to see if it really is pointless. Merely
adding more apparent instances won't suffice.

On the other hand, theists often err by implicitly assuming that since God
exists, God must really have a purpose for apparently gratuitous evils. All of
this begs the question about whether God exists. Another problem is that by
denying the factual premise while holding on to all the commitments of the
theological premise, theists hold a position on gratuitous evil's existence
which runs counter to experience. But if we consistently doubt the reliability
of our common human experience, this undermines the reliability of our per-

ception of anything in our world. That kind of skepticism about our evaluation of states of affairs in the world is too high a price to pay for solving the problem of gratuitous evil.

Another problem for theists is that too often they think that by explaining the point of certain instances of gratuitous evil, they handle all cases. This obviously isn't true. All of these considerations lead Peterson to think the better approach to solving this problem is not to deny the factual premise but to admit its truth and to reject the theological premise. In particular, Peterson argues for rejecting the principle of meticulous providence.[85] He believes this still allows theists to hold the major theological tenets of their position, while allowing them to offer a defense of theism that is experientially adequate because it admits the obvious point that gratuitous evil exists. Such a defense will find a place for gratuitous evil within the theistic system, and as a result, gratuitous evil won't disconfirm theism.[86]

Though this approach may seem strange, Peterson believes there are significant reasons for denying the principle of meticulous providence. The first has to do with free will. As Peterson elaborates this idea, it becomes clear that he merely offers the traditional free will defense. The difference is that he expands it to cover gratuitous evil. In order to allow humans significant freedom (incompatibilistic, according to Peterson), God must allow the possibility and the actuality of moral evil. But it only stands to reason that it is possible and actual that instances of gratuitous evil also result from abuse of human free will. Hence, as Peterson argues, "Those authors who agree that God should allow man significant free will and who also insist that God must not allow any gratuitous evil (specifically, moral evil in this context) are unwittingly asking for the impossible."[87] This means that we should deny the principle of meticulous providence, not because God is altogether incapable of eliminating all gratuitous evil, but only because he can't do so and still make room for significant free will.

Peterson admits that atheists might concede the connection between free will and gratuitous evil, but modify the argument slightly. They might claim that though the mere existence of gratuitous evil can be justified by appeal to human free will, the sheer number and magnitude of gratuitous evils is far more than a good God should allow.[88] Peterson has two responses.

First, Peterson says this doesn't take free will's connection to the possibility of gratuitous evil seriously enough. Given the existence of free will, how can there be any clearly defined limits to how much gratuitous evil there may be? Though things might get very bad, that is still consistent with the fact that many important things may also be achieved by allowing the possibility of free will to produce good.[89]

Second, Peterson says judgments of how much evil is too much for a good God to allow depend on personal value judgments, not on demonstrative proof. Thus, it is impossible to prove that there is too much gratuitous evil. Those predisposed against theism will think there is too much, while theists will think the amount acceptable. None of this, however, proves there is too much evil, nor can it. Hence, opinions that there is too much or just enough can't count as *evidence* against or for theism. If so, they present no problem for theism.[90]

Another reason for denying the principle of meticulous providence appeals to what Peterson calls the natural law theodicy.[91] The free will defense relates to gratuitous *moral* evil. A natural law theodicy may take one of two forms. It may focus on the importance of a natural order to free will, or it may emphasize the character of the natural order itself. In the former case, the focus is again gratuitous moral evil, but in the latter, the emphasis is gratuitous natural evil.

As to free will and the natural order, Peterson says "there must be some kind of natural order within which free creatures can operate. Free rational action requires a world of natural objects governed by natural laws."[92] Free choice involves deliberation, choosing, and then putting choices into practice. However, if there weren't a stable, predictable natural order, deliberation and action would be tremendously hampered and possibly eliminated. In addition, God wants individuals to interact with one another, but such a social structure demands a natural order as the neutral context of common life. Of course, the same natural order which sets the stage for acts of moral good, also prepares the way for moral evil. Thus, instances of gratuitous natural evil and suffering may result from the abuse of human free will. To remove them, God would have to remove the natural order altogether, but since the natural order is necessary for freedom, removing the natural order would eliminate freedom. Given what is at stake, the principle of meticulous providence had better not be true, for if it is, it would necessitate removing the natural order and human freedom with it.[93]

What about unattached natural evils like floods, famines, and earthquakes? Atheists ask why God doesn't change the parts of the natural system unrelated to free will that lead to natural evil. Atheists think God could do this either by miracle or by implementing a different set of natural laws altogether. However, Peterson thinks neither approach would work.

As to God overcoming the natural order by miraculous intervention, Peterson raises two problems. First, to do so apparently violates God's omniscience. Given divine omniscience, God would have foreseen pointless natural evils, and if he is in the business of eliminating them, he would have arranged to avoid them in the first place. Hence, miraculous removal of the evil when it occurs or is about to occur would be unnecessary. Second, Peterson thinks even these evils are important to life as we know it, though not as related to free will. Peterson explains:

> For instance, those seemingly hopeless natural evils which call forth human sympathy and moral effort, such as suffering and displacement wrought by flood, hurricane, and fire, would probably be absent in the critic's ideal world. The occasions for a number of other virtues would probably be absent or greatly diminished as well. In short, the operation of the world would verge on becoming a sham, a trivialization of the environment in which outstanding achievement as well as real disaster can occur. So, just as God cannot eliminate gratuitous natural evils which are humanly caused without jeopardizing some very important features of human existence (e.g., free will), He cannot tamper with the gratuitous effects of the ongoing world order without also jeopardizing other high values.[94]

This should sound familiar, for it is akin to the greater good defense generally, and principles raised in particular in Hick's soul-building theodicy. The same first-order evil logically attached to second-order good line of thinking is embodied in Peterson's response and these other defenses. Obviously, Peterson finds that approach compelling, so he denies that God should remove natural evils by miracles.

What if God instead simply removed natural evil by creating a different kind of natural system wherein natural evils would never occur at all? The question assumes that a different world would still contain all the valuable aspects of ours without any of its defects. Peterson, however, thinks this suggestion is problematic. He claims that it "runs the risk of trivializing the context of free human action, and for many of the same reasons that the demand for miraculous intervention does."[95] For example, if natural evil is removed, then the kinds of virtues that attach to them will also be forfeited. Moreover, there are other values we would have to forego such as natural beauty. Peterson says, "How well we know that many of the processes and objects of our world which sometimes display beauty are also the very ones which wreak havoc at other times."[96]

A further problem with suggesting that God change natural laws is that natural laws are simply descriptions of how natural objects operate. Hence, changing natural laws would mean changing the characteristics of natural objects in the system. Peterson finds this problematic, because "if alteration of the prevailing natural laws entails alteration of the relevant natural objects, we cannot be sure what kind of world we would have or how its value would compare to that of the present world."[97] Hence, eliminating the undesirable aspects of the natural order while keeping all its values by changing the system isn't clearly something that can be done. It isn't just that we can't figure out how to do this; it isn't even clear that an infinite mind could do it.[98]

In view of these considerations, Peterson concludes that the principle of meticulous providence should be rejected. When one understands the full meaning of a free moral order and of the natural order, one can see why God wouldn't remove all gratuitous evil. But if (MP) is false, the theological premise of the atheist's argument from gratuitous evil is also false, and that means the argument fails. Theism is successfully defended against the evidential problem of gratuitous evil.

Peterson notes that the preceding is merely a defensive posture for theism. He thinks the fact of gratuitous evil may actually be used to construct a positive case for theism. This can be done in three ways. First, it is clear that God's purpose in creating was to produce mature moral and rational creatures, but man as created isn't mature. Gratuitous evil, then, following Hick's soul-building theodicy, is a necessary element in an environment intended to build souls.[99]

Second, gratuitous evil also illumines certain Christian doctrines. For example, it underscores the lostness of man's fallen condition and the significance of redemption. Since man in falling exercised not merely a capacity for evil but a radical capacity for gratuitous evil, we see how truly perverse man is. This shows how desperately lost man is, and in so doing, it also highlights the need of God to redeem people. Whereas the principle of meticulous providence suggests that God has a program to compensate for every evil event or action, agreeing that there is genuine gratuitous evil allows the theologian to illustrate how lost and how much in need of a savior mankind is. Peterson also says theologians who accept (MP) frequently reject a doctrine of hell. That is, if God removes all evil, and hell is the consummate evil, then there must not be a hell. On the other hand, rejecting (MP) allows the doctrine of hell to be more palatable. In fact, someone can freely choose evil as the dominant choice of life (God can't stop this without interfering with freedom) to such an extent that "hell is simply the natural culmination of things which he has voluntarily set in motion."[100] God can't stop individual evil choices, nor can he stop the larger, cumulative evil orientation of someone's life. He can't keep people from choosing hell. Peterson thinks this line of argument about the fall, redemption, and the doctrine of hell shows that believing that there is gratuitous evil makes those doctrines more believable. In so doing, it helps to make a case for Christian theism.

Finally, Peterson asks whether God's creation of this world where gratuitous evil plays a part is really worth it. If not, then, even though gratuitous evil has a role in this world, God on the whole has acted immorally by creating this world. Has God, then, done something wrong by creating this world? Peterson thinks not and argues that the fact that God created the world with gratuitous evil in it is evidence for his existence. Peterson explains that God created a world with free moral creatures in it. Their freedom means he can't guarantee they will do what is moral. Hence,

> The real question becomes whether God's failing to provide a guarantee that the good will be done makes Him morally blameworthy. Let us ponder for a moment whether our moral structures can condemn the very being who makes it possible for us even to exist, to be able to apprehend moral values in the first place, and to have the significance of life which is lived within their ambit. Of course, we morally condemn those who lie, steal, and murder, but it is not at all clear that we must likewise condemn God for creating the context in which such evils can happen. Surely it accords with the very spirit of morality for God to create a moral context and a plurality of finite beings living within it. At the heart of morality is the principle that we should not merely avoid evil but should also seek good. We must see creation itself, then, as the supreme expression of the moral impulse to create something good, indeed to create a whole context within which finite agents are capable of achieving various goods. Is the creation not, as the Book of Genesis records, "very good"?[101]

Peterson also notes that God didn't have to create any world at all. Creating this world adds nothing to God; he created to give, not to get. The creation and preservation of our world, then, are expressions of his mercy, love, and grace. How can it be immoral to act graciously to others without any personal gain envisioned?[102]

Is our world with gratuitous evil in it really worth it? Indeed, it is, according to Peterson. And, it is consistent with belief in the God of Christian theism. Peterson contends that "only a world with the theistic origin and structure described in this chapter is capable of containing the kind of gratuitous evils we observe."[103] The world described has a free moral order and a natural order. It is a world where souls are built, and it is a world produced by a gracious and loving God who created in order to give, not to get. Indeed, this world with its gratuitous evil is positive evidence that there is a God. As Peterson says,

> Only in a game in which the stakes are incredibly high and the conditions for winning so precarious is it possible to lose in the tragic and inexplicable ways we do. The theistic character of the world provides our highest opportunities and yet makes possible our worst defeats.[104]

Peterson concludes his discussion of gratuitous evil by arguing that we should replace (MP) with what might be called the principle of gratuitous evil,

(PG) "An omnipotent, omniscient, wholly good God could allow gratuitous or pointless evil."[105] By substituting (PG) for (MP), the original evidential argument against theism becomes the following positive argument for theism:

1. If (G) is true, then assuming that (PG) is true, (E_3) could be true. (revised theological premise)

2. It is probable that (E_3) is true. (factual premise)

---

3. Therefore, it is probable that (G) is true. (logical conclusion)[106]

Interaction with Peterson

More than most contemporary writers, Peterson's focus is the problem of gratuitous evil. Though he sometimes conflates this problem and the problem of the quantity of gratuitous evil, he is to be applauded for recognizing that there are different problems of evil and for staying primarily with one of those problems. Moreover, his handling of gratuitous evil contains interesting subtleties and is most stimulating intellectually. All of this is praiseworthy, and I believe his appeal to the free will defense does justify the existence of much gratuitous evil for one committed to a free will theology like Arminianism.

In spite of these valuable contributions, parts of what he says are objectionable. I shall raise some concerns, but I also want to note that certain apparent ambiguities in Peterson's presentation serve as an introduction to a fruitful discussion and clarification of several issues involved in the problem of gratuitous evil. Specifically, his book suggests the need to answer the crucial question of how to define gratuitous evil. My contention is that "gratuitous evil" is an ambiguous notion. Until we clarify its meaning, it isn't possible to make an accurate assessment of Peterson's rejection of (MP) in particular, or his defense against the problem of gratuitous evil more generally.

Peterson divides his handling of the atheistic argument from gratuitous evil into two parts. First, he offers his defensive strategy which aims to show that atheists can't make a successful case against theism. Then, there is his offensive strategy which attempts to use gratuitous evil to build a case *for* theism. My focus is mainly his defensive strategy, but I plan to discuss his offensive strategy as well.

PETERSON'S DEFENSIVE STRATEGY

Peterson's strategy is to accept the factual premise of the atheist's argument, but to deny part of the theological premise. Much of Peterson's reason for accepting the factual premise is that common experience supports it. This is a good place to begin my interaction.

While common experience clearly affirms that there are terrible evils, it isn't so clear that they are genuinely gratuitous. My objection here has two thrusts. The first is that while there is no apparent point to these evils, that doesn't prove there is none. As many theists have argued, that which from our perspective appears pointless may, in fact, have a point from God's perspective. Had we greater knowledge (and we someday will), we would see the purpose. Hence, to accept the factual premise on appeal to common experience seems risky, since our common experience doesn't include information about all the interconnections of the evil in question to other evils or goods. Theists who raise this objection against the atheist's factual premise in essence are saying they don't think any genuinely gratuitous evil exists. Consequently, they would likely accept (MP).

My objection may be taken a second way which opens the door to an important but involved discussion. Put simply, before Peterson accepts the factual premise or his opponents reject it, we must clearly define gratuitous evil. Depending on what Peterson means by gratuitous evil, I can either agree or disagree with his contention that there is gratuitous evil, and consequently either accept or reject the atheist's factual premise.

Some may think this a tempest in a teapot. After all, isn't it abundantly clear that gratuitous evil is pointless, purposeless evil? But, what does it mean to call an evil pointless or purposeless? The meaning as seen in contemporary literature (not just in Peterson) is ambiguous. In Peterson's handling of gratuitous evil, I believe we can see some of this ambiguity. Let me illustrate.

Peterson rejects (MP), because he thinks there is gratuitous evil. What seems odd is that having called the evil pointless, Peterson then points out how that evil is connected to valuable things in the world. But if the evil is connected to something valuable, it appears that the evil does have a point. If the evil is genuinely pointless, then why present the free will defense, for example, to explain its point? If it is genuinely pointless, nothing will explain it. On the other hand, if the free will defense does explain its point (which it seems to do), then why call it pointless?

Other examples of this *apparent* confusion appear in Peterson's book.[107] But is this confusion real, or only apparent? In my opinion, it is only apparent. The reason Peterson's treatment appears to be confused stems from what he means by "gratuitous evil" and from the fact that gratuitous evil can be defined in various ways. Once we understand what Peterson means by "gratuitous evil," we can see that Peterson is fairly consistent in his use of the term.

The first real clue as to what Peterson means appears when he cites

William Rowe's explanation of the problem of gratuitous evil. Rowe repeatedly speaks of evils which don't lead to greater good. This definition, then, doesn't focus on what produced the evil but rather on the fact that the evil produces no *subsequent* good. As already noted, a non-gratuitous evil in this sense might be merely causally tied to some subsequent good (i.e., the good might arise without the evil, but on the occasion in question it was caused by the evil) or logically tied to it (i.e., the good is impossible without the evil). Neither Rowe (in the portion Peterson cites) nor Peterson distinguishes at this point between evils causally connected and evils logically connected to subsequent good. Their point is simply that an evil, regardless of its cause, is gratuitous if it is tied to no *subsequent* good. Since Peterson says this is a very clear statement of the problem and the atheist's argument, he apparently agrees with that definition.[108]

Peterson's next comment about the definition of gratuitous evil is perplexing. As he begins to analyze the atheist's argument from gratuitous evil, he raises again the principle of meticulous providence, and notes that it is widely held among theists. He then writes:

> It is also helpful to remember that no complete definition of "evil" or even of "gratuitous evil" need be given for the basic argument to stand. Virtually any definition of "gratuitous evil" could simply be substituted into the original context of debate and then the argument could proceed as before.[109]

There is a sense in which this is right, and another in which it is wrong. In a *formal* sense, for example, one might use E_1, E_2, or E_3, or any of several definitions of E_3 (gratuitous evil), and the argument can continue. But my contention is that the definition of gratuitous evil one selects makes a world of difference to the strategy the theist takes in answering the atheist's argument. On Rowe's definition, Peterson believes the proper strategy is to accept the factual premise and reject the theological premise (specifically, [MP] is the culprit). But, as I shall argue, on other definitions of gratuitous evil, it makes more sense for the theist to deny that there is any gratuitous evil, i.e., the preferred strategy is to accept (MP) and deny the factual premise of the argument. My argument for all of this will appear shortly. My point now is to note Peterson's comment and note that it is potentially confusing, for it suggests that Peterson might use "gratuitous evil" in various senses and/or that how one defines it really doesn't matter.

Several pages later Peterson offers a more detailed definition of gratuitous evil. In discussing the factual premise of the argument, he says,

> the atheist must argue that many instances of evil cannot be justified on either *extrinsic* grounds (e.g., the promotion of greater goods, the preven-

tion of greater evils, etc.) or *intrinsic* grounds (e.g., conformity to some ideal standard of goodness or meaning), and thus are gratuitous.[110]

According to this definition, gratuitous evils are unjustified evils. Evils might be unjustified on extrinsic grounds. What Peterson means here is the idea cited from Rowe that the evil doesn't produce any subsequent good. But the evil may be unjustified on *intrinsic* grounds. What Peterson means here isn't entirely clear, as even he later admits, but it says that something other than consequences provides the basis for determining whether the evil is justified or unjustified. Though an evil might be unjustified on either extrinsic or intrinsic grounds, Peterson's focus is the former. Hence, again the basic meaning of gratuitous evil, as Peterson uses it, is evil unattached to some subsequent good.

Later still, Peterson returns to this matter of definition. He elaborates his point about extrinsic and intrinsic grounds for an evil by linking those notions with consequentialist and nonconsequentialist handlings of ethics. He claims that both broad theories have their definition of gratuitous evil, but he says that in contemporary literature, the consequentialist notion is more prevalent. According to a consequentialist:

> An evil is *justified* if, and only if, it is necessary to the existence of some actual or possible greater good, or to the prevention or elimination of some greater evil; an evil is *gratuitous* if it bears no such relations. Authors who deny that there is gratuitous evil in this sense typically articulate the denial in one of the following ways: that God sees to it that every individual evil is outweighed by some good, that He insures that this world contains on balance more good than evil, that He created the best of all possible worlds, or the like. As Keith Yandell writes: "The orthodox theist is committed to the truth of some version of the greater good defense."[111]

Clearly, this is the notion of gratuitous evil Peterson incorporates into his thinking. Nonetheless, he also explains how he believes gratuitous evil is defined from a deontological (nonconsequentialist) standpoint. He writes:

> In the deontological view, an evil is regarded as *justified* or *gratuitous* on the basis of some internal property which it possesses, or fails to possess, or on the basis of its conformity, or lack of it, to some absolute standard of goodness or meaning. Thus, authors who share this perspective scrutinize evils according to whether they are somehow meaningful in themselves, and not on the basis of their consequences. This fundamental approach is echoed in the saying that no one, not even God, may do evil that good may come.[112]

This deontological notion of gratuitous evil is surely not the one Peterson or many others use. Still, this different definition underscores my point about the ambiguity of the notion.

From the preceding citations from Peterson, it seems clear that gratuitous evil is an ambiguous notion and that Peterson's presentation does little to remove the confusion. Still, I think from what I have shown it is also clear that for Peterson, the predominant sense of gratuitous evil is evil which isn't connected to some subsequent good.

It is also clear that Peterson's basic notion of a gratuitous evil is evil that is unjustified. Though this might seem definition enough, it isn't, for an evil might be unjustified in any of several respects, and each respect constitutes a different notion of gratuitous evil. From Peterson's definitions of gratuitous evil, one can say that an evil might be unjustified and thereby gratuitous in any of the following senses:

1)   an evil is gratuitous if it fails to possess some intrinsic quality or conform to some absolute standard of goodness—presumably, possessing that quality or conforming to that standard would justify the evil

2)   an evil is gratuitous if it serves no further end once it occurs, i.e., it is neither causally nor logically connected to the production of a subsequent good—presumably, that good would justify the evil

3)   an evil is gratuitous if it or its possibility has no antecedent good to which it is tied as an effect or by-product—presumably, the good that would cause it or its concomitant would justify it

We already saw the distinction between senses 2) and 3) in my discussion of Reichenbach. Unfortunately, that distinction isn't always kept in mind when philosophers talk about a good to which an evil is logically (or causally) tied, but it should be clear that there is a dramatic difference between the cause or logical concomitant of an evil and the result of an evil. As David Basinger explains, philosophers typically talk about whether an evil is outweighed by a related good without apparently recognizing that there are two possible ways to understand a good outweighing an evil. Those ways are:

(2)   The good which is *produced by* a particular occurrence of evil outweighs this evil.

(3)   The good which *makes possible* a particular occurrence of evil outweighs this evil.[113]

Basinger's (2) coincides with my 2) and his (3) is equal to my 3).

Let us return now to our original quandary over Peterson's apparently confused use of these terms. Peterson argues for the existence of genuinely gratuitous evil in the world. But he also says this evil is connected to various good things in the world (e.g., free will). That seems confused, because he appears to say, on the one hand, that there is pointless evil in the world, and then, on the other hand, he explains its point. Can we resolve this apparent confusion? My discussion on the various meanings of "gratuitous evil" lays the basic groundwork for resolving it, but to resolve it fully and provide the basis for evaluating Peterson's defensive strategy, I must raise two further key points that impact this issue, and then I can explain what is happening in Peterson and whether I agree or not.

The first point is that one must distinguish between whether an *evil* is justified and whether an *agent* is justified in doing or allowing an evil. The former evaluates the act; the latter evaluates the agent.[114] The second crucial point is that a particular *evil* could be unjustified in one of my three senses of gratuitous evil, but justified in another sense. Putting these two points together, I note that if one defines gratuitous evil in one of the three senses mentioned, and a particular evil under scrutiny is unjustified in that sense of gratuitous evil (but justified in another of those senses), then it becomes understandable how Peterson could say an *evil* is gratuitous (unjustified in sense 1], 2], or 3]), and yet offer a theodicy that says *God* is justified in allowing it.

Let me illustrate this point. Suppose one defines gratuitous evil in sense 2), as Peterson does. That means this evil is neither logically nor causally tied to some subsequent good. But suppose also that this evil was a product of the abuse of free will. In fact, without the evil's possibility, there couldn't be free will as the free will defender understands it. Had we defined gratuitous evil in sense 3), this particular evil, as a product of free will which is a great good, would *not* qualify as gratuitous evil. Thus, this one instance of evil on sense 2) is gratuitous evil, but on sense 3) is not. Now, if the theist defines gratuitous evil according to sense 2), as Peterson does, and then explains (as Peterson does) that God gave an antecedent good (free will, for example) which was used to produce it, then it should be clear that *God* is justified even though the evil is gratuitous in sense 2). But then, we can see here what Peterson means, and why it sounds strange. The evil in question, on sense 2) of gratuitous evil, is clearly gratuitous, but because of how it was introduced into the world, Peterson can say that *God* is justified in allowing this *gratuitous* evil to occur. This may sound as if Peterson is saying the evil is both justified and unjustified from the same perspective, but he isn't. From the perspective designated by 2) it is unjustified, but from the perspective of why God would allow it, *God* is justified. So, even if it is gratuitous in sense 2), one can explain how it got here so as to show that God has done nothing wrong in allowing it.

The preceding paragraph explains what Peterson means and why it isn't as confused as it may appear. But now that we understand what he means, how should we assess it, and, more fundamentally, which of the three senses of "gratuitous evil" should we adopt?

Several points suggest themselves. My first point relates to the first sense of "gratuitous evil," which Peterson calls the nonconsequentialist sense of the term. I think Peterson is confused in thinking there is a nonconsequentialist notion of gratuitous evil. The error stems from confusing what makes an act or event *evil,* which is a matter consequentialists and nonconsequentialists debate, and what makes an act or event gratuitous or pointless, which isn't what debates between teleologists and deontologists are about. Teleologists and deontologists disagree about what makes an act or event evil. The former point to consequences of the act or event; the latter point to something other than consequences. Neither points to the gratuitousness of the act or event to explain why it is evil.

To see that what makes an act or event gratuitous isn't the same thing as what makes either evil, one need only recognize that the following question makes abundant sense and doesn't contain a redundancy: Given that a particular act is purposeless or pointless, is it also an evil act? An act might be purposeless and evil, purposeless but not evil (it might be amoral, for example), or evil but have a purpose. Hence, I conclude that Peterson's distinction between teleological and deontological ways to understand gratuitous evil confuses two different issues. No wonder he has a hard time defining gratuitous evil as a deontologist might. No wonder as well that philosophers who discuss the problem of gratuitous evil do so in terms of 2) and 3), not in terms of 1). Opting for either 2) or 3) (especially 2]) doesn't turn one into a consequentialist or make one buy a consequentialist definition, even if one is a nonconsequentialist. Thinking it does confuses the issues of what makes an act *gratuitous* and what makes it *evil.*

In light of this point, we must confine our discussion of Peterson and gratuitous evil to senses 2) and 3). This brings me to my next point. Suppose one defines gratuitous evil according to sense 2), and also adopts the free will defense to explain a particular gratuitous evil's *origin* and to show that *God* is just in spite of that evil. In that case, it should be clear that nothing is lost for theism by rejecting (MP). On sense 2), there likely will be gratuitous evils, but that needn't destroy theism so long as the free will defense, Peterson's defense about the natural order, or some other defense explains the origin of these evils. Of course, one may still argue that those evils aren't gratuitous in sense 2), because they really are tied to some subsequent good, even if we don't know what it is. But that strategy for defending theism is, as Peterson says, no longer necessary; we can accept the factual premise of the atheist's argument and still defend theism.

It seems, then, that once one understands what Peterson is saying, one realizes that his strategy is an acceptable way to defend theism for those who define gratuitous evil according to sense 2). But that doesn't end the matter. Suppose someone defines gratuitous evil in sense 3). In that case, there is no reason to reject (MP) or accept the factual premise of the atheist's argument. Let me explain.

If one defines gratuitous evil in sense 3), the focus shifts from the results of an evil to the antecedents of the evil—in particular, to a good which produces the evil or at least makes the evil possible as a concomitant of the good. But with this shift in focus, if one handles moral evil with the free will defense or my defense, for example, then not only is *God* justified in allowing the evil, but the *evil* itself no longer qualifies as gratuitous on sense 3) of "gratuitous evil." But then, in virtue of any theodicy or defense (like the free will defense, my defense, and handlings of natural evil by natural law, etc.) which justifies God in terms of how evil is produced in the first place, there really are no gratuitous evils. If that is so, there is no need to reject (MP) or to accept the factual premise of the atheist's argument. Using sense 3), there is a way to argue that there are no truly gratuitous evils, so why reject (MP)?

From the preceding discussion what should we conclude? Should we conclude that either 2) or 3) is "the right definition" of gratuitous evil? I doubt that will get us very far, for the atheist might reply that we can resolve this problem on one definition of gratuitous evil, but not on another, and he thinks there are evils from this other perspective that aren't accounted for but must be.

My suggestion is that we adopt both senses, i.e., that we recognize that an evil could appear pointless (gratuitous) in either of senses 2) or 3), or in both senses. In order for it to qualify as genuinely pointless, however, it must be pointless in both senses, i.e., it is tied neither to any antecedent nor to any subsequent good. If an evil appears gratuitous in only one of those senses, then it won't really be gratuitous, because some sort of defense can be invoked to the effect that it isn't gratuitous in the other sense. Trouble arises for theism only if the theist can specify neither an antecedent good nor a subsequent good to which the evil is connected. In that case, it is hard to see how one would justify either God or the evil. In light of the many theistic defenses that focus on either the cause or the result of evil, it is dubious that atheists can find an example of an evil that is gratuitous in both senses 2) and 3).

I must also add that as long as an evil isn't gratuitous in both senses 2) and 3), (MP) need not be rejected, for by satisfying either 2) or 3) (or both), the evil has some point or purpose. Thus, the theist can accept (MP) and reject the factual premise of the atheist's argument. One needs to adopt Peterson's strategy only if one defines gratuitous evil solely in sense 2).[115]

Before leaving Peterson's defensive strategy, I must raise one further objection. In order to handle gratuitous moral evil, Peterson appeals to the free will defense. In order to handle gratuitous natural evil, he appeals to his natural order defense *and* Hick's soul-building theodicy. Now, this creates problems for his overall theological system in terms of its ethics. As I argued in chapter 4, the free will defense presupposes a nonconsequentialist ethic. Peterson's natural law/natural order defense does so as well. However, Hick's soul-building theodicy presupposes consequentialism, for God is justified in terms of the end that evil serves. Hence, Peterson offers defenses that presuppose contradictory ethical theories. We saw earlier that Hick does the same thing. This problem for Peterson is significant, for it means his whole system collapses with an internal inconsistency. Of course, this problem can be easily removed. Peterson need only drop the soul-building theodicy to maintain a consistent nonconsequentialist ethic.

In response, someone may object that my complaint is wrongheaded, since it attempts to turn the evidential problem into the logical one, which focuses on internal consistency. However, that isn't so. In regard to the evidential problem, the theist tries to show that evidence doesn't make theism improbable. But that doesn't mean the theist can explain those evils with answers that contradict one another. The internal contradiction generated by conflicting ethical systems would haunt Peterson's theism if the logical problem were under consideration. But that problem doesn't evaporate simply by changing to the evidential version of the problem. If one's views are self-contradictory, one's system collapses, regardless of what problem is under discussion. Moreover, if one's position does contain a contradiction, that would be significant evidence that one's theology is very improbable. Empirical instances of evil might lower the system's probability, but this internal inconsistency would also significantly damage its probability.

PETERSON'S OFFENSIVE STRATEGY

What about Peterson's offensive strategy? Even if one grants Peterson's definition of "gratuitous evil," there are problems. Michael Martin thinks it is flawed, because he believes Peterson's inductive argument for theism from gratuitous evil is flawed. I shall present his major objections.

Peterson's argument for theism from gratuitous evil incorporates (PG) "An omnipotent, omniscient, wholly good God could allow gratuitous or pointless evil." Earlier I presented his argument which incorporates (PG). As Martin notes, (PG) is the auxiliary assumption in Peterson's argument. Peterson's argument attempts to confirm the hypothesis (in this case, the hypothesis that God exists) by confirming the auxiliary assumption (PG) and the logical consequence of the hypothesis (in this case, that there really is gratuitous evil). Now, as Martin argues, confirming the logical consequence of a hypothesis or confirming auxiliary assumptions really doesn't confirm the hypothesis unless they would have been *false* if the hypothesis had been *false*. If one could expect either the auxiliary assumptions or the logical consequences of the hypothesis to be *true* even if the hypothesis were *false,* then confirming auxiliary assumptions or the hypothesis's logical consequences shows nothing about the truth of the hypothesis.

How does one test the hypothesis, then? According to Martin, when there is *no* independent support for the auxiliary assumptions, the following (where H represents the hypothesis, A the auxiliary assumption, and T the evidence) is the condition for a good test:

If -[(H) and (A)], then probably (-T)

If there *is* independent support for the auxiliary assumption (A), then a condition for a good test is:

If (-H) and (A), then probably (-T)[116]

Given these conditions, Martin claims Peterson's argument is in trouble, for there is no reason to think either of the following true:

If -[(G) and (PG)], then probably (-E$_3$)
If (-G) and (PG), then probably (-E$_3$)[117]

From my own perspective, I think Martin's objection is not only correct but also confirms certain intuitions about the strangeness of an inductive argument (Peterson's) that appeals to the fact of gratuitous evil as evidence for God's existence. One wonders why gratuitous evil should point to God. As Martin's tests show, in order to confirm that it does, one must prove that there would be no gratuitous evil if there were *no* God. But how can one show that? Martin's objection points precisely to this problem and demonstrates why Peterson's offensive argument is suspect.

One must be careful not to conclude too much from this point. At most Martin's objection shows that there are problems with Peterson's offensive strategy. It in no way shows that his defensive strategy fails. This is so because Peterson's defensive strategy doesn't attempt to appeal to evil as evidence *for* God. Instead, it rebuts the atheist's claim that evil is evidence *against* belief in God. To answer that charge, the theist hardly needs to turn the fact of evil into a positive evidence or argument for theism. One only needs to show that the evidence doesn't make theism improbable.

A second problem with Peterson's argument, according to Martin, is that its first premise is stated partly in terms of what could be true. Premise 1 says that if God exists, then assuming (PG), E_3 *could* be true. Indeed, that is so, but so long as we are talking about possibilities, $-E_3$ could be true also. But if both could be true, then one could write two separate arguments whose conclusions contradict one another. That is, leave the argument as Peterson wrote it, and it appears to confirm God's existence. Write another argument in which premise 1 becomes "If (G) is true, then, assuming that (PG) is true, $(-E_3)$ could be true," and premise 2 remains the same. In that case, the conclusion must be that (-G) is probably true. Is it permissible to tamper with the first premise this way? Absolutely, as Martin shows, for the first premise speaks of possibilities, and if God exists, it is *possible* that there will be gratuitous evil and *possible* that there won't be gratuitous evil. It should be obvious, then, that Peterson's argument, which incorporates into the first premise the notion of something being possibly true, is problematic.[118] Martin grants that Peterson could remove the notion of possibility from (PG) and from premise 1, and that would solve this problem, but it wouldn't solve the first and more fundamental difficulty mentioned above.[119]

In addition to these problems, I am troubled by other things in Peterson's offensive strategy. Peterson says gratuitous evil may help make a case for theism in one of three ways. One may, for example, use gratuitous evil to argue for theism via the soul-building theodicy. I have already noted the problem with this, namely, that having already adopted the free will defense with its nonconsequentialism, the soul-building theodicy then invokes consequentialism. Bringing both ethical theories into the same system produces a contradiction in the theist's position.

As to Peterson's second use of gratuitous evil, this is problematic in a different way. Peterson essentially notes a series of values he believes accrue to theism if one denies (MP). However, it is hard to see how this is an argument supportive of theism. On the one hand, the alleged benefits of rejecting (MP) in no way prove that (MP) is wrong. Nor do they prove that theistic doctrines are correct. All Peterson has shown is that if one rejects (MP) and grants that there is gratuitous evil, this all fits with certain doctrines Christians typically hold. It should be clear that none of that proves anything about the truth of (MP), those doctrines, or the existence of God more generally. The atheist may well retort that Peterson's theistic position, which includes belief in the existence of gratuitous evil, fits together without contradiction, but that in itself is no evidence that Peterson's theism is correct or even probable. Various forms of atheism are also internally consistent. That doesn't confirm them.

As for Peterson's third offensive use of gratuitous evil, I agree that ours is a good world. For an Arminian, free will and the natural order it presupposes are a major part of what makes it a good world. But as Martin's objections show, this doesn't mean gratuitous evil becomes an evidence for theism. In order for that to be so, one would have to show that if there were no God, no free will, and a different natural order, then there would be no gratuitous evil. Obviously, it will be impossible to do that. Hence, the fact that gratuitous evil can fit with these values (free will and the natural order) shows that Peterson can *defend* theism against the atheistic argument from evil, but gratuitous evil isn't evidence that argues for theism. Thankfully, it need not be in order to defend theism against the atheistic evidential attack.

In sum, Peterson's presentation shows a way to defend theism against atheistic arguments from gratuitous evil. As I have suggested, however, I think there are better defensive strategies than his. As to his offensive strategy, it is problematic.[120] Thankfully, one can build a case for theism on the grounds of other evidences. Hence, this failure is hardly devastating for theism. And, since Peterson's defensive strategy is successful, he has shown a way to defend his Arminian theology against the problem of gratuitous evil. That is no small accomplishment, and, I think, more significant than the failure of his offensive strategy.

12

EVIL AND EVIDENCE

In the four preceding chapters, I have presented various theistic and atheistic responses to the evidential argument from evil against God's existence. Now it is my turn to clarify my views as a whole. This chapter and my comments divide into three major portions, and represent two basic strategies we saw in previous chapters. Some theists claim that the nature of an evidential and probabilistic case is such that as applied to the issue of God and evil, it is impossible to formulate a meaningful problem. Hence, in view of certain factors about this kind of problem, and in light of various issues that surround the question of God and evil, the atheistic project has little or no hope of even getting off the ground, let alone succeeding.

Other theists have taken a different tack. While they are sympathetic to those who think the atheistic argument can't even get started, they aren't convinced that the atheist's program is entirely misguided. Hence, they agree that atheists raise a legitimate and troublesome problem. They turn their attention to offering explanations as to why God would allow the evil in question, explanations which they believe sufficiently raise theism's probability to meet atheists' charges that evil is evidence that makes theism improbable.

In my opinion, both strategies have merit. I find it hard to believe that atheists can pose a very convincing evidential problem. On the other hand, I think atheists are less likely to agree that theism is reasonable to hold (let alone is more probable than not), if theists offer no explanation of the evil we see about us. Hence, in this chapter I combine items from both strategies.

My first section addresses the inductive problem generally. In that section, my primary goal is to cast doubt on the atheist's ability to launch a convincing attack on theism via the evidential problem. My comments include remarks about general strategy issues that impact theistic as well as atheistic treatments of this issue. I then turn to comments that stem from the nature of inductive arguments, points based on the nature of probability arguments, and finally, remarks related to the limitations of human knowledge. What I say in that section applies to all forms of the problem, i.e., the evidential problem of evil in general, the evidential problem of gratuitous evil, and the evidential problem of the quantity of evil.

My second and third sections take the following approach: despite how difficult it is to make an evidential case against theism on the basis of evil, let us assume for the sake of argument that atheists point to evils theists must explain. Atheists raise at least two different and distinct problems of evil here, the problem of apparently gratuitous evil, and the problem of the quantity of evil. In my second section, I address apparently gratuitous evil. In the third section, I offer my answer to the problem of the quantity of evil. Though I address these two problems specifically in their evidential form, much of what I say is relevant to those problems in their logical form as well.

The Inductive Problem—How Likely Is Success?
General Strategy Issues

Before addressing directly the question raised in the section heading, I want to mention several items of strategy that are very important in handling the evidential argument from evil. The inductive problem claims theism is improbable, and challenges theists to explain why theism isn't improbable. That is, atheists don't tell theists that they really aren't sure how likely theism is, and then ask theists to build their most positive evidential case for theism. Instead, atheists believe they have positive evidence against the probability of theism. They believe that unless theists can answer their attack, the attack shows theism to be so improbable that it can't be true.

There are two basic strategies a theist can adopt in answering the atheist. Both were mentioned in earlier chapters, but I want to evaluate which is better. Theists may use either a defensive or an offensive strategy. The defensive strategy involves rebutting the atheist's charge that theism is improbable, given the fact of evil. With this strategy theists need not construct a positive argument to prove that theism is more probable than not. They need only explain why the atheist's charge that theism is improbable isn't successful.

Using the defensive strategy, theism can be defended in one of several ways. The theist may rebut the atheist's argument by arguing that the atheistic project isn't likely to succeed because there are problems with inductive and probability arguments of the sort the atheist uses. Plantinga, for example, adopts this strategy in his "The Probabilistic Argument from Evil" when he claims that no notion of probability allows the atheistic argument to achieve its goal, and when he argues that there is no way for atheist and theist to agree on probability assignments for the various items in Bayes' Theorem.

Another way to rebut the atheistic argument is to argue either that the atheist's argument is formally flawed or that one or more of its premises is faulty. In this case, the theist grants that the atheist can get the argument off the ground. The theist simply points to some flaws in the particular argument as the atheist presents it. An example here is Wykstra's claim that Rowe's early argument from evil rests on various "appears" claims which don't satisfy CORNEA.

A final defensive maneuver grants that a meaningful evidential problem can arise and that, as formulated by various atheists like Rowe, it is formally valid. That argument says that if there is a God, there is evil in the world he could have and should have removed. Hence, God has no morally sufficient reason for not removing the evil. In this case, the theist's defensive strategy is to offer a defense (or theodicy, if he thinks he has one) of God which explains why God wouldn't remove the evil in our world. The defense will claim that God can't remove evil if he is to accomplish other goals he intends to achieve. Those goals and values are tied to evil either in that they produce it, are a possible or actual concomitant of it, or stem from it (i.e., the evil is either causally or logically necessary to produce the subsequent good).

With none of these defensive postures is the theist arguing that what he says makes theism more probable than atheism, for these answers don't offer a positive evidential case for theism. Instead, the theist simply employs one of these defensive strategies to show that atheists by appealing to the facts of evil haven't made their case that theism is improbable. And that is really all that is required to meet the atheist's challenge.

In spite of these defensive strategies, sometimes theists adopt the adage that the best defense is a strong offense. Using an offensive strategy, the theist counters the atheistic argument by presenting positive evidence as to why theism is probable. If the theist succeeds, then regardless of how much the existence of evil lowers theism's probability, the positive evidences for theism will ensure that on total evidence it is more than .5 probable.

If a theist uses the offensive strategy, there are two basic ways to proceed. As Rowe noted, one way for theists to respond is to negate the conclusion of the atheist's argument and make it the first premise in the theist's argument. This means that the theist will claim that there is an omnipotent, omnibenevolent, omniscient God. The theist must then offer positive evidences for the existence of this God, and he will usually appeal to the traditional theistic arguments, arguments from religious experience, and whatever other evidence he has. With this strategy, the theist tries to establish with such a high degree of probability that there is a God that in spite of the evil in our world, there must be a way to make it fit with God's existence, even if the theist isn't entirely sure how to do that.

Michael Peterson employs a second offensive strategy. Rather than marshalling evidence for God's existence independent of the God and evil issue, Peterson argues for God's existence by appealing to evil. That is, Peterson's offensive strategy uses the fact of evil to construct a positive inductive argument for God's existence.

Either the offensive or the defensive strategy can successfully rebut the atheist's challenge, but which is the wiser route to take? One way to answer is to clarify what is ultimately under debate. The question under debate is whether or not God exists. That question has only two possible answers (yes or no), and each excludes the other.[1] But if that is so, failure to make a case for either a "yes" or a "no" answer must serve as support for the opposing option. Hence, it seems wisest for the theist not to try to prove that God's existence is probable but to make the atheist show that his nonexistence is likely. On this ground alone, then, I encourage theists to adopt a defensive strategy. If the atheist's offensive case against theism fails, then so much the better for the likelihood that theism is correct. I am not saying, of course, that simple failure of the atheist's project "proves" theism to be probable. I am only saying that because of the interdependence of the "yes" and "no" answers, failure of either side to make a positive argument for itself or to succeed in its negative argument against the opposition is beneficial to the opponent.

In addition, we must remember who "picked this fight" in the first place. It wasn't the theist who informed the atheist that he could prove by evidence that theism is more likely than not. It is the atheist who complained that the existence of evil makes theism improbable. Well, then, if the atheist believes that, let him prove it.

There are other reasons why theists would do well to adopt a defensive strategy rather than go on the offensive. It is notoriously difficult to present a convincing case for the traditional theistic arguments for God's existence. Likewise, arguments from experience are always difficult to assess, let alone demonstrate as successful. Hence, the theist will have a hard time making a convincing case for theism or against atheism. But the same is true for the atheist. He will have a difficult time making a convincing case for atheism or against theism. If this is so, let the atheist go on the offensive. The defensive strategy is far simpler to use, and since the atheist began this argument by going on the attack, let the theist "play defense."

A further point is that the atheist's strategy should help theists decide theirs. The atheist has already taken on the harder task of proving his own position by disproving his opponents'. All that is needed to meet the atheist's argument from evil is to show in some way that it doesn't work, i.e., it doesn't make theism improbable. Since the atheist has chosen an offensive strategy, why should the theist take on an equally difficult offensive strategy to defend theism?

What I am saying about the wisest strategy in this debate has clear implications for the issue of the burden of proof in this disagreement. Some atheists think the burden of proof rests on the theist. Chrzan complained that Plantinga tried to push the burden of proof onto the atheist. I suspect he would say the same thing to any theist who chooses a defensive strategy. However, the fact is that when the atheist claimed that she could prove something about theism by appealing to the evidence of evil, she assumed the burden of proof. Hence, by adopting a defensive strategy in answering the atheist's challenge, the theist isn't shifting the burden of proof. The burden of proof is already on the atheist; she took it on herself.

One further general comment is a point raised throughout this book, and it applies here as well. Throughout this book I have argued that there is no such thing as *the* problem of evil. That is so in several significant respects. For one thing, different kinds of problems can arise for theism on the basis of evil. Some problems arise in a logical form and others in an evidential form. Moreover, there are problems of moral evil and natural evil, problems about the quantity of evil, the intensity of evil, and the apparent gratuitousness of much evil. Each of these problems can be posed as a logical or evidential problem.

There is another sense, as I have argued, in which there isn't just one problem of evil. More than one theological position falls under the rubric of Christian theism, and many theological positions depart from orthodox Christian theism. But then, there will be as many problems of evil as there are theological systems with views on God and evil. For each theology the problem of evil has a distinct form, and answers must address the way the problem arises for each brand of theism.

The result of the above is that when atheists claim that evil is evidence against the probability that God exists, theists should reply, "evidence against which God?" Until the atheist specifies the conception of God under attack, and until the theist specifies the God he is defending, it will be very difficult, if not impossible, to assess the success of either the attack or the defense. Unfortunately, neither theists nor atheists seem to heed this point. They proceed merrily on their way attacking and defending, apparently thinking they are attacking and defending the same God, when in fact they are probably thinking of different conceptions of God. This accomplishes little.

Some may think it unnecessary to specify the conception of God in question, for we are dealing with the evidential problem, not the logical problem. However, this isn't so, because the evidential problem is about the probability of the theistic hypothesis, and that hypothesis takes as many forms as there are theistic positions. So, before we can evaluate whether and how the evidence of evil(s) raises or lowers the probability of the theistic hypothesis, we must know precisely which variety of theism is under consideration.

In chapter 10, I illustrated this point in regard to various free will theologies, but now I want to do the same in terms of the major forms of theism handled in this book. Initially, I looked at a theonomous conception of God. Is evil evidence against the probability that the theonomist's God exists? According to theonomy, God isn't obligated to do anything unless he chooses to be obligated. Moreover, we can't know what he or we are to do until he tells us the rules. If God reveals that the only moral obligation for anyone in the universe is to obey God's rules, then evil is defined as disobeying God's rules. God might then reveal that he personally is exempt from that obligation and any other moral obligation (he is beyond good and evil). In that case, it is hard to see how evil in our world can even begin to count as evidence against the theonomist's God.

Suppose God revealed, instead, that he must obey his own moral rules, and also revealed that he has done so. In that case, it is again difficult to see how evil in our world would be evidence against God's existence. Since he has broken no rules, and if he never reveals that it is his moral obligation to remove evil, there is no way the presence of evil can serve as evidence against his existence. There is only a problem for the theonomist's God if the theonomist says his God has revealed rules for all to follow (including himself) and then reveals that he hasn't obeyed them. In that case, the evil God did *would be* strong evidence against the theonomist's God. But until the theonomist says his God has revealed such things, it is hard to see how the presence of evil, even large amounts and apparently gratuitous instances of evil, is evidence against the theonomist's God.

Atheists may reply that this just isn't how we determine moral obligation for God or anyone else or how we assess the rightness or wrongness of anyone's actions. The theonomist should answer that this *is* the way matters are decided in regard to his God. What the atheist says may be true of any god the atheist would conceive of, but it isn't true of the theonomist's God. The atheist's evidential argument may be strong evidence against the God the atheist imagines, but it surely doesn't damage the theonomist's God.

What about Leibniz's God? Is evil evidence against his existence? It is very hard to see how it can be. Leibniz's God is morally obligated to create the best of all possible worlds, metaphysically speaking. If he doesn't, he is morally reprehensible. But Leibniz assures us that this God is intelligent enough to know what the metaphysically richest world is, good enough to want to actualize it, and powerful enough to do so. In that case, ours is the best world, metaphysically speaking. But if our world contains the greatest amount of moral evil and good and natural good and evil that are compossible, Leibniz's God dare not remove any of it. Some of it may seem too much, and other evils may appear to serve no purpose, but that is just wrong. Just the amount we have is necessary to make ours the metaphysically richest world, and apparently gratuitous evils aren't genuinely gratuitous, for they serve the end of making this the best world. Hence, evil in our world doesn't lower the probability that Leibniz's God exists. If anything, it raises it.

Moving to Modified Rationalism, this notion of God is probably more akin to the atheist's notion. But again, it isn't at all clear that evil will render the various Modified Rationalist theologies improbable. For example, an Arminian appeals to free will as that which justifies God against the moral evil in the world. In order to allow for free will, God had to allow the possibility and the actuality of evil in our world. But then, the mere fact of moral evil (and natural evil resultant from choices of God's creatures) can hardly be evidence that disconfirms God's existence. A similar point can be made with respect to John Hick's soul-building position and my Calvinistic one. In light of the reasons these positions offer for God allowing evil in the world, it will be hard to see how that evil counts as compelling evidence against God's existence or against our world as good.

The atheist may say that the values the free will defender, Hick, and I point to which necessitate or accompany evil just aren't worth it. God should have known that and created a different world that omitted those values and the evils that come with them. That he didn't is evidence against him. But this objection is misguided. The Modified Rationalist agrees that there are probably better possible worlds than ours, but he answers that God's obligation in a Modified Rationalist system isn't to create the best world or even better worlds than some good ones. His obligation is to create one of the good possible worlds, and he has done that as evidenced by free will, soul-building, or whatever. The valuable things each of these worlds contain, even though evil comes with them, serve as evidence that a good God creates them, and if our world didn't have such values, that would be evidence against God's goodness. Seen from this perspective it isn't at all clear that the atheist and theist can agree that the facts of evil in our world make it improbable that God exists.

In sum, then, when evil is cited as evidence against God, theists and atheists alike must specify which God is under discussion. It may be that atheists can make a convincing case against the theonomist's, Leibniz's, or the Modified Rationalist's God, but I doubt it for reasons already mentioned and others I shall present in the rest of this chapter. But theist and atheist alike must realize that until the God being attacked or defended is specified, this debate goes nowhere.

Comments Based on the Nature of Inductive Arguments

As already mentioned, one may adopt a defensive posture in answering the atheist's argument. One can explain why the atheist will have a hard time presenting a successful argument. This section and the next two use the defensive strategy.

There is good reason to think the atheist's evidential argument has little chance of success, because it is inductive. Certain features about inductive arguments make it hard to write a successful one. For one thing, there are different types of inductive arguments, as I explained when I first introduced this problem. The classical idea of induction moves from particular instances of a phenomenon to make a generalization about all such phenomena. If there is a large enough sampling of instances, the move to the generalization is warranted and easy to make. But as we have seen, the inductive problem of evil isn't this kind of inductive problem. If we focus solely on the evidence in the world, we find instances of various kinds, amounts, and intensity of evil. Empirically, we can observe many evils, but we can't observe the evaluation of them, nor can we observe God's relation to them, whatever it is.[2] Hence, if we proceed solely from empirical data, it appears that the most we can conclude by this sort of inductive argument is that there will likely be more instances of evil. Clearly, that inductive generalization proves nothing about God and/or his relation to evil in our world.

If the inductive argument from evil is to begin at all, it must be an argument of the form of hypothesis confirmation or disconfirmation. In that sort of argument, the only empirical data appealed to are instances of evil. Those instances in themselves contain no empirical evidence of how they should be evaluated (too much, gratuitous, etc.) nor of how they relate to God. In itself, the mere existence of evil is in no way linked to God. How then does the argument link the instances of evil to God? By postulating a hypothesis and then offering various auxiliary assumptions that are assumed true, the first premise links the ideas of the hypothesis (there is or isn't a God) to a prediction of what will probably be the case empirically (there will or won't be evil). In other words, premise 1 makes no claims about what is the case; it is a conditional sentence that speaks about what we can expect empirically if certain other things are true. Only the second premise appeals directly to empirical data, but again, it doesn't link the data to evaluation of them or to God's relation to them; it only states what is observed.

What is my point? It is that this sort of inductive reasoning involves premises that offer no empirical data for any link whatsoever between God and evil. The link between the two is made in a premise that is a conditional sentence that asserts nothing about what is actually observed in the world. That is, the connection between God and evil is made *conceptually in the argument;* it isn't observed in the world. But that should cause us to proceed with extreme caution. Since the connection between God and evil (whatever it is) isn't empirically observable, we (atheist and theist) must postulate that relation in a conditional sentence like the first premise. But since the first premise isn't an observational one and since it expresses the thinker's way of relating God and evil, it is clear that there is no *empirical* way to confirm that linkage.

As a result, not only the first premise but the whole argument is highly inferential. But inferential reasoning is notoriously difficult, especially if the reasoner must *postulate* the relation between empirical data and an explanatory theory that purports to explain them. The project becomes even more complicated when one realizes that empirical data beyond those marshaled by the argument appear to disconfirm the argument's conclusion, rather than confirm it. I am not suggesting that this sort of inductive argument can never work, regardless of what the argument is about. My point is that the inductive argument *from evil* is highly inferential and that there are more data involved (other evidences for and against theism) that affect the argument's conclusion than just those mentioned in the argument. These facts plus the lack of clear *empirical* linkage between the data and the theory make it very hard to show that one's inference is the right one or even the most likely among a series of possible inferences the data can warrant.

For those still unconvinced that the mere fact of evil allows more than one possible or even probable inference about God's connection to evil I offer the following. From the fact of evil, it is possible to construct an inductive argument of the form in question in favor of the following propositions (hypotheses): there is no God; there exists an evil God; there exists a good but impotent God; or there exists an omnipotent, all-loving God with a morally sufficient reason for allowing evil. Obviously, those propositions cancel one another out, so they can't all be correct. But then, if a piece of evidence is consistent with a series of theories, each of which excludes the others, it will be very hard to make a decisive case for any of the theories by appealing solely to the evidence in question. Thus, we should be very skeptical about how successful the atheist's argument will be.

Our skepticism should increase in light of another matter. As stated, in our world we observe evil, but we observe no connection between God and that evil. We do, on the other hand, observe humans doing evil. If we appeal only to empirical facts, we might not think that we should link what we see to God at all. We might, instead, take the evil we observe as a basis for an inductive argument of the form in question about human beings. That is, we might infer any of the following: all evil stems from human action, and all humans are radically inclined toward evil; some evil stems from human action, and all humans are radically inclined to evil; all evil stems from human action, and everyone is moderately inclined to evil; all evil stems from human action, and most are moderately inclined to do evil while some are radically inclined to do it; some evil stems from human action, and all of that comes from humans who are radically inclined to do evil, etc. Obviously, some of these hypotheses square better with the empirical data than do others, but at least more than one appears likely on the data. This again illustrates how tricky this sort of inferential reasoning can be when the same data appear to support so many mutually conflicting theories. Moreover, none of these propositions invoke or involve God at all, nor need they do so. It is possible that one might observe moral evil and natural evil that stems from human action and not connect those evils in any way to God, but connect them only to human beings. But then, the atheist must convince us that he has chosen the correct person to whom evil should be linked, and that this link is better supported by the evidence than any other connection to which this evidence might be linked. That will be very hard to do, indeed.

Beyond these problems with inductive arguments in general and with the argument from evil in particular, I must again mention Plantinga's challenge. Since atheists agree that theists can show that evil is logically consistent with theism, how likely is it that atheists can make a convincing case that evil is strong evidence against theism? This challenge is especially telling in light of what I have said above about the kind of inductive argument we have in this case. Moreover, when an atheist admits that a theist's defense can join without contradiction the existence of God and the existence of evil, it seems that a stronger inferential case can be made for the view that an omnipotent, all-loving God exists who has a morally sufficient reason for evil than for the view that there is no God. Having admitted that evil *can* fit with God's existence, how can the atheist then hope to show that evil *doesn't* fit with God and thus is evidence that makes his existence improbable?

I conclude, then, that while it isn't impossible per se to structure an inductive argument of this sort against theism, it is very hard to make a successful one. This is so because the evidence doesn't link God and evil empirically, because other evidences must be considered, and because this argument is so inferential.

Comments Based on the Nature of Probability Arguments

The chances that the atheist's argument can succeed are also slim because this inductive argument is a probability argument, and certain features of probability arguments in general increase the difficulty of success. Moreover, features of a probabilistic argument from evil against theism make it extremely unlikely that atheists can succeed in their project. To those issues we now turn.

An initial point about probability arguments is that to make as accurate a probability judgment as possible, one must base it on total evidence relevant to the theory. This point has been mentioned several times in the last few chapters, so I needn't belabor it here. However, this point significantly damages the atheist's argument from evil, because that argument appeals only to one kind of evidence in making its assessment. There are surely other evidences favoring atheism, and of course, there are plenty of evidences that favor theism. Since this is so, it isn't worth much for atheists to claim that theism is improbable in light of evil in the world. Theists can grant that evil lowers the probability of theism. In fact, they could even grant that evil lowers it below .5. But none of this particularly damages theism, since the debate about probability isn't over until theists have a chance to offer positive evidence for theism as well as rebut atheistic claims about evil by offering their explanation(s) of why evil is justified. Even if theists offer none of their positive evidences for theism but merely respond as I plan to in this chapter, it isn't at all clear that theism will be improbable at the end of the debate. Of course, atheists may think that even if theism is more than .5 probable, it is still less probable than atheism. But that too can't be decided until we see total evidence for and against each position.

Making a judgment only on the evidence of evil is also risky because of there being no empirical connection between evil and God in the world. When one couples the fact that evil may serve as evidence for any of the propositions mentioned above with the need to consider all relevant evidence, it is truly amazing that atheists would think this argument very devastating to theism. It is a start in the atheist's case, but atheists need much more than this to make a convincing case.

A second set of considerations revolves around the need to determine the prior probability of theism or atheism in order to work Bayes' Theorem and determine a theory's probability on background information and evidence. As noted in preceding chapters, it isn't easy to determine prior probability of a theory or to get an opponent to agree with one's assessment of that matter. This is so in part because assigning any numerical value to represent a probability judgment reflects the subjectivity of the assessor.

What should atheists and theists do if they disagree about prior probabilities? If they can't agree at all, it is dubious that they will agree on the probability of their theories on evidence. On the other hand, they might just arbitrarily decide to grant both theism and atheism a prior probability of .5. In this case, Bayes' Theorem can be worked, assuming they can agree on the other numerical values in the equation. If they disagree on numerical values for those other parts of the theorem, prior probability becomes unimportant, but nothing is really resolved since there is still disagreement about the other numerical values.

The net result of the subjectivity involved in determining numerical values for the various items in Bayes' Theorem is that the atheist's argument won't likely demonstrate anything more than that if one begins as an atheist, one will probably conclude that evil as evidence makes atheism probable and theism improbable. Theists will make similar judgments in favor of theism and against atheism. Obviously, this will convince no one other than those who hold the view already.

There is another respect in which it is difficult to determine the prior probability of theism or atheism. As noted when I discussed Swinburne, prior probability reflects the probability of a theory on background information. However, this raises the question of what is background knowledge for all theories and what is evidence in support of a particular theory. Theists would love to consider the traditional theistic proofs as background *knowledge,* but no atheist can grant that. If theists offer those proofs as evidence that confirms their theory, atheists won't agree. Subjective assessments of the value of these and other arguments both atheists and theists offer make it hard to decide what is background knowledge and what is evidence and how convincing the evidence (if they decide it is evidence rather than background knowledge) actually is. Of course, unless theist and atheist agree on what is background knowledge and what isn't, there is no way even to begin to calculate prior probability.

Someone may think these problems aren't crucial, because I have already shown that prior probability is nowhere near as important as someone like Swinburne thinks. Even if theism has low prior probability or if theists and atheists disagree about prior probability, if there is strong evidence for theism, that will overcome the problem. As long as on total evidence theism is .5 or more probable, prior probability doesn't matter.

Two points are appropriate by way of response. The first has to do with the mathematics of Bayes' Theorem. It is true, for example, that there are cases where prior probability makes little difference in the final outcome. Consider a case where prior probability is .9, a rather decisive positive probability. Suppose that the probability there will be a certain kind of evidence, given the hypothesis and background information, is extremely low like .1. Assign a probability in the denominator of the theorem of anything above .18, and the overall probability of a theory will be less than .5. That is, multiplying prior probability by the probability of the evidence obtaining (in the case imagined, .9 X .1—this is the numerator of Bayes' Theorem) yields .09. So long as the denominator is more than .18, when the numerator is divided by the denominator, the final outcome will be less than .5. Only if the figure in the denominator goes below .18 does the overall probability rise above .5. So, in cases like the one imagined, a high prior probability makes little difference. The theory overall will be improbable (less than .5).

Now consider another case, where the probability of the evidence obtaining on the hypothesis and background knowledge is extremely high. Let us assign that item of the numerator of Bayes' Theorem a probability of .9. Suppose we also assign the item in the denominator a .5 probability. In this case, prior probability will make a difference. If prior probability is .2, overall probability will be .36 (improbable), but if prior probability is even .3, overall probability is .54 (probable). Suppose the denominator is .3 instead of .5 and that the probability of evidence obtaining on the hypothesis and background information is still .9. Then, if prior probability is .1, overall probability is .3 (improbable), but if prior probability rises to .2, overall probability is .6 (probable).

Consider one more option, where the denominator is .7 and the probability of evidence obtaining on the hypothesis and background knowledge remains .9. In this case, a prior probability of .2 yields an overall probability of .257142 (improbable), but if prior probability rises to .5, overall probability is .642857 (probable).

The lesson from the preceding is that in some cases, prior probability makes no difference to whether the theory will overall be probable, but there are many cases where it does. In cases where prior probability does make a difference, theists and atheists must agree on the prior probability of theism in order to work Bayes' Theorem and determine the overall probability of theism. But because of the difficulties mentioned in determining prior probabilities and getting atheists and theists to agree on them, it is dubious that atheists and theists will agree on the prior probability of theism. And that just means that in those cases where prior probability does matter to the result of Bayes' Theorem, the probability of theism can't be accurately calculated. If so, in those cases, the atheist's probabilistic argument from evil can't succeed in showing theism to be improbable.

My other response to the imagined objection is that even in cases where prior probability assignments matter little, theists and atheists must still assign numerical values to the other items in Bayes' Theorem. But here there is no reason to think theists and atheists will agree any better than they did about prior probability. Take the matter of how likely it is, given the hypothesis and background information, that the evidence will obtain in the world. In the debate about God and evil, this is the question of how likely it is that there will be evil if there is an all-good and all-powerful God and if that God would remove evil insofar as he could. As is evident from the four previous chapters, there is quite a debate between theists and atheists about that matter. Not even all theists agree on this. For example, if one follows Peterson's strategy in handling gratuitous evil, one will think it very probable that there will be gratuitous evil. On the other hand, those who accept (MP) will hold that it is very improbable that there will be this evil if there is a God. Hence, differences of opinion and subjectivity abound when trying to determine the numerical values of the other items in Bayes' Theorem. That being so, it is hard to see how atheists can make a case that will convince anyone other than themselves.

In reflecting on what I have said about subjectivity in making probability judgments, one might wonder why probabilistic arguments are so prone to subjectivity. After all, isn't the same evidence available to all so that all can come to the same conclusion? In response, I think one must understand what a probability judgment actually is. A probability judgment offers an opinion about how persuasive or convincing evidence and argument for a given position are. Of course, when talking of how persuasive or convincing an argument is, two sorts of factors are involved. On the one hand, there are the facts of the case, i.e., there is the evidence and argument that can be marshaled for the truth or falsity of any position. Anyone who knows the rules of reason and argument can make a judgment on whether arguments and evidences are valid and really show the position to be true or false. But even if arguments and evidences do support the claims in question, persuasion also involves psychological factors.[3] One may grant the truth of argument and evidence, but for psychological reasons still find them unconvincing and conclude that they don't establish as true the position they support.

One can easily see how these factors apply to the issue at hand. Atheists and theists can understand one another's arguments and evidences about God and evil. They can agree about whether arguments are valid and sound and about what evidence there is and whether and how it is relevant to the issue at hand. If that were not so, the vast amount of literature on these topics would be worthless for anyone who didn't already hold a given writer's position. But despite these items of agreement, there is no guarantee that theists and atheists will agree about what those arguments and evidences suggest about the overall probability (persuasiveness) of theism or atheism. If the positions under debate made little difference to theists and atheists, then they might be able to agree about probability assignments on the basis of evidence and argument. But how probable theism and atheism are isn't an indifferent matter to those who discuss them. They are personally involved and have a definite stake in the outcome of this debate. Hence, subjectivity is likely to influence how each side evaluates the persuasiveness of arguments and evidences. No matter what theists or atheists say to convince one another that their probability assessments are right, it is unlikely that a convinced opponent will be persuaded. And that just means that the atheist's probabilistic argument won't likely convince anyone but those who are atheists already.

My point here must not be misunderstood. I am not saying that when making a probabilistic case for or against any given viewpoint, it will be impossible to get agreement on assignment of probabilities. I am only saying that assigning probabilities includes a certain element of subjectivity, because it appeals to the persuasiveness of a position, and the persuasiveness of a viewpoint depends in part on psychological factors. When the issue under debate is especially controversial and the debaters are not emotionally indifferent to the outcome, agreement on probability judgments is even harder to achieve. The God and evil issue is one of those highly controversial issues with much at stake. Hence, psychological factors are likely to play a major role in decisions about the probability of theism in light of evil. Because of those factors, it is unlikely that either side will agree with the other about probability assignments, and that just means neither is likely to offer a probabilistic argument that will convince the other.

The Evidential Problem and the Limits of Human Knowledge

Atheists make various claims about what God (if he exists) is or isn't doing and why, and about what the world would be like, if there were an all-powerful and all-loving God. However, some theists reply that our knowledge is just too limited to know if those claims are true. As a result, the evidential argument seems doomed to fail. In this section, I shall present several objections to the evidential argument from evil based on the contention that our knowledge is just too limited in one way or another to make a convincing evidential case against theism.

Garth Hallett has argued this point as forcefully as any. He begins by cit-ing Cornman and Lehrer's question about what sort of world we would cre-ate if we were all-good, all-powerful, and all-knowing. Would we create a universe like this one? Hallett says that a realistic response is that we have no way of knowing, because we aren't that kind of being. Nevertheless, Cornman and Lehrer think we would have to answer "no." Hallett complains that "these authors' failure to note the relevance of our human epistemic con-dition is symptomatic of much writing on the problem of evil; their oversight simply takes a more flagrant form than usual."[4]

Hallett explains further that even theists tend to make this error, for they agree that evil for which humans can't find a justification weighs heavily against the traditional theistic God. What they should realize, according to Hallett, is that "given our cognitive limitations, our failure to understand a given evil—or a given type, or quantity, of evil—permits no inference for or against the existence of a justifying reason, hence of God."[5]

If Hallett is right, it seems impossible for an atheistic argument from evil to succeed. Likewise, theistic attempts to defend God are in a real sense mere speculation. But how does Hallett defend his views? Hallett likens human beings' knowledge of God to a young child's understanding of his father's thinking. He then offers the following illustration:

> A young child, let us suppose, becomes excited as guests start to arrive and asks to stay up for the party. 'Just this once', he pleads. But his father insists on his going to bed. Why? Because the boy needs his sleep. Because his pres-ence would displease one of the guests or put a damper on the party. For the sake of regularity in the child's life, and so as not to favor his every whim, with the results that would have in the long-run on the development of his character. And so on. That is, the father bases his decision on facts, values, and causal connections of which he is aware but which lie outside the small child's ken. The youngster does not know the guests or what they plan to do or how his presence would affect their evening. He has probably forgot-ten the effect on his disposition and behavior the last time he stayed up late, and perhaps never connected the way he felt the day after with his lack of sleep the night before. And of course he knows nothing about child psy-chology, or the connection between early training and adult personality. The very word 'personality' means practically nothing to him, that level of val-ues, so decisive in his father's considerations, having barely appeared on his horizon. So the child is in no position to judge his father's love on the basis of this one decision or of any combination. A smile, a kiss, a tone of voice—such are the bases of his trust, not complicated calculations of his father's motivation and strategy.[6]

Hallett argues that human beings are in the same epistemic position in regard to discerning why God does what he does as is this boy in understanding his father's reasons. If the child complains that his father doesn't love him because he won't let him stay up for parties, we would think little of his complaint. It surely wouldn't reduce the probability that his father loves him to less than .5. The same is true, argues Hallett, of our inability to account for some evils in our world. That inability doesn't amount to much if our knowledge is so limited that we, like the child, are unlikely to have much idea about why God does or doesn't do things in a specific case. If we are like a little child in our understanding, then failure to understand why there is some evil is forgivable. If we are like a ten-year-old in our knowledge, the failure is less forgivable, and if like an adolescent, our failure is even more significant. As Hallett argues:

> Somewhere along the continuum between infancy and adulthood—that is, between minimal understanding and omniscience—the balance would tilt, and our failure to understand would not merely lessen the probability of God's love but (in the absence of countervailing arguments) would make it improbable. However, where that point lies and where we stand in relation to it, we have no way of knowing. This double ignorance shows the weakness of any anti-theistic argument based on the existence of evil.[7]

In other words, the child is unable to understand why his father won't let him stay up. Someday he will be old enough to understand, and at that point he will realize how little he understood when he was younger. But, as a child right now, he can't even estimate the extent of his non-understanding. The same is true for humans in regard to what evil tells us about God's existence and love for us. Not only are we not in a position to know why he would allow it, but we aren't even in a position to understand how far off we are from being able to understand. We are unable to estimate how extensive our non-understanding is.[8]

Hallett notes that since Augustine, discussion of the problem of evil by both theists and atheists has come a long way. As a result, many seem to think we are in the mopping-up stages of accounting for the last few evils and the like, but this is only because we think we know far more about these things than we do. In order to know the actual explanation for unexplained evils or to know there is no explanation, there are many pieces of information we would have to know. Again, the analogy with the child proves helpful. Hallett explains:

> Consider the range of things the child might have to know, in order to grasp its father's motivation. I have mentioned some: sleep needs, character development, the guests and their preferences, the evening's planned or probable activities. Others could be added. . . . Corresponding knowledge with regard to the problem of evil might be biological, psychologi-

cal, sociological, physical, metaphysical, conceptual, theological, eschatological. Our ignorance with regard to such matters is sufficiently evident
that our perception of the problem of evil would radically alter were it
seen, not merely as comparable to, but as being importantly affected by,
this larger ignorance.[9]

According to Hallett, the net result of this is that the problem of evil becomes
as much a problem about our understanding as a problem about evil.[10]

In reflecting on Hallett's views, I find something attractive, but I also have
some concerns. On the positive side, I agree that human beings aren't omniscient and that we really have little idea of just how far we are from omniscience. That being the case, it is excessive pride for an atheist to claim that
because we don't know the exact reason for an evil or a set of evils, there can't
be a justifying reason. Likewise, it is excessive pride for theists, barring divine
revelation, to say they know God's reason (rather than a possible reason) for
allowing certain evils. Since the atheistic argument from evil rests heavily on
whether there appears to be a justifying reason for various evils and on what
one would have done if one were God (observations that can't count for much
in light of Hallett's point about the implications of our ignorance), I must
agree in principle that it will be very hard to make a convincing evidential
argument against theism on the basis of evil. Just as I found Wykstra's
responses to Rowe about these matters (see chapter 9) compelling, I think
Hallett's basic point is correct.

On the other hand, one might conclude from Hallett's claims that debate
about God and evil is totally worthless. I think not, and it is here that I have
reservations about Hallett's views. Once one recognizes that a problem of evil
(in the logical or evidential form) isn't an attack per se on God, but rather
attacks a particular theological position, i.e., a particular conception of God
and his relation to the world, one realizes that the problem of evil in its various forms can meaningfully be posed. Granted, each theological position is
limited in its understanding of the universe, but what is at issue with either
the logical or the evidential problem is whether that theological position is
logically coherent and/or probable. And, there are things we do know that
allow us to make such judgments about specific systems. If the theological
position really does contain a contradiction (and it is possible to show that,
as we have seen), one can't rescue that system by appeal to Hallett's claims
about our ignorance. Likewise, if there is evidence that really makes one of
those systems improbable (hard as it will be to show that, I believe it can be
demonstrated for some systems), then Hallett's claims about our ignorance
can't rescue the system. If atheists can demonstrate either of these things
about a theological position, that is significant. They will have shown why

they have good reason not to hold it and why theists shouldn't either. On the other hand, if theists can answer both problems as those problems attack their systems, that is also significant, for they will have offered reasons for their belief and for others to believe.

Now, it might turn out that had we omniscience, we would see that no theological position we now know of is entirely right. That, of course, poses no problem for God's existence (if there is a God), but is a problem only for our conceptions of God. But none of this means it is futile now to evaluate the theological positions we have. Moreover, neither the atheists' decisions nor our decisions about those systems is insignificant in terms of the philosophies we adopt to guide our lives. We simply can't withhold judgment as to whether we should live like a believer or a nonbeliever just because we don't know everything we would if we were omniscient.

The upshot of this discussion is twofold. On the one hand, we must admit that we aren't omniscient. This should make us wary about thinking that either atheist or theist has proved a lot conclusively in this matter. Since the atheist has taken on the heavier burden of proof in trying to show theism improbable, his arguments are nowhere near as successful as he thinks. Inability to explain particular evils looks less significant in light of Hallett's points. As for theists, this point should show us it is wiser to speak in terms of defenses, not theodicies. Moreover, we must realize that since we aren't omniscient, our theological systems probably need at least some overhauling. I am also inclined to think Hallett's points suggest the bankruptcy of defenses which appeal to what we will know eventually (eschatologically). We cannot now know what we will know then or how we will assess the situation at that point. Hence, if we are to defend a particular theological system which is structured in terms of what we now know, it seems wisest to defend that system on the basis of what we do know, not on the basis of what we in our current ignorance think we may know someday.

On the other hand, Hallett's points don't mean atheistic evidential or logical arguments from evil are worth nothing. Atheists may be able to discredit some forms of theism via the evidential or logical problem, and if so, they will have shown why theists should abandon those positions. But in terms of a final defeat of all theistic positions, it is hard for atheists to be optimistic. Likewise, if theists can defend their systems against these attacks, they will show the reasonableness of their views and why atheists should consider those views seriously. They just need to exercise humility about how much they have conclusively demonstrated about their own brand of theism.[11]

There is yet another sense in which our limited knowledge makes it very hard to make a case against theism on the basis of evil. David O'Connor argues that there is no way to decide for or against theism empirically when arguing about the existence of natural evil. Since the evidential argument contains a factual premise that rests on empirical data, if O'Connor is correct, it is unlikely that the atheistic argument should be taken very seriously. O'Connor's point isn't that theist and atheist alike present empirical evidences which don't prove their case. Instead, his view is "that what is known in the philosophy of religion as the empirical debate over God and natural evil— when that debate is understood, as it commonly is, as an argument to a solution on the evidence of the natural world's condition—does not exist."[12]

This seems to be a rather radical view, but we must see how O'Connor argues his case. As to theism's attempts to make its case empirically, O'Connor says there are two typical methods theists use to defend theism against the atheistic attack based on evil. He argues that neither model for defending theism incorporates any empirical facts.

O'Connor calls the first model the compensation model. According to this model, the world is a proving ground for human beings. This means the world must contain difficulties to overcome even though there are no clear signs that the world has a divine origin. If there were signs that God exists, that would discourage people from doing evil, but it would also remove credit when they do good. In order for injustices of this life to be set straight, there must be a life after death, for there is far too much evidence that wrongs are not righted within this dimension of existence. This means there will be compensation for what we undergo in this life, but it won't happen in the actual world now or in any future state of the actual world. Now, it should be clear, argues O'Connor, that the only *empirical* evidence we have argues against the claims of life after death and compensation in another world for injustice here. Hence, this model appeals to no empirical evidence to prove its point.

Some may reply that there will be empirical evidence someday, but just not yet. O'Connor disagrees. His point is "that the promise of empirical evidence in a world beyond this world and in a time beyond any future time in this world is not a promise of empirical evidence in any sense in which the word 'empirical' is normally used, whether in science, philosophy, or common life."[13] Hence, for theists to say that the empirical evidence to prove their case will be available someday is to admit that it "is unavailable at all times and in all states of this, the only universe we know to exist and to which we have access." And, this means that "theism is effectively saying that it is not really participating in an empirical debate at all."[14] Thus, the compensation model is neither supported by empirical evidence nor is its story of why natural evil is justified an empirical story in any sense of what we mean when we use the word "empirical."[15]

O'Connor labels the second theistic model of explanation the suppression model. This is a possible worlds model which doesn't look to the future but to a past before this world. According to this model, there are many other possible worlds God could have created, but none where the balance of good over evil is as favorable as in the actual world. Moreover, our world and any other possible world are mutually exclusive, so God couldn't create this world and another or this and part of another. Hence, though our world contains evil, God actualized it in order to suppress all other possible worlds since all of them would have been worse worlds than ours. The problem with this explanation, according to O'Connor, is that no empirical evidence supports it. We have no access to those other possible worlds, so we can't compare them with ours. As with the compensation model, this doesn't mean there is no support for the suppression model. It only means the support isn't empirical, nor can it be. So, if theists adopt this strategy, they again don't defend theism empirically.[16]

It is clear that theists can't defend their position empirically, if they use either of these two models. Do atheists do any better empirically? Their empirical evidence is the large quantity, distribution, and variety of natural evil in the world. They say that if there were a God, this evil wouldn't exist. However, O'Connor argues that on either the compensation or suppression model, theists can show that the world is precisely as it would be if there were a God or if there were no God. Hence, for atheists to assume that natural evil proves their case is to beg the question against theism. But if that is so, then the evidence of evil really doesn't support their case, and if that is so, there appears to be no other empirical evidence available to support the atheistic argument *from evil*.[17]

O'Connor concludes that neither theism nor atheism can win the battle empirically. In fact, he goes so far as to say that theism isn't an empirical theory at all. None of this means there is no support for it or evidence against it, only that the support and objections are nonempirical.[18]

I find O'Connor's claims helpful in some respects and problematic in others. Where it is helpful, however, I think it shows again the difficulty for atheists to make a convincing evidential case against theism on the basis of evil. As to my concerns with O'Connor, I am not convinced that theists' explanations are quite so nonempirical as he claims. Consider the suppression model. It is true that many theistic defenses ultimately imply that God created our world so as to avoid other possible worlds. It is also true that those other worlds aren't empirically available to us. But this isn't the whole story. As I have argued all along, a Modified Rationalist doesn't need to show that our world is better than others or the best (i.e., he need not show what the suppression model purports to show). He merely explains that ours is one of those good possible worlds God could have created, and he does so by pointing to some feature about it (free will, human beings as created, etc.) which shows that this is true. But what is nonempirical about that? Theists and atheists may disagree about the value of that aspect of our world, and their evaluations aren't empirically observable, but they are debating about something in the empirical world. Hence, I disagree with O'Connor that there is no empirical point at all to which theists appeal when they defend their position against the atheistic argument from evil.

In addition, I certainly disagree with O'Connor's claim that theism isn't at all an empirical theory. If we move beyond the problem of evil to other evidences for and against theism, there are surely plenty of empirical evidences that are relevant to it. Think, for example, of the empirical data available to theists as they argue for the authenticity and reliability of Scripture. Think as well of empirical data relevant to the issue of Christ's resurrection.

Despite these problems, I am inclined to agree with O'Connor's assessment of atheism's case against theism on the basis of evil. O'Connor's point about the world seeming the same regardless of whether or not there is a God is similar to Wykstra's response to Rowe's atheistic argument. Since I agree with the basic points of Wykstra's argument, I can also agree with the basic point of O'Connor's claims. Hence, I agree that the atheist's use of evil as evidence does to a certain extent beg the question against theism. But then, what other empirical evidence does the atheist have when trying to make an evidential argument *from evil* against theism? There may be other empirical evidences relevant to an evidential argument from evil, but they are surely beyond our knowledge. Of course, there are probably other empirical evidences atheists can raise against theism, but they take us beyond an argument from evil.

In summing up my general comments on the inductive problem of evil, I must underscore what this doesn't mean as well as what it does mean. My comments about the nature of inductive and probability arguments and about the status of our knowledge don't mean that no inductive argument of any sort can hope to succeed. In fact, it doesn't even mean that inductive arguments that take the form of theory confirmation arguments can't succeed. What it does show is that it is generally harder to make a convincing inductive case than other kinds of cases. In particular, it shows that in view of all that is involved in the question of God and evil, it is very difficult to make a successful inductive argument from evil against theism. As long as theists stick to the basic defensive strategy of showing that atheists haven't made their case that theism is improbable because of evil, it is dubious that any atheistic argument from evil can succeed in convincing anyone but atheists. Problems stemming from the nature of inductive arguments, the nature of probability arguments, and/or the limitations of our knowledge will probably ruin the atheist's project.[19]

ON GRATUITOUS EVIL

In light of the preceding sections, one might think the chapter should end here. After all, if atheists can't even form a nonproblematic argument, why go any further? Though what I have already said would be enough to satisfy many theists and might even satisfy some atheists, none of it directly explains why there is apparently gratuitous evil in our world. I fear that unless theists offer some explanation for that evil, atheists will accuse us of escaping the force of their argument by hiding behind technicalities related to inductive arguments. Beyond that, there are things we can and should say in response to this sort of evil. Hence, in this section I plan to explain why I think gratuitous evil is only apparently so, and thereby rebut the atheist's objection that there is gratuitous evil which an omnipotent, all-loving God, if he exists, should have removed. I begin, however, by offering several objections to the argument from gratuitous evil as a whole.

Jane Trau has argued that the atheist's argument from apparently gratuitous evil is doomed to fail, because it contains several fallacies. In particular, she thinks it is guilty of three: question begging, the fallacy of ignorance, and the error of arguing from an inductive to a universal claim. As to question begging, both atheists and theists tend to do it. Claiming that there is genuinely gratuitous suffering means there is no purpose to it. To say there is no purpose is to reject one possible purpose, namely, God's. The problem with this, according to Trau, is that "both the atheist and the theist make assumptions on this issue: the former assuming that since there is no apparent purpose there is in fact no purpose; and the latter assuming that there is no apparent purpose yet there is some non-apparent purpose."[20]

Trau states the problem further for the atheist. Consider the following three propositions:

(1)   There appears to be no purpose to y (where y is any instance of apparently gratuitous suffering).
(2)   There is some non-apparent purpose to y.
(3)   There is in fact no purpose to y.[21]

Atheists argue that one should move from (1) to (3), but in so doing, they reject (2). The problem here, as Trau explains, is that this just begs the question, for in order to deny (2), one must make certain other assumptions.

Specifically, "one can never be certain that there are cases of gratuitous suffering unless one is certain that there is no God. And this would be to assume precisely what the argument is trying to prove, i.e., it begs the question."[22]

Though I think Trau's objection discredits many atheistic arguments from gratuitous suffering, I'm not sure it discredits all. An atheist might reply that (3) is too strong as stated. It would be better to say "It is highly improbable that there is in fact a purpose to *y*." In this case, the atheist might move from (1) to (3) not because she rejects belief in God, but because she simply can't find any evidence of a purpose for a given evil. Hence, for all she knows, there is none. But, to the extent that it is plausible to believe there is no purpose, it is also plausible to believe there is no God. This is especially so if one agrees that if there were a God, he would remove instances of gratuitous suffering. I don't see that the move from (1) to my revised (3) necessarily begs any questions. Of course, I think a theist can answer the atheist by explaining why this evil would likely occur, even if there were a God, but that surely won't show that the atheist begs the question in her initial argument. Hence, some atheistic arguments from gratuitous suffering are guilty of question begging as Trau suggests, but not all forms of that argument are.

Trau raises next the fallacy of ignorance. In the face of Trau's objection about question begging, the atheist might reply that he isn't constructing a deductive argument against God's existence, but only an inductive one. The inductive claim is that the most reasonable position in light of what we know is that God doesn't exist. Trau explains the atheistic argument and why she thinks it commits the fallacy of ignorance:

> it seems that unless it can be shown that all cases of apparently gratuitous suffering are in fact not purposeless, it is most reasonable to believe that they are as they appear to be; and since it cannot be shown that they are in fact not purposeless, it is reasonable to believe that they are as they appear to be; since there appear to be such cases it is more reasonable to believe that God does not exist. If this is his argument, the second premise commits the fallacy of ignorance. Thus we see that both the deductive and the inductive arguments from gratuitous suffering are fallacious.[23]

We saw this kind of objection before when discussing Reichenbach's objections to Rowe. At that point, we saw that Rowe, properly understood, doesn't commit this error. That is not to say, however, that no atheist in using the inductive argument ever commits this error. Hence, Trau has not shown that this problem afflicts all atheistic arguments from gratuitous evil, but those that do incorporate this fallacy should be rejected.

What about the third fallacy? Trau says the atheist might respond that (1) is just an inductive claim, and he has every right to make it, since the evidence justifies that there does appear to be no purpose to *y*. Trau answers that even if (1) is inductively valid, the atheist has no warrant to move from that existential claim to (3), which is a universal claim.[24]

Trau illustrates her point with a similar argument about the existence of elves. One proposition says "I have no reason to believe that there are elves," and the second is "There are no elves." The former is an inductive claim whereas the latter is a universal claim. The former is verifiable, whereas the latter is not, since it could be verified only by counting every case of non-elfdom, but this just means the second proposition can only be falsified. Hence, one really can't move from the former to the latter claim. The most one should say about the latter is that one is undecided about whether there are or aren't elves.

The same argument can be used about gratuitous suffering. The gratuitous suffering claims would be "I have no reason to believe there is a purpose to *y*" and "There is no purpose to *y*." Just as in the case of elves, the move here from the former to the latter is unjustified. The inductive claim is verifiable, but the universal is not, for it could be verified only by counting all cases of nonpurposiveness. And, obviously, that can't be done. Hence, it is most reasonable to hold that at present one cannot decide if there are cases of gratuitous suffering.[25]

I think this objection raises a significant problem with the atheistic argument from evil. However, I am not sure it amounts to much that is different from Wykstra's complaints about Rowe's move from appearance claims to claims about what is probably the case.

In turning from Trau to address gratuitous suffering directly, I believe, as I suggested when discussing Peterson, that we should begin with the definition of gratuitous evil. Depending on one's definition, one or another strategy presents itself. If we define gratuitous evil *narrowly* (as Peterson and many others do) to refer to evils which produce no subsequent good, then two strategies for defending theism are possible.

On the one hand, those fundamentally committed to a *nonconsequentialist* ethic shouldn't try to prove that there really is no gratuitous evil because the evil is tied to some subsequent good which *justifies* it. Instead, it is better to do what Peterson does, namely, grant that there is genuine gratuitous evil (and thereby reject [MP]), but then offer a defense of how that evil came to be, a defense which shows that God is justified in making a world containing that evil. An Arminian nonconsequentialist, for example, can simply appeal to the free will defense to handle moral evil, and probably something like Reichenbach's natural law defense for gratuitous natural evil. A Calvinist nonconsequentialist might use my defenses against moral and natural evil.

For a *consequentialist,* a different strategy is preferred. Consequentialist theists say that evil in our world is tied (logically and/or causally) to some subsequent good. Hence, the best strategy for a consequentialist is to accept (MP) and argue that there are no genuinely gratuitous evils in our world. All of them in fact contribute in some way to some subsequent good. If one takes this approach, then one will use some form of the greater good defense. In particular, Hick's soul-building theodicy in some form seems the most likely candidate for covering the largest amount of apparently gratuitous moral and natural evil.

What if one defines gratuitous evil narrowly as that evil which isn't the product or concomitant of some antecedent good? How should the theist then proceed? Nonconsequentialists should argue that there is no genuinely gratuitous moral evil, and offer a nonconsequentialist defense like the free will defense or my defense to show that this apparently gratuitous evil is tied to some actual or potential antecedent good which produced it or was its concomitant. Something like Reichenbach's natural law defense or my handling of natural evil could handle unattached gratuitous natural evil. Consequentialists can do either of two things. They can grant that there are genuinely gratuitous evils of this sort, but then argue that God is justified in allowing those evils, because he will use them to achieve some subsequent good like soul-building. Or, consequentialists may grant that these evils are tied to some antecedent value, but then say that the tie isn't what justifies God in allowing them. Instead, his use of those evils to accomplish some further goal is what justifies him in the face of such evils.

The first definition of "gratuitous evil" is quite commonly used in contemporary discussions. The second appears rather infrequently, if at all. However, as argued when discussing Peterson, I think the best way to define "gratuitous evil" is to combine the two notions. If one does, then the only evils that are genuinely gratuitous are those which are tied neither to an antecedent nor to a subsequent good. Those who take this route have no reason to reject (MP). They should instead maintain that apparently gratuitous evil is only apparently so, not genuinely so. To make this point, consequentialists can cover moral and natural apparently gratuitous evil by some variation of the greater good defense like the soul-building theodicy. Nonconsequentialists can make their case in regard to moral evil by appeal to the free will defense or my defense, and can cover unattached natural evil by something like Reichenbach's natural law defense or my defense.

My contention, then, is that this broader definition of "gratuitous evil" is the best way to define it, and that if one does so, there is no problem in resolving this problem evidentially or logically. But I also maintain that even if one defines "gratuitous evil" more narrowly, there are still ways to defend theism successfully against apparently gratuitous evil. Atheists like Rowe may complain that these defenses show theism to be compatible with gratuitous evil in general, but they don't explain the vast quantities of this evil. Though I think that claim is debatable, there is no need to debate it at this point. The reason is that even if it is correct, it shifts the discussion to the quantity of apparently gratuitous evil, and that is a different problem from this one. Because the defenses suggested don't necessarily handle all problems of apparently gratuitous evil, that doesn't mean they resolve none.

ON THE QUANTITY OF EVIL

Atheists frequently complain about the amount or quantity of evil in our world. As I have argued, this issue is invariably raised in the midst of discussing some other problem of evil. Confusing the issue of the amount of evil with some other problem of evil is illegitimate. However, the problem of the quantity of evil is itself a substantial problem for theism. Though I address it in the context of the evidential problem, much of what I plan to say also applies to the logical problem of the quantity of evil.

An initial point goes back to my discussion of Daniel Snyder and surplus evil. When Snyder's problem was mentioned, I suggested that it actually raises the question of the quantity of evil. I believe this is correct, and I think that in one sense the problem of the quantity of evil asserts that there is surplus evil. My point, however, is that there are different respects in which evil might be considered surplus. On the one hand, there is Snyder's serial killer. Snyder says that whatever the point for the killer's personal character development, that could have been made by the time he had killed his first five victims. The sixth and seventh murders were surplus or brought an excessive quantity of evil into the world. On the other hand, suppose those seven people were murdered by seven different people, not by a serial killer. Though we might think each killer needed that freedom to contribute to his own character development, we might still think those seven murders are too much. Whatever choices those people needed to control their own character development could have been provided, it seems, in some other way.

Just as different kinds of situations can qualify as surplus moral evil, so also critics believe the amount of unattached natural evil in our world is just too much. Whatever ends God envisions when allowing this much evil seem achievable with less evil. Even if we can't figure out how to accomplish those goals with less evil, an omniscient God should know. As all-powerful and all-loving, he can and should do so. Hence, there are different kinds of situations one can label too much evil.

In response, a theist might argue that there isn't too much evil on several different grounds, and each is a way of defending against this charge. An initial response appeals to a point I already made about specifying the God whose existence is under attack. The atheist says there is too much evil in our world for God to allow, if there is a God. I must ask which God the atheist has in mind. The theonomist's? If theonomists say their God has revealed that he is under no moral obligations whatsoever, or if they say their God has revealed that he is obligated to obey the rules he set forth for his creatures and he has, then no matter how much evil there is, there won't be too much evil to make belief in the theonomist's God improbable.

If the critic replies that God should at least remove some of this evil, theonomists need only answer that no one is obligated to do anything in a theonomous universe unless God commands it. Since God hasn't put himself under obligation to remove either moral or natural evil, God needn't remove any evil in order to prove anything about himself. The critic may reply that this is a strange and unacceptable notion of God and his moral obligations, but that amounts to little. At most, it suggests that there is something wrong with the theonomist's notion of God and/or ethics, but it doesn't prove them wrong, nor does it show that the amount of evil makes *the theonomist's* God improbable.

Is the amount of evil in our world too much for Leibniz's God to allow? Given Leibniz's claim that every instance of moral and natural good and moral and natural evil is logically necessary to produce the metaphysically richest world, how could God dare to actualize a world with less evil than we find in our world? Since Leibniz's God's moral obligation is to produce the best world, metaphysically speaking, for him to actualize a world with less evil would be to fail on his moral obligation. Given Leibniz's system, his God will be an evil God if he produces a world with less evil and/or good in it. The critic may again complain that this is a strange conception of ethics and of God, but that shows nothing other than that the critic holds different views on these issues. It doesn't show Leibnizian Rationalism logically inconsistent nor does it prove it improbable. The good and evil in our world (in whatever amounts they might occur) would only show Leibniz's God's existence to be improbable if someone could show that there is a better world, metaphysically speaking, which God didn't create but could have created. But it is hard to imagine how a critic would show that.

Perhaps the amount of moral and natural evil in our world is too much for the Modified Rationalist's God to allow. Here, I believe the atheist can make a stronger case, and the Modified Rationalist must do more explaining than the theonomist or Leibnizian Rationalist needs to do. Let me explain why. The Modified Rationalist says God needn't create any world whatsoever in order to be a good God. The critic may reply that since that is so, if God couldn't create a better world (i.e., one with much less evil than in ours), he should have created none. The Modified Rationalist also says our world is one of the good worlds God could have created, and then points to some valuable feature of the world that makes it a good world. Here the critic need not challenge the theist to prove that the good is really a great value that overbalances the evil. Instead, the critic will merely ask the theist to show why the *amount* of evil we have is necessary to have the value the theist sees in this world. Unless the theist can explain why that value (free will, humans as created, soul-building, etc.) necessitates the amount of evil in our world, the value to which the theist points won't apparently justify the quantity of evil we see. In that case, the critic will likely say that God should have created a world with less evil, since the quantity we have isn't necessary to have the value to which the theist points. And, if God didn't want to make that better world, he should have made no world at all.

In view of the preceding, it seems that both theonomy and Leibnizian Rationalism can easily handle the problem of the quantity of evil. No more is required than what I have already said. However, the very nature of a Modified Rationalist theology doesn't allow such a facile solution to this problem. Modified Rationalists may offer various reasons for thinking the amount of evil in our world isn't too much, or at least that we don't know it to be too much. I plan to raise those sorts of arguments in what follows. However, at some point it does seem that the Modified Rationalist must explain why there had to be as much moral and natural evil as there is for God to make this a world with the valuable item the Modified Rationalist points to that makes our world a good world. In what follows, I also plan to offer that sort of answer to this problem.

Before moving specifically to explanations of why the amount of evil in our world is necessary for the value(s) that make it a good world, let me raise several other items that challenge the claim that our world contains too much evil. An initial set of concerns centers around the question of how much evil we would expect to find if there is a God. Atheists are convinced there would be less than there is. In previous chapters I raised reasons for skepticism about that atheistic conclusion, and they bear brief mention here.

My initial fear is that many atheists think there is too much evil because they have concluded that, if they were God, they would create a world with less evil in it. If humans with limited goodness would make a better world, it is unthinkable that an all-good God would do less than we would. The fact that there seems to be more evil than is acceptable and expected is strong evidence against God's existence.

As I have argued previously, however, purporting to know what we would do and why if we were God really can't count for much. If we had God's perspective on things, we would understand far more than we now do, and it isn't at all clear that from that perspective we would deem it appropriate to create a different world than we have. From our dimension of knowledge, less evil may seem possible and preferable. But from the perspective of omniscience with a far clearer understanding of how evil fits into God's overall plans and purposes and of how it interconnects with goods and other evils, we can't be sure we would create any different world than the one we have. If I am right that many an atheist makes his case on the presumption of what he would do if he were omniscient, his complaint against God can't amount to much, since the atheist doesn't have the perspective of omniscience.

A second reason that it is so difficult to determine how much evil is too much was raised by Peterson. As Peterson argued, judgments about how much evil is too much for a good God to allow depend on personal value judgments. Those may stem, for example, from how comfortable we feel in the world with the evil that surrounds and befalls us at any given time. The problem, of course, as Peterson says, is that all of this is personal value judgment, not demonstrative proof. And if that is so, then we can see how such discussions will likely end. Those committed to atheism will already have concluded that there is too much evil in the world. Those committed to theism will already have decided that the amount of evil is acceptable and compatible with belief in God. Obviously, subjectivity controls these assessments, but then, it seems very hard for either side to make a convincing probability case about how much evil we should expect if there is a God.

A related reason that it is so hard to make a case against theism on the basis of the quantity of evil in our world is that we simply don't know why certain things are allowed to happen. Here I appeal to Hallett's point about our ignorance. From our perspective, there may appear to be no connection of certain evils to anything of value, but that doesn't necessarily prove there is none. Just as the child whose father won't let him stay up for the party doesn't have enough information to judge whether his father's refusal means his father doesn't love him, so we too are not in a position of knowing enough to make a judgment about whether there is just too much evil. If, then, judgments are made about too much evil in ignorance of why things are as they are, it is dubious that we can make a convincing case that there really is too much evil.

A final reason that it may be very difficult to determine that specific instances of evil are just too much also comes from Hallett. Often, we offer a general explanation for a series of similar evils, thinking the one explanation covers all those instances. Atheists may then reply that some instances really aren't covered by our explanation. Hence, there must be surplus evil. I take it that this is Snyder's point about the serial killer. But the assumption that God might have the same purpose for the sixth and seventh murders as for the first five is just that, an assumption. God may allow the last two for some reason other than his reason for the first five. In the case of the child who wants to stay up for parties, we can't assume that every time his father refuses, he does so for the same reason. One time he may refuse because the child has a cold, another time some guest may not want the child there, and another time he may refuse because the next morning the family must go somewhere early and he wants his son to have a good night's sleep.[26] Similarly, Hallett argues, we shouldn't assume for two similar evils that God's purpose in allowing them is identical. They may serve different purposes. Hallett explains:

> It is theodicists or their critics who are naive if they suppose that the workings of Providence must be sufficiently simple and uniform for humans to be able to formulate them abstractly and once for all, without regard for the many mysteries of physics, biology, cosmology, psychology, economics, philosophy, and theology, or for varied circumstances. Such simplicity and uniformity are not excluded a priori. Yet surely they cannot be assumed. 'There seems to be no reason in principle', as M.B. Ahern remarks, 'why instances of evil of the same kind should not be justified in wholly different or partly different ways. Nor does there seem to be any reason, in principle, why two instances of the same kind and degree should not be justified in ways that differ wholly or in part'.[27]

This is a very important point. The consequence of it is that evils we think are surplus or too much may not at all be, because they may have a different purpose and explanation than we think. We think the sixth and seventh murders by a serial killer are too much, because we can't see that they serve any purpose beyond that of the first five. But as Hallett and Ahern argue, that doesn't mean there is no alternate justification. Hence, before we know that certain evils are too much, we must be sure they serve no purpose in anyone's life beyond similar evils that already have been endured. Until we know that (and apart from omniscience, we aren't in a position to know that), we can't be sure they are really surplus.

What I have been saying suggests that it will be very hard for an atheist to make a convincing case against even a Modified Rationalist theology on the basis of the quantity of evil. Though I am inclined to think these comments rebut the atheistic challenge, I am willing to go one step further. As I noted above, Modified Rationalists say that the amount of evil in our world fits with or even is necessary to accomplish the valuable thing(s) God is doing with this world. Can Modified Rationalists show that this is so? I believe so, and this is where specific defenses come in.

Let me begin with my own Calvinistic system and handle moral evil and natural evil that results from moral evil. Here it is enough to appeal to my defense as offered in chapter 6. As argued, God intended to create human beings, not subhumans or superhumans, and put them in a world where they could function. Creating a world with humans definitely creates a good world, because human beings with their capacities are a value of the first order.

Now, the question is whether there must be as much evil as there is for God to have a world with human beings in it. Whoever answers negatively must then explain how God could get rid of that allegedly excess evil. My contention is that God could only get rid of that excess evil (or any moral evil at all) in one of the ways I outlined in chapter 6. But I have already shown the problems if God does any of those things. Thus, it seems clear that my defense handles not only the problem of moral evil in general but also the problem of the quantity of moral evil. If there are to be humans in this world, God cannot remove their moral evil without disrupting things in the ways I have mentioned. Moreover, the more human beings there are, the more moral evil there will be. Likewise, in cases like the serial killer where one person does multiple evil, God could stop the sixth and seventh murder but only in one of the ways I mention in chapter 6. If he allows the first five but then stops the next two in one of those ways, the negative results I have mentioned can still eventuate.

On my theological position with my defense, it seems that the only way to have less evil without getting rid of it in one of those problematic ways is to have fewer human beings. But I don't see that God should either stop people from having children (presumably, he would have to do it in one of the ways I mentioned), kill off many people now living, or reprogram us biologically so that we could reproduce only enough people to take our place when we die (this would require making us different beings than we are—I assume God could do that, but it would contradict his intention to make human beings as we know them). Moreover, even if God did reduce the number of people in some morally acceptable way, I am not convinced this would satisfy the atheist. There would still be a lot of evil in our world, and many atheists think any evil is too much.

In light of this defense, my theology has an answer to both the logical and evidential problems of the quantity of moral evil. God's existence can fit without contradiction the amount of moral evil in our world. Moreover, given the explanation of why we have the quantity of evil there is, the atheist will find it hard to convince anyone other than atheists that the amount of moral evil in our world makes this God's existence improbable.

What about unattached natural evil? Here I appeal to my handling of natural evil in chapter 7. As I argued, these evils occur because we live in a fallen world. Who can say that the amount of these evils that befall us is unjust recompense? As I argued in chapter 7, given our fallen world, it is only a matter of God's grace that more of these evils don't befall us and that they don't occur sooner than they do.

In addition, I also argued that God not only intended to create a certain sort of creature when he created humans. He also intended to put them in a world where they could function, survive, and use the capacities God gave them. It isn't at all clear that God could get rid of natural evil without changing the natural order. But, in that case, can we be sure that a new natural order where evil is avoided will be one where humans as we know them will be able to function and use their capacities as we know them? I doubt it.

Some may think these aren't good defenses since someday God will create a new heaven and new earth (according to traditional theism) where nothing ever goes wrong. Why not do that now, rather than later? My response is the same as it was when this objection was raised earlier. People who live in the new heaven and new earth will be in glorified bodies, not natural bodies. Those bodies will be attuned to that sort of world. God could have created glorified humans, but that would contradict his intention to create non-glorified human beings. Moreover, though the eternal state will be a better world, morally speaking, than ours, all a Modified Rationalist must show is that our world is a good world. He needn't show ours is the best world or even better than other good possible worlds. The presence of non-glorified humans in a world with a natural order that lets them function as they do is, I contend, a value of the first order that shows that this world, even with the quantity of moral and natural evil in it, is one of those good worlds God could have created. One may disagree, but that doesn't show any logical inconsistency in my views, nor does it show that God as I conceive him is improbable. It only shows that one chooses a different theological system or no theology at all. But none of that shows a failure to solve the logical or evidential problems of the quantity of natural and moral evil.

Some may respond that none of this explains every specific instance of evil that seems excessive. I reply that it wasn't meant to do so, since the problem of the quantity of evil in general isn't about making sure that every specific evil is explained. If pressed further on specific instances, I am inclined to respond in two ways. One is to appeal to Hallett's point that we don't have a right to claim that similar instances of evil must have the same explanation, so several instances are unnecessary. Those instances which appear extra from our perspective may have a different explanation than we imagine. Beyond that, once we begin looking at specific instances to ask if they are too much, I believe the problem in many respects has shifted to the religious problem about why specific evils happen to particular people. In other words, this objection raises other problems of evil; it doesn't refute answers to the more general question about the quantity of evil.

From the preceding, I conclude that the problem of the quantity of evil can be resolved for a Modified Rationalist theology like mine. Beyond that, I maintain that other Modified Rationalist theologies can solve this problem. For example, an Arminian should appeal to free will as to why there is the quantity of evil in our world. To get rid of much or all of that moral evil, God would have to either remove free will or remove many human beings. But this would surely contradict what the free will defender claims God is doing with this world. As to natural evil, I suspect the free will defender could respond along the lines of Reichenbach's natural law theodicy.

As to a consequentialist position like Hick's, I think it also can solve this problem. Both moral and natural evil are useful in making ours an environment in which to build souls. In response to those who believe this could be an acceptable environment for soul-building with much less evil, one might simply reply that this presumes that fewer evils would still give the same number of people the opportunity for their soul to be built, and we simply don't know that. We don't know it because we can't predict how many people any given instance of evil will touch, and we don't know it, because we can't predict how much evil must befall a given individual before she begins to take seriously this matter of growth to spiritual maturity. Sometimes people ignore what God is trying to say to them until a certain number of evils experienced finally gets their attention. Hence, the consequentialist, like myself and the free will defender, can legitimately say that the quantity of evil in our world isn't evidence which makes a convincing case that there is no God. If the amount of evil in our world is present for any of the reasons we suggest, then the amount is justified.

In summing up the discussion in this chapter, I have argued that the best way to respond to the evidential problem of evil in its various forms is to adopt a defensive strategy, not an offensive one. Then, I have used the two basic defensive strategies available. In the early part of the chapter, I offered a series of reasons to be skeptical about whether atheists can even launch a significant evidential attack against theism on the basis of evil, let alone hope to succeed in it. I believe those considerations suggest that atheists are doomed to fail if they hope to convince the theist. In the latter portion of the chapter, I directly addressed gratuitous evil and the quantity of evil, and I used the second defensive strategy against them. That is, I offered explanations of why apparently gratuitous evil isn't necessarily genuinely so and explanations of why there isn't too much evil in our world. I maintain that many traditional theistic positions can solve these problems by adopting one or both of these defensive strategies.

I believe, then, that the evidential problem, no less than the logical problem of evil, is resolvable. Those who are still uneasy about all of this probably feel that way in large part because they don't find these answers particularly comforting in the midst of some affliction they are experiencing, nor do they think others would be comforted. The problem with such complaints, however, is that they change the discussion to the religious problem of evil. Nothing said so far necessarily addresses, let alone resolves, that problem. This is undoubtedly the most painful of all problems of evil. Until one comes to grips with one's own experience of evil and suffering, all the rest is an interesting intellectual discussion, but it doesn't directly touch people where they hurt and question the most. As a result, my final chapters address that problem. Before turning to the religious problem, we should address another problem which has increasingly become the focus of attention in contemporary discussion, the problem of hell.

Section III
The Problem of Hell

13

HELL AND THE PROBLEM
OF EVIL

Previous chapters have addressed the various problems of evil. Some are more challenging for traditional theism than others. Arguably, none is more difficult than the problem before us in this chapter. The difficulty isn't just that neither theists nor their critics like the idea of retributive justice, especially when it applies to them or their friends and family. The hardest things to swallow about hell, as traditionally understood, are that it is a punishment (often even conceived of as torture) that is visited upon the majority of the human race, and it never ends!

Prior to the twentieth century, humans had seen various forms of inhumanity perpetrated against other persons. Perhaps many thought they had seen the worst that human nature could do. But then came the absolute brutality of World War I, and if that wasn't enough, World War II was even more horrible. And, it was accompanied by the Holocaust. Many have asked how there could possibly be an all-loving and omnipotent God who would allow such evils. For many, the horrors of the Holocaust were the final nails in the coffin of anything like traditional theism.

Despite the enormity of such evil, for many the existence of hell is an even worse blow to the credibility of theism. For traditional theists must be prepared not merely to explain how God could allow more than six million people to be slaughtered in the Holocaust; they must now explain how there can be a God who would torture the vast majority of mankind—*forever!* If you think it is hard to justify a holocaust in this life, just try to justify a never ending holocaust in the next life!

In *The Brothers Karamazov* Ivan decries the idea that God would allow even one small innocent child to undergo torture by others just to uphold the free will of those who do such evil. He complains that freedom isn't worth it even if only one innocent child suffers as a result.[1] If Ivan and his kin have trouble with the torture of one small child, how much more would they be repulsed by the use of free will to bring about the Holocaust! But, even worse, an eternity of hell visited upon the majority of mankind because they have used their free will to reject God would surely, in Ivan's terms, not be worth it! Any theistic position committed to the existence of hell seems out of touch with the times and seems bankrupt religiously, morally, and theologically. In the judgment of many, the traditional doctrine of hell is an embarrassment to those who hold it.

Such attitudes aren't merely confined to skeptics and critics in our day. Even within otherwise theologically conservative Christian circles, some are questioning this doctrine. In evangelical churches, one rarely hears a sermon on hell; even passing references to hell are few and far between. In a postmodern era when we need to be tolerant and accepting of others with different belief systems than ours, it seems that holding the doctrine of hell is the epitome of intolerance. As Clark Pinnock ponders this doctrine, he admits that he considers

> the concept of hell as endless torment in body and mind an outrageous doctrine, a theological and moral enormity, a bad doctrine of the tradition which needs to be changed. How can Christians possibly project a deity of such cruelty and vindictiveness whose ways include inflicting everlasting torture upon his creatures, however sinful they may have been?[2]

Pinnock's remarks are most instructive for understanding the exact nature of this evil. It isn't merely some physical affliction that befalls people. Scripture suggests that it involves that, but it also includes estrangement from God, the creator and judge of all there is. So, the types of suffering endured are substantial. And if that isn't enough, this evil endures *forever*. No matter how much the experience of hell might change a person's reaction and response to God, there is still no release from it—ever. And, Pinnock notes that this is the divine punishment for sin, regardless of how great a sinner or how virtuous one was in life. For many, it seems that this punishment for even the worst of sinners far exceeds "the crime." How can it be just to hold people accountable and to punish them *forever* for sins that are temporary and finite in nature?

The indictment of traditional theism reaches its climax with one further complaint. Not only are those who have heard of Christ but rejected him condemned to this eternal torment. Those who never heard of him are in like manner condemned. This even happens to those whom Christians would call "noble pagans." Some theologians try to soften the blow of this doctrine by arguing that while all who reject Christ go to hell, there will be different degrees of misery meted out on the basis of things like the kind of life lived, the amount of revelation of the gospel one had, and so forth. But try as one might to mollify the horror of hell, even those inhabitants of hell who were most virtuous in life will still experience unending physical and spiritual torment to some degree or other. While Scripture doesn't explicitly say that those who never heard the gospel and so never responded to Christ are clearly headed to hell, it doesn't explicitly deny it either. Moreover, passages like Acts 4:12 say of Jesus that "there is none other name under heaven given among men, whereby we must be saved"(KJV).[3] If we take this comment in a straightforward manner (as many conservative Christians do), the implications for the greater mass of humanity are staggering! How can anything like the traditional doctrine of hell be consistent with an all-powerful and all-loving God? How could there be a doctrine more repugnant than this one? And how can Christianity hope to maintain any credibility and viability as religiously adequate without a satisfactory answer to this problem?

Is there an adequate answer to this problem? How should we go about searching for it? Here I begin by underscoring some of the most central themes of this book. First, this problem is a distinct one, just as are the problems of moral evil, natural evil, apparently gratuitous evil, etc. As a distinct problem, it requires its own answer, and one's ability or inability to solve other problems of evil doesn't predetermine whether or not this problem is solvable. But theists must provide an answer that truly is relevant to this problem. It is hard to imagine that answers to the problem of unattached natural evil, for example, would offer anything of value for addressing this problem, for that natural evil doesn't arise from the actions of God's moral creatures, but stems instead from some malfunctioning of natural processes.

So, theists must offer an answer that really addresses this problem. But there is a caveat for critics as well. Since the problem of hell is a distinct problem, it is logically illegitimate for critics of theism to claim that theists haven't even touched, let alone solved, this problem, because they haven't accounted for all forms and amounts of evil. Just because a resolution to a given problem doesn't solve every problem of evil, that doesn't mean it solves none!

A second "ground rule" for handling this problem invokes another recurrent theme of this book. In addressing the problem of hell, one must first specify the particular version of theism under consideration. As we have seen in earlier chapters, there are different varieties of theism. Moreover, even when dealing with the broad variety of theism I have labeled Modified Rationalism, there isn't just one theology that aptly bears that label. Various theologies fall under that rubric, and the problem of hell must be asked and answered in relation to each one. Hence, when critics complain that the doctrine of hell generates a devastating problem for theism, we must ask which version of theism is in view.

A final guide as we delve into the problem of hell is a reminder that this question can be posed in either a logical or an evidential form. According to the former, the traditional doctrine of hell logically contradicts other beliefs the theist holds about God, evil, and human nature. According to the latter, the mere fact of hell, should it exist and have the qualities traditional theists claim it has, makes it improbable that there is an all-loving, omnipotent God. The answer to the logical problem of hell isn't necessarily the same as the answer to the evidential problem. Each must be addressed individually, and success or failure in solving the problem in one form doesn't predetermine the outcome when searching for a resolution to the other.

How should we then address these problems? Before we go much further, we must articulate the concept of hell under consideration. Some versions of hell may not raise the problems we have envisioned so far. Moreover, one way to solve the problem of hell in either its logical or probabilistic form is to so modify the concept of hell that it no longer repulses our moral sensibilities nor raises intellectual doubts. Such a maneuver (toning down the horror of hell, or so conceiving it that few if any ever wind up going there, e.g.) will definitely remove the problem, but such resolutions don't uphold the doctrine of hell as it has most frequently been held within the Christian tradition. Moreover, the most stimulating problem intellectually is the problem which conceives of hell in the traditional robust sense and then asks us to explain how *that* notion squares with the idea of an all-loving and all-powerful God.

After presenting the concept of hell under consideration along with the supports usually offered for it, we must articulate and assess the various ways this problem can be addressed. In contemporary discussions, the most frequent approach is to modify the traditional concept of hell in one way or another, and thereby remove the apparent contradiction and/or the apparent implausibility of this doctrine. But those who retain the traditional notion cannot adopt such answers. Rather, they must explain how the traditional concept of hell is logically consistent and/or plausible when wedded to a traditional understanding of God, evil, and human nature.

THE TRADITIONAL DOCTRINE OF HELL

The doctrine of hell has a long history within Christian thinking, and Christian beliefs about hell incorporate elements of Jewish thinking about the afterlife.[4] Though there have been some variations in the traditional doctrine throughout the history of Christianity, the basic perception of hell has remained stable. The traditional doctrine centers around five main points.

First, *hell is a specific place*. It isn't merely a symbol for punishment; it is an actual place of judgment. Exactly where it is located isn't entirely clear, but there is a real place of torment. Part of the uncertainty about hell's location stems from biblical language about it. In the OT, the key term is *Sheol*, but this term is used in several senses. It is used frequently to refer to the grave or physical death to which all go (e.g., 1 Sam. 2:6; Job 14:13, 14; 17:13, 14; Ps. 6:5; 89:48; 141:7). In some of the cited passages *Sheol* seems to refer to the realm of the dead. There are even believers in the OT who express their hope that their lot will be blessed when they go to the realm of the dead (this is suggested at least in part from the expressions of glad expectation or joy in the face of death. See Num. 23:10; Gen. 5:24; 49:18 [a dying Jacob says, "I have waited for thy salvation" (KJV)]; Ps. 16:9-11 ["my flesh also shall rest in hope" (KJV)]; Ps. 17:15; 49:15; 73:24-26; Isa. 25:8). However, there are also OT passages where it seems to be more than the place of the dead; it appears to be a place of punishment for the wicked who have rejected God and his ways (Job 21:13; Ps. 9:17; Prov. 5:4-5; 9:17-18; Deut. 32:22). These passages at least suggest that those involved in sin will find their ultimate abode in Sheol, and the implication seems to be that such an occurrence would be a stroke of judgment against them.

In the NT things become somewhat clearer, but not entirely. The term *Hades* is the most frequent term, and it seems to be the most typical Greek way to render the Hebrew *Sheol*. In the NT, however, it becomes very clear that this is a place of punishment for the wicked. Consider, for example, the story of the rich man and Lazarus (Luke 16:19-31). The rich man after death winds up in *Hades* (v. 23), but this can't refer merely to the place of all the dead, for Lazarus, who has also died, is taken to Abraham's bosom, a place of great joy and blessing. Moreover, the text says that there is a great gulf between Hades and Abraham's bosom, a gulf that the inhabitants of both cannot span (v. 26). The rich man in Hades experiences pain and torment (vv. 23-24). Though it isn't clear whether this is a parable or an account of two non-fictional characters, in either case we must ask what Jesus intended to teach by recounting it. At least part of his purpose seems to be to make a point about the nature of the afterlife and the relation of one's life on earth to that future place of either pain and judgment or joy and blessing.

So, the NT in various passages seems to treat Hades as a distinct place of suffering for the wicked, but that isn't the whole NT story, for the NT also speaks of Gehenna and the lake of fire. What is of most import for our purposes is Revelation 20, especially verses 11-15. This passage takes us beyond the thousand-year reign of Christ, the destruction of Satan who is cast into the lake of fire after leading one last rebellion, and the apparent destruction of the current heavens and earth (v. 11; cf. 2 Pet. 3:10-13, where we read of the destruction of the current heaven and earth and creation of a new heaven and earth). After all of these events, there will be a resurrection of the dead from all places and periods of history (Rev. 20:12-13) to stand in judgment before God at the Great White Throne Judgment. We are told that Death and Hades are cast into the lake of fire, along with any whose name is not written in the book of life (vv. 14-15). They will remain there forever along with Satan and his cohorts (v. 10).

The NT also sheds light on the ultimate destiny of the blessed. Repeatedly, we learn that those who trust Christ won't perish, but will have everlasting life (e.g., John 3:16). In addition, Paul, speaking about the physical death of believers, says that though they are absent from the body, they are present with Christ (2 Cor. 5:8). But *what* is absent from the body? Certainly nothing physical; and we know where the body goes at physical death! So this must refer to the immaterial part of human beings, and Paul is saying that in the case of believers, upon physical death their immaterial part is in the presence of the Lord. When we put these points of biblical teaching together with what we saw in the story of the rich man and Lazarus, it becomes clear that the NT teaches that after physical death, there is a place of blessing in the Lord's presence where the immaterial part of believers goes. The most logical conclusion from this is that believers go to heaven upon physical death. But that isn't the whole story about the future for believers. The NT also predicts that they, like Christ, will be resurrected from the dead (1 Cor. 15:51ff.; 1 Thess. 4:13-18; Rev. 20:4), though the passages cited suggest a resurrection prior to the kingdom age, not at its end as in the case of the Great White Throne Judgment.[5] And, once this resurrection occurs for believers in the church age, Paul says of them and himself "so shall we ever be with the Lord" (1 Thess. 4:17, KJV).

We can now summarize the NT teaching. At physical death, there is a separation of the immaterial from the material part of human nature. The material body of all people goes into the grave and decomposes. The immaterial part of believers goes immediately into the presence of God. This seems to mean that they are in heaven. The immaterial part of nonbelievers goes into punishment; it seems best to identify this with hell or Hades. Someday, however, Jesus will return for his people, and they will be bodily resurrected from the dead, their immaterial and material parts again conjoined, and their physical body will be transformed into a glorified body (1 Cor. 15:51-54). In addition, there will be a separate day on which the ungodly dead will be resurrected to stand at the Great White Throne Judgment. That resurrection will involve the reuniting of their immaterial and material parts. Scripture speaks of the resurrection of the wicked, but it never speaks of them as receiving a glorified body. In addition, Revelation 20:15 tells us that those whose name is not written in the book of life will be cast into the lake of fire, where they will remain forever.

A second element of the doctrine of hell is that it involves *both physical and spiritual death* and is a *place of torment*. This needs some clarification. In the Garden of Eden, Adam and Eve were warned that if they ate of the forbidden fruit, they would surely die (Gen. 2:17). Still, they fell to Satan's temptation and ate the fruit. Much of Genesis 3 records God's punishments for their disobedience. Genesis 3:19 states that because of disobedience, Adam and Eve would die physically ("return to the dust"). Lest we think this judgment fell only on these two, the NT teaches otherwise. In Romans 5:12, Paul affirms that through the sin of Adam, all humans became sinners. Moreover, the punishment for sin, death, passed to the whole human race. Hence, death isn't what God intended when he created us; it falls upon us because of sin.

In addition to physical death, there is also spiritual death. This, of course, doesn't mean that our immaterial part somehow ceases to exist, for immaterial substances can't die physically, and though some in our day argue that they can be ontologically annihilated, as I shall argue, that is dubious, and in any case Scripture nowhere offers that meaning of spiritual death. Instead, spiritual death refers to our alienation from God and from one another as a result of sin. We see this clearly in Genesis 3 after Adam and Eve disobey God. They first try to hide from God, and then they cover themselves with fig leaves in order to "hide their nakedness" from each other. Throughout the rest of Scripture, those who don't rely upon God for salvation from sin are alienated from him even during their earthly life. The final or ultimate result of rejecting God is that they are confined to hell and ultimately the lake of fire. In both of these places they have no relationship with God at all. Though he must be ontologically present since he is omnipresent, he isn't spiritually present to them in any way.[6] Moreover, once they die and are confronted with the consequences of rejecting God, the traditional view of hell claims that there is no second chance to repent and establish a relationship with God. Rather, in being consigned to hell and ultimately to the lake of fire, they are permanently alienated from God.

But there is more to their lost condition than this. Simply being left alone for all eternity with no fellowship with God would be horrible enough. However, the traditional understanding of hell teaches that hell is a place of torment. Scripture portrays this punishment in various ways. Often it refers to the fires of hell which never cease (Mark 9:43-48—these verses repeatedly speak of a fire that never ceases). Though hell's inhabitants experience agony from the flames, their bodies never burn up so as to stop the pain. In other portions of the NT, the judgment of hell is referred to as being cast into outer darkness where there is wailing and gnashing of teeth (e.g., Matt. 8:12; 13:42, 50). This again speaks of physical and mental pain, but some wonder how it can be so if there is also fire in hell. For, if there are flames wouldn't they emit light, light which would dispel the darkness? From our perspective of life on earth, the supposition seems very logical. What it does suggest is that we should be careful not to be "overly literal" about the exact nature of torment inhabitants of hell experience. It is enough to say that these various depictions make it very clear that hell will be a place of torment, and it will in no way be pleasant. In other passages, the torment is referred to as the worm and moth eating away at the person but without ever completely consuming him. Hence, this experience of decay and destruction continues indefinitely. Here again the major point we should take from this description is that hell isn't and won't be a pleasant place. All of this happens as a result of divine judgment upon the wicked.[7]

Some have thought that if heaven involves constantly praising God, sitting around and playing harps, etc., this will be rather boring. On the other hand, hell is seen as a place where people can do whatever they want, no matter how evil, since they can't be punished any more than they are already experiencing. Hence, at times the impression is given that there will be great fellowship in hell of like-minded people, and this will make it much more interesting than life in heaven. However, the traditional view of hell built on Scripture has nothing to do with such views. Hell isn't portrayed as pleasant or pleasurable in any sense. Moreover, nowhere in Scripture do we read that those in hell "fellowship" with one another. Rather, the full measure of their judgment for rejecting God is that they will have no relation with God or with anyone else. Regardless of what you think about life in heaven, hell isn't depicted as pleasant at all.

The third point in the traditional doctrine of hell explains *who goes there*. Roman Catholics have traditionally believed that only the exceptionally wicked wind up there. Others may require some time in purgatory before admission to heaven, but at least they won't go to hell. Hence, on such views, most people down through the centuries will wind up in heaven, and relatively few will populate hell. Universalists, of course, believe that no one ultimately winds up in hell. In one way or another, these views and others like annihilationism attempt to avoid the apparent embarrassment for Christianity if people who have sinned only a finite amount are punished infinitely. The way to avoid such a position is to claim that very few, if any, finally are consigned to hell.

But the traditional view of hell says otherwise. Throughout human history, humans have sinned and have needed a savior. At all times God has provided a means of atonement, and all that is required of sinners is to turn from their sin and accept God's provision of salvation. Throughout history, God has also revealed himself and what must be done to receive his salvation. Throughout biblical history God elaborates what he wants us to know about himself and his method of salvation, but no era has been without any revelation of God. Those people who during life on earth reject God and his salvation and never turn to him before they die go to hell after they die. In contrast, those who turn to God receive his salvation, go to heaven upon death, and will experience eternal blessedness in God's presence. No one who places his or her faith and trust in God for salvation will end up in hell.[8] Only those who reject him (and all who reject him) will inhabit hell. This is true, according to the traditional view of hell, regardless of how much or how little revelation people at any given time and place in history have had. Everyone has always had enough revelation to know at least that there is a God with certain characteristics (Rom. 1:19-20), and the impression given is that those who seek God will be given further revelation and will find him. The apostle Paul's point in Romans 1–3 is that no one, in and of their own initiative, seeks God or even lives in accord with the revelation they possess. Hence, all are guilty before God. The only way of escape is to respond to divine grace, repent of sin, and trust God for salvation. Those who refuse in this life to do so will be consigned to hell once they die physically.

Fourth, the traditional doctrine of hell is very explicit about how long this punishment lasts; hell is a *never ending punishment.* Even Roman Catholics who believe that those consigned to purgatory can eventually gain admission to heaven agree that the truly evil who do wind up in hell will be there forever. Some have tried to soften the blow of this punishment by speculating that there won't be equal degrees of torment in hell. Those who have known clearly God's law and have repeatedly and egregiously defied it will receive much more torment than, for example, noble pagans who never heard of Christ but lived good, moral lives in accord with their own religion's beliefs. Proponents of such views claim that this must be the point of opening the books at the Great White Throne Judgment and judging each person according to what is contained in the books (Rev. 20:12-13). Since those whose names are not written in the book of life are cast into the lake of fire, what would be the point of opening the books and judging them out of those books according to their deeds in life? Defenders of this view claim that the books are consulted to determine the degree of punishment each person will experience who goes to hell and the lake of fire.[9]

Regardless of whether inhabitants of hell suffer in varying degrees, one thing is still certain. Without trusting God and accepting his means of salvation, one cannot escape hell altogether. Regardless of how moderate or severe the punishment, none of it will be pleasant, none will escape it, and it will never end.

Finally, the traditional view of hell holds that being cast into hell is *an act of God's retributive justice*. It stems from God's holiness and justice.[10] The experience of hell is certainly never portrayed in the traditional conception as something that is either rehabilitative of the sinner or allows the sinner to make restitution for evil he or she has done. While the fact of hell and the preaching of it may deter some sinners from their current way of life and turn them to God, deterrence isn't the point or purpose of hell either. God has established a system of moral governance for the universe. It involves a set of rules his human creatures are to obey. Those who disobey will be punished; those who obey will be blessed. The final punishment of the disobedient is hell; that is the just retribution for those who refuse to turn to God. It is at this point, however, that many reject the traditional view of hell, for, they claim, if retributive justice is the point of hell, then God is unjust because this is a punishment that far exceeds the "crime." Proponents of the traditional view reply that whether or not we can understand whether this punishment is just, we know that God is just, so any punishment he would give must be just.

In summing up the main tenets of the traditional view, we note with Jonathan Kvanvig that it involves fundamentally four separate ideas. The first is the Anti-Universalism Thesis, according to which at least some people go to hell. Second, the Existence Thesis states that hell is a place where people assigned to that fate continue to exist. Annihilation is not an option. Third, there is the No Escape Thesis. According to this thesis, once one is sent to hell, there is no way and no time that anyone sent there can escape. There are no deeds one can do, even including "changing one's mind about God and turning to him in repentance," which will win release from hell. Finally, the Retribution Thesis claims that the justification for hell is that it is a just punishment for those whose life on earth warrants it, and in light of the previous theses, it is clear that there are those who deserve this punishment.[11]

THE LOGICAL PROBLEM OF HELL

In response, we turn first to the problem of hell in its logical form. This form of the various problems of evil accuses theism of holding accounts of God and evil that contradict one another. The critic claims that if God is both omnipotent and omnibenevolent, hell wouldn't exist.

Of course, the critic must demonstrate that the form of theism in question actually subscribes to the views that supposedly generate a self-contradictory theology. Since there are many varieties of theism, including varieties of conservative Christian theism, both theist and atheist must clarify which theology the theist holds, and then ask whether *that specific theology* contradicts itself. Moreover, since the accusation of self-contradiction means that there is *no possible way* that everything the theology claims could be true, the theist needs only to offer a possible explanation of how and why all three items (God's omnipotence, his omnibenevolence, and hell's existence) are true all at once. The critic may not find the explanation very plausible, but that is beside the point, for the logical problem isn't about plausibility; it's about the logical consistency of the theologian's views. Of course, it might be possible to make a theology internally consistent by offering an explanation which, though ridiculous, would remove the apparent contradiction if adopted by the theist. Hopefully, theists will offer explanations that are plausible, but the requirement to solve the logical problem of hell is an answer that could be true and would render the theist's system internally consistent.[12]

Basic Options for the Theist

How, then, might theists respond to the problem of hell? Several options are open to them. An initial way to address this problem is to modify one's view of God. For example, one might hold that God has the power and authority to create hell and to send people to it, and he also has so little concern for his creatures that it doesn't bother him to torment them for eternity. Such a conception of God portrays him as an evil fiend, more like the devil than the God of conservative Christianity. Or, one could claim that God isn't actually omnipotent, and that's why he doesn't remove hell. Of course, if this God is too impotent, it is dubious that he will have enough power and authority to create hell in the first place and decide that anyone should go there. But, assuming that he can set in place a system of moral governance for the universe and create hell as the final end of the wicked, the God who does this may still be conceived of as not having the power to get rid of hell once he creates it and sends the wicked there.

Modifying one's views about God can remove any hint of self-contradiction from the theist's system, but this resolution is bought with a price. The price is that one is implicitly admitting that the three key items (omnipotence, omnibenevolence, and hell) aren't mutually consistent, for if they were, there would be no reason to jettison any of them to answer the problem of hell. Various theologies do solve this problem by rejecting one or more of the traditional divine attributes. Process theology is one that does, but not the only one.

A second way to handle the logical problem of hell takes a route much less traveled. This strategy changes the system's conception of ethics so that the torment of hell is no longer deemed evil but good and even desirable. Few have taken this approach, but it isn't hard to imagine how this strategy might be used. For example, on a Leibnizian conception of ethics, it could be argued that a world with both hell and heaven is *ontologically* superior to a world with only heaven. Moreover, God knows the exact amount of torture in hell that is compossible with the various pleasurable things that can go into a world. He knows which possible world includes the greatest amount and variety of existing things, and since it is his ethical duty to create the metaphysically best of all possible worlds, he must create a world which includes hell. Hence, the existence of hell is logically consistent with an omnipotent, omnibenevolent God.

Another attempt at solving this problem by modifying one's notion of good and evil might stem from a theonomous worldview and a divine command ethic that allows God to will whatever he wants as good and evil. Here the theologian might even agree that God must work within the confines of logic (i.e., he can't actualize a contradiction), but even so, God could will the opposites of the Ten Commandments. In such a case, the kinds of torture and punishment associated with the traditional notion of hell would either be one's reward for murder, theft, lying, etc. (perhaps God could so make the world that torment and torture are deemed pleasurable, and hence are sought after) or one could receive heaven for doing those acts. In either case, actions usually considered morally evil would be morally good and even obligatory. For God to maintain the existence of hell and send people there for doing the opposites of the Ten Commandments or send people to heaven for doing such deeds would in no way reflect negatively on his love or power, and of course, there could still be a hell.

If a theologian took the imagined Leibnizian or theonomous routes to address this problem, he or she could definitely remove the apparent logical contradiction between divine goodness and power and the existence of hell as a place of pain and suffering. But to do so in either of these ways comes at a great price. The cost of the Leibnizian approach is that ethics are understood predominantly in ontological terms. This is surely not the notion of ethics usually associated with conservative theism, and so the problem of hell is solved by abandoning the typical concept of ethics. As for a system committed to theonomous ethics, hell is as horrible as usually imagined, but now it is morally good and pleasant for people to go there. Or, now they go to heaven as a reward for murder, theft, and dishonesty. Certainly, this abandons the traditional notion of hell, and so really doesn't maintain the existence of all the elements associated with traditional theism.

The preceding discussion doesn't exhaust all of the theist's options for addressing the logical problem of hell. Three more merit attention. The first maintains divine power and benevolence, but argues for universal salvation of the human race. With this strategy, the theist could agree that hell with all of its horror really exists, but it is reserved for Satan and his angelic cohorts, not for human beings. Or, one might claim that hell is for Satan and company, but also for the most obstinate, inveterate sinners. Since this describes very few people, in essence the human race as a whole goes to heaven. I note as well that one could adopt the Roman Catholic doctrine of purgatory and wed it to this answer. In that way, sin still gets recompensed, but not in such a way as to cast doubts on divine justice by making people suffer the torments of hell forever. In fact, one could even hold that most humans will spend some time in purgatory prior to entry into heaven, for few are so holy that upon death they are prepared for the beatific vision. The universalist strategy has become increasingly popular among theists. In a later section I want to consider two versions of it, that of John Hick's soul-building theodicy and the position of Thomas Talbott.

The next strategy for handling the logical problem of hell also leaves God's power and benevolence untouched. With this approach no one actually winds up in hell, although that doesn't mean that everyone is saved (universalism). Rather this view postulates conditional immortality, which it weds to annihilation. Let me explain. This approach deems hell to be so horrible a punishment that it couldn't be just for God to send anyone there. But that doesn't mean God just winks at sin. Instead, he has a way of dealing with unrepentant sinners that doesn't require them to go to hell. Proponents of this view often claim that Scripture doesn't teach the immortality of the soul; that is a remnant of Greek philosophy. Rather, Scripture teaches only the resurrection of the body, but not everyone will be raised. Those who have responded to God as Savior will be resurrected to enjoy the fellowship of God and the saints in heaven evermore. Upon physical death and before bodily resurrection, the immaterial part of these believing humans will be in God's presence to enjoy the blessings of heaven. These people will live forever, because they have met the condition for immortality, namely, turning in faith to God.

On the other hand, those who reject God to the very end of their life will also die. We know what happens to their body when they die physically. This view, however, doesn't postulate the existence of these people's immaterial

408 THE MANY FACES OF EVIL

part after physical death, and it rejects the idea that these unbelievers will be resurrected in the future. Instead, upon physical death, God destroys these people—he annihilates them. They didn't meet the requisite condition for immortality, so they are not immortal. Proponents of this view claim that it has greater plausibility than the traditional view that consigns unrepentant sinners to eternal conscious punishment, because the punishment now envisioned—annihilation—is deemed a just punishment for rejecting God. So, with this response to the logical problem of hell, God doesn't apparently wink at rebellion against himself; there will be punishment for rejecting God, and so there is indeed a good reason to turn from one's sin and accept God as Savior. However, God doesn't choose a punishment for these sinners that lasts forever and hence far exceeds the "crime."

The universalist and conditional immortality/annihilation approaches to the logical problem of hell will remove the apparent contradiction within theistic beliefs. However, they do so in effect by rejecting part of the traditional perspective on hell. Hence, it still remains to be seen whether one can hold God's power and goodness and hell's existence (and usage) without contradiction. That suggests a final way to address this problem.

The final strategy for handling this problem keeps the traditional notion of God and hell intact, but then explains God's morally sufficient reason for implementing such a punishment and sending people to it. This strategy argues that these traditional views don't generate an unresolvable contradiction, because God has a reason for not getting rid of hell, a reason that allows hell to be as horrible as traditionally conceived, and also allows God's power and goodness to be undiminished. What could that reason possibly be? In later sections we will examine the kind of explanations that have been and can be given. What follows in the next sections is a more detailed treatment of the last three strategies described, for in contemporary discussions they are the major approaches used by those who want to maintain a tie to traditional theistic beliefs about God and hell. We must see whether in fact these approaches do solve the problem of hell, and if they do, whether there is reason, independent of their logical consistency, for adopting any of them.

Universalism

Though many have held universalism, I want to address two attempts to resolve the problem of evil in general by appealing to universalism. The former (John Hick's soul-building theodicy) doesn't claim to resolve the problem of hell, but it is clearly usable to do so. The latter (Thomas Talbott's defense) is intended to address the problem of hell, and it takes a different approach from Hick's.

I turn first to Hick's approach, which I already discussed in chapter 5. Since it is has been presented already, I need not do so here in detail. Hick's soul-building theodicy comes from what he calls the Irenaean tradition in theodicy rather than the Augustinian approach (which typically invokes the free will defense). This approach doesn't require that the world as created from the hand of God contained no evil, but even if the world was created that way, Hick's defense rests on the fact of there being evil in this world.

Hick reminds us that humans are capable of growing into children of God, but at birth none of us starts out that way. Since only those whose souls are built grow spiritually into the children of God—the ultimate goal for humankind—God had to decide when he created our world what would be the best environment for building souls. Would a world where nothing ever goes wrong and where there are no obstacles to overcome be the best setting for soul-building? Or would a world in which there are challenges and evils to confront present the best opportunity for spiritual growth? According to Hick, God decided that the latter environment was the most opportune for soul-building, and so he created a world in which there are moral and natural evils for his human creatures to confront. Because it is impossible to build souls in an Edenic paradise where nothing ever goes wrong, and because soul-building is a worthwhile enterprise, our world with the evil it contains isn't inconsistent with an understanding of God as all-powerful and totally good.

Though this might be the end of Hick's theodicy, he adds another dimension to it which neither Irenaeus nor his tradition included. According to Hick, it isn't enough for our world to be an optimal venue where soul-building *can* occur; souls must actually be built in this world. Otherwise, there is still reason to think that God's power and/or love don't square with the evil in our world. In fact, more than just a few human beings must grow into children of God in order for ours to be a good world in which God's goodness, power, and justice are justified. Hick believes that only if every soul is built can the soul-building theodicy succeed as an answer to the problem of evil. And Hick affirms that every soul will in fact be built. Everyone will make it to the blessed kingdom of God, and once we all arrive there, we will see that what God has prepared for us isn't just a little better than other alternatives. It dramatically exceeds anything we have or could ever have experienced. Hence, the trials and sufferings of this life are worth it all, and we will see it that way when we arrive at the kingdom of God.

Hick's commitment to universalism may seem contrary to our experience in this life as we view how people react to problems and troubles. Rather than being stimulated to grow spiritually by their trials, more often than not people become angry at God and turn from him. So, it appears that Hick's belief in universalism can't be correct. However, Hick is aware of the problem, and so he adds that there is no reason to think the soul-building process stops with physical death. Instead, it continues into the afterlife for however long it will take God to convince everyone who hasn't already turned to God to do so. Hick isn't clear as to whether those whose souls aren't built in this life occupy purgatory, limbo, or whatever after they die until God works on them so as to bring them to turn to him. Nonetheless, given an eternity to woo the recalcitrant, God will surely win them over.

If we adopt Hick's version of the soul-building theodicy, then even if there is a hell, no one will wind up going there. And that just means that the traditional doctrine of hell need not be an embarrassment for someone who adopts Hick's soul-building theodicy. The problem of hell in its logical form is solved by denying that anyone goes to eternal hell.

What should we say to the application of the soul-building theodicy to the logical problem of hell? Since this is a problem about the consistency of views the theist actually holds, we must begin by clarifying Hick's views about God and evil. As we saw in chapter 5, Hick's brand of theism is one form of Modified Rationalism. According to this approach, there are good and there are evil possible worlds, but there is no best possible world. Hence, God's requirement if he chooses to create a world is that he choose a good possible world. The Modified Rationalist must then explain what it is about our world that makes it one of those good possible worlds that God could create.

As to Hick's ethics, we noted that he is a consequentialist; things are morally right or wrong depending on the results of what is done. Hence, it is all right to begin with a world that contains evil so long as God will use that evil ultimately to bring good. And, clearly, the building of souls is a very desirable good. A final note about the intellectual commitments that come with Hick's system is that he espouses libertarian free will. In his thinking, if people turn to God and have their souls built because they were causally determined to do so, then it is dubious that they have done what they wanted to do. Hence, Hick explains that only if a soul is built by the individual freely turning to God can we then say that spiritual growth is happening.

Given these intellectual commitments, does Hick's soul-building theodicy succeed in solving its logical problem of hell? Here I begin by commenting on the basic soul-building strategy. Is it true that the soul-building theodicy succeeds only if all souls are built? I don't believe so, because our world as a place to build souls seems to make this a good world, regardless of how many people turn to God. Who could reasonably deny that growing into mature children of God is a value of the first order? If no one's soul is actually built, then we would certainly be dubious about whether this particular possible world is really a good one. But even if only a remnant have their souls built, then God's purpose with this world is fulfilled in those cases, and what was available to those who responded positively to God is equally available to those who don't. Remember, for Modified Rationalist theologies one doesn't have to prove that our world is the best possible world, or even that our world is better than other good worlds. All that is required is that ours is a good world. So there is good reason to believe that even without Hick's universalism the soul-building strategy can solve its logical problem of evil.

But what about Hick's version of this theodicy? On the surface, it appears that adding universalism couldn't possibly defeat this theodicy as an answer to the logical problem of hell. And, if Hick holds Modified Rationalism and a consequentialist ethic, the basic claims that 1) ours is a good world, because in it souls are built and that 2) in fact all souls eventually get built in no way produce an internal contradiction when juxtaposed to Hick's metaphysics and ethics.

There is a problem, however, for Hick's soul-building theodicy when we add his commitment to libertarian free will. As we saw in chapter 5, if people have libertarian free will, there can't be any guarantees about what they will do. Try as hard as God might, there are still some who may never turn to him and enter the kingdom of God. So, Hick's libertarian free will contradicts his guarantee that everyone will eventually freely (in the libertarian sense) have their soul built. This problem means that Hick's version of the soul-building theodicy does not in fact solve its logical problem of hell; there is still a contradiction.

However, there are easy enough ways to modify Hick's system so as to remove the lingering contradiction. If one persists in holding Hick's universalism, then a way to remove the contradiction with libertarian free will is to adopt compatibilism instead. If one holds this, then it appears that God can guarantee that all will make it to the kingdom of God, assuming that is ultimately all God wants to accomplish with creation. Hick's strong adherence to libertarian free will, however, suggests that adopting compatibilism (or even some form of hard determinism) is not an acceptable way for him to solve the problem. But even if we keep Hick's libertarian free will, I think the apparent contradiction can be removed. For one thing, we don't have to stipulate (as Hick implicitly seems to do) that this is a good possible world only if all souls are built. Even if there are many whose souls are not built, ours can still be a good possible world so long as there are those who do turn to God. It is at this point that we can add the empirical claim that at this stage of history it is rather clear that more than just a few have turned to God. And if we grant that they did so using libertarian free will, then even though many have rejected God in the past and even though there will be rejecters in the future, we already have plenty of evidence that what God wanted to do with this world (build souls) has happened. In light of the total company of the redeemed down through the ages, it is hard to see that our world qualifies as an evil possible world. Since with Modified Rationalism there is no best world, God is only required to create a good world. With the modifications to Hick's soul-building theodicy suggested, then, it is possible to so construe the soul-building theodicy that it solves its logical problem of hell. As is, Hick's version has problems, but the soul-building theodicy can be salvaged. What must be clear, however, is that the method of saving the soul-building that still claims that humans have libertarian free will can no longer hold Hick's universalism. And, that just means that Hick's soul-building theodicy with its universalism doesn't solve the logical problem of hell.

Next, we turn to Thomas Talbott's version of universalism. In recent years, through a series of articles and rejoinders to his critics, Talbott has argued not only that universalism must be true and must produce an internally consistent form of theism, but also that any version of theism that incorporates the notion of hell as a place where some unbelieving people will actually go for eternity is logically inconsistent.[13]

For our purposes, I shall focus on his explanation of why universalism produces a logically consistent system and must be true, regardless of whether or not one agrees with Talbott's assessment of other versions of theism. Talbott's support for universalism fundamentally stems from two main points, one about God's nature and the other about human choices.

As to God's nature, Talbott thinks that the key to understanding the issue of hell is God's love. Though traditional theists hold that God loves every created person, they have also held that God will irrevocably reject some people and subject them to everlasting punishment. In Talbott's thinking, in order to maintain internal consistency, the theist must either reject the notion that God loves everyone or reject the claim that God will irrevocably consign some people to eternal punishment. One can't hold both claims consistently. Talbott rejects the damnation claim, but traditional theism incorporates that idea. Hence, in Talbott's thinking, these theists have really rejected the claim about God's love.[14] Talbott begins to explain his reasoning by appealing to a quote from Aquinas about God loving every person in that he wills some good to all. Aquinas adds, though, that God doesn't will every good to everyone, for he doesn't will eternal life for some people.[15] Talbott concludes that this isn't love, for "that God should will *some* good for each of them during, say, seventy years of life on earth is hardly evidence of love, not when that seventy years is followed by an eternity of separation or, as Aquinas calls it, an eternity of hatred."[16] Not only does Aquinas make this claim, but Talbott also thinks that many other key Christian theologians, including Augustine, Calvin, and current theologians, hold this same view.

But, why does Talbott think that God's loving people excludes the possibility that he might send some to hell? Talbott answers that we must understand what it means for God truly to love someone. He offers the following "principle": "Necessarily, God loves a person S (with a perfect form of love) at a time *t* only if God's intention at *t* and every moment subsequent to *t* is to do everything within his power to promote the best interest of S."[17] To amplify this point, Talbott says that it requires God to love us not for just a little while, but always. Moreover, while a loving human being doesn't do everything in his or her power to promote the interest of the loved one, an omnipotent God would do everything to promote the interests of any of us so long as doing so didn't thereby limit the interests of another human.[18]

What does it mean, however, to promote someone's best interests? Though Talbott agrees that it may be hard to tell what is in someone's best interests, he believes that a person's best interest must be connected in some way to a happy life. Such contentment must, among other things, be the kind of happiness that would last forever, and this sort of happiness the NT claims "can exist only when one is loved by others and is likewise filled with love for others."[19] Talbott affirms that whatever else we might include in this kind of happiness, it must be the type of happiness God would promote in those he loves. When we take all of these points together, the result is that God's intention is to do everything he can (within the confines of logical possibility) to promote this happiness in his creatures. But, if so, the problem of logical inconsistency for theistic positions that believe in hell should be obvious. If God loves everyone, as traditional theism claims, that means that he intends to do everything he can "to promote the best interest of and to cultivate supremely worthwhile happiness in all of them; but if he irrevocably rejects some created persons, it is *not* his intention to do all that he properly can to promote the best interest of or to cultivate supremely worthwhile happiness in all of them."[20]

The net result is that any theistic position that holds both that God is all-loving and that God sends some people to hell is logically inconsistent. The consistency of the position can be upheld only by denying that God is all-loving or by denying that anyone winds up in hell. Since love is so fundamental to God's nature (and also such a foundational attribute in our conception of God), Talbott opts for the second option, the rejection of eternal punishment. And, since the contradiction arises if even just one person goes to hell, the only way to maintain logical consistency is to reject the traditional doctrine of hell. This Talbott does, and as a result, espouses universalism.

This, however, is only half of the story, for Talbott believes that eternal damnation should be rejected as well once we think through the matter of whether any human being can and would reject God forever and thus wind up in hell. Talbott says there are theists who would hold a proposition such as the following: "Some persons will, despite God's best efforts to save them, finally reject God and separate themselves from God forever."[21] Of course, this claim incorporates the notion that such a person would *freely* reject God forever, and by "free" this view means libertarian free will. If the individual in question didn't have such freedom, God could impose a moral character on him so that he would forego rejecting God, or God might simply unilaterally, apart from the will and action of the person, save him. But if the imagined person has libertarian free will, then, despite all of God's best efforts, he might succeed in rejecting God forever.[22]

Though Talbott seems to grant this as possible in general, he doubts that it would ever happen. Of course, this needs explanation, and Talbott is forthcoming on this matter. He explains that if someone made a decision about whether or not to reject God with less than full information, then it is possible that someone would reject God and separate from him forever. However, if someone decides on his or her relationship to God when fully informed of the consequences and if God tries everything he could do to convince the person not to reject him (e.g., threaten or impose punishment, offer a crystal clear revelation about the nature of hell as a place of torment to which those who reject God go, etc.), then it is unthinkable that someone would finally and fully reject God.[23]

But, we might ask, why should this be so? Aren't there some people who use their freedom to make bad choices and gradually find themselves becoming enslaved to sin so that they can't turn from it and choose God? Talbott grants that this is possible, but claims that a loving God would intervene and release them from their bondage to sin. For those who object that this throws out libertarian free will in this instance, Talbott reminds them that someone in bondage to sinful desires has already lost libertarian free will. For God to intervene as supposed doesn't remove free will. Rather it "reinstates" it, so to speak, by removing the weight of sin that drags the person toward evil. But, once one is released from bondage to sin, if, as a rational agent, one is confronted with the option of choosing eternal misery, there is no motive for one to make that choice and every motive to choose the alternate option, eternal salvation.[24] Hence, as long as a person is fully informed and acts freely, he will reject eternal torment.

Though this assumes that every decision of this sort will be made with full awareness of the facts, Talbott knows that doesn't happen. However, if someone makes this decision in ignorance of the facts or in bondage to sinful desires, then he doesn't choose *freely.* On the other hand, a truly rational agent who is fully informed of the alternatives and their eternal implications will have no motive to choose damnation, and so he won't. So, to make a fully informed decision (without being in bondage to sin) to reject God and choose eternal damnation would be to choose irrationally. As a result, any rational being who is fully informed of all relevant data and who isn't in bondage to sin, both of which are necessary to exercise libertarian free will, "could never have a motive to choose eternal misery for oneself."[25] Such a person might occasionally freely choose what is wrong, but could not in the long run choose eternal damnation.

When we conjoin Talbott's comments about God and man, it should be obvious that all will be saved. If humans truly have free will (and they could have it only if they are fully informed and aren't enslaved to sin when they make this decision), they will choose eternity with God, not eternal damnation. On the other hand, for those who are either ignorant of the truth or are bound by their sin, a God of love would intervene to save them. He could do so either by offering a perfectly clear revelation of the truth of the matter, or he could cancel their bondage to sin. If one complains that for God to act this way would be for him to disrespect these individuals' libertarian free will, Talbott disagrees, for he believes that people who choose in ignorance or in bondage to sin aren't free in the first place. Hence, God's intervention doesn't remove their freedom but rather preserves and restores it (if it was lost). This is what we would expect of a God who loves us and looks out for our betterment. And, once we are able to act in a truly free way (fully informed and not in bondage to sin), there is no motive to choose sin and to reject God, so we won't. The net result is that everyone will ultimately be saved, and if that is so, then the apparent inconsistency between God's love and power and evil's existence is removed.[26]

What shall we say in response to Talbott's universalism? It should be obvious that it has many affinities to Hick's soul-building theodicy, though Talbott doesn't really emphasize the soul-building nature of our world. Rather, he argues that a loving God, once that love is properly understood, just couldn't condemn a person to eternal torment, and so he won't. But God has some help in this project, the free decisions of his creatures. Given the nature of a truly free choice in this matter, humans will in fact choose eternity with God. Only those who aren't truly free in the libertarian sense might choose otherwise, but in such cases a loving God would intervene to restore true freedom, and the "right" choice would be made.

Does this solve the logical problem of hell for Talbott's system? Assuming that he holds a Modified Rationalist form of theism, it should also be clear that he is a consequentialist—at least his defense of God rests on consequentialism, for the end result of universalism seems to be the only way to justify God against the evils we all endure in this world. What makes our world one of those good possible worlds the Modified Rationalist believes exist? Talbott would probably say ours is a good world because God's love is poured out in it to enhance his creatures' well-being, and it is a world in which humans may choose an eternity with God.

On the surface, this appears to be a logically consistent story, regardless of how plausible or implausible one might believe it is. However, as with Hick, there is a rub with Talbott's libertarian free will. Is it logically consistent to believe that humans, making a fully informed decision unfettered by sin, will choose God? I don't think so, and the problem stems from the nature of libertarian free will. Such freedom doesn't allow our choices to be causally determined, but it seems that Talbott's whole way of setting up the situation violates libertarian freedom at one point or another. Let me explain. For those who are ignorant, God can give them a very clear revelation that will allow them to know which is the correct choice. But if this information is strong enough to decisively move the person to choose God, then the decision is causally determined by means (at least) of that revelation. If so, then it isn't free in the libertarian sense.

There is an even more fundamental problem with libertarian freedom and Talbott's story. Talbott claims that if people are fully informed and aren't bound by sin, there will be no motive to choose eternal damnation. Presumably this also means that there will be every motive to choose eternal salvation. But doesn't this mean that the choice results from what is deemed the proper motives, and if so, doesn't that mean the choice is causally determined by our motives? Now, this must not be misunderstood. Libertarians don't deny that decisions are made in agreement with our motives. Rather they deny that there is any motive that is strong enough to decisively move the will to choose one option rather than another. And if that is so, then no matter how rational it is to choose God, there can be no guarantees that everyone will do so. Any who do choose God as a result of being moved by the motive to avoid punishment, etc., make that choice without libertarian free will.

The net result is that if libertarian free will is truly left unfettered, there can be no guarantee that everyone will choose God, and hence no guarantees about universalism. Talbott, no doubt, would retort that there is no adequate reason for people to choose damnation. But such a claim invokes again the notion that choices are made because of/in accord with one's motive(s), and that just cancels the idea that such choices are made with libertarian free will. Does this mean that Talbott's universalist theism fails to solve its problem of hell in its logical form? I believe it does mean that, because there ultimately can be no guarantees with libertarian free will. Though it may be totally irrational in the face of full disclosure to choose hell, such a choice must be possible, given libertarian free will, and who is to say that there are none who will "irrationally" (according to Talbott's definition) reject God anyway?

Though this is bad news if one wants to follow Talbott's form of theism, as with Hick's views, Talbott's defense is redeemable. That can happen by changing incompatibilism to compatibilism, for example. Moreover, Talbott doesn't say that ours is a good world only if everyone is saved, but that it is inconceivable that God would allow any other situation. However, suppose that many people in this world do respond positively to God's invitation to eternal life, while others stubbornly reject him. Why would this world, then, not be a good world? Talbott would probably reply that it isn't because God hasn't been as loving as he could be. But if we must define divine love and obligate it in the way Talbott does, then I think that obligation plus human libertarian free will produces an intolerable mix that can't succeed against the charge of internal inconsistency. On the other hand, suppose God's love doesn't obligate him to do every loving thing possible but only to act with love toward his creatures. Wouldn't that notion of divine love mesh with Talbott's libertarian free will? I think so. It would, of course, rule out universalism, but it would rule in our world as a good world, and hence, it would resolve the logical problem of evil for Talbott's system. So, Talbott's views can be "rescued" but only with some significant modifications.[27]

How should we assess these two universalist positions? As noted, in their current form neither Hick's nor Talbott's universalism solves the logical problem of hell, and the culprit in both cases is libertarian free will. However, there are ways to reform both Hick's position and Talbott's, and given such reformations, I do believe they resolve the logical problem of moral evil and the problem of hell for their respective theologies.

Should we, however, adopt either of these revised theologies? There are several grounds on which we might reject one or the other or both. First, anyone who rejects universalism cannot adopt either of these two positions. For those who adhere to biblical theism, universalism doesn't square with the text. We need not belabor the point, for there is plenty of biblical evidence against universalism. The general tenor of Scripture is that God works with a remnant in any age. It would be easy to demonstrate this by reading biblical accounts of various people who stood for God against rampant evil. Think, for example, of the days of Noah. Wickedness was so widespread that

God decided to destroy everyone on earth except Noah and his family. Or think of Elijah's complaint that he alone stood for God in his day. God informed him that there were others, seven thousand to be more exact, who hadn't bowed the knee to Baal (Rom. 11:2-4; 1 Kings 19:10-18), but that doesn't mean that most people followed Yahweh. In regard to his Jewish brethren, Paul adds that "So too, at the present time there is a remnant chosen by grace" (Rom. 11:5, NIV). Perhaps the strongest indication that universalism isn't supported by Scripture are the words of our Lord as he gave the Sermon on the Mount, "enter through the narrow gate. For wide is the gate and broad is the road that leads to destruction, and many enter through it. But small is the gate and narrow the road that leads to life, and only a few find it" (Matt. 7:13-14, NIV). As traditionally interpreted, Jesus is comparing two ways of life, a godless and a godly way of life, and he affirms that the majority of humankind is on that broader path to destruction.

In addition to outright rejection of universalism, one might simply disagree, on biblical grounds or otherwise, with Hick's picture of the kingdom of God or his belief that soul-building goes on after death. And, then, anyone who rejects consequentialist ethics and/or libertarian free will can't adopt either Hick's or Talbott's position. Moreover, as suggested above, Talbott's understanding of what divine benevolence obligates God to do may also be objectionable. And, it goes without saying that Talbott's assessment of human nature's ability and willingness to choose the right (even when what is right is perfectly clear) underestimates the devastating nature of sin (and our sin nature) and overestimates the inherent goodness of human nature. Given what Talbott says about the rationality of free actions that are fully informed, wouldn't we have to say that Adolf Hitler was unswervingly evil because he just didn't know enough to realize how wrong he was? And wouldn't it follow that if Hitler only had more light or paid more attention to it, he would have stopped what he was doing? Such assessments seem to be required by Talbott's line of argument, and yet they are far from what Scripture teaches about human sinfulness and its effects on the mind and heart of human beings (Jer. 17:9; Rom. 3:10-18).

Perhaps Talbott would reply that this only shows that Hitler was bound by sin and so "couldn't help himself." If God had just intervened to break the power of his sinfulness, everything would have been fine. But Talbott never tells us exactly what God would have to do to break the power of sin; he merely assures us that it wouldn't remove libertarian free will. Perhaps it would just destroy the penchant for sin, and leave the will free to choose or reject God, but even so, there are no guarantees about what Hitler (or anyone else) would freely choose. And from everything we know about Hitler, there was no conversion to God. If one says it happened on his deathbed, how do we know that? But even if we grant that, why, when Hitler was destroying so many lives—lives which a benevolent God wouldn't want handled as Hitler and the Nazis did for he would will what is in their best interests, too—didn't God intervene to stop Hitler and convert him much sooner?

Talbott's assessment of how likely it is that everyone, fully informed and free from sin, would choose God, and his comments that God's love for everyone would move him to save us all, are simply off the mark. One of the most fundamental problems with his proposal is that it underestimates the power of sin. It assumes that the key to right living is knowing all the facts correctly. But none of that will matter if one's will is perverse and depraved. The problem with a Hitler (and all sinners) isn't lack of knowledge, but perversity of heart and will. And, contra Talbott, these people aren't forced to sin against their wishes; they do so willingly and happily (see, e.g., Rom. 1:32). Talbott would say they don't do it freely, but that begs the question by assuming that the only actions that count as free (in the libertarian sense or any other sense) are ones that are good. It also rejects the biblical portrait of the perversity and stubbornness of evil hearts. Hence, even if one modified Talbott's position as suggested above to remove the apparent contradiction, that still wouldn't necessarily be reason enough to adopt his overall position.

And, finally, one might reject both Hick's and Talbott's universalist theologies because one doesn't agree that the only way to build souls is to overcome evils (Hick). Or one doesn't see why God's love and concern for everyone's best interests result only in their choosing eternal life rather than damnation, and doesn't also result in removal of moral and physical evil altogether from our world. All of the reasons raised in the last few paragraphs are reasons to reject either of these universalist theologies altogether, but none of this shows that they can't solve their logical problem of hell. There is a way for Hick and Talbott to tell logically consistent stories about God and hell, but the resultant theologies aren't necessarily ones that we should adopt.

Annihilation/Conditional Immortality

THE VIEW

Another way to address the logical problem of hell appeals to annihilation and conditional immortality. Though these two items are often considered corollaries and taken together, they represent two distinct lines of argument. As to annihilation, various theologians and philosophers have argued that once humans die, that completely ends their existence. We know that the body is placed in the grave and over time decomposes. Various thinkers disagree on what happens to the immaterial part of human nature. Some reject the notion of immaterial substances and hence see human nature only in physical terms. Those who believe in immaterial substances address this issue in one of two ways. Some firmly believe that at physical death human life, including our immaterial part, completely ends. God simply destroys it. Others believe that the immaterial part of some people lives on, while those who reject God suffer complete annihilation.

This final point raises the issue of conditional immortality, and it involves several ideas, depending on the thinker in question. There are some who claim that the soul isn't naturally immortal. For example, Clark Pinnock proposes that belief in the natural immortality of the soul is a vestige of Greek philosophy, but it isn't taught in Scripture.[28] According to the notion of natural immortality, all souls live on after individuals physically die, regardless of whether their life was pleasing or displeasing to God. Of course, if one holds to the natural immortality of souls, one wonders what happens to all of these souls that live on. At this point the Christian doctrine of the two possible destinies of human souls comes in. If all souls are naturally immortal, then the only way to distinguish between their destinies seems to be what traditional Christian doctrine has done. Those who established a relationship with God during their life on earth spend eternity in his presence and are blessed beyond measure. Those who rejected God must be punished, and since there is no way to "kill" the immortal soul, their punishment must be eternal.[29]

But what if souls are not "naturally" immortal? Then everyone seems headed toward future annihilation when their life ends on earth. But is annihilation the only option? A number of Christian thinkers have thought that it isn't. If immortality isn't natural to the soul, perhaps, then, it is a gift. But, a gift to whom? Everyone? If so, that's universalism, and proponents of conditional immortality reject universalism. No, according to these thinkers immortality is a gift given by God to his people who have established a saving relationship with him. They become immortal on the condition that they trust God as their Saviour. As to the rest of mankind, they don't receive the gift of immortality; their existence ceases with physical death.

If one adopts this view, it is argued, it solves the problem of hell. God's love and power are both upheld, because no one actually winds up in hell. Though the nonbelieving are annihilated, this is thought to be a better destiny than eternal conscious punishment. Moreover, those who do place their faith and trust in God will be granted the gift of immortality and will live with him forever. God, as omnipotent, can make a soul immortal just as he is able to resurrect a body from the dead.

Now, it is worth noting that one could believe in annihilation without also holding conditional immortality. In that case, one would hold that everyone, believer and unbeliever, ceases to exist entirely at death. One who held this view might believe that souls are naturally immortal, but God just snuffs them out at death. Or one might reject the natural immortality of the soul and hold that God needs to do nothing more than allow the person to die. While believers in annihilation aren't logically required to adopt conditional immortality, it is hard to imagine how one would hold conditional immortality without also holding that souls which fail to meet the condition are destroyed.

It is also noteworthy that in recent years various theologians working broadly within the evangelical spectrum have adopted one version or another of this view or have, at least, seen it as a possible way to handle the problem of hell. Adopting such views is thought to be an especially good way to handle the question of what happens to those who have never heard of Christ. Traditionally, Christian theology has said that there is salvation only in Christ, but is this also true for those who have never heard of Christ? Some believe that such an eventuality would be unjust on God's part, and so they are attracted to the conditional immortality/annihilation viewpoint.

SUPPORT FOR THE VIEW

Many of these same theologians believe their views are supportable by various biblical and theological arguments. The biblical arguments can be divided into four basic categories. The first is biblical language itself. Edward Fudge asks whether the OT tells us anything about the fate of the wicked, and he replies that

> it overwhelmingly affirms their total destruction. It never affirms or even hints at anything resembling conscious unending torment. The OT uses about 50 different Hebrew verbs to describe this fate, and about 70 figures of speech. Without exception they portray destruction, extinction or extermination.[30]

In turning to the OT we note the kind of language that speaks of destruction. The wicked are likened to smoke that vanishes (Ps. 37:20), thorns and stubble in the fire (Isa. 33:12), ashes trodden underfoot (Mal. 4:3), and a vanished dream (Ps. 73:20). Even more directly, we find in Psalms various passages that say the wicked will die, they won't be remembered, and it will be as though they never existed; in contrast, the righteous will be rescued from death and will enjoy God eternally (Ps. 9; 21:4-10; 36:9-12; 49:8-20; 52:5-9; 59; 73; 92). Similarly, we read in Proverbs that the wicked will be cut off and will be no more (Prov. 2:21-22; 10:25; 12:7; 24:15-20).[31]

Then, some passages speak about the alternate destinies of the wicked and the righteous. As explicit as any are Daniel 12:2 and Isaiah 66:22-24.[32] And finally, several note the story of the demise of Sodom and Gomorrah (Gen. 19:24-29). God brought fire and brimstone on these wicked cities. It destroyed the people living there and even the vegetation. This was such a horrible judgment that at various points in Scripture this event is seen as the prototype of divine judgment on the wicked in history and at the end of the world (Deut. 29:23; Isa. 1:9; 13:19-22; Jer. 49:18; 50:40; Lam. 4:6; Amos 4:11; Zeph. 2:9; Luke 17:28-33; 2 Pet. 2:6; Jude 7, 23).[33]

As to the NT, Fudge reminds us that we must understand its language against the backdrop of the OT. For example, in Mark 9:43, 48 Jesus speaks of the place of punishment as a place with unquenchable fire. John the Baptist, speaking of doomed sinners as he announced the coming of the Messiah (Matt. 3:12), says they will be burned with unquenchable fire. When the OT speaks of unquenchable fire, it means that it can't be put out or extinguished (e.g., Ps. 118:12). The writer of Hebrews 11 speaks of OT heroes of faith who were able to "quench the violence of fire" (Heb. 11:34, KJV).[34]

According to Fudge, we see the same sort of thing in relation to the phrase "gnashing of teeth." This phrase appears in various places in the OT (Job 16:9; Ps. 35:16; 37:12; Lam. 2:16), and it invariably portrays someone who is so angry with another person that he grinds his teeth in anger (see also Acts 7:54). Those who hold the traditional account of hell understand this gnashing to refer to pain eternally experienced by the disembodied spirits of the lost. However, Fudge explains that in a passage like Psalm 112:10, the point is horrible rage on the part of the wicked who are "frustrated by the wicked's own inexorable destruction."[35]

A second line of biblical evidence appeals to the imagery Scripture uses to portray hell. The primary portrait of hell is given in terms of fire. Since this is so, some have argued that the point isn't unending pain but rather destruction. Fire, in our experience, completely consumes the object on fire. Hence, this imagery fits better with annihilation than with unending suffering from the flames of hell.[36]

Then, we find the argument here that we have seen motivating much of the attack on the traditional doctrine of hell. Some holding the annihilation/conditional immortality viewpoint reject the traditional doctrine of hell on the grounds that inflicting this punishment is unjust. Sins committed in time (even the grossest sins) don't merit an eternity of punishment. The point here is not that sins should go unpunished, but that they require a just punishment. Eternal conscious torment seems to far exceed the sin, while annihilation seems to be more equitable, according to those holding this view.[37]

A final line of argument from Scripture appeals to passages that seem to be universalistic in nature (e.g., Eph. 1:10; Col. 1:20; Phil. 2:10-11; 1 Cor. 15:28). Of course, the theologians under consideration can't adopt a universalistic reading of these passages unless they switch their views from annihilation to universalism. Instead, some who appeal to these passages have claimed that these texts "are easier to reconcile with the awful realities of hell if hell means the destruction of the impenitent and not their continuing rebellion against God and God's corresponding continuing infliction of punishment upon them."[38]

ASSESSMENT

What should we say about whether this approach solves the logical problem of hell for theologies that adopt it? We must remember that there are variations of this viewpoint. Some hold only that all people cease to exist when they die—no one is naturally immortal and God grants conditional immortality to no one. There is also the view that everyone is naturally immortal, but God annihilates all of us when we die. A further variation says that we are all naturally immortal, but God annihilates nonbelievers upon their death. A final option is that no one is naturally immortal, but God grants conditional immortality to those who trust him; the rest simply die and cease to exist.

The first option allows no one to go to hell, so God's power and love can't be inconsistent with the existence of hell. However, is annihilation consistent with divine power and love? If one believes that God is obligated to give believers immortality, then, of course, this theology is in significant trouble with respect to handling the logical problem of hell. But if one doesn't hold that God must grant conditional immortality, and if one doesn't believe that God lacks love or power because of creating a creature (humans) who isn't naturally immortal, then there seems to be no contradiction left for this theology. Of course, if one believes that it is unjust and/or unloving for God not to grant immortality (and also believes that God has the power to give anyone immortality), then this attempted resolution to the logical problem of hell is unsuccessful. Moreover, if extinction without conditional immortality is viewed as a punishment for sin, then whether or not this is a logically consistent position depends on whether one believes that annihilation is a just punishment for sin. If so, then this approach can solve its logical problem of hell; if not, the problem is unsolved.

What about the option that everyone is naturally immortal, but God annihilates us all at death? Here it all depends on whether you think annihilation results from all of us being sinners and whether you think extinction is a just penalty for sin. If one grants both points, then this approach solves its logical problem of hell. If one grants the former but not the latter, then it fails to solve its problem.

Suppose, however, that one holds that all are annihilated (though naturally immortal), but not because they are sinners. Would that produce a logically consistent theology? Here the answer seems to depend on whether God has promised anyone eternal life and on what his reason is for annihilating us. If he does this for some reason other than our sinfulness, it is hard to imagine that he would have a just reason for annihilating people who are naturally immortal, and hence it is dubious that this imagined theology can solve its logical problem of hell.

As to the third view (all are naturally immortal and God annihilates only nonbelievers), assessment again depends largely on whether or not one thinks extinction is a just punishment for nonbelievers. If it is deemed fair, then theologies that adopt this approach both get rid of hell and substitute for it a punishment that is just. On the other hand, if annihilation is a punishment that exceeds the sin of nonbelief, then even though this theology jettisons the notion of hell, it still has a problem of logical consistency, because it holds that God is just but then claims that he exacts an unjust penalty on nonbelievers.

The final option (none are naturally immortal, and God grants conditional immortality to believers) again rejects the notion of hell, but it still isn't clear that there are no leftover internal contradictions. Is extinction a just punishment for rejecting God? If so, then this theology can solve its logical problem of hell. If not, then the contradiction isn't entirely removed, and the theology collapses under the weight of internal inconsistency.

This may seem to be all we can say in assessing this answer to the problem of evil, but it isn't, because some of these options become just if one thinks annihilation and/or conditional immortality are just. If one couples the free will defense with annihilation and/or conditional immortality, one can argue that the punishment of annihilation is just, because a person freely chooses this destiny herself. She freely decides that she doesn't want reconciliation to God and eternal fellowship with him. If the sinner is clear about the results of her decision on this matter and then, using libertarian free will, chooses to reject God, then a case can be made that this is a just punishment and hence, God is exonerated; the problem is indeed solved. Remember that those annihilated don't *experience* an eternal punishment. That is, while they never live again, they at least are not *consciously experiencing* this punishment; as extinct, they experience nothing whatsoever.

In sum, there are some circumstances under which adopting annihilation and conditional immortality does remove the apparent contradiction in a theology that adopts belief in hell. But, even so, should we adopt such beliefs as our theology? There are at least two major reasons one might reject this theology as a whole, despite its ability to solve the logical problem of hell. The first is that one believes that the biblical concept of hell is conscious punishment. Despite the biblical evidence produced in favor of annihilation, some key biblical passages are omitted. For example, the apostle Paul, speaking about what happens to believers after death, says that to be absent from the body is to be present with the Lord (2 Cor. 5:8). But what is present with the Lord? Surely not the body, since one is absent from it. Hence, the correct answer must be our disembodied immaterial part. Proponents of annihilation/conditional immortality would probably affirm that this is consistent with conditional immortality of the righteous, but in no way does it prove that the ungodly won't be extinguished. That is true, but such a Scripture at least shows that it is unbiblical to hold a view that says everyone will be annihilated at death, regardless of spiritual condition.

What about the wicked? Will they just be annihilated? Scripture seems to teach otherwise. It is true that many passages talk about the ungodly perishing or being destroyed, but it is question begging to assume that this can only mean annihilation, rather than condemnation to eternal punishment. We must ask whether Scripture ever portrays the wicked as consciously suffering in hell, and a case can be made that it does. A passage that is often cited is Luke 16:19-31, the story of the rich man and Lazarus. Some call this a parable, and it may be, but it doesn't say that in the text. Even if it is a parable, what does the parable teach? Does it teach that nonbelievers are extinguished at physical death? If so, why then does the rich man, suffering in hell, plead for Abraham to send Lazarus to give him relief? It is hard to see this as signifying annihilation, since those extinguished feel no pain and can't ask for any relief.

But there is more. Think of the Great White Throne Judgment predicted in Revelation 20:11-15. Those condemned at this judgment are cast into the lake of fire. In verses 7-10 we are told that Satan will lead one last rebellion toward the end of the millennial kingdom, but he and his forces will lose. Satan will be cast into the lake of fire, where he will join the Beast and the False Prophet (see Revelation 13 for more information about them). Verse 10 says they will be tormented day and night forever. Verse 15 says that those whose names are not written in the book of life will be cast into the lake of fire; and verse 14 explains that this is the second death. Those so condemned will join Satan, the Beast, and the False Prophet. Now it is surely possible that these three will be consciously tormented while the ungodly dead will be extinguished, but that is unlikely. Remember, the annihilationist position says that nonbelievers are destroyed at physical death. If so, how then can they be resurrected to stand at the Great White Throne Judgment? Will God recreate them again, just to inflict the lake of fire on them? Or will God recreate them, cast them into the lake of fire and annihilate them a second time in the lake of fire? If so, why? Since their ultimate end is extinction, why not do that once and for all at physical death? Surely a second extinction in the lake of fire makes little sense.

Suppose, however, that it is only when they are cast into the lake of fire that they are annihilated. That is possible, but then what happens to their immaterial part between physical death and the Great White Throne Judgment? They can't be with God. Are they in limbo—but what does that even mean? Are they in hell during that time? If so, many people have already been in hell for thousands of years awaiting resurrection to stand at the Great White Throne Judgment. Those who believe eternal conscious punishment in hell is an unjust recompense for sin shouldn't then agree that hell for several thousand years is acceptable. The motivation behind the annihilation/conditional immortality option (at least in part) is the belief that hell is an inappropriate punishment for a loving God to inflict on us, regardless of how long it lasts.

Other passages also suggest conscious punishment of the wicked, but the above will suffice. Those who hold the *biblical* portrait of hell will likely reject the annihilationist/conditional immortality strategy as their way to solve the problem of hell. The other main reason for rejecting the annihilation/conditional immortality approach is that even if one adopts it, it isn't entirely clear that this is a just punishment for the ungodly. Proponents of this view assume that it is, but total extinction forever may also be a punishment that far exceeds the crime. At least proponents of this view haven't shown that it isn't. Hence, one might reject this theology altogether on the grounds that it doesn't properly uphold God's justice. Any punishment, including this one, that lasts forever arguably exceeds the "crime" that brought such punishment.

In sum, there are theologies which incorporate this resolution to the logical problem of hell and thereby solve that problem. However, that in itself isn't good enough reason to adopt any of those theologies because of the intellectual commitments they include.

A Morally Sufficient Reason for Hell

A final way to address the problem of hell maintains its existence and unending conscious torment, and it also accepts divine omnipotence and omnibenevolence. Proponents of this approach believe that they can show that God has a morally sufficient reason for not removing hell, or that in systems like theonomy God has no obligation to remove it. Clearly, the *logical* problem of hell must be posed against the backdrop of some specific theological position; it can't merely be a "cannon blast" aimed indiscriminately at all theistic systems at once. With that in mind, let us address this problem from the perspectives of the major theological systems set forth in this book.

How might a theonomist respond to this problem? He might say any of several things. For one, given God's absolute sovereignty, he has the right to implement and enforce any system of moral governance in our universe that he wants. Hence, if he wants to send disobedient people to hell for eternal torture, that is his right. In addition, God could reveal a set of moral laws which must be obeyed by all, including himself, with the proviso that those who disobey will merit hell and will eventually receive it. Since in this scenario God only obligates himself to obey the moral rules he chooses for all beings, and since he reveals that he has never broken any of them, God doesn't deserve hell. But something more must be said. Given the theonomous system imagined, God is nowhere obligated to keep people from disobeying him (unless, of course, he reveals that he has placed himself under that rule, but he hasn't), and hence, he isn't obligated to remove hell or keep people from going there. There is nothing intrinsically good or evil about hell per se for a theonomous ethic; it is simply the instrument God uses to punish the disobedient. Now, undoubtedly other versions of theonomy might argue the case differently. But any theonomist following the basic approach I have outlined can affirm that he or she has produced a logically consistent theonomous theology, and hence has solved the logical problem of hell.

As for a Leibnizian rationalist, the resolution to the problem of hell is rather straightforward. Since God must create the metaphysically richest possible world, if hell contributes to that richness (and it does because it adds more variety to a world already rich in existing things), God is obligated to create it. Remember that Leibniz believed that God surveys all possible worlds and knows which is the richest, metaphysically speaking. He has the power to create it, and Leibniz assures us that he is morally good, which means he will fulfill his moral duty to create the best world. Moreover, Leibniz believed that everything happens in accord with the principle of sufficient reason. Hence, if there isn't a sufficient reason to create a world, God won't do so. But the only sufficient reason to create a world is that it is the metaphysically best world. The fact that God has created a world and included hell in it assures us that it is the metaphysically best of all possible worlds. Hence, God has met his moral obligation, and as a result, the logical problem of hell for Leibniz's rationalistic system is solved.

Next we turn to Modified Rationalist theologies. We have discussed several in earlier chapters. Here I propose to offer the defenses against the problem of hell that fit free will theologies, soul-building theologies, and my own moderate Calvinist theology. Since each of the theologies is a Modified Rationalist system, they needn't show that ours is the best possible world but only that it is a good world. We have already seen how each of these theologies solves its problem of moral evil, and since moral evil (sin) is what merits hell, it is likely that the basic defense of each system against the problem of moral evil can be applied to the problem of hell. But more is needed than simple transference of one defense to a second problem. This is so, because, as noted all along, hell is an evil that befalls people as a punishment. Hence, we must ask of these theologies and their defenses why they believe hell is a just punishment for rejecting God.

It might also help to explain why hell is a more just punishment than, for example, annihilation. Such an explanation isn't required to show that these Modified Rationalist theologies hold that ours is a better possible world than any other God might have created. One might agree that a world in which recalcitrant sinners are annihilated is a better world (presumably because this is a more just punishment, in one's opinion) than a world with hell as punishment for rejecting God, but that is beside the point, for the Modified Rationalist is only required to show that a world with hell is a good possible world. The theologian, however, might explain anyway why hell is a more just punishment than annihilation in order to make the defense more plausible and thereby prepare the way for handling the evidential problem of hell.

In sum, the defenses envisioned must first show that God has a morally sufficient reason for creating a world with hell as punishment for sin and that this reason does qualify our world as a good world. In addition, these theologies should also explain why hell is a just punishment for evil. Otherwise, hell may be deemed such a great evil that it counterbalances or even overbalances the good thing(s) God has done with our world and thereby makes ours one of those evil possible worlds that Modified Rationalists speak about.

THREE DEFENSES

How might a free will defender answer the logical problem of hell? The free will defender will point to libertarian free will as that which makes ours a good world. But the free will defender will likely say more, adapting ideas from the basic free will defense to the problem of hell. Free will defenders always claim that libertarian free will is a value of such worth that even though with free will people can and do act in sinful ways, it is worth the risk that they will sin just to have the possibility that they will freely choose the good. Free will defenders also affirm that God would prefer humans to love and obey him because they want and choose to do so, rather than because they are made to do so. They also claim that anything less than libertarian free will is subhuman, and of course, anyone who thinks a world with humans is a good world won't prefer a world with people who are subhuman.[39] So, God's morally sufficient reason for creating our world with hell as a final punishment is that he gave his creatures libertarian free will, a value of great worth. Of course, if people have this kind of freedom, no one can guarantee what they will do with it. Sadly, many people use it to reject God, even when they fully understand that doing so without repentance will eventuate in their going to hell. The possibility of going to hell is a high price for maintaining the integrity of human free will, but free will defenders believe that it is worth it.

There is more to the free will defense as it is applied to the problem of hell. The other part involves whether hell is a just punishment for those who refuse to turn to God. The free will defender might explain that as moral governor of the universe, God has the authority and right to ordain any sort of punishment he chooses for those who ultimately reject him. And, because we know that God as revealed in Scripture is just, we can be sure that this is a just punishment, even if we can't explain why it is just. Of course, few theists would deny that God has every right to choose any punishment he wants, but that in itself doesn't prove his punishments to be just. We still need an explanation of how and why it is just.

Though a free will defender might handle the justice issue as just mentioned, I suspect that most would offer a further explanation of why they think this is a just punishment, and I can sketch what a free will defender could and probably should say about this. Consider what people who wind up in hell have done to merit that punishment. They have rejected a relationship with God. No matter how many times they have been called to repent and turn to God, by refusing to do so they have in effect said that they would prefer not to have a relationship with God. Many of these sinners fully understand that the punishment for rejecting God is eternal separation from God, but they still prefer that to having a relationship with God. In other cases, those involved don't know the full extent of punishment for rejecting God, but they believe it would be better than being forced to have a relationship with him. And it is certainly possible that even if they knew the extent of the punishment for rejecting God, they would do so anyway. Sinful human nature coupled with libertarian free will just turns out in many instances to be unredeemable. There can be no guarantees of repentance; the risk God takes in giving us such freedom results in those who reject God spending eternity in hell. But the risk is worth the freedom that goes along with it.

So, God has given humans free will to choose whether to love and obey him or reject him. Hell is a just punishment, because those who go there choose to do so. As C. S. Lewis says, "The doors of hell are locked on the inside."[40] In effect, God is saying that if you really don't want to have a relationship with him, he won't force you to do so. How can it be unfair to keep people from something they really don't want, a relationship with God?

Does the free will defense as I have adapted it to the problem of hell solve the logical problem of hell for theologies that use it? Here we must remember that "solving" means offering a *possible* explanation of how God's power and goodness fit consistently with the existence of hell. From my own perspective, if the basic free will defense solves the logical problem of moral evil, I see no reason why it won't work for the problem of hell. Moreover, as I have sketched how it might be applied to the specific question of hell, I believe it does allow theists holding such a theology to tell a logically consistent story. Of course, those who reject libertarian free will won't adopt this theology and its answer to any of the problems of evil, but that in itself shows no internal inconsistency in this theology's answer to the logical problem of hell. Of course, one might also hold that the "trade-off" of getting libertarian free will but also getting the real chance of using it to inflict upon oneself eternal separation from God isn't worth it. But that again shows no logical inconsistency internal to the free will defender's theology. It only suggests that there are reasons external to the system that would cause some to reject the theology with its various intellectual commitments (Modified Rationalism, libertarian free will, etc.) altogether. So, this defense does solve the logical problem of hell for a theology committed to libertarian free will.

What about the soul-building theodicy? Can it be used to solve the problem of hell? I believe so. In fact there are several ways this theodicy can solve its theology's problem of hell. The first is one we have already talked about—universalism. Regardless of what one believes about how horrible hell is, that doesn't count against God's power or benevolence, because God won't send anyone there. Of course, in this section of the chapter we are discussing solutions that maintain traditional beliefs about hell, so the universalism answer won't help.

What if many don't get their souls built during this life, and soul-building ends at physical death? Can this theodicy resolve its theology's logical problem of hell? I believe it can to a certain extent. As to God's morally sufficient reason for not removing hell altogether or not saving people from it, the reason is that evils, including hell, are being used by God to get people's attention and help them grow spiritually. It is possible that as some hear of hell as punishment for "unbuilt" souls that refuse to turn to God, those people will understand how serious God is about the need to grow spiritually and put away sin from one's life, and they will decide to yield to God and grow closer to him. If that should happen, then those who trust God in the midst of the realization of hell's significance are fulfilling God's purposes for not removing hell or other evils altogether; they are growing into spiritually mature individuals who know and love God better. Ours is one of those good possible worlds God could create, because in it, as a result of confronting and contemplating the evils around us, including the ultimate evil of hell for those who reject God, souls are built and prepared for an eternity of communion with God. To be sure, not everyone's soul is built, but those who couple libertarian free will with the soul-building theodicy can affirm that with this sort of freedom, one can't guarantee that everyone will choose God. Still, the fact that many souls are built justifies God in the face of evil.

So, the basic soul-building theodicy can handle part of the problem of hell. But how does it do in regard to showing that hell is a just punishment for those whose souls are not built? It is here that I believe the problem arises. Nothing per se about our world as a venue for soul-building explains why one of its evils, namely hell, is a just punishment for rejecting God. It seems that in order to make that case one must depart from the soul-building theodicy and move to another defense. For soul-building theodicists who believe in libertarian free will, the most likely refuge will be the free will defense as applied above to the problem of hell. Soul-building theodicists who hold compatibilistic free will could move to an approach like my defense, assuming that I can show that my defense can handle this problem.

The net result is that the soul-building theodicy per se can offer a morally acceptable reason for God not removing evil altogether, but it can't explain why hell is a just punishment for those who refuse to grow into children of God. Adding the free will defense or my approach (assuming that it explains why hell is a just punishment) to the soul-building theodicy can produce a successful answer, but the success ultimately comes not from the soul-building theodicy but from another defense. It appears, then, that in itself the soul-building theodicy doesn't solve the logical problem of hell.

What about my theological system? Is it possible to solve the problem of hell while holding the metaphysical and ethical beliefs of my system? I believe so, but there are several parts to my defense against the problem of hell. As already noted, my system is a Modified Rationalist theology that holds a non-consequentialist account of ethics and a compatibilistic notion of freedom. I have argued that what makes our world one of those good possible worlds God could create is that it contains non-glorified human beings. I also argued that even though these creatures have compatibilistic free will, God cannot maintain the integrity of human nature as created and still remove all evil (the reader may review the details of why this is so by reading chapter 6). And this just means that even with compatibilism, God can't get everyone always to do good, if he wants to maintain the integrity of humans as created. Sadly, one of the things he cannot do is guarantee and/or bring it about that everyone will choose to have a relationship with him. Some who initially reject God can be redeemed later in life, but not everyone. It isn't unlikely that at least some have decided to turn to God as a result of knowing that hell is the ultimate punishment for those who finally reject him. The fact that many have established a saving relationship with God shows that what God intended to do with our world (including the reality of hell for those who refuse to turn to God) has succeeded; ours is a good world. Moreover, anyone who thinks non-glorified humans are of significant value can agree that God has not erred in making such creatures.

So, my defense can handle the question of whether God has a morally sufficient reason for not removing hell, but can it convincingly explain why hell is a just punishment for those who reject God? I believe it can, but this requires further explanation. For one thing, I do agree that God as revealed in Scripture is a just God, and as omniscient and morally perfect it is hard to imagine that he wouldn't know what punishment(s) are just or that, knowing the just punishment, he would choose an unjust punishment for those who reject him or commit any other sin. Still, I recognize that many will see the appeal to the Scriptural portrait of God as just as question begging, since what is at issue now is whether or not hell is a just punishment. If it isn't, then that would cast grave doubts about the biblical teaching that God is just. So, we must do more than cite Scriptures that say God is just, holy, and omniscient.

There are two major considerations that lead me to conclude that hell is a just punishment. Moreover, I must further explain how my arguments relate to the question of whether hell is a just punishment for those who never heard the gospel. The first major consideration was already voiced when offering a defense of the free will defender's answer to the problem of hell. Though I hold compatibilism, not libertarian free will, that doesn't mean that free creatures' choices aren't their own or are forced upon them against their will. They are free to consider the evidence and argument for trusting God and the reasons for rejecting him. Whatever people do with the message, they choose in accord with their wishes and desires.[41] Hence, as with libertarian free will and the free will defense, in my system people wind up in hell because they have decided that they don't want a relationship with God. While God can bring into the lives of many factors which, upon reflection, cause those people to decide without being constrained that they want a relationship with God, given my defense against the problem of moral evil, there can be no guarantee that God can persuade *everyone* to choose him. Of course, if some people finally decide that they don't want a relationship with God for eternity, despite the consequences of that choice, it isn't unjust to give them what they want. God has warned humankind of the consequences of rejecting him. Those who hear that warning via Scripture, a missionary, or some other avenue and still prefer an eternity without God won't be forced to have a relationship with him. It isn't unjust to give informed people what they both deserve and want.

Some may reply that regardless of whether or not a person chooses hell, hell as traditionally understood is just too terrible. God should never have chosen such a devastating punishment. Even the worst of sinners sins only a finite amount, and yet this is an eternal punishment. How can a punishment that lasts forever be just recompense for a finite amount of evil? Some think that annihilation would be more just than consigning someone to eternal torment.

In comparing annihilation to hell as punishment for those who reject God, I don't think it is entirely clear that annihilation is any more just than hell. Annihilation also lasts forever. Anyone who thinks that life, even lived in the most meager of circumstances, is preferable to not existing at all won't be convinced that annihilation is more just than hell. To be sure, annihilation stops or avoids punishment and suffering altogether, but it isn't clear even so that this makes it more just than continued existence in hell. Perhaps it is more just, but I have yet to see the argument to that effect. Remember that if those who reject God are annihilated at death and if they know that this will happen, they must live their whole life with the knowledge that by rejecting God, they will become extinct upon death. For many, such knowledge could be absolutely terrifying, and it isn't clear that it would be less terrifying (and as well a more just punishment) than knowing that rejecting God would result in eternal conscious punishment (hell). Remember as well, that if the punishment for rejecting God is annihilation and one chooses it, there are no guarantees that those who reject God will have a long and enjoyable life before dying and extinction. It is fully possible that someone who chooses annihilation will live only into his teenage years. Given all of these considerations, is it clear that the kind of loss annihilation involves is fairer than the kind of punishment given to those in hell? I am unconvinced that it is, and I don't know how to show that it is fairer, if indeed it is.

Regardless of one's assessment of the comparative justness of hell and annihilation, many still think that hell is just too severe a punishment. But why? It is because they think the punishment (hell) far outweighs the crime (sin in general and in particular the sin of rejecting God). I believe the appropriate reply is that this objection rests on a misconception of how serious sin is. Humans as fallen creatures can be quite comfortable with sin. In fact, many who reject God altogether do so because they believe (rightly) that trusting God will mean that they have to change their conduct/lifestyle, and they are unwilling to stop committing certain sins which they especially enjoy. So, people react against hell as unjust not only because they think sin isn't so significant a problem that God should send someone to hell for it; many believe sin (at least some sins) is actually fun and desirable and hence should have no penalty whatsoever attached to it.[42]

All of this shows how far we have strayed from God's perception and assessment of sin. Those who think sin is bad but not so bad as to merit eternal punishment don't demonstrate the injustice of hell or the insignificance of sin; rather they show their own perversity and comfort with sin. Those who think sin isn't bad but rather is desirable are even further divorced from God's perspective. Indeed, humans living in a fallen world with sin all around may not like sin (at least when its negative results fall on them), but they are still used to it and have become to a certain extent anesthetized to its true nature. But sin, seen from the perspective of someone who is absolutely morally perfect and who has never had any evil thoughts, never made any evil choices, never done any evil deeds, and who doesn't dwell amidst sin so that he becomes "accustomed to it," is a much greater outrage than we humans can ever imagine.

I can make this point by way of an illustration. Consider the following: many of us are married and have children. Each child is born absolutely helpless. A newborn can't work to earn a living, can't speak to express his or her needs, can't clothe, feed, or house itself, or protect itself from danger. That baby is entirely dependent upon its mother and father. Those parents feed, clothe, protect, guide, and love that child; they do everything necessary to take care of the baby. What does any of this cost the baby? Nothing. All the parents ask is that their child obey certain rules that her parents set forth. Unfortunately, children don't always obey their parents. But when they don't do what Mom and Dad ask, their disobedience in many instances seems rather insignificant to them—no big thing. But do the child's parents perceive the child's disobedience as "no big thing"? Of course not! In many families, parents believe it is a serious thing for their child to disobey their rules. Some even think that obedience to parents is the least a child can and should do in light of everything her parents have done and are doing for her. So, depending on whether you have the perspective of a child or that of its parents, you will view disobedience to rules as quite significant or relatively unimportant. Moreover, from the child's perspective certain punishments the parents mete out for disobeying rules also seem excessive, but that doesn't mean the punishments are actually too much. A lot depends on one's perspective.

If this is true for human parents and their children, how much more so must it be true of the creator and sustainer of our universe and his human creatures! Sin isn't all that big a thing to us, but it is quite significant to a creator who has given us everything we have and asks only that we obey his rules. Just as the child believes that disobeying his parents is no big thing, so we judge sin not to be that big of a problem. Moreover, since we see sin as much less horrible than God does, we find ourselves offended at his punishments for various sins, just as the child thinks his parents are unfair to punish his "slight" misdeed with, in his opinion, a severe punishment. As in the case of children and their parents, so it is with God and his creatures; perspective makes a whole lot of difference. But once we realize this, it isn't at all clear that eternal separation from God in hell is an inappropriate punishment for someone who spurns God's love altogether. Humans tend to think otherwise, but that doesn't make it so. That only shows how different our perspectives are from God's. Hence, when one considers God's absolute holiness plus the creature's inability to appreciate how inappropriate sin is, it isn't clear that sin is as insignificant as we treat it or that hell is as unjust a punishment for rejecting God as many think it to be.

Some may still be unconvinced, but with the logical problem of hell all that is needed is a possible explanation which, if adopted, would remove the apparent inconsistency in the theology in question. The defense I have offered above certainly is possible, and if adopted by a theology like mine, it would produce an internally consistent theology. One can disagree with any of the parts of my defense and reject my theology altogether. But that doesn't prove the defense to be altogether inadequate. It does solve the logical problem of hell for my theology.

One issue remains. What I have said so far presumes that those who reject God are either fully informed or informed enough about the rules to understand what they are doing. What about those who have never heard the gospel? Can it be fair to send them to an eternity of hell? This seems to be the most difficult issue, but I think it can be answered. However, I must admit that whatever one thinks on this issue is based on inference; nowhere does Scripture clearly tell us why it is just to condemn the ignorant, but neither in Scripture nor beyond its borders is there a clear statement of why and how this is unjust. All sides must to some extent engage in inferential reasoning.

My explanation begins with Romans 1–2. In Romans 1:18-32 Paul affirms that all people at all times have had some revelation about God. They have it through the natural world around them (1:20), and through God's law written on their hearts (2:11-15). What may be known through these avenues of revelation? In Romans 1:20 Paul says that from the natural world it is possible to know that God exists, and to know something of his attributes, his power in particular. In addition, in our conscience there is a basic sense of right and wrong that everyone knows, regardless of whatever further written or oral law code they have. I don't think this means that every person on the basis alone of the law written in his heart has the exact same "do's" and "don'ts" as everyone else, though there is some overlap. The main thing that seems universal is that everyone has the concept that some things are morally right and others are morally wrong, and when they do things that are morally wrong, their conscience condemns them (2:15).

So, everyone has enough revelation to know that there is a God, something of what he is like, and a sense of right and wrong. Paul adds that as a result, they are without excuse. In other words, no one will tell God on judgment day (and be acquitted) that he would have believed in God but he had no idea whatsoever that there is a God. In Romans 1:21ff. Paul explains what humankind has done with that revelation of God. He says that humans sinfully refused to glorify God as God and rejected the revelation he had given of himself and of his moral will (1:21-23, 25, 28, 32). How did God respond? Did he withdraw or cut off this revelation? Not at all. Nothing in Romans 1–2 suggests that God ceased to reveal himself once people rejected the truth about him. God did judge them in various ways ("he gave them over," 1:24, 26, 28), but that judgment didn't include cutting off revelation to them. In fact, rather than withdrawing what he had revealed or ceasing to reveal more, natural revelation continued, and God added to it special revelation. Specifically, Paul notes that God gave the Jews the Mosaic Law, and we know as well that throughout history God has given various revelations of his law beyond natural revelation for humans of each era (see, for example, Gen. 2:16-17;12ff. [Abraham]; etc.). In addition, in spite of Jews and Gentiles alike rejecting God's revelation of himself in various forms, rather than withholding further information, God sent his Son into this world. The writer of Hebrews tells us that Christ is the highest form of revelation God has given of himself (Heb. 1:1-3); Jesus says that whoever has seen him has seen the Father (John 14:9), and Paul affirms that Christ is the exact image of the invisible God (Col. 1:15) and that in him dwells all the fulness of the Godhead in bodily form (Col. 2:9). The reaction to God's revelation of himself in Christ was rejection by most Jews and Gentiles. In response, did God cut off further revelation? On the contrary, he gave further revelation of himself in the pages of the fully inspired NT.

In sum, God has given various forms of revelation to various groups and some forms of revelation to all people. Moreover, when those receiving revelation rejected it, God didn't discontinue revelation; he gave more.

Now, if God continued to give more revelation when those receiving it rejected it, it stands to reason that he would have given more to anyone who accepted the revelation already given and attempted to live in accord with it. One of Paul's main points in Romans 1–3, of course, is that no one on their own apart from divine enablement has any concern to obey and live in accord with the revelation God has given. This is so, because all people are sinners who are unrighteous and go their own way, rather than obey God (Rom. 3:10-12). All are guilty before God whether they possess God's written law (Rom. 3:19) or only the law written in their hearts (2:15). Paul offers the answer to this problem, and it isn't more attempts to impress God by obeying his law so as to obligate God to grant us salvation. Rather the answer is to put on the righteousness of Christ which comes only by trusting Christ as one's personal Savior (Rom. 3:19-28).

Do not miss the point here for my defense against the problem of hell. Everyone has some revelation of God and is without excuse if they reject it (Rom. 1:20). In addition, God has given further amounts and forms of revelation over the centuries of history, in spite of the fact that humans have routinely rejected any and every piece of revelation given by God, and certainly they are guilty for doing so. Moreover, it only makes sense that if God gave more revelation to those who rejected it, he surely would give more revelation to those attempting to live in accord with it (by divine enablement, even if they didn't fully understand that such was the means of moving them to live in agreement with the revelation they had). So, at any time in history, information about God, including whatever God had revealed to that age and people about how to establish a relationship with him, was and is available to anyone who wants it. Those who don't get that information don't fail to get it because it was impossible to attain it; rather, they fail to get it because they reject even the truth they have and don't seek further truth about God. Hence, it is just to condemn even those who have never heard the gospel, because they have rejected the truth they do possess, and because more is available if they would ask God for it.

Some will, of course, deny what I have just said, because they think it impossible for someone to get revelation of God up to and including the message of salvation without possessing and reading a Bible or hearing a missionary explain the gospel. But that is wrong, because Scripture teaches that God has other ways of communicating his truth to someone who has never heard. Think, for example, of Job 33:13-18. Elihu is the speaker, and he and Job's other friends say a lot of things that are wrong—at least they aren't true of Job's situation, even if they are accurate statements about God's general providences. However, there is no indication that what Elihu says in verses 13-

18 is false. He says: "Why dost thou strive against him? For he giveth not account of any of his matters. For God speaketh once, yea twice, yet man perceiveth it not. In a dream, in a vision of the night, when deep sleep falleth upon men, in slumberings upon the bed; then he openeth the ears of men, and sealeth their instruction, that he may withdraw man from his purpose, and hide pride from man. He keepeth back his soul from the pit, and his life from perishing by the sword" (ᴋᴊᴠ).

What does this mean? Elihu is saying that God has ways of getting information to people who are in need of it. God can give information by means of dreams and visions, and that information can include what man needs to know in order that his soul will be kept from the pit. Is Elihu right, or is this just one of the many inaccuracies that he and his friends expound? Elihu is absolutely right, and we know that simply by reading the pages of Scripture. For in them we find many portions which were revealed to the writer in a dream or a vision (e.g., Daniel 7; 8; 9:23-27; Ezek. 40:2ff.; most of the book of Revelation). In other cases, God sent an angel to deliver a message (e.g., Matt. 1:20; 2:13; 28:5). In yet other cases, God spoke directly to someone in need of revelation (e.g., Saul on the Damascus Road—Acts 9:4-7). We should also remember that most of the writers of Scripture didn't get the majority of the ideas and words they put into their books from reading other books of the Bible or from talking to a missionary. Revelation of Scripture first went to the writers who, for most of the content of their writings, had no way of getting that information except by God himself giving it to them by any of the means (and more) mentioned in this paragraph. So, if God in the past could transfer his truth to people in times and at places where they had no access to other parts of the Bible or to missionaries, why can't he do the same thing in our day? Some may answer that everything changed when the canon of Scripture closed. Once God's written Word was complete, that was to be the sole means of revealing God's truth. That works as an answer if all people have access to the Bible, but we know they don't. Nor do they in some cases ever come in contact with a missionary. Their situation isn't unlike that of many biblical writers who had none of the Bible in their possession (in part because it hadn't been written yet) and who had no contact with a missionary. So, why is it impossible for God to get them information? He could send a missionary, but that isn't his only means, as we have seen above.

The upshot of this discussion is that not only do all people at all times have some revelation of God, but more, up to and including a message about salvation of their souls, is available, if they genuinely seek God. A God who gave more revelation to those who rejected it surely would give more to someone who sought it and lived in accord with what he already had. Even if we don't see how this can be true, God does have his ways; Elihu's general point about God's ability to communicate information in various ways is correct.

As a result, even those who never heard the gospel are guilty before God. They are guilty because they have some revelation of God already (and have rejected it), and could have much more, including the message of salvation, if they wanted. But no one on their own wants more truth or wants to live in accord with the truth they have, according to Paul. Hence, the fact that they don't get this further information isn't God's fault; it is their choice. God is just in holding them accountable for not turning to him; their condemnation and consignment to hell are fair, because they could have had more truth about God, but chose not to seek it and rejected even the amount they had.

Some will complain that this still isn't fair because God does enable some to seek him, and he does give more revelation to them so as to bring them to salvation. If he does this for some, why not for everyone else? It's unfair that only some get this further help from God. Actually, it isn't fair, and it isn't unfair either; it's gracious that God saves any of us. Being fair means being just and giving what is earned and deserved, but if justice is what we want, God's Word clearly says that all have sinned and so deserve punishment. So, what is fair, just, deserved is condemnation and punishment for all of us. But some are saved anyway, so why not others? That anyone is saved is a result of God's grace. Grace is unmerited favor. That means you get something good that you didn't earn, aren't owed, and don't deserve. Given the nature of grace, it can never be owed, so if God doesn't give grace to some, there is no obligation that he has failed to meet. Why does he extend grace to some and not to all? The answer is hidden in God's ultimate purposes for our world, but nothing obligates him to give grace to all; nothing obligates him to give grace to any. Hence, if he extends saving grace only to some, he hasn't failed to do anything he was obligated to do.

In light of these various aspects of my defense (my defense against the problem of moral evil, the point about unbelievers willingly choosing to reject a relationship with God, the further point about the horrendous nature of sin, and my answer to the condition of those who never heard), I believe that when taken together, they produce a theology that is logically consistent on these matters. Hence, the logical problem of hell for my theology is solved. Of course, one may reject my theology and its defense against the problem of hell because one disagrees with its intellectual commitments. But that is a rejection on grounds external to the system; no internal contradiction has been demonstrated by offering evidence against one or more of the claims of my defense and/or my theology in general.

The Evidential Problem of Hell

In addressing the evidential problem, I can be much briefer because of the work already done in chapters 8-12 and the previous material in this chapter. Readers can apply much of what was said in those chapters (especially my response in chapter 12 to the evidential problem) to the problem of hell. In this section, however, my focus is four main items. First, I want to direct readers' attention to my discussion (chapter 12) of strategies that can be used in addressing the evidential problem. I argued that one might adopt an offensive strategy which puts the burden of proof on the theist to show that theism in general is more probable than not, in spite of evidences of evil. Theists may use such a strategy when addressing the evidential problem of hell. However, I argued that given the nature of what is at issue (the relative probabilities of atheism and theism), one would be hard pressed to show conclusively (from the perspectives of both broad positions) that either atheism or theism of any sort is more probable. Hence, it is wiser to take a defensive posture which explains why the theist doesn't believe the atheist has made the case that atheism is more probable than theism (and/or that theism is actually improbable—i.e., its probability is less than .5). This is true whether considering the evidence of evil in general, the quantity of evil in our world, the intensity of some evils, the evil of hell, or any other evils found in our world.

Is adopting a defensive strategy rather than setting forth one's evidence for theism a cowardly maneuver? I don't think so, for several reasons. First and foremost, who picked this fight? Certainly it isn't the theist who claimed that he could show that theism is more probable than atheism, despite the existence of various evils, including hell. Rather, the atheist took upon himself the offensive strategy by attacking theism as improbable on the evidence of evil (hell, in this case). Atheists are certainly allowed to offer whatever probability judgments they want to make about theism, but that doesn't mean they can actually demonstrate either that theism is improbable or that atheism is more probable than theism by pointing to hell and other evils and by offering whatever other evidence for atheism they have. By picking this fight, the atheist has taken upon himself the burden of proof. Why should the theist shift that burden to himself? Why not just let atheists present their case and then explain why, if theists can, that case doesn't make theism improbable?

Another reason for theists to take a defensive posture even on the problem of hell comes from considerations Plantinga raised about the problematic nature of probability judgments. When you couple those concerns with the problems I raised in chapter 12 about the nature of probability assessments and about the nature of the sort of inductive argument involved in the evidential argument from evil, those problems still mitigate against the atheist convincingly making the case that evil, including the evil of hell, shows theism to be improbable. As explained in chapter 12, these considerations make it dubious that the atheist can even get this argument off the ground, so it is even less likely that such arguments, should one offer them, can succeed in confirming the atheist's point about theism.

My second point about the evidential problem of hell is that it is dubious that the atheist can make the case against theism on the basis of hell because of Plantinga's point (illustrated by his example of Feike the Frisian) that an evidential argument of the sort we are considering must be made on total evidence, not just on the basis of one piece of evidence. *Prima facie*, hell seems to be significant evidence against theism, especially if one overlooks various explanations we saw earlier in this chapter about what morally sufficient reason God might have for allowing it. But even though the existence of hell can be significant evidence in a case against God, it isn't total evidence. If we consider total evidence, we must include all of those defenses and theodicies theists propose, including the ones about hell offered in this chapter, which render their theologies logically consistent. Those defenses and theodicies serve as counterevidence to atheists' claims that theism in conjunction with evil is improbable. This is also true for the evidential problem of hell. In this chapter we have seen a variety of ways that theists can show their theologies to be internally consistent. Some of them incorporate the traditional teaching on hell and yet still wind up with a logically consistent theology. So, given the requirement that an evidential argument must consider total evidence, and in light of the ways we have seen in this chapter that theists can show hell to be consistent with their theologies, it is highly dubious that atheists can make a successful evidential case against theism on the basis of hell.

Third, a further set of problems arise for the evidential problem of hell in light of how difficult it is to make a successful probability argument about something as contentious as the relative merits and demerits of atheism and theism. Moreover, when this argument is cast in the form of Bayes' Theorem, a whole host of problems arise. How can atheists and theists alike agree on the prior probability of theism, or the posterior probability of theism upon evidence, and what counts as background knowledge and what counts as evidence? These issues arise whether one is considering the problem of hell or any of the other intellectual problems of evil. In chapter 12, I argued that there is an objective element to probability judgments, but also a subjective aspect. That subjective element makes it hopeless to think that theists and atheists can agree on numeric assignments for the various items in Bayes' Theorem. And if they can't, then the numeric result from working the math problem contained in Bayes' Theorem can't be one that atheists and theists can agree on. The good news for theists is that they aren't trying to prove that theism is more probable on evidence than not or more probable than atheism; they are only rebutting the atheist's claim that she can demonstrate on the basis of the existence of evil, including hell, that theism is improbable. If that case can't be made because atheists and theists can't agree on the numeric values in Bayes' Theorem, so much the worse for the atheist's project. Theism is in no way damaged; the theist didn't pick this fight and isn't attempting to prove evidentially that theism is probable or is more probable than atheism.

A final reason that atheism can't make a successful evidential case against theism on the basis of hell invokes a central theme of this book. Before we can assess whether evil, including hell, is conclusive evidence against theism, we must specify which conception of God is under scrutiny. As we have seen throughout this book, there are different forms of theism (even of what might be labeled traditional or evangelical theism), and depending on the intellectual commitments of a given theology, how the problem of evil even arises, let alone how it should be answered, depends on the nature of the theology under consideration. So we must again look at the major forms of theism considered in this book and see whether the evil of hell is conclusive evidence against theism. Here we can be brief, because most of the work has already been done in the earlier part of this chapter. We turn first to theonomy.

Can the existence of hell be conclusive evidence that theonomous theism is improbable? As we noted repeatedly in discussing theonomy, a lot depends on what God reveals concerning our obligations and his. God has the right and power to stipulate any moral rules he wants us to follow and to attach whatever penalty he chooses to disobedience. If God reveals that those who reject obedience to his law go to an eternity of conscious punishment in hell, he has done nothing wrong. When he sends to hell those who disobey him, he does nothing wrong. So, with this version of theonomy, the existence of hell can't serve as evidence that theonomy's God doesn't exist. Perhaps there are other evidences which show that theonomy as a whole is improbable, but the evidence of hell alone can't make such a case.

Suppose, however, that God obligates himself 1) to save every individual or 2) to use hell as punishment only for Satan and his demons. Suppose as well that he also reveals 3) that he has decided to send especially recalcitrant sinners to hell along with Satan and his minions. If God revealed all of 1)-3), then the existence of hell populated by such individuals would serve as strong evidence that the theonomous God doesn't exist. Of course, there is no reason to think that theonomists will inform us that their God has revealed anything whatsoever about obligating himself to remove hell or to keep everyone or even anyone from it. Since God isn't obligated to do these things, the fact that there is hell and that many people will experience unending conscious punishment there in no way proves it unlikely that he exists. Again, the atheist may reply that there is ample evidence against theonomy altogether, so the existence of its God is improbable. That may be so, but it would be beside the point of whether the existence and use of hell alone demonstrate that it is unlikely that theonomy's God exists.

What about Leibniz's God? Here the existence of hell not only doesn't count as conclusive evidence against Leibniz's God but instead, the existence and use of hell are arguments for believing in the moral goodness of Leibniz's God. For Leibniz's concern is that God create the metaphysically richest of all possible worlds. Such a world contains the maximal number of things, people, actions, events, etc., compossible. A world without hell is metaphysically poorer than one with it. The only issue then can be whether hell is compossible with everything else in our world, and it seems that it is. So, it is hard to see how the existence of hell serves as strong evidence against the existence of Leibniz's God. Of course, atheists may believe that on total evidence the basic tenets of Leibniz's views are improbable, but that in itself won't prove that the existence of hell alone renders his view of God improbable.

In turning to Modified Rationalist theologies, we must remember that there are three basic ways of responding to the problem of hell: universalism, annihilation/conditional immortality, and offering a morally sufficient reason for the existence of hell. As for the first option, a universalistic theology may be objectionable on biblical grounds, but it cannot be improbable on the grounds of hell. For according to universalism, there either won't be a hell at all, or it will exist but no one goes there. In either case, hell's existence won't make God's existence improbable.

Some who reject both the traditional doctrine of hell and universalism opt for annihilation/conditional immortality. On this view no one goes to hell; nonbelievers' lives are just entirely extinguished at death, while believers are granted immortality and an eternity of fellowship with God. Now there may be reasons to judge annihilation and the theologies that adopt it untenable (e.g., biblical evidence that there is ongoing conscious existence of the wicked after physical death), but such theologies can't be improbable solely because of the existence of hell, because with the annihilation/conditional immortality view, no one goes there.

What about the Modified Rationalist theologies that keep the traditional doctrine of hell and attempt to justify it by arguing that God has a morally sufficient reason for not removing it? Surely the existence of hell must count as evidence against these conceptions of God, but a probability judgment must be made on total evidence. Part of that evidence is the defense the theologian offers which explains God's reason for allowing hell to exist. As noted earlier in this chapter, the free will defense and my own defense, when adapted to the problem of hell, can produce a logically consistent theology.[43] In light of that, can the atheist be absolutely sure that these defenses don't raise the probability of these theologies to more than .5 probable? Atheists will probably think these theologies, even with their defenses against the problem of hell included, are still improbable. If that judgment stemmed entirely from objective evidences and arguments, presumably the atheist could convince the theist that his theology is improbable, or the theist could convince the atheist that it is probable. But as we have seen, probability judgments involve a subjective element. Since that is so, it is dubious that the atheist, when all evidence (including the theology's defense against its problem of hell) is considered, can convince the theist that the theist's view is improbable. Likewise, it is unlikely that the theist, when all evidence (including his theology's defense against its problem of hell) is considered, can convince the atheist that the theist's view is probable. What this means is that even when all evidence, including each theology's defense against the problem of hell, is considered with respect to the free will defender's theology and my theology, it is unlikely that the atheist's evidential case from the evil of hell can succeed. But then, so much the worse for atheism, since it was the atheist who picked this fight, but who can't successfully convince all sides that the existence of hell renders these theologies improbable. If theists had no defense against the problem of hell, then atheists' complaint against theism would be more believable. As we have seen, however, many Modified Rationalist theologies offer a morally sufficient reason for hell's existence and explain why hell is not unjust punishment. By doing so, they render inconclusive atheists' complaints that theism is improbable because of its belief in hell.

CONCLUSION

In this chapter, I have considered extensively the problem of hell. As we have seen, there are various ways one might address it, and many of those approaches do resolve it for the theologies involved. Some answers successfully resolve the problem at the expense of rejecting the traditional doctrine of hell. This will cause some no concern, but for those committed to biblical authority, they will seek another solution. Thankfully, as shown in this chapter, there are ways to maintain the traditional doctrine of hell and solve the problem of hell in its logical and evidential forms. This very difficult doctrine doesn't sound the death knell for traditional Christian theologies.[44]

Section IV
The Religious Problem of Evil

14

THE RELIGIOUS PROBLEM
OF EVIL

Why do bad things happen to good people? If God really loves us, why doesn't he stop the bad things that befall us? How can I serve or even worship a God who rewards my faithfulness with affliction? Most of us have probably asked these questions at some time or other. In fact, these are issues that for most of us begin our thinking about God and evil. They raise the personal dimension of the problem of evil.

Some years ago Alvin Plantinga wrote about the religious problem of evil in his work *God, Freedom, and Evil*. After writing of the more abstract theological/philosophical problem of evil, he noted that there is also a religious problem that confronts theists:

> in the presence of his own suffering or that of someone near to him he may find it difficult to maintain what he takes to be the proper attitude towards God. Faced with great personal suffering or misfortune, he may be tempted to rebel against God, to shake his fist in God's face, or even to give up belief in God altogether. But this is a problem of a different dimension. Such a problem calls, not for philosophical enlightenment, but for pastoral care.[1]

I read that statement many years ago. Intellectually, I agreed with it, but experientially, I didn't fully understand it. I had always viewed the problem of evil as a major hindrance that keeps unbelievers from turning to Christ and causes believers to turn away. I thought that as long as one had intellectual answers that explained why God allowed evil in the world and as long as one could point to specific benefits that might accrue in the life of the sufferer, the sufferer would be satisfied in his struggles with affliction. When I saw others struggle over their relationship with God because of some tragedy, I naively thought that if I could just talk with them and offer some of the answers contained in the earlier chapters of this book, that would resolve everything. I was somewhat impatient with those who seemed unable to move past these struggles. In principle, I agreed that sufferers need pastoral care, but I thought that a lot of that care involved explaining intellectually God's purposes in allowing evil. Maybe the religious problem isn't about philosophical enlightenment, but a healthy dose of philosophy couldn't hurt. Or so I thought.

More than fifteen years ago my perceptions on this matter changed dramatically as a result of experiences of evil that befell my family. Before these things happened, I couldn't have written this chapter, for I operated under the misguided ideas already mentioned. For a long time after these things occurred, I found it too painful to speak about this, let alone write about it. I offer it as an illustration of my point that the religious problem of evil is a different kind of problem than the others we have discussed. But my primary reason for writing about this isn't to evoke sympathy or pity, but hopefully to help those who suffer and those who minister to the afflicted.

Like many people, I grew up, went to school, got married, and began a career in relatively trouble-free circumstances. I had problems and afflictions as most people do, but nothing you would consider catastrophic or truly tragic. I knew that those who take a stand for Christ can expect to suffer, so I figured there were more troubles coming. But I figured that they would be like the rest I had endured—annoying, frustrating, and painful to a certain degree, but nothing totally devastating. After all, I reasoned, once one goes a certain distance with Christ and reaches a certain level of spiritual maturity, even really big problems aren't likely to derail spiritual growth. There might be temporary disruption in one's relation to the Lord, but that would soon be put to rest.

All of that changed for me on November 4, 1987, when we learned something far beyond my worst nightmare. For some years my wife Pat had experienced certain physical difficulties, though they weren't painful, and we didn't think they were real physical problems. They were symptoms of something, but we had no idea of what. As the years passed, they became more pronounced. We decided that we had to find out what the problem was and get it corrected. My wife eventually wound up at a neurologist who made the diagnosis. When she came home, I could tell something was wrong, but I never could have imagined what she was about to tell me. The doctor had diagnosed her as having Huntington's Chorea.

I had no idea about what that was, and you may not either. Huntington's Disease is a genetically transmitted disease. It involves the premature deterioration of the caudate nucleus of the brain. Symptoms are both physical and psychological. On the physical side, it involves gradual loss of control of all voluntary bodily movement. Psychologically, it involves memory loss and depression, and as the disease progresses, it can lead to hallucinations and paranoid schizophrenia. Symptoms do not begin until around thirty years of age at earliest, though some who have it show no signs of it until their later thirties or into their forties. It is a slowly developing disease, but over ten to twenty years or so it takes its toll, and it is fatal. Currently, there are some medications to help with symptoms, but there is no known cure. Only a few years prior to my wife's diagnosis had doctors even discovered the chromosome involved. At the time of her diagnosis, the exact genetic marker was unknown, but through ongoing research doctors and scientists have isolated the gene for this disease. Still, we are a good distance from a cure.

As bad as that news is, the story gets even worse. Huntington's Disease is controlled by a dominant gene. This means that only one parent needs to have it in order to transfer it to their children. Each child has a fifty-fifty chance of getting it, but as mentioned, symptoms don't show up until about thirty at earliest. We have three children, all born prior to Pat's diagnosis.

Since Huntington's is controlled by a dominant gene, those who have the gene get the disease. If they don't get the disease, they can't be a carrier. There are now tests that accurately tell whether someone at risk for the disease has the gene and will get the disease. However, there is a real dilemma over whether one should take this test or remain in the dark about this matter. If one takes the test and learns that one will get the disease, it may be impossible to get health insurance or employment. And, some who have found that they will get the disease have committed suicide rather than endure this lengthy and difficult disease. On the other hand, if one doesn't know, one must make decisions about career, marriage, and children in the dark.

After this news came, my initial reaction was shock and confusion. How could this be happening? Before we were married, we knew that my wife's mother had mental problems. At the time of our wedding, she had been in a mental institution for five years. We asked several people, including doctors, how likely it was that this might happen to my wife, believing all along that it was a purely psychological problem. Psychologists assured us that if my wife were to have such problems, they would have already surfaced. Since she was in her twenties and nothing had happened, there was no need to worry. We never imagined that there was a physiological base to my mother-in-law's problems or that the difficulty could be passed genetically to my wife. Nor did anyone else. Immediate family members knew nothing about this, and others who might have known said nothing. My father-in-law had at one time heard the name of the disease, but didn't ask for details about what it was. Everyone who might have known the truth either didn't know or did but withheld the information. Before we started our family, we checked again to see if anything hereditary that might harm the children could be passed on. Again, we were told there was nothing to fear.

So, none of this could possibly be happening, but it was. People who were supposed to know had said it wouldn't, but it did. I found it all very hard to believe. It was also unbelievable because of the doctor's basis of diagnosis. He did nothing more than observe Pat's symptoms and ask about her family history. No other tests were done that day, but the diagnosis was given. I complained that this was all too inferential. Such minimal data didn't warrant that conclusion. No philosopher would accept that kind of argument. For several months I was torn between hope that it wasn't true and fear that Pat's problems could be nothing else. A second opinion by a specialist doing research on the disease confirmed the diagnosis. All hope that it wasn't true was lost.

INITIAL REACTIONS

After the initial diagnosis and later confirmation, I was besieged by a host of emotions. Even to this day, I still wrestle with those feelings. I believe others who experience tragedy undergo similar reactions. If we are to minister to those who are hurting, we must understand how they feel. The predominant reaction I experienced was a feeling of hopelessness and helplessness. There had been problems before, but usually there was some way out. In fact, usually, I could figure out something to do and do it. But not this time. When no one knows the exact cause of the problem, no one can offer a solution.

I felt that the situation was absolutely hopeless. I would have to watch my wife whom I dearly love slowly deteriorate and die. Maybe as the disease progressed, she wouldn't even know me. Or possibly worse, she would know me but would turn against me as she imagined that I had turned against her. After all, my mother-in-law had misjudged my father-in-law's reasons for putting her in a mental institution for the last years of her life. Then, Pat would eventually be gone, and yet it still wouldn't be over. The same thing could happen to each of our children. I remember thinking that this threat of doom would hang over me and my family every day for the rest of our lives. There was no morally acceptable way out. There was only one person who could do anything about this, and it appeared at that time that he wasn't. The situation seemed hopeless. I realized how dismal life can seem when there is no hope.

Beyond the hopelessness, I felt helpless to do anything. I was experiencing physical problems myself that were only exacerbated by the stress from this news. Before long I came to a point where I was barely able to do my work. And I wasn't much help to my family either. I wanted at least to comfort my wife and help her deal with this distressing news. But all along she has handled this situation far better than I. Somehow God gave her strength and victory over the situation, and she didn't seem to need my help. I felt locked out of her life at this most critical time, and I felt as though I could be of little help. Whatever therapeutic value there might be for me in comforting her was lost.

Though your situation is probably different than mine, if you have confronted this sort of affliction, I suspect that you have had similar feelings of hopelessness and helplessness. Along with those feelings comes as well the sense of abandonment. At a time like this, one feels as though there is no answer and no one to help. Yes, there are friends and family, but what can they do? They aren't doctors, but even the doctors don't have a cure for this disease, so what could others do? Anyway, they have their own families to care for and their own problems.

Something else heightens the feeling of abandonment. Invariably when news like this comes, people are very concerned, but they tend to stay away. They are afraid they will say the wrong thing at a time like this. Nobody wants to be like Job's comforters who over time became his accusers! Better to stay away than take the chance of sticking one's foot in one's mouth. But staying at a distance only serves to confirm the worst fears of the person suffering. He feels abandoned, and by keeping your distance you communicate that he is. And the problem isn't just that one feels abandoned by friends at this point. The deeper fear and pain is that God is no longer there. It doesn't matter how much you have sensed God's presence in your life before. At a time like this, he seems absent. And when you know that he is the only one who can do anything about your problem, it is especially painful to sense his absence.

It goes without saying as well that these emotions are accompanied by anger. The anger may not be particularly rational, but it is real. I was angry that this was happening to us. I never expected exemption from problems just because I am a Christian, but I never thought something like this would happen. In one fell stroke, we learned that my whole family was under this cloud of doom. That kind of catastrophe wasn't supposed to happen. I was angry. Since I had known before I married that God wanted me in the ministry, and having been raised in the home of a well-known Christian educator and minister, I had a pretty good idea about the nature of the life I would lead. It would require lots of time and effort, but it was what God wanted me to do. Given that mindset, had I known the truth about my wife's family medical history, I wouldn't have married her. Pat has said that had she known, she probably wouldn't have married at all. If we had known, we wouldn't have had children. Nobody wants to put people they most love in this kind of jeopardy! I was angry at family members who knew and didn't tell us. I was angry at the doctors who knew and never explained it to the family. And I was angry at family members who didn't know but could have asked the doctors for an explanation but didn't. If anyone had given us the information before we married, I could have avoided this situation.

Though I didn't want to admit it, I was also angry at God. I knew that was foolish. After all, God hadn't done this. Nor could I think of anything in or out of Scripture that obligates God to keep this from happening. Beyond that, it was foolish to be angry at the one person who could do anything about it. Anyway, who was I, the creature, to contest the creator? As Paul says (Rom. 9:19-21), the creature has no right to haul the creator into the courtroom of human moral judgments and put him on trial as though he has done something wrong. God has total power and authority over me. It was foolish to be angry with one who has such total control over my every move.

Still, it is human nature to be angry and expect something different from God. In my case, it wasn't just that he had allowed this to happen to us. I felt that God had somehow misled me, even tricked me. When Pat and I first met, we were sure there was no way we would marry. I was headed into teaching, and she was headed to the mission field. This could never work out. Our relationship grew, but I feared that we were headed for trouble if we continued, because it seemed God was leading us in different directions. One night I went to break off the relationship, because I was sure God couldn't want us to fight his will to send us in different directions. As Pat and I talked, we began to realize that she had a definite call to full-time ministry, but there was no clear call to missions. We continued to see each other and prayed about this whole thing, telling the Lord to break it off (as painful as that would be) if he didn't want us together. Rather than destroying the relationship, the Lord made it abundantly clear in various ways that he wanted us to marry.

With that background, perhaps you can sense why I felt I had been misled. The Lord knew I was going into a very demanding ministry. He knew that I needed a wife to help me, and he knew that if I was really to give myself to the ministry he was giving me, I would need at least a relatively healthy wife. My mom had suffered with various physical problems, and I had seen the strain that had put on Dad and his ministry. But Mom was never incapacitated so that she couldn't function in the home on a consistent basis. I reasoned that God knew all of that, so he would give me at least a relatively healthy wife. Beyond that, the Lord had so clearly led us to marry, and those who had been asked about whether Pat could have the same problems as her mother had assured us there was nothing to worry about. Now I had learned the horrible truth, and I felt that I had been tricked. I had been led down a path only to learn that I wasn't getting what I thought I was.

I remember thinking at the time that none of this made any sense. God is the supremely rational being, and yet it seemed that he was actualizing a contradiction in my life! The news of my wife's illness seemed to contradict the Lord's leading in my life over the previous fifteen years. I didn't know what to do, and I didn't even know what to think. At one point, I thought about Abraham. God had given him Isaac, the child of promise, only to tell him to sacrifice Isaac on Mount Moriah. That must have made no more sense to Abraham than my situation made to me. And yet Abraham had believed, anyway. He believed that if he sacrificed Isaac, God would resurrect Isaac from the dead (Heb. 11:19).

What incredible faith! I thought. I should be more like Abraham. Surely, his situation should comfort and encourage me. But it didn't. I remembered only too quickly that it was reasonable for Abraham to believe, because God had made very specific promises about this son (Gen. 12:1-3; 15:4-6; 17:15-19). God had made no such promises to me about my wife and children. He had made it clear that Pat and I should marry, and he had seen to it that information that would have kept us from having children was hidden. But he had never promised that there would be no catastrophic illness. There had never been any promises about how long or healthy a life any of us would live. Yes, God could perform a miracle (as Abraham expected in Isaac's case) and heal all of them, but there were no guarantees that he would—no promises that necessitated a miraculous healing. As instructive as the Abraham and Isaac case is, I had no right to take comfort from it.

None of this made sense to me, and I was confused. I was also confused for another reason. I was raised around people who suffered greatly. As I mentioned, my mother had one physical problem after another. I can't remember a time when there wasn't some significant problem. In part, I am sure, because of her experiences, I became interested at an early age in the problem of pain and suffering. As I grew up, I thought about it repeatedly. In seminary, I wrote my Master of Divinity thesis on Job. Later, my Master of Theology thesis was on God's sovereign control of all things and how that relates to human freedom. Then, my doctoral dissertation comprises many of the chapters of this book. If anyone had thought about this problem and was prepared to face real affliction, surely it was I. And yet when the events I have recounted happened, I found little comfort in any of it. I couldn't figure it out. I had all these intellectual answers, but none of them made any difference in how I felt. The emotional and psychological pain were unrelenting, and the physical results from the stress and mental pain were devastating.

Why didn't all the years of study, reflection, and writing on the problem of evil help at this moment of personal crisis? I was experiencing a religious crisis, and none of this information I had stored away seemed to
matter. As I reflected on this, I came to what for me was a very significant
realization. All my study and all the intellectual answers were of little help
because the religious problem of evil isn't primarily an intellectual problem.
Instead, it is fundamentally an emotional problem! People wrestling with
evil as I was don't need an intellectual discourse on how to justify God's
ways to man in light of what's happening. That's what is needed to solve
the abstract theological/philosophical problem of evil and the other problems handled earlier in this book. This, on the other hand, is a problem
about how someone experiencing affliction can find it in himself to live with
this God who doesn't stop it.

This doesn't mean that no spiritual truths or intellectual answers can help
the sufferer. It means that many of those answers won't help with this problem and that others that do won't help at all stages in the sufferer's experience. They must be used at times when the emotional pain has healed enough
so that the sufferer is in a frame of mind for them to make a difference.

It was at this point that I understood experientially Plantinga's point
about the religious problem requiring pastoral care, not philosophical discussion. And I would urge you to take this very seriously, if you want to help
those struggling with the religious problem. I can illustrate the point by a simple example. Think of a young child who goes out to play on a playground.
Sometime during her play, she falls and skins her knee. She runs to her mother
for comfort. Now, her mother can do any number of things. She may tell her
daughter that this has happened because she was running too fast and not
watching where she was going. She must be more careful the next time. The
mother, if she knew them, might even explain to her child the laws of physics
and causation that were operating to make her child's scrape just the size and
shape it is. The mother might even expound for a few moments on the lessons
God is trying to teach her child from this experience.

If she then pauses and asks her daughter, "Do you understand,
Sweetheart?" don't be surprised if the little girl replies, "Yes, Mommy, but it
still hurts!" All the explanation at that moment doesn't stop her pain. The
child doesn't need a discourse; she needs her mother's hugs and kisses. There
will be time for the discourse later; now she needs comfort.

The same is true for each of us as we struggle with the religious problem
of evil. We don't want or need immediately a lengthy lecture to appeal to our
mind, because this isn't primarily an intellectual matter. What we need is
something to take away the pain. And a very big part of that pain is not

knowing what these events mean about how God feels about us or how we should feel toward him.

THINGS THAT DON'T HELP

If the religious problem of evil isn't primarily about justifying God's ways to man but about how one can live with this God, how can we help people through this difficult time in their life? I can only answer in terms of things that weren't helpful to me, and things that did make a difference. Hopefully, this will help you whether you are struggling with suffering or only hoping to minister to those who are.

Invariably, people will try to say something they hope will help. Sometimes it does, but often it is extremely insensitive and only drives the sufferer into further despair. Let me mention some things that are inappropriate to say. Someone may say, "There must be some great sin you've committed; otherwise this wouldn't be happening to you." I am very thankful that no one said this to me or my family, though it is a common reaction when others hear of severe affliction. This was the reaction of many of Job's miserable comforters. They didn't really know what was happening, but they were sure it wouldn't look good for God if a righteous man suffered. So they reasoned that God would allow this to happen only to the guilty.

While it is true that God punishes sin, and the wicked will have a day of judgment, Scripture is very clear that sometimes the ungodly prosper (Psalm 73) and the righteous suffer (Job 1:8; 2:3; 1 Pet. 4:12-19). The truth is that in most instances we don't really know whether someone suffers as a righteous person or as a sinner. Outwardly moral people may be great sinners, and even those who seem righteous may be guilty of some hidden sin. The story of the rich man and Lazarus (Luke 16) is a vivid reminder that outward appearances aren't a good basis for judging spirituality. If someone is suffering in punishment for sin, that person will likely know it without our saying a thing. If that person doesn't realize it, it is still probably better to ask him what he thinks God is saying through the affliction, rather than to offer our opinion. And, if someone is suffering for righteousness' sake, as was Job, it won't help if those who aren't suffering assume an attitude of moral superiority and accuse the sufferer of sin.

Another mistake is to focus on the loss of things rather than the loss of people. I don't speak from personal experience, but from that of a relative. Some years ago a relative was on vacation. While on vacation, she learned that her home had burned to the ground, trapping and killing her son who was unable to escape. Her pastor tried to be of help, but made some significant mistakes in handling her situation. For one thing, he made very little attempt to see her and allow her to talk out her feelings. And then, the few times he did say something, he expressed concern over the loss of her house and possessions. You can imagine how hurt she was. The loss of one's home and possessions is not insignificant, but in one way or another, those things can be replaced. The loss of a loved one is the greatest loss. How does one replace a son? That pastor missed the point of her grief. By his insensitivity, he missed the opportunity to minister to her in her time of crisis, and hindered rather than helped the healing process in her life.

Sometimes when we lose a loved one people will try to comfort us by convincing us that what has happened spares us from other problems. Here I relate the experience of one of my students. He and his wife had their first baby, and he was in my class for the term just after the baby's birth. About midway through the term, the baby very suddenly and unexpectedly died. After the funeral and toward the end of the term, he shared with the class some of what he had learned. Part of what he told us focused on things not to say to someone experiencing such grief. He told us how some people had said, "You know, it's probably a good thing that your son died. He probably would have grown up to be a problem. Maybe he'd have been a drug addict or would have refused to follow Christ. God knows these things in advance, and he was probably just saving you from those problems."

I trust that no one thinks this is an appropriate thing to say. It may be true that the child would have been a problem, but it is hard to see how that information is a comfort at the time of loss. Parents and relatives love that child, and they love him regardless of whether or not he is or would be a problem. Their loss is extremely painful, and the pain isn't eased, let alone removed, by insensitive speculations about the future. Moreover, the comment is wrong, because it in effect says that it is good that evil has happened. I don't see how that can ever be an appropriate attitude for a Christian. Yes, James says we are to count it all joy when we fall into various afflictions (James 1:1-2), but we must not misunderstand this. The affliction is not joy; it is evil. The cause for joy is that in spite of the evil, God is with us and can accomplish positive things in our life even in the midst of affliction. But the affliction isn't a good thing. If it were, we might be inclined to seek suffering. Obviously, nothing in Scripture suggests that we should do that. Anyway, we don't have to seek affliction; it has a way of finding us.

There are other comments that don't help either, and here I do speak from personal experience. Not long after we learned the truth about my wife's condition someone said to me, "Well, you know, everyone's going to die from something. You just know in advance what it is in your wife's case."

Even if this were true, in what respect can it be a comfort? Does the thought of your own death bring you comfort? If you knew in advance the *cause* of your own death, would you be inclined to say, "Ah, well, very good; now I can rest easy knowing what will get me"? No one likes to reflect on their own or a loved one's demise. That it will happen to all of us is no encouragement, nor is knowing the manner of our death. That is true even if ours will be an "easy death," let alone if we face death from a catastrophic disease. At the time of someone's grief, don't think you will help them by reminding them that others will also die someday or that at least they know in advance how they will die.

The other problem with this comment is that it isn't necessarily true. Indeed, the likelihood that my wife will die of Huntington's Disease is great, but it isn't absolutely certain. She could die of a heart attack, in a car accident, or some other way. None of that is cause for rejoicing either, but it does show that the comment in question is neither helpful nor necessarily correct.

Likewise, it doesn't help to remind me or my wife that despite her disease and despite the fact that it takes people when they are relatively young, I might still die before she does. That could be true as well, but I don't find it comforting to think that at a time when she is least able to function and most needs my help, I might not be there. And that is no encouragement for her either.

One of the most typical comments is one I have made myself at times when visiting the sick or the bereaved. As we fumble for something to say that will comfort our friend or loved one, somehow it seems appropriate to say, "I know how you must feel at a time like this." Through my experiences, I have learned how inappropriate and unhelpful this comment can be. The problem is really twofold. On the one hand, the problem is that it isn't true, and the sufferer knows it. Hence, it sounds phony when you say it. Even if you think you know how I feel, and even if the same thing happened to you, you don't and you can't know how I feel. You can't, because you are not me with my particular personality and emotions, with my background and experiences, with my particular family and the relations to one another we share. Nor can I know exactly how you feel when suffering comes your way. Telling me that you know how I feel sounds insincere, a cheap way to try to comfort me, because I know it can't be true.

Now, it may be, especially if something similar has happened to you, that you tell me this, because you think I might be encouraged by seeing that others have suffered greatly and yet have survived it. If that is your point, then why not simply say that, rather than saying you know how I feel? What you say may still not comfort me, because I may be in too much pain at the time to think I'll ever make it through this crisis. You can say this from the vantage point of looking back at the crisis and seeing that you survived. I am still in the midst of the crisis. Your experience is no guarantee that I'll make it.

So your reassurance that others have survived tragedy may not comfort me. But at least that comment, if you make it, is true. You aren't telling me you know how I feel when I know you can't know how I feel. You are simply saying that though these things are hard, others like yourself have experienced tragedy and still survived. Unless I am totally different from everyone else, it is possible for me to make it, too.

The other problem with saying you know how I feel is that it really doesn't matter whether you know how I feel. For one thing, do you think I would rejoice in knowing that you feel as miserable as I do? I wouldn't wish my feelings of grief on my enemies, let alone my friends. To know that you feel as bad as I do would make me feel worse, not better. But beyond that, the fundamental reason it doesn't matter if you know how I feel is that this information alone won't help me. What helps is not knowing you feel like I do, but knowing that you care!

Look at it this way. Suppose some horrible tragedy happened to you, suppose I had experienced the same thing, and suppose I know you. Suppose I tell you, "You know, friend, I know exactly how you feel. I've been there myself. But, you know what? I know how you feel, but I don't really care about what's happening to you." Would that comfort or help you? Of course not! But if I tell you I don't know how you feel, but I do care, and I want to be of help, that will make a difference. Remember, the sufferer feels helpless, hopeless, and abandoned. He doesn't need us to identify with his situation or "feel his pain." He needs us to care and to show that care by helping however we can. He doesn't need us to share his feelings; he needs us to share his burdens!

Here it is very important to recognize the difference between "I know how you feel" and "I really feel for you." The former identifies with the sufferer. The latter shows our concern. It doesn't matter whether you know how I feel. You can't really know, anyway. What does matter is that you care!

Let me mention a final set of comments I found thoroughly unhelpful. As the months wore on after my wife's diagnosis, I longed to have someone to talk to about how I felt. A dear, godly colleague who has been a friend for many years offered to listen. I began to explain how perplexed I was because of how things had happened. It seemed that God had hidden information from us about my wife prior to our marriage and prior to having children. I noted that, on a Calvinistic conception of God that sees God in control of all things, this was especially troublesome. But even if I were more inclined toward an Arminian notion of God, it still seemed God should have intervened in our behalf. After all, hadn't we prayed that God would lead us and keep us from making a wrong decision about whether to marry? My friend replied that I was talking about this concept of God and that model of God. What I really needed to do was stop such talk and recognize that God is bigger than all those conceptions.

There is something right about what my friend said. Surely, we can never hope to understand our majestic and mighty God thoroughly through human thought forms. Yet I found my friend's comments unhelpful. For one thing, he failed to see that his comment about God being bigger than all our conceptions of him is itself another conception of God. But that wasn't the real problem. The real problem was that my friend in essence was saying that things would be better for me if I just changed my notion of God. Now, it is true that a sufferer who is an atheist needs to change her perception of God. A Christian who has little training in theology might also need a better understanding of God. In fact, even a theology professor could hardly be hurt by adjusting his views to a more accurate picture of God.

But there is still a major problem in thinking that this will resolve the religious problem of evil. The problem with telling someone in this situation that all they really need to do is just change their view of God is that the comforter is treating what is fundamentally an emotional problem as if it were an intellectual problem. Please do not misunderstand this. The sufferer may have a wrong notion of God, and at some point in dealing with her, we must help her get a better picture of God. But if the religious problem is, as I suggest, at root an emotional hurt, that must be handled first. And you don't handle that problem by telling someone to adjust her idea of God. You can change your view of God and still find that the pain remains!

There are other forms of this error that are just as common among Christians. One is, "You know, if you were a Calvinist, you'd see that God is in control of all of this, and then you could rest in him." Another is, "If you weren't so Calvinistic, you wouldn't think God has his hand so directly in everything, and then you'd stop blaming him for what's happened to you." Perhaps the most common is, "When things like this happen, aren't you glad you're a Calvinist? Isn't it great to know that God is ultimately in control of it all, and he's already planned the way out of your problem?"

The first two of these comments are really saying that this whole thing will be all right, if you just change your view of God. The third doesn't tell the sufferer to get a new concept of God, but tells him to take comfort in his beliefs about God. But don't assume this will in fact comfort everyone. I am a Calvinist, and I found that comment distressing, not helpful. Because of my belief in God's control of all things and because of what I thought about how it appeared that God had misled me, I took no comfort in the fact that I was a Calvinist. In fact, I remember thinking quite frequently that everything that had happened to me and my family would be easier to take if I were an Arminian. At least then I wouldn't see God so actively and directly in control of what had happened.

What was the problem here? Was it that I really needed to discard my Calvinism as inadequate? Not at all. Had I been an Arminian, what had happened would still hurt terribly. The problem was that others who made the comment, and I as well, thought this deep emotional wound could be salved by simply reflecting on this intellectual concept. Indeed, there is a time for explanation and reflection upon what one knows to be true of God. If one's ideas about God are wrong, there is also a time for changing them. But not when the hurt is so deep and so new! Remember the little girl with the skinned knee. In answer to her mother's explanations she says, "Yes, Mommy, but it still hurts."

Remember as well Plantinga's point. This isn't a problem that requires philosophical (and, I would add, theological) discourse; it requires pastoral care. In any given case, no one can predict how long it will take for the pain to subside to the point where the sufferer is ready to think seriously about concepts of God. But until it does, it won't help the afflicted to tell them to change their view of God or simply meditate on what they believe about him.

There was one other thing I found unhelpful in the midst of this emotional and spiritual turmoil and upheaval. I was concerned about my response to our situation, and I felt guilty that I was not on top of things. After all, Christians are supposed to rejoice in all things and persevere no matter what. Beyond that, as one in a position of Christian leadership, people would be looking all the more closely at me to see how I handled this. Still, I was finding it hard to cope. I preach quite frequently, but for about six months I was physically and emotionally unable to preach. Even more, I felt that anything I would say would be hypocrisy, since I wasn't living whatever I might preach.

All of this was disturbing enough, but my uneasiness increased. One day I was listening to a Christian radio program. A husband and wife who had lost a daughter in her twenties in an automobile accident were giving their testimony. They recounted what had happened to their daughter and how, as a result of these events, various people had come to know the Lord. They concluded that even though the loss of their daughter was hard, it was all for the best. It was good that this had happened. I heard that and I only felt more guilty. It seemed the height of Christian maturity to take life's harshest blows and say that it was good that this had happened. If that was what it meant to be victorious in the midst of affliction, I knew I was far from that. I couldn't rejoice over the evil that had befallen and would befall my family. But I thought I was supposed to, so my sense of inadequacy increased.

When I went to talk with my friend and colleague, as I suggested above, some things he said weren't helpful. But what he said on this matter was most helpful. I told him I knew I was supposed to respond Christianly in this situation. But did that mean I had to like what was happening? Without batting an eyelash he responded, "You do have to learn to live with this, but that doesn't mean you have to like it!"

This may sound like heresy to some. Popular Christian belief reminds us to rejoice in everything and count it all joy when trials come our way. One isn't really "with it" spiritually unless he can say the affliction was a good thing—or so we are told. But I beg to differ. Thinking that way won't help you cope with your grief; it will only add to it as you feel guilty about your inability to do what you think we are called to do.

My friend was right, and I came to see why as I reflected on this over the following weeks and months. Those verses don't say the affliction is good or that it is a cause for rejoicing. They say that we are to rejoice when these things happen, because God is sufficient in the midst of trials. We are to rejoice because we can see what God is accomplishing in spite of the trial. Affliction may prove to be the occasion for God to do good things in our life, but the suffering isn't good. It is still evil.

Because the affliction is evil I am neither required to like it nor should I. We live in a fallen world. That is why it is even possible for these things to happen. Scripture is very clear that people die because of sin (Rom. 5:12). If people are going to die, they must die from something, and that means there will be diseases that take life. But if what is happening to my wife (and will happen to all of us in some way or another, barring the Rapture) is ultimately the consequence of living in a sinful, fallen world, how can I applaud it? As a Christian, I am called to resist sin and its consequences in all forms. How, then, can I like it when the consequences of sin befall anyone, let alone a loved one? No, you don't have to like it, and if you properly understand why this is happening, you had better not like it!

It is wrong in another respect to suggest that the sufferer like what is happening. It is wrong because it ignores our humanness. Grief and sorrow in the face of tragedy are very human emotions. Unless they are admitted and expressed, they will remain inside us and destroy us. Healing can't come if we deny what we are feeling and act as though it is good that evil has occurred. Those negative feelings must be admitted, expressed and dealt with, not hidden so that the sufferer *acts* as though everything is all right. We can't help the afflicted if we expect them to deny their humanness.

Realizing that I didn't have to like what was happening relieved a great burden from me. But other things helped me as well. In the rest of this chapter I want to turn from things that didn't help to things that did. The things I shall mention didn't all happen at once, and in some cases it took a while after they occurred for their import to sink in. If you are wrestling with the religious problem of evil, I trust that you will read these comments with that in mind. None of it may help you now, but don't hesitate to come back to part or all of it later.

Things That Helped

Though many things didn't help me, others did. One thing that did help over time came in a conversation with my father several weeks after we first received my wife's diagnosis. I was bemoaning the fact that the situation looked so hopeless. I couldn't see how I would be able to handle it as Pat got worse. And on top of that there was the prospect of having to go through the same thing with one or more of our children. I didn't know how I could take it. At that point Dad said, "John, God never promised to give you tomorrow's grace for today. He only promised today's grace for today, and that's all you need!"

How true that is! In that one comment I was reminded both of God's grace and of my need to take each day one at a time. As I have thought about those truths, God has impressed upon me the fact that I don't have to live my tomorrows today. I don't know how I'll cope when my tomorrows come, but I know that they will come only one day at a time, and with each day, even as now, there will be grace to meet each new challenge. That doesn't mean it will be fun, but it does mean that for each day God will provide the strength needed.

As a result of those truths, I began to readjust my focus from the future to the present. I would begin each day asking God for just the grace needed to sustain me that day. As that prayer was answered day after day, I gained more assurance that God would be there when things got worse. As a result, I found that I worried less about the future and focused more on the present day and its responsibilities.

Another major factor in helping me to cope, though I didn't realize it at the time, was seeing that God and others really do care. I spoke earlier of the sense of abandonment and helplessness one feels. There is a sense that an incredible burden has been put on one's shoulders, and no one is there to help carry it. In the midst of those feelings, God used various people to show me that he and others knew what I was going through and cared.

Several incidents in particular were especially meaningful. Shortly after the news came about my wife, my brother came to encourage me. I remember him saying that though I might feel abandoned at that moment, God hadn't abandoned me, and neither had he or the rest of my family. At that point I was still in such shock that I didn't realize enough to know that I was feeling a sense of abandonment. But God knew it, and sent my brother to reassure me.

I remember as well an important visit from my pastor. No one told him to come, and we hadn't asked that he come. He knew we were hurting, and he cared enough to come. I remember well what his first words to me were. He told me that he couldn't begin to know how I felt, but he wanted me to know that he really cared about what was happening, and he and the church wanted to help in any way possible. At the time, he may not have realized how right what he said was, but it was what I needed to hear. He didn't say much more, but he was willing to be there and listen. His presence said enough; he cared. At a time when it seems impossible to survive the trial and when everything appears hopeless, we need to know that someone cares and will help.

After that first visit, there were other visits, and words were matched with actions. My pastor had noticed that our home was in need of some decorating. He took it upon himself to get together a group of people from the church to come over and do it. It was his way and theirs of saying they loved us, were sorry about what had happened, and wanted to do something tangible to express that care. I remember thinking at the time that this was God's way of showing me that in a future day when I needed more involved help to care for my wife, his people would be there as well.

Not only have people at my church been helpful and caring, but so have colleagues and students at school. Students on their own initiative set aside special times each week to pray for us. Colleagues also pray for us, and both express their concern by asking periodically how we are doing and if they can help.

Those in administration at my school also showed in various ways that they cared and were willing to help. It was difficult for me to teach many of my classes at that time. Rather than scolding me or threatening to take my job, those in administration responded with patience and understanding. I was scheduled for a sabbatical that first academic year when the news came, and I didn't know how I would fulfill my responsibilities. I was in sufficient physical pain, let alone emotional stress, that I didn't know how I would be able to write during my sabbatical. I mentioned this to the president and dean, suggesting that perhaps I should postpone the sabbatical. They took a more compassionate approach. The president and board told me to take the quarter off, and to consider it a combination sabbatical and medical leave of absence. I was told not to worry about how much writing I would accomplish. Though I did in fact get much done that sabbatical, that didn't overshadow their care, concern, and compassion toward me at this difficult time.

All these events and more showed me that there were people who cared and would be there when things got worse. I also saw these things as God's sign that he cared as well. All of this ministered to me greatly and helped to overcome the feeling of abandonment, hopelessness, and helplessness.

But I realized through this in an even fuller way that God did care for me. There is part of the story I have left until now. After my wife was first diagnosed, and before we went for a second opinion, we requested a copy of my mother-in-law's chart from the hospital in New York. Because she had died some ten years earlier, and because of my wife's situation, they sent us the chart.

When the chart came, I began to look through it. My mother-in-law had been admitted to that hospital in 1967, five years before my wife and I met and married. As I read the chart, I didn't understand much of it, but one thing I saw horrified me. Within a few months of her arrival at the hospital, the family medical history and the diagnosis of Huntington's Disease were recorded in her chart. The information that could have saved me from this situation was there for five years before I even met my wife. The information that could have kept us from having children and saddling them with this burden was right there from 1967 onward. It had been there for twenty years, and no one had told us about it, even though we had sought answers. Even when we did learn the truth, it wasn't from that chart.

When I saw that information, I was furious. You can understand better why I was so angry and why I felt so cheated and misled. You can understand as well why comments about it being great to be a Calvinist at a time like this didn't comfort me but repulsed me.

But in the months and years that have passed since that revelation, I have come to see this in a different way. For twenty years that information had been there, and at any time we could have found it out. Why, then, didn't God give it to us until 1987? As I wrestled with that question, I began to see his love and concern for us. God kept it hidden because he wanted me to marry Pat. She is a great woman and wife. My life would be impoverished without her, and I would have missed the blessing of being married to her had I known earlier. God wanted our three sons to be born. Each is a blessing and a treasure, but we would have missed that had we known earlier. And God knew that we needed to be in a community of brothers and sisters in Christ at church and at the seminary who would love us and care for us at this darkest hour. And so he withheld that information, not because he accidentally overlooked giving it to us, and not because he is an uncaring, evil God who delights in seeing his children suffer. He withheld it as a sign of his great care for us. There is never a good time to receive such news, but God knew that this was exactly the right time.

I have written many words in this chapter about the need to care and show it, because I am so convinced of how crucial it is. We must show those who are hurting that we really do care. We must show it not only by saying it but also by our deeds. And, by all means, we must show it by not avoiding those who suffer. We must be there, even if only to listen. It is human nature to stay away for fear that we may say the wrong thing. Be there, anyway, even if you say nothing. Your presence and willingness to listen and help say enough. They say you care. When we keep our distance from those who suffer, we confirm their worst fears that no one cares and no one will help. Show them that someone cares. Show them not only when the initial shock comes. Show them in the weeks and months and years that follow. There is a sense in which one never completely recovers from tragedy. The need for the love and concern of others is always there.

In the midst of these problems, I was vividly reminded about how difficult it is to go on without hope. I didn't really begin to feel much relief from my pain until I began to see some rays of hope. The fact that God and others cared was reason for hope, as was the realization that God would give grace for each new day. But beyond that, friends who knew about our situation and about this disease could point to specific reasons for hope. For one thing, research on this disease continues. With advances in genetic engineering in the area of gene therapy, there is legitimate reason for hope. Of course it is possible that neither a cure nor even much help will come in time to help my wife, but research continues on this disease, and there is reason to be hopeful in regard to our children. Five to ten years in medical science is a long time.

Are these false hopes? I think not. I believe it is crucial that we give people reason for hope if we can. We must be careful not to offer false hope, but when there are real grounds for hope, we should be quick to point those out. Some of my colleagues are especially sensitive to this need. When a newspaper or journal article appears which chronicles some advance in research on Huntington's, no matter how small or insignificant the development, they make a point to show me the article. They realize that it is difficult to go on without hope, so when there are legitimate grounds for hope, they bring them to my attention.

Something else that helped me was focusing on the fact that in spite of what has happened, God is good. One particular incident made me focus on that. A little over a year after we first received news of my wife's condition, I was being considered for tenure where I teach. In the tenure review interview, I was asked a question that really stopped me in my tracks. One of the members of the committee asked, "In light of what you've been through, can you still say that God is good?" Though I answered affirmatively, I did so somewhat hesitantly. I realized that I had been focusing so much on the problems and on what God had *not* done, that I really hadn't paid enough attention to all the evidence of his goodness in my life.

In the months that followed, I thought a lot about how many things were going well for us. I believe that no matter how much pain and turmoil there is, it helps the sufferer to focus on ways God has shown his goodness in spite of the problems. Even if a situation seems absolutely terrible, upon reflection one can probably imagine ways for it to be worse. Counting one's blessings may seem trite, but it does in fact give a different perspective on what is happening to you.

In our case, there were many evidences of God's goodness. For one thing, for many years the disease progressed very slowly in my wife's case. Given the nature of this disease, God is the only one who can do anything about it. I have come to see that contrary to appearances, he is. At least for many years, he retarded the course of the disease. There are no guarantees for its future progression, but I can always be thankful for those extra years of relative normality in my wife's condition.

I have already mentioned the love and concern shown to us by other Christians. That continues, and periodically I am again reminded of God's goodness as I hear of people literally all over the world who somehow have heard about this and are praying for us. In addition, I have often thought that since this has happened, what a blessing to live at this time in history! During much of the nineteenth and early part of the twentieth century (let alone earlier), little was known about this disease. Now it is known that there is a physiological base to this disease, not a psychological one. Moreover, within the last decade or so the chromosome involved has been identified, and even the exact genetic marker has been isolated. My wife could have lived at any other time in history and still had this disease. That she and our children live now is a sign of God's goodness.

When I look at these and many other things, I can truly say that God has been and is good to us. It is easy to focus on what is going wrong. But when you stop to think about it, it is truly amazing that in a world where Satan is so dominant and sin so rampant anything ever goes right. That much does go right is ample evidence of God's grace and goodness to us. Surely we don't deserve it, and he isn't obligated to give it, but he does.

In recent years, I have continually been reminded of 1 Peter 5:7, which tells us to cast all our cares on him, because he cares for us. Usually, we focus on the first part of that verse as we remind one another not to worry about what is happening. But the latter part of the verse explains why we should do this, and I believe it is most instructive. Peter could have written, "Cast all your cares on him, for he is powerful enough to do something about it." That would be equally true as what he wrote, but I'm glad Peter wrote what he did. It's as if Peter is saying, "Of course, he's powerful enough to do something about our problems. He wouldn't be God if he weren't. What we want to know, though, is whether he cares enough to help us. And he does."

Indeed, he does care. Everywhere in our life, in spite of what may be happening, we can find ample signs that God cares if we only look for them. God does care, because he is so good, and focusing on those truths as well as reflecting on the many expressions of his goodness to us helps the sufferer feel more comfortable with this God.

In spite of all these encouragements in the midst of affliction, there will still be the nagging question of how this could happen to us. After all, it isn't just that my wife is a Christian and has given her life in service to the Lord. The question of why this should happen to her is especially nagging because it couldn't be God's retribution upon her for any sin she committed in her life. That she would get this disease was decided at the moment she was conceived!

As I thought about that, I was reminded of an unpopular but very important biblical truth I mentioned when dealing with natural evil. It is that things like this happen because we live in a fallen world. God told Adam and Eve that if they disobeyed him, they would die (Gen. 2:17). They disobeyed, and the curse fell on them, and Paul tells us that it fell on all of us as well (Rom. 5:12). Adam's sin and its consequences have been imputed to the whole race. But if people are to die, they must die of something. There are many possible causes of death, and disease is one of them. When one realizes this, one understands that though my wife committed no specific sin after birth that brought this upon her, this has happened because of sin. It is her sin in Adam, though she is no more responsible than the rest of us. That isn't the most comforting thought, but it is a healthy reminder that this isn't God's fault, but ultimately ours. And the human race was warned.

The main lesson to learn from this, however, is the enormity of sin and the need to hate it. Shortly after the news of my wife's disease came, I received what I thought a rather strange note of condolence from a friend who was teaching at another seminary. He expressed his sorrow over the news. But then he wrote, "I can imagine how angry you must be right now at sin." Frankly, I thought at the time this was a rather odd way to console someone. I knew as well that sin was the last focus of my anger, if it was a focus at all.

As I thought about what my friend wrote, I realized that he was absolutely right. This has happened and other tragic events occur, because we live in a fallen world. We may think our sins are a trifling matter, and to us they may be. But when you hear the diagnosis of a terminal disease, or when you stand at the grave of a loved one, as we did at my mother's grave and then at my father's, you get a vivid illustration of how terrible sin is. God has told us it will lead to this, but we don't take him as seriously as we should until something like this happens to us.

We may think sin is really a trivial thing, but that's what Adam and Eve thought, too, and look at the mess that resulted! We may also think the punishment (disease, troubles, and death) far outweighs the crime, a little sin. But that only underscores how far we are from God's perspective on these things. In light of our relative comfort with sin, a little sin doesn't seem so bad. From the perspective of an absolutely perfect God who has nothing to do with sin, it must be atrocious.

Think of it in the terms we considered in the last chapter. If you are a parent, you brought children into the world. You have nurtured them and provided for their needs. You have loved them deeply, and expressed that love in many different ways. In return, you simply ask that they obey you. How do you feel when they disobey? Surely their disobedience seems far more serious to you than to them. But then, how much more must it hurt God, who has given us so much and who moment by moment sustains us in existence, when we disobey him! Viewed from our perspective, sin isn't so bad, but this analogy reminds us that we need a different perspective altogether.

My friend was right. We need to see sin as God does, and hate it. When we see it from the perspective of where it ultimately leads, we begin to understand how truly serious it is and how much we must resist it. I can't say this will be of great comfort to you. But it may help you to focus your anger in the right direction. It may also help you to feel more comfortable with God as you realize that ultimately all of us, not God, have brought these things on ourselves. God warned us, but we didn't listen. Thank God that now in our troubles *he* will listen, forgive, and restore!

There were yet other things that happened which helped me to cope with our situation. I mentioned earlier that I also had physical problems and that the stress from my wife's situation only made matters worse. Within a few months I came to a point where I was in great pain and was of little use to anyone. I didn't have the physical stamina to preach, nor the energy to make it through my classes. I not only felt that our situation was helpless and hopeless. I felt that I was useless and that I was adding to the problem by requiring attention that should have been placed elsewhere. As with many people, my feelings of self-worth are tied in large part to my work and productivity. When I could do little to function, that only made my sense of hopelessness worse.

In the midst of this dilemma, the Lord gave me some opportunities to do things that helped other people. This was just what I needed at the time. It gave me a chance to get my focus off of our problems and on someone else's needs. Even more, it showed me that I still could be useful. Gradually, as I regained strength and was able to do more, I became increasingly thankful that I could do anything, let alone help others who had shown us so much love and concern.

For those wrestling with affliction, I would encourage the same. As you are able and when you are able, seek out ways to help others. There is therapeutic value in getting your eyes off your problems and in seeing again that you can help others. I found that this helped to lift the burden somewhat, and it showed me that when others, including my family, needed me, through God's enablement I would be able to help them.

Somewhere in the process of dealing with my emotions and my problems, something else happened that helped me greatly. I began to ask myself what my options were for handling this problem long range. Somewhere in the grieving process I think each of us must ask ourselves what the options are for addressing our problem. In my case, there were few, but they were radically diverse. On the one hand, I could continue to grieve and fall apart. But I had already done that, and it had solved nothing. I saw little improvement in my own outlook, and I was of little help to anyone else. This approach would in no way solve our problems. Beyond that, my wife still needed a husband, my children a father, and my students a teacher. Falling apart wouldn't help any of them. As Scripture says, there is a time to mourn, but then one must get on with one's life.

Well, perhaps, instead, I would get on with my life, but just exclude God from it. Many people choose this option in the face of affliction. They conclude either that there is no God or decide that there is but they will fight him. None of this was acceptable for me. I had seen too many evidences of God's working in my life to think there was no God. It made no sense to devote my life to propagating the view that there is no God. Even if that were true, there were surely more productive things I could do with my life.

Rejecting God's existence was totally unsatisfactory, but choosing to fight him was no better. God's goodness throughout my life and even now in our circumstances didn't warrant my turning from him. Moreover, it is lunacy to pick a fight you can't win. Even more, it is beyond lunacy to fight someone who, rather than being the cause of your problems, is the only possible answer to them.

Maybe I should take a Kierkegaardian leap of faith that somehow this all made sense, though I could explain none of it. In other words, I could simply ignore and bypass intellect and throw myself on God in hopes that he was there. But this didn't seem a live option for me. Some might find it attractive, but it isn't my nature to sacrifice intellect so totally. I knew there would still be the questions and that there would be no peace until they were settled. I didn't expect to find all the answers, but I knew I had to find many of them.

The only real option for me was clear. I had to continue trusting, and yes, worshiping God, and I had to get on with my life. I needed to stop the seemingly interminable deep grieving and allow emotional healing to continue by focusing on the things I have already shared and will share in this chapter. I had to focus on answers that would satisfy the emotional dimensions of my struggle and would at the same time give enough intellectual answers to warrant peace of mind. And I realized that I couldn't wait until all those answers arrived to continue with life. Too many people needed my help, and I needed to help them.

As I began to take this approach to my problems (and at some point all of us must decide how we will handle our problems), I began to focus more on the positive things I have already mentioned as well as others I shall mention. The healing and coping process continues to this day as it will through the rest of my life. I still wrestle with these issues. But God has allowed me to function again, and there is progress in dealing with these problems. I am so thankful God led me to choose the option I did for handling my situation.

God is not only there when the shock of tragic news first comes. At various points along the way when we are ready to hear it, he adds a further word. One of those words of help comes from a passage in Ecclesiastes. The passage is Ecclesiastes 7:13-14, and the thrust of the passage is that God hides the future from us so that we will trust him. Though this might seem a rather strange source of comfort, let me share it with you. The passage reads:

(13) Consider the work of God,
For who is able to straighten what He has bent?
(14) In the day of prosperity be happy,
But in the day of adversity consider—
God has made the one as well as the other
So that man may not discover anything that will be after him.

The context of these verses is significant. Commentators agree that chapter 7 contains a series of aphorisms, though they don't always agree on how they fit together. Generally, much of chapter 7 focuses on things that at first appear undesirable in order to show that in fact they have a certain benefit. Chapter 6 shows that things that look good also have a down side. The ultimate message is that we can't always take things at face value, nor should we think we can always understand them. And if this is true of things we do and experience, how much more is it true of God and his ways! This is the context of verses 13-14.

In the passage itself, the writer begins by emphasizing the sovereign power of God (v. 13). Verse 13b is a rhetorical question, and the answer is obvious. Some think this verse means that if God brings something we consider evil, we can't make it good (straighten it). We can't overturn God's powerful hand. While this interpretation surely fits verse 14 and its teaching about God's bringing of adversity, I think the writer's point is even more general. That is, just as no one can straighten what God bends, no one can bend what he straightens. No one can overturn what God does; man must simply submit to God's providence.

All of this suggests that adversity and prosperity are all under God's hand. Verse 14 confirms that, for it says God sends both good and bad. The writer tells us to be happy in the good days. Out of fear of the future, we might be troubled even when things are going well. That worry will help us learn nothing about the future, but it may destroy the happiness in the present that we should be and could be having.

The writer then says that in evil days, we should consider. He doesn't say that in evil days we should be sad, for he doesn't need to. That comes naturally. Instead, we should consider. We should think about what has happened, think about the alternation of good and bad, and realize that no one knows when which will come. In fact, what appears to be good may turn out evil and vice versa. Things aren't always as they seem.

Why does God give this alternation of good and bad? Why doesn't he always reveal how things will turn out? The writer says God does this to conceal the future ("so that man may not discover anything that will be after him"). But why would God do that? Though the answer isn't explicit in the text, I think it is implicit. If we don't know what to expect, we must just wait on the Lord for what will come next and entrust it all to him. We may want to change what he will do, but verse 13 reminds us that we can't. We must submit to his providence and simply trust him. If we knew the details of our future, we might think we could figure out what we would need to do. In short, we might think there was no need to trust God.

God conceals the future, so we must trust him. You can see how this truth fit so specifically our situation. It wasn't only relevant to us before we learned the news that was for so long available but untouched. It is relevant now as we contemplate the course of this disease and our children's futures as well.

What are the implications of this truth? If God conceals the future so that we must trust him, doesn't that mean God manipulates us and events to get us to love him? Maybe he can't get our love and trust any other way, so he manipulates things to force us to trust him. If that is so, this is no God worthy of praise and worship! This isn't a good God! This is a conniving, manipulative God who has created us solely for his benefit, and really doesn't care about us after all.

As I thought about the implications of this truth, I realized that God isn't an evil God. By concealing the future, God does make us trust him, but I submit that this isn't manipulative, but compassionate! It is compassionate in a number of ways.

It is compassionate, because knowing the details of our future would be harmful to us. Suppose our future would be good. No doubt we would be relieved, but the joy of discovery would be gone. What should be great when it happens would lose its excitement as a surprise. We might even be bored. The joy of anticipation would be gone. Revealing a good future might also make us complacent in our relation to God, and that would be bad. We might conclude that we don't need him, but obviously we do.

Suppose our future would be evil. Barring the return of the Lord for the church, Scripture and common sense teach that the ultimate end of this life is death, and that is evil. But if we knew how or when it would end or even what evils would befall us along the way, we might be totally horrified and unable to act as fear paralyzed us. Hiding the future is compassionate, because knowing the future could easily harm us.

Hiding the future is also compassionate because we must not ignore the present, but we might if we knew the future. If the future is good and we know what it will be, we might become impatient with the present. Think of how things are now even without knowing the future specifically. When we anticipate an exciting summer vacation, we become impatient with the present. In essence, we overlook the good things that are happening now, and lose the present. On the other hand, if our future is evil, we might spend much of our time worrying about it or grieving over our anticipated misfortune. The net result in either case could well be a wasting of the present and never really "living" at all.

One of the things that our experiences have done for me is to focus my attention on the present. I have always been a goal-oriented person with a focus on the future. I still plan for the future, but now for the near future, not the distant future. I don't want to know any more about the distant future than I already do. I find myself focusing more on the present and enjoying it more. In fact, I am better able to cope when I focus on where my wife is today, rather than on where she may be in her condition somewhere down the road. I don't have tomorrow's grace yet, and I don't need it until tomorrow! We must not be so overly occupied with the future that we lose today. God has hidden the future so that we might trust him. He is compassionate in doing so.

God is compassionate in hiding the future as well because we would probably try to change it if we knew it. This is especially true if it is evil, but even if it is good we might try to change it to make it better. But as verse 13 suggests, it is impossible to change what God has decided to do. Why waste the present trying to change something you can't change? In the process, you may drive yourself crazy.

God's hiding of the future is also compassionate because we couldn't handle the information in some cases if we had it. Especially if the future is evil and if we see it all at once, it could be too horrifying for us to take. On November 4, 1987 I caught a glimpse of the future that just about destroyed me. I am more than willing now to take the future one day at a time. In most cases God compassionately reveals the details of our futures moment by moment, and that is enough. As Scripture says, "Sufficient unto the day is the evil thereof" (Matt. 6:34, KJV). We don't need to know tomorrow's evil today!

Though all the things I have shared were sources of comfort and encouragement, something still seemed wrong. There seemed to be a basic unfairness about what was happening. And, frankly, I believe this is a sticking point for many people which makes it so difficult for them to live with God. Put simply, why was this happening to us, and not also to other people? Wasn't it unjust of God to ask us to bear this burden, and not others? Please do not misunderstand. I wouldn't wish this on anyone, but it seemed only fair that if others escape, we should, too. If God could keep others from this fate, why couldn't he keep us from it? It's not that he owes any of us anything per se, but justice seems to show that he owes us at least as good a shake as the next person.

I suspect that most who experience significant tragedy in their life have thought this way at some point. I surely had those thoughts, but I came to see that they contain an error. In philosophical discussions of justice, there is a distinction between what is called distributive justice and egalitarian justice. Distributive justice refers to rendering each person what is their due. If you do good, in strict justice you are owed good. If you do evil, in strict justice you deserve punishment. Egalitarian justice, however, is giving everyone the same thing, regardless of merits or deserts.

Now I saw where the source of the problem was. It isn't just that we think distributive justice mandates a better fate for us since we think we have done good. Our complaint is that we expect God to deal with the world with egalitarian justice. We expect him to treat everyone the same, and that means I should escape an affliction if others do!

Once I realized this, I immediately asked why God is obligated to operate in these matters on the basis of egalitarian justice. Given the demands of distributive justice, all of us as sinners *deserve* nothing but punishment. Why, then, is God obligated to respond to us in egalitarian terms? I could not answer that. I realized that if God really did handle us according to egalitarian justice, we would all either experience the same torture or be equally blessed. Neither of those ideas squares with the God of the Scriptures. It was a tremendous help to realize that part of my anger stemmed from thinking that God is obligated to treat us with egalitarian justice, even though he isn't. Once I realized that he has no such obligation, I understood that much of my anger rested on a misunderstanding of what God is expected to do.

But even this principle doesn't solve the problem. Even if God isn't obligated to give any of us more than we deserve, and even if what we deserve is punishment for sin, still God has chosen to be gracious to some. If you are suffering from some affliction, you may feel that God should have extended equal grace to you as he has to those who never confront your affliction. God must be unjust for not extending as much grace to you as to the next person.

Though this objection is understandable, it is still wrong. The objection now has moved from a demand that God treat us with egalitarian *justice* to a demand that God dole out egalitarian *grace*. This is wrong in two respects. In the first place, God is no more obligated to give the same grace to everyone than he is to give the same justice to all. He is obligated only to distribute what we deserve. The other point is that since we are talking about grace, the charge of *injustice* on God's part (and that is really what the sufferer means by this complaint) can't even arise. Grace is unmerited favor. That means you get something good that you don't deserve. But if I don't merit it at all, it can't be unjust that my neighbor gets more grace than I do. It can be unjust only if God is obligated to treat us with egalitarian grace, and he surely isn't. In fact, He isn't *obligated* to treat us with any kind of grace. That's why it's grace, and not justice. And that is also why it can't be unjust if someone gets more grace than another. God owes none of us any grace. If he graciously chooses to give some of us a better (by our evaluation) lot than others, that is his right. He has done nothing wrong. There can't be any requirements placed on grace lest we turn it into justice.

Though these principles about grace and justice won't relieve the pain of what you are experiencing, if they are properly understood, they can help dissipate anger toward God. I have found it to be liberating, and I frequently remind myself of these principles when I am inclined to lament that God has given others an easier lot than I.

I close this chapter hoping that what you have read will minister to your needs and will help you minister to others who are hurting. It hasn't been an easy chapter to write, and I would give anything not to have learned what I have learned in the way I did. But if the chapter is helpful to you, then it has been worth my effort to write it.

I close as well with a final thought. It is especially relevant to those who are believers and suffer as righteous individuals. It was something I needed to see, and it helped me as well when I realized it. John says the world didn't understand Christ, so we who are the children of God and follow Christ can expect to be misunderstood and persecuted as well (1 John 3:1). Jesus told his disciples that following him means bearing a cross (Matt. 16:24). Scripture is also very clear that those who follow God are engaged in a war with those who don't (Eph. 6:12; 1 Pet. 5:8-9).

Yes, we are engaged in a spiritual war. But did you think you could go to war, even be in the front lines of the battle, and never get wounded?

I did. At least, I never expected a wound like the one we got. But I have come to see that this was unrealistic. The enemy is very real, and has many ways of attacking those who would follow God. Knowing that there will be attack and battle wounds doesn't mean the wounds don't hurt. But it does help us assess more accurately what has happened. One may wish exemption from the battle, but that isn't possible. One may even contemplate changing sides as many do when confronted with tragedy, but that option isn't the answer to our problems for either time or eternity.

There were other afflictions that came during the trials I have mentioned, just as I know there will be others in the future. The story isn't finished yet. Just as there have been some surprises already (some welcome, some unwelcome), God has others in store. When the wounds of battle come, and they will come, we need the comfort and care of God. I am so thankful God is there to give it!

15

THE RELIGIOUS PROBLEM: USES OF SUFFERING

In chapter 14, I shared something of my own struggles with the religious problem of evil. As I suggested throughout that chapter, the religious problem isn't primarily an intellectual struggle, but an emotional one. However, that doesn't mean there is no intellectual dimension to it, for of course, what one thinks affects how one feels. As a result, I have shared a variety of concepts which I found very comforting at one point or another.

There is yet another line of intellectual answers that can help in ministering to those who are hurting. I am thinking of the uses of affliction in our life. Though God isn't the author of evil and affliction, he does allow it to happen. When it does and we suffer, God isn't helpless to put affliction to positive use in our life. While the affliction isn't good, it can serve as an occasion for God to work in our lives to bring some good out of evil. The fact that God does this and that we can see him doing so can reassure us that God's hand is still upon us. He isn't angry at us, and he hasn't abandoned us. When we realize that God didn't bring this affliction but is doing something positive in the midst of a bad situation and doing so to our benefit, it can remind us that God is good and that he is worthy of our worship.

In this chapter I want to present a series of things God can do in the life of the sufferer as a result of that affliction. I have found these principles encouraging, though they weren't particularly helpful in the earlier stages of my struggles. When someone is still reeling from the shock of tragedy, it won't likely help to tell her, "Take heart, there are many positive things God can do through this affliction, and I want to share them with you." At that point, the sufferer is too hurt, too angry, and too much in shock to grasp fully the import of what you would say. If you begin to rehearse the beneficial uses of suffering, the afflicted may quickly inform you that she would gladly forego any of that since it must come through affliction. Or she may simply ask why, if God can bring good out of evil, he can't bring good out of good.

So allow the sufferer time to begin healing. Share the things I mentioned in the previous chapter as opportunities arise. Then, at some point in the healing process the sufferer will be ready to hear the things I am going to present in this chapter.

Before turning to the positive uses of suffering, I must first address an initial conceptual matter. Some might respond to what I plan to do in this chapter by saying, "All along, you've told us that you hold a nonconsequentialist ethical theory. Now you are going to look at uses of suffering. Isn't that appealing to consequentialism? Aren't you contradicting your overall ethical stance?"

This is an understandable reaction, but it is incorrect. For one thing, nonconsequentialists don't say that consequences of actions are unimportant. They only hold that consequences aren't the basis for determining whether an act is right or wrong. But the results of our actions do matter. As this applies to the problem of evil, we must again distinguish between justifying God and living comfortably with him. If I were to offer these uses of suffering as my *justification* of God in the face of evil, then I would be invoking a consequentialist defense of God's ways. That would, indeed, contradict my nonconsequentialist defenses presented earlier in the book. But I'm not doing that. Rather, I offer this material not to defend God in the face of evil, but to help the sufferer feel more "at home" with God, in spite of affliction. As shown in the previous chapter, many things can help the sufferer live with God. None of those things justify God[1] and thereby solve the more abstract logical and evidential problems of evil. But they do help the afflicted to live with the God who permits these evils. What I offer in this chapter is more of the same, i.e., helps for healing the breach in the sufferer's relation to God.

How, then, might God use affliction in the life of the righteous sufferer?[2] There are many ways he can use it, and those uses divide into ten basic categories. Before turning directly to them, however, I must note that it is natural to think that in any given instance of suffering, God is working to accomplish only one thing in the life of the sufferer. If we don't immediately sense what that is, frustration arises. However, in any given case, God may intend to accomplish a whole series of things, not just one, and not just in the life of the sufferer alone. In allowing affliction, God may intend to accomplish something in the sufferer's life, something in the lives of those who know the sufferer, and something in regard to angelic and demonic forces.

It goes without saying as well that my list of the uses of suffering isn't meant to be exhaustive. In a particular instance of suffering, God may intend some use beyond those I mention. But just because nothing in my list fits a particular case, that doesn't mean God isn't working. It only shows that sometimes God's purposes are beyond our comprehension. Even if nothing I mention fits a specific case, hopefully it will be encouraging to see that there are things God can accomplish through suffering. These uses of suffering may in part also explain why God allows the affliction to befall us.

What possible good, then, might God accomplish in our lives through the afflictions we endure? First, God may allow affliction for the same end as in the case recorded in John 9:1-3. In that situation, affliction *provided an opportunity for God to manifest his power.* In John 9, the disciples asked Jesus concerning a man blind from birth, "Who sinned, this man or his parents, that he should be born blind?" Jesus rejected the common belief that all suffering must be a recompense for some specific sin. He answered, "It was neither that this man sinned, nor his parents; but it was in order that the works of God might be displayed in him." To the amazement of those who saw it, Christ then performed a miracle to restore the man's sight. Likewise, sometimes God may allow affliction in the life of the righteous as a basis for some future working in that person's life, a work that demonstrates the power and glory of God.

Earlier in my wife's dealing with Huntington's Disease, we saw this happen to a certain extent. For many years, my wife's disease progressed rather slowly. Doctors repeatedly mentioned how wonderful it was that the disease was developing so slowly in her case. On more than one occasion, we have used those comments as an opportunity to state our belief that this is evidence of God's hand upon her life. Even though deterioration is now substantial, that can't negate the display of God's power in her life to this point.

Second, God may use affliction to *remove a cause for boasting.* When things go smoothly in life, we tend to feel self-sufficient. Affliction reminds us that we aren't, and that we must rely on God. A classic illustration of this principle comes from the life of Paul. Paul had a thorn in the flesh, some sort of physical ailment whose exact nature commentators debate. In 2 Cor. 12:7, Paul wrote that though he asked God to remove it, God didn't. Paul then says that if God hadn't left that problem, he might have thought too highly of himself in view of the significance of the revelations God had given to him. His thorn in the flesh was a constant reminder that there was no room for boasting. Sometimes God may use affliction similarly in our lives.

In the first two chapters of Job, we see a third possible use for righteous suffering. God allowed Job's afflictions at least in part to *demonstrate true or genuine faith to Satan.* Satan claimed that the only reason Job served God was that it was worth Job's while. If God removed his hand of blessing from Job, Job would no longer serve him. God answered that Job served him out of genuine love, and he decided to demonstrate that to Satan. Through Job's afflictions and through his faithfulness to God, Satan saw that there are those who serve God out of genuine love, not because "it pays to do so."

Likewise, God may use affliction in our life to accomplish some purpose *for us,* and at the same time use our response to show Satan and his cohorts that there are still those who love and serve God regardless of their personal circumstances in life. Not only will Satan see this, but others will as well. And this is extremely important. As Christians, we claim to have the ultimate answers to life's problems. But of course, it is in a sense easy to be a Christian when everything is going well. What non-Christians want to know is whether Christianity works when things go wrong. That's the true test of this religion. If we turn from God in the midst of affliction, in effect we communicate to those watching that at times of stress Christianity offers no more of an answer than any other religion or ideology. God still needs people today who will show others that they love and serve God, not because it pays to do so, but because he is worthy of their devotion.

This is also why Peter tells us that in the midst of affliction we must be ready to explain why we continue to hold on to our hope in God (1 Pet. 3:15). This verse is frequently taken out of context to show that Christians should do apologetics in general. That is neither the point nor the context of the verse. Peter discusses the suffering of the righteous, and says that in that circumstance we must be ready to defend our continued belief in God and faithfulness to him, when others challenge us to explain why we do so in light of the affliction that has befallen us. Our response must be both verbal and non-verbal (1 Pet. 3:15-17). We must not only explain why we have hope and why Christianity makes a difference. We must live as people for whom Christianity makes a difference. We dare not use our affliction as warrant to contradict Christian principles by disobeying God's Word.

Fourth, sometimes God uses affliction as an opportunity to *demonstrate to believers and nonbelievers the Body of Christ concept.* According to 1 Corinthians 12:12-26, each believer in Christ as Savior is a member of the Body of Christ. We are related to one another through Christ, and we need one another. Moreover, verse 26 says we are sympathetically related to one another, i.e., when one suffers, all suffer, and when one rejoices, all rejoice. This is the ideal, but it doesn't always match our experience. Too often Christians treat one another as if there were total isolation of members within the Body of Christ. Consequently, God may on occasion use affliction of one member to show other members that believers must help one another.

Through affliction the Body of Christ concept may be demonstrated to several groups of people. Suffering allows the afflicted person to experience the compassionate love of God through other believers. It allows sufferers to understand experientially what it means to have one's burdens borne (Gal. 6:2). These truths have been vividly reinforced in our minds through the words and deeds of other believers who care.

In addition, suffering gives other believers the chance to express Christian love to those in need. When we help others in the Body of Christ, we understand more fully how deeply we need one another. We experience as well what it means to show Christian love and compassion to other believers. In order to give us that opportunity to minister, God may allow affliction to strike another member of Christ's Body. Moreover, Christ said people would know that believers are his disciples if they love one another (John 13:35). Helping a suffering brother or sister is a tangible way to show one another and the world that we are Christ's disciples, because we love one another.

A fifth broad category encompasses a number of uses of affliction in the life of the righteous. It is the matter of sanctification. Scripture teaches a number of ways in which afflictions *promote sanctification*. For example, Scripture says the experience of suffering helps believers to put away sin. Peter writes (1 Pet. 4:1-2, KJV),

> Forasmuch then as Christ hath suffered for us in the flesh, arm yourselves likewise with the same mind; for he that hath suffered in the flesh hath ceased from sin; that he no longer should live the rest of his time in the flesh to the lusts of men, but to the will of God.

The Greek for "ceased from sin" is *pepautai hamartias*. Commentators agree that *hamartia* in 1 Peter always means a sinful act. Hence, Peter isn't suggesting that by suffering the believer is completely removed from the power, influence, or guilt of sin. As John suggests in 1 John 1:8, such a removal of sin's influence is impossible for anyone in this life. Instead, Peter means that afflictions have a way of driving a believer from committing specific acts of sin, i.e., afflictions cause us to exercise restraint in regard to the temptations that surround us, rather than yielding to them.

In my own experience, I have found this to be true. In light of my family's situation, certain things that enticed me before pale in significance in light of facing ultimate issues of life and death. That is not to say that those things never tempt me or that I never sin. Rather, what has happened to us has helped tremendously to put those tempting things in proper perspective. Life isn't about such enticements; much more important things are at stake. Of course, if affliction does drive one from committing specific acts of sin, one will in the process draw closer to his Lord, view things more with the significance that Christ puts on them, and in so doing show that one is being sanctified.

Another way affliction promotes sanctification is to *refine one's faith*. 1 Peter 1:6-7 says,

> Wherein ye greatly rejoice, though now for a season, if need be, ye are in heaviness through manifold temptations: that the trial of your faith [*to dokimion humon tes pisteos*], being much more precious than of gold that perisheth, though it be tried [*dokimazomenou*] with fire, might be found unto praise and honour and glory at the appearing of Jesus Christ (KJV).

The emphasis of the phrase "trial of your faith" is not on the test itself but on the outcome of the test, i.e., the residue of faith that remains when the test is over. As Charles Bigg explains (*Epistles of St. Peter and of St. Jude*), the verse's point is not that the test itself is precious, for the test is suffering, and that isn't more precious than gold. Rather it is the residue of faith left over after the test that is precious. Therefore, as Peter says in verse 6, believers can rejoice in the midst of affliction, because through these experiences God is refining their faith so that at Christ's appearing the residue of their tested faith will be found unto praise and honour and glory. Of course, if faith is refined through testing, the believer is thereby being sanctified.

Sanctification is also promoted by suffering because God uses it to *educate believers* in ways that cause them to grow closer to the Lord and be more Christlike. For example, James 1:3-4, Romans 5:3-4, and 1 Peter 5:10 say that God teaches perseverance or endurance through afflictions. Likewise, Hebrews 5:8 indicates that even Christ in his humanity learned obedience through suffering. The point is that if God is to teach us anything, he must have our attention. When there is no affliction in our life, it is easy to become overly self-sufficient, and not to pay attention to what the Lord wants to teach us as he desires to draw us closer to himself. But when affliction comes, we may be inclined to rebel against God, but instead we may realize that we need to pay attention to what God is trying to teach us, things that we might not otherwise be open to hear.

Through experiences of affliction believers can also draw closer to the Lord by *catching a glimpse of his sovereignty and majesty* such as they have never seen before. Job 42:2-4 records the response of a man who had suffered greatly. Even though Job was a righteous man (Job 1:8, 21-22; 2:3, 10), he still suffered, and he sought God to understand why. God finally answered Job (chapters 38–41), and overwhelmed him with a sense of his power and majesty. As a result, Job exclaimed (42:2-4) that he finally understood that God could do anything. In our case as well, sometimes our view of God is too small, and God corrects that by sending afflictions and then proving himself to be the all-powerful One in our behalf. As a result, like Job, we draw closer to the Lord as we come to know him better.

Suffering also produces sanctification in that it *gives intimacy with God.* Again, Job's case is instructive. Even though Job had grown in the Lord before his experiences of suffering, he still needed to draw closer to God. At the end of his ordeal, Job's comments show that his experiences had given him a knowledge of God that he had never had before. In Job 42:5 he says, "I have heard of thee by the hearing of the ear: but now mine eye seeth thee" (KJV). Job traded mere hearsay knowledge of God for firsthand experiential knowledge. There is nothing like affliction to take concepts such as the majesty and sovereignty of God (as well as the comfort and concern of God) and change them from doctrinal theories to concrete realities in the sufferer's life.

There is yet another regard in which affliction can relate to sanctification. God may use affliction to *challenge the righteous to growth, rather than to fall into sin.* My point arises from an interesting set of facts about the first chapter of James. In James 1:1-12 the topic is clearly affliction, whereas in verses 13 and following the topic is temptation to sin. The typical Greek word for tribulation, affliction, or suffering is *thlipsis. Thlipsis* never appears in the NT in a context where it means temptation. On the other hand, the noun *peirasmos* and the verb *peirazo* are the usual words for temptation and to tempt. In several instances, they indicate a trial or testing (cf. 1 Pet. 4:12; Acts 9:26; 16:7; 24:6; Rev. 2:2, e.g.). However, those verses don't focus on affliction or suffering, but on putting someone to a test.

In light of these basic uses of *thlipsis* and *peirasmos,* one would expect to find *thlipsis* in James 1:1-12 and *peirasmos* in 1:13ff. Instead, *peirasmos* is used throughout the chapter, and *thlipsis* doesn't appear at all. This leads me to raise the following questions: 1) Is James suggesting that afflictions are temptations or trials? 2) Are all temptations afflictions? 3) Are all afflictions temptations?

The answer to the first question is debatable, but the second and third are easier to answer. As to whether all temptations are afflictions, obviously, they aren't. Some temptations come in the midst of afflictions (e.g., the temptation to curse God which confronted the afflicted Job), but many times temptation arises without any accompanying suffering at all. As to whether afflictions are temptations, the answer is that all afflictions are potentially temptations. That is, afflictions provide an occasion for us to be tempted, for example, to be angry at God and turn from him. We may yield to that temptation, but we may instead respond positively in faith to God and resist the temptation that arose as a result of affliction. When we do resist, the trial has served as a basis for growing closer to the Lord, rather than for falling to the temptation to turn from him. Perhaps this is implicitly James's point in using *peirasmos* when *thlipsis* would seem to be the more natural choice of words.

A final way affliction promotes sanctification is that it offers the sufferer tremendous opportunities to *imitate Christ*. Those who suffer for righteousness may suffer unjustly and for the sake of others. In so doing, they imitate the Savior's example (1 Pet. 3:17-18). Moreover, those who suffer as righteous may be required to bear that affliction and persecution without complaint. In so doing, they again follow the Lord's pattern (1 Pet. 2:23). Christ himself put in perspective the whole matter of what his disciples should expect. He said, "The disciple is not above his master, nor the servant above his lord. It is enough for the disciple that he be as his master, and the servant as his lord" (Matt. 10:24-25, KJV).

This is a general principle which, when applied to Christ's sufferings, indicates that if the world hated and persecuted Christ, those who would follow him can expect the same. In fact, the more Christlike we become, the more we can expect to be out of step with the world and to incur the world's and Satan's wrath (1 John 3:1). Of course, as we imitate Christ, our sanctification is promoted.

Moving beyond the general category of sanctification, we come to a sixth category of uses of suffering. Sometimes God permits affliction into the life of the righteous because of the *ministry that is possible in suffering*. There are several ways afflicted believers can minister in spite of and even because of their afflictions. Those who experience affliction can have a tremendous testimony to those who don't know Christ as personal Savior. As already mentioned, many nonbelievers observe how Christians react when they undergo affliction. When they see the righteous experience affliction and remain faithful to the Lord, they are positively impressed. As Peter says (1 Pet. 3:15-16), their persevering faith and the positive testimony it gives not only put to silence the negative thoughts of evil men but also serve as a positive witness to those who don't know Christ.

Just as there is a testimony to nonbelievers, there is a ministry to believers as a result of affliction. Those who remain true to the Lord during affliction serve as an encouragement to others to remain faithful in spite of their own problems. Moreover, God uses suffering to prepare us to minister to other believers (and nonbelievers) who undergo affliction (2 Cor. 1:3-4).

There is also a sense in which those who remain true to God amidst affliction are actually ministering to themselves. That is, as we persevere in the midst of our suffering, God uses these experiences to prepare us for even further and greater ministry. Here I think of the role affliction played even in

Christ's life to prepare him for further and greater ministry. In Hebrews 2:10 we read, "For it became him, for whom are all things, and by whom are all things, in bringing many sons unto glory, to make the captain of their salvation perfect through sufferings" (KJV).

The words "make perfect" (from *teleioo*) don't refer to sinless perfection. That would make no sense in Christ's case, for he has always been perfect! Instead, the words mean "to be brought to completeness or maturity." In other words, Jesus Christ in his humanity was prepared to be the complete Savior (the Savior who is everything a Savior should be) by means of enduring various afflictions even before he went to the cross. If God could use afflictions to prepare Christ to be the "captain of our salvation," surely he can use suffering to prepare believers for greater ministry.

God also uses affliction to *prepare us for further trials.* Just because one difficult trial hits us, that is no reason to think we have had our lifetime quota. Since we live in a fallen world, we can expect to face further troubles. In fact, there may be even greater and more severe trials yet to come. Had they come sooner, they would have destroyed us. But God in his goodness and grace prepares us for each new test. Part of that preparation involves confronting and enduring the current pains and sorrows.

Think of Abraham. Suppose his first request from God had required him to offer up his son Isaac (cf. Genesis 22). No doubt that would have been too much for him. But God knew that, so he didn't give Abraham the most difficult trial until he had brought him safely through other trials. Faith and endurance, like other Christian virtues, can grow and develop. One of the ways God can help those virtues to grow in us is through sustaining us successfully through our current trials. God knows exactly how much we can endure at any given moment. Part of God's program of giving us grace for each day is to prepare us to receive that grace. And part of that preparation may involve enduring affliction.

An eighth broad use of suffering in the life of the righteous is to *prepare them for judgment of their works for rewards.* According to 1 Peter 1:7, affliction helps to prepare the believer for the coming of Christ. After Christ returns for the church, believers will give Christ an account of what they have done in their Christian walk (2 Cor. 5:10 and 1 Cor. 3:10-15). In 1 Peter 1:7, Peter says that affliction helps to prepare sufferers for that judgment so that their faith and actions will be "found unto praise and honour and glory at the appearing of Jesus Christ" (KJV).

The connection here between suffering and reward may be unclear, but I believe it can be explained. As we endure afflictions, we should become more Christlike. If we do, then, indeed, our lives are likely to be filled with deeds that please God. At judgment time it will be evident that we have built a life of gold, silver, and precious stones, not wood, hay, and stubble (1 Cor. 3:12-15). If our lives are pleasing to God, there will be reward. So, rather than interpreting affliction as a sign of God's displeasure with us, we should realize that God may be using it to prepare us for the day of judgment when our endurance under fire serves as the basis of reward.

Ninth, God may use the afflictions of the righteous as a *basis for ultimately exalting them.* First Peter vividly and repeatedly teaches the theme of suffering and glory (cf. 1 Pet. 1:6-7, 11, 21; 2:12, 15, 19-21; 3:9, 14-22; 4:1, 4, 12-16, 19; 5:1-6, 9-10). The message is quite clear that whoever would be great in God's economy must first be brought low. Affliction has a way of bringing us low so that God may someday exalt us. As a result, Peter says, "Humble yourselves therefore under the mighty hand of God, that He may exalt you in due time" (1 Pet. 5:6). Affliction helps to humble us, but regardless of how much we need to humble ourselves or be humbled, affliction endured for righteousness' sake is clearly a prelude to exaltation. A beautiful example of this truth is Christ himself (1 Pet. 2:22; cf. Phil. 2:5-11).

Finally, God may use affliction *as a means to take a believer to be with himself.* As life comes to an end, the final affliction will usher us into God's presence. This may not seem like a positive use of affliction, but that may be because we don't entirely agree with Philippians 1:21, "For to me, to live is Christ, and to die is gain." I am not suggesting that anyone should wish to die, or that death itself is good. The reason for it (sin) and the event itself aren't good. But for the believer death is the doorway to everlasting blessing in the presence of God. Therefore, we shouldn't always and only evaluate death as a sign of God's displeasure. Affliction leading to death may just be God's way of "promoting" someone to his presence.

These are some of the uses of affliction. In a given instance, one or more may explain in part God's reasons for allowing evil to befall his people. Perhaps God is doing none of these things in a particular case. Perhaps he is doing several. Whatever the case may be, when someone experiences affliction and is angry that God doesn't stop it, I believe that pointing to these uses of evil can help to assuage the sufferer's feelings of confusion and anger. Even if it is impossible to determine exactly why God allows affliction on a particular occasion, that might be the reason itself. That is, God may simply want to teach us that his ways are ultimately beyond our scrutiny. At some point all of us need to recognize that we must let God be God and know a few things we don't!

We have seen, then, in discussing the religious problem of evil, that it is different from any of the other problems of evil. If you have suffered or are suffering greatly, you know that already. If we are to survive these experiences with victory and if we are to minister in ways that really help those who suffer, we must recognize the different nature of this problem. And, while we must have something to say, we must be sensitive to the right timing for anything we would say. I trust that what you have read in these two chapters on the religious problem will be beneficial to that end.

I close with the following. Often, it is natural to ask God to keep us from afflictions. When that doesn't happen, it is easy to become angry and wonder why God doesn't answer that prayer. But if we take seriously the fact that ours is a fallen world and that we are engaged in a spiritual war, we realize better why God doesn't always answer our prayers. Instead of requesting exemption altogether from the battle and the wounds that come with it, Phillips Brooks's advice is wiser counsel:

> Do not pray for easy lives; pray to be stronger people! Do not pray for tasks equal to your powers, pray for powers equal to your tasks. Then the doing of your work shall be no miracle, but you shall be a miracle. Every day you shall wonder at yourself, at the richness of life which has come to you by the grace of God.

Appendix:
Strategy of Theodicy and
Defense-Making

In this book, I have examined various problems of evil and various answers to those problems. Many of those answers include a theodicy or defense which tries to explain why an omnipotent, all-loving God might or would allow evil in our world. In reflecting on these theodicies and defenses, I detect that they follow a certain strategy. In fact, I believe that with the exception of the defense for theonomy, all the successful defenses discussed adopt this basic strategy. Even many unsuccessful defenses generally follow this approach. If so, it would be instructive to sketch that strategy, especially for the sake of those who would defend their own theology by constructing a defense against the various problems of evil in either their logical or their evidential form.

The strategy involves four basic steps. The theologian begins by adopting a notion of divine omnipotence according to which God can do only what is logically possible. This, of course, means he can't actualize a world that contains contradictory states of affairs.

The second step is to argue that in creating a world, God had to choose between actualizing one of two good things. The two are mutually contradictory, so God couldn't do both, because the theist's notion of omnipotence doesn't allow God to actualize a contradiction. Regardless of the theology, one of the two options will be removing evil. Depending on the theology, the other option will specify some other valuable thing God could do in creating a world. For Leibniz, it is creating the best of all possible worlds, metaphysically speaking. The free will defender says God's second option was to create a world with incompatibilistically free creatures. For Hick that second option was to create a world where souls are built. For my own theology, the second option was creating a world with non-glorified human beings in it.

Once the theist sets up these two options, he argues that God cannot do both conjointly. If he removes evil, he cannot create the best of all possible worlds, metaphysically speaking. If he gives us free will, he can't also remove evil. To build souls there must be evil, so he can't both build souls and remove evil. If he removes evil, he can't create human beings and let them function as they were intended to function in our world. In each case, one option logically excludes the other.

The third step in the strategy of defense and theodicy-making appeals to a commonly held ethical principle. This principle says that no one can be held morally accountable for failing to do what they couldn't do or for doing what they couldn't fail to do. In other words, no one is morally accountable unless they act freely. But in all of the cases in question, God isn't free both to remove evil and to accomplish the other positive goal in our world. Hence, he isn't guilty for failing to do both. For example, God can either remove evil or give us free will. If he removes evil, he isn't guilty for failing to give us free will. If he gives us free will, he isn't guilty for failing to remove evil. He can't do both conjointly, so he isn't guilty for failing to do both.

Some might agree that God isn't guilty for failing to actualize both options, but still wonder why God chose the option he did, rather than the option of removing evil. If the option God chose is something evil or at least a good which is a lesser good than removing evil, then it still seems that God did something wrong. This brings us to the final step in the strategy of defense and theodicy-making. The theist grants that if God had chosen to remove evil, he would have done something very good. However, the theist argues that the option God chose is a value of such magnitude that it is at least as valuable as removing evil. It either counterbalances or overbalances the evil present in our world. Hence, in choosing this option rather than removing evil, God has done nothing wrong.

In sum, the basic strategy of theodicy and defense-making is to argue that God is a good God, despite the evil in our world, because he cannot remove it. He cannot, that is, if he wants to do more with our world then simply remove evil. God could either remove evil or do something else of value with our world, but not both conjointly, because the two contradict each other. Since he can't do both, he isn't guilty for failing to do both. Moreover, what he did choose brought a value of the highest order into our world. God has fulfilled his moral obligation; he is a good God.

Πotes

1: INTRODUCTION

1. David Hume, *Dialogues Concerning Natural Religion,* part X, in *The Empiricists* (Garden City, N.Y.: Doubleday, 1974), 490.

2. J. L. Mackie, "Evil and Omnipotence," in Basil Mitchell, ed., *Philosophy of Religion* (Oxford: Oxford University Press, 1971), 92.

3. Peter T. Geach, *Providence and Evil* (Cambridge: Cambridge University Press, 1977), 29.

4. For a detailed explanation and defense of this theology, see my *No One Like Him: The Doctrine of God* (Wheaton, Ill.: Crossway, 2001).

5. What I call a religious problem of evil coincides with what Ahern calls a specific concrete problem, a problem which arises from the actual world as experienced by an individual. See M. B. Ahern, *The Problem of Evil* (New York: Schocken, 1971), 8. Brian K. Cameron speaks of an existential problem of evil as he discusses Marilyn McCord Adams's response to the problem of evil. As Cameron describes this problem, it is in the main what I am calling the religious problem of evil. See Brian K. Cameron, "A Critique of Marilyn McCord Adams' 'Christian Solution' to the Existential Problem of Evil," *American Catholic Philosophical Quarterly* 73 (Summer 1998): 420-424. The work by Marilyn Adams to which Cameron refers is "Redemptive Suffering: A Christian Solution to the Problem of Evil," in Robert Audi and William J. Wainwright, eds., *Rationality, Religious Belief, and Moral Commitment* (Ithaca, N.Y.: Cornell University Press, 1986).

6. Ahern (*Problem of Evil*) calls this problem the general problem (p. 4). He also delineates what he calls specific abstract problems, problems that deal with specific kinds (moral and physical, for example), degrees, and numbers of evils that do or might exist (pp. 7-8).

7. Or someone might say that once one sees that "evil" should be interpreted on an emotivist account of ethics, one comes to understand that evil really doesn't exist. According to an emotivist account of ethics, ethical claims don't assert facts about the world. They merely express the utterer's feelings about something. Hence, "It's not right that I have to suffer so terribly," on an emotivist rendering of ethics means little more than that the speaker doesn't like pain. It doesn't assert that his afflictions are truly unjust.

8. Alvin Plantinga, *God, Freedom, and Evil* (New York: Harper & Row, 1974), 63-64.

9. In recent years a problem related to the wastefulness of the evolutionary process has been raised. Those who think evolution gives the correct account of origins and that God is in some way in control of evolution wonder why the process has taken such a long and destructive (of individual life forms) route to form the various species we have today. An article which discusses this problem and gives a very helpful bibliography relevant to this topic is Christopher Southgate, "God and Evolutionary Evil: Theodicy in the Light of Darwinism," *Zygon* 37 (December 2002). If this issue raises a difficult issue, so much the worse for theistic evolution and evolution in general. Traditional Christian theism hasn't embraced Darwinian evolution, and hence it is understandable that this is not a problem of evil that is raised against traditional theism.

10.　Bertha Alvarez, "How the Problem of Evil Poses an Obstacle to Belief in God," *Dialogue* 41 (April 1998): 23.

11.　Richard Schoenig, "The Free Will Theodicy," *Religious Studies* 34 (1998): 470.

12.　Plantinga, *God, Freedom, and Evil,* 28.

2: THEONOMY AND THE PROBLEM OF EVIL

1.　Such a universe is called theonomous. "Theonomy" comes from two Greek words, *theos* (God) and *nomos* (law). The idea is that God (his will in particular) is law in this universe.

2.　Peter T. Geach, *God and the Soul* (New York: Schocken, 1969), 126-127.

3.　For a discussion of some theologians whose views on ethics fit theonomy see G. Stanley Kane, "The Concept of Divine Goodness and the Problem of Evil," *Religious Studies* 11 (1975). As Kane shows, for example, John Calvin held the basic theonomous notion that whatever God wills to be righteous is righteous by that fact alone (p. 68).

4.　For an extensive discussion of the whole issue of divine providence and its relation to human freedom and moral responsibility, see my *No One Like Him: The Doctrine of God* (Wheaton, Ill.: Crossway, 2001).

5.　For discussion of this issue consult David W. Clark, "Voluntarism and Rationalism in the Ethics of Ockham," *Franciscan Studies* 31 (1971): 72-87; and Linwood Urban, "William of Ockham's Theological Ethics," *Franciscan Studies* 33 (1973): 310-350.

6.　Heiko A. Oberman, *The Harvest of Medieval Theology* (Grand Rapids, Mich.: Eerdmans, 1967), 37.

7.　Gordon Leff, *Medieval Thought* (Baltimore: Penguin, 1970), 288.

8.　Philotheus Boehner, "Introduction," in William of Ockham, *Philosophical Writings,* introduction and trans. Philotheus Boehner (New York: Bobbs-Merrill, 1964), xlvi.

9.　Ibid., xlix.

10.　Oberman, *Harvest of Medieval Theology,* 99. The view that results when applied to ethics is a position like a modified version of divine command ethics. God, rather than choosing ethical rules in a totally arbitrary way, chooses whatever he wants, but what he wants is governed by his nature. I note that one can hold a modified divine command theory of ethics without adopting divine simplicity. For example, I hold a modified divine command theory of ethics (see John Feinberg and Paul Feinberg, *Ethics for a Brave New World* [Wheaton, Ill.: Crossway, 1993], chapter 1), but I also reject the doctrine of divine simplicity (see Feinberg, *No One Like Him,* chapter 7).

11.　William of Ockham, *"Sententiarum* IV," *Opera Plurima, Vol. 4:1494–1496* (London: Gregg, 1962), q. 9, E and F. Hereafter cited as Ockham, *Sent.* IV.

12.　William of Ockham, *"Sententiarum* II," *Opera Plurima, vol. 4:1494–1496,* q. 19, O. Hereafter cited as Ockham, *Sent.* II.

13.　Ockham, *Sent.* IV, q. 8 and 9, E and F.

14.　Ockham, *Philosophical Writings,* 163.

15.　Ibid., 162.

16.　Clark, "Voluntarism and Rationalism," 79-80.

17.　Gabriel Biel, *Lect.* (Basel, 1510), 23E.

18.　Ockham, *Sent.* II, q. 19, O.

19.　Ibid., q. 19, H. For further clarification of some of the key points in Ockham's ethical theory, see Kane, "Concept of Divine Goodness," 63-64.

20.　I have been discussing Ockham's ethics in this section of the chapter, and they clearly fit with the theonomous metaphysic Ockham also holds. In fact, it might seem that commitment to a theonomous metaphysic automatically entails adopting a theonomous meta-ethic, but this is not so. Obviously, doctrines about the meaning of "good" and "evil" like G. E. Moore's view that "good" stands for a nonnatural property don't fit theonomy's views on what kinds of things are good or evil, because according to theonomy, no property (nonnatural or otherwise) intrinsic to any action is the reason for calling it "good" or "evil." Likewise, a natural law meta-ethic doesn't fit theonomy, because natural law theory guarantees that some things are always good and others are always evil because of the nature of the universe. There are, however, other meta-ethical positions theonomists could hold. They might hold any modern nonrealist or nonobjectivist view about the meaning of ethical terms. For example, a theonomist who held that God's omnipotent will is the constant for the universe could also hold meta-ethically either Hare's universal prescriptivism or Firth's and Brandt's ideal observer theory. By combining theonomy and universal prescriptivism, for example, one could derive the view that any rational non-fanatical prescriber must universally prescribe what his creator has set forth as universal moral law. Though few, if any, universal prescriptivists or ideal observer theorists hold a theonomous metaphysic, that just describes things as they are, not as they *could be*. My meta-ethical point is that a theonomous metaphysic doesn't necessarily bind one to a theonomous meta-ethic.

21. James King, "The Meta-ethical Dimension of the Problem of Evil," *The Journal of Value Inquiry* 5 (Summer 1971): 178; James King, "The Problem of Evil and the Meaning of Good," *Proceedings of the Catholic Philosophical Association* 44 (1970): 188.

22. Ibid.

23. This doesn't mean that the problem of evil in its logical form is irrelevant to God's existence. My point is that what is under attack is a particular theological conception of God. Insofar as that theology squares with the God who actually exists, the attack on that theological system also attacks God. Showing that a given conception of God squares with how things actually are, i.e., showing that a given theology is correct in its portrayal of God and the world, is a task that goes beyond the scope of this book. And it is important to understand why that is so!

24. For further refutation of theonomous ethics, see Kane, "Concept of Divine Goodness," 68ff.

3: LEIBNIZ AND THE PROBLEM OF EVIL

1. Roughly, the principle of sufficient reason is that for everything that occurs or is there must be a sufficient reason that it occurs or exists as opposed to something else happening or existing. If two options seem equal with nothing preferable about either, there won't be a sufficient reason to choose one over the other. Hence, neither will be chosen.

2. Nicholas Rescher, "Leibniz on Possible Worlds," *Studia Leibnitiana* 28 (1996): 158-160.

3. Gottfried W. Leibniz, "The Freedom of Man in the Origin of Evil," *Theodicy*, trans. E. M. Huggard (New York: Bobbs-Merrill, 1966), part 1, sec. 21, 40. Hereafter cited as Leibniz, *Theodicy*, "Evil."

4. Leroy T. Howe, "Leibniz on Evil," *Sophia* 10 (October 1971): 15.

5. Leibniz, *Theodicy*, "Evil," part 1, sec. 20, 40.

6. Ibid., part 3, sec. 241, 124.

7. Ibid., part 1, sec. 21, 40.

8. As Joseph Owens explains, a *pros hen* equivocal term is used equivocally, but despite its equivocal usage, all its uses in one way or another *refer to one thing*. See Joseph Owens, *The Doctrine of Being in the Aristotelian 'Metaphysics'* (Toronto: Medieval Studies of Toronto, 1963), 117. See also the detailed discussion of Leibniz's understanding of metaphysical evil in Michael Latzer, "Leibniz's Conception of Metaphysical Evil," *Journal of the History of Ideas* 55 (January 1994).

9. Rescher, "Leibniz on Possible Worlds," 148-151.

10. Leibniz, *Theodicy*, "Evil," part 1, sec. 37, 47.

11. Benson Mates, "Leibniz on Possible Worlds," in *Leibniz*, Harry G. Frankfurt, ed. (Garden City, N.Y.: Doubleday, 1972), 337.

12. Ibid.
13. Leibniz, *Theodicy,* "Evil," part 2, sec. 173, 102.
14. Ibid., part 3, sec. 349, 153.
15. Ibid., part 3, sec. 367, 157-158.
16. Ibid., part 3, sec. 335, 148-149.
17. Ibid., part 3, sec. 275, 133-134. See also Leonard J. Russell, "Possible Worlds in Leibniz," *Studia Leibnitiana* 1 (1969): 161-162.
18. E. M. Curley, "The Root of Contingency," in *Leibniz,* Harry G. Frankfurt, ed. (Garden City, N.Y.: Doubleday, 1972), 93. See also Mates, "Leibniz on Possible Worlds," 338.
19. Leibniz, *Theodicy,* "Evil," part 1, sec. 52, 51-52.
20. Ibid., part 1, sec. 9, 36. See also Mates, "Leibniz on Possible Worlds," 340.
21. Ibid., part 1, sec. 8, 35.
22. Ibid.
23. Ibid., part 1, sec. 1, 31. Put differently, Leibniz tries to show that the world isn't metaphysically imperfect, but also that there is an answer to the problems of moral and physical evil generated by the presence of those evils in the world.
24. Leibniz, *Theodicy,* "Evil," part 1, sec. 1, 31.
25. Specifically, they resolve the problem of evil with the free will defense, but understand God's sovereignty in relation to human freedom as a Calvinist might. The difficulty is that the free will defense incorporates a notion of free will that contradicts some basic concepts in a Calvinistic theology. For details on this issue, see my chapter 4.
26. Ibid., part 2, sec. 120, 77.
27. Ibid., part 2, sec. 120, 77-78.
28. Ibid., part 3, sec. 319, 144.
29. Henry J. Schuurman, "Two Concepts of Theodicy," *American Philosophical Quarterly* 30 (July 1993), has an interesting take on Leibniz's project. Schuurman distinguishes between what he calls a strong and a weak theodicy. A strong theodicy claims that the actual world is the best world God can actualize. A weak theodicy holds that there isn't a best that God can do (pp. 210, 212). Both of these differ from Leibniz's actual position, which claims that there is a best possible world, God is morally obligated to create it, and he not only can do so, but has.
30. Leibniz, *Theodicy,* "Evil," part 1, sec. 78, 60.
31. For an explanation of Leibniz's views on monads (foundational to his metaphysics) see his "Monadology," anthologized in *Monadology and Other Philosophical Essays,* The Library of Liberal Arts, trans. Paul Schrecker and Anne Martin Schrecker (Indianapolis: Bobbs-Merrill, 1965).
32. Leibniz, *Theodicy,* "Evil," part 1, sec. 84, 62.
33. Ibid., part 2, sec. 225, 120-121.
34. Ibid., part 1, sec. 9, 35-36; ibid., part 2, sec. 121, 79-80; Gottfried W. Leibniz, "Preliminary Dissertation on the Conformity of Faith with Reason," *Theodicy,* trans. E. M. Huggard (New York: Bobbs-Merrill, 1966), sec. 38, 18. See also Rescher, "Leibniz on Possible Worlds," 158-160.
35. Leibniz, *Theodicy,* "Evil," part 2, sec. 130, 86. See also, ibid., part 2, sec. 125, 84.
36. For example, Voltaire's *Candide* gleefully pillories this seemingly ridiculous idea.
37. Leibniz, *Theodicy,* "Evil," part 2, sec. 209, 116.
38. Ibid., part 2, secs. 212 and 213, 117.
39. Ibid., part 2, sec. 128, 85.
40. Ibid., part 1, sec. 22, 40-41.
41. Ibid., part 1, sec. 22, 41.
42. Ibid., part 1, sec. 24, 41-42.
43. Ibid., part 1, sec. 25, 42.

44. For those who think it is impossible to do what a) and b) state, see my lengthy discussion of a soft determinist specific sovereignty model of providence in *No One Like Him: The Doctrine of God* (Wheaton, Ill.: Crossway, 2001), chapters 13-14. I am not suggesting that Leibniz holds my model of providence, nor even that he holds a compatibilistic account of human free will as I do. I am only saying that for those who think it altogether impossible to do what Leibniz wanted to do, there is at least one way to accomplish it. Interested readers can consult the details in *No One Like Him*.

45. Leibniz, *Theodicy,* "Evil," part 1, sec. 23, 41.

46. There is another angle to this issue about God's knowledge of and control over the future that is worth mentioning. Leibniz might also respond that this objection rests on a wrong conception of God's relation to time. It seems to incorporate the notion of time as real temporal succession. However, for Leibniz, from God's perspective there is no temporal succession. Hence, he would deny that God's choice of a world binds him for the future. God merely chooses a complex of events that constitutes a possible world, and that's all we can say. Those who hold divine atemporal eternity would be sympathetic to such ideas, whereas proponents of divine temporal eternity wouldn't be, but that is a subject that goes beyond the scope of this book.

47. John Hick, *Evil and the God of Love* (London: Macmillan, 1966; Fontana Library Edition, 1975), 167-168.

48. Ibid., 169-170.

49. In what follows, I shall offer what seem to me the most telling objections to Leibniz's views, but I shall not present the case in favor of those objections. To do so would involve trying to build a conclusive case against the Leibnizian system and for an alternate system. That is a valuable project, but it goes beyond the scope of this book. The point in discussing the logical problem of evil is not to see which theological position best squares with the data of reality. The point is to see whether various theological systems are objectionable on the grounds that they contradict themselves. Hence, the other project goes beyond the purpose of this book.

50. Hick, *Evil and the God of Love,* 173-174.

51. For a further discussion of why it may not be possible, or if possible not desirable, for God to create the best world see Richmond Campbell, "God, Evil, and Humanity," *Sophia* 23 (July 1984): 21-27. Some of what Campbell says does pertain to Leibniz's concept of a best possible world. However, Campbell in general fails to understand the full thrust of Leibniz's views, for he interprets Leibniz's best possible world as a best world, morally speaking. I think his refutation of that notion of a best world is telling, but too much of what he says doesn't touch the concept of a best world, metaphysically speaking.

52. Consequentialism and nonconsequentialism are two broad kinds of ethical theories. The former holds that what makes an action right or wrong are the consequences of that action. Results that promote a desired value (e.g., increase of pleasure and decrease of pain) become morally right and obligatory. Nonconsequentialist ethical theories claim that what makes an act morally right or wrong is something other than its consequences. The fact that the act is mandated by God or deemed to be one's duty, for example, is an example of some of the many reasons (other than consequences) that deeds are considered morally right or wrong. For a further explanation of such ethical theories, see John Feinberg and Paul Feinberg, *Ethics for a Brave New World* (Wheaton, Ill.: Crossway, 1993), chapter 1.

53. See my *No One Like Him: The Doctrine of God* (Wheaton, Ill.: Crossway, 2001).

4: THE FREE WILL DEFENSE

1. For an interesting, though at times confused, discussion of whether God must create a world and the sort of world that was open for him to create see William Rowe, "Evil and God's Freedom in Creation," *American Philosophical Quarterly* 36 (April 1999).

2. Consequentialism (known also as teleological ethics) claims that what makes an action good or bad, right or wrong are the consequences that result from it. Nonconsequentialism (often referred to as deontological ethics) says that whatever makes an action right or wrong (e.g., it keeps a promise or obeys a divine command) is something other than the consequences of the action.

3. Augustine, *On Free Choice of the Will,* trans. Anna Benjamin and L. H. Hackstaff (New York: Bobbs-Merrill, 1964), book II, chapter 1, 36.

4. Ibid., book I, chapter 1, 3.

5. Ibid., book I, chapter 3, 6-8; ibid., book I, chapter 15, 29-33.

6. Ibid., book I, chapter 16, 34.

7. Ibid., book II, chapter 3, 40.

8. Ibid., book II, chapter 19, 80-81.

9. Ibid., 81.

10. Ibid., book II, chapter 1, 36; ibid., book II, chapter 18, 79.

11. Ibid., book III, chapter 3, 90-93.

12. Ibid., book III, chapter 4, 94-95.

13. Ibid., book III, chapter 17, 125-126.

14. Ibid., book III, chapter 23, 140-141.

15. For a discussion of Augustine's and Aquinas's understanding of the cause of evil, see Carlos Steel, "Does Evil Have a Cause? Augustine's Perplexity and Thomas's Answer," *Review of Metaphysics* 48 (December 1994). For an interesting study on how Augustine, given his views prior to converting to Christianity, came to hold the free will defense in the form presented in my text, see Rowan A. Greer, "Augustine's Transformation of the Free Will Defence," *Faith and Philosophy* 13 (October 1996).

16. For other expressions and defenses of the free will defense see Bruce R. Reichenbach, "The Deductive Argument from Evil," *Sophia* 20 (1981); G. Stanley Kane, "The Free-Will Defense Defended," *New Scholasticism* 50 (1976); Michael P. Smith, "What's So Good About Feeling Bad?" *Faith and Philosophy* 2/4 (October 1985); Thomas F. Tracy, "Victimization and the Problem of Evil: A Response to Ivan Karamazov," *Faith and Philosophy* 9 (July 1992); Edward J. Khamara, "Mackie's Paradox and the Free Will Defence," *Sophia* 34 (1995); Sung-Keun You, "Why Are There Sinners? Augustine's Response to Mackie," *International Journal for Philosophy of Religion* 37 (1995); and Gene Fendt, "God Is Love, Therefore There Is Evil," *Philosophy and Theology* 9 (1995). Further discussions of the free will defense appear in C. Mason Myers, "Free Will and the Problem of Evil," *Religious Studies* 23 (1987); William Hasker, "Providence and Evil: Three Theories," *Religious Studies* 28 (1992); J. L. Schellenberg, "Claims and the Problem of Evil," *Sophia* 32 (1993); Michael P. Levine, "Pantheism, Theism and the Problem of Evil," *Philosophy of Religion* 35 (1994); A. M. Weisberger, "Depravity, Divine Responsibility and Moral Evil: A Critique of a New Free Will Defence," *Religious Studies* 31 (1995); Sandra Menssen, "Maximal Wickedness vs. Maximal Goodness," *American Catholic Philosophical Quarterly* 71 (1997); Ryan Nichols, "Actions, Their Effects and Preventable Evil," *International Journal for Philosophy of Religion* 46 (December 1999); Donal P. O'Mathuna, "'Why Me, God?' Understanding Suffering," *Ethics and Medicine* 15 (1999); Tom Mawson, "The Problem of Evil and Moral Indifference," *Religious Studies* 35 (September 1999). Articles that attack the free will defense in general and Plantinga's expression of it in particular in one way or another are Fred Chernoff, "The Obstinance of Evil," *Mind* 89 (1980); Frederick W. Kroon, "Plantinga on God, Freedom, and Evil," *International Journal for Philosophy of Religion* 12 (1981); Hugh LaFollette, "Plantinga on the Free Will Defense," *International Journal for Philosophy of Religion* 11 (1980); James E. Tomberlin and Frank McGuinness, "God, Evil, and the Free Will Defence," *Religious Studies* 13 (1977); Evan Fales, "Should God Not Have Created Adam?" *Faith and Philosophy* 9 (April 1992); David Lewis, "Evil for Freedom's Sake?" *Philosophical*

Papers 22 (1993); John Bishop, "Evil and the Concept of God," *Philosophical Papers* 22 (1993); Richard Shoenig, "The Free Will Theodicy," *Religious Studies* 34 (1998); Daniel Howard-Snyder and John O'Leary-Hawthorne, "Transworld Sanctity and Plantinga's Free Will Defense," *International Journal for Philosophy of Religion* 44 (1998); and K. H. A. Esmail, "Plantinga's Defence of the Free Will Defence in Chapter Nine of the *Nature of Necessity*," *Sophia* 41 (2002). Examples of articles written in defense of Plantinga against these attacks are Del Ratzsch, "Tomberlin and McGuinness on Plantinga's Free Will Defense," *International Journal for Philosophy of Religion* 12 (1981); Barry L. Gan, "Plantinga's Transworld Depravity: It's Got Possibilities," *International Journal for Philosophy of Religion* 13 (1982); Jonathan N. Evans, "Lafollette on Plantinga's Free Will Defense," *International Journal for Philosophy of Religion* 14 (1983); and William L. Rowe, "In Defense of 'The Free Will Defense'," *International Journal for Philosophy of Religion* 44 (1998). For an application of Plantinga's free will defense to the problem of hell and universalism see Jerry L. Walls, "Can God Save Anyone He Wills?" *Scottish Journal of Theology* 38 (1985). For a discussion of the free will defense as it relates to natural evil and a broad conception of theism called Orthodox Christian Theism (as opposed to a more meager version of theism that might be held by various Christians, Jews, and Muslims and by philosophical theologians interested in discussing the problem of evil apart from a specific religious tradition) see David O'Connor, "A Reformed Problem of Evil and the Free Will Defence," *International Journal for Philosophy of Religion* 39 (February 1996). Finally, a defense of the free will defense against Antony Flew's charges appears in Richard L. Purtill, "Flew and the Free Will Defence," *Religious Studies* 13 (1977).

17. Antony Flew, "Divine Omnipotence and Human Freedom," in *New Essays in Philosophical Theology,* ed. Antony Flew and Alasdair MacIntyre (New York: Macmillan, 1973), 145. Hereafter cited as Flew, "Omnipotence and Freedom." Consult also Antony Flew, "Compatibilism, Free Will and God," *Philosophy* 48 (July 1973): 231-232. Hereafter cited as Flew, "Compatibilism."

18. Flew, "Omnipotence and Freedom," 145. This is the third move in Flew, "Compatibilism."

19. Flew, "Omnipotence and Freedom," 145-146. This is the second and part of the third move as expressed in Flew, "Compatibilism."

20. Flew, "Compatibilism," 232; Flew, "Omnipotence and Freedom," 146.

21. Flew, "Omnipotence and Freedom," 149; Flew, "Compatibilism," 233.

22. Flew, "Compatibilism," 233.

23. Ibid., 234-235.

24. Ibid., 239.

25. Ibid., 233.

26. Ibid., 233 and 234.

27. Ibid., 234.

28. For a fuller description of compatibilistic free will, along with examples that actually illustrate this kind of free will, see my *No One Like Him: The Doctrine of God* (Wheaton, Ill.: Crossway, 2001), chapter 13.

29. Flew, "Compatibilism," 235.

30. Even if one adopts Flew's concept of compatibilism so that a compelled action is free (the Bank Manager), his main point about the free will defense is still clear enough. What Flew and other compatibilists would have to accept in principle is that an act can be free though causally determined, so apparently God could give us free will and still guarantee that we won't use it for anything but good. The difference of opinion between Flew and other compatibilists about the exact way to define compatibilism doesn't undercut Flew's point about the free will defense.

31. J. L. Mackie, "Evil and Omnipotence," in Basil Mitchell, ed., *The Philosophy of Religion* (London: Oxford University Press, 1971), 98.

32. Ibid.

33. Ibid., 99.

34. Ibid., 100.

35. Philip Bennett refers to Mackie's argument this way in Philip W. Bennett, "Evil, God, and the Free Will Defense," *Australasian Journal of Philosophy* 51 (May 1973): 39-50.

36. Mackie, "Evil and Omnipotence," 100-101.

37. Actually, they are thinking of incompatibilism or libertarian free will. Libertarians deny that their view of free will involves randomness, but determinists such as Mackie obviously think it does. While Mackie's description of incompatibilism would be rejected by incompatibilists, it is clear that what he describes couldn't be said of compatibilism or some harder form of determinism. He is clearly referring to incompatibilism.

38. Mackie, "Evil and Omnipotence," 101.

39. As I shall note in my discussion of the evidential problem of evil, Mackie later in life admitted that the free will defense can solve the logical problem of evil. However, even in that discussion in *The Miracle of Theism,* he wavers back and forth about whether or not the free will defense works. At the stage in his thinking represented by "Evil and Omnipotence," he was convinced that it didn't work.

40. Ninian Smart, "Omnipotence, Evil and Supermen," in *God and Evil,* ed. Nelson Pike (Englewood Cliffs, N.J.: Prentice Hall, 1964), 103-104.

41. Ibid., 104.

42. J. L. Mackie, "Theism and Utopia," *Philosophy* 37 (1962): 153-154.

43. Ibid., 154.

44. Alvin Plantinga, *God, Freedom, and Evil* (New York: Harper & Row, 1974), 26.

45. I must interject at this point that what Plantinga says is true, if one is dealing with a Modified Rationalist theology of some sort. What he says must be done isn't what a theonomist or a Leibnizian Rationalist must do, because their problems of evil arise differently than does the Modified Rationalist's, and their problems require a different approach to solve them.

46. Plantinga, *God, Freedom, and Evil,* 29-30.

47. Ibid., 30.

48. Ibid., 31.

49. Alvin Plantinga, "The Free Will Defence," in *The Philosophy of Religion,* ed. Basil Mitchell (London: Oxford University Press, 1971), 108-109; Alvin Plantinga, *God and Other Minds* (Ithaca, N.Y.: Cornell University Press, 1967), 134-135.

50. Plantinga, *God and Other Minds,* 136-138.

51. Ibid., 138.

52. Ibid.

53. Ibid.

54. Ibid.

55. Ibid.

56. Ibid., 138-139.

57. Ibid., 137.

58. Ibid., 139. As we shall see later, (5c) still troubles Plantinga even if it is only contingently true. He introduces the notion of transworld depravity, and if everyone suffers from it, that is a reason for thinking that (5c) isn't even contingently true. More on transworld depravity later.

59. Ibid.

60. See the passage cited from Mackie and numbered as note 36 in this chapter. That passage demonstrates this point.

61. Plantinga, *God and Other Minds,* 141.
62. Plantinga, *God, Freedom, and Evil,* 34-36.
63. Plantinga, *God and Other Minds,* 140-141.
64. Plantinga, *God, Freedom, and Evil,* 39-40.
65. Ibid., 42-44. Note again that all of this assumes that we interpret Plantinga's (5) as (5b). As already argued, compatibilism versus incompatibilism is at issue with (5b). Moreover, note that none of this is relevant to (5) as (5c). Transworld depravity handles that interpretation of (5).
66. As Plantinga explains, the error isn't believing that there are possible worlds in which free human beings never do anything wrong. Rather, the error comes in accepting Leibniz's Lapse and hence thinking that under any circumstances imaginable God could actualize such a possible world. See Plantinga, *God, Freedom, and Evil,* 44.
67. Plantinga, *God, Freedom, and Evil,* 45-47.
68. Ibid., 47.
69. Ibid., 48.
70. Ibid.
71. Ibid., 58-59; Plantinga, *God and Other Minds,* 151-152.
72. Plantinga, *God, Freedom, and Evil,* 27-28.
73. Ibid., 58-59.
74. Alvin Plantinga, "Reply to the Basingers on Divine Omnipotence," *Process Studies* 11/1 (Spring 1981): 26-27, as cited in David Ray Griffin, *Evil Revisited* (Albany: State University of New York Press, 1991), 42.
75. Griffin, *Evil Revisited,* 43-44. Relatedly, Matt Ingraham also thinks Plantinga should offer a theodicy if he hopes to convince his contemporaries. However, Ingraham thinks that any attempt to turn the free will defense into a free will theodicy isn't likely to succeed. See Ingraham's "Why Plantinga's Free Will Defense Cannot Be Expanded into a Theodicy," *Dialogue* 36 (April 1994).
76. Griffin, *Evil Revisited,* 42-48 passim.
77. Ibid., 46ff.
78. Ibid., 45, 46. Griffin (44-45) argues that in a court case a jury is asked to acquit only if there is a *reasonable* doubt of innocence, not just a *possible* doubt. He then imagines a case where someone is accused of theft, but pleads innocent because of having been abducted by aliens on the morning in question. Even though the story is consistent with the defendant's innocence, that wouldn't be enough to acquit him, because the story is so unbelievable. The problem with Griffin's example is that the defendant isn't accused of a contradiction, but of robbery. Direct evidence will be necessary to show that claim plausible or implausible. Hence, his story which shows his innocence *consistent* with the facts is irrelevant, because there is no direct evidence to prove his story. On the other hand, the logical problem of evil accuses theistic systems of contradicting themselves. The charge isn't that there is direct evidence that makes a given theology implausible. If that were so (as it is with the evidential problem), the theist had better either offer evidence that makes his system plausible, or explain why the atheist's challenge doesn't make theism implausible. But the complaint with the logical problem of evil is a different one. This complaint says there is no possible way to fit God's existence together with evil without contradiction. This challenge requires a different kind of response than does Griffin's court case.
79. See others who apparently think so since they complain about the same thing. Their complaint is specifically with Plantinga but more generally with theists whose only concern is to meet the logical theoretical dimensions of this problem. See, for example, David Basinger and Randall Basinger, "Divine Omnipotence: Plantinga vs. Griffin," *Process Studies* 11/1 (Spring 1984); and Kenneth Surin, *Theology and the Problem of Evil* (Oxford: Basil Blackwell, 1986). On pages 70-78 Surin makes the point in regard

to Plantinga. His introduction and chapters 1 and 2 make the point more generally about all attempts to solve the problem of evil. For an example of someone who sees the same need and thinks he has found a theodicy that suits modern needs see Charles Pinches, "Christian Pacifism and Theodicy: The Free Will Defense in the Thought of John H. Yoder," *Modern Theology* 5/3 (April 1989).

80. Alvin Plantinga, "Reply to the Basingers on Divine Omnipotence," *Process Studies* 11/1 (Spring 1981): 26. See also his comments on pages 27-28 which Griffin cites (*Evil Revisited,* 44) and then rejects as inadequate, because he thinks a defense which only proves logical consistency isn't a successful defense even of the consistency of the propositions involved if it is an implausible defense.

81. As I shall point out in later chapters, I'm not at all convinced that the free will defense is inadequate in handling various of the evidential problems of evil where the question is the probability of theism. As to the religious problem, I understand it as an entirely different problem from a problem requiring a theodicy or defense, but more on that later.

82. If the complaint is, instead, that even though there is a spirit world, there is little evidence that evil spirits are the ones who produce much natural evil, that is another question. It is clear, however, that Griffin's complaint isn't this, but the mere fact that the defense appeals to spirit beings. But then, as I say, it is illegitimate to rule out evidence that spirit beings exist on question-begging, anti-supernaturalistic grounds.

83. Those interested in the debate between these two views of free will can consult my *No One Like Him,* chapters 11, 13-14 for a thorough presentation of arguments for and against these positions.

84. I am indebted to Alan Donagan, who first clarified this point for me. Though Donagan was an indeterminist, he held that both views are possible.

85. Griffin, *Evil Revisited,* 15.

86. Ibid., 16.

87. Ibid.

88. Ibid., 18-19.

89. Ibid., 19.

90. Griffin also complains (*Evil Revisited,* 19) that the free will defense may promote callousness toward others' suffering. God apparently doesn't think suffering is a very serious matter since he creates conditions which produce it in order to use it to stimulate spiritual growth. Since that is so, we might easily conclude that the suffering of others isn't really something we should try to assuage. Again, this complains about the soul-building theodicy, not the free will defense.

91. Griffin, *Evil Revisited,* 19.

92. Ibid., 20.

93. Ibid., 21.

94. Ibid.

95. Ibid., chapters 1, 4, and 5.

96. Ibid., 17-18.

97. I should add here that I would make the same reply to others who reject various Modified Rationalist theologies, including my own, on the grounds that God could have created a better world. That objection misses the point of how a logical problem of evil arises for a Modified Rationalist theology and what the theologian must do to answer it.

98. Griffin, *Evil Revisited,* 20.

99. Steven E. Boër, "The Irrelevance of the Free Will Defence," *Analysis* 38 (1977): 110-112.

100. Frank B. Dilley, "Is the Free Will Defence Irrelevant?" *Religious Studies* 18 (1982): 355.

101. In defense of Boër, see, for example, Robert McKim, "Worlds Without Evil," *International Journal for Philosophy of Religion* 15 (1984). Opposing viewpoints are found in the work of Michael Coughlan and Frank Dilley. See, for example, Michael J. Coughlan, "In Defence of Free Will Theodicy," *Religious Studies* 23 (1987); Frank

B. Dilley, "Is The Free Will Defence Irrelevant?"; and Frank B. Dilley, "The Free-Will Defence and Worlds Without Moral Evil," *Philosophy of Religion* 27 (1990).

102. Dilley, "Free Will Defence," 3.

103. As Dilley also explains, this will make it nonsensical to try to do evil, since one can't succeed, but it will also make it meaningless to try to do good, since whatever one does will turn out good. Hence, by cutting the nerve between intentions and consequences of actions, one apparently removes meaningful bases for assessing moral praise or blame for actions. But, a view that truncates the notion of moral responsibility is hardly a friend to human freedom. See these objections as Dilley expounds them in "Is the Free Will Defence Irrelevant?" 357-359.

104. Dilley, "Is the Free Will Defence Irrelevant?" 360-361.

105. Dilley, "Free Will Defence," 9.

106. Of course, this problem arises for those libertarians who think God doesn't know the future. Many libertarians believe that God does know the future, even though his creatures' actions are free (incompatibilistically). Toward the end of this chapter, I shall discuss and evaluate various indeterminist attempts to accommodate divine foreknowledge to future free human actions. Suffice it to say now that for those who believe God doesn't know the future, Dilley's objections are formidable.

107. Harry G. Frankfurt, "Alternate Possibilities and Moral Responsibility," *The Journal of Philosophy* 66 (December 1969).

108. Andrew Eshleman, "Alternate Possibilities and the Free Will Defence," *Religious Studies* 33 (1997): 269.

109. Flew, "Divine Omnipotence and Human Freedom," 150.

110. Eshleman, "Alternate Possibilities and the Free Will Defence," 268.

111. Ibid., 269.

112. Feinberg, *No One Like Him,* chapter 14.

113. Joseph Runzo, "Omniscience and Freedom for Evil," *International Journal for Philosophy of Religion* 12 (1981): 131. For a further expression of this problem see Frederick W. Kroon, "Plantinga on God, Freedom, and Evil," *International Journal for Philosophy of Religion* 12 (1981): 90.

114. Runzo, "Omniscience and Freedom for Evil," 132. For a thorough definition and discussion of this divine attribute see my *No One Like Him,* chapter 7.

115. Ibid., 133-139.

116. Ibid., 139-141.

117. For a presentation of presentism by those who espouse it, see Clark Pinnock, Richard Rice, John Sanders, William Hasker, and David Basinger, *The Openness of God* (Downers Grove, Ill.: InterVarsity Press, 1994); and John Sanders, *The God Who Risks* (Downers Grove, Ill.: InterVarsity Press, 1998). For a thorough discussion and critique of open theism and presentism in particular, see my *No One Like Him.*

118. Runzo, "Omniscience and Freedom for Evil," 144.

119. See Thomas V. Morris, *Our Idea of God* (Downers Grove, Ill.: InterVarsity Press, 1991), 97-99, for a lengthier explanation of and interaction with this view. See also Norman Geisler's essay in Basinger and Basinger's *Predestination and Free Will* (Downers Grove, Ill.: InterVarsity Press, 1986) for an example of someone who resolves the problem of freedom and foreknowledge this way.

120. David P. Hunt, "Divine Providence and Simple Foreknowledge," *Faith and Philosophy* 10 (July 1993): 398.

121. William Hasker, *God, Time, and Knowledge* (Ithaca, N.Y.: Cornell University Press, 1989), 56.

122. Ibid., 59.

123. This is an adaptation of an option Basinger proposes in his discussion of David Hunt's attempt to support simple foreknowledge. See David Basinger, "Simple Foreknowledge

and Providential Control: A Response to Hunt," *Faith and Philosophy* 10 (July 1993): 423ff.

124. Thomas Kapitan, "Providence, Foreknowledge, and Decision Procedures," *Faith and Philosophy* 10 (July 1993): 416. Kapitan offers an earlier version of the doxastic principle, but settles on the revised version mentioned in my text as more defensible.

125. See the rest of Kapitan's article for elaboration of this point. Hunt attempts a response to Kapitan's argument, but it doesn't seem particularly convincing. See David P. Hunt, "Prescience and Providence: A Reply to My Critics," *Faith and Philosophy* 10 (July 1993): 428-431.

126. Hunt, "Divine Providence and Simple Foreknowledge," 398. See also the preceding pages for development of this illustration.

127. Hasker, *God, Time, and Knowledge,* 58-62. Hasker offers two illustrations of this point, an imagined future marriage of Susan and Kenneth, and the encirclement of the Allied armies in World War II by the Germans at Dunkirk in 1940. Anything God would know in advance about either of those events by means of simple foreknowledge wouldn't make it possible for him to help either side by enhancing weather conditions, for example, for if God doesn't see himself doing this already, he couldn't decide to do it and change a future he has already foreseen as occurring.

128. Ibid., 62-63.

129. David Hunt believes that he can answer this, but I believe his suggestion is incoherent. For further discussion of this argument see Hunt, "Divine Providence and Simple Foreknowledge," 404-405. See also Basinger's response to Hunt, "Simple Foreknowledge and Providential Control: A Response to Hunt," and Hunt's rejoinder in "Prescience and Providence: A Reply to My Critics."

130. Morris, *Our Idea of God,* 95.

131. For further discussion of middle knowledge, see Robert M. Adams, "Middle Knowledge and the Problem of Evil," *American Philosophical Quarterly* 14 (April 1977); Bruce Reichenbach, "The Deductive Argument from Evil," *Sophia* 20 (1981): 35-36; Richard Otte, "A Defense of Middle Knowledge," *Philosophy of Religion* 21 (1987); William L. Craig, *The Only Wise God: The Compatibility of Divine Foreknowledge and Human Freedom* (Grand Rapids, Mich.: Baker, 1987); Peter Hutcheson, "Omniscience and the Problem of Evil," *Sophia* 31 (1992); R. Gaskin, "Conditionals of Freedom and Middle Knowledge," *The Philosophical Quarterly* 43 (October 1993); and Kenneth Perszyk, "Molinism and Theodicy," *International Journal for Philosophy of Religion* 44 (1998).

132. Thomas Morris takes a slightly different tack on this whole matter. According to him, God does in fact know the exact future for the following reason: "Knowing how every individual he could possibly create would freely act in every complete set of circumstances he could possibly be placed in, God, by deciding who [sic] to create and what circumstances to create them in, completely provides himself with the knowledge of everything that will happen" (p. 96). The problem here is that if God actually chooses one of the foreseen sequences, then there is a guarantee that the actions in that sequence will occur. And, if that is so, the same problem for incompatibilism arises again, for incompatibilism doesn't seem to admit of guarantees in advance about what will occur.

133. Morris, *Our Idea of God,* 94.

134. William of Ockham, *Ordinatio,* I, Prologue, q. 6.

135. Not even all determinists would say the action in question was the only action that might have occurred. Even strong determinists would say that given antecedent causal conditions at time *t,* x must occur, but before any possible world is chosen, nothing dictates that the world as we will know it at *t* must be actualized. Only on a fatalistic view is there only one world that could be chosen. For a fatalist, there is no possible world in which conditions will be otherwise at *t* than they will be in our world, and that just means that there is no possible world that excludes x at time *t.* Hence, the

notion of accidental necessity rules out fatalism, but it doesn't necessarily rule out all forms of determinism. Moreover, it fits with both incompatibilism and compatibilism.

136. In my exposition of the differences between soft and hard facts, I am relying primarily on Alvin Plantinga's description and explanation of the concepts as he presents them in "On Ockham's Way Out," *Faith and Philosophy* 3/3 (July 1986): 245-248. See also William P. Alston, "Human Foreknowledge and Alternative Conceptions of Human Freedom," *International Journal for Philosophy of Religion* 18 (1985): 21-22. Moreover, my understanding of the Ockhamist strategy for handling the issue of freedom and foreknowledge is greatly indebted to Plantinga's article and to Marilyn Adams's and Norman Kretzmann's introduction to Ockham's treatise *Predestination, God's Foreknowledge, and Future Contingents* (trans. Marilyn McCord Adams and Norman Kretzmann [New York: Appleton-Century-Crofts, 1969]).

137. Here my choice of "believes" rather than "knows" isn't significant. Since God is omniscient, if he really believes something, then it is true. Hence, once we know what he really believes, believed, or will believe, we know that he knows it as well.

138. Ockham, *Predestination, God's Foreknowledge, and Future Contingents,* 50. The passage quoted is in the discussion of question I, assumption 6. See also Adams's and Kretzmann's helpful introduction to the volume.

139. Smart, "Omnipotence, Evil and Supermen," 104-105.

140. Ibid., 105.

141. Ibid., 106.

142. Ibid., 108-109.

143. Ibid., 109-110.

144. Ibid., 110.

145. Ibid.

146. Ibid., 110-111.

147. For an elaboration of this point see my "And the Atheist Shall Lie Down with the Calvinist: Atheism, Calvinism, and the Free Will Defence," *Trinity Journal* 1NS (Fall 1980): 142-152.

148. For elaboration of this point and demonstration that Augustine does incorporate contradictory notions in these areas see Gerard O'Daly, "Predestination and Freedom in Augustine's Ethics," in Godfrey Vesey, ed., *The Philosophy in Christianity* (Cambridge: Cambridge University Press, 1989).

5: SEVERAL CONTEMPORARY MODIFIED RATIONALIST THEOLOGIES

1. G. Schlesinger, "The Problem of Evil and the Problem of Suffering," *American Philosophical Quarterly* 1 (July 1964): 244.

2. Ibid.

3. Ibid., 246.

4. Ibid.

5. Ibid.

6. Ibid.

7. Ibid.

8. Ibid.

9. Ibid.

10. Ibid.

11. Ibid.

12. Schlesinger offered a revised version of his views in *New Perspectives on Old-Time Religion* (Oxford: Clarendon, 1988), 53-76. One notable response to this version comes from Stephen Grover, "Satisfied Pigs and Dissatisfied Philosophers: Schlesinger on the Problem of Evil," *Philosophical Investigations* 16 (April 1993).

13. Jay F. Rosenberg, "The Problem of Evil Revisited: A Reply to Schlesinger," *The Journal of Value Inquiry* 4 (Fall 1970): 214.

14. Ibid., 214-215.

15. Ibid., 215.

16. Ibid.

17. Ibid., 215-216.

18. Ibid., 217.

19. Ibid.

20. Winslow Shea, "God, Evil, and Professor Schlesinger," *The Journal of Value Inquiry* 4 (Fall 1970): 219.

21. Ibid.

22. Ibid., 220.

23. He quotes Schlesinger (p. 221 in Shea's article) and shows that a mathematical concept is in view.

24. Shea, "God, Evil, and Professor Schlesinger," 222.

25. Ibid.

26. Ibid., 222-223.

27. Ibid., 223.

28. Ibid.

29. Ibid.

30. Ibid., 224.

31. Ibid., 226.

32. Ibid., 227.

33. Ibid., 228.

34. In *New Perspectives on Old-Time Religion*, 53-76.

35. Ibid., 54.

36. Ibid., 53.

37. Ibid., 53-54.

38. Stephen Grover, "Satisfied Pigs and Dissatisfied Philosophers," 214-215.

39. Ibid., 215-216.

40. Ibid., 217.

41. Ibid., 217-218.

42. Ibid., 218-219.

43. Ibid., 220.

44. Schlesinger, *New Perspectives on Old-Time Religion*, 55.

45. Grover, 223-225. Readers may also find interesting an exchange in *Faith and Philosophy* about a perfect being creating a surpassable world. This isn't the exact issue Schlesinger is raising, but it does discuss the question of whether there is a best world and whether God is obligated to create it if he creates at all. The relevant literature is Daniel Howard-Snyder and Frances Howard-Snyder, "How an Unsurpassable Being Can Create a Surpassable World," *Faith and Philosophy* 11 (April 1994); and William Rowe's response in "The Problem of No Best World" in the same edition of *Faith and Philosophy*. Also of interest in relation to whether God is obligated to create the best possible world are Charles B. Daniels, "God vs. Less than the Very Best," *Sophia* 35 (March–April 1996); Mark L. Thomas, "Robert Adams and the Best Possible World," *Faith and Philosophy* 13 (April 1996); and Bruce Langtry, "God and the Best," *Faith and Philosophy* 13 (July 1996).

46. Schlesinger, "Problem of Evil and the Problem of Suffering," 246.

47. Ibid.

48. Keith E. Yandell, "The Greater Good Defense," *Sophia* 13 (October 1974): 1.

49. Ibid.

50. Ibid., 3.
51. Ibid. Consult also Keith E. Yandell, "Ethics, Evils and Theism," *Sophia* 8 (1969): 20-21.
52. Yandell, "The Greater Good Defense," 4.
53. Ibid. The last sentence would seem to make better sense if it read that the being created or permitted *E* for the sake of *G*. However, it reads just the opposite. I suspect that this may be a printer's or editor's error; nonetheless, I have quoted Yandell's article as it reads.
54. Ibid.
55. Ibid., 1.
56. Ibid., 5-6.
57. Ibid., 7-8.
58. Ibid., 10; Yandell, "Ethics, Evils and Theism," 22.
59. G. Stanley Kane, "Theism and Evil," *Sophia* 9 (March 1970): 17.
60. Ibid., 16.
61. Keith E. Yandell, "Theism and Evil: A Reply," *Sophia* 11 (January-June 1972): 1.
62. Ibid.
63. Yandell, "Greater Good Defense," 11; Yandell, "Ethics, Evils and Theism," 22.
64. Yandell, "Greater Good Defense," 11.
65. John Hick, *Evil and the God of Love* (London: Macmillan, 1966; Fontana Library edition, 1975), 262-266.
66. Ibid., 262.
67. Ibid., 263.
68. Ibid., 289-290.
69. Ibid., 290.
70. Ibid.
71. Ibid., 291.
72. Ibid., 293-294.
73. Ibid., 308.
74. Ibid., 308-309.
75. Ibid., 310.
76. Ibid., 310-311. For an article that sees Hick's soul-building theodicy as subsuming and presupposing Plantinga's free will defense see George Panthanmackel, "Problem of Evil: Hick's Sublimation of Plantinga," *Journal of Dharma* 23 (1998).
77. Ibid., 344-345.
78. Ibid., 367-369. Hick discusses the option and gives his reasons for rejecting it.
79. Ibid., 372.
80. Ibid.
81. Ibid., 376.
82. Ibid., 377.
83. When I originally wrote this book in the mid-1970s Hick's revised edition hadn't quite come out. Hence, I didn't have access to it. Kane's articles had been published, but for some reason I hadn't come across them. Nonetheless, they are certainly worthy of consideration, especially since Hick himself thought so. My original objections to Hick's theodicy contain one of Kane's complaints, though I stated the point in a slightly different way.
84. G. Stanley Kane, "The Failure of Soul-Making Theodicy," *International Journal for Philosophy of Religion* 6/1 (Spring 1975): 4.
85. Ibid., 15.
86. Ibid., 4ff. For a further discussion of this whole issue of epistemic distance and its relation to theodicy see C. Robert Mesle, "Does God Hide from Us? John Hick and Process Theology on Faith, Freedom and Theodicy," *Philosophy of Religion* 24 (1988).

87. John Hick, *Evil and the God of Love*, rev. ed. (San Francisco: HarperCollins, 1977), 380.

88. Kane, "Failure of Soul-Making Theodicy," 8-9.

89. William Hasker, "Suffering, Soul-Making, and Salvation," *International Philosophical Quarterly* 28 (March 1988): 11.

90. Ibid., 12.

91. Hick, *Evil and the God of Love*, rev. ed., 382.

92. Kane, "Failure of Soul-Making Theodicy," 2.

93. Ibid., 2-3.

94. Hick, *Evil and the God of Love*, rev. ed., 377-378.

95. Ibid., 378-379.

96. G. Stanley Kane, "Soul-Making Theodicy and Eschatology," *Sophia* 14 (1975): 27. Hick raises this objection himself on page 384, and then says his response is in his book *Death and Eternal Life*, chapter 13.

97. John Hick, *Death and Eternal Life* (San Francisco: Harper & Row, 1976), 251.

98. Ibid., 254.

99. Ibid., 255.

100. Ibid., 256-257.

101. Ibid., 257.

102. Ibid., 253.

103. Ibid., 254.

104. John Hick's article "Theology and Verification" in *Philosophy of Religion: Selected Readings,* ed. William L. Rowe and William J. Wainwright (New York: Harcourt Brace Jovanovich, 1973), 437-452, presents his concept of eschatological verification.

105. As argued above, the soul-building theodicy can succeed in solving the logical problem of evil without this eschatological dimension. As to the evidential problem, where plausibility is at stake, it seems that a system that can make its case in terms of evidence now available is likely to be more plausible than a system that tells us to wait for proof until some distant future.

106. For further interaction with Hick's approach see R. Douglas Geivett, *Evil and the Evidence for God: The Challenge of John Hick's Theodicy* (Philadelphia: Temple University Press, 1993).

107. Marilyn Adams, "Horrendous Evils and the Goodness of God," in Marilyn Adams and Robert Adams, eds., *The Problem of Evil* (Oxford: Oxford University Press, 1990), 210-213.

108. Marilyn Adams, "Redemptive Suffering: A Christian Solution to the Problem of Evil," in Robert Audi and William J. Wainwright, eds., *Rationality, Religious Belief, and Moral Commitment* (Ithaca, N.Y.: Cornell University Press, 1986), 249f.; see also Adams, "Horrendous Evils," *passim.*

109. Adams, "Redemptive Suffering," 252-253.

110. Ibid., 253.

111. Ibid., 253-254.

112. Ibid., 256-257.

113. Ibid., 257.

114. Ibid., 259.

115. Ibid., 259-260.

116. Ibid., 262-264.

117. Ibid., 262-265.

118. Ibid., 265.

119. Ibid., 267.

120. Ibid., 252 and 264. See also Adams, "Horrendous Evils," 215-216.

121. Still, at one point early in her presentation she claims that there are answers to the logical and factual problems of evil, but she thinks they are embedded within the Christian theological tradition and that they must be extracted indirectly. See Adams, "Redemptive Suffering," 250.

122. For further interaction with Adams's approach readers may find helpful Brian K. Cameron's "A Critique of Marilyn McCord Adams' 'Christian Solution' to the Existential Problem of Evil," *American Catholic Quarterly* 73 (Summer 1998). For an even more recent presentation of her views see Adams's *Horrendous Evils and the Goodness of God* (Ithaca, N.Y.: Cornell University Press, 1999). See also her "Horrors in Theological Context," *Scottish Journal of Theology* 55 (2002), along with William Placher's response in "An Engagement with Marilyn McCord Adams's *Horrendous Evils and the Goodness of God,*" *Scottish Journal of Theology* 55 (2002).

123. Further attempts to resolve the problem of evil, to discuss others' solutions, or to reflect on the nature of the problem may be found in Michael Torre, "God and Evil: A Classical View," *Dialogue and Humanism* 1 (1991); Marilyn M. Adams, "God and Evil: Polarities of a Problem," *Philosophical Studies* 69 (1993); Mark T. Nelson, "Temporal Wholes and the Problem of Evil," *Religious Studies* 29 (September 1993); Bruce Langtry, "Some Internal Theodicies and the Objection from Alternative Goods," *International Journal for Philosophy of Religion* 34 (1993); Frank J. Murphy, "The Problem of Evil and a Plausible Defence," *Religious Studies* 31 (June 1995); Linda Zagzebski, "An Agent-based Approach to the Problem of Evil," *International Journal for Philosophy of Religion* 39 (June 1996); Sandra L. Menssen and Thomas D. Sullivan, "Does God Will Evil?" *The Monist* 80 (1997); Robert Oakes, "Creation as Theodicy: In Defense of a Kabbalistic Approach to Evil," *Faith and Philosophy* 14 (October 1997); Eleonore Stump, "Saadia Gaon on the Problem of Evil," *Faith and Philosophy* 14 (October 1997); Kenneth J. Perszyk, "Stump's Theodicy of Redemptive Suffering and Molinism," *Religious Studies* 35 (June 1999). Though the authors don't tell us their account of metaphysics, these articles seem to be written from within the Modified Rationalist perspective.

6: God and Moral Evil

1. For an example and explanation of this sort of position, see Robert M. Adams, "A Modified Divine Command Theory of Ethical Wrongness," in Paul Helm, ed., *Divine Commands and Morality* (Oxford: Oxford University Press, 1981).

2. William K. Frankena, *Ethics* (Englewood Cliffs, N.J.: Prentice-Hall, 1963), 81.

3. Here I should add that even if it is decided that God can remove evil, there is still a debate about whether he is obligated to do so. Though I am inclined to think that he isn't obligated to remove all evil, I'm not sure that debates about whether God is or isn't so obligated are entirely fruitful. Thankfully, that debate needn't be settled before we proceed. Most Modified Rationalist positions, including my own, build their case in terms of God's inability to remove evil if he is to accomplish some other goal. And, of course, if God can't remove evil under those circumstances, he isn't obligated to do so.

4. As noted earlier, it might also produce a theology according to which one of God's attributes is contradicted and/or according to which a state of affairs would be produced that we would neither expect nor desire God to produce, because it would be a greater evil than any existent evil.

5. Joseph B. Mayor, *The Epistle of St. James,* in the Classic Commentary Library (Grand Rapids, Mich.: Zondervan, 1954), 54-55.

6. Carl F. H. Henry, *God, Revelation and Authority,* vol. 6, part 2, *God Who Stands and Stays* (Waco, Tex.: Word, 1983), 272. See also Henry's comment (p. 274) that "Feinberg's concentration on human desire as the ultimate source of moral evil, moreover, overlooks Scripture's attribution of some of the radical evil in the world to satanic forces, even if the Bible always bounds these forces by God's creative power and will."

7. In this case, people wouldn't need to be able to have such knowledge, since God would take care of any possible problems by means of miracles.

8. It almost seems that the only other way God could make us so that he wouldn't have to eliminate evil by miracle is to make us incapable of acting at all or at least acting in ways that produce evil, but I have already discussed the problems with doing that.

9. My point here is similar to Dilley's response to Steven Boër's proposal (see my chapter 4). For God to get rid of evil in any of the ways imagined would produce a much different world from ours than we might imagine.

10. This must not be misunderstood. Were I a consequentialist, the decision about which actions are evil would depend on the consequences of those actions. But, even here, I might intend to do an act whose consequences would be beneficial to others, and yet there might be unforeseen consequences that make the results of my act other than I had intended. The evil is unintentional, but it is still real. God would have to stop those acts, too. Moreover, reflex actions which are preceded by neither good nor evil intentions but lead to evil consequences would have to be stopped. As a nonconsequentialist, I determine rightness or wrongness of an act otherwise than by consequences. The point about involuntary and reflex actions, however, still applies. I may intend to do and perform an act that obeys God's command. Even so, there may be unforeseen results that are negative toward the well-being of others. Even though I'm not guilty of evil, the evil that befalls others unintentionally is still real. Hence, God would have to stop my good-intentioned act in that case. Likewise, reflex actions which attach to neither good nor evil intentions but produce evil for others would have to be stopped.

11. The point to which I allude here is that regardless of the kind of free will one thinks humans have, sometimes we can be forced to do something evil against our wishes. In those cases, however, we aren't acting freely. For example, the bank teller faced by a gunman who demands the teller's money or life, really doesn't want to choose either option, but she will likely give up the money. While it's not good to aid a thief, in this case she certainly didn't do so freely according to any account of freedom.

12. Henry, *God, Revelation and Authority*, 272.

13. Ibid., 272-273.

14. A key issue here is whether one can do otherwise than one does when confronted with a choice. As I have argued elsewhere (see my "God Ordains All Things" in Basinger and Basinger, eds., *Predestination and Free Will* [Downers Grove, Ill.: InterVarsity, 1986]; and *No One Like Him: The Doctrine of God* [Wheaton, Ill.: Crossway, 2001], chapter 14), there are various senses of the phrase "the agent could have done otherwise." In every one of those senses except the contracausal sense, a compatibilist can legitimately claim, just as an incompatibilist can, that the agent could have done otherwise. If being able to do otherwise is the key to genuine freedom, then compatibilism describes a genuine sense of freedom. And, if there is genuine freedom, then it is wrong to think sin is inescapable. Hence, I conclude that my position doesn't make sin inevitable. As also discussed in *No One Like Him,* a case can be made that even if the agent could not do otherwise, that is irrelevant to whether or not he is morally responsible for his deeds. See chapter 14 of *No One Like Him* for details.

15. Bruce R. Reichenbach, "Evil and a Reformed View of God," *Philosophy of Religion* 24 (1988): 75.

16. For examples of some of the differences in our physical capabilities, compare Scriptural descriptions about Jesus' abilities in his resurrected and glorified body as opposed to his natural body.

17. Reichenbach, "Evil and a Reformed View of God," 75-76.

18. Ibid., 76.

19. Obviously, the degree or intensity of evil hasn't necessarily been justified, but that is unnecessary for the sake of finding an answer that removes the alleged logical

contradiction in regard to a theological/philosophical problem of evil, a problem about the existence of moral evil in general.

20. Here I should add as well that the professors who first read this agreed that it succeeded in removing any apparent inconsistency in my system. They rejected the theology as a whole in light of commitment to incompatibilism or to another notion of God. But they agreed that if one held this sort of theology, this defense would solve its logical problem of evil.

7: GOD AND NATURAL EVIL

1. John Stuart Mill, *Nature and Utility of Religion* (Indianapolis: Bobbs-Merrill, 1958), 20-21.
2. Reichenbach doesn't divide natural evils as I have, but considers them all together. Still, I believe some of his basic points are applicable specifically to the problem of unattached natural evils.
3. I realize that those committed either to atheistic or theistic evolution aren't likely to take the Genesis account very seriously. Nevertheless, there is a point in what I am saying that is relevant to them. Typically, those who believe in evolution say that death is simply natural. I take it, however, that this claim doesn't mean they think death is good. But, if people die, they must die from something—hence, the natural evils I have delineated. I raise this point to show that my analysis of the relation of these natural evils to death is something about which even atheists can agree. Of course, once that point is made, agreement ceases, for our explanations of why there is death differ.
4. Bruce Reichenbach, *Evil and a Good God* (New York: Fordham University Press, 1982), 111-112.
5. F. R. Tennant, *Philosophical Theology II* (Cambridge: Cambridge University Press, 1928), 201; cited in Reichenbach, *Evil and a Good God,* 111. Reichenbach offers further illustrations (p. 111) of this point. For example, fire's ability to warm us and cook our food are the very qualities about it that can also make it very harmful in certain circumstances. Likewise, the hardness of wood is responsible for the pain it inflicts when someone hits us with a piece of it. But unless it is hard and impenetrable, it isn't very useful as building material.
6. Reichenbach, *Evil and a Good God,* 101-107.
7. Ibid., 103-107.
8. Ibid., 107-108.
9. For other discussions of natural evil see Gijsbert van den Brink, "Natural Evil and Eschatology," in Gijsbert van den Brink, Luco J. Van den Brom, and Maral Sarat, eds., *Christian Faith and Philosophical Theology* (Kampen, Netherlands: Kok Pharos, 1992); and Wayne Ouderkirk, "Can Nature Be Evil? Rolston, Disvalue, and Theodicy," *Environmental Ethics* 21 (Summer 1999).

8: EVIL AS EVIDENCE

1. J. L. Mackie, *The Miracle of Theism* (Oxford: Oxford University Press, 1982), 154. Mackie's comment on 154 doesn't relate directly to Plantinga's free will defense, though as the discussion proceeds, he appears to grant that Plantinga's free will defense in relation to both moral and natural evil is formally possible. However, he then argues that it doesn't provide a real solution for reasons already explained in the chapter on the free will defense. Here again we see Mackie's misunderstanding of the nature of the problem of evil. Objections he raises show no internal inconsistency in the free will defender's theological system. Hence, the free will defense as formally possible (which Mackie admits) does solve the logical dimensions of the problem for its theology. Mackie's objections are on grounds external to the theist's beliefs, but those objections only explain why he rejects that kind of theology. Mackie's confusion about what constitutes a solution to the logical problem causes him, I believe, to be very

inconsistent in his whole discussion of whether theists can solve the problem of evil. As he begins his discussion of the problem of evil, he says the existence of evil can be shown to generate a logical contradiction for the theist (p. 150). But later he says theists have solved this problem (via the free will defense), and later still he says the solution is not a *real* solution. Throughout his discussion he seems to vacillate back and forth between the idea that theists have and haven't solved the logical problem. For further discussion of this point see Kelly J. Clark, "Evil and Christian Belief," *International Philosophical Quarterly* 29 (June 1989): 180-183 (especially 180). It is also noteworthy that other critics of theism have also admitted that theists can solve the logical problem of evil. See, for example, William Rowe's claim in "The Problem of Evil and Some Varieties of Atheism," *American Philosophical Quarterly* 16 (October 1979): 335, footnote 1. Interestingly, though, it is hard to find someone who thinks any defense other than Plantinga's free will defense solves the logical problem. As I have demonstrated, many theologies do.

2. Hence, the frequent appeal to Plantinga's distinction between a defense and a theodicy, with the realization that most, if not all, answers to logical problems of evil are defenses, not theodicies.

3. Mackie, *Miracle of Theism,* 154.

4. It is also called the *a posteriori* problem by Alvin Plantinga in *God and Other Minds* (p. 123), but this designation is the least frequent way of referring to the problem.

5. See Max Black, "Induction," in Paul Edwards, ed., *The Encyclopedia of Philosophy,* vol. 4, 169-170 (New York: Macmillan, 1972), for explanation of different types of inductive argument.

6. Ibid., 169.

7. Michael Peterson, *Evil and the Christian God* (Grand Rapids, Mich.: Baker, 1982), 62-63.

8. Ibid., 65. Here I modify Peterson slightly. In his schema (T) represents the factual *test,* whereas I use it to represent factual *data,* i.e., the facts. Peterson uses "appears to be true" both because he refers to a test rather than simple data, and also to note that empirical observation may be wrong. More frequently, however, when critics of theism cite the facts of evil, they don't say there appears to be evil; they say there is evil.

9. I am not suggesting that other kinds of inductive arguments (like concluding the sun will rise tomorrow) aren't inferential, nor do I think inferences are suspect just because they are inferences. I note only that the inference in this case is a rather complex one whose truth depends on a number of different things (some of which are very hard to prove) being true.

10. Alvin Plantinga, "The Probabilistic Argument from Evil," *Philosophical Studies* 35 (1979): 2-3. I have made slight changes in Plantinga's numbering scheme, but otherwise the point is his.

11. Ibid., 3.

12. See Bruce Reichenbach, *Evil and a Good God* (New York: Fordham University Press, 1982), chapter 2; Bruce Reichenbach, "The Inductive Argument from Evil," *American Philosophical Quarterly* 17 (July 1980); and Plantinga, "The Probabilistic Argument." What this means to the structure of the inductive argument set forth above in the text is that additional premises calculating theism's probability are relevant to premise 1 and the whole argument. In fact, premise 1 turns out to be a probability judgment of the following sort: It is probable that there will be no evil, given the hypothesis that there is an omnipotent, omniscient, all-benevolent God and the background evidence (assumption) that such a God eliminates evil insofar as he can.

13. I adapt these notations from Reichenbach, "Inductive Argument from Evil," 221. He also includes notation representing 1) the prior probability that the hypothesis is false, and representing 2) the probability that there will be no relevant evidence, given the truth of the hypothesis and the background information.

14. Plantinga, "Probabilistic Argument," 3.

15. Ibid., 5.

16. Of course, the same is true of inductive, probabilistic arguments in favor of theism. In addition, it is also worth noting that the argument from design (teleological argument) is the "flip side" of the probabilistic argument from evil against theism. The teleological argument claims that evidences of design and purpose in our world make it probable that God is the designer. Critics of the argument typically respond that if evidences of design increase the probability of God as creator of the world, evidences of disorder (evil) must count against the probability that he is creator/designer. This objection to the teleological argument is, in essence, the substance of the atheist's evidential argument from evil against theism.

17. It is worth noting at this point that there is some ambiguity in the way philosophers use the term "gratuitous." This will be explained more fully in a subsequent chapter, but for now suffice it to say that some use the term "gratuitous evil" to refer to evil that doesn't seem tied to any good which *produced* it, whereas others use the term to refer to evil which is not logically (and even causally) necessary to any future good that might *result from* it.

18. This is the general trend of discussions by both theists and atheists. For example, the focus of discussions by theists like Plantinga and Reichenbach and atheists like Mackie and Rowe is natural evil. This doesn't mean that no one discusses moral evil as evidence against God, but only that the emphasis has primarily been on natural evil.

9: ATHEISTIC ARGUMENTS FROM EVIL

1. J. L. Mackie, *The Miracle of Theism* (Oxford: Clarendon, 1982), 150. David Conway, "The Philosophical Problem of Evil," *Philosophy of Religion* 24 (1988): 16, notes that this is basically equivalent to Mackie's earlier formulation of the problem, and he says it is too strong. It involves the claim that any evil whatsoever is incompatible with the existence of an omnipotent, all-loving God. Conway says all the theist must do is show one instance of evil that is compatible with God's existence, and he meets Mackie's charge. On the other hand, if the atheist proposes the more modest claim that there are evils which are preventable by this God, he is more likely to make his case, and the conclusion that there is no God follows just as easily from this claim as from the claim that God's existence is incompatible with any evil whatsoever.

2. Mackie, *Miracle of Theism,* 152.

3. Ibid., 153.

4. For a more detailed analysis of this idea, see my discussion of Mackie's point in my chapter 4, and see the use of the notion as well by Yandell in his greater good defense (discussed in my chapter 5). Here as well it is important to distinguish this approach from the preceding one Mackie raises. According to the first theistic approach to the problem of evil, evil isn't logically necessary to any specific good, i.e., it is possible to attain that good without that evil. However, there are certain circumstances in which a given evil may cause a particular good to arise. Because of that causal connection, sometimes humans are willing to put up with that evil as a means to producing that good. However, there is nothing inherent in either the good or the evil which demands that if the good occurs, the evil, as logically tied to it, is inescapable. In this case, there is no logical tie, even though there is a causal connection.

5. Mackie, *Miracle of Theism,* 154.

6. Ibid., 155.

7. Ibid., 159, 162-176.

8. Though I am taking Mackie's discussion in this direction, I only note that others who appeal to the evidential problem (pro and con) begin their discussion by appealing to Mackie's notion of unabsorbed evils. Many think instances of natural evil are examples of such unabsorbed evil, and they think those evils can be cited as evidence against

God's existence. See, for example, Kelly J. Clark, *Return to Reason* (Grand Rapids, Mich.: Eerdmans, 1990), 77-81, who uses Mackie's comments about unabsorbed evils as a springboard to pose the evidential problem of evil. See also Kelly J. Clark, "Evil and Christian Belief," *International Philosophical Quarterly* 29 (June 1989); and Conway, "Philosophical Problem of Evil," 46-50.

9. William Rowe, "The Problem of Evil and Some Varieties of Atheism," *American Philosophical Quarterly* 16 (October 1979): 335.

10. Ibid.

11. Ibid., 336. Though this argument isn't stated in the exact form I set forth earlier in chapter 8, it clearly could be. Premise 2 can be seen as a different way of expressing the theistic hypothesis and the assumption that an omnipotent, omniscient, wholly good being would remove evil insofar as he could, both of which lead to the conclusion that there will be no intense suffering (or at least it is improbable that there will be any). Premise 1 is the evidential claim, and premise 3 the conclusion which could just as easily be stated in terms of probability. In fact, Rowe later says that all of this makes it rational to be an atheist, even though we don't know for sure that God has no reason for permitting such evil. This clearly shows we are working with a probability argument.

12. Ibid., 336-337. Rowe explains that the premise offers a *necessary* condition but doesn't claim to state a *sufficient* condition for an omniscient, wholly good being to permit intense suffering.

13. Ibid., 337.

14. See Conway, "Philosophical Problem of Evil," 59-60, where he argues for precisely the same interpretation of Rowe as I am taking.

15. Rowe, "Problem of Evil and Some Varieties of Atheism," 337.

16. Ibid.

17. In an article published in 1986, Rowe used the suffering caused by the Lisbon earthquake as an example of intense human suffering. See his "The Empirical Argument from Evil," in Robert Audi and William J. Wainwright, eds., *Rationality, Religious Belief, and Moral Commitment: New Essays in the Philosophy of Religion* (Ithaca, N.Y.: Cornell University Press, 1986).

18. Rowe, "Problem of Evil and Some Varieties of Atheism," 338.

19. Ibid.

20. Ibid., 338-339.

21. Rowe refers to this as the "G. E. Moore shift" in honor of Moore, who used it in dealing with arguments of skeptics to the effect that no one can know that material objects exist. See Rowe, "Problem of Evil and Some Varieties of Atheism," 339.

22. Ibid.

23. In his "God and Evil," *Philosophic Exchange* 28 (1997-1998): 13-14, Rowe entertains this third strategy again, and seems even more positive than in the 1979 essay that it is the best of the possible theistic approaches.

24. Rowe, "God and Evil," 6-7. As Rowe notes, Stephen Wykstra has developed at some length this argument against Rowe's evidential argument. I shall present the exchange between Rowe and Wykstra in the next section of the chapter.

25. Ibid., 7.

26. Ibid.

27. Ibid., 8.

28. Ibid., 10-11.

29. Ibid., 11-12. Rowe notes that this fullest expression of Hick's theodicy, including the items about excessive amounts of evil, appears in the 1996 edition of Hick's *Evil and the God of Love.*

30. I note here again that Rowe believes he's dealing with one problem, whereas he blurs together two distinct problems, the problem of the amount of evil, and the problem of the intensity of some evils. Still, his objection would apply equally well to either problem.
31. Rowe, "God and Evil," 12.
32. Rowe, "Problem of Evil and Some Varieties of Atheism," 340. Rowe explains that a theist may have grounds for believing in God, but not be aware of the atheist's reasons for unbelief. In such a case, the atheist holds his atheism, because he believes the theist's arguments and evidence don't actually prove God's existence, but since he also knows the theist is unaware of his arguments for atheism and at least has some evidence for his theistic belief, the atheist can afford to be charitable and believe those theists are rational in their belief. Friendly atheism becomes more difficult to maintain when the atheist thinks the theist knows all the evidence for atheism that the atheist knows and yet maintains his theistic belief. At that point can he still think the theist is rational in his belief? Even here, Rowe thinks the atheist can remain friendly, if the atheist thinks he has grounds for believing the arguments for theism to be less compelling than the theist does.
33. Stephen Wykstra, "The Humean Obstacle to Evidential Arguments from Suffering: On Avoiding the Evils of 'Appearance'," *International Journal for Philosophy of Religion* 16 (1984): 74-76.
34. Ibid., 77. Wykstra explains that evidence weakly supports a claim when it makes the claim to some degree more likely to be true than it would be on the antecedent evidence.
35. Ibid., 79.
36. Ibid., 80. Wykstra says this sense of "appears" is somewhat close to what Swinburne, following Chisholm, calls its "epistemic" sense (as distinct from its "comparative," "phenomenal," and "hedging" senses). See Richard Swinburne, *The Existence of God* (New York: Oxford University Press, 1979), 245ff.
37. Wykstra, "Humean Obstacle," 81.
38. Ibid., 85.
39. Ibid., 87-89. Wykstra notes that Hume's *Dialogues* makes the same point. Philo, the atheist, considers whether suffering constitutes *negative* evidence against Cleanthes' theism, and answers no. The reason is that someone assured that the universe is a creation of a God such as Cleanthes' "might, perhaps, be surprised at the disappointment, but would never retract his former belief, if founded on any very solid argument; since such a limited intelligence must be sensible of his own blindness and ignorance, and must allow, that there may be many solutions of those phenomena, which will forever escape his comprehension" (Wykstra, "Humean Obstacle," 89, quoting Hume).
40. William L. Rowe, "Evil and the Theistic Hypothesis: A Response to Wykstra," *International Journal of Philosophy of Religion* 16 (1984): 95.
41. Ibid., 95-96.
42. Ibid., 97.
43. Ibid.
44. Ibid., 98.
45. Ibid., 99-100.
46. Ibid., 100. For a further discussion of the issues involved in the distinction between restricted standard theism and expanded theism see Stephen Napier, "Is Rowe Committed to an Expanded Version of Theism?" *Sophia* 41 (October 2002).
47. For details here, readers should consult Stephen J. Wykstra, "Rowe's Noseeum Arguments from Evil," in Daniel Howard-Snyder, *The Evidential Argument from Evil* (Indianapolis: Indiana University Press, 1996), 126-139.
48. Wykstra, "Rowe's Noseeum Arguments," 140.

49. William Rowe, "The Empirical Argument from Evil," 238. Wykstra, "Rowe's Noseeum Arguments," 141 cites (1) and (2). I have adjusted Rowe's numbering to make his argument simpler to comprehend.

50. Rowe, "Empirical Argument from Evil," 238.

51. Wykstra, "Rowe's Noseeum Arguments," 141.

52. Ibid., 141-142.

53. William Rowe, "Ruminations About Evil," *Philosophical Perspectives* 5 (1991): 79.

54. Wykstra, "Rowe's Noseeum Arguments," 142.

55. Ibid., 142-143.

56. Ibid., 143-144.

57. Ibid., 143-145.

58. Bruce Reichenbach, *Evil and a Good God* (New York: Fordham University Press, 1982), 38.

59. Wykstra, "Humean Obstacle," 81-83, presents this whole line of argument in support of Rowe and against Reichenbach's interpretation of him. It is Swinburne's Principle of Credulity that Wykstra modifies in favor of CORNEA.

60. Reichenbach, *Evil and a Good God,* 38.

61. Delmas Lewis, "The Problem with the Problem of Evil," *Sophia* 22 (1983): 29.

62. Ibid., 30.

63. Ibid.

64. Ibid. The similarities between Lewis's argument against the Epistemological Slide and Wykstra's argument against Rowe (invoking CORNEA) should be obvious.

65. Ibid., 32. Here I have modified the numbering of the premises of this argument for the sake of the clarity of my own text. That is, what I label 1 and 2, are premises 4 and 5 in Lewis's article, but I don't want to use his numbering and confuse readers into thinking they should search my text for premises 1-3.

66. Ibid., 33.

67. Ibid.

68. Ibid.

69. Ibid.

70. Ibid., 34.

71. Ibid.

72. Ibid. Lewis's actual numbering is from 7 to 11, but to avoid confusion, I have again changed the numbering.

73. Rowe, "Empirical Argument from Evil," 241-242.

74. Ibid., 243-244.

75. Ibid., 244.

76. Ibid., 244-245.

77. Shane Andre, "The Problem of Evil and the Paradox of Friendly Atheism," *International Journal for Philosophy of Religion* 17 (1985): 212.

78. Ibid., 213.

79. Ibid., 214.

80. Ibid., 211.

81. Ibid., 215.

82. Ibid., 216.

83. Daniel T. Snyder, "Surplus Evil," *Philosophical Quarterly* 40 (January 1990): 80.

84. Ibid., 81.

85. By this I mean that it answers the logical problem of moral evil. Whether it also works when dealing with the problems of the quantity, intensity, and the apparent gratuitousness of evil is another story.

86. Here I note that in later versions of his argument from evil, Rowe does include an instance of moral evil (the rape and killing of the five-year-old little girl). Hence, Snyder's supposition about how Rowe might respond seems to raise a possible line of response that Rowe wouldn't take, in virtue of his appealing to instances of moral evil as examples of gratuitous, horrendous suffering.

87. Snyder, "Surplus Evil," 81.

88. Ibid.

89. Ibid.

90. Rowe cites two of his articles as articulating his handling of the argument from evil prior to his "second look" article. Those two are "Evil and Theodicy," *Philosophical Topics* 16 (1988); and "Ruminations About Evil," *Philosophical Perspectives* 5 (1991).

91. William Rowe, "The Evidential Argument from Evil: A Second Look," in Daniel Howard-Snyder, ed., *The Evidential Argument from Evil* (Indianapolis: Indiana University Press, 1996), 263.

92. Ibid., 265-268. Rowe calculates the probability of P (P/k) by using the rule of elimination (p. 268): $Pr(P/k) = [Pr(G/k) \times Pr(P/G\&k)] + [Pr(-G/k) \times Pr(P/-G\&k)]$.

93. Ibid., 268-270.

94. Ibid., 272. Rowe is citing and interacting with Wykstra's "Rowe's Noseeum Arguments from Evil."

95. Ibid., 273.

96. Ibid., 276.

97. Ibid., 276-277. Rowe agrees that various defenses and theodicies attempt to explain the value for which God allows evils like E1 and E2. Rowe considers the free will defense in this regard (as the defense theists most frequently invoke), and argues that free will isn't a great enough value to justify permitting horrendous evils. Even if God shouldn't interrupt all evil deeds because that would remove freedom, he should at least do so if that is the only way to stop E1 and E2 evils from occurring. Maintaining freedom at such costs isn't justified. See his pages 278-282.

98. Alvin Plantinga, "Degenerate Evidence and Rowe's New Evidential Argument from Evil," *Noûs* 32 (December 1998): 532-536. I believe that part of what Plantinga has in mind, for example, about determining the prior probability of theism is as follows: isn't it possible that some theist holds that based on background knowledge alone, the prior probability of theism is less than .5? If so, we might wonder why that person is a theist at all. The answer might well be that the theist in question knows a number of arguments in favor of theism and believes that even though without those arguments and evidences theism is more improbable than probable, *with* those evidences theism becomes probable. Hence, she believes in God. Possibilities such as this suggest why, even though Rowe is trying to be fair to all sides by assigning .5 as the prior probability of theism or atheism, that decision doesn't make as much sense as Rowe thinks.

99. Ibid., 536.

100. Ibid., 536-537.

101. Ibid., 538-539.

102. Ibid., 540.

103. Ibid., 540-543.

104. William Rowe, "Reply to Plantinga," *Noûs* 32 (December 1998): 549.

105. Ibid., 549-550.

106. Ibid., 550.

107. Ibid., 551.

108. Ibid., 548, 549, 550.

109. Plantinga, "Degenerate Evidence," 536, 537.

110. Ibid., 532.

111. For further discussion of Rowe's evidential argument (and its respondents) see Terry Christlieb, "Which Theisms Face an Evidential Problem of Evil?" *Faith and Philosophy* 9 (January 1992); Daniel Howard-Snyder, "Seeing Through CORNEA," *International Journal for Philosophy of Religion* 32 (August 1992); James F. Sennett, "The Inscrutable Evil Defense Against the Inductive Argument from Evil," *Faith and Philosophy* 10 (April 1993); Bruce Langtry, "Eyeballing Evil: Some Epistemic Principles," *Philosophical Papers* 25 (1996); James Beilby, "Does the Empirical Problem of Evil Prove That Theism Is Improbable?" *Religious Studies* 32 (1996); John Beaudoin, "Evil, the Human Cognitive Condition, and Natural Theology," *Religious Studies* 34 (1998).

112. Michael Martin, "Is Evil Evidence Against the Existence of God?" *Mind* 87 (1978): 429. Martin defines *prima facie* evidence as follows: if E stands for the evidence, H for the hypothesis, and A for the auxiliary assumptions, then "E is *prima facie* evidence against H if E and H do not entail a contradiction and E and A do not entail a contradiction and E and H and A do entail a contradiction" (p. 430).

113. Ibid., 430.

114. Ibid.

115. Ibid.

116. Ibid., 430-431.

117. Ibid., 431.

118. Ibid., 431-432.

119. Ibid., 432.

120. Ibid.

121. Ibid.

122. Ibid.

123. David Basinger, "Evil as Evidence Against God's Existence: Some Clarifications," *The Modern Schoolman* 58 (March 1981): 176-177.

124. Ibid., 177.

125. Ibid., 178-179.

126. Ibid., 180-181.

127. Ibid., 181.

128. Ibid., 183.

129. Ibid., 184.

130. Snyder, "Surplus Evil," 82.

131. Ibid., 82-83.

132. Ibid., 83.

133. Ibid.

134. Ibid., 83-84.

135. Ibid., 84.

136. Ibid.

137. Ibid., 85-86.

138. For further discussion of evidential arguments from evil see Daniel Howard-Snyder, "On the A Priori Rejection of Evidential Arguments from Evil," *Sophia* 33 (July 1994); Keith Chrzan, "An Atheistic Argument from the Quantity of Evil in the World," *Philosophia* 27 (March 1999); Richard Schoenig, "The Argument from Unfairness," *International Journal for Philosophy of Religion* 45 (1999).

10: THEISTS AND THE EVIDENTIAL ARGUMENT FROM EVIL

1. Plantinga discusses this third approach in his "Reason and Belief in God," in Alvin Plantinga and Nicholas Wolterstorff, eds., *Faith and Rationality* (Notre Dame, Ind.: University of Notre Dame Press, 1983). In other works (*The Nature of Necessity* and

"The Probabilistic Argument from Evil") he discusses the issue of evil as evidence head-on. He calls his strategy in "Reason and Belief in God" the "high road" approach. Rather than trying to calculate probabilities of theism and atheism and evaluate the force of evil as evidence directly, he argues that belief in God is properly basic for the theist. If that is so, the theist is within his epistemic rights in maintaining belief in God in spite of evil's existence and in spite of what the atheist thinks about how improbable the evidence of evil makes theism. See here Chrzan's reconstruction ("Plantinga on Atheistic Induction," *Sophia* 27 [1988]: 10) of Plantinga's different approaches to the probabilistic problem of evil. Of course, Plantinga has further developed what is called reformed epistemology in his major works *Warrant: The Current Debate* (Oxford: Oxford University Press, 1993); *Warrant and Proper Function* (Oxford: Oxford University Press, 1993); and *Warranted Christian Belief* (Oxford: Oxford University Press, 2000). For an interesting interaction with these ideas in relation to the evidential problem of evil see David Silver, "Religious Experience and the Evidential Argument from Evil," *Religious Studies* 38 (2002).

2. Alvin Plantinga, *The Nature of Necessity* (Oxford: Oxford, 1974), 193-194.
3. Ibid., 194.
4. Ibid.
5. Ibid., 195.
6. Ibid.
7. Keith Chrzan, "Plantinga on Atheistic Induction," *Sophia* 27 (1988): 10.
8. Ibid., 11.
9. Ibid.
10. Ibid.
11. Ibid., 12.
12. Ibid.
13. Ibid.
14. Ibid.
15. Ibid.
16. Ibid.
17. Ibid., 12-13.
18. Ibid., 13.
19. Ibid. The first line of this quote must contain a printing error, for it says just the opposite of what Chrzan explains in the rest of the cited portion. As printed, it says p disconfirms q if q is *less* probable by itself than it would be if p pertained. Actually, if q is *less* probable by itself than it is if p pertains, then p confirms, not disconfirms q. Hence, I conclude that (1') should read: p disconfirms q if $P(q) > P(q/p)$.
20. Ibid. Chrzan makes this point by saying that Plantinga must show that $P(G) < P(G/E)$ is false.
21. Bruce Langtry, "God, Evil and Probability," *Sophia* 28 (1989): 32-33.
22. Ibid., 32-34. This is the way Langtry sets forth the issues addressed by the arguments raised by Plantinga and cited in the text.
23. Ibid., 34.
24. Ibid.
25. Ibid., 35.
26. Ibid., 36. Langtry also considers Chrzan's objection that Plantinga appeals to a premise Chrzan labels 1.5 to persuade us that premise (b) in Langtry's reconstruction of Plantinga ("therefore it is not the case that -[4] is more probable relative to [2] than [4] is") is true. Langtry grants Chrzan that premise 1.5 is false. However, Langtry sees no reason for Plantinga to appeal to 1.5 to prove (b). God's existence might still be probable even though 1.5 is false. Langtry concludes (p. 36) that since Chrzan "fails to investigate these questions further, his criticism of Plantinga has little weight."

27. Ibid., 36-37.
28. Ibid., 38.
29. Ibid.
30. Ibid.
31. Ibid., 39.
32. Ibid.
33. Ibid.
34. Terrence Tilley, "The Use and Abuse of Theodicy," *Horizons* 11 (1984): 305-310, makes the same kind of point I am making in regard to Langtry in response to various critics of Plantinga like Hick. As he notes, many of the objections to Plantinga's program in regard to either the logical problem of evil or the evidential problem fall flat when one recognizes that Plantinga offers a defense, not a theodicy, and when one recognizes the logical difference between the two.
35. For a further comment on Langtry, Plantinga, and the issues involved in Chrzan's interchange with them see Keith Chrzan, "Comment on Langtry's 'God, Evil and Probability'," *Sophia* 32 (1993).
36. Harold Moore, "Evidence, Evil and Religious Belief," *International Journal for Philosophy of Religion* 9 (1978): 241-242.
37. Ibid., 243. Here there appears to be a misprint in 10'. In order for it to make sense, it should say "since H_2 entails the denial of E_2."
38. Ibid., 242. Moore labels this proposition 6, and on page 243 he claims that Plantinga holds what I've called C, probably because he holds something like 6.
39. Ibid., 243.
40. Ibid.
41. Ibid., 244.
42. Ibid.
43. Edward Wierenga, "Reply to Harold Moore's 'Evidence, Evil, and Religious Belief'," *International Journal for Philosophy of Religion* 9 (1978): 246.
44. Ibid., 247.
45. Ibid.
46. Ibid., 248.
47. Ibid.
48. Ibid.
49. Ibid., 249. Wierenga labels this proposition 13.
50. Ibid. Wierenga also discusses Moore's third complaint about needing background information before evil can count as evidence against theistic belief. Wierenga complains that "Plantinga's argument presupposes that for every pair of propositions p and q, the conditional probability of q on p is defined, without reference to any background knowledge" (p. 250). He then notes some problems that arise if one holds this view (pp. 250-251). I have chosen not to discuss this matter here, for Plantinga's later work on the probabilistic argument from evil shows that he believes one must include the background information. In fact, part of his complaint about the probabilistic argument from evil is that it tends to rest solely on an appeal to the evil in the world, whereas if one is to assess theism's probability, one must assess it on the basis of total evidence.
51. Harold Moore, "Evidence—Once More," *International Journal for Philosophy of Religion* 9 (1978): 252-253. Moore concludes by saying that he still agrees with Plantinga's basic conclusion that evil doesn't count against theism, but for a different reason. Moore believes it doesn't count against theism because we don't know how to assess beliefs about God and his existence in terms of evidence at all (p. 253).
52. Of course, Moore may reply that he is well aware of the free will defense as Plantinga presents it. He just doesn't think it makes theism plausible, because he doesn't think it

is plausible. If Moore were to respond this way, it would demonstrate the problem of subjectivity that encumbers many attempts to make probability arguments. As we shall see, in Plantinga's later work, he points to this problem as a major obstacle against atheists successfully arguing from evidence against theism. However, as Moore raises the requirement in his analysis of Plantinga's *Nature of Necessity* argument, he gives the impression that Plantinga has offered no reason to think the premises of his argument plausible. My point is that the free will defense is the reason. One may reject the free will defense as implausible, but one must admit that Plantinga has met the requirement of offering an explanation of why the premises of his argument are plausible.

53. Alvin Plantinga, "The Probabilistic Argument from Evil," *Philosophical Studies* 35 (1979): 3.
54. Ibid., 4-5.
55. Ibid., 7.
56. Ibid., 8.
57. Ibid., 11-15.
58. Ibid., 15.
59. Ibid., 17.
60. Ibid.
61. Ibid., 15.
62. Ibid., 18.
63. Ibid., 21.
64. Ibid., 21-25, for Plantinga's arguments against both suggestions.
65. Ibid., 30. See also 25-30 for other problems with this interpretation of probability.
66. Ibid., 31.
67. Ibid., 35.
68. Ibid., 36.
69. Ibid., 44-47. In summarizing this whole issue, Plantinga says (pp. 47-48), "What we have seen so far is that none of the main interpretations of probability provide the atheologian with resources for a decent objection to theism based on the premiss [*sic*] that $P(G/E)$ is low. On the logical view, this claim involves extremely dubious suggestions about the probability of tautologies of G, E, and (12^*)—suggestions that were doubly dubious, since in the first place there is good reason to deny that such propositions *have* such probability on such evidence, and, in the second, even if they did there isn't the slightest reason to think these *a priori* probabilities have the values the atheologian says they have. The personalist view, on the other hand, makes no such dubious claims: but on that view '$P(G/E) < 1/2$' carries an implicit subscript and simply measures $P(G \& E)/P(E)$ for some person or other—perhaps the atheologian. But then it constitutes a piece of atheological autobiography rather than an objection to theism. The advocate of the frequency view encounters substantial difficulty in construing probability as a relationship among propositions in frequentist terms. If, however, we try to work out such an interpretation, keeping to the spirit of frequentism, we find that prior probabilities in an application of Bayes' Theorem are to be assigned in the light of what one already knows or believes. Here, then, just as with personalism, prior probabilities are relative to noetic structures. Of course there is no reason to think theist and atheist need agree about these prior probabilities; there is therefore no reason to think they either will or should agree about the value of $P(G/E)$."
70. Ibid., 48.
71. Ibid., 49.
72. Ibid., 51.
73. Ibid.
74. Robert M. Adams, "Plantinga on the Problem of Evil," in James E. Tomberlin and Peter van Inwagen, eds., *Alvin Plantinga* (Boston: D. Reidel, 1985), 237.

75. Ibid., 240.

76. Ibid.

77. Ibid., 241.

78. Ibid.

79. Ibid., 242.

80. Ibid., 242-243.

81. Ibid., 243.

82. Ibid.

83. Ibid., 243-245. Adams adds the same basic point as follows in regard to the logical problem of evil (p. 245): "It is worth remarking that the theist does not *need* a Defense against the logical arguments from evil any more than against the probabilistic argument from evil. Our not knowing any reason that could, logically, have been morally sufficient for an omnipotent God to permit the evils that occur would no more prove that such a reason is logically impossible, than our not knowing any good reason that God may, plausibly, have had for permitting the evils would prove that He had no such reason in fact. The disproportion between an infinite intellect and our own gives grounds for some distrust of any argument or judgment about what good reasons God could, logically, have had, just as it gives grounds for some distrust of any conjecture about how much more or less likely something would be to happen if God existed than if He did not."

84. Ibid., 246.

85. Ibid., 247.

86. Ibid., 248.

87. Ibid., 249.

88. Ibid.

89. Ibid.

90. Ibid., 250.

91. Ibid.

92. Ibid., 251.

93. Ibid.

94. Ibid.

95. At this point, I should make a comment about the other side of the equation. Suppose a determinist atheist tries to convince an indeterminist theist that the theist's position is improbable, given the existence of evil. The theist, being a theist, won't likely be impressed by the atheist's argument from evil, but beyond that, once he realizes that the attack presupposes determinism, he will be even less impressed. We have already seen, for example, how unimpressed Plantinga and other free will defenders are by complaints like Mackie's that God could have made it the case that man always freely chooses to do good and that since God didn't, evil counts as evidence against theism.

96. I am much less certain that Plantinga would be negative toward a theology that incorporates the Ockhamist strategy. This is so because he seems positive toward it in his article "On Ockham's Way Out."

11: THEISTS AND EVIL AS EVIDENCE (II)

1. Richard Swinburne, "The Problem of Evil," in Stuart C. Brown, *Reason and Religion* (Ithaca, N.Y.: Cornell University Press, 1977).

2. Richard Swinburne, "Natural Evil," *American Philosophical Quarterly* 15 (October 1978).

3. Richard Swinburne, "Does Theism Need a Theodicy?" *Canadian Journal of Philosophy* 18 (June 1988): 287-312.

4. Richard Swinburne, *The Existence of God* (Oxford: Clarendon, 1979), chapter 2.

5. Ibid., 64-69. Swinburne's explanation of the various factors and the overall function of the theorem is very helpful.

6. Ibid., 52.

7. Ibid.

8. See ibid., 90, for the idea that simplicity is the key and 106 for Swinburne's summary of his chapter 5, which contains his arguments that theism has considerable simplicity, more than its competitors.

9. Ibid., 94.

10. Ibid.

11. Ibid., 97.

12. Ibid., 97-101.

13. Ibid., 104.

14. Ibid., 105. His objections to materialism appear in his chapter 9.

15. Ibid., 105-106.

16. Ibid., 106.

17. Swinburne, "Does Theism Need a Theodicy?" 301.

18. Ibid., 303.

19. Ibid., 305. Swinburne is interacting with Plantinga's objections raised in "The Probabilistic Argument from Evil."

20. See ibid., 305-307, for further explanation of why Swinburne thinks Plantinga's arguments don't destroy his program or the ability to assess the probability of theories.

21. Ibid., 309.

22. Ibid.

23. Swinburne doesn't use "theodicy" in a sense distinct from "defense" as others do, but synonymously. One senses that he thinks of theodicies and defenses both as attempts to explain God's possible reason (not necessarily his actual reason) for allowing evil, but Swinburne really doesn't clarify that matter.

24. Swinburne, "Does Theism Need a Theodicy?" 309-311.

25. Though Swinburne wouldn't deny that moral evil is related to the problem of evil, he discusses the problem of natural evil and its quantity as the major concern for theism. This is an example of how in recent years discussions of the problem of evil have shifted focus from the logical problem with emphasis on moral evil to the evidential problem with emphasis on natural evil. Of course, as we shall see, free human action and its relation to moral evils which cause natural evils figure prominently in Swinburne's views.

26. Swinburne, *Existence of God*, 202-203.

27. Ibid., 203-205. The basic example is Swinburne's, but I have used it with minor adaptation.

28. Ibid., 207.

29. Ibid., 211.

30. Ibid., 211-212.

31. Ibid., 212.

32. Ibid., 213-214.

33. Ibid., 215.

34. Ibid., 219. I note here that the emphasis on the quantity of evil makes this part of the discussion focus clearly on the evidential problem (though I believe his earlier discussion of the existence of natural evil in general, put in the context of a book where he is trying to determine the probability of theism on the evidence, also handles the evidential problem). Moreover, the last sentence of this quote which speaks about counting against theism is typical of language used in respect to the evidential argument.

35. Ibid., 219-220.

36. Ibid., 220.

37. Michael Martin, "The Coherence of the Hypothesis of an Omnipotent, Omniscient, Free and Perfectly Evil Being," *International Journal for Philosophy of Religion* 17 (1985): 186.

38. Ibid., 187. Martin refers to the belief aspect as reason$_B$ and the intentional aspect as reason$_I$.

39. Ibid., 188-189.

40. Ibid., 190.

41. Ibid., 190-191.

42. Ibid., 190.

43. Ibid., 191.

44. Ibid. Of course, theism may still have greater posterior probability, but that's a different matter.

45. Eleonore Stump, "Knowledge, Freedom and the Problem of Evil," *International Journal for Philosophy of Religion* 14 (1983): 52-53. For another way in which God might provide the necessary information without directly revealing it, see Paul K. Moser's suggestion as he raises the same objection to Swinburne in "Natural Evil and the Free Will Defense," *International Journal for Philosophy of Religion* 15 (1984): 53. For further discussion of and objection to Swinburne's argument, see pages 49-53 of Moser's article.

46. Stump, "Knowledge, Freedom and the Problem of Evil," 53.

47. Ibid., 53-54.

48. Ibid., 54.

49. Ibid., 55.

50. Ibid., 55-56.

51. Ibid., 57.

52. Ibid.

53. It is also clear that in the case mentioned, if the theistic arguments are considered as knowledge, that knowledge seems far more important for establishing a high prior probability for theism than does theism's simplicity.

54. As we shall see later in this chapter, Michael Peterson applies the free will defense to the problem of apparently gratuitous moral evil and natural evil resultant from the abuse of human free will. Normally, the free will defense isn't invoked to cover natural evil in general (gratuitous or otherwise) or natural evil unrelated to free agency. The notable exception is Plantinga's suggestion that natural evil results from the abuse of angelic free will. Of course, Plantinga employs this only in regard to natural evil in general, not directly in regard to gratuitous natural evil, and he uses it as a defense, not a theodicy.

55. Here the appeal to Auschwitz appears to shift the focus of the discussion to the intensity of evil away from the quantity or amount of it. But Stump's basic point is correct. Even if all instances of man-made natural evil are equally evil, God could accomplish the goals Swinburne says God has with much less of this kind of evil.

56. See, for example, Bruce Reichenbach, "The Inductive Argument from Evil," in *Evil and a Good God* (New York: Fordham University Press, 1982), 25 and *passim*. See also Bruce Reichenbach, "The Inductive Argument from Evil," *American Philosophical Quarterly* 17 (July 1980): 221 and *passim*.

57. Ibid., 26; and ibid., 221.

58. Ibid., 28; and ibid., 222.

59. Ibid.; and ibid.

60. Ibid.; and ibid.

61. Ibid., 29; and ibid., 223.

62. Ibid., 29-30; and ibid.

63. Ibid., 31; and ibid.

64. Ibid.; and ibid., 224.
65. Ibid., 32; and ibid. Reichenbach illustrates his point about a belief being more probable on all evidence (or all background evidence) with the following illustration. Proposition (M) "Mary Carter completed a college degree" is improbable on proposition (N) "Mary Carter is an adult resident of Rochester, and 3 out of 10 adult residents of Rochester completed a college degree." However, it is probable on (N) and proposition (O) "Mary Carter is a business executive, and 95 out of 100 business executives in Rochester completed a college degree" (32; and 224).
66. Ibid., 32-33; and ibid.
67. Ibid., 33; and ibid.
68. Ibid., 34; and ibid., 225.
69. Ibid.; and ibid.
70. Ibid., 34-35; and ibid.
71. Ibid.; and ibid., 224-225.
72. Ibid., 225. Reichenbach states this slightly differently in his book, but it amounts to the same thing. He claims that the theist could argue that if God didn't exist, we would expect more evil than there is. "Thus, (Q) lends support to (W) $P(E/N\&G) > P(E^*/N\&G)$ ... What this suggests is that the position one adopts in this regard vis-a-vis (U) or (V) depends on one's noetic structure, for it would seem that it is one's noetic structure which would account for the fact that from (Q) one draws (V) rather than (W) or vice versa" (p. 36). In the journal article (W) is $P(E^*/N\&G) < P(E^*/N\&-G)$. Reichenbach's conclusion is that which is stated in my text. Even a quick examination of the two readings shows that though the form is different, the meaning is the same.
73. Ibid.; and "Inductive Argument," in *Evil and a Good God,* 36.
74. Ibid., 36-37; and "Inductive Argument," in *American Philosophical Quarterly,* 225-226.
75. Ibid., 37-38; and ibid., 226.
76. Ibid., 39; and ibid.
77. Ibid.; and ibid., 226-227.
78. Ibid., 40; and ibid., 227.
79. Ibid., 40-41; and ibid.
80. Michael Peterson, *Evil and the Christian God* (Grand Rapids, Mich.: Baker, 1982). Peterson covers the general evidential problem on pages 68-70 and the problem about the quantity of evil on pages 70-73. His answers are cryptic.
81. Rowe's work is his *Philosophy of Religion: An Introduction* (Belmont, Calif.: Dickenson, 1978), which contains the substance of his article "The Problem of Evil and Varieties of Atheism." As to Cornman and Lehrer, Peterson cites them as saying: "At this stage of the discussion we seem warranted in concluding that the existence of what surely seems to be unnecessary evil in this world provides inductive grounds for the belief that God does not exist, because it is probable that if he once existed he would have created a different world and that if he now exists he would control the course of nature so as to avoid many pernicious events that occur" (p. 347 in James Cornman and Keith Lehrer, *Philosophical Problems and Arguments: An Introduction* [New York: Macmillan, 1970]; cited on 74-75 in Peterson, *Evil and the Christian God*).
82. Peterson, *Evil and the Christian God,* 76-77.
83. Ibid., 77.
84. An example of this sort of strategy appears in Keith Yandell's "Gratuitous Evil and Divine Existence," *Religious Studies* 25 (1989). Though this isn't Yandell's only attack on the atheistic argument, it does occupy a major portion of his paper. He argues, as others have, that what may appear to us as gratuitous isn't necessarily so. Yandell makes this point in a more complex way in terms of a distinction between 1) not appearing to have property P and 2) appearing not to have property P. The two are not the same. Atheists typically complain that some evils don't appear to serve a morally

adequate end, but that isn't the same as saying that they appear not to serve a morally adequate end (p. 19). As Yandell explains, a man with a bag over his head doesn't appear to have a moustache, but the bag makes it impossible for him to appear to have any facial qualities. What is more important is whether, with the bag off, he appears not to have a moustache. Hence, 2) is more significant than 1), and the atheist has only shown 1) in regard to many evils. But the fact that they don't appear to have a purpose is no proof that they don't. Yandell later argues that in order for an evil to be genuinely gratuitous, the person who suffered it wouldn't consider it outweighed by any or all other factors in her life. Hence, if it would be better for her to live than not to live at all, even though living includes suffering that evil, then the evil isn't gratuitous (23ff.). Yandell uses these kinds of considerations to argue against the factual premise. But to illustrate Peterson's point of why the debate often gets stuck in the mud if one challenges the factual premise, one need only read Keith Chrzan's response to Yandell in "God and Gratuitous Evil: A Reply to Yandell," *Religious Studies* 27 (1991): 102-103. Among other things, Chrzan challenges Yandell to show that there really have never been any lives that shouldn't have been lived. Yandell argues that despite how much and how intense evil has befallen various people, it is still rational for those people to have wanted to live rather than to wish they had never lived at all. Hence, the evil they suffered is outweighed by the value of life, and thus, the evil isn't gratuitous. Chrzan replies that "Yandell's premise is false if a single human ever experienced a life worse than not existing, and they seem to be innumerable" (p. 102). If Chrzan is right, then there is genuinely gratuitous evil. Who is right? More to the point, how could we ever decide who's right in a way that would satisfy both atheist and theist? But if they disagree on that matter, the debate is stuck in the mud. And that is Peterson's point. The theist can deny the factual premise, and offer various reasons like Yandell's that it is false. The atheist can simply counter as Chrzan and others have, and then the debate is at a standoff. As a result, Peterson thinks there is a better strategy for theists in responding to the atheist's argument from evil.

85. Peterson, *Evil and the Christian God*, 79-93. I have summarized Peterson's discussion as he presents it in these pages.
86. Ibid., 94.
87. Ibid., 105. Peterson appeals to Plantinga's formulation of the free will defense. It is interesting to note, however, that the points appealed to in Plantinga and Peterson's general approach really invoke the free will defense as structured to meet the logical problem of evil. Peterson clearly thinks this is sufficient for the evidential problem, and he may be right, but one must be careful not to reduce the evidential problem to the logical problem.
88. Ibid., 106.
89. Ibid., 106-107.
90. Ibid., 107.
91. Here the relation to Reichenbach's handling of natural evil is obvious. Peterson cites Reichenbach and fundamentally adapts his defense against the problem of gratuitous evil.
92. Peterson, *Evil and the Christian God*, 108.
93. Ibid., 108-111.
94. Ibid., 112-113. Peterson notes that this doesn't preclude miracles altogether, but only the consistent use of miracles in the way suggested by the critic.
95. Ibid., 114.
96. Ibid.
97. Ibid., 115.
98. Ibid., 115-116.
99. Ibid., 118-119. In the following pages (120-122), Peterson goes on to explain, invoking Hick's views, that our epistemic distance from God which allows for genuine human

free will also makes certain things that happen appear gratuitous. But that is just as we would expect in a world where God has given man free will and expects him to use it to overcome evil so as to build his soul into spiritual and moral maturity.

100. Ibid., 124.

101. Ibid. 127.

102. Ibid., 128-129.

103. Ibid., 129.

104. Ibid.

105. Ibid., 132.

106. Ibid.

107. Let me offer several. Peterson offers two main reasons for rejecting (MP), and both embody this confusion. First, Peterson claims God gave man free will, but because man abuses it, sometimes gratuitous evil results. But then, God has a good reason for not removing all gratuitous evil, because to do so would eliminate free will. Hence, (MP) is false. However, if gratuitous evil is tied to free will as Peterson claims, then it isn't pointless. If God has a morally sufficient reason for allowing it in the universe, then it seems hard to think it purposeless. But then, (MP) is correct, i.e., God has removed genuinely pointless evil. So, it appears that there both is and is not genuinely gratuitous evil in our world, and it seems that (MP) must be both false and true. This just illustrates the confusion I have been speaking about.

Peterson offers a second reason for rejecting (MP), namely, appeal to the natural order. The natural order must be present, argues Peterson, for us to exercise free will. However, some gratuitous evil will result from the malfunctioning of the natural order. But then, if the natural order is tied to free will and gratuitous evil is tied to the natural order, God has a morally sufficient reason for not removing this gratuitous evil. Again, (MP) can be rejected along with the theological premise of the atheist's argument, so the atheist's argument fails. However, if gratuitous evil is tied to the natural order and the natural order is necessary for free will, then apparently gratuitous evil has a point. But if Peterson's argument shows that there is a point to this evil, then how can it be genuinely gratuitous? Isn't (MP) upheld again by Peterson's line of argument?

One more illustration of this apparent confusion in Peterson will suffice. Peterson considers how much gratuitous evil is too much. His basic response is that no one can say, because depending on whether one is a theist or atheist, his value judgment about how much is too much will vary. But then there is no objective way to tell how much is too much, and the atheist's subjective opinions about this can't count as evidence against theism. At first glance, this appears cogent until one recognizes that Peterson is speaking not about evil for which there is a purpose or point, but about genuinely purposeless evil. But if there is no purpose or point to the evil, how can God have a morally sufficient reason for any of it? To have such a reason would give the evil a point and purpose. But then, it seems rather clear that if there is really no point or purpose to any instance of evil, God shouldn't allow it! On the other hand, if one can explain how some of it serves a purpose, then why call it gratuitous? Again, the apparent confusion is evident.

Finally, in regard to Peterson's treatment, Chrzan notes this ambiguity, but uses it to accuse Peterson of equivocating. He thinks this equivocation ruins Peterson's attempts to handle the evidential problem. As I shall point out, it may appear that Peterson is equivocating, but something else is going on which Chrzan hasn't caught. For Chrzan's analysis of Peterson, see Keith Chrzan, "When Is a Gratuitous Evil Really Gratuitous?" *Philosophy of Religion* 24 (1988): 90-91.

108. Peterson, *Evil and the Christian God*, 75, citing Rowe, *Philosophy of Religion*, 89. What Rowe describes as gratuitous evil is close, if not identical, to Mackie's unabsorbed evil.

109. Peterson, *Evil and the Christian God*, 81.

110. Ibid., 84.

111. Ibid., 96.

112. Ibid., 97.

113. David Basinger, "In What Sense Must God Do His Best: A Response to Hasker," *International Journal for Philosophy of Religion* 18 (1985): 162. Basinger writes in response to William Hasker who very clearly thinks of gratuitous evil as evil that isn't tied to some subsequent greater good. However, Hasker recognizes the connection between the evil and good only as one wherein the evil produces the good, not one where the good makes possible the particular evil. To see that Hasker does in fact understand gratuitous evil this way (the same way Peterson does), see William Hasker, "Must God Do His Best?" *International Journal for Philosophy of Religion* 16 (1984): 215-217.

114. Keith Yandell makes a similar point, though his purposes require him to develop it more fully. In order to understand more fully the difference between justified evils and justified agents, I quote Yandell's helpful explanation: "It is one thing for an evil to be justified, and another for an agent to be justified in allowing it. Suppose that, unknown to John, if he allows an evil E to occur, or brings it about, then E will not be gratuitous (and so will be justified). John, however, intends to permit or produce a gratuitous evil and allows E or brings E about only because he believes that E will be gratuitous. Then E is non-gratuitous or justified though John is not justified in allowing it or in bringing it about. It is also one thing for an evil to be gratuitous and another thing for an agent's allowing it or bringing it about to be gratuitous. If Jane believes that an evil E will, if it occurs, be justified, and therefore allows E or brings E about, then even if E will, if it occurs, be unjustified or gratuitous then Jane will be justified in allowing E to occur or in bringing E about, always supposing that Jane is not culpable in having the false belief that E will be justified" (pp. 15-16). Though this clearly shows the distinction between justified agents and justified evils, one wonders how Yandell will apply it to God, since God can't be mistaken about whether an evil he allows will be gratuitous, and since as good, he can't intend to produce a gratuitous evil, nor as all-powerful and omniscient, does it seem that he can fail to produce one, if he intends to. However, Yandell does have a specific use for this distinction. In much of his paper, as noted in an earlier footnote, he argues that there really are no gratuitous evils. Hence, God hasn't allowed any. But, Yandell applies this distinction between unjustified evil and unjustified agents to his discussion of the atheistic argument's premise that "if there are gratuitous evils, then there is no God." Yandell writes, "The latter portion of this paper has mainly dealt with the claim *If there are gratuitous evils, then there is no God* by way of considering what sort of evil God could not allow without sullying his goodness. It is not obvious what this is. An evil that is not gratuitous cannot be one that God could be gratuitous in allowing, for if an evil is justified then one can be gratuitous in allowing it only if one mistakenly thinks that it is not justified, and omniscience will preclude this mistake. Once one recognizes that even if it is clear that there are gratuitous evils, it does not follow that God would be gratuitous to allow them, and that the fact that a good human being could not allow something to occur without sullying her goodness does not entail that God cannot allow it to happen without sullying His goodness, part of whatever initial force the root argument, and its successors, possesses is lost" (pp. 29-30; the root argument to which Yandell refers is the basic atheistic argument from evil against the probability of God's existence).

115. It goes without saying, of course, that if Peterson defined gratuitous evil only in sense 3), something might be gratuitous in that sense, but we could still find some value the evil leads to that would justify God in allowing it. In that case, one could reject (MP), accept the atheist's factual premise, and still exonerate God by pointing to some subsequent value that is connected to the evil. I didn't raise this point in the text, however, because Peterson doesn't define gratuitous evil in sense 3), and because in virtue of my own defenses against the problems of moral evil and natural evil, I'm not

convinced that there is any genuinely gratuitous evil in sense 3). Hence, though Peterson might still reject (MP) and the like even if he defined gratuitous evil in sense 3), I wouldn't follow that strategy.

116. Michael Martin, "A Theistic Inductive Argument from Evil?" *International Journal for Philosophy of Religion* 22 (1987): 82-83. Martin takes these rules from Ronald N. Giere, *Understanding Scientific Reasoning* (New York: Holt, Rinehart, and Winston, 1977), 91-94.

117. Martin, "Theistic Inductive Argument from Evil?" 83.

118. Ibid., 83-84.

119. Ibid., 85. Martin also shows how, using Peterson's pattern of inductive reasoning, one could write an argument to the effect that it is probable that fairies exist (H), even though normal human beings fail to see fairies dancing on moonbeams (T), and even though there is an auxiliary assumption that fairies could prevent normal humans from seeing them. The problem with this argument, of course, would be the same as the first problem I noted from Martin. The fact that normal humans fail to see fairies dancing on moonbeams is consistent with fairies who deceive us so we can't see them, but it also fits with there being no fairies at all. Hence, the argument really doesn't work, but then, neither does Peterson's, which uses the same form.

120. For further discussion of using gratuitous evil to make a positive case for theism see William Hasker, "The Necessity of Gratuitous Evil," *Faith and Philosophy* 9 (January 1992).

12: EVIL AND EVIDENCE

1. Answering as an agnostic that we don't know is a way to respond to this question. But it doesn't actually answer the question about God's existence. It answers a question about our knowledge of God's existence. Strictly speaking, there are only two answers to the ontological question of whether God exists. Saying we don't know addresses an epistemological issue.

2. Here my point is akin to Wittgenstein's point in the *Tractatus Logico-Philosophicus* (6.41; 6.421). As Wittgenstein argues, in the world, we find states of affairs. Those states of affairs don't include evaluations of themselves. They may include activities of unseen agents like God or angels, but we can't know that from empirical observation. I agree with these points from Wittgenstein, though I don't buy the implications of this worldview about whether God is at all an object of knowledge or can be spoken of.

3. An example might be memory of some affliction one suffered or one's friend or relative suffered that leaves one so bitter toward God that regardless of what evidence there is in favor of his existence, one won't likely evaluate it as very significant. Because of that bad experience and the bitterness that resulted from it, the individual is likely to think theism improbable, regardless of anything the theist says. That feeling may even affect one's ability to understand an argument or judge its validity or soundness.

4. Garth L. Hallett, "Evil and Human Understanding," *Heythrop Journal* 32 (1991): 467.

5. Ibid.

6. Ibid., 468. Hallett cites his own work *Darkness and Light: The Analysis of Doctrinal Statements* (New York: Paulist Press, 1975), 82-83.

7. Ibid., 469.

8. Ibid.

9. Ibid., 470.

10. Ibid., 468.

11. Hallett's point is not unlike Wykstra's response to Rowe about there not appearing to be any purpose for certain evils. I agree with Wykstra that Rowe's "does not appear" claims really don't satisfy CORNEA. As he explains, too much is beyond our knowledge to be certain that Rowe interprets correctly the lack of apparent explanation

of certain evils. One says things appear exactly as they would if there were a God, and the other says they appear different than they would if there were a God. At this point, Hallett would probably say we really don't have enough knowledge to know how the world would appear if there were or weren't a God. If there were a God, for example, how do we know the world would appear any different than it does? But it is also possible that if there were a God, things would appear quite different than they do. We just aren't in a position to know.

12. David O'Connor, "On Failing to Resolve Theism-Versus-Atheism Empirically," *Religious Studies* 26 (1990): 92.

13. Ibid., 96.

14. See ibid. for both quotes, which are parts of the same sentence.

15. Ibid., 98. O'Connor then notes that this doesn't mean that the compensation model has no supporting evidence at all; it only means its support isn't empirical.

16. Ibid., 99-100.

17. Ibid., 101-102.

18. Ibid.

19. I must add that this doesn't mean atheists are irrational in their atheism. If "rational" means holding a position on the basis of argument and evidence, the atheist is rational in holding atheism. Likewise, theists are rational (in this sense of "rational") in holding theism. However, being rational (in this sense) in holding theism or atheism in itself shows nothing about which position is correct. Hence, I'm not claiming that atheists are irrational, but only that their argument from evil won't likely succeed.

20. Jane Mary Trau, "Fallacies in the Argument from Gratuitous Suffering," *New Scholasticism* 60 (Autumn 1986): 486.

21. Ibid., 486-487.

22. Ibid., 487. Trau also says theists move from proposition (1) to (2) rather than to (3), because they are already convinced there is a God. Hence, they also beg the question. However, the theist doesn't try to use this line of reasoning as proof for God's existence, so this error isn't particularly serious. On the other hand, atheists beg the question and commit other logical errors in an argument meant to demonstrate God's nonexistence. Since their argument incorporates these fallacies, it can't work (p. 489). I am not entirely sure theists beg the question as Trau suggests. Theists offer defenses of why various evils aren't necessarily gratuitous. They don't say they are sure they have offered the justifying reason for the evil's existence, but they need not give *the* reason to resolve either the logical or evidential problem. Stating a possible reason for the evil shows that it is logically compatible with God's existence. It also indicates that the evil in question doesn't necessarily make theism improbable. I don't see that theists who handle matters this way necessarily beg the question in their move from (1) to (2), for they are just trying to explain how evil might fit with God's existence, if there is a God.

    I also suspect this is pretty much what Trau might say to Rowe's move from "there appears to be no purpose for certain evils" to "there is no purpose for this evil." Wykstra argued that Rowe's claims don't meet the requirement of CORNEA. Hence, the world would look the same as it does, regardless of whether there is or isn't a God. I think Trau would say that, given what Wykstra has said, for Rowe to reject (2), he would have to have a reason. But what could that reason be other than a rejection of the idea that God exists, and as Trau says, that begs the question.

23. Ibid., 487-488.

24. Ibid., 488.

25. Ibid.

26. Hallett, *Darkness and Light,* 472.

27. Ibid., 472-473. Hallett cites M. B. Ahern's *The Problem of Evil* (New York: Schocken, 1971), 55-56.

13: HELL AND THE PROBLEM OF EVIL

1. Fyodor Dostoyevsky, *The Brothers Karamazov* (New York: The New American Library, 1964), 223, 225-226.

2. Clark Pinnock, "The Destruction of the Finally Impenitent," *Criswell Theological Review* 4 (1990): 246-247. Pinnock's comments are typical of both theists and atheists who have problems with the traditional doctrine of hell. See also Pinnock, "The Conditional View," in William Crockett, ed., *Four Views on Hell* (Grand Rapids, Mich.: Zondervan, 1996), 135-137.

3. Of course, this also raises the question of the salvation of people before Christ. Would Gentiles, for example, living during the OT era be hopelessly consigned to hell when even Jews never heard the name of Jesus Christ? Would believing Jews during that era also be headed for hell because they didn't believe specifically in Jesus? These are significant theological issues which have significance for a Christian philosophy that attempts to justify the power and goodness of God in the face of evil. For a discussion of salvation in the OT, see my "Salvation in the Old Testament," in John Feinberg and Paul Feinberg, eds., *Tradition and Testament: Essays in Honor of Charles Lee Feinberg* (Chicago: Moody, 1981).

4. For help with the historical development of the doctrine of hell, see such works as David W. Lotz, "Heaven and Hell in the Christian Tradition," *Religion in Life* 48 (1979); Alan Bernstein, "Thinking About Hell," *Wilson Quarterly* 10 (1986); John D. Kronen, "The Idea of Hell and the Classical Doctrine of God," *The Modern Schoolman* 77 (November 1999); Hiroshi Obayashi, "Death and Eternal Life in Christianity," in Hiroshi Obayashi, ed., *Death and Afterlife: Perspectives of World Religions* (New York: Greenwood Press, 1992); John R. Sachs, "Current Eschatology: Universal Salvation and the Problem of Hell," *Theological Studies* 52 (1991); and Lawrence R. Hennessey, "Origen of Alexandria: The Fate of the Soul and the Body After Death," *The Second Century* 8 (1991).

5. Here our concern isn't with precise eschatological systems. However, I am articulating a position known as premillennialism. For a discussion of various conceptions of the kingdom, see Robert Clouse, ed., *The Meaning of the Millennium* (Downers Grove, Ill.: InterVarsity Press, 1977), or the more contemporary Darrell L. Bock, ed., *Three Views on the Millennium and Beyond* (Grand Rapids, Mich.: Zondervan, 1999).

6. In *No One Like Him: The Doctrine of God* (Wheaton, Ill.: Crossway, 2001) I have defined ontological and spiritual presence as follows: "Ontological presence means that some entity or being is actually present at a given place in space. If the being is physical in nature, the being that is really there (ontological presence) will also be physically present. However, if the being is immaterial, then it can still actually be somewhere (ontological presence), but as immaterial it cannot be present physically. . . . To say that someone is morally, spiritually, or ethically present to someone else means that they have a relationship of fellowship with one another. As this relates to God and his people, it means that God has a spiritual relationship by means of saving faith with an individual and that no sin blocks fellowship and communion between God and that person" (p. 250).

7. See Kronen, "Idea of Hell," 14-15 for a summary of this point about hell's nature.

8. As some have noted, there have been those in the history of the church who claimed not only that the wicked suffer in hell but also that the "blessed in heaven eternally witness, and rejoice over, the sufferings of the damned in hell." Lotz, "Heaven and Hell," 89.

9. See, for example, Jonathan L. Kvanvig's discussion of this view in *The Problem of Hell* (New York: Oxford, 1993), 62-63.

10. See Kronen's brief discussion of this point, "Idea of Hell," 15; and also the major emphasis given to this issue in Kvanvig's *The Problem of Hell*.

11. Kvanvig, *Problem of Hell*, 25.

12. In relation to this point, we should remember that theists may offer either a theodicy or a defense of their theology. The former purports to explain the actual reason for God allowing the existence of hell; the latter offers a possible way for the existence of hell to be consistent with the existence of an all-loving and all-powerful God.

13. See, for example, Thomas Talbott, "The Doctrine of Everlasting Punishment," *Faith and Philosophy* 7 (January 1990); "Craig on the Possibility of Eternal Damnation," *Religious Studies* 28 (December 1992); "Providence, Freedom and Human Destiny," *Religious Studies* 26 (1990); and "The Love of God and the Heresy of Exclusivism," *Christian Scholar's Review* 27 (Fall 1997).

14. Thomas Talbott, "Doctrine of Everlasting Punishment," 21.

15. Ibid.

16. Ibid.

17. Ibid., 25.

18. Ibid., 26.

19. Ibid., 27.

20. Ibid., 28.

21. Ibid., 35.

22. Ibid.

23. Ibid., 35-36.

24. Ibid., 36-37.

25. Ibid., 37-38. See also Talbott, "Craig on the Possibility of Eternal Damnation," 500-501.

26. A further example of a solution to the problem of evil that opts for universalism is Marilyn Adams's position. This view was described in chapter 5 of this book, and it is a position she has elaborated most fully in her *Horrendous Evils and the Goodness of God* (Ithaca, N.Y.: Cornell University Press, 1999). Adams ultimately adopts the position of universalism, which means for her that even perpetrators of horrendous evils will be saved. Hence, Hitler, though he will experience great suffering in an attempt to cure him of his evil (his punishment will be curative, not retributive), will eventually be saved as well. For further discussion of her views see Marilyn Adams, "Horrors in Theological Context," *Scottish Journal of Theology* 55 (2002)—here note in particular her comments about Hitler and others who have committed horrendous evils (p. 476). See also William C. Placher, "An Engagement with Marilyn McCord Adams's *Horrendous Evils and the Goodness of God*," *Scottish Journal of Theology* 55 (2002).

27. For further interaction with Talbott and his views see William L. Craig, "Talbott's Universalism," *Religious Studies* 27 (1991); William L. Craig, "Talbott's Universalism Once More," *Religious Studies* 29 (1993); Charles Seymour, "On Choosing Hell," *Religious Studies* 33 (1997); Thomas Talbott, "Providence, Freedom, and Human Destiny," *Religious Studies* 26 (1990); and Thomas Talbott, "Craig on the Possibility of Eternal Damnation," *Religious Studies* 28 (December 1992).

28. Clark Pinnock, "Destruction of the Finally Impenitent," 253.

29. Ibid.

30. Edward Fudge, "The Final End of the Wicked," *Journal of the Evangelical Theological Society* 27 (September 1984): 326.

31. Ibid.

32. Robert L. Reymond, "Dr. John Stott on Hell," *Covenant Seminary Review* 16 (1990): 45.

33. Fudge, "Final End of the Wicked," 326.

34. Ibid., 328-29.

35. Ibid., 330. See also Fudge's handling of phrases that speak of undying worms, smoke that ascends, the cup of God's wrath, etc. (pp. 329-333).

36. Reymond, "Dr. John Stott on Hell," 56-57.

37. Ibid., 57.

38. Ibid., 58. Reymond cites David L. Edwards and John Stott, *Evangelical Essentials: A Liberal-Evangelical Dialogue* (Downers Grove, Ill.: InterVarsity Press, 1988), 319. See also Pinnock, "Destruction of the Finally Impenitent," 250-257, for similar arguments that appeal to various scriptural and theological points to argue in favor of annihilationism.

39. Of course, God could have created us as superhuman, but then we would likely be glorified and sin would be an impossibility for us. Free will defenders don't deny that such a situation (free will defenders believe in the eternal state wherein believers will be glorified) is better morally than our current world with non-glorified human beings. However, a Modified Rationalist theology doesn't need to show that our world is a better world than other possible worlds. It only needs to explain why our world is a good possible world, and of course, free will defenders believe that ours is a good world because it contains humans with libertarian free will.

40. C. S. Lewis, *The Problem of Pain* (New York: Macmillan, 1962), 127.

41. For an explanation of how this works and a defense of compatibilistic free will see my *No One Like Him,* chapters 13-14.

42. Here one thinks of what it would take and what it would be like for Hugh Hefner to turn from his sexual practices, enter a totally monogamous relationship, disassemble his *Playboy* empire (and the millions of dollars a year it generates), and preach premarital abstinence from sex and marital faithfulness of spouses. Is it reasonable for us to imagine this happening without some radical action on God's part? The point is that Hefner either doesn't consider his lifestyle and philosophy of life to be sinful, or he does think these things are sinful but refuses to turn from them. Why? At least in part because he enjoys these sins and the results (financial, etc.) of his lifestyle. Hefner isn't the only example of someone who enjoys sin, but he is a very blatant example of the point I am making that sin isn't viewed as meriting eternal punishment.

43. We also noted that the soul-building theodicy by itself doesn't solve the problem of hell. However, when joined to either the free will defense or my defense, this theodicy can both offer God's morally sufficient reason for not removing hell and also explain why hell isn't an unjust punishment for rejecting God.

44. The following otherwise uncited works were helpful in the preparation of this chapter: David Moore, *The Battle for Hell* (Lanham, Md.: University Press of America, 1995); Jerry L. Walls, *Hell: The Logic of Damnation* (Notre Dame, Ind.: University of Notre Dame Press, 1992); Marilyn M. Adams, "Hell and the God of Justice," *Religious Studies* 11 (1975); Edward Fudge, "Putting Hell in Its Place," *Christianity Today* 6 (August 6, 1976); Vernon Grounds, "The Final State of the Wicked," *Journal of the Evangelical Theological Society* 24 (1981); Paul Helm, "Universalism and the Threat of Hell," *Trinity Journal* 4NS (1983); J. D. O'Donnell, "Hell: The Bible's Most Solemn Subject," in F. Leroy Forlines, ed., *Contending for the Faith: Practical Answers for Perplexing Problems* (Nashville: Commission on Theological Liberalism, 1984); Grace M. Jantzen, "Do We Need Immortality?" *Modern Theology* 1 (1984); Evan Fales, "Antediluvian Theodicy: Stump on the Fall," *Faith and Philosophy* 6 (July 1989); William L. Craig, "'No Other Name': A Middle Knowledge Perspective on the Exclusivity of Salvation Through Christ," *Faith and Philosophy* 6 (April 1989); Ronald L. Hall, "Hell, Is This Really Necessary?" *Philosophy of Religion* 25 (1989); Ronald Lindsay, "Thomas Aquinas's Complete Guide to Heaven and Hell," *Free Inquiry* 10 (1989–1990); Leon Morris, "Hell: The Dreadful Harvest," *Christianity Today* 21 (May 27, 1991); Timothy R. Phillips, "Hell: A Christological Reflection," in William V. Crockett and James G. Sigountos, eds., *Through No Fault of Their Own? The Fate of Those Who Never Heard* (Grand Rapids, Mich.: Baker, 1991); Scot McKnight, "Eternal Consequences or Eternal Consciousness?" in William V. Crockett and James G. Sigountos, eds., *Through No Fault of Their Own? The Fate of Those Who Never Heard* (Grand Rapids, Mich.: Baker, 1991); Kerry S. Walters, "Hell, This Isn't Necessary After All," *Philosophy of Religion* 29 (1991); William Hasker, "Middle

THE MANY FACES OF EVIL

Knowledge and the Damnation of the Heathen: A Response to William Craig," *Faith and Philosophy* 8 (1991); Mark Stephen Pestana, "Radical Freedom, Radical Evil and the Possibility of Eternal Damnation," *Faith and Philosophy* 9 (October 1992); David Basinger, "Divine Omniscience and the Soteriological Problem of Evil: Is the Type of Knowledge God Possesses Relevant?" *Religious Studies* 28 (1992); Keith E. Yandell, "The Doctrine of Hell and Moral Philosophy," *Religious Studies* 28 (1992); Geoffrey Rowell, "Heaven and Hell: (3) In Victorian Times," *Epworth Review* 19 (1992); Paul T. Jensen, "Intolerable But Moral? Thinking About Hell," *Faith and Philosophy* 10 (April 1993); David Cheetham, "John Hick, Authentic Relationships, and Hell," *Sophia* 33 (March 1994); and Tan Tai Wei, "Justice and Punishment Without Hell," *Sophia* 35 (March–April 1996). See also, Charles Seymour, "Hell, Justice, and Freedom," *International Journal for Philosophy of Religion* 43 (1998); Wilko Van Holten, "Hell and the Goodness of God," *Religious Studies* 35 (1999); and James Cain, "On the Problem of Hell," *Religious Studies* 38 (2002).

14: THE RELIGIOUS PROBLEM OF EVIL

1. Alvin Plantinga, *God, Freedom, and Evil* (New York: Harper & Row, 1974), 63-64.

15: THE RELIGIOUS PROBLEM: USES OF SUFFERING

1. At this point, I must add that if I were a consequentialist, I might, indeed, see the material for this chapter as more than helps in living with God. I might view it as justification of his ways. In fact, given an approach to justification like the soul-building theodicy, I might claim that these uses of evil illustrate the point that God has done nothing wrong, because he will bring good out of evil. However, since I'm not a consequentialist, I in no way intend for the material in this or the preceding chapter to serve as justification of God's ways to man. That is, I don't see any of this as a solution to the theological/philosophical problem, the problem of natural evil, the problem of the quantity of evil, etc., in either their logical or evidential forms.

2. The questions of why the unrighteous suffer and how God uses affliction in their lives are also important. However, the more troublesome religious problems focus on righteous suffering. By "righteous" I don't mean sinlessly perfect, but rather that their basic pattern of life is to follow God and avoid evil. While God may use affliction in unbelievers' lives to accomplish some of the same goals he intends for believers, he might also use affliction of the unbelieving as punishment for their sin.

İndex

Adams, Marilyn McCord, 491n. 5, 507nn. 121, 122, 530n. 26; Feinberg's assessment of, 159-164; redemptive suffering defense of, 155-159

Adams, Robert M., 212, 286-292, 520n. 83

affliction. *See* suffering

Ahern, M. B., 387, 491nn. 5, 6

Andre, Shane, 239-241

animal suffering, 23, 94, 217-219

annihilation/conditional immortality, 402, 407-408, 419-421, 433, 443; Feinberg's assessment of, 423-426; support for the view, 421-423

Aquinas, Thomas, 412-413

argument from design. *See* teleological argument

Arminianism, 187-188, 295, 296, 301, 355, 390

atheism: arguments from evil, 215-259; evidential case against, 336; "friendly," 222-223, 513n. 32; and human and animal suffering, 217-220; on the improbability of theism, 207-209; "indifferent," 222; paradoxical atheism (PA), 239-241; as "rational," 528n. 19; special grounds atheism (SGA), 239-241; "unfriendly," 222

"Atheistic Argument from the Quantity of Evil in the World, An" (Chrzan), 516n. 138

Augustine, 67, 122, 150, 503n. 148; on free will, 69-72, 104

"Augustine's Transformation of the Free Will Defence" (Greer), 496n. 15

Basinger, David, 109, 348, 501n. 117, 501-502n. 123, 526n. 113; response to Martin's argument, 253-257

Bayes' Theorem, 210-212, 245, 247, 249-250, 282, 286-287, 300, 304, 325, 367-370, 441-442

Bennett, Philip, 498n. 35

Biel, Gabriel, 40

Bigg, Charles, 482

Black, Max, 208, 510n. 5

Body of Christ, 480-481

Boehner, Philotheus, 38

Boër, Steven, 99-102, 202

Boethius, 107

Brooks, Phillips, 487

Brothers Karamazov, The (Dostoyevsky), 395-396

Calvin, John, 492n. 3

Calvinism, 166, 296, 459-460; and the glory of God, 185-187

Cameron, Brian K., 491n. 5, 507n. 122

Campbell, Richmond, 495n. 51

"Can Nature Be Evil?" (Ouderkirk), 509n. 9

"Christian Pacifism and Theodicy" (Pinches), 500n. 79

Chrzan, Keith, 263-265, 361, 516n. 138, 517nn. 1, 20, 26, 518n. 35, 524n. 84, 525n. 107

Clark, Kelly J., 510n. 1, 512n. 8

"Coherence of the Hypothesis of an Omnipotent, Omniscient, Free and

Perfectly Evil Being, The" (Martin), 522n. 38

Coherence of Theism, The (Swinburne), 303

"Comment on Langtry's 'God, Evil and Probability'" (Chrzan), 518n. 35

compatibilism, 74-76, 78, 91-92, 103, 122, 141, 152, 411, 502-503n. 135, 508n. 14

"Compatibilism, Free Will and God" (Flew), 73-75

Compatibility Thesis, 78, 118

"Concept of Divine Goodness and the Problem of Evil, The" (Kane), 492nn. 3, 19, 493n. 24

conditional immortality. See annihilation/conditional immortality

consequentialism. See ethics, consequentialist

Conway, David, 511n. 1, 512n. 14

Core Naturalism, 232-233

Core Theism, 230-233

CORNEA (Condition of Reasonable Epistemic Access), 224-226, 230, 359, 514nn. 59, 64

Cornman, James, 338, 372, 523n. 81

creation, 342-343

"Critique of Marilyn McCord Adams' 'Christian Solution' to the Existential Problem of Evil, The" (Cameron), 491n. 5, 507n. 122

Curley, E. M., 51-52

death, 195, 509n. 3

Death and Eternal Life (Hick), 150

defense, 72, 510n. 2; basic strategy for, 489-490; definition of, 29, 164, 530n. 12; marshaled against evil in general, 156; need for, 337; Plantinga's concept of, 86-87, 88; value of for theists over theodicy, 375

"Degenerative Evidence and Rowe's New Evidential Argument from Evil" (Plantinga), 246-247, 515n. 98

Descartes, René, 34

"Destruction of the Finally Impenitent" (Pinnock), 529n. 2, 531n. 38

determinism. See compatibilism

Dialogues Concerning Natural Religion (Hume), 17-18, 513n. 39

Dilley, Frank, 99, 100-101, 501n. 103

"Divine Providence and Simple Foreknowledge" (Hunt), 502n. 129

Doctrine of Being in the Aristotelian 'Metaphysics,' The (Owen), 493n. 8

"Does Evil Have a Cause?" (Steel), 496n. 15

"Does God Hide from Us?" (Mesle), 505n. 86

"Does Theism Need a Theodicy?" (Swinburne), 303, 307-308, 521nn. 19, 20

Donagan, Alan, 500n. 84

Doxastic Problem, 109, 110

election, 36

"Empirical Argument from Evil, The" (Rowe), 238-239, 512n. 17

"Engagement with Marilyn McCord Adams's Horrendous Evils and the Goodness of God, An" (Placher), 507n. 122

epistemic distance, 146-147, 505n. 86

Eshleman, Andrew, 102-103

ethics: consequentialist, 65, 68, 124, 382, 495n. 52, 496n. 2, 508n. 10; deontological, 496n. 2; divine command theory of, 492n. 10; emotivist account of, 491n. 7; nonconsequentialist, 68, 165-166, 381-382, 495n. 52, 496n. 2, 508n. 10; teleological, 496n. 2; theonomous, 165-166

Ethics for a Brave New World (Feinberg and Feinberg), 492n. 10, 495n. 52

"Evidence, Evil, and Religious Belief" (Moore), 518n. 38

"Evidence—Once More" (Moore), 518n. 51

"Evidential Argument from Evil, The" (Rowe), 244-246

evidential problem of evil, 20, 24, 207-208, 295, 362, 499n. 78, 500n. 81, 506n. 105, 521n. 25; evaluation of, 89; forms of, 213-214; and the limits of human knowledge, 371-379; nature of the problem, 208-213; strategies for handling, 358-364, 440-441. *See also* inductive problem of evil; first-order good and evil; Plantinga, Alvin, on the evidential problem of evil; probabilistic problem of evil; second-order good and evil

evil. *See* animal suffering; evidential problem of evil; hell; natural evil; problem of evil; problem of gratuitous evil; problem of the intensity of evil; problem of moral evil; problem of natural evil; problem of the quantity of evil; unattached natural evil, Feinberg's defense against

"Evil and Christian Belief" (Clark), 510n. 1

Evil and the Christian God (Peterson), 337-342, 523n. 80, 524nn. 87, 94, 524-525n. 99

Evil and the God of Love (Hick), 142, 146, 512n. 29

"Evil and God's Freedom in Creation" (Rowe), 495n. 1

Evil and the Good God (Reichenbach), 325

"Evil and Omnipotence" (Mackie), 18, 498n. 39

"Evil and Theodicy" (Rowe), 219, 515n. 90

"Evil, God, and the Free Will Defense" (Bennett), 498n. 35

Evil Revisited (Griffin), 92-93

evolution, 94; and death, 509n. 3; wastefulness of, 491n. 9

Existence of God, The (Swinburne), 303-306, 308-313, 521nn. 5, 8

existential problem of evil, 491n. 5

"Failure of Soul-Making Theodicy, The" (Kane), 146-148

Faith and Reason (Swinburne), 303

fall, the, 168, 401; consequences of, 194-195, 401, 467; and man's sin nature, 173, 180, 194, 324, 342

"Fallacies in the Argument from Gratuitous Suffering" (Trau), 528n. 22

Farmer, H. H., 145

Feinberg, John, 491n. 4, 492nn. 4, 10, 495nn. 44, 52, 497n. 28, 500n. 83, 501n. 114, 508n. 14, 511n. 4, 529nn. 3, 6, 531n. 41; answer to the objection that God could have made humans who never sin, 181-182; answer to the objection that he is presenting a form of the greater good defense, 180-181; answer to the objection that his view emphasizes God creating human beings, not subhuman or superhuman beings, 183-184; answer to the objection that since his view holds that God will create a better world eventually why not sooner, 187-190; answer to the objection that his view makes sin inescapable, 183; answer to the objection that human beings are instrumentally valuable, not intrinsically valuable, 185-187; comments on the inductive problem and the likeliness of success, 358-379; defense against unattached natural evils, 194-203; on gratuitous evil, 379-383; on how sin/moral evil arises, 169-172; and the problem of hell, 431-439, 444; on the quantity of evil, 383-391; seven theses of, 19-20; theory of ethics, 492n. 10; thesis 1, 21-27; thesis 2, 27-29; on what man is, 167-169; on why it would be undesirable for God to turn our world into a utopia, 172-180; and wife's battle with Huntington's Chorea, 448-475, 479. *See also* problem of gratuitous evil, Feinberg on; problem of moral evil, Feinberg on; problem of natural evil, Feinberg on; problem of the quantity of evil, Feinberg on; *Feinberg's assessment of various positions passim*

Feinberg, Paul, 492n. 10, 495n. 52

"Final End of the Wicked, The" (Fudge), 530n. 35

first-order good and evil, 76-77, 135-136, 138-140, 192-193, 216

Flew, Antony, 67, 497n. 30; Feinberg's assessment of, 91-92; on the free will defense, 72-76, 102, 497n. 30

Frankena, William K., 166

Frankfurt, Harry, 102-103

"Free Will Defence, The" (Plantinga), 80

free will defense, 24, 26, 54, 93, 96, 167, 181, 187-188, 189, 241-243, 257-259, 297, 301, 354, 494n. 25, 509-510n. 1, 522n. 54; Augustine's formulation of, 69-72; Boër's objection to, 99-102; compatibilist's objection to, 76; contemporary writings/works on, 496-497n. 16; as a defense, not a theodicy, 271; Feinberg's rejection of, 121-122; Flew's attack on, 72-76; and freedom, 67; Griffin's objections to, 92-99; in Leibnizian Rationalism, 61; Mackie's attack on, 76-79; not a form of the greater good defense, 180-181; Peterson on, 339-340; Plantinga's development of, 24, 26, 67, 79-87; presupposition of a nonconsequentialist ethic, 352; and

the problem of hell, 428-430, 444; rejection of on the ground of incompatibilism, 121; theists' inconsistency in holding the defense, 122

freedom: Flew's concept of, 73-76; free will defense and, 64; Griffin's concept of, 96-97; Hick's concept of, 151; Plantinga's concept of, 79-80; as randomness, 77-78. *See also* compatibilism; free will defense; freedom/foreknowledge problem; incompatibilism

freedom/foreknowledge problem, 104-107; Boethian answer to, 107, 296; Molinist (middle knowledge) answer to, 112-113; Ockhamist answer to, 113-118; simple foreknowledge answer to, 107-112

Fudge, Edward, 421-422, 530n. 35

"G. E. Moore shift," 220, 512n. 21

Geach, Peter T., 19, 34-35

Geisler, Norman, 501n. 119

Giere, Ronald N., 527n. 116

God, 465-475 and compatibility with evil, 242-244; evil and existence of, 251-257, 259, 267-274, 326-330, 335, 365-366, 447-448; infinity of, 305; knowledge of the future, 62-63; omnibenevolence of, 228-229; omnipotence of, 18, 166-167, 169, 228-229; omniscience of, 104-105, 169, 305, 503n. 137; perfection of, 64; *potentia absoluta*, 37-39; *potentia ordinata*, 37-39; purposes in creating, 65; rejection of, 431-435; retributive justice of, 404; revelation of, 436-439; theological conception of, 21. *See also* grace, of God; justice, of God

"God and Evil" (Rowe), 220-221, 229, 512n. 23

"God and Evolutionary Evil" (Southgate), 491n. 9

"God and Gratuitous Evil" (Chrzan), 524n. 84

God and Other Minds (Plantinga), 80, 268

God and the Soul (Geach), 34

"God, Evil, and Humanity" (Campbell), 495n. 51

"God, Evil, and Probability" (Langtry), 517nn. 22, 26

God, Freedom and Evil (Plantinga), 26, 80, 83, 447

"God Ordains All Things" (J. Feinberg), 508n. 14

God Who Risks, The (Sanders), 501n. 117

God Who Stands and Stays (Henry), 507n. 6

grace, of God, 196, 439, 474; sufficiency of, 462

Graham, Harrison, 257-258

"Gratuitous Evil and Divine Existence" (Yandell), 523-524n. 84

greater good defense, 135-137, 161, 180-181, 382; Feinberg's assessment of, 137-138, 139-141; Kane's objection to, 138-140

"Greater Good Defense, The" (Yandell), 135-137

greatest happiness argument, 123-125; Feinberg's assessment of, 132-135; Grover's criticism of, 130-132; Rosenberg's criticism of, 125-126; Shea's criticism of, 126-128

Greer, Rowan A., 496n. 15

Griffin, David, 499n. 78, 500nn. 80, 90; definition of genuine evil, 96; objection to the free will defense in general, 92-99, 499n. 78; objection to Plantinga, 88-91

Grover, Stephen, 130-132, 503n. 12

Hallett, Garth, 372-374, 386-387, 389-390, 527n. 6, 527-528n. 11; Feinberg's assessment of, 374-375

hard/soft facts distinction, 114-117, 503n. 136

Hasker, William, 107-108, 110-111, 148, 501n. 117, 502n. 127, 526n. 113, 527n. 120

hell, 20, 23, 342; as conscious punishment, 425; as a distinct problem, 397; evidential problem of, 440-444; and God's retributive justice, 404; and the Great Throne Judgment, 425-426; logical problem of, 404-439; morally sufficient reason for, 426-428, 443-444; as a never ending punishment, 403-404; and physical and spiritual death, 401; as a place of torment, 401-402; in the rich man and Lazarus parable, 425; a specific place, 399-401; traditional doctrine of, 398-404; who goes there, 402-403. *See also* annihilation/conditional immortality; free will defense, and the problem of hell; Feinberg, and the problem of hell; Leibnizian Rationalism, and the problem of hell; Modified Rationalism, and the problem of hell; soul-building theodicy, and the problem of hell; theonomy, and the problem of hell; universalism

Henry, Carl F. H., 171, 181-182, 183, 507n. 6

Hick, John, 63-64, 65, 138, 506nn. 96, 104, 512n. 29; Feinberg's assessment of, 152-155, 417-419; Hasker's defense of, 148; Kane's objections to, 146-148, 149-150, 154; soul-building theodicy of, 94, 138, 142-146, 167, 187, 188, 222, 342, 352, 363, 382, 390, 409-412

Hobbes, Thomas, 34

Horrendous Evils and the Goodness of God (M. Adams), 155, 507n. 122, 530n. 26

"Horrors in Theological Context" (M. Adams), 507n. 122

Howard-Snyder, Daniel, 516n. 138
human beings: as instrumentally
    valuable, 185-187; ontological
    constituents of, 167-169; as a value
    of the first order, 179. See also fall,
    the, and man's sin nature
Hume, David, 17-18, 143
"Humean Obstacle to Evidential
    Arguments from Suffering, The"
    (Wykstra), 223-228, 514n. 59
Hunt, David, 109-110, 502nn. 125,
    129, 513n. 39

ideal observer theory, 493n. 20
"In What Sense Must God Do His
    Best" (Basinger), 526n. 113
incompatibilism, 74-76, 78, 91-92, 101,
    102, 141, 152, 498n. 37, 502-503n.
    135; and divine omniscience, 104-
    118, 501n. 106
indeterminism. See incompatibilism
"Induction" (Black), 510n. 5
inductive problem of evil, 209-210,
    212, 510n. 12; definition of
    induction, 213; general issues, 358-
    364; nature of, 364-367; as a
    probability argument, 367-371
inference, 210, 510n. 9
infinity: mathematical conception of,
    126-127; Schlesinger on, 123, 124-
    125
Ingraham, Matt, 499n. 75
Irenaeus, 143, 409
"Irrelevance of the Free Will Defence,
    The" (Boër), 99
"Is Evil Evidence Against the Existence
    of God?" (Martin), 516n. 112
"Is the Free Will Defence Irrelevant?"
    (Dilley), 501n. 103
"Is Rowe Committed to an Expanded
    Version of Theism?" (Napier), 513n.
    46

Job, 17, 21, 35-36, 156, 195, 479-480,
    482-483

justice, of God, 196

Kane, G. Stanley, 138-140, 146-148,
    492nn. 3, 19, 493n. 24
Kapitan, Thomas, 109, 502n. 125
King, James, 41-42
Kingdom of God, 78-79, 118, 153;
    Hick on, 145; Mackie's concept of,
    118
knowledge, 105; background
    knowledge, 319-321, 334; free
    knowledge, 112; human beings' lack
    of omniscience, 375, 386; middle
    knowledge, 108, 112; natural
    knowledge, 112; and senses of
    "know," 104-105; simple
    foreknowledge, 107-108, 108-109
Kroon, Frederick W., 501n. 113
Kvanvig, Jonathan, 404

Langtry, Bruce, 265-270, 517nn. 22,
    26
Latzer, Michael, 493n. 8
Leff, Gordon, 38
Lehrer, Keith, 338, 372, 523n. 81
Leibniz, Gottfried, 233-34, 384, 443,
    489. See also Leibnizian Rationalism
"Leibniz's Conception of Metaphysical
    Evil" (Latzer), 493n. 8
Leibnizian Rationalism, 33-34, 45-46,
    362-363; on the best possible world,
    46, 48, 52-53, 56-60; 62-64, 65,
    494n. 29; defense of God in, 54;
    distinction between God's
    antecedent and consequent wills, 60;
    distinguished from theonomy, 45,
    50; on evil, 46-48, 384; Feinberg's
    assessment of, 62-66; free will
    defense of, 61; on God's purpose in
    creating, 54-56, 65; on metaphysical
    and moral necessity, and the
    absolutely arbitrary, 49; on moral
    evil, 60-61; on natural evil, 61-62;
    on necessity, contingency, and
    logical possibility, 48-49; on possible

existents, 49-52; and the principle of sufficient reason, 46, 55, 63, 493n. 1; priority of logic in, 45; and the problem of evil, 53-62; and the problem of hell, 406, 427; on time, 495n. 46

Leibniz's Lapse, 84, 499n. 66

Lewis, C. S., 212, 430

Lewis, Delmas, 235-239; on the Epistemological Slide, 235-237, 514n. 64; and the Inductive Slide, 235-237

logical problem of evil, 20, 24, 90, 133-134, 138, 295, 493n. 23, 499n. 78, 500n. 97, 506n. 105, 510n. 1, 521n. 25; evaluation of, 89; ground rules for handling, 27-29; and the internal consistency of theological positions, 91-92; of Leibnizian Rationalism, 53-62; point in discussing the problem, 495n. 49; of theonomy, 41-43

Mackie, J. L., 18-19, 66, 67, 180, 190, 191, 498nn. 37, 39, 509-510n. 1, 511nn. 1, 8; arguments from evil, 215-217; Feinberg's assessment of, 18-19, 91-92; first-order evil/second-order good analysis of, 76-77, 216; on the free will defense, 27-28, 76-79, 180, 207; "good choosing argument" of, 77; on the utopia thesis, 118, 120

Martin, Michael, 250-253, 313-315, 352-355, 516n. 112, 522n. 38, 527nn. 116, 119; Basinger's response to, 253-257

Mascall, E. L., 212

McCloskey, H. J., 190

Mesle, C. Robert, 505n. 86

metaphysical moralism, 166

Mill, John Stuart, 191-192

Miracle of Theism, The (Mackie), 207, 215-217, 498n. 39, 509-510n. 1

miracles, 200, 202, 203; coincidence miracles, 99, 100, 101

Mitchell, Basil, 212

Modified Divine Command theory, 166

Modified Rationalism, 64, 67, 97, 99, 363, 364, 390, 397, 500n. 97; distinguished from Leibnizian Rationalism, 68; distinguished from theonomy, 67-68; ethics of, 68; on God and the removal of evil, 507n. 3; and good possible worlds, 68, 97, 99, 133, 179, 182, 188, 189-190, 299, 377-378, 410, 416; and the problem of evil, 67-69, 133; and the problem of hell, 427-439, 443-444; and the problem of the quantity of evil, 384-385, 388-390

Molina, Luis de, 112-113

Moore, G. E., 492n. 20

Moore, Harold, 275-280, 518nn. 38, 51, 518n. 51, 518-519n. 52

Morris, Thomas, 112, 113-114, 501n. 119, 502n. 132

Moser, Paul K., 522n. 45

"Must God Do His Best?" (Hasker), 526n. 113

Napier, Stephen, 513n. 46

natural evil, 254-255, 308-312, 316-319, 324, 333, 341-342, 382, 389; as unabsorbed evil, 511-512n. 8. *See also* problem of natural evil

"Natural Evil" (Swinburne), 303, 308

"Natural Evil and Eschatology" (van den Brink), 509n. 9

"Natural Evil and the Free Will Defense" (Moser), 522n. 45

natural law theory, 493n. 30

Nature of Necessity, The (Plantinga), 261-262, 270, 300, 516-517n. 1; Chrzan's response to, 263-265; Feinberg's assessment of the Plantinga/Chrzan/Langtry exchange, 270-275; Feinberg's assessment of the Plantinga/Moore/Wierenga

exchange, 279-281; Langtry's
response to, 265-270; Moore's
response to, 275-277, 279;
Wierenga's response to, 277-279
"Necessity of Gratuitous Evil, The"
(Hasker), 527n. 120
New Perspectives on Old-Time Religion
(Schlesinger), 503n. 12
No One Like Him (Feinberg), 491n. 4,
492n. 4, 495n. 44, 497n. 28, 500n.
83, 501nn. 114, 117, 508n. 14,
529n. 6, 531n. 41
nonconsequentialism. See ethics,
nonconsequentialist

Oberman, Heiko, 37
O'Connor, David, 375-377, 528n. 15;
Feinberg's assessment of, 377-379
O'Daly, Gerard, 503n. 148
"On the A Priori Rejection of Evidential
Arguments from Evil" (Howard-
Snyder), 516n. 138
"On Failing to Resolve Theism-Versus-
Atheism Empirically" (O'Connor),
528n. 15
On the Free Choice of the Will
(Augustine), 69-71
"On Ockham's Way Out" (Plantinga),
503n. 136, 520n. 96
Openness of God, The (Pinnock et al.),
501n. 117
Ouderkirk, Wayne, 509n. 9
Our Idea of God (Morris), 501n. 119
Owens, Joseph, 493n. 8

Panthanmackel, George, 505n. 76
perfect being/surpassable world debate,
504n. 45
Peterson, Michael, 209, 323, 360, 381,
386, 510n. 8, 522n. 54, 523n. 80,
524n. 87, 524-525n. 99, 524nn. 91,
92, 525n. 107, 526-527n. 115;
Feinberg's analysis of , 344-352 (on
Peterson's defensive strategy), 352-
355 (on Peterson's offensive
strategy); on gratuitous evil, 337-
344; Martin's response to, 352-355
"Philosophical Problem of Evil, The"
(Conway), 511n. 1, 512n. 14
Philosophical Problems and Arguments
(Cornman and Lehrer), 338, 523n.
81
philosophical/theological problem of
evil, 21-22, 23-24, 134, 138, 508-
509n. 19; and Leibnizian
Rationalism, 53-62
Philosophy of Religion (Rowe), 523n.
81
Pinches, Charles, 500n. 79
Pinnock, Clark, 396, 420, 501n. 117,
529n. 2, 531n. 38
Placher, William, 507n. 122
Plantinga, Alvin, 22, 358-359, 361,
366, 440, 441, 447, 460, 499n. 66,
503n. 136, 510n. 4, 515n. 98, 516-
517n. 1, 519nn. 52, 69, 520n. 96,
522n. 54, 524n. 87; on degenerate
evidence, 247-250; on the evidential
problem of evil, 209, 212, 213; on
the free will defense, 24, 26, 67, 207;
Griffin's objection to, 88-91;
Leibnizian notions and, 82-85;
Nature of Necessity discussion, 261-
281; and the pluralistic problem
from evil, 281-301, 518n. 50; on the
probabilistic problem of evil, 518n.
50; reconstruction of Mackie's
argument, 80-82; response to
Rowe's new argument, 246-250,
282; on transworld depravity, 86-97,
498n. 58, 499n. 65. See also
probabilistic argument from evil
"Plantinga on Atheistic Induction"
(Chrzan), 517nn. 1, 20
"Plantinga on God, Freedom, and Evil"
(Kroon), 501n. 113
"Plantinga on the Problem of Evil" (R.
Adams), 520n. 83

"Predestination and Freedom in Augustine's Ethics" (O'Daly), 503n. 148

"Prescience and Providence" (Hunt), 502n. 125

presentism, 105-106

principle of credulity, 235

principle of gratuitous evil (PG), 214, 343-344

principle of meticulous providence (MP), 338, 342, 382; Peterson's argument for the rejection of, 339-342

principle of sufficient reason, 46, 55, 63, 493n. 1

probabilistic argument from evil, 281-286, 444; Feinberg's assessment of the discussion, 292-301; R. Adams's response to, 286-292

"Probabilistic Argument from Evil, The" (Plantinga), 517n. 1

"Probabilistic Problem from Evil, The" (Plantinga), 300, 358-359

probabilistic problem of evil, 208, 210-212, 281-301, 367-371; definition of probability, 213

problem of evil, 18; fundamental questions concerning, 166; many problems of evil, 19, 20-21, 26-27, 89-90, 95, 132, 361 (*see also* specific problems of evil by category). *See also* evidential problem of evil; hell; logical problem of evil; philosophical/theological problem of evil; religious problem of evil

Problem of Evil, The (Ahern), 491nn. 5, 6

"Problem of Evil" (Panthanmackel), 505n. 76

"Problem of Evil, The" (Swinburne), 303, 308

"Problem of Evil and Some Varieties of Atheism, The" (Rowe), 217, 510n. 1

problem of gratuitous evil, 23, 96, 214, 217, 218, 238-239, 379-383;

definition of gratuitous evil, 344-351, 511n. 17; Feinberg on, 381-383; Peterson's views on, 337-352; Rowe's explanation of, 346; theistic strategy for handling, 235; Trau on, 379-381

problem of the intensity of evil, 22-23, 99

problem of moral evil, 22, 95, 194, 214; Feinberg on, 122, 165-190, 388-389; and the free will defense, 87; Leibnizian Rationalism on, 60-61. *See also* sin

problem of natural evil, 22, 95, 194, 214, 511n. 18; Feinberg on, 191-203, 389; and the free will defense, 87; Leibnizian Rationalism on, 61-62; unattached natural evils, 193-203; varieties of natural evils, 190-194

problem of the quantity of evil, 22, 213-214, 217; Feinberg on, 383-391; Hick on, 153; Swinburne on, 324-325

prophecy, biblical, 106-107

pros hen equivalent terms, 47, 493n. 8

providence, 343

"Providence, Foreknowledge, and Decision Procedures" (Kapitan), 502n. 124

purgatory, 402, 403

"Reason and Belief in God" (Plantinga), 516-517n. 1

redemption, 342, 403; before Christ, 529n. 3

"Redemptive Suffering" (M. Adams), 155, 491n. 5, 507n. 121

redemptive suffering defense, 155-159

reformed epistemology, 517n. 1

Reichenbach, Bruce, 380, 509nn. 2, 5, 510n. 13, 523nn. 65, 72, 524n. 91, 532nn. 65, 72; Feinberg's assessment of, 334-337; on the inductive problem of evil, 325-334; natural law defense of, 198-202, 381, 382, 390; objections to Feinberg's argument, 183-187; objections to Rowe's argument, 234-235

"Religious Experience and the Evidential Argument from Evil" (Silver), 517n. 1

religious problem of evil, 20, 21, 160, 194, 220, 447, 491n. 5, 500n. 81; evaluation of, 89; as fundamentally an emotional problem, 156, 160, 454-455, 459; things that don't help people through this difficult time, 455-462; things that help people through this difficult time, 462-475. *See also* suffering

"Reply to Harold Moore's 'Evidence, Evil, and Religious Belief'" (Wierenga), 518n. 50

Return to Reason (Clark), 512n. 8

revelation, 435-439; theonomy's view of, 42

Rice, Richard, 501n. 117

Rosenberg, Jay, 125-126

Rowe, William L., 282, 338, 359, 380, 381, 383, 495n. 1, 510n. 1, 512nn. 11, 12, 17, 23, 24, 29, 513nn. 30, 32, 515nn. 86, 90, 92, 97, 523n. 81, 525n. 108, 527n. 11; Andre's response to, 239-241; arguments from evil, 217-223, 244-246; Feinberg's assessment of, 219-220; Feinberg's assessment of the Rowe/Plantinga exchange, 249-250; Feinberg's assessment of the Rowe/Wykstra exchange, 228-230, 233; on gratuitous evil, 346; Lewis's response to, 235-239; Plantinga's response to, 246-248; Reichenbach's response to, 234-235; Snyder's response to, 241-244; works discussing his evidential argument (and its respondents), 516n. 111; Wykstra's response to, 223-228, 230-233

"Rowe's Noseeum Arguments from Evil" (Wykstra), 230-233, 246

"Ruminations About Evil" (Rowe), 515n. 90

Runzo, Joseph, 104-105, 106

salvation. *See* redemption

"Salvation in the Old Testament" (J. Feinberg), 529n. 3

sanctification, suffering's promotion of: by challenging the righteous to growth, rather than to fall into sin, 482-484; by educating believers, 482; by giving believers a glimpse of the Lord's sovereignty and majesty, 482-483; by giving believers intimacy with God, 483; by helping believers to put away sin, 481-482; by offering believers opportunities to imitate Christ, 484; by refining believers' faith, 482

Sanders, John, 501n. 117

Satan, 87, 90, 171-172, 479-480

"Satisfied Pigs and Dissatisfied Philosophers" (Grover), 503n. 12

Schleiermacher, Friedrich, 142

Schlesinger, G.: Feinberg's assessment of, 132-135, 503n. 12; greatest happiness argument of, 123-125; Grover's criticism of, 130-132; Rosenberg's criticism of, 125-126; Shea's criticism of, 126-128

Schoenig, Richard, 26

Schuurman, Henry J., 494n. 29

second-order good and evil, 76-77, 135-136, 138-140

Shea, Winslow, 125, 126-128

Silver, David, 517n. 1

"Simple Foreknowledge and Providential Control" (Basinger), 501-502n. 123

sin: Jesus' teaching on, 170; seriousness of, 433-435, 467-468; ultimate source of, 169-172. *See also* fall, the, and man's sin nature; problem of moral evil

Smart, Ninian, 78; on the Utopia Thesis, 118-121

Snyder, Daniel, 241-244, 514n. 86; and surplus evil, 257-259, 383, 387

soul-building theodicy, 93, 96, 161, 410-411, 506n. 105; and the problem of hell, 430-431

"Soul-Making Theodicy and Eschatology" (Kane), 150

Southgate, Christopher, 490n. 9

specific abstract problems, 491n. 6

specific concrete problem, 491n. 5

Steel, Carlos, 496n. 15

Stump, Eleonore, 313, 315-319, 522n. 55

suffering, 94, 217-219, 477-479, 486-487; as a means God uses to take believers to be with himself, 486; ministry possible in, 484-485; as an opportunity for God to manifest his power, 479; and the positive value of mystery, 145; "righteous" suffering, 532n. 2; used as a basis for ultimately exalting the righteous, 486; used to demonstrate to believers and nonbelievers the Body of Christ concept, 480-481; used to demonstrate true or genuine faith to Satan, 479-480; used to prepare the righteous for further trials, 485; used to prepare the righteous for judgment of their works for rewards, 485-486; used to promote sanctification, 481-484; used to remove a cause for boasting, 479. *See also* animal suffering

Surin, Kenneth, 499-500n. 79

Swinburne, Richard, 235, 284, 303, 368, 513n. 36, 521nn. 5, 8, 19, 20, 23, 24, 522n. 55; Feinberg's assessment of, 319-325; Martin's response to, 313-315; Stump's response to, 315-319; on theism and prior probabilities, 303-306; on theism and probability, 306-308; on theodicy and the probability of theism, 308-313

Talbott, Thomas, 412-417; Feinberg's assessment of, 417-419

Taylor, A. E., 212

teleological argument, 511n. 16

Tennant, F. R., 199, 212

theism: all-determining theism, 96; atheists' attack on, 207-208; avoidance of contradictions, 27-29; core theism (à la Rowe), 230-233; and Darwinian evolution, 490n. 9; and defensive strategy, 358-361; expanded theism (à la Rowe), 225-228, 230; multiple forms of, 18, 20; and offensive strategy, 359-361; open theism, 105-106 (*see also* presentism); probability of, 211-213, 246; process theism, 96, 97, 98, 405-406; as "rational," 528n. 19; restricted theism (à la Rowe), 225-228; standard theism (à la Rowe), 225-228; traditional free-will theism, 96. *See also* Core Theism; Swinburne, on theism and prior probabilities; Swinburne, on theism and probability; Swinburne, on theodicy and the probability of theism; theonomy

theodicy, 86, 222, 510n. 2; Augustinian Tradition, 142-143, 145; basic strategy for defense-making, 489-490; definition of, 29, 165, 530n. 12; Irenaean Tradition, 142-143; marshaled against evil in general, 156; natural law theodicy, 340-343; need for, 336, 337; strong theodicy, 494n. 29; weak theodicy, 494n. 29. *See also* soul-building theodicy

Theodicy (Leibniz), 49, 57

theological systems: evaluation of, 89; and future issues, 154

Theology and the Problem of Evil
(Surin), 499-500n. 79
"Theology and Verification" (Hick),
506n. 104
theonomy, 33, 45, 50, 165, 362; broad
forms of, 36-37; ethics of, 165-166,
492-493n. 20; etiology of the word,
492n. 1; Feinberg's assessment of,
43-44; overview of, 34-36; and the
problem of evil, 41-43, 384; and the
problem of hell, 406-407, 427, 442-
443; scriptural support for, 35-36;
theonomous metaphysics and
theonomous meta-ethic, 492-493n.
20. *See also* William of Ockham
theory: and background knowledge,
319-321; and simplicity, 319
Tilley, Terrence, 518n. 34
transworld depravity, 86-97, 498n. 58,
499n. 65
Trau, Jane, 379-381, 528n. 22
"Two Concepts of Theodicy"
(Schuurman), 494n. 29

unattached natural evil, Feinberg's
defense against, 194-203
Understanding Scientific Reasoning
(Giere), 527n. 116
universal prescriptionism, 493n. 20
universalism, 402, 407, 420, 443;
Talbott's version of, 412-417. *See
also* Hick, soul-building theodicy of
"Use and Abuse of Theodicy, The"
(Tilley), 518n. 34
utopia, 172-174; undesirability of, 179-
180; ways in which God could create
it, 174-178
Utopia Thesis, 78; Mackie on, 118,
120; Smart on, 118-121

van den Brink, Gijsbert, 509n. 9
voluntarism. *See* theonomy

Warrant (Plantinga), 517n. 1
Warrant and Proper Function
(Plantinga), 517n. 1
Warranted Christian Belief (Plantinga),
517n. 1
"When Is a Gratuitous Evil Really
Gratuitous?" (Chrzan), 525n. 107
"Why Plantinga's Free Will Defense
Cannot Be Expanded into a
Theodicy" (Ingraham), 499n. 75
Wierenga, Edward, 275-280, 518n. 50
William of Ockham, 37, 296; approach
to the freedom/foreknowledge
problem, 115-118; ethical theory,
39-41; foundational notions, 37-39
Wittgenstein, Ludwig, 527n. 2
Wykstra, Stephen, 223-228, 230-233,
234, 359, 378, 381, 512n. 24,
513nn. 34, 36, 39, 514nn. 59, 64,
527n. 11

Yandell, Keith, 347, 511n. 4, 523-524n.
84, 526n. 114; Feinberg's assessment
of, 137-138, 139-141; greater good
defense of, 135-137; Kane's
objection to, 138-140

Made in the USA
San Bernardino, CA
13 February 2020